PENGUIN  CLASSICS

THE RISE OF THE ROMAN EMPIRE

ADVISORY EDITOR: BETTY RADICE

The Greek statesman and historian POLYBIUS (c. 200–118 B.C.) played a prominent part in the Achaean League, which strove to maintain a friendly but independent policy towards the Romans. After the defeat of Macedon in 168 B.C., Polybius was removed to Rome for indefinite detention on political grounds. There he met Scipio Aemilianus, a son of the conqueror of Macedon, and became the young man's friend and adviser. This gave Polybius entry to the aristocratic Scipionic circle and the freedom of movement to visit Africa, Spain and Gaul. In 150 B.C. his detention ended and he returned to Greece, but he remained closely associated with Scipio and accompanied him to Carthage in the Third Punic War.

Polybius drew upon a variety of written and oral sources which are no longer identifiable, as well as employing documentary evidence, such as the treaties between Rome and Carthage. His aim was partly to assess the achievement of the Roman domination and partly to write a history of practical benefit to future statesmen. For the latter purpose he insisted that the historian must himself have participated in war and politics at first hand. As a work of scientific history, written by a man of great intelligence who commanded a wide experience of political and military affairs, and who is largely free from national prejudices and dedicated to the search for truth, it is of inestimable value.

FRANK W. WALBANK was educated at Bradford Grammar School and Peterhouse, Cambridge, where he is now an Honorary Fellow. He is a past President of the Classical Association and of the Roman Society, and a Fellow of the British Academy. He was successively Professor of Latin and of Ancient History and Classical Archaeology in the University of Liverpool for thirty-one years. His published works include *The Awful Revolution* (1969), *Polybius* (1972), *A Historical Commentary on Polybius* (three volumes; 1957, 1967 and 1979), *The Hellenistic World* (1981), *Selected Papers* (1985) and numerous articles and reviews.

POLYBIUS
THE RISE OF THE ROMAN EMPIRE

*   *   *

TRANSLATED BY IAN SCOTT-KILVERT

SELECTED WITH AN INTRODUCTION BY

F. W. WALBANK

*

PENGUIN BOOKS

PENGUIN BOOKS

Published by the Penguin Group
Penguin Books Ltd, 80 Strand, London WC2R 0RL, England
Penguin Putnam Inc., 375 Hudson Street, New York, New York 10014, USA
Penguin Books Australia Ltd, 250 Camberwell Road, Camberwell, Victoria 3124, Australia
Penguin Books Canada Ltd, 10 Alcorn Avenue, Toronto, Ontario, Canada M4V 3B2
Penguin Books India (P) Ltd, 11 Community Centre, Panchsheel Park, New Delhi – 110 017, India
Penguin Books (NZ) Ltd, Cnr Rosedale and Airborne Roads, Albany, Auckland, New Zealand
Penguin Books (South Africa) (Pty) Ltd, 24 Sturdee Avenue, Rosebank 2196, South Africa

Penguin Books Ltd, Registered Offices: 80 Strand, London WC2R 0RL, England

www.penguin.com

First published 1979
33

Translation copyright © Ian Scott-Kilvert, 1979
Introduction copyright © Frank W. Walbank, 1979
All rights reserved

Printed in England by Clays Ltd, St Ives plc
Set in Monotype Fournier

ISBN-13: 978-0-14-044362-2

TABLE OF CONTENTS

TABLE OF CONTENTS

LIST OF MAPS

INTRODUCTION

1 The Background

The conquest of the largely Greek eastern Mediterranean was a major step in Rome's rise to world power. The decisive years were from 200 to 167 B.C., and we owe our knowledge of them to the Greek historian Polybius. His own lifetime overlapped part of the period, and it was his fortune to be brought into intimate contact with some of the most influential Romans. For contemporary Greeks the impact of Rome was a terrifying and disheartening experience, fraught with problems. Even after the predominance of Rome was no longer in doubt, not everyone fully understood the harsh realities of the new relationship. It was therefore primarily to elucidate to his fellow-countrymen that invincible combination of manpower, military skill and might, intimidating toughness in adversity and moral scrupulousness (sometimes compounded with self-deception) which formed the basis of Roman domination, that Polybius composed his *Histories.* Such knowledge, he hoped, would help them to cope with the political problems of a world in which they now had to learn to live with their Roman masters.

In its final form his work covered the years from 264 to 146 B.C. At the beginning of this period the Hellenistic system of sovereign states was still intact, roughly in the shape in which it had emerged from the struggles which followed the death in 323 B.C. of Alexander the Great of Macedonia, who had conquered the east from Greece to India. There were three major monarchies, in Macedonia, Syria and Egypt. Macedonia was ruled by a native dynasty, the Antigonids. Monarchy in Macedonia was less absolute than elsewhere, and retained several primitive features. Macedonian nobles prided themselves on their tradition of speaking and behaving with frankness towards their King. Elsewhere, Macedonian Kings ruled over conquered populations of a different stock. In Egypt Alexander's general, Ptolemy, had seized the lands and throne of the Pharaohs.

9

His descendants exploited the wealth of Egypt with the aid of a Greco–Macedonian ruling class and a highly-organized bureaucracy. Syria was ruled by the descendants of Seleucus, another of Alexander's generals. It was a sprawling, rather ramshackle amalgam of cities, principalities, feudal domains and temple states, inhabited by a multitude of different peoples. At first the Seleucid kingdom had stretched from Asia Minor to India; but by 264 many of the eastern provinces had become detached. In the west, too, in Asia Minor, there were several independent kingdoms such as Bithynia, Cappadocia and Pergamum. In the course of the third century Pergamum rose to be a major power. Its rulers, the Attalids, acquired wealth, territory and prestige, following their victories over a group of marauding Galatian tribes, who were terrorizing the Greek cities of Anatolia. Later they figure in Polybius' pages as loyal collaborators of Rome. Pergamum, their capital, and Alexandria in Ptolemaic Egypt, were the two great cultural centres of the Hellenistic world, rivalling and outstripping Athens as patrons of art, literature, science and scholarship.

Greece proper remained divided among a number of independent city-states, which lived under the constant threat and at times the reality of Macedonian domination. Athens, Thebes and Sparta, famous in earlier centuries, still tried to pursue an independent policy (though Thebes was in decay and for much of the third century Athens was held by a Macedonian garrison). Across the Aegean the maritime republic of Rhodes, relatively secure on its island, cultivated the friendship of the Kings and grew rich on commerce and on their benefactions. Politically, however, the most important Greek states were now the confederacies. In north-west Greece the backward state of Aetolia expanded during the third century to win control over Delphi with the prestige of its famous oracle and festival, and to incorporate the areas eastward as far as Thermopylae. Since 279 B.C. the Aetolians, whom Thucydides in the fifth century had characterized as barely Greek, enjoyed considerable and much advertised popularity for having preserved Delphi from an incursion of Celtic marauders, kinsfolk to those later defeated by the Attalids of Pergamum in Asia Minor.

The Aetolian League was rivalled by that of Achaea in south Greece. There, along the southern shore of the Corinthian Gulf, an ancient but moribund league of Achaean cities enjoyed a revival in the early part of the third century. In 251 Aratus incorporated his native Dorian city of Sicyon in Achaea and subsequently directed the expansion of the League, until it covered much of the Peloponnese.

This, in brief outline, was the shape of the Hellenistic world, and its dissolution was to be Polybius' theme. But the event with which he opened his two introductory books happened far away from Greece. In the year 264 B.C. war broke out between Rome and Carthage over the city of Messana on the Sicilian Straits. Situated on the north African coast near the site of Tunis, the powerful commercial city of Carthage at this time controlled a loosely held empire embracing Tripolis, the coast of Numidia and Mauretania as far as Spain, and much of Sicily. For their part the Romans had recently completed the conquest of the whole Italian peninsula, including the Greek cities of the south, and now controlled it with the help of a well-linked network of colonies and allied states. Only a narrow strip of water separated their two spheres of power, and it needed only a conflict in Messana, in the course of which rival parties called in the help of the two governments of Rome and Carthage, to start the First Punic War (264–241 B.C.).

Polybius saw the Punic Wars as a major step on the road to world conquest by Rome. That of 264–241 B.C. was only a prelude, for it remained confined to the west. But with the Hannibalic War (218–202 B.C.) the Greek east was also drawn in. Hannibal's alliance with Philip V of Macedonia (215 B.C.) was soon countered by a Roman alliance with the Aetolian League (211 B.C.). From then on a succession of causally related events led the Romans forward to domination over virtually the whole Hellenistic world. It was therefore the years 220–216 B.C., the 140th Olympiad by Greek reckoning, which saw the beginning of the war with Hannibal, that Polybius chose as the starting-point for his *Histories* proper. His main narrative begins in Book III. It was preceded by two books in which he briefly recounted the events of the First Punic War, the subsequent war between Carthage and her mercenary army in revolt, the building of a Carthaginian empire in Spain, and then, switching to Greece, the rise of Achaea and the war between the Achaean League and Cleomenes of Sparta, which led to Macedonia's once more gaining a foothold in southern Greece. This introduction was intended to provide readers with the information necessary to enable them to embark on the main narrative in Book III.

Polybius wrote as a Greek and mainly (though not exclusively) for Greeks. As one of the defeated he could analyse the problems of Greek statesmen working within limitations imposed by the hegemonic power. Besides, during a critical period of his career he experienced the advantages and disadvantages of detention, mainly in Rome, over a period of sixteen years (167–150 B.C.) and, in consequence of this, a close association with various leading Roman statesmen – in particular Scipio Aemilianus. He was thus exceptionally well-placed for writing a contemporary history.

2 *Polybius' Life*

Polybius was born towards the end of the third century B.C. – the exact date is uncertain. His birthplace was Megalopolis among the wild mountains of Arcadia, which at that time formed part of the Achaean League. His father Lycortas was eminent in Achaean politics and from his youth onward Polybius was likewise marked out for a political career. There was something a little old-fashioned about Megalopolis, with its emphasis on musical education, held to be a civilizing antidote to the relatively harsh mountain climate, its vivid historical memories of the great events of the fourth century and its slightly sentimental attachment to the Macedonian ruling house. Polybius' own training was practical rather than academic. The son of a rich landowner, he naturally rode and hunted, diversions that were later to commend him to his noble Roman friends and indeed were to claim his attachment down to the time of his death. Of other aspects of his studies something can be deduced from his work. He learnt to read with a critical eye the historians of his own and earlier generations. He also had the usual acquaintance with the standard literary and philosophical writers, but these he studied only superficially, and some perhaps only at second hand. He was especially attracted to political theory and, either in his youth or later, he actively followed several of the current controversies about such questions as the habitability of the equatorial regions, or how far Homer's account of Odysseus' journeys could be adjusted to fit geographical realities.

In 182 B.C., as a young man, he was accorded a signal honour. He was chosen to bear the funeral urn containing the ashes of Philopoemen, the most illustrious Achaean of his generation. Later Polybius wrote Philopoemen's *Life* in three books (x.21.6). The work is lost, but it was probably used by Plutarch as a source for his own *Life of Philopoemen*. In 181 B.C. Polybius was selected to serve on an embassy to Egypt but this was cancelled owing to the King's sudden death. Of his activities during the next ten years we know virtually nothing; but by 170/69 B.C. he had grown sufficiently important to be elected hipparch (cavalry leader), an Achaean federal office which normally paved the way to election to the annual *strategia*, or post of general, the highest office in the League. It was a critical time for all Greek states. Since 172 the Romans had been at war with Philip V's son and successor, Perseus, and the struggle had dragged on and frayed tempers. The Romans had become highly sensitive to Greek behaviour. Only complete commitment to Rome was now felt to be satisfactory and in this respect Achaea along with several other states seemed to fall short. In 168 Perseus was defeated at Pydna and dethroned. The Romans now felt free to act, and they at once instituted a political purge throughout the Greek cities. Polybius was among a thousand Achaeans who were denounced by Callicrates, a pro-Roman politician, summoned to Italy for examination, and kept there for sixteen years without either accusation or trial.

Most of these men were lodged in the cities of southern Etruria; but Polybius was more fortunate. Perhaps as a result of an acquaintance begun in Greece and, as he himself records (p. 528), following a conversation about books after he had come to Rome, he had the good luck to strike up a close friendship with the young Publius Scipio, the son of Aemilius Paullus, who had commanded the Roman army at Pydna. Through the influence of this young aristocrat, who was connected with two leading families, the Aemilii Paulli and the Cornelii Scipiones (into which he had been adopted),

Polybius unlike his fellow-detainees was granted permission to remain in Rome. There he became Scipio's mentor and close friend, indeed, one might almost say, his political manager. Through Scipio he could meet members of leading Roman families; but he also saw a good deal of his fellow-Greeks, many of whom lived in or visited Rome. In addition, he probably kept in touch with the other detainees, since his movements do not seem to have been seriously circumscribed. We hear of hunting trips in southern Latium, and it was probably during the later of these years that he visited Locri in southern Italy and made many of the journeys which he speaks of 'through Africa, Spain and Gaul, and voyages on the sea which adjoins these countries on their western side' (p. 231). When in 151 B.C. Scipio Aemilianus volunteered for service in Spain, Polybius went with him. It must have been then that he accompanied Scipio to north Africa, where he met and talked to Masinissa, the aged King of Numidia, about Hannibal and other matters (p. 402). On his way back to Italy he made a detour through the Alps 'to obtain,' he says, 'first-hand information and evidence' concerning Hannibal's celebrated crossing nearly seventy years earlier (p. 222).

In 150 B.C. the remnants of the Achaean detainees were allowed home. Of the original thousand only three hundred were still alive; they included Polybius. But shortly after his return he received a friendly summons to join Scipio at Carthage, now under siege. The Romans were in the middle of their third and last war against the old enemy. Polybius was valued both as a friend and as a military expert. Whether he had already published his lost treatise on *Tactics* is unknown; but Plutarch tells of his giving military advice to Scipio during the assault on the city. He stayed on to witness the capture and burning of Carthage and then, soon after, undertook a voyage of exploration beyond Gibraltar and well down the coast of Africa – though attempts to reconstruct the details and extent of his voyage have on the whole been unsuccessful. For this expedition he used ships put at his disposal by Scipio.

In Greece, meanwhile, a sudden war had flared up between Rome and the Achaean League. Events there moved swiftly, and by the time Polybius had returned home, all was over. Achaea had been overwhelmingly defeated, and Corinth deliberately destroyed on the Senate's orders. Polybius had nothing in common with the radical leaders who had led Achaea into this catastrophe; indeed he attacks them in the strongest terms. But for the next two years (146–144 B.C.) he acted as intermediary between the Romans and the Achaeans. The League was dissolved, but when the Romans removed their army they left Polybius the task of regulating relations between the cities and solving the many problems to which the new constitutional position gave rise. His services to Achaea were widely recognized. Statues were erected in his honour in many cities, at Megalopolis, Tegea, Pallantium, Lycosura, Cleitor and Mantinea. The topographer Pausanias (*Description of Greece*, VIII.37.2) quotes the inscription at Lycosura, which declared that, 'Greece would never have come to grief, had she obeyed Polybius in all things, and having come to grief, she found succour through him alone.' At Megalopolis it was recorded that 'he had roamed over all the earth and sea, had been the ally of the Romans, and had quenched their anger against Greece'.

Of Polybius' later career little is known. He visited Alexandria, and Sardes too (if that visit was not earlier), and he still kept in touch with his Roman friends. Cicero (*De republica*, 1.34) describes how Scipio, Polybius and the Stoic philosopher, Panaetius of Rhodes, used to hold discussions on the Roman constitution; this must have been after 146 B.C. In 133 B.C. Scipio summoned his many friends to support him when he was appointed to the command against the Spanish city of Numantia, and it is likely that Polybius was among them. He later wrote a monograph on the war (Cicero, *Ad familiares*, V.12.2). When he died is unknown. A reference to the measuring of the Via Domitia in southern Gaul (p. 212) must be later than 118 B.C., and though it has the marks of an interpolation, it may well have been taken by the posthumous editor from Polybius' manuscript notes. According to the anonymous author of a work on long-lived men (Ps. – Lucian, *Macrobioi*, 23) Polybius died as a result of a fall from his horse at the age of eighty-two.

3 The Writing of the Histories

When he arrived in Rome in 167 B.C. it is likely that Polybius was already the author of more than one work. The *Life of Philopoemen* was probably composed early; the *Tactics* too may have been written already, but could belong to the Roman period. There are also good grounds for thinking that Polybius had already written or begun a history of the rise of Achaea, which he never published, but part of which, at a very late stage in the preparation and revision of his *Histories*, was incorporated in the introductory Book II, to form the present Achaean chapters. However it is clear that the stimulus to write his *magnum opus* came at Rome, when his friendship with Scipio had opened up new perspectives on the ruling power.

His main theme is simple and frequently stated. 'There can surely be nobody so petty or so apathetic in his outlook that he has no desire to discover by what means and under what system of government the Romans succeeded in less than fifty-three years in bringing under their rule almost the whole of the inhabited world, an achievement which is without parallel in human history' (p. 41). The fifty-three years cover the period from 220 B.C., the beginning of the Olympiad in which the Second Punic War began, to 167 B.C., the aftermath of Pydna. But lurking at the back of Polybius' mind were the fifty years during which the Macedonians had risen from anonymity to become the conquerors of the Persian Empire, an event which had inspired the philosopher and statesman Demetrius of Phalerum to prophesy that one day Macedon in turn would suffer a fate similar to that of Persia. Polybius believed (and tells us: XXIX.21) that in his own lifetime he had seen that prophecy fulfilled by the Romans.

Originally then, the *Histories* were to explain the reasons for the Roman achievement, and they were planned to occupy thirty books. Later Polybius resolved to add a further ten books, and so carry the story down to 145 B.C. In Book III he offers an explanation of why that had proved necessary. Judgements on states and individuals based on the actual struggle are, he says, inadequate. One needs to be able to see how they both react to subsequent success or disaster; and it is only by considering how Rome exercised her hegemony that we can decide whether she merits praise or blame. In choosing 146/5 B.C. as his new terminal point, however, these were not the only considerations Polybius had in mind. The period immediately preceding that year appeared to him one of great confusion; yet he was anxious to incorporate an account of it in his *Histories*, since he himself had played an important part during those years, as witness, as active participant or in some cases as the man in control of events. This section, he tells us, will be almost the equivalent of a fresh work (pp. 181–2).

Polybius' explanation of why he has extended his original programme in this way is not entirely satisfactory. He claims to be concerned with judging the Romans' imperial performance; but his own attitude towards Rome is ambiguous. Where he is dealing with events that coincided with his forced stay in Rome, he is usually highly critical of the Senate's motives. His remarks frequently seem to reflect the bitterness and the cynicism of the Achaean exiles. But when he reaches the wars against Carthage, Macedonia and Achaea, and the events in which he had himself played a distinguished part, not unnaturally his sympathies are clearly enlisted on the Roman side. The detail and emphasis of these later books suggest that an important reason for the extension – which was very likely planned and written after the death of Scipio Aemilianus in 129 B.C. – was to transmit an account of his own personal achievements and to celebrate the great deeds of his friend and patron. The material which he had assembled from the years 168 B.C. to 152 B.C. provided a convenient bridge to the period of the great wars of 151–146 B.C., and gave some kind of plausibility to his remarks about passing judgement on the ruling power. But the comparative unimportance of this claim can perhaps be seen from the epilogue (pp. 540–41) in which Polybius, rounding off his whole *Histories*, simply reaffirms his original programme – to explain the rise of Rome to world power in almost fifty-three years.

The final edition, with its forty books – Book XL was a kind of index volume and is now lost – was published posthumously. It contained two books which, at any rate in their final form, were additional to the original plan. Book XII is really an extended digression devoted to a general attack on Polybius' third-century predecessor, Timaeus, who came from Tauromenium in Sicily. It is a substantial piece of polemic, in which Polybius does not appear at his best; indeed it displays something of the carping criticism of which he accuses Timaeus himself. No doubt many of his complaints are just – Timaeus was certainly given to cavilling and fault-finding, and some of his stories seem to have been childish and credulous – though indeed in assessing these we are a little at the mercy of his accuser. There was probably a fundamental opposition in temperament and method between the two men, the one a typical armchair historian, working in Athenian libraries for fifty years, the other an active statesman, general and explorer. But in addition Polybius resented Timaeus' reputation as the historian of the western Mediterranean and even as the first writer on Rome; and the importance which he attributed to Sicily in his *Histories* was unacceptable to the Achaean writer. Timaeus had nothing to say on the period which Polybius was writing about; indeed by opening his first book at 264 B.C. Polybius proclaimed himself to be Timaeus' continuator. Thus Book XII holds up the narrative. Nonetheless it throws valuable light on the controversies of Greek historians and no less on Polybius' personality.

The other book which interrupts the historical narrative is XXXIV, which was devoted to geographical matters. It has survived only in the form of discussion of Polybius' views in later writers such as Strabo and Pliny, and its general structure has to be reconstructed from their remarks. It probably contained a general physical sketch of the world as Polybius knew it, a more detailed account of the distances and dimensions of Europe and a description of its lands, and finally a survey of Africa, which must have incorporated the results of Polybius' coastal voyage of 146 B.C. This geographical excursus is not only an indication of Polybius' growing interest in geography, following on his own journeys. It also provides a kind of demarcation line between Books XXX–XXXIII, in which Polybius had recounted the events from 168 B.C. to 152 B.C., and Books XXXV–XXXIX which, when still intact, contained the narrative of the wars of 151–146 B.C., and the events in which Polybius had himself been personally involved. Coming appropriately at this point, Book XXXIV draws upon Polybius' own discoveries and criticizes the work of earlier geographical writers, such as Pytheas of Marseilles and the great Eratosthenes of Alexandria. Even in its present form Book XXXIV tells us a great deal about the geographical knowledge and speculation of the Hellenistic age. It also touches on many of the subjects which exercised Alexandrian critics, such as the credibility of Homer's description of Odysseus' wanderings, or the consistency and reliability of the maps of the world constructed by Dicaearchus and Eratosthenes. The disappearance of the original text of this work is a great loss, which must be attributed to a lack of interest in such matters at the time that Polybius' writings were being excerpted.

4 The Character of the Work

Polybius may have been inspired to write his *Histories* by his amazement at the supposed fulfilment of Demetrius' 'prophecy'. But his aims in writing them were much more practical. In the earliest English translation of Polybius (1568) Christopher Watson describes his work as 'containing holsome counsels and wonderful devices against the inconstances of fickle Fortune'. This fairly reflects its purpose. For in addition to offering useful, vicarious experience to the active politician – and politics did not disappear from Greece with the setting up of the Roman hegemony – it was also intended to teach the reader how to bear the vicissitudes of Fortune. This lesson was to be inculcated by a description of the disasters that had befallen others (p. 41). Thus the detailed account of the Gallic invasions of Italy demonstrates to Greek statesmen how such attacks can be met (pp. 146–7); and on a more personal level the well-merited disasters of Regulus in Africa and the triumph of his opponent, the mercenary captain Xanthippus, illustrate the part played in history by the unexpected element, and the way in which sheer determination can sometimes lead to a successful outcome. These events are described 'in the hope that the readers of this history may profit from them' (p. 80).

Who were these readers? Primarily they were Greeks, but Romans were also envisaged, for by the mid second century upper-class Romans were largely bilingual, and the earliest Roman historians had opted to write their own works in Greek. Apart from that, Polybius expects to cater for readers with various expectations, for not everyone was out to learn. This had long been recognized by Greek literary critics. The fourth-century historian Ephorus had insisted that a historian's prime duty was to furnish useful patterns of behaviour, but others thought of history as an entertainment, in which the reader's interest would be titillated and his emotions stirred by the description of pathetic and colourful incidents. Polybius admitted the validity of both views, but it is clear that the scales come down sharply on the side of 'the useful' rather than 'the pleasurable' (cf. p. 45, p. 357, p. 387, p. 493, p. 534) and he rarely loses an opportunity to press home to the reader the precise lesson that is to be drawn. In one place it is a point of geography, in another the vital importance of understanding the causes of events or the lessons implicit in the lives of great men; and he does not shrink from humdrum topics, such as the proper use of fire-signalling in war-time – Polybius had himself perfected a new technique – or making sure, when planning a surprise attack on a city, that one's ladders were not too short.

Given these two general aims – profit and pleasure – there were still many different ways of writing history, in order to satisfy various tastes (p. 386). The casual reader enjoys genealogies; those with antiquarian interests enjoy reading about colonization and the foundation of cities. But the student of politics – and he is clearly the kind of reader Polybius prefers – will want to hear about the affairs of peoples, cities and rulers, for it is from this that he can learn most. Polybius calls this sort of history *pragmatike historia*, a phrase which has often been misunderstood. It means 'political and military history' and in practice (though this is not a meaning inherent in the word) 'contemporary history'; and finally it seems, in Polybius' hands at least, to carry the idea of some didactic purpose. 'Pragmatical history', in this sense, is austere and factual. Though it can include references to contemporary developments in the arts and sciences and such topics as the cycle of constitutions as described by philosophers, it concentrates mainly on war and politics, and it is in direct reaction against the sensational and emotional history widely practised in the Hellenistic period.

In Polybius' opinion, to write history that way was to confuse it with tragedy. Many so-called historians were guilty of this, including those who told fantastic tales about Hannibal's crossing of the Alps (p. 221) or retailed fabulous stories of Phaethon's chariot and of the changing of his sisters into Lombardy poplars (p. 127). Among such writers Polybius' chief *bête noire* is Phylarchus, whom he undoubtedly disliked for espousing the cause of the Spartan King Cleomenes, the enemy of Achaea, but whom he attacks with polemical fervour for his meretricious and emotional account of the sufferings of the people of Mantinea, after the Achaeans had recovered and punished that rebel city. 'In his eagerness to arouse the pity of his readers and enlist their sympathy through his story,' Polybius writes (p. 168), 'he introduces graphic scenes of women clinging to one another, tearing their hair and baring their breasts, and in addition he describes the tears and lamentations of men and women accompanied by their children and aged parents as they are led away into captivity.' The great fault of this kind of writing is that, like tragedy, it tries to create an immediate effect by thrilling the audience. But it is the real business of history to be seeking to confer permanent benefits on serious students of politics by recounting what really happened and recording the speeches that were actually delivered (p. 168).

The dramatization of history is a fault which, Polybius believed, was especially characteristic of writers of historical monographs. That was because, having a limited theme, they felt obliged to make up for the meagre and restricted character of their material by rhetorical exaggeration. They therefore included very detailed topographical descriptions and elaborated their accounts of sieges (always a good subject for lively writing, as were land and sea battles: xiv.12.4). The fault, then, lay partly at least in their subject. Polybius himself was writing a different kind of history: history on a large canvas, covering the whole inhabited world. Universal history in this sense was new, or almost new. No one hitherto had attempted it except Ephorus. Yet, in Polybius' view, it was only through the study of universal history, world history, that one could reach a proper appreciation of cause and effect and so come to understand the part played by Fortune in human affairs; and that was essential if one wanted to learn the lessons of history.

Polybius regards universal history as inherently superior to separate monographs. But he makes a still greater claim for it. For the period with which he is concerned, that of the rise of Rome to world power, it is the only feasible kind of history, since no other sort can properly describe the gradual coalescing of all the different parts of the known world to form an organic whole. 'Now in earlier times the world's history had consisted, so to speak, of a series of unrelated episodes, the origins and results of each being as widely separated as their localities, but from this point onwards history becomes an organic whole: the affairs of Italy and of Africa are connected with those of Asia and of Greece, and all events bear a relationship and contribute to a single end' (p. 43). The notion that a work of art or literature should constitute a unity had been formulated in the school of Plato and in more detail in that of Aristotle, and it had become part of the common currency of Hellenistic literary criticism, which had applied it to works of historical writing. Essentially it implied a history of limited scope, in fact a monograph. One cannot therefore but admire the audacity with which Polybius transfers this concept to his universal history and the way in which he accomplishes this, seizing on the idea of organic unity, which really belonged to the written history, and superimposing it on the actual events described. In doing this he not only justified his method, he also produced a highly sophisticated version of the historian's traditional boast that his theme was inherently greater and more important than that of any of his predecessors.

5 The Techniques of the Historian

Polybius is unusual among ancient historians in the extent to which he enjoys discussing the techniques of his trade. Altogether he gives the reader a very full account of what has to be done before one can write 'pragmatical history'. The good historian should study and compare memoirs and other writings; but he must also make himself familiar with cities, districts, rivers, harbours and geographical features generally, and above all he must have personal experience of political life (pp. 442–3). It is these last two activities – knowing the country and practising politics (which in ancient times included warfare) – that Polybius rates highest. Real history cannot be properly written in a library. The historian must get about; he must visit sites, test the various accounts of the battle on the spot and cross-question those who took part in it. This, says Polybius (p. 431), is the most important part of history. As a technique, such interrogation of eye-witnesses could of course be applied only to a period within living memory; naturally it was no good for events of a century ago. But the main part of Polybius' *Histories* – apart from the two introductory books – fell within the memory of his own or the previous generation, for like Thucydides, Xenophon and Theopompus before him, Polybius had chosen to write the history of contemporary and recent events.

Personal experience, personal enquiry – these constituted the basic foundations of the historian's task. History, writes Polybius (pp. 448–9), adapting to his own ends Plato's famous remark about the ideal state being one in which the kings have become philosophers or the philosophers kings, 'should be undertaken by men of action ... or alternatively those who set out to write history must understand that the experience of affairs is an essential qualification for them.' It is clear that Polybius believed himself to qualify in both cases, for he was a man of action turned historian and as a historian he spared himself no pains in making journeys of discovery and questioning such eye-witnesses as were available.

The purpose of this restless programme was quite simple and straightforward: it was to discover the truth about what had happened. For only by means of the truth could history fulfil the ambitious practical and moral aims which Polybius assigned to it. Truth was all-important. 'For,' he insists, 'just as a living creature, if it is deprived of its eyesight, is rendered completely helpless, so if history is deprived of the truth, we are left with nothing but an idle, unprofitable tale' (p. 55, p. 432). Truth can of course be distorted in all sorts of ways. Since history is to provide moral lessons, it is very important that praise and blame should be correctly assigned where they are due. The rosy hues of panegyric are quite unsuited to history. What is permissible in the one is wholly out of place in the other – even when the same man is writing both, as Polybius was in his two accounts of Philopoemen, treating him objectively in the *Histories* and 'somewhat exaggeratedly' in the lost biography.

One reason for Polybius' dislike of Phylarchus is that his itch to write in a sensational manner is incompatible with honest composition (p. 168). Similarly, the authors of monographs, working on a small subject, get things out of perspective. They cannot take the broader view of the events they are dealing with and so they obscure the causal relationship between one event and another – even when they do not deliberately exaggerate the importance of their own chosen theme (p. 208, p. 357). True, the universal historian who has to cover so vast an area may also make an occasional factual slip or misstatement; but if he does, his errors, says Polybius, should be treated charitably.

Unfortunately Polybius is more ready to ask for charity than to accord it to others. The charge he brings against Timaeus of making carping and unfair criticisms of his predecessors (XII.4a, 7.6, 8.1, 11.4, p. 432) is frequently – though not always – justified. But Timaeus' malice finds a match in that displayed from time to time by Polybius himself. For example, his criticisms of Timaeus as an armchair historian and also as a pioneer of epigraphical research (XII.11.2) land Polybius himself in some inconsistency. Timaeus had certainly been harsh and virulent in his attacks on Ephorus, Theopompus and Aristotle; but when Polybius wrote to his own contemporary, the Rhodian historian Zeno, to point out some of his grosser errors, one may wonder whether his sole aim was the single-minded pursuit of truth.

One must, however, concede that in general Polybius meets a strict criterion of honesty and truthfulness. He is prepared to accept a slight deviation from that standard in only two situations. The first concerns religion. Polybius' attitude towards religion is not easy to define. He has been called irreligious, but although his attitudes towards the gods are inconsistent and incoherent, that is true of many other writers too: Herodotus, for example. Certainly Polybius adopts a critical and almost rationalist attitude towards the cruder forms of superstition. Certain historians had stated that no snow or rain ever fell on the statue of Artemis Cindyas at

Bargylia, and Theopompus, the fourth-century historian, had asserted that anyone entering the inner shrine of Zeus on Mount Lycaeum in Arcadia lost his shadow. 'To believe things that are beyond the limits of possibility,' Polybius comments, 'reveals a childish simplicity or is the mark of a limited intelligence.' Nevertheless, where such stories help to sustain feelings of piety towards the gods among the common people, one should excuse those who purvey them, provided that they do not go too far – for a line must be drawn somewhere (XVI.12.3–11). The difficulty was of course to know where. In fact, Polybius approves the use of religious pageantry at Rome to overawe the people and he describes superstition (*deisidaimonia*) as the force that holds together the Roman state (p. 349). Approval of religion as an efficacious political device, regardless of its truth, had had a long previous history in Greece. One of its main exponents was Critias, an Athenian oligarchic leader, who towards the end of the fifth century asserted that religion was a deliberate imposture devised by some cunning man for political ends. In practice this concession to political expediency had little effect on Polybius as a historian, except perhaps in his account of Scipio Africanus the elder, whom he misrepresents as a man who cynically exploited the religious credulity of his troops, in order to confirm their allegiance and inspire them with confidence at the assault on New Carthage, the stronghold of Carthaginian power in Spain (cf. pp. 406–15).

It is more relevant to his standing as a truthful writer that he makes concessions to the claims of patriotism; but even that is suitably qualified. 'I would admit,' he writes, 'that authors should show partiality towards their own country, but they should not make statements about it that are false' (XVI.14.6). True, patriotism seems to warp his judgement in certain contexts. He is certainly charitable – though not uncritically so – towards Achaea, and a good deal less than charitable towards the Aetolians, the perennial foe of the Achaean League. His account of Cleomenes III, the Spartan revolutionary leader, is based mainly on sources hostile to Sparta. His criticism of social conditions in contemporary Boeotia (XX.5–7) seems also to be in some degree distorted by Achaean hostility. Elsewhere too his assessment of a situation or his judgement of a person seems to be coloured by the attitudes of those concerned towards Achaea – or, in his later books, to-wards Rome. But he is nowhere deliberately untruthful, and by and large, his history can justly claim the reader's confidence.

One field in which Polybius' impartiality and honesty have sometimes been impugned is in his speeches. The inclusion of speeches in history was a long-established tradition among Greek historians (which was to be followed by their successors down to the time of Clarendon), and Polybius inserted such speeches at intervals throughout his work. Thucydides had used this device in order to introduce historical comment on a situation, and the degree to which his 'speeches' really echo the words and sentiments of the persons who deliver them is still a subject of controversy. His successors in the Hellenistic age present fewer problems, for it is agreed that such writers as Timaeus exploited the convention to produce mere rhetorical exercises (see p. 440). Polybius has a pro-found contempt for that kind of thing. He upbraids two of hispre-decessors, Chaereas and Sosylus, for recording speeches allegedly delivered in the Roman Senate on the eve of the Hannibalic War, which are 'pitched at the level of the common gossip of the barber's shop'. (p. 197). The historian's task, he affirms (p. 168), 'is, first and foremost, to record with fidelity what actually happened and was said, however commonplace this may be;' and elsewhere he remarks that 'it is not the historian's business to show off his ability to his readers, but rather to devote his whole energy to finding out and setting down what was really and truly said, and even of this only the most vital and effective parts' (XXXVI.1.6–7). Of the speeches in the *Histories* thirty-seven survive, and we can deduce the existence of others from passages in Livy, where he is following Polybius and includes speeches which clearly match those included at the corresponding point in the original. Not all Polybius' speeches achieve the standard of historical reality which he envisages: for example, some of the pairs of speeches delivered by the generals on each side before a battle. But there is no reason to think that he actually improvised. On the contrary, he went to considerable pains to obtain authentic versions when they existed. Noteworthy examples of this are his account of the conference held in Locris in 198 between the Roman commander Flamininus and Philip V of Macedonia, for which he evidently had access to a verbatim account (pp. 494–503), or the speech which the Aetolian Agelaus delivered at the conference of Naupactus in 217 (pp. 299–300). But where he lacked such information he would occasionally fall back on written sources containing rhetorical compositions which he accepted at their face value. In the main, however, and especially in his versions of speeches delivered in Greece, he lets his readers hear the authentic tones of Greek statesmen as they disputed with each other, sharing with us their dilemmas and their fiercely argued clashes of policy. In this way he adapts a traditional ingredient of history to reinforce the purpose of his own work as a handbook of political and moral instruction.

6 *The Problem of Fortune*

A different issue is raised by Polybius' treatment of Fortune, *Tyche*, that unforeseeable and incalculable element in human affairs, which Greeks of the Hellenistic world liked to personify as a goddess. Polybius' theme – the unification of the known world under the guidance and control of Rome – could hardly avoid coming to terms with the problem of Fortune. To deal with that theme only one kind of history was adequate – universal history – for it is only in universal history that the synoptic view of the historian matches the organic character of the historical events themselves. 'Now my history,' writes Polybius (p. 44), 'possesses a certain distinctive quality which is related to the extraordinary spirit of the times in which we live, and it is this. Just as Fortune has steered almost all the affairs of the world in one direction and forced them to converge upon one and the same goal, so it is the task of the historian to present to his readers under one synoptical view the process by which she has accomplished this general design. It was this phenomenon above all which originally attracted my attention and encouraged me to undertake my task.'

This passage is important both for the role which it assigns to Fortune and because in it Polybius asserts that it was through pondering on the part played by Fortune in the rise of Rome that he was led to undertake the writing of his *Histories*. As we have seen (p. 19), these were intended, in Christopher Watson's words, to proof the reader against 'the inconstances of fickle Fortune'. Is it this same 'fickle Fortune' that has contrived the rise of Rome? Or does Fortune mean more than one thing to the historian? The question is important, since the value of history as a storehouse of examples and as a source of practical lessons is diminished if the normal working of cause and effect is at the mercy of an incalculable and capricious power. Yet such, in the eyes of most men living in the Hellenistic age, was the divine power worshipped under the name of *Tyche*.

How far Polybius shared the common belief is a question not easily answered, for it is clear that he does not always use the word *Tyche*, 'Fortune', in one and the same sense. A phrase such as 'Fortune brought it about' is often no more than a loose way of saying that something 'chanced to happen'. But in other passages *Tyche* seems to be a positive power or force exercising an objective influence upon the historical process. Polybius, by temperament a rationalist (see above, pp. 24–5) is aware of the dangers, and in one of his later books (pp. 537–9) he discusses in detail the part that can properly be assigned to *Tyche* and fate in human affairs. His conclusion is that where no cause can be discovered, for instance in the case of floods, drought and frost, leading to famine and plague, one may fairly invoke Fortune as a cause – rather in the same way that we describe certain events as 'acts of God'. Furthermore, when people act in an inexplicable manner – for example, the Macedonians, when they were infatuated by the pretender known as the Pseudo-Philip – their behaviour, since it cannot be explained rationally, may be attributed to *Tyche*. But when we are dealing with events for which there are determinable causes, such as the achievements of Scipio Africanus (x.5.8), the rise of the Achaean League (pp. 149–50), and the success of the Romans in battle (pp. 508–9) to invoke *Tyche* as an explanation is a cheap and worthless procedure.

In practice, however, Polybius does not always observe this distinction. *Tyche* figures frequently in his pages, and not always after other attempts at explanation have been exhausted. In particular, he calls in the aid of *Tyche* in situations where two lines of

development, each in itself explicable in rational terms, intersect
to produce a new, quite unforeseen situation. An example occurs in
the account of Scipio's early career in Spain when a Spanish leader,
Abilyx, persuaded the Carthaginian Bostar to release some Spanish
hostages and then promptly handed them over to Scipio (III.97.5–
99.9). Abilyx acted quite rationally in the light of his own private
calculations. But this sudden advantage was wholly unforeseen in
Scipio's plans, and from his point of view was an intervention of
Fortune. *Tyche* is also frequently invoked as the cause of events
which are capricious or sensational, and where issues are decided
by a narrow margin: for instance, the defeat of Cleomenes who, had
he waited a few days, must have been saved by an Illyrian invasion
of Macedonia (pp. 175–6). Alternatively, there are examples of
an unexpected, and often ironical, reversal of roles, such as occurred
when the Aetolians who were attacking Medion debated whether
the name of the incoming or outgoing general should be attached to
the dedication of the booty which they expected to win, but *Tyche*
stepped in to bring about their defeat, and it was the victorious
Medionians who dedicated the spoils – which they then recorded
as won from *both* generals (p. 114)! The caprice of Fortune lets
no one prosper indefinitely, and Polybius is especially concerned
to preach the sermon of moderation in times of prosperity, because
of what will surely come hereafter. Moderation now cannot avert
the blow; but it is more fitting for a human being and may one day
be remembered in one's favour.

Tyche is not always capricious. Occasionally she intervenes to
punish wrongdoing (pp. 482–3), and in such instances she seems to
take on a personality not very far removed from the modern concept of Fate or Providence. The *Tyche* which had brought about
the rise of Rome to world-power in less than fifty-three years, and
so occupied a central position in the *Histories*, seems to fall within
this definition; and this presents difficulties, since the whole work
is based on Polybius' assumption that the success of Rome is to be
explained in rational terms. 'The supremacy of the Romans,' he
writes (p. 109), 'did not come about, as certain Greek writers have
supposed, either by chance or without the victors knowing what
they were doing. On the contrary, since the Romans deliberately
chose to school themselves in such great enterprises, it is quite

natural that they should not only have boldly embarked upon their pursuit of universal dominion, but that they should actually have achieved their purpose.' There is indeed a contradiction here. But it is not – as some scholars have argued – to be solved by assuming a change and a development in Polybius' philosophical beliefs. The fact is rather that the contradiction lies at the heart of Polybius' work, because it is unresolved in his own thinking. That is because he does not clearly differentiate between the various shades of meaning covered by the word *Tyche*, which by reason of its history and everyday usage had become unsuitable for conveying precise ideas. Faced by the unparalleled rise of Rome to world domination, Polybius seems to have blurred the distinction between what had happened and what had *had* to happen, between *Tyche*, chance, and *Tyche*, fate. Thus Roman success was an expression of the design of *Tyche* – and yet, at the same time, the result of the Romans' own qualities of drive and discipline. In fact, the contradiction is not so fundamental as it at first sight appears. The notions of divine aid and virtue rewarded are not necessarily contradictory or exclusive. Our own proverb 'God helps those who help themselves' suggests lines along which Polybius' dilemma could be and was resolved. Roman success was the fitting reward and outcome of Roman merit.

7 The Roman Constitution

The merit of Rome lay partly in her high principles, partly in her superbly organized and disciplined army, but above all – in Polybius' eyes – in her well-balanced constitution. All these three aspects of Roman excellence are given special emphasis in Book VI, which forms an extended digression placed at that point in the *Histories* where Rome was depicted at the nadir of her fortunes in the war against Hannibal, following the three defeats of Trebbia, Trasimene and Cannae. Book VI is fundamental to Polybius' central theme, which was, as we saw (p. 16), to describe 'by what means and what system of government' the Romans had attained their position of supremacy in the whole civilized world. The book ends with an anecdote taken from this very time of the Second Punic War after Cannae, which is intended to illustrate the integrity and high morale of the Roman government (pp. 351–2). The central part of the book, moreover (pp. 318–38), is devoted to a detailed description of the Roman army, its method of mobilization, its constituent parts, its armament, uniforms, method of encampment, and disciplinary system. But the most striking feature of the book is its account of the Roman mixed constitution.

It was a widespread Greek belief that the form of its constitution was all-important to the success or the failure of any state. Polybius analyses the constitution of Rome in terms of the Greek theory of the mixed constitution: a combination of kingship, aristocracy and democracy, which from the fifth century onwards was held up as the best and most stable of all constitutional forms, and exemplified in the traditional Lycurgan constitution at Sparta. In his sixth book Polybius did far more than define the Roman constitution as it existed at the time of the war with Hannibal. He also expounded a kind of political cycle, in which the three simple constitutional forms – kingship, aristocracy and democracy – together with their corrupt counterparts – tyranny, oligarchy and ochlocracy (or mob rule) – follow each other in a circular sequence to which he gives the name *anacyclosis*. In this political cycle, which Polybius regarded as the natural pattern of political development, monarchy is the first form to arise in primitive society and it becomes kingship when the monarch puts his strength behind moral ideas and justice. But in time kingship deteriorates into tyranny, the best men expel the tyrant and set up an aristocracy, which in turn is soon corrupted and so becomes an oligarchy. When this happens the people drive out the oligarchs and establish a democracy, which however in its turn lapses into mob rule and eventually into utter chaos. At this point salvation comes only in the form of a new monarch – and the process begins all over again.

In a now lost section of Book VI Polybius described how by a series of happy choices the Romans had succeeded in converting oligarchy, not into democracy (as the *anacyclosis* would require), but into a mixed constitution; and this release from the cycle he puts after the overthrow of the Decemvirate of 450/49 B.C. He then goes on to show how the three elements in the state – the consuls or royal element, the Senate representing aristocracy, and the popular or democratic element – are so evenly balanced that to the outsider it is difficult to define the constitution at all. Book VI also contains a comparison of the Roman 'mixed' constitution with the constitutions of Athens, Thebes, Crete, Sparta and eventually Carthage, and an explanation of why it is superior to them all; though since all things by their nature decay, the same will be true one day of the Roman mixed constitution too.

As an analysis of Rome in the third and second centuries B.C. Polybius' theory is too formal and too abstract. It fails, surprisingly in view of Polybius' personal experience at Rome, to comprehend the elaborate texture of Roman political life, which secured the domination of the noble families, substituting instead this highly elaborate and theoretical model. But it gives full weight to the Roman ability to grow and innovate and to adapt to changing circumstances, taught by experience in adversity. This acute diagnosis gets close to the heart of Roman success and affords some justification for Polybius' claim to be the interpreter of Rome to the Greek world.

8 *Polybius' Sources*

It has already been explained that Polybius regarded personal enquiry as the most important part of a historian's task (p. 23), and he chose the year 220 B.C. for the opening date of his main history because 'I should be able to speak as an eyewitness concerning some of the events and from the information of eyewitnesses concerning others' (IV.2.2). This clearly implies that for the two introductory books (I and II), which cover the years from 264 B.C. to 220 B.C., such sources of information were not available, but in fact he makes a discreet and proper use of written sources for the main period of his *Histories* as well. For the introductory books he mentions four third-century authors on whom he certainly drew: for Greek events the *Memoirs* of the Achaean Aratus and the *Histories* of Phylarchus, who wrote from the point of view of the Spartan King Cleomenes, together with Fabius Pictor and the pro-Carthaginian Philinus of Agrigentum, whom he used for his account of the First Punic War. His critical discussion of these writers (pp. 54–6, p. 167, pp. 203–4) is interesting as evidence of his independent and critical attitude to his predecessors, even when he draws upon them; it is at the same time a warning not to be over-optimistic about our ability to identify the written sources behind the detailed part of his narrative where such have clearly been used. It was not the practice of Greek historians to name their sources except occasionally – and then usually to express disagreement. It is therefore likely that even in Books I and II and still more in his main narrative Polybius used sources whom he did not name and who are no longer identifiable. For instance, his account of the events leading up to the First Punic War probably drew on Timaeus of Tauromenium, the Sicilian historian whom he attacks in Book XII, and for some of his digressions on earlier events it is likely that he followed the fourth-century historians, Ephorus and Callisthenes.

The Hannibalic War aroused great interest throughout the Mediterranean world and many authors, Greek and Roman, wrote about it. Apart from Fabius Pictor, Polybius mentions only Chaereas and Sosylus, and then in a most contemptuous way (see above, p. 26). For the affairs of the Greek east, he clearly uses written sources, but these can no longer be identified. Zeno and Antisthenes of Rhodes were contemporaries of Polybius and Zeno may be used for the history of other states besides Rhodes; but in the main we are reduced to conjecture, and in the few places where it is possible to analyse the sources Polybius followed with any confidence – for instance in his account of Cleomenes' death (pp. 292–7), for which an alternative version exists in Plutarch's *Life of Cleomenes* (33 ff.), and where the original sources seem to be Phylarchus and Ptolemy of Megalopolis, who wrote a scandalous history of Ptolemy IV – the complicated picture which emerges discourages any hope of naming Polybius' written sources for the greater part of the *Histories*. However, published works were not the only sources available. There was in addition other material, for instance Scipio Africanus' letter to Philip V of Macedon, describing his campaign against New Carthage (p. 409), typical of a genre of such letters written nominally to kings but perhaps intended for wide circulation. It was also possible to use published speeches and official archives, like those of the Achaeans at Aegium, to which Polybius will certainly have had access, and he may have been able to consult some documentary material at Rome, such as the senatorial decree on the peace with Philip (pp. 513–14). He may also have consulted the Carthaginian treaties in the 'treasury of the Aediles' (p. 203) but on the whole it is more likely that he had access to a privately circulated version. Like most ancient historians, Polybius did not make systematic use of inscriptions; an exception is the bronze tablet set up by Hannibal at the temple of Hera on the Lacinian promontory, which Polybius discovered there (p. 210, pp. 228–9), and which recorded Hannibal's numbers and troop formations.

In fact, Polybius believed that the real business of historical research lay in the cross-examination of witnesses. One or two names have come down: C. Laelius talking about his old friend the elder Scipio Africanus (pp. 405–6), and Masinissa, the King of Numidia, recalling in extreme old age the characteristics – including the avarice – of Hannibal (p. 402). But Rome, where Polybius was detained for sixteen years, had become, as it were, the capital of the civilized world, visited sooner or later by almost everyone who mattered. There or in the vicinity he could meet not only the other Greek detainees – mostly men of importance in their own states – but also a steady stream of envoys from all over the known world. We can fairly assume that as many as possible of these were avidly questioned on such matters as were germane to Polybius' work, and that he eventually developed a skilful technique of eliciting information. The names of his informants for the most part can only be guessed at, but it is mainly to them that Polybius owes the subject matter of his narrative, and the fact that it is so comprehensive and reliable.

THE SURVIVAL OF POLYBIUS

9 The Survival of Polybius

Of Polybius' long history, amounting to forty books, only a fraction has survived – Books I to V complete, much of Book VI, and fragments of the remaining thirty-four (though virtually nothing has come down from Books XVII, XIX, XXVI and XXXVII, which were all lost as early as the ninth century, nor have we anything from Book XL, the index volume). For this there are several reasons. To those more interested in a good Attic style than in the contents of a book the *Histories* had little appeal. Indeed Dionysius of Halicarnassus reckons them among the works no one ever managed to finish. The subject, too, grew less relevant as the position of Rome became more established. Diodorus and Livy both followed Polybius extensively, but they saw Rome in a different perspective from his. In the second century A.D. Plutarch took material from Polybius for several of his *Lives*, but adapted it of course to the needs of biography. Cicero was interested in the political discussion of Book VI and followed Polybius to some extent in Book II of his *De republica* (*On the State*), but the setting up of the Empire rendered Polybius' political theory obsolete. Tacitus sneered at the mixed constitution as something easier to describe than to attain (*Annals*, 4.33), and the writers of the later empire were almost all indifferent to Polybius – with the exception of Zosimus who, writing in the fifth century A.D., set out to chronicle the fall of Rome, and so naturally looked back with interest to the historian of her rise to power.

Polybius lived on at Constantinople, where his *Histories* were excerpted – to the detriment of the work itself. In the tenth century the Emperor Constantine VII Porphyrogenitus had a collection of excerpts made from a large number of Greek historians including Polybius, arranged under such headings as *On Embassies*, *On Gnomic Sayings*, *On Virtue and Vice*, *On Plots* and *On Stratagems;* and about the same time another collection of Polybian excerpts was prepared from Books I–XVI and XVIII and has come down to us under the title of the *Excerpta antiqua* ('ancient excerpts').

It was not however until the early fifteenth century that texts of

Polybius appeared in the west, first of all at Florence, where Leonardo Bruni Aretino used him (*circa* 1418–19) for an account of the First Punic War and some later events. Books I–V were translated (rather inadequately) into Latin in about 1450 by Niccolò Perotti at the instigation of Pope Nicholas V, but, if we ignore the military part of Book VI, which Janus Lascaris edited in Latin, with the Greek added 'for comparison', in 1529, there was no edition of the Greek text until 1530, when V. Opsopaeus brought out Books I–V at Haguenau. Shortly afterwards, in 1549, the *Excerpta antiqua* were published by Hervagius at Basel. This comparatively late publication does not however mean that there was ignorance of the Greek text previously. Clearly Book VI was being discussed in Florence for some time before Machiavelli began his *Discorsi*, which reveal its influence, in 1517, and it has recently been pointed out that Bernardo Rucellai was familiar with Book VI at the time he wrote his pamphlet *De urbe Roma* ('On the city of Rome') somewhat before 1505. There is evidence too that the *Excerpta antiqua* were known in Urbino from about 1482 onwards.

The sixteenth century saw a great flowering in Polybian studies, with translations into French, Italian, English and German. I have already mentioned (p. 19) that the first English translation was Christopher Watson's in 1568. Towards the end of the century Flavius Ursinus' publication of the Constantinian excerpts *On Embassies* in 1582 greatly extended the amount of Polybius known, and this additional material was incorporated in Casaubon's edition in 1609.

Polybius was studied at this time not only for his narrative history, but also for his political wisdom and as a theorist and practitioner of warfare. Of many works inspired by his account of the Roman army in Book VI the most famous is Justus Lipsius' *De militia Romana libri quinque* ('Five books on the Roman military system') published in 1594. Lipsius has been described as 'the spiritual and technical guide behind the military reforms of Maurice of Orange', who had sat under him at Leiden. Despite new perspectives created in warfare by the use of gunpowder, Polybius was still read and valued as an author who could assist in the organization of armies – and in the defence of Christendom against the Turk. Moreover, in the seventeenth century he continued to attract even greater popularity as a political teacher, especially in England, where he influenced William Camden, the historian of Elizabeth I (1615). The mixed constitution had figured in the work of Machiavelli's contemporary, Guicciardini, and also in the constitutional theories of John Calvin. But it made its greatest impact in Montesquieu's *Esprit des lois* (1750), which Bryce called the bible of eighteenth-century political philosophy. Through him, indirectly, Polybius thus played a part – or at least helped to provide the background – in the burst of political thinking which created the American Constitution of 1787 and several American state constitutions from about the same time.

Since then Polybius has continued to be read, but perhaps more by those interested in Hellenistic Greece and the rise of Rome to world empire than as a guide to political reform or military success. This more recent chapter in his fortunes has been associated with extensive work on the Greek text and, more recently, with a detailed investigation into his historical method and his technique of writing.

10 Recent Work on Polybius

This section must begin at the end of the eighteenth century, when Johannes Schweighaeuser of Strasbourg produced his monumental edition of Polybius (1789–95), with text, commentary and a lexicon. Some parts of our present-day text had still to be published – the excerpts *On Gnomic Sayings* (Mai, 1827), those *On Treachery* (Müller, 1848) and those *On Stratagems* (Woescher, 1867). Otherwise Schweighaeuser included virtually everything now known to us as the text of Polybius, and he made a magnificent start on recovering the original structure of the work out of the excerpts, and added many extracts from later writers, lexicographers, grammarians and the like which could fairly be identified as fragments of Polybius. Since then there have been several important editions: Bekker (1844), Dindorf (1866–8), Hultsch (1867–92) and Büttner-Wobst (1882–1905). A Loeb edition by W. R. Paton appeared in 1922–7, and a Budé edition, with a French translation, by P. Pédech, J. de Foucault, R. Weil and C. Nicolet, is in process of publication (1961–   ). J. de Foucault has also published a useful study of Polybius' style and language: *Recherches sur la langue et le style de Polybe* (Paris, 1972). On the manuscript tradition there is now a full study by J. M. Moore, *The Manuscript Tradition of Polybius* (Cambridge, 1965); and a new *Polybios-Lexicon* edited by A. Mauersberger (Berlin, 1956–   ) has reached the letter O.

In recent years there has been a large output of specialized studies of various aspects of Polybius' work, though unfortunately for readers of English most of these are written in other European languages. The most convenient introduction to the historian – in addition of course to reading him – is *Polybius* (Berkeley and London, 1972) by F. W. Walbank; this gives the text of the Sather Lectures delivered in the University of California in 1971, and contains a full bibliography of the main recent studies. Of these, readers of French or German may wish to consult especially P. Pédech, *La Méthode historique de Polybe* (Paris, 1964) and G. A. Lehmann, *Untersuchungen zur historischen Glaubwürdigkeit des Polybios* (Munster, 1967); to these add K. Meister, *Historische Kritik bei Polybios* (Wiesbaden, 1975). There is an excellent study of Polybius (in German) by K. Ziegler in Pauly-Wissowa, *Real-Encyclopädie der classischen Altertumswissenschaft*, vol. XXI.2 (1953), cols. 1440–578; this also contains a very full bibliography up to 1950. For work written since 1950 there is a sound critical survey (in Italian): 'Polibio negli studi dell' ultimo ventennio (1950–70)' by D. Musti in *Aufstieg und Niedergang der römischen Welt*, ed. Temporini (Berlin–New York), II.1 (1972), 1114 ff. Finally, for detailed study, see F. W. Walbank, *A Historical Commentary on Polybius* in three volumes: Oxford, 1957, 1967, 1979).

In 1973 a conference on Polybius was held at the Fondation Hardt at Vandoeuvres near Geneva. The proceedings have appeared as vol. XX of the *Entretiens sur l'antiquité classique: Polybe* (ed. E. Gabba: Vandoeuvres–Geneva, 1974), and include lectures by ten Polybian scholars. The last of these, by A. Momigliano, deals with 'Polybius' Reappearance in Western Europe', and this, along with Momigliano's J. L. Myres Memorial Lecture, 'Polybius between the English and the Turks' (Oxford, 1974), constitutes the best introduction to the historian's later fortunes.

11 The Present Selection

There have been several translations of Polybius into English, including those of Christopher Watson (1568), and Sir H. Shears, with an introduction by Mr Dryden (1693), and more recently E. Shuckburgh (1889) and W. R. Paton (1922–7). But fashions in language change substantially even in half a century, and the present volume, with a new translation by Ian Scott-Kilvert, presents Polybius in the rhythms and vocabulary of contemporary English. The text used is that of Büttner-Wobst. The passages selected cover the whole of the First Punic War from Book I; the whole of Book II with its account of the Gallic invasion of Italy, the First Illyrian War and the history of the Achaean League down to the war with Cleomenes of Sparta, his defeat at Sellasia and the re-establishment of Macedonian power at Corinth; almost all Book III, which recounts the events of the Hannibalic War down to the Roman catastrophe at Cannae; and virtually all Book VI with the description of the Roman army and camp, and Polybius' discussion of the Roman constitution. From the later books there is the siege of Syracuse with Archimedes' counter-measures, Hannibal's famous but abortive march on Rome, the taking of New Carthage in Spain by the young Scipio Africanus, a selection from the criticism of Timaeus in Book XII, the violent events in Alexandria which followed the accession of the boy-king Ptolemy V, the comparison between the Roman legion and the Macedonian phalanx, the Roman proclamation of Greek freedom in 196 B.C., the strange story of how Demetrius of Syria escaped from Rome (with Polybius' help) to seize the Seleucid throne, the debate among the Greeks concerning the destruction of Carthage in 146 B.C. and, finally, Polybius' epilogue to the whole work.

To keep the selection within the scope of a single volume some passages had inevitably to be excluded; but it has been possible to include virtually all the most interesting and most typical parts of what has survived of the original *Histories*.

F. W. WALBANK

TRANSLATOR'S NOTE

In preparing this translation, I am deeply indebted to Professor Walbank's Commentary on *The Histories* and to his personal assistance in providing much helpful and constructive criticism and advice for the text and notes.

IAN SCOTT-KILVERT

BOOK I

Introduction

1. If earlier chroniclers of human affairs had failed to bear witness in praise of history, it might perhaps have been necessary for me to urge all readers to seek out and pay special attention to writings such as these; for certainly mankind possesses no better guide to conduct than the knowledge of the past. But in truth all historians without exception, one may say, have made this claim the be-all and end-all of their work: namely that the study of history is at once an education in the truest sense and a training for a political career, and that the most infallible, indeed the only method of learning how to bear with dignity the vicissitudes of Fortune is to be reminded of the disasters suffered by others. We may agree, then, that nobody at this time need feel himself obliged to repeat what has been so often and so eloquently stated by other writers. Least of all does this apply to my own case, for here it is precisely the element of the unexpected[1] in the events I have chosen to describe which will challenge and stimulate everyone alike, both young and old, to study my systematic history. There can surely be nobody so petty or so apathetic in his outlook that he has no desire to discover by what means and under what system of government the Romans succeeded in less than fifty-three years[2] in bringing under their rule almost the whole of the inhabited world, an achievement which is without parallel in human history. Or from the opposite point of view, can there be anyone so completely

1. The element of the unexpected plays an important part in Polybius' approach to history. The idea derives from the Hellenistic historians, who in turn borrowed it from Greek tragedy; Aristotle defines its function as the arousing of fear and pity. In the context of the rise of the Roman Empire it is the unseen and irrational factor, controlled by *Tyche* (Fortune), which often works in favour of Rome.

2. From 220 B.C. – the start of the Second Punic War – to 167 B.C.

absorbed in other subjects of contemplation or study that he could find any task more important than to acquire this knowledge?

2. The arresting character of my subject and the grand spectacle which it presents can best be illustrated if we consider the most celebrated empires of the past which have provided historians with their principal themes, and set them beside the dominion of Rome. Those which qualify for such a comparison are the following. The Persians for a certain period exercised their rule and supremacy over a vast territory, but every time that they ventured to pass beyond the limits of Asia[1] they endangered the security not only of their empire but of their own existence. The Lacedaemonians after contending for many years for the leadership of Greece at last achieved it, but were only able to hold it unchallenged for a bare twelve years.[2] The rule of the Macedonians in Europe extended only from the lands bordering the Adriatic to the Danube, which would appear to be no more than a small fraction of the continent. Later, by overthrowing the Persian Empire, they also became the rulers of Asia;[3] but although they were then regarded as having become the masters of a larger number of states and territories than any other people before them, they still left the greater part of the inhabited world in the hands of others. They did not even once attempt to dispute the possession of Sicily, Sardinia or Africa, and the most warlike tribes of western Europe were, to speak the plain truth, unknown to them. The Romans, on the other hand, have brought not just mere portions but almost the whole of the world under their rule, and have left an empire which far surpasses any that exists today or is likely to succeed it. In the course of this work I shall explain more clearly how this

1. Both Aeschylus and Herodotus associate this overstepping of the frontier with *hubris* (mortal arrogance) which attracts *nemesis* (retribution). The events in question were Darius' Scythian expedition and his and Xerxes' invasions of Greece.

2. Polybius, who was not favourably disposed to Athens, makes no mention of the preeminence of the Athenians in the fifth century B.C. The Spartan hegemony is reckoned from 405 B.C. (Lysander's defeat of the Athenians at Aegospotami) to 394 B.C. (the defeat of the Spartans by Conon the Athenian at Cnidos with the help of a Persian fleet).

3. After Darius' death in 330 B.C. Alexander became the Great King and ruler over Egypt, Syria, Asia Minor and the eastern provinces of the Persian Empire.

supremacy was acquired, and it will also become apparent what great advantages those who are fond of learning can enjoy from the study of serious history.

3. The starting point for my history will be the 140th Olympiad,[1] and the events with which it begins are these. In Greece the so-called Social War, the first which was waged by Philip of Macedon, the son of Demetrius and father of Perseus, in alliance with the Achaeans against the Aetolians; in Asia the war for the possession of Coele–Syria,[2] fought between Antiochus and Ptolemy Philopator; and in Italy, Africa and the neighbouring countries the war between Rome and Carthage, which most historians call the Hannibalic War.[3] These events immediately follow those which are recorded at the end of the history of Aratus of Sicyon.[4] Now in earlier times the world's history had consisted, so to speak, of a series of unrelated episodes, the origins and results of each being as widely separated as their localities, but from this point onwards history becomes an organic whole: the affairs of Italy and of Africa are connected with those of Asia and of Greece, and all events bear a relationship and contribute to a single end. This, then, is the reason why I have chosen that specific date as the starting-point for my work. For it was after their victory over the Carthaginians in the Hannibalic War that the Romans came to believe that the principal and most important step in their efforts to achieve universal dominion had been taken, and were thereby encouraged to stretch out their hands for the first time to grasp the rest, and to cross with an army into Greece and the lands of Asia.

Now if we Greeks were familiar with these two states which disputed the rule of the world, there would perhaps have been no need for me to write of their previous history, or to explain what purpose impelled them or upon what resources they relied in embarking upon such an immense undertaking. But the truth is that most of the Greeks know little of the former power or the history

1. 220–216 B.C.

2. The fourth Syrian War, 219–217 B.C.

3. i.e. most Greek historians; they wrote from a pro-Carthaginian point of view and centred their account upon the personality of Hannibal. The Romans referred to the conflict as the Second Punic War.

4. This Greek statesman wrote a series of memoirs which occupied over thirty books.

either of Rome or of Carthage, and so I believed it necessary to prefix this and the succeeding book to the main body of my work. I was anxious that nobody, once he had become engrossed in the narrative proper, should find himself at a loss and have to ask what the Romans had in mind, and what were the forces at their disposal when they ventured upon that enterprise which finally made them the masters by land of our part of the world. On the contrary, I intended that these two books and the introduction they contain should leave my readers in no doubt that the Romans had from the outset sufficient reason to entertain the design of creating a world empire and sufficient resources to accomplish their purpose.

4. Now my history possesses a certain distinctive quality which is related to the extraordinary spirit of the times in which we live, and it is this. Just as Fortune has steered almost all the affairs of the world in one direction and forced them to converge upon one and the same goal, so it is the task of the historian to present to his readers under one synoptical view the process by which she has accomplished this general design. It was this phenomenon above all which originally attracted my attention and encouraged me to undertake my task. The second reason was that nobody else among our contemporaries has set out to write a general history; certainly if they had done so I should have had far less incentive to make the attempt myself. But as it is I notice that while various historians deal with isolated wars and certain of the subjects connected with them, nobody, so far as I am aware, has made any effort to examine the general and comprehensive scheme of events, when it began, whence it originated, and how it produced the final result. I therefore thought it imperative not to overlook or allow to pass into oblivion this phenomenon – the achievement of Fortune which is the most excellent and profitable to contemplate. For although Fortune is forever producing something new and forever enacting a drama in the lives of men, yet she has never before in a single instance created such a composition[1] or put on such a show-piece as that which we have witnessed in our own times.

It is impossible for us to achieve this comprehensive view from

1. Polybius' conception of Fortune here is of a force in the universe which takes pleasure in change for its own sake, and also acts as a dramatic producer, fashioning a design out of men's destinies.

those histories which record isolated events: one might as well try to obtain an impression of the shape, arrangement and order of the whole world by visiting each of its most famous cities in turn or looking at separate plans of them, an approach which is not in the least likely to yield the right result. It has always seemed to me that those who believe they can obtain a just and well-proportioned view of history as a whole by reading separate and specialized reports of events, are behaving like a man who, when he has examined the dissected parts of a body which was once alive and beautiful, imagines that he has beheld the living animal in all its grace and movement. But if anyone could reconstruct the creature there and then, restoring both its shape and its beauty as a living being and show it to the same man, I believe he would immediately admit that his conception was nowhere near the truth, and was more like something experienced in a dream. The fact is that we can obtain no more than an impression of a whole from a part, but certainly neither a thorough knowledge nor an accurate understanding. We must conclude then that specialized studies or monographs contribute very little to our grasp of the whole and our conviction of its truth. On the contrary, it is only by combining and comparing the various parts of the whole with one another and noting their resemblances and their differences that we shall arrive at a comprehensive view, and thus encompass both the practical benefits and the pleasures that the reading of history affords.

5. In this book I shall take as my starting-point the first occasion on which the Romans crossed the sea from Italy. This event occurs at the point where Timaeus' history leaves off, namely in the 129th Olympiad.[1] It will therefore be my task to describe first of all how and at what date the Romans established themselves in Italy, and what considerations impelled them to cross to Sicily, which was the first country beyond the shores of Italy on which they set foot. The actual cause of their crossing must be stated without comment, for if I were to pursue the cause of the cause, I should fail to establish either the starting-point or the fundamental principle of my history. The starting-point, then, must be fixed at a moment

1. 264–260 B.C. For Timaeus of Tauromenium (c. 350–c. 255), see Introduction, pp. 18, 24, 26, 33.

which is agreed and recognized by all, and can be clearly identified from events, even though this may require me to retrace my steps for a short period and summarize the intermediate happenings. For if the facts on which the commencement of the history is based are unknown or are open to dispute, it will be impossible to win approval or credibility for what follows, but once the reader's agreement has been secured on that point, the rest of the narrative will be readily accepted.

6. The date I have chosen, then, to mark the beginning of the establishment of Roman power in Italy falls in the nineteenth year after the naval battle of Aegospotami,[1] and the sixteenth before the battle of Leuctra.[2] In the same year the Spartans ratified the so-called Peace of Antalcidas[3] with the King of Persia; Dionysius the elder, the tyrant of Syracuse, defeated the Italian Greeks at the river Elleporus and laid siege to Rhegium; and the Gauls captured Rome by storm and were occupying the whole city except for the Capitol. However the Romans were able to negotiate a peace on terms which were acceptable to the Gauls. So when they found themselves, contrary to all their expectations, once more in possession of their native land, they began from that moment to enlarge it, and in the years that followed they waged a succession of wars against their neighbours. Through their martial valour and their consistent success in the field they subdued all the Latin tribes; after this they fought the Etruscans, then the Celts and then the Samnites, whose frontiers bordered the territory of the Latins to the east and to the north. Some years later the Tarentines insulted a delegation from Rome, and then, taking fright at the consequences of their action, they appealed for help to King Pyrrhus of Epirus. This happened in the year before the invasion of Greece by the Gauls, some of whom perished at Delphi, while others

1. In this action the Spartans surprised and almost wiped out the Athenian fleet and at a stroke brought the Peloponnesian War to an end (405 B.C.). The year Polybius chose is 387/6 B.C.

2. The battle in which the Spartan army was defeated by the Thebans under Epaminondas and the hegemony of Greece passed to Thebes (371 B.C.).

3. This settlement ended the war between Sparta and the forces of Athens, Thebes, Argos and Corinth supported by the Persians. It also restored the authority of the Persian King over the Greek states of Asia Minor (387/386 B.C.).

crossed into Asia Minor. The Romans had already, as I have mentioned, subdued the Etruscans and the Samnites and defeated the Italian Celts in many battles. They now for the first time made war upon the rest of Italy, not as if its inhabitants were foreigners, but rather as if the country were already rightfully their own. The trials of strength they had already experienced with the Samnites and the Celts had made the Romans veritable champions in the art of war. They showed great courage in withstanding the invasion of Pyrrhus, and after they had finally driven him and his army out of Italy, they continued to fight and to subdue those who had taken his side. They succeeded, contrary to expectation, in overcoming all these adversaries, and when at length they had subjugated all the peoples of Italy except for the Celts, they laid siege to the city of Rhegium, which was at that moment in the hands of a number of Roman citizens.

7. I must explain that the two cities of Messana and Rhegium, which face each other across the Sicilian Straits, had suffered a peculiar but similar fate. A contingent of Campanian mercenaries in the service of Agathocles[1] had for some time cast greedy eyes upon the wealth and beauty of the city of Messana, and shortly before the events I have just described, they had seized their opportunity and captured the place by treachery. They insinuated themselves into the city under the guise of friendship, and then at once took possession of it. They followed up this action by expelling some of the citizens, massacring others and taking prisoner the wives and families of their dispossessed victims, each man keeping those whom he happened to have found at the moment of the outrage. Lastly they divided among themselves the ownership of the land and all the remaining property. Once they had so quickly and so easily appropriated such a fine city and its adjoining territory, others were quick to imitate them. When King Pyrrhus soon afterwards crossed over from Italy to Sicily, the people of Rhegium believed they were threatened by a double danger. It was not only an attack by Pyrrhus that they feared, but also an invasion by the

1. Agathocles, who ruled as tyrant of Syracuse from 317–289 B.C., had captured Messana about 315. He had settled these mercenaries in Syracuse and they had agreed to leave Sicily after his death. It was between 288 and 283 that they seized Messana.

Carthaginians who controlled the sea, and so they appealed to Rome to support them and send a garrison. The force which the Romans dispatched numbered 4,000. It was commanded by one Decius, a native of Campania, and for a time his troops carried out their undertaking of protecting the city. But in the end they were tempted to follow the example of the Mamertines.[1] They became envious of the beautiful situation of Rhegium and of its inhabitants' prosperity and private wealth, and having made the mercenaries their accomplices, they broke their word to the people of Rhegium. They expelled or massacred the citizens and took possession of the place, just as the Mamertines had done at Messana. In Rome the people were outraged at their compatriots' action, but at that moment they were powerless to prevent it, because they were too deeply involved in the other wars which I have mentioned. But as soon as they were free to act, they surrounded the city and laid siege to it, as I have related above. When Rhegium fell,[2] most of the garrison were killed in the assault, during which they defended themselves desperately, since they knew the fate that was in store for them, but more than 300 were captured. These prisoners were sent to Rome, the consuls had them all marched into the Forum, and there, according to the Roman custom, they were first scourged and then beheaded; the object of inflicting this punishment was to restore, so far as possible, the good name of Rome among the allies. The city and the territory of Rhegium were immediately restored to the inhabitants.

8. All this while the Mamertines, so long as they could count on the alliance of the Romans and of the Campanians who had seized Rhegium, not only remained in undisturbed possession of the city and territory of Messana, but also harassed the Carthaginians and the Syracusans in the neighbouring territories,[3] and levied tribute from many parts of Sicily. But when the outlawed Roman garrison in Rhegium was closely besieged by their compatriots, the Mamer-

1. The name which the Campanian mercenaries assumed after they had captured Messana. It is derived from Mamers, the Oscan version of Mars.
2. In 270 B.C.
3. In 270 B.C. Carthage possessed western and central Sicily, the Mamertines the north-east corner, and Syracuse the east coast from Tauromenium to Cape Pachynus with the hinterland to Agyrium. The Mamertines were more in conflict with the Syracusans than with the Carthaginians.

tines lost this support and were quickly compelled in their turn to take refuge within their city from the Syracusans. This happened as follows. Not long before, the Syracusan armed forces had fallen out with the civil authority. The troops were at that time stationed near Mergane, and they elected two commanders from their own ranks: one of these was Artemidorus and the other Hiero, who later became the ruler of Syracuse.[1] Hiero was still quite a young man, but he was well fitted by natural character for some kind of royal position and political authority. Having taken over the command, he used some of his family connections to gain entry to the city. Once inside, he quickly got the upper hand over his opponents, but proceeded to administer affairs with such tolerance and generosity that the Syracusans unanimously acclaimed him as their general, even though they were by no means well-disposed towards leaders chosen by the army. However from the very first measures that he introduced, it immediately became clear to all intelligent observers that his ambitions extended beyond the position of general.

9. Hiero had observed that the dispatch of a Syracusan army on an expedition under the command of the supreme magistrates invariably resulted in quarrels among the leaders and the outbreak of revolutionary activity of some kind. He also knew that of all his fellow Syracusans it was a certain Leptines who commanded most supporters and the highest prestige and was particularly popular with the masses. He therefore made a family alliance with Leptines by marrying his daughter, so that whenever he had to go away on active service he could count on leaving Leptines behind as the guardian of his interests at home. Meanwhile he had come to the conclusion that the veteran mercenaries were an unreliable and potentially mutinous element in the army. He therefore led them out against the city of Messana, ostensibly to attack the Campanians who had seized it. He pitched camp against the enemy near Centuripa and drew up his troops near the river Cyamosorus. His battle order was so arranged that the infantry and cavalry which consisted of Syracusan citizens were grouped under his personal command and held in reserve, as if he intended them to

1. The evidence for the date of Hiero's assumption of power is conflicting the alternatives are approximately 275/4 or 270/69 B.C. The earlier date is the more probable.

attack from another quarter. The mercenaries on the other hand were ordered to make an advance, in which he allowed them to be cut to pieces by the Campanians. While they were being routed, he retired, and withdrew safely with the Syracusans to the capital.[1] Then, when he had effectively achieved his purpose and rid the army of its unruly and seditious elements, he proceeded to enrol a considerable body of mercenaries whom he picked himself, and thereafter continued in secure control of affairs. Before long he noticed that the Mamertines, as a result of their success, were acting in a reckless and overbearing manner, so he proceeded to arm his citizen levies and put them through a hard period of training. Then he led out his troops, engaged the enemy near the river Longanus in the plain of Mylae,[2] defeated their army decisively and captured their leaders. This action put an end to the Mamertines' aggressive conduct, and when Hiero returned to Syracuse he was saluted by all the allies as king.

10. Thus the Mamertines after losing the support they had enjoyed from Rhegium, as I have mentioned above, next suffered a crushing defeat on their own territory for the reasons that I have described. At this point some of them turned to the Carthaginians and offered to put themselves and the citadel in their hands, while another party sent a delegation to Rome to appeal for help as Campanians and so as a kindred people, and they likewise proposed to surrender the city. For a long while the Romans could not make up their minds, since it was all too clear that to give the help required would be thoroughly inconsistent. Only a little while before, the Romans had inflicted the death penalty on a number of their fellow citizens because they had broken faith with the people of Rhegium. To try now to help the Mamertines, who had committed an identical offence, would be an act of injustice that would be very hard to defend. The Romans saw this clearly enough, but they saw too that the Carthaginians had brought not only Africa but also large parts of Spain under their rule, and that they were the masters of all the islands in the Sardinian and Tyrrhenian Seas. If the Carthaginians gained control of Sicily, they would prove the most vexatious and dangerous of neighbours, since they would en-

1. This battle was probably fought in 274 B.C.
2. On the north coast of Sicily, a few miles west of Messana.

circle Italy on every side and threaten every part of the country, and this was a prospect which the Romans dreaded. It seemed clear that this would be the fate of Sicily unless help were given to the Mamertines: for the Carthaginians had already subdued the greater part of the island, and once Messana had fallen into their hands it would not be long before they brought Syracuse under their domination as well. The Romans foresaw all these possibilities and considered it imperative that they should not abandon Messana, and thus allow the Carthaginians to secure a bridgehead for the invasion of Italy, and so they debated the question at length.[1]

The First Punic War

11. Even after long consideration, the Senate did not approve the proposal to send help to Messana; they took the view that any advantage which could result from relieving the place would be counterbalanced by the inconsistency of such an action. However, the people, who had suffered grievously from the wars that had just ended and were in dire need of rehabilitation of every kind, were inclined to listen to the consuls. These men, besides stressing the national advantages I have already mentioned which Rome could secure if she intervened, also dwelt on the great gains which would clearly accrue to every individual citizen from the spoils of war, and so a resolution in favour of sending help was carried. When this decree had been passed by the people, one of the consuls, Appius Claudius, was appointed to command the expedition, and was given orders to cross to Messana. After this the Mamertines, partly through threats and partly by spreading false information, contrived to persuade the Carthaginian commander,[2] who had

1. It is doubtful whether Carthaginian power presented a serious threat to Italy at this date. More probably the wars with Pyrrhus had alerted the Romans to the dangers of foreign intervention in southern Italy and the Mamertines played upon these fears, as did the Massiliots before the Second Punic War.

2. His name was Hanno.

previously established himself in the citadel, to move out; they then invited Appius to enter and handed the city over to him. The Carthaginians crucified their general for what they regarded as his cowardice and lack of judgement in leaving the citadel. They then stationed their fleet near Cape Pelorias[1] and used their land forces to press the siege vigorously from the direction of Suneis. At this point it seemed to Hiero that the moment had come for the barbarians who had occupied Messana to be driven out of Sicily once and for all, and so he formed an alliance with the Carthaginians, marched out of Syracuse, and advanced upon Messana. He pitched his camp near the mountain of Chalcidicus on the opposite side to the Carthaginian lines, and so cut off this route of escape from the city as well. Meanwhile Appius, the Roman consul, performed the dangerous operation of crossing the straits by night and making his way into Messana. But he found that the enemy were pressing the siege vigorously from all sides, and since he considered it both dangerous and humiliating for him to be encircled in this way with the enemy in control equally of the sea and the land, he tried to come to terms with the Syracusans and the Carthaginians in the hope of taking the Mamertines out of the war. Both sides ignored his proposals, however, and at length he decided, out of sheer necessity, that he must risk a battle and that he would attack the Syracusans first. So he led out his troops and drew them up in battle order, whereupon Hiero eagerly followed suit and engaged him. There was a long and hard-fought struggle, but in the end Appius gained the upper hand and drove the whole of the opposing army back to their camp, after which he stripped the enemy's dead and returned to Messana. To Hiero this action gave a foreboding as to how the whole campaign was likely to end, and so he disengaged his troops under cover of darkness and retired with all speed to Syracuse.

12. The next day Appius was greatly encouraged when he learned of the outcome of the battle, and he decided to attack the Carthaginians without delay. He ordered his troops to stand to at an early hour and at first light led them out to battle. He engaged the enemy, killed large numbers of their troops, and forced the rest to retreat in disorder to the towns in the vicinity. These successes

1. A few miles north of the city.

enabled him to raise the siege of Messana and then to move over to the offensive, ravaging the territory of the Syracusans and their allies and scouring the country without meeting any resistance. Finally he turned the tables by encamping before Syracuse and laying siege to the city.

This, then, was the first occasion on which the Romans crossed the sea with an army, and it was for these reasons and in the context which I have described that they did so. It seemed to me that this was the most suitable point of departure for my whole narrative, and so it is upon these episodes that I have based my main theme, though I also went some way further back in summarizing the course of events, so that in my exposition of the general causes there should be no matters left in doubt. For those who desire a complete and comprehensive account of the development of Rome's present supremacy, it is vitally important, I believe, to trace this earlier phase of her history. In other words, they must acquaint themselves with the period and with the process whereby the Romans began to advance towards better fortunes after the defeat they had suffered on their own soil,[1] and with the details of how and when, after becoming the masters of Italy, they applied themselves to the conquest of countries further afield. My readers should not, therefore, be surprised if in the course of this work, I sometimes digress to explain some of the earlier history of the most famous states. I shall do this to give them a starting-point, and thus enable them to understand the origins and the circumstances from which each of these states reached its present position. In other words I shall use the same approach as I have adopted for the Romans.

13. After these explanations it is time to present my main theme, but first of all I must summarize the episodes which are dealt with in these introductory books. To mention these in order, we come first to the events of the war which was fought between Rome and Carthage for the possession of Sicily. There follows the war in Africa, and after that the achievements of the Carthaginians in Spain, first under Hamilcar and later under Hasdrubal; the latter campaigns coincide with the first incursion by the Romans into Illyria and that region of Europe, which was shortly followed by

1. The invasion by the Gauls in the early fourth century B.C.

their struggles within Italy against the Celts. At the same time the war named after Cleomenes, the King of Sparta, was being fought in Greece, and with this I shall conclude my general introduction and the second volume of my history.

There is no need for me to relate all these developments in detail, nor would this be useful to my readers; my plan does not require me to record them in full, but merely to refer to them in passing by way of introduction to those events which form my principal theme. I shall therefore do no more than recapitulate them briefly in due order so as to make the end of the introduction fit into the beginning of my history proper. In this way my narrative will follow an uninterrupted sequence, and it will be seen that I have good reason to touch upon certain matters even though others have already recorded them; at the same time this arrangement will make the approach to later events intelligible and easy to follow for the student of history. I shall, however, try to give a rather fuller account of the first war which was fought between Rome and Carthage for the possession of Sicily. This is because it would be difficult to find any contest which was longer in its duration, more intensively prepared for on both sides, or more unremittingly pursued once begun; or one which involved more battles or more decisive changes of Fortune. The two states concerned were still at that time uncorrupted in their customs and institutions, both received no more than moderate help from Fortune and both were equal in strength; in consequence we can form a more accurate picture of the national qualities and resources of each by comparing their conduct in this war than in any subsequent one.

14. There was also another reason, no less influential than those I have already mentioned, which persuaded me to pay especial attention to this war, namely the fact that Philinus and Fabius,[1] the historians who are reputed to be the most expert authorities on

1. Quintus Fabius Pictor, the oldest Roman historian, lived through the Hannibalic War. His history, which traced the story of Rome from the foundation of the city to his own time, was written in Greek and was aimed at justifying Roman policy to the Greeks. Philinus of Agrigentum lived during the First Punic War and wrote its history from a pro-Carthaginian standpoint. It is generally agreed that Fabius and Philinus are Polybius' exclusive sources for the First Punic War.

it, have failed, in my opinion, to report the truth as they should have done. Now, if we may judge by the lives and principles of these men, I do not suggest that they deliberately set out to mislead their readers; on the other hand both seem to me to have behaved in the way that men do when they are in love. Thus because of his partisan zeal and his persistent devotion to the one side Philinus insists that the Carthaginians acted with wisdom, virtue and courage on every occasion and that the Romans behaved in the contrary fashion, while Fabius gives us a diametrically opposite version. Now in other spheres of human life we should perhaps not rule out such partiality. A good man ought to love his friends and his country, and should share both their hatreds and their loyalties. But once a man takes up the role of the historian he must discard all considerations of this kind. He will often have to speak well of his enemies and even award them the highest praise should their actions demand this, and on the other hand criticize and find fault with his friends, however close they may be, if their errors of conduct show that this is his duty. For just as a living creature, if it is deprived of its eyesight, is rendered completely helpless, so if history is deprived of the truth, we are left with nothing but an idle, unprofitable tale. We must therefore not shrink from accusing our friends or praising our enemies, nor need we be afraid of praising or blaming the same people at different times, since it is impossible that men who are engaged in public affairs should always be in the right, and unlikely that they should always be in the wrong. We must therefore detach ourselves from the actors in our story, and apply to them only such statements and judgements[1] as their conduct deserves.

15. The truth of what I have just said is borne out by an example from one of these histories. At the beginning of his second book Philinus tells us that the Carthaginians and Syracusans made war against Messana and laid siege to the city; that the Romans then arrived by sea, entered the town, and promptly made a sortie to attack the Syracusans, but that after suffering heavy losses in the fighting, they fell back upon Messana. Next they marched out against the Carthaginians, and were not only repulsed but lost a large number of men who were taken prisoner. This is Philinus'

1. i.e. statements of facts, and judgements on matters of opinion.

account, but he then goes on to say that after the battle Hiero, the ruler of Syracuse, completely lost his head, that he not only set fire to his camp and his tents and hurried back to Syracuse the same night, but also abandoned all the forts which had been built to threaten the territory of Messana. In the same way he reports that the Carthaginians after their battle immediately evacuated their entrenchments, dispersed among the various towns of the neighbourhood, and made no attempt to contest the possession of the open country. He further tells us that the Carthaginian commanders, recognizing that their troops had become demoralized, decided not to put matters to the test of a battle, and that the Romans, following on their heels, ravaged both Carthaginian and Syracusan territory and proceeded to lay siege to Syracuse. This account, it seems to me, is a mass of inconsistencies and does not need to be examined in detail. The same troops whom Philinus describes at the outset as besieging Messana and as successful in all their operations are seen a little later as retreating in headlong rout, abandoning the open country, and finally as having become demoralized and encircled in their turn. On the other hand, the men whom he represented as defeated and beleaguered are suddenly reported as having broken out, pursued their enemies, taken control of the open country, and finally placed Syracuse under siege. It is impossible to reconcile the two versions of events, so it follows that either his account of the earlier or else of the later operations must be false. It is the former which is inaccurate. The Syracusans and the Carthaginians actually did abandon the open country, and the Romans immediately began to make war on Syracuse, and, as he says, on Echetla too, a town which lies between Syracusan and Carthaginian territory. We must therefore admit that the first part of Philinus' report is false, and that this historian represents the Romans as having been defeated in the fighting in front of Messana, whereas in fact they had been victorious. We shall find that this fault is repeated throughout Philinus' history, and the case is similar in that of Fabius, as I shall show when the occasion arises. At any rate I have made my point in respect of this digression, and shall now return to the matter in hand and do my utmost to give a true picture of this war, taking a short road and confining my narrative strictly to the order of events.

16. When the news of the victories won by Appius and his legions reached Rome, the people elected Manius Otacilius and Manius Valerius as consuls and dispatched the whole of their armed forces[1] and both these generals to Sicily. The Romans possess four legions in all which consist of full citizens, as distinct from the units provided by the allies. Each of the legions is enrolled annually and comprises 4,000 infantry and 300 cavalry. When these troops arrived in Sicily, most of the cities rose against the Carthaginians and Syracusans and came over to the Romans. Hiero took note of the mood of terror and dismay which had seized the Sicilians, and when he contrasted this with the numbers and the strength of the Roman forces, he concluded that the Romans' prospects were far brighter than those of the Carthaginians. So, since his reason urged him to take the side of the Romans, he sent messages to the consuls with a view to concluding peace and a pact of friendship with them. The Romans responded readily to his proposals especially in view of the problem of provisioning themselves, for since the Carthaginians commanded the sea, they were afraid of being cut off on all sides from their essential supplies; they remembered that their troops which had crossed to Sicily before had suffered badly from such shortages. They judged that Hiero could do them great service in this respect, and so they welcomed his offer of friendship.

A treaty was then drawn up according to the conditions of which the King undertook to hand over his prisoners to the Romans without a ransom and, in addition, to pay them 100 talents of silver. When these terms had been agreed, the Romans henceforth treated the Syracusans as friends and allies. For his part Hiero, once he had placed himself under the protection of the Romans, kept them provided at all times with their essential supplies, and for the rest of his life he reigned securely over the Syracusans, treating the Greeks with such consideration that he earned crowns and many other honours from them. He may fairly be regarded as one of the most outstanding of rulers, and as the one who enjoyed for the longest time the fruits of his own wisdom, both in particular cases and in general policy.

1. The year was 263/2 B.C. The dispatch of both consular armies shows the gravity of the occasion: in all some 40,000 men were sent.

17. After the terms of the agreement had been referred to Rome and the people had accepted and confirmed the treaty with Hiero, the Romans decided not to maintain their whole army on the island but to keep only two legions there. They calculated that with the King on their side the size of their commitment had decreased, and also that in this way their troops would be better supplied than before. The Carthaginians, on the other hand, when they understood that Hiero had become their enemy and that the Romans were becoming more and more deeply involved in Sicily, concluded that their own numbers must be reinforced if they were to be strong enough to confront their opponents and maintain control over Sicilian affairs. Accordingly they recruited mercenaries from across the sea, many of them Ligurians and Celts, and even larger numbers of Iberians, and dispatched them all to Sicily. They noted that Agrigentum possessed the greatest natural advantages for their preparations, and as it was also the most important city in their province, they concentrated their troops and supplies there, and decided to use it as a base for the war.

On the Roman side the consuls who had originally negotiated the treaty with Hiero had now left, and their successors in command, Lucius Postumius and Quintus Mamilius, had arrived in Sicily with their legions.[1] When they became aware of the plans of the Carthaginians and of the preparations they were making at Agrigentum, they decided to seize the initiative and attempt a bolder stroke. They broke off all other operations, concentrated their entire force for an advance against Agrigentum, encamped at a distance of about a mile from the city, and confined the Carthaginians within their walls. At that moment the harvest was at its height, and as the siege was expected to be a long one, the Roman soldiers began to gather the corn, showing rather more enterprise than prudence. The Carthaginians saw that their enemies were scattered about the countryside, made a sortie and attacked the foragers. They easily routed them, and then some of them pressed on to plunder the Romans' fortified camp, while others attacked the covering force. But here, as so often in the past, it was the excellence of their institutions that saved the Romans. According to their customs it is a capital offence for a man to desert his post or to

1. In 262 B.C.

58

retreat in any way when he is on guard duty. And so on this occasion, as on so many others, they gallantly stood their ground against opponents who far outnumbered them, and although they lost many men, they killed even more of the enemy. Finally they succeeded in surrounding the Carthaginians just as they were on the point of tearing up the palisade. They slaughtered many of them on the spot and pursued the rest back to the city, cutting them down as they fled.

18. After this action the Carthaginians were less inclined to be venturesome in launching any sorties, while the Romans took stricter precautions in their foraging. When the Roman generals found that the Carthaginians would not venture beyond skirmishing range, they divided their army into two bodies. One division remained in its original position near the temple of Asclepius outside the walls, while the other pitched camp on the side of the city which faces Heracleia. The Romans then fortified the ground between the two camps on each side of the city: they dug an inner trench to protect them against any sallies by the garrison, and an outer one to repel any attack from outside and also to prevent any men or supplies from being infiltrated into the city, as is often attempted during a siege. The spaces between the trenches that joined the camps were patrolled by pickets, which were protected by strong-points placed on suitable ground at some distance from one another. The food supplies and other stores were collected for the Romans by their Sicilian allies and brought to the town of Herbesus. As this city was conveniently close, they could visit it frequently to transport livestock and other provisions to the camp, and in this way they were well provided with all their necessities. For five months, then, a stalemate prevailed with neither side being able to obtain a definite advantage over the other, and scarcely any action took place apart from such minor successes as resulted from skirmishing. By this time, however, the Carthaginians were beginning to suffer from hunger, for there were at least 50,000 people shut up in the city. Hannibal [1] who had been placed in command of the besieged army, became seriously alarmed at this situation and

1. This general had accepted the offer of the Mamertines to instal a Carthaginian garrison in Messana, and had sent the Hanno who was subsequently crucified to command it (see p. 51).

sent one dispatch after another to Carthage explaining his plight and begging for reinforcements. Thereupon the Carthaginian government embarked the fresh troops they had assembled, and their elephants, and sent them to Sicily to join Hanno, their other general on the island.[1] Hanno concentrated his troops and stores at Heracleia [2] and his first move was to make a surprise attack on Herbesus; the attempt succeeded, and he was able to capture the city and cut off the Romans from their essential supplies. In this way the Romans found themselves both besiegers and besieged at once, and they were reduced to such severe shortages and privations that they considered more than once the prospect of raising the siege. In fact in the end they would have done so but for the efforts of Hiero, who by using every possible resource and contrivance succeeded in providing them with a sufficient quantity of essential supplies.

19. At this point Hanno again took the initiative. He learned that the Romans had been weakened by disease as well as by hunger, since an epidemic had broken out amongst them. He felt confident that his own troops were strong enough to give battle, and so he mobilized his whole force, including the elephants, which numbered about fifty, and made a swift advance from Heracleia. He had sent out his Numidian cavalry as an advance guard, and they had orders when they approached the Romans' fortified camp to try to draw out their cavalry and lure them into action; once they had achieved this, they were to give way and fall back on the main body. The Numidians carried out these orders and rode up to one of the camps, whereupon the Roman cavalry at once made a sortie and boldly engaged them. The Libyans retreated according to plan until they reached Hanno's army; then they wheeled about, encircled the enemy, charged them, killed great numbers and pursued them back to their camp. After this action Hanno occupied the hill called Torus and pitched camp there at a distance of about ten furlongs from the enemy. For two months both sides remained in these positions without attempting anything more decisive than skirmishing actions every day. But all this while Hannibal was making fire-signals and sending messages to remind his colleague

1. He had made the alliance with Hiero (see p. 52).
2. This port was some twenty miles north-west of Agrigentum.

that the population could not endure the famine any longer, and that more and more of his men were deserting to the enemy for lack of food. At last the Carthaginian commander determined to risk a battle, while the Romans for the reasons which I have explained were no less eager, and so both armies advanced into the space between the camps and engaged. The fighting was long drawn-out, but in the end the Romans succeeded in driving back the front line of Carthaginian mercenaries, and as they retired on to the elephants and the other units stationed behind them, the whole Phoenician army was thrown into confusion. The rout became general and the greater part of the Carthaginians were slaughtered on the field, though some escaped to Heracleia. The Romans captured most of the elephants and all the baggage. But after darkness had fallen, the Romans, who were at once exultant and exhausted, failed to keep watch as strictly as usual. Then Hannibal, who up to that moment had despaired of his plight, suddenly saw his chance to save the situation, and at about the hour of midnight he broke out of the city with his mercenaries. He had the Roman entrenchments filled up with baskets that were tightly stuffed with straw, and managed to withdraw his force safely and unobserved. When day broke the Romans discovered what had happened; there was a brief skirmish with Hannibal's rearguard, and then the Romans advanced in full force to the gates. There they found nobody to resist them and so they burst into the city and sacked it, enslaving great numbers of the inhabitants[1] and taking huge quantities of booty of every description.

20. When the news of the events at Agrigentum was received in Rome, the Senate was almost beside itself with rejoicing. In this exultant mood their aspirations soared far above their original designs, and they were no longer content with having rescued the Mamertines nor with what they had gained in the fighting. They now cherished the hope that they could drive the Carthaginians out of Sicily altogether, and that once this goal was attained their own power would be greatly increased; accordingly they made this their prime objective and gave their whole attention to plans designed to bring it about.

So far as the war on land was concerned, they considered that

1. Diodorus estimates the number at 25,000.

their forces were achieving all that could be hoped for, as the consuls elected after those who had laid siege to Agrigentum, namely Lucius Valerius Flaccus and Titus Otacilius Crassus, were handling the operations in Sicily capably enough. But so long as the Carthaginians held unchallenged control of the sea, the issue of the war still hung in the balance. In the months that followed[1] many of the inland cities came over to the Romans for fear of their army now that they were in possession of Agrigentum, but at the same time many of the coastal cities deserted them because they were overawed by the Carthaginian fleet. So when the Romans saw that the balance of advantage continually oscillated from one side to another for this reason, and that while the Italian coasts were repeatedly raided and devastated those of Africa suffered no damage, they were filled with the desire to take to sea and meet the Carthaginians there.[2] It was this factor among others which persuaded me to describe the war at greater length than I would otherwise have done. I was anxious that my readers should not remain ignorant of an important initiative of this kind: that is, how and when and for what reasons the Romans first ventured upon the sea.

It was, therefore, because they saw that the war was dragging on that they first applied themselves to building ships – 100 quinqueremes and twenty triremes. They faced great difficulties because their shipwrights were completely inexperienced in the building of a quinquereme, since these vessels had never before been employed in Italy. Yet it is this fact which illustrates better than any other the extraordinary spirit and audacity of the Romans' decision. It was not a question of having adequate resources for the enterprise, for they had in fact none whatsoever, nor had they ever given a thought to the sea before this. But once they had conceived the idea, they embarked on it so boldly that without waiting to gain any experience in naval warfare they immediately engaged the Carthaginians, who had for generations enjoyed an unchallenged supremacy at sea. One piece of evidence of their extra-

1. 261 B.C.
2. Other evidence suggests that while the Romans' motives were no doubt mixed, the need for defensive measures to protect the Italian coasts was the first consideration.

ordinary daring, and of the truth of my account, is this. When they first ventured to transport their forces to Messana, not only had they no decked ships, but no warships at all, not so much as a single galley. They merely borrowed penteconters and triremes from the Tarentines, the Locrians and the people of Elea and Neapolis, and ferried the troops across at great risk. It was on this occasion that the Carthaginians sailed out to attack them as they were crossing the straits, and one of their decked ships, in their eagerness to overtake the transports, ventured too near the shore, ran aground, and fell into the hands of the Romans. It was this ship which they proceeded to use as a model, and they built their whole fleet according to its specifications; from which it is clear that but for this accident they would have been prevented from carrying out their programme for sheer lack of the necessary knowledge.

21. As it was, those who had been given the task of ship-building occupied themselves with the construction work, while others collected the crews and began to teach them to row on shore in the following way.[1] They placed the men along the rowers' benches on dry land, seating them in the same order as if they were on those of an actual vessel, and then stationing the *keleustes*[2] in the middle, they trained them to swing back their bodies in unison bringing their hands up to them, then to move forwards again thrusting their hands in front of them, and to begin and end these movements at the *keleustes*' word of command. When the crews had learned this drill, the ships were launched as soon as they were finished.[3] After this they spent a short time on rowing practice actually at sea, and then the ships cruised along the Italian coast as the consul had ordered them. The consul, Gnaeus Cornelius Scipio, who had been placed in command of the fleet, a few days previously had instructed the captains to make for the Straits of Messana as soon as the ships were fitted out. Meanwhile he himself had put to sea with seventeen vessels and sailed on ahead

1. This practice was necessary because the method of rowing a quinquereme (five men to each oar) is different from that of a trireme (one man per oar); the latter was the largest vessel of which the Romans hitherto had had any experience.

2. The *keleustes* called the time, and so regulated the pace and rhythm of the rowing.

3. Within sixty days, according to the tradition in Pliny.

to Messana, since he was anxious to obtain the stores and materials which the fleet urgently needed. While he was there, an opportunity presented itself of capturing the town of Lipara[1] by treachery. Scipio seized the chance with more haste than prudence, put to sea with the squadron I have mentioned, and anchored off the town. News of his movements reached the Carthaginian general Hanni-bal[2] at Panormus, and he dispatched Boödes, a member of the Carthaginian Senate, with a force of twenty ships. Boödes sailed to Lipara by night and trapped Scipio in the harbour. When it was daylight, the Roman crews abandoned their ships and fled ashore, while Scipio, who was seized by panic at this turn of events and was in any case powerless to act, surrendered to the enemy. The Carthaginians at once sailed off to join Hannibal, taking with them the captured ships and their commander. But only a few days later, even though the example of Scipio's blunder was so glaring and so recent, Hannibal himself very nearly fell into the same error with his eyes open. He had heard that the Roman fleet was close at hand on its voyage down the Italian coast, and as he was anxious to observe its numbers and dispositions, he shaped a course in their direction with a fleet of fifty ships. As he was rounding the Cape of Italy[3] he suddenly came upon the enemy, who were sailing in good order and formation. He lost most of his ships, but was able to make his own escape with the remainder; in the event this was more than he had either expected or hoped for.

22. Soon after, as the Romans neared the Sicilian coast, they learned of the disaster which had befallen Scipio; they immediately sent word to Gaius Duilius, the commander of the land forces in Sicily, and waited for his arrival. They also learned that the enemy's fleet was in the vicinity, and began to prepare for action. As their ships were poorly fitted-out and difficult to manoeuvre, it was suggested to them that they could obtain an advantage in fighting at sea by using the device which afterwards came to be known as the 'raven'. This was constructed as follows. A round pole about twenty-four feet high and ten inches in diameter was erected on the

1. Situated on the island of that name, the largest of the Aeolian group; it was then in the hands of the Carthaginians.
2. The same general who had escaped from Agrigentum (see p. 61).
3. Possibly the modern Capo Vaticano, near the toe of Italy.

prow of the ship. At the top of this pole was a pulley, and at its base a gangway four feet in width and thirty-six in length made of planks which were nailed across each other. Twelve feet from one end of the gangway an oblong slot was cut, into which the base of the pole was fitted, and each of the long sides of the gangway was protected by a rail as high as a man's knee. At the outboard end of the gangway was fastened an iron spike shaped like a pestle; this was pointed at one end and had a ring at the other, and looked like the appliance which is used for pounding corn. A rope was passed through the ring and thence through the pulley at the top of the pole. When the ship charged an opponent, the 'raven' would be hauled up by means of the pulley and then dropped on to the deck of the enemy vessel; this could either be done over the bows, or the gangway could be swivelled round if the two ships collided broadside on. As soon as the 'raven' was embedded in the planks of the deck and fastened the ships together, the soldiers would leap into the enemy vessel. If the two ships were alongside, they could board from all the way down the hull, but if they had collided bows on, the men stayed on the gangway and advanced down it two abreast. The leading pair then protected their front by holding their shields before them, while the files who followed guarded their sides by resting the rims of the shields on the top of the railing. So having adopted this device, they waited for their opportunity to engage at sea.

23. As soon as Gaius Duilius learned of the disaster which had befallen Scipio, he handed over the command of the legions in Sicily to the military tribunes and went to join the fleet. Then he received intelligence that the enemy were ravaging the region of Mylae,[1] and sailed there with his whole force. No sooner had the Carthaginians sighted him than they eagerly put to sea with their fleet of 130 sail; their spirits were high, for at this stage they felt nothing but contempt for the inexperience of the Romans. They steered straight for the enemy and thought they could risk an attack without keeping any formation, as though they were seizing a prize which was already theirs for the taking. They were com-

1. Mylae, the modern Milazzo, was situated on a promontory about twenty-five miles west of the north-eastern tip of Sicily; the battle took place in the summer of 260 B.C.

manded by the same Hannibal who had extricated his troops from Agrigentum by means of a withdrawal under cover of darkness, and whose flagship was a single-banked vessel with seven men to each oar, which had once belonged to King Pyrrhus. As they neared the enemy and saw the 'ravens' hoisted aloft in the bows of several ships, the Carthaginians at first did not know what to make of these devices, which were completely strange to them. However, as they still felt an utter contempt for their opponents, the leading ships attacked without hesitation. Then, as they came into collision, the Carthaginians found that their vessels were invariably held fast by the 'ravens', and the Roman troops swarmed aboard them by means of the gangways and fought them hand-to-hand on deck. Some of the Carthaginians were cut down and others were thrown into confusion by these tactics and gave themselves up, for the fighting seemed to have been transformed into a battle on dry land. The result was that they lost every one of the first thirty of their ships which engaged, crews and all. These included the flagship, but Hannibal himself, by means of a daring action and a stroke of good luck, managed to escape in the ship's pinnace. The rest of the Carthaginian fleet bore up as if to attack; but as they came close, they saw what had happened to their leading vessels, and so sheered away and avoided contact with the 'ravens'. Instead they relied on their speed and circled round the enemy, hoping that they could safely ram them either broadside on or from astern. But the Romans swung their gangways round so as to meet an attack from any direction and then dropped the 'ravens', so that any ship which came to close quarters found itself inescapably grappled. Then at last the Carthaginians turned and fled, for they were completely unnerved by these new tactics, and in all they lost fifty ships.

24. In this way the Romans, contrary to all expectations, had made good their hopes to win control of the sea, and their determination to continue the war was redoubled. For the present they made another descent on the Sicilian coast, raised the siege of Segesta, where the inhabitants were almost at their last gasp, and on their return captured the city of Macella by storm.

After the naval battle Hamilcar,[1] the Carthaginian general who

1. He succeeded Hanno in command after the fall of Agrigentum; he is not the Hamilcar Barca who was the father of Hannibal.

commanded the land forces and was stationed near Panormus, received a report that the Romans and their allies had quarrelled concerning the award of prizes and decorations for the fighting, and that the allies were encamped apart from the Romans between the town of Paropus and the hot springs of Himera.[1] He launched a surprise attack on them with his whole force while they were engaged in striking camp, and killed some 4,000 men. After this action Hannibal sailed away to Carthage taking with him those ships which had escaped capture at Mylae, and soon after crossed to Sardinia with a reinforced fleet, which included some of the best of the Carthaginian naval officers. A little later he was blockaded by the Romans in one of the island's harbours. He lost many of his ships, and was arrested on the spot by the surviving Carthaginians, who crucified him. I should explain that as soon as the Romans had begun to take an interest in the sea, they tried to gain control of Sardinia.

During the following year[2] the Roman troops in Sicily achieved no important success, but at the end of it, after the arrival of the consuls Aulus Atilius and Gaius Sulpicius who were to hold office in the following year, they took the offensive against Panormus, where the Carthaginians were in their winter quarters. The consuls took up position close to the city and offered battle with their whole army, but as the enemy did not come out to meet them, they marched away and attacked the town of Hippana, which they captured by storm. They also took Myttistratum, which had long resisted a siege because of the strength of its natural position, and Camarina, which had recently revolted from its allegiance to Rome; here they brought up siege engines and made a breach in the city wall. They went on to occupy Enna and a number of other fortresses belonging to the Carthaginians, and after completing these operations they laid siege to Lipara.

25. In the following year the consul Gaius Atilius Regulus, who commanded the fleet, was anchored off Tyndaris[3] when he sighted the Carthaginian fleet sailing past without any attempt to keep formation. He gave orders to his main body to follow the leading

1. On the north coast of Sicily, about thirty miles east of Panormus.
2. 259 B.C.
3. About fifteen miles west of Mylae; the date was 257 B.C.

ships, and himself sailed out ahead, taking an advance guard of ten ships which could all make an equal speed. The Carthaginians saw that some of the enemy were still only getting aboard, while others were already under way, and that the advance guard had far outdistanced the rest, and so they turned and engaged them. They surrounded the squadron, sank nine of them, and came near to capturing the consul's ship with its crew. This vessel, however, was both fast and well fitted-out, and was able to foil their hopes and escape from danger. Meanwhile the rest of the Roman fleet arrived and soon took up a close formation. Once they had formed a line they attacked the enemy, sank eight of them and captured ten ships with their crews. The rest of the Carthaginian fleet withdrew to the Liparean Islands.

The result of this battle was that both sides now considered themselves equally matched, and both threw themselves with redoubled energy into the task of building up their fleets and contesting the command of the sea. In the meanwhile the land forces achieved no decisive success, but spent their time upon such minor or random operations as chance threw in their way. Accordingly the Romans, as I have mentioned, once their naval preparations for the coming summer were complete, put to sea with a fleet of 330 decked warships[1] and touched at Messana. From there they resumed their voyage keeping Sicily on the starboard side, and after rounding Cape Pachynus sailed on to Ecnomus,[2] because their land forces were stationed there at that time. The Carthaginians, setting out with a fleet of 350 decked ships, put in at Lilybaeum and proceeding south-eastwards from there, came to anchor off Heracleia Minoa.[3]

26. Now the Romans' plan of campaign was to sail to Africa and shift the whole scene of operations to that country: they wished to make the Carthaginians feel that the war no longer threatened Sicily but their own territory. The Carthaginians, on the other hand, were determined to prevent this. They knew that Africa was extremely vulnerable to attack, and that the population would offer

1. Modern estimates put the Roman strength at about 230 vessels and the Carthaginian at 200.
2. Midway along the southern coast, about twenty miles east of Agrigentum.
3. About twenty-five miles west of Agrigentum.

little resistance to any invader who succeeded in getting ashore; this was a situation which they could not allow to arise and they were eager to risk a battle at sea. Since the one side was determined to force a landing and the other to prevent one, it was clear that this inexorable clash of purposes would produce the struggle that followed.

The Romans had made preparations for both eventualities: that is, for a naval battle and for a sea-borne invasion of the enemy's territory. For the second they had chosen the pick of their land troops and organized the invading force into four divisions. Each of these had alternative titles, the first being known as the first legion or the first squadron and the others accordingly; the fourth, however, had a third title, that of the *triarii*, after the term used for that part of the army.[1] The whole force which was carried on the ships amounted to about 140,000 men, each vessel carrying 300 rowers and 120 marines. The Carthaginians, on the other hand, had made their preparations almost exclusively with the intention of fighting at sea, and to judge by the number of their ships, their manpower must have exceeded 150,000.[2] These figures are bound to strike not only an eye-witness but even the reader with amazement at the vast scale of the encounter and the enormous outlay and resources of the opposing states, if these are calculated from the numbers of men and ships; they must have been far more awe-inspiring to the eye-witnesses who could actually see the forces ranged against one another.

The Romans had to reckon with two difficulties: first that their course lay across the open sea, and secondly that their enemies possessed the faster vessels, and they therefore took great pains to devise a formation that would remain unbroken and would be difficult to attack. Their two largest galleys, in which the consuls

1. The Roman army was traditionally grouped into four classes, *velites*, the skirmishing troops, *hastati*, men in the flower of youth, *principes*, those in the prime of manhood, and *triarii*, the seasoned veterans. Here the *triarii* may have been a nickname for those to whom amphibious warfare was new, 'the oldsters' in other words.

2. Polybius' totals are based on his estimate of the ships present. This would give a manpower of nearly 100,000 rowers and 40,000 marines. But as there were only four legions in Sicily, the total of picked men must have been smaller, about 18,000 by modern estimates.

Marcus Atilius Regulus and Lucius Manlius were sailing and whose oars required six men apiece, were stationed in front of the convoy and alongside one another. Astern of each of these came a column of ships in single file; these were grouped in echelon, so that each successive vessel was further and further away from its opposite number in the column and had its bows pointing to the open sea. The first and second squadrons thus formed the two sides of a wedge, while the ships of the third squadron were stationed side by side in a straight line at the base. In this way the whole fleet presented the appearance of a triangle. Astern of the line which formed the base sailed the horse-transports, which were attached by tow-ropes to the ships of the third squadron. Finally in the rear of these they placed the fourth squadron, the *triarii*. These ships were again positioned in a single line, which was extended so as to overlap the line in front of it at each end. When every ship had taken up position in the manner I have described, the whole order of battle had the shape of a wedge; the point of this was open, the base compact and strong, and the whole formation was effective and easy to maintain, but also difficult to break up.

27. At about the same time the Carthaginian commanders made short speeches to their men. They explained to them that if they were victorious in this battle, they would thenceforth be fighting for the control of Sicily, but that if they were defeated, they would be obliged to fight for their homeland and their possessions; and with these words they gave the order to embark. All the crews responded at once and boarded their vessels with alacrity, for their generals' message had given them a clear understanding of the alternatives which faced them, and so they put to sea with high spirits and in a fighting mood. Then the commanders, as soon as they could make out the enemy's order of battle, adapted their own to meet it. Three-quarters of their fleet were drawn up in a single line; all their vessels faced the Romans, but the right wing was extended towards the open sea so as to outflank the enemy. The remaining quarter of the fleet was posted so as to form a left wing which pointed towards the shore, at an angle to the main body and extending beyond it. The Carthaginian right wing was commanded by Hanno, the general who had been defeated in the

battle outside Agrigentum.[1] His squadron included beaked vessels which could ram the enemy and also the fastest of the quinqueremes, which had the speed required for an outflanking manoeuvre. The officer in charge of the left wing was Hamilcar,[2] who had commanded the Carthaginians in the sea-battle at Tyndaris, and as he also occupied the centre of the line, he used on this occasion a tactic which I shall now describe. The action began when the Romans, seeing that the Carthaginian line was only thinly held because of its great length, launched an attack on the centre.[3] The ships in this sector had orders to give ground immediately in the hope of breaking up the Roman formation, and so they retired at a brisk speed hotly pursued by the Romans. The result was that while the first and second Roman squadrons chased after the retreating enemy, the third and fourth became separated from them: the third was slowed up because it had to tow the horse-transports, and the *triarii* because they remained with them and formed the reserve. When the Carthaginians judged that they had lured the first and second squadrons far enough away from the rest, a signal was hoisted on Hamilcar's flagship and the whole Carthaginian force swung round at once and engaged their pursuers. The battle that followed was fiercely fought. The Carthaginians' superior speed allowed them to sail round the enemy's flank as well as to approach easily or to beat a rapid retreat. But for their part the Romans were equally confident of victory; as soon as the vessels came to close quarters the contest became one of sheer strength, since their 'ravens' grappled every ship the moment it arrived within striking distance, and besides this they were fighting under the eyes of both their consuls, who were taking part in the battle in person. This at any rate was the state of affairs in the centre.[4]

28. Meanwhile Hanno, in command of the right wing, which had kept its distance when the Romans first attacked the centre,

1. See p. 61.
2. See p. 68.
3. The sea-battle of Ecnomus has been described as 'Cannae with the result reversed'. On this occasion the Punic centre proved too weak to hold the Romans.
4. The battle became a contest between one navy built for ramming and the other for boarding.

sailed across the open sea, attacked the squadron of the *triarii* and caused them much difficulty and distress. At the same time the Carthaginian left, which had been posted near the shore, abandoned their original formation, deployed into line with their bows facing the enemy, and attacked the Roman squadron which was towing the horse-transports, whereupon these ships cast off their tow-ropes and engaged the enemy. The battle had now resolved itself into three separate actions, each of which was being fought at a considerable distance from the others. Because of the disposition of the fleets at the outset the forces in each sector were fairly evenly matched, and so in each case the battles were fought on equal terms. The outcome of these engagements was much as might have been expected, given that the fleets opposed to each other were so similar in strength. Those who had first joined battle were also the first to break off, for Hamilcar's squadron was finally driven back and took to flight. Manlius then set about taking his prizes in tow, and Regulus, when he saw the struggle in which the *triarii* and the horse-transports were engaged, hurried to the rescue with all the ships of the second squadron that were still able to fight. As soon as he reached Hanno's squadron and joined in the action the *triarii* were immediately encouraged, and although they had by then suffered severely, they threw themselves with renewed spirit into the battle. It was then the Carthaginians' turn to find themselves hard-pressed. They were attacked both from the front and the rear and discovered to their surprise that they were being encircled by the relieving force, and so finally they gave way and retired towards the open sea. Meanwhile Manlius, who was now on his way back to the battle, saw that the third Roman squadron had been hemmed in by the Carthaginians close to the shore.[1] Both he and Regulus, who had by then left the *triarii* and the horse-transports in safety, made all speed to relieve the pressure on their comrades who were in great danger. They were surrounded as effectively as if they were besieged and would all have been destroyed long before, if the Carthaginians had not been afraid of the

1. Since it was the custom to hug the coast whenever possible, a decisive victory meant driving the enemy ashore. The arrival of the consuls' squadrons turned the tables on the Carthaginians, and of the sixty-four ships captured, fifty were from this Carthaginian left wing which could not escape to the open sea.

'ravens' and merely kept them penned in close to the land; as it was they made no attempt to ram for fear of being grappled. So the two consuls came up rapidly, surrounded the Carthaginians in their turn and captured fifty ships together with their crews; only a few succeeded in slipping away and escaping by keeping close inshore. This was how the various individual actions ended. The general outcome of the battle was in favour of the Romans. Twenty-four of their ships were sunk, but more than thirty of the Carthaginians'. Not a single Roman ship was captured with its crew, but sixty-four Carthaginian vessels suffered this fate.

29. After the battle the Romans revictualled their fleet, repaired the captured ships, and tended their own crews with the care that such a success deserved. Then they put to sea and continued their advance towards Africa. A squadron sent ahead of the main body made a landfall just below the promontory which is called the Hermaeum; this forms the eastern tip of the Gulf of Carthage and projects into the sea in the direction of Sicily.[1] There they waited for the rest of the ships to arrive, and when the whole fleet had joined them they sailed along the coast until they came to the city of Aspis. Here they disembarked, beached the ships and constructed a trench and a palisade to protect them. The garrison of the town refused to surrender, and so the Romans set about besieging it. Meanwhile the remnants of the Carthaginian fleet which had escaped from the battle arrived home. They thought it certain that the enemy must be full of confidence from their recent victory and would at once attack Carthage from the sea, and they therefore took men from both their land and their naval forces and organized a system of forward defences to guard the various approaches to the capital. However, when the news reached them that the Romans had landed safely and were besieging the city of Aspis, they abandoned these precautions for guarding against the approach of the fleet. Instead they united all their forces and concentrated their efforts upon the defence of the capital and its surroundings on the landward side.

Meanwhile the Romans had captured Aspis and posted a garrison to hold the town and the surrounding region. After this they sent envoys to Rome to report on the progress of the campaign and ask

1. The modern Cape Bon.

73

for instructions as to what action they should take next, and how they were to handle affairs in Carthaginian territory. They then made a swift advance with the whole army and set about plundering the country. They met no resistance, destroyed a number of luxuriously furnished houses and captured a large quantity of cattle; they also took more than 20,000 slaves whom they brought back to the ships. At this point messengers arrived from Rome with orders that one of the consuls should remain on the spot with a sufficiently strong force, while the other should return with the fleet. It was Regulus who remained, keeping a squadron of forty ships and an army of 15,000 infantry and 500 cavalry. Manlius then embarked the ships' crews and all the prisoners, sailed safely along the Sicilian coast, and in due course arrived in Rome.

30. The Carthaginians now saw that the Romans were preparing for a long occupation of their country. They therefore elected two generals from among their own citizens, Hasdrubal the son of Hanno, and Bostar, and sent a dispatch to Hamilcar at the Sicilian port of Heracleia ordering him to return forthwith. He arrived in Carthage with a force of 5,000 infantry and 500 cavalry and was appointed the third general. He then held a conference with Hasdrubal as to how they should deal with the immediate crisis. They decided that they should go to the help of those in the countryside and not allow it to be plundered without resistance. A few days later Regulus marched out on one of his marauding expeditions, storming and sacking the unwalled towns and laying siege to those which were fortified. When he reached Adys, a town of some size, he pitched camp around it and energetically set about investing it with siege-works. The Carthaginians were eager to relieve the town, and as they had decided to challenge the Romans for the control of the countryside, they led out their troops. They occupied some high ground which had the advantage of overlooking the enemy, but was otherwise unsuitable for their forces. Their principal advantage lay in their cavalry and their elephants, but by abandoning the level country and confining themselves to rocky and inaccessible ground, they ran the risk of showing their enemies how best to attack them, and this was exactly what happened. The Roman commanders' experience of war at once suggested to them that their enemies' most effective and formidable arm had

been rendered useless to them by their choice of ground. So they did not wait for the Carthaginians to come down and offer battle on the plain, but themselves seized the initiative and at first light advanced on the hill from both sides. In the battle which followed the elephants and the cavalry could play no part at all, but their mercenary troops delivered a gallant and vigorous charge, and forced the first legion to give ground and take to flight. But then the mercenaries advanced too far; they were encircled and routed by the Roman division which attacked from the other side of the hill, and the whole Carthaginian army was quickly driven out of its encampment. The cavalry and the elephants, once they had reached the plain, succeeded in withdrawing without loss. The Romans pursued the infantry for a short distance, but then broke off the chase, returned and destroyed the Carthaginian camp. After this battle they were free to overrun the country and sack the towns with impunity, and among these they captured the city named Tunis. This provided a useful starting-point for their raiding expeditions, and was also excellently placed to serve as a base for operations against the capital and its surroundings, and the Romans set up their headquarters there.

31. The Carthaginians now found themselves in a critical situation. They had suffered two major defeats, the first at sea and the second on land, and these had been brought about not through any lack of courage on the part of their fighting men, but rather through the inefficiency of their commanders. Apart from the misfortunes I have already described they also had to contend with an invasion from the Numidians. This people attacked them at the same time as the Romans and inflicted even more damage upon the countryside. The inhabitants fled in terror to the capital, where they found nothing but famine and despair, the first being caused by over-crowding and the second by the prospect of a siege. Regulus, on the other hand, had anxieties of a different kind. He knew that the Carthaginians had suffered crushing defeats both at sea and on land, and he counted on taking the city in a very short time, but he was afraid that his successor as consul might arrive from Rome before Carthage fell and thus deprive him of the glory of its capture, and so he invited the enemy to open negotiations. The Carthaginians were more than ready to listen to proposals and sent

out a delegation of their most prominent citizens to meet him. But when the conference took place, the envoys discovered that they were far from willing to meet the terms which Regulus offered; indeed the conditions were so harsh that they could hardly bring themselves even to listen to them.[1] Regulus took the attitude that he was already virtually master of the city, and hence that any concessions on his part must be regarded as a personal favour and an act of grace. The Carthaginians concluded that even if they became subjects of Rome, they could be no worse off than if they yielded to the present demands, and so they went home not only hostile to the terms he had proposed, but offended by the implacable attitude he had taken up. Thus although the Carthaginian Senate had almost abandoned any hope of deliverance, yet when the Roman commander's terms were reported to them they behaved with manly dignity and resolved that they would suffer any extremity and try every resource rather than submit to a settlement which was so ignoble and so unworthy of their past achievements.

32. At about this time one of the recruiting officers whom they had earlier dispatched to Greece returned to Carthage. He brought with him a large body of soldiers, and among them an officer named Xanthippus of Lacedaemon. This man had been brought up in the Spartan system of discipline and had gained a wide experience of war. When he learned of the defeats the Carthaginians had recently suffered and of the circumstances in which they had occurred, he carried out a review of the country's remaining resources and of their strength in cavalry and elephants. The conclusion which he quickly reached and which he confided to his friends was that these reverses must be attributed not to the superiority of the Romans but to the inexperience of the Carthaginians' own commanders. Because of the state of crisis which then prevailed, the gist of Xanthippus' remarks quickly spread among the people and became known to the generals, whereupon the government decided to send for him and question him. He appeared before

1. According to Dio (frag. 43.22–3) they required the payment of an indemnity, the surrender of Roman and the ransoming of Carthaginian prisoners, the evacuation of Sicily and Sardinia, the surrender of the entire navy except for one ship, and an undertaking to provide fifty vessels for Rome at any time upon demand.

them and reported his view of the situation, explaining the reasons why they were now suffering so many defeats. He went on to argue that if they would trust his advice and take advantage of the level country equally to march, to encamp and to engage the enemy, they would find it easy not merely to ensure their own safety but to defeat the Romans. The generals accepted his criticisms and decided to follow his advice, and thereupon placed their forces under his command.

Now even when Xanthippus' remarks on this subject had first been spread abroad they had caused a stir and given rise to hopeful rumours among the populace, and these impressions were confirmed as soon as he began to handle the troops. His decisive manner of leading out the army, drawing it up in regular formation in front of the city, manoeuvring the various detachments and giving his commands in the correct military terms, stood out in striking contrast to the inept performance of his predecessors. The soldiers demonstrated their feelings with loud cheers and showed themselves impatient to engage the enemy, for they were convinced that no harm could come to them so long as Xanthippus was in command. As soon as the generals noticed this extraordinary revival of spirit among their troops, they seized the moment to address them with words that matched the occasion, and a few days later they took the field.[1] Their army consisted of 12,000 infantry, 4,000 cavalry and nearly 100 elephants.

33. When the Romans noticed that the Carthaginian troops now always marched through the plains and encamped on level ground, they were surprised and a little alarmed by this change in strategy, but their prevailing desire was still to engage the enemy. So when the two armies had made contact, the Romans pitched camp on the first day a little over a mile away from the enemy. The next day the Carthaginian leaders held a council of war to decide what they should do in the present situation. At this the soldiers who were eager to chance a battle, collected in groups, began to shout out the name of Xanthippus, and demonstrated unmistakably that they wished him to lead them against the Romans at once. When it became clear to the generals that their troops were in high spirits and full of ardour, while at the same time Xanthippus urged them

1. Probably in May 255 B.C.

not to let the opportunity slip, they gave orders to prepare for action and entrusted to Xanthippus the power to conduct operations as he thought best. Xanthippus used this authority at once. He ordered the elephants forward and stationed them in a single line in front of the whole army, with the phalanx consisting of Carthaginian citizens[1] at a suitable distance behind them. He placed some of his mercenaries on the right wing, while those he considered most mobile were grouped with the cavalry in advance of both wings. The Romans, when they saw the enemy drawn up to offer battle, moved forward eagerly to meet them. They were alarmed by the prospect of a charge by the elephants, and so they stationed the *velites*[2] in the front line; behind them were drawn up the legionaries in a formation many maniples[3] deep, and the cavalry were divided between the two wings. These dispositions meant that the Roman line was at once shorter and deeper than usual. This order of battle was well enough designed as a defence against the elephants, but it failed to take sufficient account of the Carthaginian cavalry, which far outnumbered their own. At length all these arrangements were complete – both the general dispositions and the particular tactical groupings which best suited the operational plans of either side – and for the moment each held their formation, while they looked for a favourable opportunity to attack.

34. As soon as Xanthippus gave the order to the elephant-drivers to advance and break the enemy's line, and to the cavalry on each wing to perform an outflanking movement and charge, the Roman army also moved forward, clashing their shields and spears together, as is their usual custom, and shouting their battle-cry. The Roman cavalry, which was far outnumbered, was quickly routed on both wings. As for the infantry, those who were stationed on the left wing, partly to avoid the charge of the elephants and partly because they despised the mercenaries who opposed them,

1. These citizen levies were only mobilized when Carthaginian territory was invaded.

2. Light-armed troops, whose weapon was the throwing-javelin.

3. Originally the word *manipulus* meant 'a handful'; then, as in early days a pole with a handful of hay twisted round it was used as a standard, *manipulus* came to signify this, and hence a company of soldiers belonging to the same standard.

charged the Carthaginian right, drove it back and pursued it as far as the enemy's camp. Of the remainder of the Roman line which faced the elephants, the maniples in front fell back before the weight of the charge, were trampled underfoot and perished in heaps in the fighting, but the main body of the legionaries, because of its great depth, was able for a while to hold its formation unbroken. But at last the maniples in the rear were encircled on all sides by the cavalry and found themselves compelled to face about and engage them; on the other hand, those who had managed to force their way to the front through the elephants and regroup behind them were faced by the Carthaginian phalanx of heavy infantry, which was completely fresh and in unbroken order, and were cut to pieces. From this point the Romans came under terrible pressure from all sides. The greater number were trampled to death by the enormous weight of the elephants, while the rest were shot down in their ranks as they stood by the overwhelming numbers of the Carthaginian cavalry. Only a small body tried to save themselves by flight, and for these the only line of retreat lay across level ground. Some were dispatched by the elephants and the cavalry, while a body of about 500 who retreated with Regulus were soon afterwards captured, their commander with them.

The Carthaginians lost about 800 of their mercenaries, those who had faced the Roman left wing, while of the Romans only about 2,000 survived. These were the troops on the left who, as I have described above, pursued the mercenaries to their camp, and had thus moved out of range of the main battle. All the rest perished except for Regulus and those who fled with him. The surviving maniples escaped with remarkable good fortune to the town of Aspis. The Carthaginians stripped the corpses and marched back to the capital, exultant at this change in their fortunes and taking with them Regulus and the rest of the prisoners.

35. These events carry in them many lessons for those who can read them aright[1] and wish to be guided in the conduct of their lives. The disaster which befell Regulus offers us the clearest possible illustration of the principle that we should not rely upon the favours of Fortune, above all when we are enjoying success.

1. A prime example of the kind of lessons to which Polybius refers on p. 41.

Here we see the very man, who only a little while before had refused any pity or mercy to the vanquished, himself led captive and pleading before his victims for his own life. And that saying of Euripides,[1] which has long been acknowledged as just,

One wise head can outmatch a score of hands

is once more confirmed by the facts in this instance. One man and one brain overcame that host which until then had seemed invincible and capable of accomplishing anything, restored the fortunes of a state which had seemed irretrievably ruined, and raised up the spirits of its soldiers which had sunk to the depths of despair. I have recorded these events in the hope that the readers of this history may profit from them, for there are two ways by which all men may reform themselves, either by learning from their own errors or from those of others; the former makes a more striking demonstration, the latter a less painful one. For this reason we should never, if we can avoid it, choose the first, since it involves great dangers as well as great pain, but always the second, since it reveals the best course without causing us harm. From this I conclude that the best education for the situations of actual life consists of the experience we acquire from the study of serious history. For it is history alone which without causing us harm enables us to judge what is the best course in any situation or circumstance. Enough, then, on this subject.

36. Now that all the Carthaginians' hopes had been fulfilled, they indulged their feelings of joy to the limit, not only making thank-offerings to the gods but celebrating their victory and entertaining among themselves. It was of course Xanthippus who had been responsible for this extraordinary transformation and recovery in the fortunes of Carthage, but quite soon after the battle he sailed off home, and by this action proved that he was a man of rare wisdom and good sense; for the truth is that it is precisely the most brilliant and exceptional achievements which give rise to the most intense jealousies and the most poisonous slanders. A native citizen may be able to resist these for some time, if he enjoys the support of his kinsmen and possesses plenty of friends, but a foreigner will quickly succumb and find his position immediately

1. A fragment from Euripides' *Antiope*.

threatened. However there is yet another account which is sometimes given of Xanthippus' departure, and this I shall try to explain at a more suitable moment in my history.

When the news of this unexpected disaster reached the Romans, they at once began preparations to fit out a fleet to rescue what remained of their army in Africa. After their success the Carthaginians pitched camp before Aspis, since they were eager to capture the survivors of the battle, but these men defended the city with such courage and daring that the Carthaginians failed to capture it, and at length abandoned the siege. Then, when they learned that the Romans were preparing their fleet and intended to sail again to Africa, the Carthaginians set to work to repair the ships they still possessed and to construct new ones, and before long they had manned a fleet of 200 vessels. With these they put to sea and patrolled the coast against the arrival of the enemy.

By the beginning of the summer the Romans had launched 350 ships,[1] which they dispatched under the command of Marcus Aemilius and Servius Fulvius, and this fleet sailed along the coast of Sicily making for Africa. They met the Carthaginian fleet near the Hermaeum, attacked and easily routed them, and captured 114 ships with their crews. They then took on board from Aspis the remaining Roman troops in Africa and sailed again for Sicily.

37. They had safely crossed the straits and were off the Sicilian coast near Camarina when they ran into a fearful storm and suffered a disaster on a scale which almost beggars description. Of their 364 ships only eighty survived: the rest either foundered or were hurled by the waves against the rocks and headlands, where they broke up, leaving the shore heaped with corpses and wreckage. There is no record in all history of a greater catastrophe having taken place at sea on any one occasion, and for this it was not Fortune which was to blame so much as the commanders themselves. Time and again their pilots had tried to persuade them not to sail along the southern coast of Sicily where it faces the Libyan

1. This total is consistent with Polybius' figures as given on p. 69, these were derived from his sources for the battle of Ecnomus, and modern estimates have reduced them to about 200 ships. Allowing therefore for an over-estimate of about 100 and for the forty vessels left at Aspis, the relieving fleet would have numbered about 210 ships.

Sea,[1] as it is a rocky shore which possesses few safe anchorages. They had also warned them that of the two constellations which herald bad weather the one was not yet past and the other was close at hand, for the voyage had been begun between the rising of Orion and of Sirius.[2] In spite of this, the commanders completely disregarded their advice: they chose a course which was threatened by the full force of the open sea, because they hoped to overawe a number of the cities which lay along their route with the spectacular victory they had gained, and so win them over. At any rate these commanders, who for the sake of such a trivial advantage exposed themselves to such an overwhelming disaster, were compelled to recognize the folly of their action.

Now in general the Romans rely upon force in all their undertakings, and consider that having set themselves a task they are bound to carry it through, and similarly that nothing is impossible once they have decided to attempt it. It often happens that this spirit inspires them to succeed, but sometimes it involves them in total disaster, and this is especially the case at sea. The reason is that on land they are contending with other men and with the products of men's labour; hence they are usually successful because they are applying one kind of force against another which is essentially similar – although even here their efforts have on rare occasions miscarried. But when they are contending with the sea and the atmosphere and try to overcome these by force, they meet with crushing defeats. So it turned out on this occasion, and the process will no doubt continue until they correct these preconceptions about daring and force, which make them believe that they can sail and travel whenever they choose at any season of the year.

38. When the Carthaginians learned of the destruction of the Roman fleet, they decided that they were now a match for their enemies both on land, in the light of their recent success, and at sea, because of this disaster, and so they took heart and began to

1. By this Polybius means sailing anti-clockwise so as to round Cape Pachynus at the south-eastern extremity of Sicily. In fact the Roman commanders had no choice, given the ancient practice of hugging the coast, since the western ports were in Carthaginian hands.

2. 'Rising' signifies the date when the star becomes visible on the eastern horizon, before the rising sun makes it disappear. The rising of Orion is conjectured to have been on 4 July, that of Sirius on 28 July.

make more ambitious military and naval preparations. They at once ordered Hasdrubal to Sicily, and placed under his command not only the troops they had previously mobilized but also a force which had joined them from Heracleia, together with 140 elephants. After they had sent him on his way, they began to fit out 200 ships and to make all the other preparations necessary for a naval expedition. Hasdrubal, having safely made the crossing to Lilybaeum, at once began to train the elephants and the rest of his troops, and made it plain that he intended to challenge the Romans for the possession of the open country.

When the Romans learned the full extent of the catastrophe from the survivors, they took the news greatly to heart, but they were determined that on no account would they surrender, and so they resolved to lay down yet another 220 ships. The work was finished in three months, an almost incredible feat, and as soon as the new consuls Aulus Atilius and Gnaeus Cornelius had completed the fitting-out of the fleet, they once more put to sea.[1] As they passed through the straits they were joined at Messana by those vessels of the original fleet which had escaped shipwreck. Then, with a combined force of 300 sail, they descended on Panormus, the strongest city in the Carthaginian province of Sicily, and began an assault on it. They erected siege-works at two separate points, and after making the necessary preparations brought up their battering rams. The tower which stood by the sea shore was easily demolished, the soldiers forced an entry through the breach, and the quarter known as the New Town was carried by storm. Soon afterwards, since this success threatened the so-called Old Town, the inhabitants quickly surrendered it. The consuls took possession of the city, and after posting a garrison sailed back to Rome.

39. At the beginning of the summer of the following year[2] the new consuls Gnaeus Servilius and Gaius Sempronius again put to sea with their whole fleet, and after touching at Sicily crossed over to Africa. They sailed along the coast, landed at a number of places where they accomplished nothing of importance, and reached the legendary island of the Lotus Eaters, which is named Meninx and is not far from the Lesser Syrtes. Here, because of their ignorance of the coastal waters, they ran upon some shoals; the tide then

1. In the summer of 254 B.C.   2. 253 B.C.

retreated, the ships went aground and the whole fleet was in a position of great danger. However, after a while the tide unexpectedly flowed back, and by throwing overboard all their heavy belongings they succeeded with difficulty in lightening the ships. After this lucky deliverance their return voyage was more like an escape from disaster than anything else. They reached Sicily, and after rounding the promontory of Lilybaeum anchored at Panormus. But then, as they shaped their course for Rome, they rashly ventured across the open sea and once more encountered such a terrible storm that they lost 150 ships.

At this point the Roman government, in spite of their habitual and inflexible determination to succeed in all their undertakings, were compelled in view of the gigantic scale and the frequency of the disasters they had suffered to abandon the idea of building yet another fleet. They decided to rely exclusively upon their land forces, dispatched an army under the command of the consuls Lucius Caecilius and Gaius Furius, and manned no more than sixty ships, to serve as supply vessels for the legions. These reverses suffered by the Romans greatly improved the prospects of the Carthaginians. They now held unchallenged command of the sea, since the Romans had virtually withdrawn from it, and they had high hopes of their army. These expectations were not unfounded, for the reports of Xanthippus' victory in Africa had in due course reached the Romans, and they had then learned that the elephants had broken their line and killed the greater part of their troops. The news created such terror of these animals that for the next two years the Romans, although in the neighbourhood of Lilybaeum or Selinus they were often drawn up no more than five or six furlongs from the enemy, never dared to launch an attack; in fact they would not even descend to level ground to meet the enemy's infantry, so much did they dread a charge by the elephants. During this period their only successful actions were the reducing of the towns of Therma and Lipara by siege, and in these operations they clung to mountainous country and to ground that was difficult to cross. The Roman government could not fail to notice the timidity and lack of spirit which now prevailed in the army, and in the end they changed their minds and decided to try their fortunes once again at sea. Accordingly during the consulship of Gaius Atilius and

Lucius Manlius they built fifty ships, and threw every effort into the task of enrolling sailors and assembling a fleet.

40. Meanwhile Hasdrubal, the Carthaginian commander-in-chief, had noticed the lack of spirit which the Romans had shown in their encounters with the enemy. He discovered that one of the consuls had returned to Italy taking half the Roman army in Sicily with him, while Caecilius had been left at Panormus with the remainder to protect the corn crops of the allies, for the harvesting season was now at its height:[1] Hasdrubal therefore marched out his troops from Lilybaeum and pitched camp on the border of the territory of Panormus. Caecilius noticed Hasdrubal's evident confidence, and kept his troops inside the gates in the hope of luring him into making an attack. When Hasdrubal saw this, he was all the more encouraged, as he concluded that Caecilius was afraid to come out, so he boldly pressed on with his whole force and descended through the pass into the territory of Panormus. Caecilius continued to follow his plan and allowed Hasdrubal to ravage the crops right up to the walls, until he had drawn his opponent forward to cross the river which flows in front of the town. As soon as the Carthaginians had got their elephants and the rest of their army across, he began to harass them with light-armed troops until he had compelled them to deploy their whole force. Then, as he saw that his tactics were taking effect, he stationed some of his light-armed troops before the wall and the trench in front of the city. Their orders were to discharge their missiles against the elephants once they came within range; next, as they were driven back, they were to take refuge in the trench, and then again dart out and shoot at any elephants which charged them. He also arranged that the camp-followers drawn from the civil population should bring the missiles from the market-place and stack them at the foot of the wall; at the same time he himself with his maniples took up position at the gate which faced the enemy's left wing and sent frequent reinforcements to support the skirmishers.

As the action between the Carthaginians and the light-armed troops became more general, the drivers of the elephants were fired with the impulse to show off their prowess to Hasdrubal. They

1. The date of the ensuing battle was June 250 B.C.

were anxious to play the leading part in the victory, and so, charging the front ranks of the light-armed troops, they easily drove them back and pursued them to the trench. But when the elephants attacked this obstacle, they were at once wounded by the archers who were shooting at them from the wall, while at the same time volleys of spears and javelins were poured upon them from the fresh troops who were drawn up in front of the trench. The animals found themselves pierced and riddled with missiles and before long they stampeded. They turned on their own troops, trampling and killing them, breaking their ranks, and throwing them into utter confusion. As soon as Caecilius saw this he led out his force in a vigorous charge, attacking the enemy on the flank. His troops were fresh and well disciplined, the Carthaginians in disorder; the result was that he routed the enemy, killed many men and drove back the rest in headlong flight. He captured ten elephants with their Indian drivers and after the battle he succeeded in rounding up the remainder, who had thrown their mahouts, and capturing them all. By achieving this success it was generally agreed that he was responsible for restoring to the Roman troops the will to fight and to regain control of the open country.

41. When the news of this victory was received at Rome the people were overjoyed, not so much because of the reverse the enemy had suffered in the loss of their elephants, as because of the confidence their own troops had gained in overcoming them. The Romans were thus again encouraged to send out the consuls to campaign with a fleet and a naval force in accordance with their original plan, for they were anxious to use every means in their power to finish the war. When all the necessary preparations had been made, the consuls set sail for Sicily with a fleet of 200.[1] It was by then the fourteenth year of the war.[2] They dropped anchor off Lilybaeum, and joining forces with the army proceeded to blockade the city, for they calculated that with this port in their hands it would be easy to carry the war into Africa. On this point at least the Carthaginian leaders were of the same mind as the Romans and held a similar view of the importance of Lilybaeum. They therefore abandoned all other operations, concentrated their whole

1. Modern estimates give a figure of 120.
2. 250 B.C.

effort upon the relief of the city, and prepared themselves to accept any risk or sacrifice to this end; they knew that if it fell, no military base would be left to them in Sicily, since all the rest of the island except for Drepana was now in Roman hands.

The account I shall give of this campaign requires some knowledge of the topography of the island, and so I shall now try to give a brief explanation of the geographical position and the special advantages of the places with which we are concerned.

42. Sicily occupies a position in relation to Italy and her southern extremity similar to that of the Peloponnese towards the rest of Greece. The difference is that the first is an island, while the second is a peninsula, so that the communication with the former is by sea and with the latter by land. The shape of Sicily is a triangle, the points of each of the three angles taking the form of a cape. The cape which looks southwards and projects into the Sicilian Sea is called Pachynus. The northerly cape forms the western boundary of the Strait of Messana; the distance between it and the Italian coast is about a mile and a half, and it is called Pelorias. The third cape is turned towards Africa itself and is well situated as a base for attacking the promontories that protect Carthage, from which it is about 115 miles distant. This cape faces south-west, separates the Libyan from the Sardinian Sea and is named Lilybaeum; on it stands the city of the same name, to which the Romans were now laying siege. Lilybaeum is strongly protected not only by its walls and by the deep moat which encircles it,[1] but also by the lagoons which lie on the seaward side; it is a task demanding great skill and much practice to find the channel through these into the harbour.

The Romans built two camps, one on each side of the town, and fortified the space between them with a ditch, a palisade and a wall. They then began to move forward siege-works against the tower which was nearest to the sea on the Libyan side. They advanced slowly, adding a little at a time to their structures, and in this way they managed to extend their siege-works both forwards and sideways until they had demolished the six towers which adjoined the seaward one; at the same time they attacked all the other towers at

1. According to Diodorus, *History*, XXIV.I.2, this was ninety feet wide and sixty feet deep.

once with battering rams. By this time the siege was being pressed with tremendous energy and at an alarming speed. Each day saw some of the towers being shaken or reduced to rubble, while the Roman siege-works were pushed further and further towards the centre of the city. The result was that a mood of confusion and terror descended upon the whole besieged population, although there was a garrison of about 10,000 mercenaries[1] in the town. However, their general, Himilco, resisted the Romans by every means that was in his power, and by building a new wall behind the demolished towers and counter-mining the enemy's siege-works he caused them great difficulties. Every day he would make a sortie, attack the siege-engines and try to set them on fire; these counter-attacks were launched both by day and by night, and were pressed home with such bitter fighting that at times the losses were heavier than would normally be suffered in a pitched battle.

43. At about this time some of the senior officers of the mercenary force had discussed among themselves a plan to hand over the city to the Romans. They were convinced that the men under their orders would obey them, and so they stole out of the city by night to the Roman camp and put their proposals for surrender to the consul. Now on an earlier occasion the mercenaries of Syracuse had hatched a plot to betray the citizens of Agrigentum, but they had been saved by an Achaean named Alexon, and now again this man was the first to discover the conspiracy, which he reported to the Carthaginian commander. As soon as Himilco heard this, he at once summoned the remaining officers and appealed to them with all the eloquence he could command. He promised them lavish rewards and favours if they would stand by their engagement to him and not go over to those who had already left the city. The officers responded enthusiastically to his words, whereupon he ordered them to return at once to their men. He sent with them Hannibal, the son of the Hannibal who had been executed in Sardinia, to join the Celtic contingent, choosing this officer because the Celts had served under him and knew him well. Alexon was assigned to the other division of mercenaries, because he was both liked and trusted by them. The officers then called the whole mercenary force together and made an appeal to them.

1. It consisted of Celts and Greeks.

They pledged their word that every man would receive the reward the Carthaginian commander had promised, and in the end they easily prevailed upon the troops to remain loyal. The result was that when the officers who had gone over to the enemy approached the walls openly and tried to gain a hearing and explain the promises offered by the Romans, not only did they fail to make any impression, but the men would not even listen to them and drove them away from the walls with volleys of stones and other missiles. In this way the Carthaginians came very near to losing everything they had in Lilybaeum through the treachery of their mercenaries, and it was that same Alexon – whose loyalty had previously saved not only the territory and the city of the Agrigentines but also their constitution and their freedom – who was now responsible for rescuing the Carthaginians from complete disaster.

44. Meanwhile the Carthaginian authorities at home were quite unaware of these events. But they had in any case to consider the needs of a besieged city, and so they manned fifty ships, filled them with troops, and after giving instructions suitable to the operation in hand, dispatched them at once under the command of Hannibal, the son of Hamilcar, who was both a trierarch and the trusted colleague of Adherbal.[1] Hannibal's orders were that he should on no account delay but should seize the first opportunity to make a bold attempt at relieving the beleaguered city. Accordingly he put to sea with 10,000 troops on board, anchored off the Aegates Islands which lie between Lilybaeum and Carthage, and there waited for favourable weather. As soon as he had a good breeze from astern he hoisted all sail and running before the wind made straight for the mouth of the harbour, with his men drawn up on the decks armed and ready for action. The Romans were taken unawares by the sudden appearance of his fleet, and they were also afraid of being swept by the force of the wind into their enemies' harbour in the midst of a hostile force, and so they made no attempt to bar the entry of the relieving fleet; instead they remained standing out at sea, still half lost in amazement at the audacity of the Carthaginians.

1. It seems probable that Adherbal was the commander of the expedition and that he went on to Drepana (see p. 91), leaving Hannibal at the Aegates Islands to relieve Lilybaeum.

Meanwhile the whole population of Lilybaeum had crowded on to the walls. They were in an agony of anxiety for the outcome, yet at the same time overjoyed at the unexpected prospect of rescue; then, as the fleet sailed into the harbour they greeted it with loud cheers and clapping of their hands. Then Hannibal, having brought off this daring and risky feat of entering the harbour, dropped anchor and safely disembarked his troops. As for the citizens, they were overjoyed not so much at the fact that relief had arrived – although this did much to revive their hopes and increase their strength – as that the Romans had not dared to prevent the Carthaginians from sailing in.

45. Himilco, the commander of the garrison, saw that his whole force was now full of confidence and eager for action: the original garrison because of the presence of reinforcements, and the new arrivals because they were still unaware of the dangers that threatened them. He was anxious to take advantage of this fresh spirit which inspired both divisions of his army, and make another attempt to fire the enemy's siege-works. Accordingly, he paraded the whole army and appealed to them with a speech that matched the mood of the occasion. He stirred his listeners to a high pitch of enthusiasm by promising generous bounties to soldiers who performed individual acts of bravery, and he assured them that the whole army would be treated with favour and handsomely rewarded by the Carthaginian government. The troops applauded him as one man, and there were loud shouts that he should delay no longer but lead them straight into action. Himilco showed his pleasure at their response, and praised their spirit; then he dismissed them, ordering them to take an early rest and await their officers' instructions. Soon afterwards he sent for the commanders, assigned to each of them his place in the assault, and then gave out the password and the exact time for the attack. He ordered all the officers to have their units at full strength and in the assault positions at the morning watch.

His orders were carried out to the letter, and at first light he led out his troops and attacked the siege-works at several places simultaneously. The Romans had anticipated his intention, and were neither unprepared nor slow to respond. They instantly ran to defend the threatened points and resisted the enemy strongly.

In a short while the fighting became general and a desperate battle developed along the whole length of the walls, for the besieged had thrown 20,000 men [1] into the attack, and the Romans were even more numerous. The battle had been joined in an irregular fashion, with neither side taking up a strict formation, but each man using his weapons as his judgement directed; this made the struggle fiercer still, for the reason that even with such large numbers engaged, the fighting was carried out man against man or rank against rank, so that something of the spirit of single combat pervaded the whole battlefield. But it was above all round the siege-works that the noise of the battle was loudest and the action the hottest. Here was the heart of the fighting, since it was the prime task of the attackers to drive the enemy from the works and that of the defenders to hold them, and each side resisted with the utmost fury and determination, the former straining every nerve to dislodge their opponents, while the latter clung indomitably to their positions; in the end both sides fought themselves to a standstill and perished on the ground where they had first stood. At the same time other combatants mingled with the fighting men, bringing up torch-wood, tow and firebrands, and these auxiliaries attacked the siege-engines from every side, hurling their incendiary missiles with such daring that the Romans, who were unable to contain this assault, found themselves in a situation of great danger. But at this point the Carthaginian commander, recognizing that he was suffering heavy losses and had still not achieved his objective of carrying the siege-works by storm, ordered his trumpeters to sound the retreat. The Romans had come very near to losing their entire siege-train, but in the end they held their ground and remained in possession of the works.

46. As for Hannibal, he sailed out with his ships after the battle, unobserved by the enemy and while it was still dark, and made for Drepana to join the Carthaginian admiral Adherbal. Drepana is about fifteen miles from Lilybaeum and because of its convenient situation and the advantages of its harbour, the Carthaginians had always paid great attention to its defence.

1. This figure implies that the entire Carthaginian force was engaged, i.e. the original garrison of 10,000 (see p. 88) plus Hannibal's troops of the same number.

The Carthaginian government was anxious to find out what was happening at Lilybaeum, but had no means of receiving news, since their own forces were shut up in the town and the Romans were maintaining a strict blockade. Accordingly one of their leading citizens, a certain Hannibal who was nicknamed 'The Rhodian', volunteered to sail into Lilybaeum and make a full report at first hand. The authorities were very willing to listen to his proposal, but doubted whether he could succeed, since the Roman ships were moored outside the entrance to the port. However, Hannibal fitted out his own vessel, set sail and crossed to one of the islands lying off Lilybaeum. The next day he found the wind in the right quarter, and sailed straight through at about 10 o'clock in the morning in full view of the enemy, who were dumbfounded at his effrontery. On the following day Hannibal lost no time in making his ship ready to return. But meanwhile the Roman commander, who was determined to guard the harbour entrance more carefully, had fitted out overnight a patrol of ten of his fastest ships, while he himself watched from the land, where the whole army was drawn up waiting to see what would happen. The ten ships were lined up as close to the shoals as they could approach on either side of the harbour mouth; there they floated, their oars stretched out like wings, ready to strike the water, all prepared to run down and capture the ship which was about to sail out. 'The Rhodian' for his part got his ship under way in full view of the enemy, and so far surpassed the Romans both in speed and in the audacity of his manoeuvring, that he not only brought out his ship and its crew unscathed leaving his enemy standing, but then sailing a little way ahead he hove to and waited, without shipping his oars, as if to challenge the Romans. Then, as nobody ventured to advance and attack him because of the speed of his rowing, he made off, having successfully defied the entire Roman fleet with his single ship. After this he several times repeated the same exploit and performed a service that was of great value both to the government and the besieged city. He kept the Carthaginian authorities continually informed of the most urgent news and raised the spirits of the defenders, while at the same time his audacity served to dishearten the Romans.

47. The factor which contributed most to Hannibal's confidence

in these attempts was that he had accurately plotted from experience the course he should steer through the shallows, and discovered the landmarks for it. As soon as he had crossed the open sea and arrived in sight of the harbour, he would steer as though he were coming from Italy, keeping the seaward tower on his bows, so that it covered the whole line of the city's towers in the direction of Africa. It is only by steering along this course that a vessel sailing with the wind astern can make the mouth of the harbour. This display of daring on the part of 'the Rhodian' encouraged several others who had local knowledge of the coast to follow his example; these efforts were particularly galling to the Romans, who tried to counter them by filling up the mouth of the harbour. Most of their efforts in this direction failed completely: the sea was too deep at this point, and none of the material which they threw down would either stay in its place or hold together as a solid mass. The rubble, as they emptied it in, would be swept away and scattered by the waves and by the force of the current before it could reach the bottom. However, at one place where the sea-bed was shallow, they succeeded after immense labour in piling up a mound, and here a quadrireme ran aground one night as it was leaving the harbour and fell into the Romans' hands. The vessel was of exceptionally fine construction, and the Romans, after taking possession and manning her with a picked crew, kept a special watch for blockade runners and above all for 'the Rhodian'. It so happened that he had entered the harbour that very night, and later sailed out in his usual, deliberately open fashion. Then, when he saw the quadrireme put to sea at the same time, he recognized her and took fright. At first he made a spurt in an effort to pull away, but when he found that he was being overtaken by the greater rowing power of his pursuers, he was forced at last to turn and engage. When it came to boarding, his crew were no match for the marines, who were superior in numbers and were all picked men, and he was taken prisoner. The Romans found when they took possession of her that his ship was likewise exceptionally well-constructed; they fitted her out for these special duties, and thus put an end to the operations of all those who were daring enough to try to run the blockade of Lilybaeum.

48. Meanwhile the besieged garrison were still hard at work

building counter-fortifications, although they had abandoned hope of damaging or destroying the enemy's siege-engines. But while these efforts were still in progress, a steady wind arose, which blew with such violence and strength on the apparatus for moving the engines forward that it shook loose the penthouses[1] from their foundations and swept away the wooden towers which had been erected to cover them. As the gale continued, it occurred to some of the Greek mercenaries that this was a perfect opportunity to destroy the siege-works, and they explained their plan to the commander of the garrison. The Carthaginian seized upon the idea, and lost no time in making all the necessary preparations. The younger soldiers of the garrison gathered at three separate points and there threw lighted brands on to the siege-works. The whole apparatus was so old that it was highly inflammable, and with the strong wind blowing the conflagration directly against the towers and the siege-engines the flames took hold swiftly and with immediate effect, while the efforts of the Romans to check the blaze and save the works were made correspondingly difficult, in fact almost impossible. The would-be rescuers were so overwhelmed by the sudden outbreak that they could neither grasp nor properly see what was happening. They had to face flames, sparks, and dense clouds of smoke, which blew into their faces and blinded them; many of them were overcome by the fumes and collapsed, unable to come near enough to fight the fire. At the same time all the factors which hindered the Romans in their efforts to control the blaze, combined for the reasons I have mentioned to help the incendiaries. Anything which could obscure the vision or injure the Romans was blown towards them or thrust into their faces; but the defenders had a clear view of the space immediately in front of them, and so could take careful aim with the missiles which they discharged at the rescuers as they ran up, or with the brands which they hurled to destroy the works, and whatever they discharged at either target was made more destructive by the force of the wind behind. In the end the destruction was so complete that the very foundations of the towers and the beams of the battering rams were rendered useless by the flames. After this

1. These were sheds with sloping roofs, which protected the besiegers against missiles from above.

catastrophe the Romans abandoned the attempt to capture the town by means of siege-works. Instead they invested the place by digging a moat and building a stockade around it. At the same time they fortified their own camp with a surrounding wall and left further developments to time. For their part, the garrison of Lilybaeum re-built the sections of their walls which had been destroyed, and settled down in good heart to await the outcome of the siege.

49. The news duly reached Rome and was later confirmed from other quarters that the greater number of the crews of the fleet had lost their lives either through the fire or in the siege operations. The government made haste to enlist more sailors, and when they had recruited some 10,000, they sent them to Sicily; the men were ferried over the Straits of Messana, and from there they marched to the camp. Soon after their arrival the consul Publius Claudius Pulcher summoned a meeting of the military tribunes and told his audience that the time was ripe for the whole fleet to attack the Carthaginian base at Drepana. Adherbal, who was in command there, knew nothing, he explained, of the arrival of the fresh crews, and was convinced that the Roman fleet was incapable of putting to sea because of the losses of men it had suffered during the siege. The tribunes enthusiastically supported his plan, whereupon he at once embarked both the men who had already served in the fleet and the new arrivals. The marines were selected from the best troops in the army, who readily volunteered for the expedition, since the voyage was only a short one, and there were excellent prospects of picking up booty at the end of it.

After completing these preparations he put to sea unnoticed by the enemy at the hour of midnight, and for the first part of his voyage he sailed in close formation with the coast of Sicily on his starboard bow. By daybreak the leading ships of his fleet were sighted advancing on Drepana, and at first Adherbal was thoroughly disconcerted, as their appearance came as a complete surprise. But he quickly recovered his self-possession, grasped the meaning of his adversary's approach, and at once determined that he would make every effort and risk any danger rather than allow his force to be shut up by the blockade which now threatened him. He therefore immediately mustered his sailors on the beach and sent out a proclamation to summon the mercenary troops from the city. When his force was assembled, he addressed them and strove to impress on their minds in a few words what an excellent chance of victory they would have if they risked a battle now, and what a certain prospect of hardship if they shrank from it and allowed themselves to be besieged. His men soon made it clear that they still possessed the spirit to fight at sea and they urged him with shouts of approval to lead them into action without delay. Adherbal thanked them for their response and praised their courage, then he ordered them to embark immediately, keep their eyes fixed on his ship, and follow in her wake. Once he had made these instructions clear, he got under way with all speed and led his fleet out to sea, steering close to the rocks on the opposite side of the harbour to that by which the Romans were entering it.

50. Pulcher, the Roman commander, had assumed that the enemy would be so dismayed by his arrival that they would avoid an action; but when he saw that on the contrary the Carthaginians were determined to fight and that some of his own vessels were by now inside the harbour, others in the entrance, and others still approaching it, he gave orders for the whole fleet to put about and make for the open sea. Because of the abruptness of the turn, the result of this manoeuvre was to cause some of the ships inside the harbour to foul those which were entering it; it also created great confusion among the crews, and a number of vessels had the blades of their oars snapped as they collided with one another. However, as soon as the ships had cleared the harbour, the captains were able to bring them into line and drew them up near the shore with their bows facing the enemy. Pulcher himself had originally sailed in the rear of the fleet, but now while the manoeuvre was still in progress he steered for the open sea, and took up position on the extreme left wing. At the same time Adherbal had succeeded in outflanking the Romans' left with five ships that were fitted with rams, and manoeuvred his own vessel into a position opposite the enemy and facing the shore. As each of the other four joined him, he ordered them through his staff officers to take station alongside him, until all five were in line facing the enemy. When they all presented a united front, he gave the agreed signal to advance and bore down in line upon the Roman ships, which were still close

inshore, waiting to be joined by their comrades who were returning from the harbour. This position near the shore proved a great
disadvantage to them in the action which followed.

51. As the two fleets drew closer the battle signals were hoisted
on the flagships of both admirals, and the vessels engaged. At first
the fighting was evenly balanced, since both sides had the pick of
their land troops serving as marines. Gradually, however, the many
advantages with which the Carthaginians had commenced the
action began to tell in their favour. The construction of their ships
and the superior training of their rowers made them much faster
than the Romans, and the position they had chosen also helped
them, since they had deployed their line in the open sea. This meant
that if any of their ships were hard-pressed by the enemy, they
could use their superior speed to retire in safety to open water.
There they could put about and attack the foremost of their
pursuers, either working round astern of them, or attacking them
from the beam; the Romans were then obliged to turn, and were
at once in difficulties because of the weight of their hulls and the
inexperience of their rowers, whereupon the Carthaginians often
rammed and sank many of them. If any of the Carthaginian ships
were in danger, they could come to one another's rescue with no
risk, since they could sail in open water and unmolested past the
sterns of their own line. For the Romans the situation was exactly
the opposite. Those who were in difficulties were too close to the
land to have any room to retire, so that their ships, if they were
hard-pressed by the enemy in front, either ran on to the shallows
stern foremost, or made for the shore and went aground. One of
the most effective manoeuvres in sea battles, that of sailing through
the enemy's line and reappearing astern of ships which are already
engaged with others, was ruled out for the Romans because of the
weight of their vessels and the inferior training of their crews.
And unlike the Carthaginians they could not sail round behind
their own line to help their comrades, because they were hemmed
in so close to the shore that there was no space left for the passage
of a ship that wished to come to the rescue. This, then, was the
adverse situation in which the Roman fleet found itself in every
part of the battle, with some ships sticking fast in the shallows
and others running aground, and when the Roman consul saw

what was happening he took to flight. He made his way out on the port side of the fleet, hugging the shore and accompanied by some thirty of the ships, which happened to be the nearest to him. The remaining ships of the fleet, which numbered ninety-three, were all captured by the Carthaginians together with their crews, except for those who ran their vessels ashore and managed to escape.

52. As a result of this action Adherbal won himself a high reputation at Carthage, since it was his foresight and daring which were credited with the success. Pulcher, on the other hand, fell into disgrace among the Romans and he was attacked on all sides for his conduct of the battle. It was felt that he had acted without due caution or judgement, and that so far as it lay within the power of one man he had brought a great disaster upon Rome. He was therefore put on trial, condemned, heavily fined and barely escaped the death penalty.

Yet despite this catastrophe such was the determination of the Romans to win the war that they in no way slackened the effort that was now required, but put in hand all the necessary measures to continue the campaign. It was now the time for the elections, and as soon as the new consuls had been appointed they sent one of them, Lucius Junius Pullus,[1] to take charge of a consignment of corn for the besiegers of Lilybaeum together with the provisions and stores required by the army, and manned sixty warships to escort the convoy. On arriving at Messana, Pullus added to his fleet a number of ships which had come from Lilybaeum and others from elsewhere in Sicily, and from there coasted with all speed to Syracuse; he now had a fleet of 120 warships to escort the 800 transports which were carrying the supplies. There he handed over to the quaestors half the transports and a number of warships and sent them ahead, as he was anxious that the supplies should be delivered to the army without delay. He himself remained at Syracuse waiting for the ships which had still to arrive from Messana and collecting further supplies of corn from Rome's allies inland.

53. Meanwhile Adherbal had sent the prisoners taken in the naval battle and the captured warships to Carthage. He then placed his colleague Carthalo in command of a fleet of thirty vessels in addition

1. Polybius' dating is incorrect. Pullus was the colleague of Publius Claudius Pulcher in 249, not his successor in 248.

to the seventy which he had brought to Drepana, and dispatched him with orders to make a surprise attack on the Roman fleet which was anchored off Lilybaeum, capture all he could, and set fire to the rest. Carthalo followed these orders, and carried out his attack at dawn; he set fire to some of the ships and had begun to tow away others, by which time his action had caused a tremendous commotion in the Roman camp. Then, as the soldiers rushed to rescue the ships, Himilco, who was on the watch inside Lilybaeum, was aroused by the noise. As day was now beginning to break, he could see what was happening, and sent out his mercenaries to attack the Romans from the landward side. The Romans were now threatened from every quarter and found themselves in no ordinary difficulty. However, the Carthaginian admiral, after towing away a few ships and breaking up others, soon afterwards left Lilybaeum; he then coasted along for some distance in the direction of Heracleia and there remained on the watch, since his real intention was to intercept the transports which were on their way to supply the army. When his look-outs reported that a large convoy of vessels of every variety was approaching and was already close at hand, he stood out to sea and sailed to meet them, for the success he had just gained had made him feel contemptuous towards the Romans, and he now felt eager to engage. In the same way the approach of the Carthaginian fleet was reported to the quaestors who had been sent on in advance from Syracuse by the light reconnaissance craft which normally cruise ahead of the fleet. As they did not reckon themselves strong enough to risk a battle at sea, they anchored off a small fortified town which was subject to the Romans; this place possessed no proper harbour, but had roadsteads enclosed by headlands which ran out from the coast and afforded some shelter. Here they disembarked, set up a number of catapults and mangonels which they obtained from the fort, and awaited the enemy's approach. The Carthaginians, when they neared the town, at first conceived the plan of blockading the enemy, as they assumed that the Romans would be frightened into withdrawing behind the defences and that they could then capture the ships without opposition. However, these hopes were disappointed, the Romans put up a determined resistance, and as the situation of the place presented them with a number of difficulties they towed away a few of the ships which were laden with stores, sailed to a nearby river where they anchored, and lay in wait for the enemy to resume their voyage.

54. Meanwhile Pullus, the consul who had stayed behind in Syracuse, completed his business there, put to sea, and rounded Cape Pachynus on his way to Lilybaeum; all this time he knew nothing of what had happened to his advance force. The Carthaginian look-outs then once more reported to their commander that the enemy were in sight, whereupon the admiral put to sea and made with all speed towards the main body, as he was anxious to engage them as far away as possible from their comrades. Meanwhile Pullus had sighted the Carthaginian fleet from a considerable distance and had taken note of its strength; he did not dare to offer battle, but by then they were too close for him to escape. He therefore altered course, put in near a rock-bound and altogether dangerous part of the coast, and anchored there, for he thought it better to run any risk from the weather rather than to allow his entire force and its ships to fall into the enemy's hands. The Carthaginian admiral saw what he had done, and decided that he would not venture to approach such a dangerous shore; instead he gained the shelter of a nearby cape, anchored off it and remained on the alert between the two Roman fleets, keeping both under observation. Presently the weather worsened and it became clear that a heavy gale was blowing up from the open sea; at this the Carthaginian pilots, who from their familiarity with the locality and the weather signs could predict what was likely to happen, persuaded Carthalo to avoid the storm by rounding Cape Pachynus. He had the sense to listen to them, and after skirting the cape with great toil and difficulty, they were able to anchor in safety. The two Roman fleets, however, were caught by the storm off a stretch of coast which offered no shelter whatever and were annihilated, the destruction being so complete that not even one of the wrecks could be salvaged. In this totally unforeseen fashion, then, the Romans had both of their fleets put out of action.

55. The destruction of the Roman fleet put fresh heart into the Carthaginians and caused their hopes to revive once more. The Romans, on the other hand, although they had met with various partial misfortunes before, had never suffered such a total disaster.

The result was that they gave up any attempt to carry on naval operations and confined themselves to holding their positions ashore, while the Carthaginians not only enjoyed the complete mastery of the sea [1] but had by no means abandoned hope of winning back their possessions on land. Yet, although both the Roman people and their army at Lilybaeum were deeply disheartened by these reverses, they persisted in their determination to carry on the siege; the government continued without hesitation to send supplies by land, and the troops kept up as close a blockade as they could. After the wreck of the fleet the consul Pullus returned to the army and, tormented though he was by the catastrophe, he at once set himself to devise some new and effective venture to retrieve as best he could the ground that had been lost. He seized the first vestige of an opportunity that came his way by surprising and taking possession of Eryx, where he occupied both the town and the temple of Venus.

Eryx is a mountain [2] near the coast on the side of Sicily which faces Italy; it lies between Panormus and Drepana, but is closer to the latter, indeed it adjoins the boundaries of the city and is by far the largest mountain in Italy after Etna. On its flat summit stands the shrine of Venus Erycina, [3] which is without doubt the richest and most splendid of all the temples in Sicily. The city is spread out along the slopes below the crest, and the approach to it is both long and steep on every side. Pullus installed a garrison on the summit and also at the foot of the road which leads to Drepana. He kept a strict guard on both points, but especially on the latter, since he believed that by this means he could secure possession not only of the city of Eryx but of the whole mountain.

56. After this the Carthaginians appointed Hamilcar Barca as their commander and placed him in charge of naval operations. He began by ravaging the Italian coast in the eighteenth year of

1. The Carthaginians failed, however, to exploit this superiority, perhaps because their resources were weakened by the civil war in Africa.

2. The modern Erice near Trapani. It is some 2,250 feet high, and so neither the highest nor the largest mountain after Etna.

3. The temple was very ancient and maintained a system of temple prostitution which suggests an Eastern origin. The Phoenicians identified the goddess with Astarte; Roman legend attributed the foundation of the shrine of Venus to Aeneas.

the war. Then after devastating the territory of Locri[1] and the Brutti, he crossed to Sicily and descended with his whole fleet on the territory of Panormus. Here he took possession of the stronghold near Hercte[2] – both the hill and the fortress bear the same name. It is situated on the coast between Eryx and Panormus and was considered to possess the best situation in the whole region on which to establish a well-protected and permanent camp. The place consists of a hill, which rises to a considerable height from the surrounding plain, with steep slopes on every side. The top measures over twelve miles in circumference and the soil of this plateau provides good pasture and is also suitable for agriculture; it is well-protected against the sharp sea winds and entirely free of dangerous animals. Both to seaward and on the side facing inland the slopes are sheer and inaccessible; the other sides of the plateau require only a little work to fortify, and in the centre there is a knoll which serves both as an acropolis and as an observation post that provides an excellent view over the surrounding country. Hercte also commands a harbour, which is well-placed to receive ships sailing to Italy from Drepana or from Lilybaeum, and it possesses an abundant supply of water. There are only three approaches to the hill, two from the landward side and one from the sea, and all of them are difficult. Here, then, Hamilcar established his base, but in choosing it he was running great risks:[3] there was no city in the vicinity on which he could rely as an ally, and he had no prospect of help from elsewhere, but had planted himself in his enemies' midst. On the other hand his presence constituted a serious threat to the Romans, and eventually involved them in a whole series of difficulties and trials of strength. Before long he was to sail with his fleet from this port and ravage the coast of Italy as far as Cumae. Then, after the Romans had established a camp against him in front of Panormus and a little over half a mile from his own position, he harassed them by keeping up a variety of attacks and offensive patrols by land over a period of almost three years. How-

1. On the south-east coast of Bruttium, the modern Calabria.

2. Polybius' description of Hercte as lying between Panormus and Eryx is inaccurate; modern scholars identify the hill with the present Monte Castellaccio, some seven miles north-west of Palermo.

3. Hamilcar's arrival marks a new and more active phase in the war, his seizure of Hercte being a counterstroke to the Roman occupation of Eryx.

ever it is impossible for me to describe these operations in detail here.

57. Hamilcar's campaign in Sicily against the Romans might be compared to a boxing match in which two champions, both in perfect training and both distinguished for their courage, meet to fight for a prize. As the contest develops and the two exchange blow after blow, without a moment's pause, it is out of the question either for the combatants or the spectators to anticipate or to keep count of every attack and every hit; nevertheless it is possible from the general activity of the two and from the determination which they display to obtain a sufficiently clear impression of their skill, their strength and their courage. So it was with these two commanders. The various causes which prompted their daily operations and the tactical details of these are far too numerous for any writer to describe, and would prove both tedious and unprofitable to read, since every day brought its ambushes on the one side or the other, and its sorties and counter-attacks. But a general summing-up of the leadership of the two men and of the results of their rival efforts may provide a clearer picture of the facts. Certainly no stratagems were left untried – whether orthodox tactics, ruses occasioned by some local factor or pressure of circumstances, or the kind of operation which is inspired by a forceful and adventurous initiative. However, there were several reasons why the campaign could not be brought to a decisive issue.

In the first place, the forces on either side were equally matched; secondly their respective entrenchments were so strongly fortified as to be virtually impregnable; and lastly the two camps were pitched only a very small distance apart from one another. This was the main reason why the two armies, although they clashed repeatedly at certain places, never ventured a decisive battle. The losses in these actions were confined to the men who fell in hand-to-hand fighting. The troops who gave ground were accustomed to getting themselves immediately out of trouble by retiring behind their defences, from which they would later sally forth and resume the fighting.

58. But Fortune, like a good umpire[1] in the games, suddenly brought about an unexpected change in the contest: the theatre

1. i.e. in order to obtain a decision between two equally matched opponents.

of action was shifted from the locality I have just described, and confined to a narrower field, which rendered the struggle even more desperate. The Romans, as I have mentioned, occupied the mountain of Eryx with garrisons posted both on the heights and at the foot of the slope, but Hamilcar managed to capture the town which lay between these positions. The Romans who were holding the crest thus found themselves trapped, but endured the hardships and dangers of the ensuing siege with extraordinary courage. At the same time the Carthaginians, hemmed in between two Roman forces, also held out with a determination which almost passes belief; their supplies could only be brought up with great difficulty since they held only one outlet to the sea and a single road which connected it with their position. Here again both sides employed every resource, every stratagem and every effort that the siege demanded, endured every kind of hardship, and resorted both to pitched battles and every other variety of fighting. In the end, the contest was left drawn; this did not mean, however, that both sides were completely exhausted or demoralized, as Fabius Pictor has represented it, but rather that they left the field like two champions, still unbroken and unconquered. What happened was that before either side could overcome the other – and the contest in this theatre lasted for another two years – the war was decided by other means and in another place.

This was the state of affairs, then, at Eryx, so far as concerned the land forces. And in general the struggle between the two nations might be compared to a fight to the death between two game-cocks. It often happens that when the two birds have lost the use of their wings from sheer exhaustion, their courage remains high to the end, so that they go on striking blow after blow at one another, until at last without any intervention from outside they fall into a mortal grapple, and once this has happened one or the other will drop dead.[1]

Such was the situation of the Romans and the Carthaginians. They were worn out with the strain of an unbroken succession of hard-fought campaigns and were being driven to despair. Their

1. The metaphor is precisely worked out. The loss of the use of the birds' wings refers to the five-year duel on land, and the final grapple to the change in Roman strategy which culminated in the battle of the Aegates Islands.

strength was beginning to fail and their resources had been drained by taxes and military expenses which continued year after year.

59. And so, like the victorious fighting-cock, the Romans braced themselves for a final life or death effort. For the previous five years they had withdrawn completely from naval operations, partly because of the disasters they had suffered, and partly because of their belief that they could win the war by means of their armies alone. They now recognized that chiefly because of Hamilcar's daring leadership they were failing to achieve the results on which they had counted by land, and so they decided for the third time to risk their fortunes upon the sea. They believed that this strategy, if they could strike the enemy a mortal blow, offered the only prospect of finishing the war successfully. And this in fact they finally achieved. At their first attempt they had been forced to abandon the sea through sheer misfortune. The second time they had failed because of their defeat at the battle of Drepana. Now in their third effort they at last succeeded.

The naval victory at Aegusa enabled them to cut off the sea-borne supplies to the Carthaginian army at Eryx and eventually to finish off the war. Yet the effort sprang from sheer resolution rather than material resources. There were no funds in the treasury to finance the enterprise; but in spite of this, thanks to the patriotism and generosity of a number of leading citizens, the money was found. Single individuals or syndicates of two or three, according to their means, each undertook to build and fit out a quinquereme, which was fully equipped on the understanding that they would be repaid if the expedition was successful. In this way a fleet of 200 quinqueremes was quickly made ready, all of them constructed on the model of the ship originally captured from Hannibal, 'the Rhodian'. The Romans then appointed Gaius Lutatius to the command and sent him out at the beginning of the summer.[1] His sudden appearance off the coast of Sicily took the enemy completely by surprise. The whole Carthaginian fleet had sailed home, and he at once took possession of the harbour at Drepana and the roadsteads near Lilybaeum. He then erected siege-works around Drepana and made other preparations to blockade the city. But while he pursued these operations by every means in his

1. 242 B.C.

power, he foresaw that the Carthaginian fleet would return, and he never lost sight of the prime object of his expedition: namely that it was only by a victory at sea that the war as a whole could be decided. So he did not allow the time to be wasted or his men to be left unemployed. The crews were rehearsed and drilled every day in the manoeuvres that would be needed for the battle. He also paid particular attention to the training and discipline of his sailors, and by these methods he raised them in a very short time to the condition of trained athletes for the coming contest.

60. The news that the Romans had launched a fleet and were again preparing to fight for supremacy at sea came as a shock to the Carthaginians, but they at once fitted out their own ships, loaded them with corn and other provisions, and dispatched them to Sicily, for they were greatly concerned that the troops at Eryx should be kept well-supplied. This fleet was placed under the command of Hanno, who immediately set sail from Carthage and reached the so-called Holy Isle. His plan was to sail on as soon as possible to Eryx without the Romans' knowledge; there he would unload his stores and so lighten the ships, take on board those of the mercenary troops who were best trained to fight as marines – together with Hamilcar Barca himself – and then engage the enemy. However, Lutatius received intelligence of Hanno's arrival and anticipated his intentions. He too embarked the best troops in the Roman army to fight as marines, and sailed to the island of Aegusa which lies off Lilybaeum. There he made a speech to his troops that was well chosen for the occasion, and warned his captains that the battle was likely to take place the next day. At daybreak the next morning he saw that the strong breeze which was blowing up was favourable to the enemy, and that it would be difficult for his ships to beat up against the wind, as the sea had turned rough and boisterous. At first he could not decide what was the best course in these circumstances, but after a while he reflected that if he risked an attack now while the weather was stormy, at least he would be fighting Hanno and his sailors alone and before they had received any reinforcements. If he waited for calm weather and allowed the Carthaginians to cross to Eryx and link up with the land forces he would have to contend with ships that had been lightened and were

more manoeuvrable, with the pick of the Carthaginian troops, and above all with the aggressive presence of Hamilcar, which the Romans dreaded more than anything else. For these reasons he decided that he must not lose the present opportunity, and when he saw the enemy vessels under full sail, he at once put to sea. Thanks to their excellent condition his crews easily mastered the high sea that was running, and in a short while he had manoeuvred his fleet into a single line with the ships' prows facing the enemy.

61. When the Carthaginians saw that the Romans intended to oppose their crossing, they lowered their masts, and cheering one another on from each ship, they closed with the enemy. This time the state of preparation of each force was exactly the opposite of what it had been at the battle of Drepana, and since the conditions were the opposite, the results of the battle were the opposite. The Romans had reformed their methods of ship-building and had also removed all heavy equipment from their vessels, leaving only what was required for the battle. Their rowers worked in complete unison and gave excellent service, while their marines were all men selected from the legions for their indomitable spirit and thoroughly seasoned in battle. With the Carthaginians it was the reverse. Their vessels were heavily loaded and so difficult to manoeuvre in action, their crews had been enlisted for the emergency and were quite untrained, while their marines were raw recruits who were undergoing their first experience of hardship or dangerous service. The Carthaginians had assumed that the Romans would never again challenge their naval supremacy, and so in their contempt for their opponents they had neglected their own navy. The result was that immediately the battle was joined they were worsted at one point after another, and were swiftly put to flight: fifty ships were sunk outright and seventy captured with their crews. The remainder raised their masts and, running before the wind – which fortunately for them veered round in the nick of time to help their escape – they made their way back to the Holy Isle. The Roman consul sailed to Lilybaeum to join the army and there busied himself with disposing of the men and the ships he had captured; this was a large undertaking as the Romans had taken nearly 10,000 prisoners in the battle.

62. When they learned of this unexpected defeat, the Carthaginians, so far as resolution and the will to conquer were concerned, were still ready to fight on, but when it came to calculating their resources, they found themselves in an impasse. First of all, the enemy had now gained control of the sea, which made it impossible for them to supply their own troops in Sicily; secondly, if they were to abandon and as it were betray these forces, they would be left without either the men or the leaders to continue the war. Accordingly they immediately sent a message to Barca giving him full powers to handle the situation, whereupon Hamilcar acted like the good and prudent commander that he was. So long as there had been some reasonable chance of success, he had left no stratagem untried, however bold or dangerous it might seem, and if ever there was a general who tested every prospect of victory to the full, it was he. But when Fortune had turned against him and he was left with no other possibility of saving the troops under his command, he showed his good sense and practical capacity in yielding to the inevitable and sending a delegation to negotiate for peace; for it is after all the duty of a commander to know when he is beaten, no less than when he is victorious. Lutatius for his part readily agreed to negotiate, for he understood that the Romans were by this time worn out and exhausted by the war, and so he succeeded in putting an end to the hostilities by a treaty which was expressed in some such terms as the following:

'There shall be friendship between the Carthaginians and the Romans on the following terms, provided that they are ratified by the Roman people. The Carthaginians shall evacuate the whole of Sicily; they shall not make war upon Hiero, nor bear arms against the Syracusans nor their allies. The Carthaginians shall give up to the Romans all prisoners without ransom. The Carthaginians shall pay to the Romans 2,200 Euboean talents of silver over a period of twenty years.'

63. However, when these terms were sent to Rome, the people did not accept them, but dispatched ten commissioners to examine the whole question. On their arrival they made no important changes in the terms, but introduced a few minor alterations which imposed more severe conditions on the Carthaginians. They reduced, for example, the time allowed for the payment of the

indemnity to ten years, added 1,000 talents to the total, and demanded that the Carthaginians should evacuate all the islands lying between Sicily and Italy.

So ended the war between the Romans and the Carthaginians, and such were the conditions upon which peace was concluded. It had lasted uninterruptedly for twenty-four years, and is the longest, the most continuous and the greatest war of which we have knowledge. Apart from all the other battles fought and preparations made which I have described in the earlier chapters of my history, there were two naval actions in which on the one occasion more than 500 quinqueremes took part, and on the other nearly 700.[1] In the course of this war, if we include those vessels destroyed by shipwreck, the Romans lost some 700 quinqueremes and the Carthaginians 500. Those who are impressed by the great sea battles of an Antigonus, a Ptolemy or a Demetrius[2] would doubtless be amazed, if they were to read the account of this war, at the vast scale of the operations which it involved. Again, if we consider the size of these quinqueremes compared with that of the triremes with which the Persians fought against the Greeks, and the Athenians and Spartans against each other, we shall find that never before in the history of the world have two such immense forces been ranged against one another at sea. These facts confirm the proposition which I put forward at the beginning of my history, namely that the supremacy of the Romans did not come about, as certain Greek writers have supposed, either by chance or without the victors knowing what they were doing. On the contrary, since the Romans deliberately chose to school themselves in such great enterprises, it is quite natural that they should not only have boldly embarked upon their pursuit of universal dominion, but that they should actually have achieved their purpose.

64. Why is it then, some of my readers may wonder, since the Romans are now the masters of the world and wield far more power than they did in the past, that they can no longer in our time man so many ships or put to sea with such large fleets? Those who

1. In the battles at C. Hermaea and Ecnomus respectively.

2. These were among the most prominent of the Macedonian commanders who inherited the empire of Alexander the Great, and fought to carve out Hellenistic kingdoms for themselves.

are perplexed by this apparent contradiction will be able to understand the reason clearly when we come to describe Rome's political institutions. This subject forms a most important part of my work: it must not be treated cursorily by the writer, and it demands the full attention of the reader. It provides a noble spectacle, and yet one which until now has remained quite unfamiliar, thanks to the incompetence of the writers who have attempted the subject, some of whom have failed for lack of knowledge and others by giving a confused and quite useless account of it. As for the war of which we have just been speaking, it will be found, I believe, that so far as their scope of action was concerned, the two states were evenly matched in the enterprises they undertook, the lofty spirit which they displayed in pursuing them, and above all in their ambition to gain the upper hand. In respect of individual courage the Romans were far superior, but the general who must be acknowledged as the greatest on either side, both in daring and in genius, was Hamilcar, surnamed Barca. He was in fact the father of that Hannibal who later made war on the Romans.

BOOK II

Affairs in Spain

1. In the preceding book I explained at what point in their history the Romans, after subduing the whole of Italy, began to take a hand in the affairs of the countries beyond, and then I described how they crossed to Sicily and the reasons which made them embark upon the war with Carthage for the possession of that island. Next I related how and when they first built a navy, and I reported the principal events of the war on both sides down to its end, when the Carthaginians withdrew completely from Sicily, and the Romans took possession of the whole territory except for the regions which were ruled by Hiero. After this I set myself to describe the mutiny of the mercenaries against Carthage which kindled the so-called Libyan War, the fearful atrocities which were committed in that struggle, and the various unexpected events and shifts of fortune which marked its progress before Carthage finally gained the upper hand. I shall now try to summarize, according to my original plan,[1] the events which immediately succeeded this conflict.

As soon as the Carthaginians had brought the situation in Africa under control, they assembled a sufficiently strong expeditionary force, appointed Hamilcar to command it, and despatched it to Spain.[2] When Hamilcar took up the command of these troops he was accompanied by his son Hannibal, who was then nine years old. He at once crossed the straits by the Pillars of Hercules and proceeded to establish the power of Carthage over the peoples of Iberia. He spent nearly nine years[3] in the country, during which time he brought many tribes under Carthaginian sway, some by

1. As set out on pp. 44–5.
2. In this book Polybius touches on the reconstruction of the Carthaginian empire in Spain in three chapters – 1, Hamilcar; 13, Hasdrubal; 36, Hannibal – which serve as a chronological frame.
3. 238–229 B.C.

force of arms and some by diplomacy, and he ended his career in a manner which formed a fitting climax to his achievements, for he lost his life after fighting gallantly and with complete disregard for his personal safety in a battle against one of the strongest and most warlike of the tribes. The Carthaginians appointed as his successor his son-in-law Hasdrubal, who had previously commanded Hamilcar's fleet.

The Romans in Illyria

2. It was at about the same time[1] that the Romans first invaded Illyria and that region of Europe. This was a significant event and deserves to be studied closely by those who wish to grasp the purpose of my history and to understand the formation and growth of the Roman Empire. The reasons which made them decide to cross to Illyria were the following. Agron, its king, was the son of Plevratos and possessed a stronger army and navy than any Illyrian ruler before him.[2] Demetrius, the father of Philip V of Macedon, had hired Agron to go to the help of Medion;[3] this was a city which was being besieged by the Aetolians, who since they could not persuade the Medionians to join their League, had determined to force them to do so. The Aetolians accordingly mobilized their whole army, encamped all round the city, and launched an immediate assault, at the same time bringing siege-engines into action and using every possible means to force an entry. These operations coincided with the date of their annual elections, at which the Aetolians had to choose another general.[4] As the besieged town was in dire straits and its fall was expected daily, the officer who was then in command appealed to the Aetolians. He argued that it was he who had undergone all the dangers and hardships of the

1. The Roman intervention in Illyria took place in the spring of 229 B.C. Hamilcar was killed in the winter of 229/8.

2. He ruled a group of tribes round Scodra and the Bay of Rhizon (the modern Kotor), who lived by piracy carried out in light galleys.

3. A town on the frontier of central Acarnania.

4. Probably in the autumn of 231 B.C.

siege during his term of office, and therefore that it was only fair that when the place fell he should have charge of distributing the spoils of war and the privilege of inscribing his name upon the shields which would be dedicated to commemorate the victory. His claim was opposed, especially by those who were standing as candidates, and these men urged the people not to pre-judge the issue but to leave it to Fortune to decide whom she would honour in this way. Thereupon the Aetolians passed a resolution that whoever was general when the city fell should share with the previous holder of the office the distribution of the spoils and the honour of inscribing the shields.

3. It so happened that this decree had been passed on the day before the election was due to be held, and it is the custom of the Aetolians that the new general should immediately take up his command. But that very night 100 boats with 5,000 Illyrians on board arrived at the point on the coast which lay nearest to the city. They anchored there and as soon as it was daylight quickly disembarked the men without attracting attention. The troops then formed up in the order[1] which is customary in their country, and advanced in small groups upon the Aetolian camp. The Aetolians, when they learned of the enemy's presence, were at first amazed at the unexpectedness and the audacity of their landing, but since they had for many years held a high opinion of their own military qualities and felt confident of the present strength of their forces, they were not unduly dismayed. They drew up the main body of their cavalry and heavy infantry on the level ground in front of their camp; next they quickly occupied some high ground which was situated a little further forward and was easy to defend, and posted part of their cavalry and their light infantry there. The Illyrians charged these light-armed troops, and thanks to their superior numbers and the weight of their formation they succeeded in dislodging them from the heights and forcing the cavalry to fall back on the heavy infantry. In this way they could use the higher ground to launch their second charge against the Aetolians' main body which was drawn up on the plain. They quickly put their

1. These may have been groups based on kinship, of the kind which were found among the Greeks of Homeric times, or more recently among the Albanians.

opponents to flight, their attack being supported by the Medionians, who at the same time made a sortie from the city. They killed many of the Aetolians, captured an even larger number of prisoners, and seized all their arms and their baggage train. The Illyrians, having thus fulfilled their King's orders, carried off the baggage and the rest of the spoils to their boats and immediately sailed home.

4. After this unexpected deliverance the Medionians held an assembly, and debated among other matters the question of an appropriate inscription for the shields. They decided to parody the decree the Aetolians had passed by representing the shields as having been won *from* instead of *by* the Aetolian commander and the candidates who had stood for office in the following year. Certainly the turn of events which befell the Medionians might have been expressly designed by Fortune to demonstrate her power to mankind in general;[1] for overnight she had enabled them to inflict on their enemies the very fate which they believed the latter were about to inflict on them. As for the Aetolians, the unexpected disaster which they suffered should serve as a lesson never to make plans concerning the future as though it were already an accomplished fact, and never to cherish confident hopes about an event which may still turn out quite differently. We are no more than mortal men, and we should at all times make due allowance for the unexpected, and especially in time of war.

As for King Agron, when his ships returned and his officers reported to him on the battle he was so overjoyed at the idea of having defeated the Aetolians, the very people who held the most exalted opinion of themselves, that he at once gave himself over to drinking parties and other convivial celebrations, with the result that he contracted a pleurisy from which he died in a few days.[2] He was succeeded on the throne by his widow, Teuta, who entrusted the details of government to a council of friends in whom she had confidence.[3] She suffered from a typically feminine weakness, that of taking a short view of everything; she could see no further

1. This figure of speech continues the metaphor, which Polybius uses on p. 44, of Fortune as a play-producer.
2. In the autumn of 231 B.C.
3. Teuta followed the practice, which was normal in Hellenistic kingdoms, of working through a council of friends.

than her people's recent success, and thus had no eyes for events elsewhere. First of all she granted permission to the privateers who plied off the Illyrian coast to plunder any ships they met, and next she collected a fleet and a body of troops of as large a size as the earlier expedition, and sent it out with orders to the commanders that they should treat all states alike as their enemies.

5. The expedition set off and chose as its first objective the territories of Elis and Messenia, which the Illyrians had been in the habit of raiding from time immemorial. This was because both states possessed a long sea-board, and since their principal cities were situated far inland, any forces sent to protect the coastal districts had a long distance to cover and were slow to arrive; thus the Illyrians could always overrun and plunder these regions with impunity. However, on this occasion, when the Illyrian fleet arrived off Phoenice[1] in Epirus, they put in to obtain supplies. There they found a body of Gauls some 800 strong, employed in the Epirot service, and approached them with a proposal that they should betray the town. The plot was agreed, whereupon the Illyrians landed, attacked the city and captured it and its inhabitants with the aid of the Gauls, who gave help from within the walls. As soon as this news reached the Epirots, they quickly gathered their whole army and marched to the rescue. When they arrived close by, they pitched their camp so as to have the river which flows past Phoenice between them and the enemy, and to protect their front they tore up the planks of the bridge which crosses it. They then received a report that Scerdilaidas[2] with a force of 5,000 Illyrians was approaching them overland by way of the pass near Antigoneia,[3] and so they detached a body of troops to protect that city. Meanwhile they proceeded to take their ease, helping themselves generously to the resources of the country, but neglecting to post guards or arrange their night watches. The Illyrians discovered that their opponents had divided their forces and allowed their security to become thoroughly lax, and so they made a sortie under cover of darkness. They repaired the planks of the bridge, got their men safely across the river, took up a strong position, and rested

1. A town in Chaonia, near the modern Saranda.
2. Probably a brother of King Agron.
3. About twenty miles south of the modern Tepeleni in Albania.

there for the remainder of the night. At daybreak the two armies formed up in front of the town and engaged. In the battle which followed the Epirots were defeated, a large number of their men were killed, and even more taken prisoner; the remainder fled in the direction of the country of the Atintanes.

6. As a result of these misfortunes the Epirots lost all confidence in themselves and sent delegations to the Aetolians and the Achaean League to beg for help. These states took pity on their plight, responded to their appeal, and dispatched a relief force which soon afterwards arrived at Helicranum. Meanwhile the Illyrians, who had occupied Phoenice, first joined forces with Scerdilaidas, and then marched upon Helicranum. There they pitched camp opposite the rescuing army whom they were eager to engage. However, they found that the terrain was by no means in their favour, and at that very moment a dispatch arrived from Queen Teuta ordering them to return home with all possible speed, because some of the Illyrians had seceded to the Dardanians.[1] They therefore ravaged the neighbouring Epirot territory and then concluded a truce with the Epirots. By the terms of this agreement they handed back the city of Phoenice and its free citizens in return for a ransom. But they carried off the slaves and other movable property in their boats, and while the original Illyrian army sailed home, Scerdilaidas and his force returned overland by way of the pass near Antigoneia. This Illyrian expedition had spread dismay and terror among the Greeks who were settled in the coastal region. They had seen the city, which was both the strongest and the best protected by nature in all Epirus, unexpectedly plundered, and henceforth they became anxious not, as in the past, for the mere fate of their crops, but for the security of their cities and of their own lives.

The Epirots had been unexpectedly rescued from danger, but so far from attempting to retaliate against the aggressors or show their gratitude to their deliverers, their next action was to send an embassy to Queen Teuta and enter into a joint pact with the Illyrians and the Acarnanians. According to this they engaged in future to ally themselves with the Illyrians and against the

1. A neighbouring tribe whose territory lay on the upper Axios, the modern river Vardar.

Achaean and Aetolian Leagues. In this course of action they showed not only an extraordinary lack of judgement towards their benefactors,[1] but also a foolish disregard for their own interests which had indeed been evident from the very beginning.

7. Now, human nature is always fallible, and to meet with some unpredictable mishap is not the fault of the victim, but rather of ill-fortune, or of those who have inflicted it on him. But when we err with our eyes open and involve ourselves in great tribulations through sheer lack of judgement, then everyone agrees that we have nobody to blame but ourselves. It follows therefore that if a people's failures are due to ill-fortune, they will be granted pity, pardon and assistance, but if to their own folly, then all men of sense will blame and reproach them. Certainly in this case the Greeks would have had every reason to find fault with the Epirots. In the first place, anybody who knows the general reputation of the Gauls would hesitate to entrust to them the security of a wealthy city when they had both the opportunity and the incentive to betray it. Secondly, anyone should have been on his guard against the reputation and the conduct of this particular band. They had originally been expelled from their native land through an outburst of feeling on the part of their fellow-countrymen, because they had betrayed their own friends and kinsmen. Later, when the Carthaginians – who needed their help because of the exigencies of war – had received them and posted them to garrison the city of Agrigentum (where they were over 3,000 strong), they seized on a dispute about pay between the soldiers and their generals as an excuse to pillage the place. Subsequently when the Carthaginians again employed them on garrison duty in Eryx, which was then blockaded by the Romans, they tried to betray the city and those who were besieged in it with them; and when this plot failed, they deserted in a body to the enemy. The Romans in turn entrusted them with the task of guarding the temple of Venus Erycina, which again they pillaged. As a result of this clear proof of their impious character the Romans, as soon as the war with Carthage was over, made it their first concern to disarm them; they then put the Gauls on board ship and forbade them ever to set foot again

1. Polybius was particularly indignant at this action, since he was an Achaean himself.

in any part of Italy. These were the men whom the Epirots made the protectors of their republic[1] and the guardians of their laws, and to whom they entrusted their most prosperous city. Thus they can hardly be acquitted of the charge of having brought about their own misfortunes. I thought it necessary to deal with this subject at some length not only to demonstrate the folly of the Epirots, but also to point out that no people ought, if they are wise, to admit a garrison which is stronger than their own forces, above all when such a force consists of barbarians.

8. Now to return to the Illyrians. For some time previously it had been the custom of this people to prey upon vessels sailing from Italy, and at this moment, while they were occupying Phoenice, a number of them, operating independently of the Illyrian fleet, had attacked Italian traders; some of these they had robbed, some they murdered, and a large number were carried off into captivity. In the past the Roman government had always ignored complaints made to them about the Illyrians. But now, as more and more people approached the Senate on this subject, they appointed two commissioners, Gaius and Lucius Coruncanius, to travel to Illyria and inquire into what was happening.

In the meanwhile Queen Teuta had been so delighted by the quantity and the magnificence of the spoils which her fleet had brought back from Epirus (since Phoenice was at that time by far the most prosperous city there) that she redoubled her determination to plunder the Greeks. For the moment she had been obliged to put off such adventures because of the disturbances within her own territory. She had quickly put down the revolt of the Illyrians, but was engaged in besieging Issa,[2] the only city which still held out against her, when the Roman commissioners arrived by sea. They were granted an audience and proceeded to complain of the wrongs which had been committed against Roman citizens. Teuta listened to them with an arrogant and contemptuous air throughout the interview. When they had finished speaking, she told them she would see to it that Rome suffered no public wrong at the hands of Illyrians, but that so far as private wrongs were concerned, it was

1. The reference is to the democratic confederation of Epirus, which resembled that of the Achaean and Aetolian Leagues.
2. The modern Vis, an island off the southern Dalmatian coast.

not the custom of the Illyrian Kings to prevent their subjects from taking plunder at sea. The younger of the Roman ambassadors was angered at her words, and spoke out with a forthrightness which had ample justification, but was hardly well-timed. 'Queen Teuta,' he said, 'the Romans have an excellent tradition, which is that the state should concern itself with punishing those who commit private wrongs, and with helping those who suffer them. With the gods' help we shall do our utmost, and that very soon, to make you reform the dealings of the Kings of Illyria with their subjects.' After this plain speaking, the Queen gave way to a fit of womanish petulance, and was so furious at the ambassador's words that she cast aside the civilized convention which governs the treatment of envoys, and as the delegation were leaving on their ship, she sent agents to assassinate the Roman who had uttered the offending speech. When the news reached Rome, public opinion was violently roused by this outrage on the Queen's part, and the authorities immediately began to enrol legions, assemble a fleet, and prepare for an expedition.

9. When the campaigning season arrived, Queen Teuta fitted out a larger fleet of galleys than in the previous year and dispatched them to the Greek coast;[1] some of them sailed straight across the high sea to Corcyra, while others put in to Epidamnus. They touched there ostensibly to take on water, but really in the hope of surprising and capturing the town. The people of Epidamnus received them unsuspectingly and without taking any precautions. The Illyrians landed, dressed in their tunics and without armour as if they were going to fetch water, but they carried swords hidden in the water-jars; then they suddenly cut down the guards on the city gates and seized the gate tower. More men were swiftly disembarked from the ships, according to a pre-arranged plan, and with these reinforcements they easily seized possession of the greater part of the walls. The people of Epidamnus were taken by surprise and completely unprepared, but they quickly rallied and fought with great courage, with the result that the Illyrians, after holding out for a long while, were finally driven out of the town. In this way the Epidamnians all but lost their native city, but thanks to their courage they came out unscathed and were taught a useful

1. In the spring of 229 B.C.

lesson for the future. After this the Illyrian commanders hastily put to sea, rejoined the rest of their fleet which had sailed on ahead of them, and bore down upon Corcyra. There they landed, and to the dismay of the inhabitants proceeded to besiege the city. These events threw the Corcyraeans into the depths of despair, and they joined with the people of Apollonia and Epidamnus in sending a delegation to the Achaeans and Aetolians; they begged these states to hurry to their rescue, and not to stand by and see them driven from their homes by the Illyrians. The two Leagues gave audience to the envoys, decided to respond to their appeal, and both of them joined forces in manning the ten decked ships which belonged to the Achaeans. The squadron was fitted out in a few days, and then sailed for Corcyra in the hope of raising the siege.

10. Meanwhile the Illyrians had been reinforced in their turn by seven decked ships which the Acarnanians had sent in accordance with the terms of their alliance. With these vessels they put to sea and met the Achaean squadron off the Paxi Islands.[1] There the Acarnanians and those ships of the Achaeans which had been detached to engage them fought an indecisive action, in which they suffered no damage apart from having a few of their sailors wounded. The Illyrians, however, lashed their light galleys together in groups of four and engaged the enemy in this formation. They ignored the risk of damage to their vessels and presented them broadside on so as to offer an easy target for their opponents to ram. Once the collision had taken place, their enemies found themselves entangled by the bows and were momentarily in a difficult situation, as their rams were embedded and the four galleys lashed together were suspended on the beaks. Then the Illyrian marines leaped on to their opponents' decks and overwhelmed their crews by weight of numbers. In this way they captured four quadriremes and sank a quinquereme with all hands; this ship carried Margus of Caryneia, a man who had all his life served the Achaean League with complete loyalty. When the ships of the Achaean squadron which were engaged with the Acarnanians saw the success of the Illyrians, they decided to rely on their speed, and hoisting their sails to a favouring wind, they reached home in safety. After this, the Illyrians, who were exultant at their victory, were able to continue

1. A few miles south-east of Corcyra.

the siege of Corcyra without interference and with increased confidence. The Corcyraeans, however, whose hopes had been dashed by the defeat of their allies, were reduced to despair; and after holding out for a little longer, they came to terms with the Illyrians, and allowed a garrison to be installed in the town under the command of Demetrius of Pharos. After making these arrangements, the Illyrian commanders sailed away, anchored off Epidamnus and prepared to blockade the city once again.

11. At about the same time[1] one of the consuls, Gnaeus Fulvius, sailed from Rome with a fleet of 200 ships, while the other, Aulus Postumius,[2] set out with the land forces. Fulvius' original plan had been to sail for Corcyra, as he expected to find that the siege was still in progress there. However when he learned that he was too late, he decided nevertheless to sail for the island; he wanted first of all to discover exactly what had happened there, and secondly to test the accuracy of the messages sent him by Demetrius of Pharos. This officer was suspected by the Illyrians, and since he was afraid of what Queen Teuta might do to him, he had made contact with the Romans and offered to hand over the city and the rest of his command. The people of Corcyra were delighted at the arrival of the Romans, and immediately surrendered the Illyrian garrison to them by agreement with Demetrius. They also unanimously accepted the Romans' offer of protection, as they were convinced that this was the only way to ensure their safety for the future against the lawless raids of the Illyrians. The Romans, having admitted Corcyra into the number of states with which they were on friendly terms, then sailed for Apollonia, while Demetrius acted as their guide for the rest of the campaign. At the same time the other consul, Postumius, was engaged in transporting the land forces from Brundisium; these consisted of some 20,000 infantry and 2,000 cavalry. The two armies joined forces at Apollonia, whose people also agreed to accept Roman protection, but at this point news arrived that Epidamnus was under siege, and the army at once set off for that city. No sooner did the Illyrians learn that the Romans were approaching than they abandoned the siege in disorder and withdrew. The Romans also placed Epidamnus under

1. The spring of 229 B.C.
2. An error for Lucius Postumius.

their protection, and from there advanced into the interior of Illyria, subduing the tribe of the Ardiaeans on the way.

Many delegations now approached them, including one from the Parthini which came offering unconditional surrender. This tribe was admitted to the friendship of the Romans, as also were the Atintanes, and the army then advanced towards the island of Issa, which had earlier been placed under blockade by the Illyrians. The Romans forced the enemy to raise the siege, and here too they took the Issaeans under their protection. The fleet also captured a number of Illyrian cities by storm as they cruised along the coast, but at Nutria they suffered a reverse, losing not only a large number of soldiers but also several of the military tribunes and their quaestor. They captured at the same time twenty of the Illyrian galleys, which were carrying plunder taken from the countryside. Of the Illyrian troops who had been besieging Issa, those who were now on the island of Pharos were allowed to remain there unharmed as a favour to Demetrius;[1] the others scattered and took refuge at Arbo. Queen Teuta, accompanied by only a few attendants, escaped to Rhizon, a small town some distance from the sea, which was strongly fortified and situated on the river of the same name. After having accomplished these various missions and placed the greater part of Illyria under the authority of Demetrius, thus making him the ruler of a large territory, the consuls returned with the fleet and the army to Epidamnus.

12. Gnaeus Fulvius then sailed for Rome[2] with the greater part of the land and sea forces, while Postumius was left with a fleet of forty ships. He proceeded to enrol an army from the neighbouring cities, and spent the winter at Epidamnus to guard the Ardiaeans and the other tribes who had placed themselves under the protection of Rome. Then in the early spring Teuta sent a delegation to the Romans and concluded a treaty. According to its terms she agreed to pay whatever sum of tribute they imposed,[3] to give up the whole of Illyria with the exception of a few places, and – the condition which was of the greatest importance to the Greeks – she undertook not to sail beyond Lissus with more than

1. It was his native island.
2. He celebrated a naval triumph in Rome in 228 B.C.
3. This was probably an indemnity to be paid in instalments.

two galleys, which were to be unarmed. When this treaty had been concluded, Postumius sent envoys to the Aetolian and Achaean Leagues. On their arrival these officers first explained the reasons which had led to the war and caused the Romans to cross the Adriatic, next they gave a report of what had been accomplished in the campaign, and lastly they read out the treaty which they had made with the Illyrians. The envoys were received with due courtesy by both the Leagues, after which they returned by sea to Corcyra. The conclusion of this treaty had delivered the Greeks from a fear which had hung over them all, for the Illyrians were not merely the opponents of this people or that, but the common enemies of all alike. These, then, were the circumstances of the Romans' first armed intervention in Illyria and those parts of Europe, and of their first diplomatic mission to Greece, and the reasons which brought them about. Having taken the first step they immediately afterwards sent other envoys to Athens and to Corinth, and it was on this occasion that the Corinthians first invited them to take part in the Isthmian Games.

Affairs in Spain

13. During this period we have digressed from affairs in Spain, to which we now return. Throughout these years Hasdrubal had distinguished himself by his wise and practical handling of the province. He had made great progress in promoting Carthage's interests in general, and in particular he had strengthened them by his foundation of the city which some called Carthage and others the New Town. Since the place was admirably suited as a base for operations either in Africa or in Iberia itself, I shall find a more suitable occasion to describe its geographical situation and explain the advantages it can offer to both these countries. The Romans suddenly perceived that Hasdrubal had gone far towards creating a larger and more formidable empire than Carthage had possessed before, and they determined to take a hand in the affairs of Spain. They became aware that during these years they had been

fast asleep and had allowed Carthage to build up and equip a large body of troops, and so they now tried to make up the ground they had lost. For the present they did not venture to impose conditions or to make war on Carthage, because at this time the threat of a Celtic invasion was hanging over them, and an attack was expected almost from day to day. They therefore decided to try to mollify and conciliate Hasdrubal in the first place, and then to attack the Celts and put the issue to the test of war, for they were convinced that so long as they had an enemy such as the Celts threatening their frontier not only would it be impossible to control the affairs of Italy, but they would not even be able to live in safety in Rome itself. So they first sent envoys to Hasdrubal and concluded a treaty. According to its terms nothing was said about the rest of Spain, but the Carthaginians undertook not to cross the Ebro under arms. Then the Romans at once threw themselves into the struggle against the Italian Celts.

Rome and the Gauls

14. It will, I believe, be useful for me to give some account of these peoples, which must however be no more than a summary one, if I am to follow the original plan of this work as I explained it in my preface. To describe their situation I must go back to the period when they first took possession of these regions. I think the story is worth knowing and keeping in mind, not only for its own interest but because it is also essential to my larger design, in order for us to understand the nature of the men and the regions on which Hannibal later relied in his attempt to destroy the Roman Empire. First of all I must deal with the character of the country in which the Celts live and its position in relation to the rest of Italy, for if we have a clear picture of the special features both of its various parts and of the area as a whole, we shall be better able to grasp the main events of the war.

Italy seen as a whole is shaped like a triangle, the eastern side of which is bounded first by the Ionian Straits and then continu-

ously by the Adriatic Sea, and the southern and western by the
Sicilian and Tyrrhenian Seas. These sides converge to form an
apex at the southernmost promontory of Italy[1] known as Cocyn-
thus, which separates the Ionian from the Sicilian Sea. The remaining side, which constitutes the frontier of the interior to the north,
is formed by the chain of the Alps which stretches continuously
across the country; this mountain range begins at Marseilles[2] and
the northern shore of the Sardinian Sea, and extends in an unbroken
line to within a short distance of the head of the Adriatic Sea.
At the foot of this chain, which we should regard as the base of the
triangle, and to its south, lies the most northerly plain of the
Italian peninsula. This is the area with which we have now to
deal, and in respect of size and fertility this plain surpasses any
other in Europe with which I am acquainted. In this instance too the
general shape of the lines which bound it is triangular. The apex is
formed at the point where the Alps and the Apennines converge
above Marseilles, and not far north of the Sardinian Sea. The
northern side, as I have mentioned, is formed by the Alps themselves
and extends for some 250 miles in length, the southern by the
Apennines for some 400, and the base by the coast of the Adriatic,
its length from the city of Sena to the head of the gulf amounting to
more than 280 miles. The combined length of the three sides of the
plain is thus nearly 925 miles.

15. The fertility of this region is not easy to convey in words.
It yields such an abundance of corn that often in my time the price
of wheat was four *obols* for the Sicilian *medimnus*[3] and two for the
same quantity of barley, while a *metretes*[4] of wine cost the same
as a *medimnus* of barley. There is also a huge production of millet[5]
and of panic,[6] and the quantity of acorns that grow in the oak
forests throughout the region may be reckoned from the fact that

1. This is a somewhat forced and artificial description. Book XXXIV
indicates that Polybius was better informed as to the real shape of the
peninsula.
2. Polybius evidently believed that the Po valley extended to a point above
Marseilles.
3. About 1½ bushels or 51·5 litres.
4. About 8½ gallons or 38 litres.
5. The Greek word used is *elymos*, which signifies Italian millet.
6. The Greek word used is *kenchros*, which signifies common millet.

while very large numbers of pigs are slaughtered in Italy every year both for domestic consumption and to feed the army, a great proportion of them are reared on this plain. The cheapness and abundance of all food-stuffs may best be illustrated by the fact that travellers in this region when they stop at an inn do not bargain for the price of individual items, but simply ask what is the charge per head for their board. The inn-keepers, generally speaking, provide an inclusive tariff at half an *as* a day, in other words a quarter of an *obol*, and seldom charge more than this. As for the size of the population, the stature and good looks of the inhabitants and their courage in war, there is evidence enough in their history.

Those parts of the Alps which are not too rocky and possess a certain depth of soil are inhabited on both sides – on the northerly side the slopes overlook the Rhône and on the southerly the Italian plains which I have just described. The former region is inhabited by the Transalpine Gauls, the latter by the Taurisci, the Agones and other barbarian tribes. The adjective Transalpine does not, of course, denote an ethnic group, but is derived from the Latin preposition *trans*, meaning beyond, and is applied to those peoples who live beyond the Alps. The summits of the Alps are completely uninhabited on account both of their rugged character and of the depth of the snow which covers them all the year round.

16. The slopes of the Apennines are inhabited from the point where they join the Alps above Marseilles – that is both the slopes which overlook the Tyrrhenian Sea and those which face the inland plain. The first region is the home of the Ligures, whose territory stretches on the seaward side as far as Pisae, the first city[1] of western Etruria, and on the landward as far as Arretium. Next to them come the Etruscans and south of them both slopes are inhabited by the Umbrians. For much of its length the Apennine range runs at a distance of about sixty miles from the Adriatic, but south of the territory of the Umbrians it veers to the right and passes down the centre of Italy as far as the Sicilian Sea. The remaining low-lying part of the triangle, that is the plain which

1. The first city you come to, not the most important.

continues towards the Adriatic coast, extends as far as the city of Sena Gallica.[1] The river Po,[2] which poets have celebrated as the Eridanus, rises in the Alps near the apex of the triangle and begins by flowing south towards the plain. Then it makes a bend in an easterly direction, and passing through the plain discharges its waters by two mouths into the Adriatic. It thus divides the plain into two parts, the larger of which lies between it and the Alps and stretches to the head of the Adriatic. It carries a larger volume of water than any other river in Italy, since it is fed by all the mountain streams which descend to the plain from the Alps and the Apennines and they flow into it from either side. The river runs highest and looks at its most beautiful at the time when the Dog-star rises,[3] because it is then swollen by the melting of the snows in both mountain ranges. It is navigable for some 250 miles upstream from the mouth which is known as Olana,[4] for the river which has a single channel at its source divides into two at a place called Trigaboli;[5] one of the mouths is named Padua and the other Olana, the latter providing a harbour which is as safe as any in the Adriatic. The local name of this river is the Bodencus. There are various myths which the Greeks have recorded concerning the Po; I am thinking now of those which refer to Phaethon and his fall, and of the black clothes which it is said the inhabitants of this neighbourhood wear to this day in mourning for Phaethon. All the material which is of a tragic character and similar to this legend I leave aside for the present, since the nature of my introduction makes it unsuitable for a detailed criticism of the so-called 'tragic historians'. But I shall return to the subject in a more

1. The modern Sinigaglia, a few miles north of Ancona.
2. The passage which follows is the earliest accurate description of the Po. The name Eridanus is first found in Herodotus, *Histories*, III. 115, where it refers to a fabulous amber-producing river in northern Europe. In reality several rivers in this plain have separate mouths, but Polybius is presenting a simplified picture to Greek readers who were quite unfamiliar with the region.
3. In late July.
4. The northern mouth.
5. Until about A.D. 1150 the Po flowed into the Adriatic by two channels, the river dividing near Ferrara.

suitable context, especially since Timaeus[1] has shown himself to be so ignorant concerning these regions.

17. In ancient times this northerly plain was inhabited by the Etruscans at the same period as they occupied the Phlegraean plain in the neighbourhood of Capua and Nola. The latter region acquired the greatest reputation for fertility because it lay in the path of many peoples and thus became well-known. Those who are interested in learning something of the period of Etruscan supremacy should not study the region which they now inhabit, but should rather turn their attention to the northerly plains and the resources which they derived from them. The Celts, who were much associated with the Etruscans because they were their neighbours, cast envious eyes upon the beauty of their country, and suddenly seized upon some trivial pretext to attack them with a large army, drove them out of the valley of the Po and occupied the area themselves. Those who first settled in the district near the source of the Po were the Laevi and Lebecii; after them came the Insubres, the largest tribe of all, and finally the Cenomani, who lived along the banks of the river. The part of the plain which borders the Adriatic had always belonged to another very ancient tribe, that is the Veneti; in their customs and their dress they scarcely differed from the Celts, but they spoke a different language and the tragic poets have many fabulous tales to tell about them. On the southern bank of the Po, that is the side nearer the Apennines, the first settlers beginning from the west were the Anares and later the Boii. Eastwards of them in the direction of the Adriatic lived the Lingones, and beyond these and near the sea the Senones.

These are the names of the principal tribes which took possession of this region. They lived in unwalled villages and had no knowledge of the refinements of civilization. As they slept on straw and leaves, ate meat and practised no other pursuits but war and agriculture, their lives were very simple and they were completely unacquainted with any art or science. Their possessions consisted of cattle and gold, since these were the only objects which they could easily take with them whatever their circumstances and

1. Timaeus of Tauromenium composed a history of the western Greeks, Rome and Carthage; although a careful historian, he showed excessive credulity and superstition.

transport wherever they chose. It was of the greatest importance to them to have a following, and the man who was believed to have the greatest number of dependents and companions about him was the most feared and the most powerful member of the tribe.

18. When they first arrived in Italy the Celts not only took possession of this northern region, but subjugated many of the neighbouring peoples and terrified them by their audacity. Not long afterwards they defeated the Romans and their allies in a pitched battle, pursued their routed opponents, and three days later occupied the whole of Rome with the exception of the Capitol.[1] But at that moment an invasion of their own territory by the Veneti diverted their attention, and so they made a treaty with the Romans, handed back the city and returned home. Later they became involved in domestic wars, for a number of the neighbouring Alpine tribes often joined forces against them and made raids on their territory when they saw what prosperity the Celts had achieved compared with their own situation. In the meanwhile the Romans were able to recover their strength and re-establish their authority over the region of Latium. Thirty years after their occupation of Rome, the Celts again advanced with a large army as far as Alba.[2] On this occasion the Romans did not dare to meet them in battle because the invasion took them by surprise, and they had no time to organize resistance and bring together the forces of their allies. However, twelve years later the Celts made another attempt to invade in force,[3] and this time the Romans had intelligence of their attack. They mustered their allies and marched out confidently to meet them, for they were eager to engage and fight a decisive battle. The Gauls took fright at their enemies' advance, and meanwhile dissensions broke out within their own ranks; finally, as soon as darkness fell, they made off for home, and indeed their withdrawal was hardly distinguishable from a rout. After this alarm they kept quiet for thirteen years, and then as they saw that the power of the Romans was growing fast, they concluded a formal treaty with them and faithfully observed its terms for thirty years.

19. At the end of that time a new migration began among the Transalpine Gauls,[4] and the Celts began to fear that a dangerous

1. In 386 B.C.   2. In 356 B.C.
3. 344 B.C.   4. 299 B.C.

war was threatening them. So they diverted the advance of the invading tribes from their own territory by means of bribes and by pleading their ties of kinship with the Gauls; next they incited their compatriots to attack the Romans, and even took part themselves in the expedition. They marched first through Etruria where they were joined by the Etruscans, and after they had seized great quantities of plunder they returned safely from Roman territory. But no sooner had they arrived home than they began to quarrel about obtaining a larger share of the spoils, and in the end destroyed the greater part of their own army and even of the plunder itself. This is a common occurrence among the Gauls after they have appropriated a neighbour's property, and it usually arises from their undisciplined habits of drinking and gorging themselves.

Four years later[1] the Gauls formed an alliance with the Samnites, fought a pitched battle in the territory of Camerinum,[2] and inflicted heavy losses on the Roman troops. The Romans, nothing daunted, showed a victorious spirit in the face of their reverse: a few days later they marched out with their whole army[3] and attacked the Gauls and Samnites in the neighbourhood of Sentinum. They annihilated the greater part of the invading army and scattered the rest in headlong flight, so that each contingent took refuge in its separate territory. Ten years later the Gauls again attempted an invasion and laid siege to Arretium.[4] The Romans went to the help of the town, attacked the enemy before the walls and suffered a defeat. In this battle their praetor Lucius Caecilius was killed, and they appointed Manius Curius in his place. But when Curius sent a delegation to negotiate for the return of prisoners, the Gauls treacherously broke the truce and massacred the envoys, whereupon the Romans were roused to such anger that they immediately took the offensive and invaded the enemy's territory, where they were confronted by the Gallic tribe called the Senones.[5] They defeated them in a pitched battle in which

1. In 295 B.C.
2. The Romans had divided their forces and it was the advance guard which was defeated.
3. This signifies the two consular armies, totalling over 30,000 men.
4. In 284 B.C.
5. It was this tribe which had undertaken the siege of Arretium.

the greater number of the Gauls were killed and the rest driven from their homeland, the whole of which was then occupied by the Romans. This was the first place in Gaul where they planted a colony, and they named it Sena after the Gallic tribe which had previously inhabited it. This is the city which I mentioned above and which is situated near the Adriatic at the south-eastern corner of the northern plain.[1]

20. When the tribe known as the Boii saw the Senones expelled from their territory, they were afraid that they might suffer a similar fate, and so they mobilized all their fighting men, called in the help of the Etruscans and marched out to battle.[2] The combined armies engaged the Romans near Lake Vadimon,[3] with the result that most of the Etruscan army was wiped out and only a few of the Boii escaped. Despite this disaster the two peoples again joined forces in the very next year; they armed even those who had barely reached manhood, and once more challenged the Romans in a pitched battle. They suffered a total defeat, and it was only then that their spirit was sufficiently chastened to make them send a delegation to the Romans to sue for peace and conclude a treaty. These events took place three years before Pyrrhus, the King of Epirus, crossed into Italy and five years before the destruction of the Gauls at Delphi, and at this time it almost seemed as if Fortune had afflicted the whole race of the Gauls with a kind of epidemic of aggression.[4] But however that may be, there were two great advantages which the Romans gained from these struggles. In the first place, once they had grown accustomed to suffering great losses at the hands of the Gauls, there was no more terrifying experience than this which they need expect either to undergo or to fear. Secondly, by the time that they had to meet Pyrrhus they came to the contest like trained and seasoned athletes in military operations. They were able to crush the aggressive spirit of the Gauls[5] while there was still time to do so; then, having disposed

1. See note 1, p. 127.   2. In 283 B.C.
3. Some forty-two miles north of Rome, the modern Lago di Bassano.
4. Polybius often offers such synchronisms to support generalizations. Pyrrhus' crossing was in May 280; the disaster at Delphi in the autumn of 279 B.C.
5. This mention of the subjugation of the Gauls echoes and reverses the words which Polybius uses to describe the early Gallic invasions on p. 129.

of this threat, they could give their undivided attention first to the war with Pyrrhus for the possession of Italy, and later to the war with Carthage for the possession of Sicily.

21. After suffering these defeats the Gauls remained quiet and at peace with Rome for forty-five years. But as time went on, and those who had actually witnessed these terrible battles passed away, they were replaced by a younger generation, men who were filled with an unreflecting desire to fight and who were completely without experience of suffering or of national peril, and their impulse, not surprisingly, was to destroy the equilibrium which had been imposed by the treaty. They interpreted the slightest action of the Romans as a provocation, and they invited the Alpine Gauls to join them in an alliance. At first these approaches were carried out secretly by their chieftains without the knowledge of the people: thus when a force of Transalpine Gauls arrived at Ariminum,[1] the Boii became suspicious of them, quarrelled with their own leaders as well as with the strangers, killed their own Kings Atis and Galatus, and fought a pitched battle with their Transalpine compatriots in which both sides suffered heavy losses. The Romans had already been disturbed by the advance of the Gauls and had dispatched a legion to the north, but when they learned of this act of self-destruction by the enemy they returned home. Five years after this alarm[2] the Romans, during the consulship of Marcus Aemilius Lepidus, divided among their own citizens the Gallic territory known as Picenum, the region from which they had expelled the Senones when they conquered them.[3]

This policy of colonization was a demagogic measure introduced by Gaius Flaminius, which may be said to have marked the first step in the demoralization of the Roman people,[4] as well as pre-

1. The modern Rimini.
2. In 237 B.C.
3. See p. 131 above.
4. Flaminius was a plebeian and a *novus homo*. His scheme was designed to give the Roman proletariat a stake in the land, and was strongly opposed by the Senate, whose members had profited from the occupation of land acquired by conquest, so that Flaminius eventually carried his measure as a tribune in the popular assembly. Polybius' sweeping statement about demoralization probably refers to this particular phase of democratic assertiveness, which coincided with Flaminius' career. In the eyes of Polybius' senatorial friends

cipitating the war with the Gauls which followed. For the truth is that many of the Gauls and especially the Boii, whose territory bordered that of Rome, went to war because they were convinced that the Romans were no longer fighting to establish their sovereignty over the Gauls, but to expel them and finally to exterminate them altogether.

22. The two largest tribes, therefore, the Insubres and the Boii, immediately banded together and sent messengers to the Gallic tribes who lived among the Alps and near the Rhône. These peoples are known as the Gaesatae because they serve as mercenaries.[1] The envoys urged the rulers of the Gaesatae, Concolitanus and Aneroestes, to join in attacking the Romans. They offered them a large sum of gold, to be paid at once, and as for the future they dwelt upon the great prosperity which Rome enjoyed, and the vast wealth which would fall into their hands if they were victorious. They had little difficulty in winning over the Kings, as in addition to all these inducements they pledged themselves to be loyal allies and reminded their listeners of the exploits of their own ancestors. These heroes had not only conquered the Romans in battle, but after their victory had attacked and captured Rome itself and taken possession of all it contained; they had remained masters of the city for seven months, had then given it up of their own accord and as an act of grace, and had finally returned home with their spoils, unconquered and unscathed. These arguments so roused the enthusiasm of the Kings that the invading force was the largest which that region had ever sent out, and contained more leaders and celebrated warriors than ever before.

Meanwhile the Romans had received reports of these preparations, had surmised what was likely to happen, and so were kept in a state of continual alarm and suspense. At times we find them enrolling legions and laying in stocks of corn and other stores, and at other moments moving up troops to the frontier as if the enemy had already crossed into their territory, whereas the fact

---

democratic reforms at home were inseparably linked with the election of demagogic candidates such as Flaminius and Minucius to positions of military command, which led to the disasters of Trasimene and Cannae.

1. An incorrect statement; the name is derived from *gaesum*, a throwing-spear.

was that the Celts had not yet set foot outside their own. It was largely because of this unrest among the Gauls that the Carthaginians were enabled to establish their power in Spain without interference. The Romans, as I have mentioned above, regarded the threat from the north as by far the most pressing of their problems because it endangered their flank, and so they were compelled to ignore what was happening in Spain, and to devote their attention to dealing with the Celts. They therefore secured their relations with the Carthaginians by negotiating a treaty with Hasdrubal, the terms of which I have set out above,[1] and then concentrated all their resources upon the struggle with the enemy in Italy, for they considered it vital to bring this to a decisive conclusion.

23. The Gaesatae, then, having mobilized a strong and lavishly equipped army, crossed the Alps, and in the eighth year[2] after the distribution of the lands at Picenum, they descended into the valley of the Po. The Insubres and the Boii stood loyally by the pledge they had given their allies, but a Roman delegation succeeded in persuading the Veneti and the Cenomani to take their side; and so the Celtic chiefs were obliged to detach part of their forces to guard their territory against an attack by these tribes. They then struck camp, marched out in high spirits with their main army which consisted of some 50,000 infantry and 20,000 cavalry and chariots, and advanced on Etruria. The Romans, as soon as they learned that the Gauls had crossed the Alps, dispatched one of the consuls, Lucius Aemilius Paullus, to Ariminum to bar the enemy's route and one of the praetors to Etruria. The other consul, Gaius Atilius,[3] had already set off for Sardinia with his legions. Meanwhile in Rome itself the people were filled with dread; the danger that threatened them was, they believed, both great and imminent, and these feelings were natural enough, since the age-old terror inspired by the Gauls[4] had never been altogether

1. See p. 124.
2. 225 B.C.
3. He was the son of the celebrated Regulus of the First Punic War (see pp. 74–80). The move to defend Sardinia may well have been to ward off a possible Carthaginian attack.
4. i.e. the invasion of 387 B.C.

dispelled. Their thoughts always returned to this possibility, and the authorities were continuously occupied with calling up and enrolling the legions, and summoning those of the allies who were liable for service to hold themselves ready. All Roman subjects in general were required to provide lists of men of military age, since the authorities were anxious to know the total strength that was available to them, and meanwhile stocks of corn, of missiles and of other warlike stores had been collected on a scale which exceeded any such preparations within living memory. Help was readily provided on all sides, for the other inhabitants of Italy were so terror-stricken by the invasion of the Gauls that they no longer thought of themselves as allies of Rome, nor regarded this as a war undertaken to uphold the Roman hegemony. On the contrary, every people saw the danger as one which threatened themselves and their own city and territory. For this reason they responded to the orders from Rome without a moment's hesitation.

24. Here I should like to demonstrate from the actual facts of the situation how great was the power which Hannibal later ventured to attack, and how mighty was the empire which he boldly faced when he almost achieved his objective, and in any case inflicted great disasters on Rome. So, to make my point clear, I must explain what were the resources of Rome and the forces at her disposal at this moment. Each of the consuls had taken the field with two legions of Roman citizens, each legion consisting of 5,200 infantry and 300 cavalry. Besides these, the allied forces for the two consular armies numbered 30,000 infantry and 2,000 cavalry. The cavalry of the Sabines and the Etruscans, who had rallied at once to the support of Rome, numbered 4,000 and their infantry over 50,000. The Romans formed these levies into an army and posted them on the Etrurian frontier under the command of a praetor. The Umbrians and Sarsinati, hill-tribes of the Apennine mountains, raised a force of some 20,000, and with them were a further 20,000 men provided by the Veneti and the Cenomani. These troops were placed on the frontier of the Gauls' territory, so as to create a diversion by invading the lands of the Boii. These were the forces which protected the boundaries of Roman territory.

In Rome itself was stationed a strategic reserve, held ready for any contingency which might arise, and this numbered 20,000 infantry and 1,500 cavalry, all drawn from the Roman citizen body, together with 30,000 infantry and 2,000 cavalry provided by the allies. The lists of men capable of bearing arms that were supplied to the authorities read as follows. Latins, 80,000 infantry and 5,000 cavalry; Samnites, 70,000 infantry and 7,000 cavalry; Iapygians and Messapians, 50,000 infantry and 16,000 cavalry; Lucanians, 30,000 infantry and 3,000 cavalry; Marsi, Marrucini, Frentani and Vestini, 20,000 infantry and 4,000 cavalry. In Sicily and Tarentum there were two reserve legions, each consisting of about 4,200 infantry and 200 cavalry. The total number of Romans and Campanians whose names appeared on the roll amounted to 250,000 infantry and 23,000 cavalry. Thus the number of Romans and their allies able to bear arms totalled more than 700,000 infantry and 70,000 cavalry, whereas Hannibal invaded Italy with an army of less than 20,000 men. I shall deal with this subject in greater detail at a later stage in this work.

25. The Celts, then, descended on Etruria and overran the whole region, plundering the country as they chose, and as they met no opposition, they advanced upon Rome itself. When they had arrived at Clusium, a city only three days' march from Rome, news reached them that the army which the Romans had posted in Etruria was coming up in their rear and was close upon them, whereupon they turned back to meet it, full of ardour to engage the enemy. At sunset the two armies were almost in contact, and they encamped for the night with only a short distance separating them. When it was dark the Celts lit their camp-fires. They left their cavalry there with orders that they should wait for daybreak, and then as soon as they became visible to the enemy they were to follow the route which the infantry had already taken. In the meanwhile the Celts withdrew their main body under cover of darkness towards a town named Faesulae[1] and took up their positions. Their plan was to wait for the cavalry, and at the same time to disconcert any attack by the enemy by confronting them with an unforeseen situation. When the Romans sighted the cavalry at daybreak and saw them unsupported, they concluded that the Celts had fled, and so pursued the cavalry along the line of the enemy's sup-

1. Faesulae (Fiesoli) is some eighty miles from Clusium (Chiusi): clearly the Gauls did not march there overnight, but only in that direction.

posed retreat. Then, as they approached, the main body of the Celts sprang forward from their positions and charged them A fierce battle followed, which was stubbornly contested on both sides, but in the end the courage and superior numbers of the Celts prevailed. The Romans lost 6,000 men, and the rest took to flight, most of these retreating to a hill which offered them a naturally strong position. The Celts at first tried to take the hill by assault, but they were exhausted by their march of the previous night and by the suffering and hardship caused by the fighting, and so they made haste to rest and refresh themselves But they left a detachment of cavalry to guard the hill, and determined to attack the fugitives next day unless they offered to surrender.

26. Meanwhile the other consul, Lucius Aemilius Paullus, who was in command of the second Roman army near the Adriatic, had been informed that the Celts had invaded Etruria and were nearing Rome. He hurried southward to help, and fortunately reached the battlefield at the critical moment. He encamped near the enemy, and the Romans on the hill, as soon as they caught sight of his camp-fires, understood what had happened. They took heart again and under cover of darkness sent off some unarmed messengers to find their way through the forest and report to the consul. On receiving the news, Paullus decided that no alternative was left him but to fight, and he gave orders to his military tribunes to march out the infantry at daybreak, while he led the way with the cavalry towards the hill on which his comrades had taken refuge. The commanders of the Gauls, who had also seen the camp-fires, concluded that the enemy had arrived and held a council of war. At this King Aneroestes argued that since they had by now captured so much booty (for the numbers of prisoners and cattle and the quantities of plunder they had taken were enormous) they should not give battle again and thus put all their gains at risk, but should return home in safety. After they had disposed of the plunder and freed themselves of all these encumbrances they should march back, and then if the prospects seemed favourable try conclusions with the Romans. The council decided in the circumstances to follow Aneroestes' advice. They agreed on this during the night, broke camp before daybreak and marched through Etruria along the coast. Paullus then rescued the surviving remnant

of the Roman army from the hill and united it with his own force. He decided that this was not the moment to risk a pitched battle, but chose to follow the enemy's rear and watch for a favourable place or moment to harass him, or recover some of the plunder.

27. At the same time the other consul, Gaius Atilius, had crossed from Sardinia with his legions and arrived at Pisae on his way to Rome, and was thus marching in the opposite direction to the enemy. When the Celts reached the vicinity of Telamon in Etruria, their foragers encountered Atilius' advance guard and were captured. They were interrogated by the consul and informed him of what had happened in the battle; they also revealed the presence of both the opposing armies, explaining that the Gauls were close by and Paullus in their rear. This news astonished Atilius but also raised his hopes, because he believed that he had trapped the Gauls between the two Roman armies while they were on the march. He gave orders to the military tribunes for the legions to prepare for action and to move forward at marching pace, so far as the nature of the ground allowed them to advance in line. By a fortunate chance he had noticed some high ground which dominated the road along which the Celts had to pass, and so taking the cavalry with him he galloped forward, as he was anxious to occupy the crest of the hill before the Celts came up. The move would enable him to begin the battle, and in this way he counted upon securing the greatest share of the credit for the result.

The Celts at first knew nothing of Atilius' arrival, and supposed that Paullus' cavalry must have outflanked them during the night and were occupying positions ahead of their line of march. They therefore immediately sent out some of their own cavalry and light-armed troops to oppose the move to occupy the hill. But they soon learned of Atilius' presence from a prisoner who was brought in. At this they hastily deployed their infantry so that the army then faced in both directions, to the front and the rear; for both the information that reached them and the movements which they could see now made it clear that one army was behind them and that they must expect to meet the other in front.

28. Meanwhile Paullus had received news that Atilius' legions had landed at Pisae, but he had never supposed they were so near him. However, when he saw the fighting in progress round

the hill it was clear that the other Roman army was close at hand. He at once sent forward his cavalry to support Atilius' attempt to capture the heights; then he drew up his infantry in their usual order and advanced against the enemy who barred his way. The Celts had posted the Alpine tribe of the Gaesatae to face their rear, the direction from which they expected Paullus to attack, and behind them the Insubres; on their front, to meet the attack of Atilius' legions, they had stationed the Taurisci and the Boii, who came from the northern bank of the Po. Their waggons and chariots had been placed at the end of either wing, and the spoils they had captured had been collected and placed under guard on one of the neighbouring hills. This Celtic order of battle which faced both ways was not only awe-inspiring to see but was also well suited to the needs of the situation.

The Insubres and the Boii wore their trousers[1] and light cloaks, but the Gaesatae had been moved by their thirst for glory and their defiant spirit to throw away these garments, and so they took up their positions in front of the whole army naked and wearing nothing but their arms. They believed that they would be better-equipped for action in this state, as the ground was in places overgrown with brambles and these might catch in their clothes and hamper them in the use of their weapons. At first the conflict was confined to the fighting round the hill, and because of the great numbers of cavalry which were locked in battle the rest of the three armies stood by and watched the contest. In this encounter the consul Gaius Atilius lost his life, fighting with desperate courage in the thick of the action, and his head was brought to the Celtic King. But the Roman cavalry fought on stubbornly, and at length overcame their opponents and took possession of the heights. By this time the infantry were almost in contact, and the battlefield provided a strange and marvellous spectacle, not only to those who were actually present, but to all those who could afterwards picture it in their imagination from the reports.

29. In the first place, as the battle was fought between three armies, it is clear that the appearance and the movements of the

1. The barbarian garment which is seen in the reliefs on Trajan's column in Rome: the trousers were loose-fitting, but fastened close at the ankles.

forces arrayed against one another must have been strange and unusual in the extreme. Secondly a spectator must have asked himself – as we do to this day – whether the Celts were in the more dangerous position with the enemy advancing upon them from both sides, or in the more favourable one, because they could fight both armies and had their rear protected from each, and above all because they were completely cut off from retreat or from any possibility of escape if they were defeated; for this is the peculiarity of adopting an order of battle which faces both ways.

For their part the Romans felt encouraged at having trapped the enemy between their two armies, but at the same time dismayed by the splendid array of the Celtic host and the ear-splitting din which they created. There were countless horns and trumpets being blown simultaneously in their ranks, and as the whole army was also shouting its war-cries, there arose such a babel of sound that it seemed to come not only from the trumpets and the soldiers but from the whole surrounding countryside at once. Besides this the aspect and the movements of the naked warriors in the front ranks made a terrifying spectacle. They were all men of splendid physique and in the prime of life, and those in the leading companies were richly adorned with gold necklaces and bracelets. The mere sight of them was enough to arouse fear among the Romans, but at the same time the prospect of gaining so much plunder made them twice as eager to fight.

30. However, when the Roman javelin-throwers, following their regular tactics in Roman warfare,[1] advanced in front of the legions and began to hurl their weapons thick and fast, the cloaks and trousers of the Celts in the rear ranks gave some effective protection, but for the naked warriors in front the situation was very different. They had not foreseen this tactic and found themselves in a difficult and helpless situation. The shield used by the Gauls does not cover the whole body, and so the tall stature of these naked

1. The Roman legion contained 3,000 heavy infantry, who fought in three main lines: in front the *hastati* (1,200), next the *principes* (1,200) and lastly the *triarii* (600) in reserve. These ranks were arranged in ten spaced-out groups (maniples) of 120 men each – sixty for the *triarii*, each space being covered by a group in the rank behind. The javelin-throwers (*velites*) often opened the action by advancing in front of the heavy infantry and discharging their missiles, then they retired through the spaces in the ranks.

troops made the missiles all the more likely to find their mark. After a while, when they found themselves unable to drive off the javelin-throwers who were out of reach and continued to pour in their volleys, their nerve broke under the unbearable ordeal. Some of the men rushed forward in a blind fury and threw away their lives as they tried to close with the enemy, while others gave ground and fell back step by step into the ranks of their comrades, where they created confusion since they were evidently backing away from the enemy. In this way the martial ardour of the Gaesatae was broken by an attack with the javelin. However, when the javelin-throwers stepped back into the ranks of the infantry and the whole Roman line advanced upon the enemy, the Insubres, the Boii and the Taurisci met their charge head-on and held their ground in fierce hand-to-hand fighting. Although the tribesmen were almost cut to pieces, yet they stood firm and proved that they were equal to their enemies in courage, and inferior only in their weapons, in which the Romans had the advantage, both individually and collectively. The Roman shields, I should explain, were far better designed for defence, and so were their swords for attack, since the Gallic sword can only be used for cutting and not for thrusting. The end came when the Celts were attacked by the Roman cavalry, who delivered a furious charge from the high ground on the flank; the Celtic cavalry turned and fled, and their infantry were cut down where they stood.

31. Some 40,000 of the Celts were killed and at least 10,000 taken prisoner, among them their King, Concolitanus. The other King, Aneroestes, fled from the battlefield with a few of his followers, and found a refuge where he and his whole retinue took their own lives. The spoils and trophies of the Celts were collected by the surviving consul, Lucius Aemilius Paullus, who sent them to Rome; at the same time he returned to its local owners the property which the Gauls had seized from them. Then he took command of the legions, marched along the frontier of Liguria and invaded the territory of the Boii. There he allowed his troops to take their fill of plunder, and after a few days led them back to Rome.[1] He sent the standards and the gold necklaces worn by the Gauls to

1. Aemilius' campaign took longer than this: he did not return to Rome until the autumn of the year (225 B.C.).

decorate the Capitol;[1] the rest of the spoils and the prisoners were reserved to adorn his entry into Rome and his subsequent triumph.

This was how the most formidable of the Celtic invasions, which had placed all the Italians and above all the Romans in mortal danger, was finally destroyed. The victory encouraged the Romans to hope that they could clear the Celts from the entire valley of the Po, and so in the following year[2] they sent out both the consuls, Quintus Fulvius and Titus Manlius, with a strong and well-equipped force. Their attack took the Boii by surprise and frightened them into making submission to Rome. But the rest of the campaign produced no practical results; this was partly owing to the onset of heavy rains, and partly to the outbreak of an epidemic in the army.

32. In the following year[3] the consuls Publius Furius and Gaius Flaminius again invaded Celtic territory, this time advancing through the country of the Anares, who live not far from Marseilles.[4] After receiving this tribe into friendly relations with Rome, they marched into the territory of the Insubres at a point near the junction of the Po with the river Adda. The Romans suffered some losses both in crossing the frontier and in setting up a camp beyond it. They occupied this position for some time, but later concluded a truce, by the terms of which they agreed to leave Insubrian territory. From there they made a roundabout march in a north-easterly direction for some days, crossed the river Clusius, and entered the territory of the Cenomani. This people who were allies of Rome, again joined forces in invading the lands of the Insubres, this time from the district at the foot of the Alps. From there they descended to the plains and began to ravage the country and plunder some of the Insubrian settlements. The chieftains of that tribe, seeing that the Romans were determined to attack them,

1. According to Dio, frag. 50.4, the Gauls had sworn an oath not to take off their sword-belts or breast-plates until they had entered the Capitol (which they did not capture in 387). The oath was therefore fulfilled, with dramatic irony, by those who appeared in Aemilius' triumph.

2. In 224 B.C.

3. In 223 B.C.

4. This geographical error is explained by Polybius' belief that the Alps begin a little north of Marseilles; hence he places the territory of the Anares near that city. In fact it was near Placentia, the modern Piacenza.

resolved to stake everything on bringing their enemies to a decisive battle. They gathered all their forces, took down the golden standards which are known as ' the immovables' from the temple of Minerva,[1] and made all the other necessary preparations for war; then in high spirits they set out with a force of 50,000 men and encamped in a challenging position opposite the enemy. The Romans, seeing themselves greatly outnumbered, were anxious to appeal for help to their Celtic allies. But at the same time they remembered the habitual treachery of the Gauls and the fact that their allies were the fellow-nationals of their opponents, and so they hesitated to call upon men of such unpredictable loyalties to fight beside them in a battle where so much was at stake In the end, however, they overcame their misgivings. They themselves remained on the right bank of the river, dispatched their Celtic allies to the other side and destroyed the bridges. They did this partly as a precaution against their allies, and partly so as to leave themselves no prospect of safety except through victory, since the river, which was now impassable, lay to their rear. After making these dispositions they were ready for action.

33. The Romans are considered to have shown great skill in this battle because of the instructions which the military tribunes gave to the soldiers both for hand-to-hand fighting and for general tactics. They had learned from previous battles that the Gauls are at their most dangerous in their first onslaught while their ardour is still fresh, and also that because of the way their swords are forged, as has already been mentioned, it is only the first slash which takes effect. After this the edges are immediately blunted and the blades become so bent both lengthways and sideways that unless the men are given time to straighten them with the foot against the ground, the second blow has virtually no effect.[2] Accordingly the tribunes issued to the men in the front ranks the

1. The Celts worshipped a goddess of war and victory, corresponding to the Roman Minerva; the temple may have been at the Insubrian capital of Mediolanum (Milan). The Insubres were taking down the standards as a source of divine protection.

2. The same details concerning the soft edge of the Gallic sword are found in Plutarch's account of Camillus' victory over the Gauls in 377 B.C.; it may have become a traditional legend.

thrusting spears normally carried by the *triarii*,[1] who are stationed in the rear, and ordered them not to use their swords until after the spears had done their work. Then they formed up opposite the Celts and engaged them. As soon as the enemy had delivered their first sword cuts against the shafts of the spears and so put their weapons out of action, the Romans closed with them and rendered them helpless by leaving them no room to raise their arms to slash;[2] this is the stroke which is peculiar to the Gauls, and the only one they can make, as their swords have no points. The Romans, on the other hand, made no attempt to slash and used only the thrust, kept their swords straight and relied on their sharp points, which were very effective. They inflicted one wound after another on the breast or the face, and in this way killed the greater number of their opponents. This success must be credited entirely to the foresight of the military tribunes, for the consul Flaminius is considered to have made a serious error in his dispositions for the battle. By deploying his troops along the very edge of the river bank he made it impossible to carry out a manoeuvre which is particularly characteristic of Roman tactics, that is to say, he left no room for the maniples to fall back within limits. If his troops had been compelled in the course of the battle to give ground even to the very smallest extent, they would have been forced, through this oversight of their commander's, to throw themselves into the river. But as the event turned out they gained a brilliant victory thanks to their own valour, and returned to Rome laden with great quantities of spoil and many trophies.

34. In the following year the Celts sent a delegation to sue for peace, which they undertook to accept on any terms, but the new consuls, Marcus Claudius and Gnaeus Cornelius, were uncompromising in insisting that peace should not be granted. So having failed in this attempt they decided to put their last hope to the test: they once more approached the Gaesatae, the Gallic tribe which lives on the Rhône, and hired from them a host of some

1. See note, p. 140, on the order of battle of the legion. The *hastati* and the *principes* were normally armed with the *pilum*, a short throwing-spear, and a sword; the *triarii* with the *hasta*, a longer thrusting-spear.
2. The Romans came in so close that the enemy had no room to swing their blades.

30,000 men; then, having engaged these warriors, they kept them in readiness and waited for the Romans to attack. When the campaigning season came round, the consuls took command of their forces and marched them into the territory of the Insubres. They pitched their camp around a city named Acerrae, which lies between the river Po and the Alps, and laid siege to it. It was impossible for the Insubres to help their compatriots, because the Romans had seized in advance all the commanding positions in the neighbourhood; but as they were determined to make the enemy raise the siege they detached part of their forces and crossed the Po. From there they entered the territory of the Anares and laid siege to a town named Clastidium. When the Roman generals learned of this move Marcus Claudius set off with his cavalry and a small body of infantry and made a forced march to try to rescue the besieged. As soon as the Celts received warning of his approach, they raised the siege, marched out to meet him and drew up their army in battle order. The Romans began the fighting with a furious charge launched by the cavalry alone; the Celts held their ground, but before long they found themselves encircled both on the flank and in the rear, and in the end they were put to flight without the Roman infantry having been engaged at all. Many of them plunged into the river and were swept away by the current, but the greater number were cut down where they stood. The Romans went on to capture Acerrae, which contained large stocks of corn, while the Gauls fell back upon Mediolanum, which was the most important settlement in the territory of the Insubres. Cornelius pursued them closely and suddenly appeared before Mediolanum. At first the Gauls stayed in their positions, but once the consul had begun his march back to Acerrae they made a sortie and launched a bold attack on his rearguard; in this action they killed many of his men and even routed a part of his force, until Cornelius brought back his vanguard and called upon his troops to stand fast and engage the enemy. The Romans responded to his order, rallied and fiercely counter-attacked their opponents, whereupon the Celts, although they were elated by their brief success and held their ground with spirit for a while, were soon put to flight and scattered among the mountains. Cornelius harried their retreat, ravaging the country as he marched, and he went on to capture

Mediolanum by storm. After this the chieftains of the Insubres gave up all hope of winning safety through their own efforts, and made complete submission to the Romans.

35. So ended the war against the Celts. If we consider it in terms of the audacity and the desperate courage displayed by those taking part and of the numbers who fought and died in the battles, this conflict is unsurpassed by any war in history; but from the point of view of the planning of the various offensives or of the judgement shown in executing them, the standard of generalship was beneath contempt. For not only in the majority of their actions, but in every single instance the Gauls were swayed by impulse rather than by calculation. Not long afterwards I was to see these tribes completely expelled from the valley of the Po, except for a few districts at the foot of the Alps, and accordingly I felt that it would have been wrong to pass over either their original invasion, or their behaviour after it, or their final expulsion.[1] For I believe that it is the proper function of history to hand down to posterity such episodes in the drama of Fortune, so that our successors may not through sheer ignorance of the facts be overcome by terror at these sudden and unexpected incursions of the barbarians, but should understand how short-lived and easily extinguished such movements may prove to be. If they are fortified with this knowledge they can face the invader and try their prospects of safety to the very limit before they yield an inch of their most vital interests.

Indeed I consider that those writers who recorded and handed down to us the story of the invasion of Greece by the Persians and the attack by the Gauls on Delphi made a great contribution to the Greek peoples' fight to preserve their common liberty. For there is no reason why the enemy's superiority in numbers or in weapons or supplies need terrify a man into abandoning his ultimate hope – that is to fight to the last for his native land – so long as he keeps steadily in view the knowledge of how great a part the unexpected has often played in these campaigns, and remembers how many myriads of troops, what immense armaments and what overweening confidence have been defeated by the resolution and the ability of men who faced the danger with intelligence and cool calculation. And it was not only in those far-off days but more

1. Cisalpine Gaul was pacified between 200 and 180 B.C.

than once in my own times that the Greeks have been seized by the fear of a Gallic invasion. It was for this reason in particular that I have given an account of the Gauls, which although no more than a summary, traces their history back to its beginnings.

Affairs in Spain

36. In following this theme we have digressed from events in Spain. There the Carthaginian commander Hasdrubal, who had governed the province for eight years, was assassinated in his lodgings at night by a certain Celt on account of private grievances. He had done much to strengthen the Carthaginian presence in the country, not so much by military achievements as by the friendly relations he had established with the local chieftains. To succeed him the Carthaginians appointed Hannibal as supreme commander in Spain; they chose him, notwithstanding his youth,[1] because he had already shown that he combined a daring spirit with a quick and fertile brain. As soon as he took up his command it became clear from the measures[2] which he put in hand that his purpose was to declare war on Rome, as indeed he ended by doing, and that with little delay. From this point onwards in the dealings between Carthage and Rome friction and mutual suspicion followed one another in perpetual sequence. The Carthaginians continued to lay plans against Rome, since they longed to revenge themselves for their defeats in Sicily, while the Romans, as they observed these schemes, grew increasingly mistrustful. It thus became clear to all those who had eyes to see that a war between the two peoples could not be far away.

1. He was then twenty-five (221 B.C.).
2. This assertion is not borne out by Hannibal's immediate actions, but in this analysis of the causes of the war Polybius lays great stress on the anger of the Barca family, to which Hannibal belonged, and their determination to wipe out the humiliation of the settlement which followed the First Punic War.

Events in Greece

THE ACHAEAN LEAGUE

37. It was at about the same time that the Achaeans and King Philip of Macedon, together with their allies, began the war against the Aetolians which is known as the Social War.[1] We have now traced the outline of affairs in Sicily and in Africa and the developments which ensued; accordingly next in the series of events described in my introduction we come to the beginning of the Social War and of the second war between the Romans and the Carthaginians, which is generally known as the Hannibalic War. It is at this point, as I explained in my opening chapters,[2] that I plan to begin my own narrative. I therefore leave for the present the affairs of Rome and Carthage and turn to events in Greece so as to bring all the sections of my introduction to the same point in time, after which I shall embark upon my detailed history.[3] For I do not confine myself, as earlier writers have done, to the history of one nation alone, such as Greece or Persia, but have set myself to describe what was happening in all the known parts of the world at once. There is indeed something in the nature of our times which is especially favourable to my present purpose,[4] and this theme I shall develop more explicitly elsewhere in my history. And so in view of the broad scope of my survey I ought before entering upon my main theme to touch upon the state of the most important and best-known peoples and countries of the world. So far as Asia and Egypt are concerned there is no need for me to retrace events beyond the starting-point of my book. Their earlier history has been described by many writers and is familiar to all the world, nor in our own times has Fortune brought about any such dramatic

1. In the late spring of 220 B.C.

2. As stated on p. 43.

3. i.e. history which includes evidence and argument as distinct from a mere assertion or a summary statement of events, such as is contained in his introductory survey.

4. See pp. 44–5 in which Polybius argues for the importance of a synoptic presentation of history and for the principle that truth resides in a panoramic rather than a local view of events; in a word, 'Only connect!'

change in their situation as to make it necessary to recall their past.

But in the case of the Achaean nation and the royal house of Macedon[1] it will be quite consistent with my plan to give a brief recapitulation of events, since in our day the Macedonian dynasty has become extinct, while the Achaeans, as I mentioned above, have achieved a growth of power and an internal political harmony which are altogether remarkable. There have been many attempts in the past to persuade the Peloponnesians to adopt a common policy for the general advantage, but none of them ever succeeded because each of the promoters of such a union was always striving not for the general liberty but for his own supremacy. Yet in our day these ideals have made so much progress and achieved such a degree of fulfilment that not only have the Achaeans created an allied and friendly community, but they also share the same laws, weights, measures and currency, and besides these the same magistrates, council and law courts. An area which embraces almost the whole Peloponnese only differs from the situation of a single city in the sense that its inhabitants are not encircled by a single wall; in other respects whether the region is considered as a whole or city by city its institutions are virtually identical.

38. In the first place it is worth investigating how the name of Achaeans first came to be applied to the Peloponnesians, and was later adopted by all of them. The people who originally bore this ancestral name were not pre-eminent among the rest either for the size of their territory, the number of their cities, their wealth or their prowess in war. The Arcadian and Laconian nations far exceed them in area and in population, and certainly neither of these could ever agree that any Greek people was their superior in warlike valour. How then do we explain the fact that both these peoples[2] and the rest of the Peloponnese have been willing to exchange not only their political institutions but even their name for those of the Achaeans? Clearly we ought not to say that this is the

1. Polybius is contrasting the survival of the ruling dynasties of Syria and Egypt with the fall of the Antigonids in Macedon

2. The Arcadians joined the Achaean League in 235 B.C. The Spartans were forcibly incorporated by Philopoemen in 192, subsequently seceded, and were re-admitted in 182–181 B.C.

work of chance,[1] for that would be a very inadequate explanation. We must rather seek a cause, since no chain of events, whether expected or unexpected, can reach its conclusion without a cause. The cause, then, in my opinion is something like this. It would be impossible to find anywhere a political system or a guiding principle which allowed more equality and freedom of speech, or which was more genuinely representative of true democracy, than that of the Achaean League.

This constitution found some of the Peloponnesians ready to adopt it of their own free will; many others were induced by persuasion and argument to take part, while those who were obliged to accept it by force when the time came soon found themselves appreciating its benefits. For the community reserved no special privileges for its original members, but equal rights were granted to all states as they joined it, and in this way it soon achieved the aim it had set itself, since it was supported by two very powerful allies: the sense of humanity and of equality. It is this system, then, which we must regard as the foundation and the prime cause of the harmony which prevails in the Peloponnese, and hence of its prosperity.

These principles and this constitution had existed in their particular local form in Achaea from an early date. There is plenty of evidence of this, but for the present purpose it will be enough to quote one or two examples.

39. At the time when the houses belonging to the Pythagorean associations were burned down, there followed a general revolutionary upheaval, as was natural since the most prominent members of each city-state had thus been unexpectedly massacred, and the Greek communities in that region of southern Italy[2] became the

1. Polybius' patriotic pride in the League here proves stronger than the consistency of his philosophy of history. There are many passages in the *Histories* where the strength of chance or fate is acknowledged, e.g. p. 146 above, where he dwells on the part played by chance in the repulse of the barbarian invasions.

2. Pythagorean influence in southern Italy had begun with the philosopher's migration from Samos to the city of Croton in about 530 B.C., and his disciples had gradually obtained positions of influence in many cities. There is little positive evidence as to the nature of their political influence, but by the time of the risings to which Polybius refers, which took place in the middle of the fifth century B.C., they were regarded as a reactionary element.

scene of murder, revolutionary warfare and every kind of civil disturbance. At that time delegations were sent from many parts of Greece to offer their services as mediators, but it was the Achaeans in whom these cities felt most confidence, and to whom they entrusted the task of finding a solution for their disorders. And it was not only at this period that they showed their preference for the Achaean political system: only a few years later they decided to adopt the Achaean constitution as a model for their own.[1] The first states to take the initiative were Croton, Sybaris and Caulonia. They summoned a conference, formed a league, and began by erecting a common temple and centre of worship dedicated to Zeus Homarios[2] in which to hold their meetings and debates, and thereafter they adopted the customs and laws of the Achaeans and resolved to carry on their own government according to these principles. It was only when they fell under the domination of Dionysius of Syracuse[3] and also came under pressure from the neighbouring barbarian tribes that this purpose was frustrated and they were compelled to abandon these institutions – and even then they did so much against their will. Later on when the Spartans, against all expectations, were defeated at Leuctra,[4] and the Thebans, equally unexpectedly, claimed the hegemony of Greece, all the other states were plunged into uncertainty, and above all the two peoples directly concerned, since the Lacedaemonians refused to admit that they had lost, while the Thebans were not entirely convinced that they had won. Here again the Achaeans were the one people in all Greece to whom both parties turned for arbitration on the matters in dispute. This could not have been on account of their strength, for they were at that time almost the weakest state in Greece, but rather on account of the general faith in their trustworthiness and high principles, and there is no doubt that this opinion of the Achaeans was universally held.

Up to that time, however, these political principles had done no more than exist among the Achaeans. There had been no

---

1. Dionysius' invasion of Italy and his victory at Elleporus (389 B.C.) ended the influence of Croton and the alliance on the Achaean model.
2. 371 B.C. The title probably means 'who unites together'.
3. After 389 B.C.
4. 371 B.C.

practical application of them and no significant effort to increase the power of the country, since it had not hitherto produced a statesman worthy of the system; whenever anyone had shown signs of fulfilling this role, he had been thrust into the background and hampered, either by the Lacedaemonian government, or still more effectively by that of Macedon.

40. But when in due course the country did find leaders of sufficient stature, its potentialities for good were immediately revealed by the fulfilment of that most glorious purpose, the union of the Peloponnese. The originator and creator of the project was Aratus of Sicyon.[1] Philopoemen of Megalopolis championed it and finally established it, while Lycortas and his party secured its continuance for a considerable time. I shall try to describe how and at what date each of these statesmen contributed to the result, introducing them from time to time in such a way as will not conflict with the scheme of this work. As for the measures carried out by Aratus, I shall touch upon these only briefly both now and hereafter, since he has published an honest and lucid memoir of his own career, but I shall deal with the achievements of the other two at greater length and in fuller detail. I think that the easiest procedure for me to adopt and for my readers to follow will be to begin from the period when the cities of the Achaean League began to approach one another so as to restore it after it had been broken up by the Kings of Macedon. After that point the League continued to grow, until within my own lifetime it reached the state of completion which I have just been describing.

41. The first step was taken by the cities of Patrae and Dyme, which formed a league during the 124th Olympiad.[2] This four-year span also witnessed the deaths of Ptolemy the son of Lagus,[3]

1. Aratus of Sicyon (271–213 B.C.) founded the League in the form in which it played an important part in the third and second centuries B.C. Philopoemen (252–182) reformed the Achaean army, defeated the Spartans in 206, and became the most famous Achaean statesman of the second century. Lycortas of Megalopolis was Polybius' father and supported a policy of neutrality towards Rome and of alliance with the Ptolemies of Egypt and the Attalids of Pergamum.

2. 284–280 B.C.

3. Ptolemy, who became King of Egypt, Seleucus and Lysimachus were all Macedonian generals who had served under Alexander the Great and became

Lysimachus, Seleucus and Ptolemy Ceraunus. The state of the Achaean nation before this date may be summarized as follows. Their first King was Tisamenus, the son of Orestes, who had been expelled from Sparta on the return of the Heraclidae, and who then proceeded to occupy Achaea. The Achaeans continued to be ruled by his descendants down to the time of Ogygus, whose sons aroused so much hostility among the people by their tyrannical and unconstitutional methods of government that a revolution broke out and a democracy was set up.[1] After this and up to the time when Philip of Macedon and Alexander established their supremacy the fortunes of the Achaeans varied according to circumstances, but they always strove to preserve their democratic institutions within the Confederation.[2]

Their League consisted of twelve cities which exist to this day, with the exception of Olenus and of Helice, which was engulfed by the sea, shortly before the battle of Leuctra. These cities are named Patrae, Dyme, Pharae, Tritaea, Leontium, Aegium, Aegira, Pellene, Bura and Caryneia. Between the end of Alexander's reign and the 124th Olympiad, and chiefly on account of the efforts of the Kings of Macedon, these cities became so ill-disposed and even hostile to one another that they all broke away from the League and began openly to act against one another's interests. The result was that some of them were garrisoned by Demetrius Poliorcetes[3] and Cassander, and later by Antigonus Gonatas, while others even had to accept the rule of tyrants whom he

---

the direct heirs of his empire. Seleucus defeated and killed Lysimachus in 281, but was himself assassinated by Ptolemy Ceraunus in the same year. The date of Ptolemy Ceraunus' death is uncertain. Such synchronisms often feature in Hellenistic histories as illustrations of the workings of Fate.

1. It was rare in Greek history for a democracy to succeed a monarchy without an interval of aristocratic rule. Ogygus' dates are not known.

2. In the fifth century the Achaean states were democracies, but the evidence suggests that during the fourth their political institutions were controlled by the governments of Sparta or of Thebes.

3. Demetrius Poliorcetes (the 'besieger of cities') was intermittently powerful in Greece and Macedonia at the end of the fourth century, and ruled Macedonia from 294 to 287. Cassander, the son of Alexander the Great's viceroy Antipater, ruled Macedonia from 317 till his death in 297. Antigonus Gonatas, Demetrius' son, was King of Macedonia from 283 to 240.

installed there, for no man ever set up more absolute rulers in Greece than Antigonus. However, as I have mentioned, at about the time of the 124th Olympiad the cities underwent a change of heart and began once more to regroup themselves in leagues. This took place at about the time when King Pyrrhus of Epirus invaded Italy.[1] The first cities to act were Dyme, Patrae, Tritaea and Pharae, and because they had not entered the League but had formed it, we do not find any inscription to record that a League had been established. Some five years later the people of Aegium expelled their Macedonian garrison and joined the League, and the people of Bura, after putting their tyrant to death, followed their neighbours' example, while the next to join, almost at the same time, was the state of Caryneia. Its tyrant Iseas had seen the garrison driven out of Aegium and the tyrant of Bura killed by Margus and the Achaeans, and when he recognized that all the neighbouring cities were about to make war on him, he abdicated. He received a guarantee of his personal safety from the Achaeans and formally consented to the admission of Caryneia to the League.

42. Now why, the reader may ask, do I retrace the history of this period? My purpose is first of all to explain which of the Achaean cities took the initiative in the re-creation of the League and at what dates, and secondly to show that the claims which I made concerning the political principles of the League are borne out by the facts. The point at issue is first that the Achaeans always followed one consistent policy: this was to invite other cities to share in their equality and freedom of speech, and to make war on and subdue all those who either on their own account, or with the help of the Kings,[2] tried to enslave any of the states within their borders; and secondly that in this manner and pursuing this purpose they finally achieved this aim, partly through their own efforts and partly with the help of their allies. It is important that we attribute to the Achaean political principle in the first place all due credit for the results to which in later years their allies also con-

1. 280 B.C.

2. From the middle of the fourth century onwards the democratically governed states of Greece were under incessant threat, first from Macedonia and later either from local tyrants or from the nominees of 'the Kings', that is, the great Hellenistic dynasties such as the Ptolemies of Egypt and the other inheritors of Alexander's empire.

tributed. For although the Achaeans played a prominent part in the enterprises of others – especially in many conducted by the Romans which were conspicuously successful – yet they never showed the least desire to exploit any of these successes to the advantage of any one state; in return for all the ardent support which they gave to their allies they bargained for nothing but the freedom of all states and the union of the Peloponnesians. All this will be more clearly understood when we come to examine the efforts of the League in action.

43. For the first twenty-five years after the re-constitution of the League among the cities I have mentioned,[1] a secretary and two generals were elected by each city in turn.[2] After this they decided to elect only one general and to entrust him with the management of all the League's affairs.[3] The first man to receive this honour was Margus of Caryneia. Then, in the fourth year after Margus' generalship, Aratus of Sicyon, who was still only twenty years of age, liberated his city from its tyrant through his personal valour and daring. He had always been a passionate admirer of the Achaean political system, and he now made his own city a member of the League. Eight years later, during his second term of office as general of the League, Aratus successfully planned an operation to seize the Acrocorinth, which at that time was held on behalf of Antigonus, the King of Macedon. By this stroke he not only delivered all the inhabitants of the Peloponnese from a great source of fear, but he persuaded the newly liberated city of Corinth to join the League as well. Then during the same term of office he contrived to bring Megara into the League by similar means. These events took place in the year before the defeat of the Carthaginians at the Aegates Islands, as a result of which they evacuated Sicily and were obliged for the first time to pay tribute to Rome.[4]

Aratus had achieved remarkable progress in his aims within a very short space of time, and thereafter he continued to direct the affairs of the League. His designs and projects were all concerted towards one end: to expel the Macedonians from the Peloponnese,

1. From 280 till 255 B.C.
2. Chosen by rota each year, probably each from a separate city.
3. This change probably meant a decrease in the secretary's importance.
4. 242 B.C.

155

to sweep away the tyrannies, and to re-establish the freedom of the League both as a communal and an ancestral right for each member.[1] So long as Antigonus Gonatas lived, Aratus opposed Macedonian interference in Greek affairs and resisted the perpetual lust for plunder of the Aetolians; he effectively upheld both policies, even though these two powers were so unscrupulous and aggressive that they entered into an agreement for the express purpose of dissolving the Achaean League.[2]

44. However, on the death of Antigonus,[3] the Achaeans went so far as to make an alliance with the Aetolians and they supported them ungrudgingly in their war against Demetrius of Macedon.[4] So for the time being their estrangement and hostility were appeased and a somewhat more sociable and friendly sentiment grew up between the two peoples. Demetrius only reigned for ten years. He died at the time that the Romans made their first expedition to Illyria,[5] and after this the tide of events seemed for a while to be flowing in favour of the policy for which the Achaeans had striven all along. The local tyrants of the Peloponnese were in despair, alike at the death of Demetrius, who had acted so to speak as their patron and paymaster, and at the pressure which Aratus now brought to bear upon them. He demanded that they should lay down their authority, offering generous rewards and honours to those who agreed to abdicate, and holding over those who refused the fear of what they would suffer at the hands of the Achaeans. And so there was a general move to grant Aratus' demands, vacate the seats of power, set free the various cities, and join the League. Lydiades, the tyrant of Megalopolis, had shown rare foresight and practical sense in anticipating while Demetrius was still alive what

1. These represented Aratus' aims up to the outbreak of the Social War. At that point he was forced to change them, and when obliged by Cleomenes of Sparta to fight, he recalled the Macedonians to the Peloponnese and handed over the Acrocorinth.

2. In 245 B.C. Antigonus reoccupied Corinth, and the Aetolians invaded the Peloponnese.

3. 239 B.C.

4. Demetrius II, the son and successor of Antigonus. The Aetolians were trying to annex the Epirote half of Acarnania, whereupon Demetrius sent help to his mother-in-law Olympias, the Queen of Epirus.

5. 229 B.C.

was likely to happen, and had of his own free will laid down his authority and given his allegiance to the League. Later Aristomachus, the tyrant of Argos, Xenon, the tyrant of Hermione, and Cleonymus, the tyrant of Phlius, all likewise laid down their authority and joined the League.

45. These events substantially increased both the size and the power of the League, but they also aroused the resentment of the Aetolians. This people, who possess an innate lack of scruple and an insatiable appetite for the possessions of others, may have acted out of envy of their neighbours, but it is more likely that they hoped to divide the cities of the League,[1] as they had partitioned those of Acarnania with Alexander,[2] and were planning to do in Achaea with Antigonus Gonatas. They now had the effrontery to enter into negotiations and form an alliance with both Antigonus Doson, the regent of Macedonia and guardian to Philip, who was still a child, and with Cleomenes, the King of Sparta.[3] They saw that Antigonus had established his authority securely in Macedonia, and also that he was an open and avowed enemy of the Achaeans, because the latter had seized the Acrocorinth in a surprise attack. They calculated that if they could first arouse the Lacedaemonians to take hostile action against the League and secure their support for their own designs, they could easily overcome the Achaeans by choosing a favourable moment for their attack and delivering it from all quarters at once. And it is very likely that they would have quickly succeeded in their plans, but for the most important factor which they had left out of account. They had failed to reckon with the fact that their opponent would be Aratus, and that they would find in him a man capable of grappling with any set of circumstances. And so the result of all their carefully laid schemes and unscrupulous aggression was that they not only failed to achieve any of their objects, but that they actually strengthened the power of the League and the authority of Aratus, who was then its general and who skilfully parried and frustrated all their efforts. The following account will show how he contrived this.

1. This assertion is not supported by the facts: Polybius is giving Aratus' version of the origins of the war.

2. The reference is to Alexander II of Epirus, who succeeded Pyrrhus in 282 B.C., not to Alexander the Great.

3. He had succeeded his father Leonidas in 235.

46. Aratus had noted that the Aetolians were ashamed to make an open declaration of war, because it was only very recently that the Achaeans had supported them in their campaign against Demetrius. But he also observed that they were so deeply implicated with the Lacedaemonians and so envious of the Achaeans that they not only showed no indignation when Cleomenes made a treacherous attack upon the cities of Tegea, Mantinea and Orchomenus, but even confirmed his occupation of these places. And yet these cities were not only allies of the Aetolians, but members of their own League. In the past, because of their lust for plunder, the Aetolians had thought almost any excuse good enough to justify attacking those who had done them no wrong, but now they allowed treaties to be broken, themselves to be attacked, and some of the largest cities in their confederation to be taken from them simply in order to see Cleomenes become a dangerous opponent for the Achaeans. Aratus and the other officials of the League took note of all these events and determined that they would not take the initiative in going to war with any power, but would defend themselves against attack from the Spartans. That, at least, was their first decision, but soon afterwards Cleomenes made the provocative move of fortifying the fortress of the Athenaeum in the territory of Megalopolis against the Achaeans, and began to show a bitter and undisguised hostility towards them. Thereupon Aratus and his colleagues summoned an extraordinary meeting of the Achaean assembly, which passed a resolution to declare war openly upon Sparta. These were the origins of the so-called Cleomenean War, and this was the date when it began.[1]

47. At first the Achaeans resolved to face the Lacedaemonians

1. In the autumn of 227 B.C. Cleomenes completed the anti-aristocratic revolution unsuccessfully initiated by Agis IV, who had been put to death in 241. In his coup, Cleomenes immediately had four of the ephors killed, the ephorate was abolished, and eighty of his principal opponents were exiled. A 'Lycurgan' social programme was carried through, which included the cancellation of debts, the transfer of property to a common pool, the revival of the traditional and austere training for the young, and the organization of the citizen body into communal 'messes'. The word 'tyranny' can only, in justice, be applied to the abolition of the dual monarchy and the use of violence; in general terms Cleomenes' programme was far from tyrannical. Plutarch in his *Life of Cleomenes* shows much more enthusiasm for these reforms than Polybius.

entirely on their own. In the first place they considered it more honourable not to look to others for their safety, but to defend their cities and their territory with their own hands, and secondly they were anxious to maintain their friendship with King Ptolemy of Egypt; they were already in his debt for certain earlier services and they did not wish to give the impression that they were appealing to others for help.

The two states had been at war for some time when the Spartan King suddenly revolutionized his country's traditional political system, and turned its constitutional monarchy into a tyranny, while at the same time showing himself a bold and vigorous commander in the conduct of the war. At this point Aratus foresaw what might well happen, and since he dreaded the reckless daring of the Aetolians, he determined that he would frustrate their plans by taking action in advance. He had satisfied himself that Antigonus, the regent of Macedon, was both energetic and intelligent, and also that he represented himself to be a man of honour. But he was also well aware that kings do not look on anyone either as an ally or as an enemy of account on their personal qualities, but always reckon friendship or hostility in terms of advantage. So he decided to open conversations with Antigonus and build up a relation of confidence with him, and in this way explain to him the results which the present course of events would probably produce. But for a variety of reasons he decided that it would be unwise to do this openly. In the first place he would be likely to arouse the opposition both of Cleomenes and of the Aetolians to his enterprise, and secondly he would undermine the courage of the majority of the Achaeans if he gave the impression that he was now turning to the enemy for help, and had thus completely abandoned all the hopes he had placed in them. This was the very last idea that he wanted to put in their minds, and so having formed this plan he decided to pursue the negotiations in secrecy. He was thus often obliged to act and to speak in public in a way which was quite inconsistent with his real intention: in other words he could only keep his design concealed by creating the opposite impression. For this reason there are some details of this period which he does not record in his memoirs.

48. Aratus knew that the people of Megalopolis were suffering

severely from the war. The fact that their country bordered upon Lacedaemonia left them more exposed to attack than other states, while the Achaeans, who were hard-pressed by difficulties and dangers of their own, were unable to provide all the help that should have been due to an ally. He also understood clearly that the Megalopolitans had harboured friendly feelings towards the royal house of Macedon ever since the benefits they had received from Philip,[1] the father of Alexander the Great, and so he concluded that they would be very ready to appeal to Antigonus and place their hopes of safety in the Macedonians. So he approached Nicophanes and Cercidas of Megalopolis and after pledging them to secrecy he unfolded his plan. These men were family friends of his own who were well-qualified to undertake such a mission, and with their support he had no difficulty in persuading the people of Megalopolis to send a delegation to the League with the object of calling upon Antigonus for help. The Megalopolitans chose Nicophanes and Cercidas as their envoys, and instructed them to proceed first of all to Achaea, and then if the League supported this proposal, to Antigonus. The Achaeans agreed that the people of Megalopolis should send the delegation, and Nicophanes and his colleagues lost no time in visiting the Macedonian King. On the subject of the local problems of Megalopolis they merely outlined the essential facts, but on the general situation in Greece they spoke at greater length, and here they relied on the instructions they had been given by Aratus.

49. These had been to emphasize the scope and the significance of the common action which had been undertaken by the Aetolians and Cleomenes, and to stress the point that both the Achaeans, and even more Antigonus, needed to be on their guard against it. It should be obvious to all that the Achaeans could not resist an attack from both quarters at once, and even more apparent to any man of sense that if the Aetolians and Cleomenes were victorious, they would not confine themselves to this acquisition. The greed of the Aetolians would not be limited by the frontiers of the Peloponnese, or even those of Greece; as for Cleomenes' personal ambitions,

1. These were additions to their territory granted them after the battle of Chaeronea (338 B.C.) and the subsequent invasion of the Peloponnese by the Macedonians.

his whole effort for the present was aimed at making himself master of the Peloponnese, but once he had achieved that goal his next would be the hegemony of Greece itself, and this prize he could never obtain without first destroying the supremacy of Macedon.[1] So the envoys urged the King to look to the future and consider which course was the more advantageous for him: to join forces with the Achaeans and Boeotians and oppose Cleomenes in the Peloponnese in a contest for the supremacy of Greece, or to abandon the greatest of the Greek nations[2] to its fate and then stake the dominion of Macedon on a battle in Thessaly, in which he would be fighting the Spartans, Aetolians, Boeotians and Achaeans all at once. If the Aetolians were to make a pretence of keeping the peace, as they were doing at present[3] out of regard for the goodwill the Achaeans had shown them at the time of their war with Demetrius,[4] then the Achaeans would undertake to fight Cleomenes alone, and if Fortune were on their side they would need no further help. But if luck went against them and if they were also attacked by the Aetolians, then they begged the King to watch the course of events with care and not let matters deteriorate too far, but to rescue the Peloponnesians while they could still be saved. As for the good faith of the Achaeans and the return which they could offer for his support, they believed that he could rest assured; once the Achaeans' need was met, they promised that Aratus would find guarantees which would satisfy both parties, and he would also make it clear at what date the help would be needed.

50. After listening to these arguments Antigonus concluded that Aratus had presented an accurate and realistic view of the situation. He considered carefully what action was required, and his first step was to write a letter to the people of Megalopolis in which he promised to help them if that was what the Achaeans also wished.[5]

1. It seems probable that this is an *ex post facto* version of the talks. In reality the prospect of Spartan domination of the Peloponnese would not have represented any serious threat to Macedon.

2. The reference is to the Achaean League.

3. Here Polybius reveals the real situation, namely that the Aetolians at this date were still neutral.

4. See p. 156.

5. It was important that the invitation should come from the League as a whole, not merely from Megalopolis alone.

When Nicophanes and Cercidas returned home, delivered the King's letter, and at the same time reported his goodwill and his readiness to help them, the people were greatly encouraged; they declared their wish that the Achaean assembly should be approached and requested to call in the aid of Antigonus, and to entrust the direction of the war to him without delay. Meanwhile Aratus had been privately informed by Nicophanes that the King was well-disposed towards both the League and himself, and he was greatly relieved to find that his plan had been well conceived and that the King was by no means antagonistic to him, as the Aetolians had hoped that he would be. He thought it an important point in favour of his scheme that the Megalopolitans were so ready to deal with Antigonus through the Achaeans. He would have liked best, as I have already explained, not to have to ask for help at all, but if from sheer necessity he had to resort to this, he was anxious that the appeal should come from the League as a whole and not only from himself. He feared that if Antigonus should arrive in the Peloponnese, and after defeating Cleomenes and the Spartans in the field, should take any steps which were contrary to the League's wishes, then he himself would be blamed on all sides for the outcome; it would be argued that the King had right on his side, because of the wrong which Aratus had committed against the house of Macedon by his seizure of the Acrocorinth.[1]

The envoys from Megalopolis duly presented themselves in the council chamber of the League, showed the Macedonian King's letter which assured them of his goodwill, and appealed to the Achaeans to invite the King's immediate intervention. As soon as Aratus saw that the sense of the meeting was in favour of this course he rose to speak. He began by expressing his pleasure at the King's readiness to assist them, and his approval of the cooperative mood of the assembly. Next he embarked upon a long speech in which he urged the Achaeans to use every means to save their cities and their territory by their own efforts if this were possible, since this was the most honourable as well as the most expedient course. But if Fortune went against them, it should only be after they had exhausted all hope of succeeding by their own efforts that they should turn to their friends for help.

1. This had happened in 243 B.C. when Achaea and Macedon were at peace.

51. The people applauded his speech and a resolution was passed that they should abide by their present undertakings and carry on the war unaided. But then they suffered a series of misfortunes. First King Ptolemy abandoned the League and began to provide financial aid to Cleomenes, with the object of encouraging him to attack Antigonus; Ptolemy calculated that the Lacedaemonians could be more effective allies than the Achaeans in his policy of restraining the ambitions of the Macedonian Kings. Next the Achaeans suffered three defeats at the hands of Cleomenes: the first as they were on the march near Mount Lycaeum, a second in a pitched battle at a place named Ladoceia,[1] and finally at the Hecatombaeum in the territory of Dyme,[2] where the whole Achaean army was decisively defeated. This situation gave the Achaeans no prospect of a respite in which they might recover, and so they were compelled to appeal with one voice to Antigonus. In this crisis Aratus dispatched his son as envoy to the King and confirmed the details of assistance to be sent. There was, however, one particularly intractable problem, which caused them great difficulty and uncertainty. It was generally believed that Antigonus would not send help except on the condition that the Acrocorinth should be restored to him and he should be enabled to use the city of Corinth as a base for the war; on the other hand the Achaeans could not bring themselves to hand over the Corinthians to Macedon against their will. For this reason the Achaeans were obliged at first to adjourn their deliberations so as to examine the question of what guarantees they could offer the King.

52. Cleomenes' successes, which I have described, had spread dismay throughout the Peloponnese, and the King proceeded to make an unopposed advance through the cities, some of which he won over by persuasion and others by threats. In this way he took possession of Caphyae, Pellene, Phoneus, Argos, Phlius, Cleonae, Epidaurus, Hermione, Troezen and finally Corinth.[3] Next he laid siege to Sicyon[4] and took personal command of the operations, but during this campaign he also relieved the Achaeans of their greatest problem. The Corinthians, by ordering the Achaean garrison and

1. Both in 227 B.C. 2. 226 B.C.
3. In the summer of 225. 4. Probably in January 224.

its commander Aratus[1] to leave their city, and by sending letters to Cleomenes inviting him to enter it, had provided Aratus with the opportunity to offer Antigonus the Acrocorinth and a sufficient reason for doing so. Aratus was quick to seize his opportunity, and in this way he not only made amends for his earlier offence against the royal house, but also delivered a sufficient guarantee for their future association, and provided Antigonus with a base for his war against the Lacedaemonians.

When Cleomenes discovered that an agreement had been reached between Antigonus and the Achaeans, he left Sicyon and pitched camp near the Isthmus of Corinth. He constructed a trench and a palisade to join the Acrocorinth with the fortification which is known as the Ass's Back, and confidently began from this point to regard the whole of the Peloponnese as subject to his rule. For his part Antigonus had long been making his preparations as Aratus had advised him, and was only awaiting the right moment to attack. He now concluded from the progress of events that Cleomenes was on the point of advancing into Thessaly, and he therefore sent envoys to Aratus and the Achaeans invoking the terms of their alliance. He then took his forces through Euboea[2] and arrived at the Isthmus. He followed this route because the Aetolians, apart from the other efforts they had made to prevent him from helping the Achaeans, had forbidden him to pass with his army beyond Thermopylae, and had threatened that if he advanced they would oppose his march. Thus the armies of Antigonus and of Cleomenes were now face to face, the one determined to enter the Peloponnese and the other to keep his adversary out.

53. Meanwhile the Achaeans, despite the heavy defeats they had suffered, were not deterred from their purpose, nor did they depart from their principle of relying upon their own efforts. So when Aristoteles of Argos rose in revolt against Cleomenes' supporters, they sent a force under the command of the League's general Timoxenus[3] to help him, and these troops made a surprise

1. This apparently was a special command for Aratus. The League's official general was Timoxenus (see note 3).

2. This route avoided Thessaly, which was in Aetolian hands.

3. Timoxenus was general either in 225/4 or 224/3. Aratus was still supreme commander, but probably occupied with strategic rather than tactical command.

attack and succeeded in entering and capturing the city. This enterprise, indeed, should be seen as the principal cause of the recovery in the Achaeans' fortunes which followed, for later events clearly showed that it was this reverse at Argos which checked Cleomenes' ardour and daunted the spirits of his troops. Although he was occupying a stronger position than Antigonus, was better furnished with supplies, and temperamentally speaking was driven by stronger forces of courage and ambition, yet no sooner was the news received that Argos had been taken by the Achaeans, than he immediately broke off contact with the enemy, abandoned all his superior positions, and withdrew from the Isthmus in headlong retreat for fear of being encircled on all sides by the enemy. He attacked Argos and gained possession of a part of the city, but the Achaeans put up a fierce resistance and were stoutly supported by the Argives, who fought with no less valour for having changed sides. So the attempt to recapture Argos also failed, whereupon Cleomenes marched back by way of Mantinea and returned to Sparta.

54. Meanwhile Antigonus advanced unopposed into the Peloponnese, took possession of the Acrocorinth, and without losing any time pushed on to Argos. There he praised the Argives for the help they had given, and after making arrangements for the security of the city at once set off for Arcadia. He drove out the Spartan garrisons from a number of fortified posts which Cleomenes had built in the territory of Aegys and Belbina,[1] handed these positions over to the Megalopolitans, and then returned to Aegium, where the Achaeans were in session. He gave the council a report on the operations he had undertaken and agreed with them on the arrangements for the future conduct of the war. The council appointed him commander-in-chief of all the allied forces,[2] and he then moved into winter quarters near Sicyon and Corinth.

Early in the following spring[3] Antigonus moved southwards with his army and reached Tegea in three days; there he was joined by the Achaeans, pitched camp and proceeded to lay siege to the

1. South of Megalopolis and near the border between Laconia and Messenia; among these posts was the Athenaeum fortress (see p. 158).
2. This gathering included more states than the Achaean League.
3. 223 B.C.

city. The Macedonians pressed the siege operations vigorously, especially by mining, and the Tegeans soon despaired of holding out any longer and surrendered. After making the necessary arrangements for the security of the city, Antigonus moved on to the next objective in his plan of campaign, and advanced with all speed upon Laconia. He found Cleomenes' army drawn up on the frontier to defend his territory, and began to test his strength with a few skirmishing operations. But when his scouts brought the news that the garrison of Orchomenus had marched out to join Cleomenes' troops, he immediately broke camp and made a forced march to the town. His move took the place by surprise and he was able to capture it by storm, after which he surrounded and laid siege to Mantinea. That city was likewise soon frightened into submission, whereupon he again broke camp and advanced against Heraea and Telphusa, whose inhabitants surrendered to him of their own accord. By this time winter was approaching, and Antigonus travelled to Aegium to attend the assembly of the Achaean League. He dismissed his Macedonian troops to allow them to winter at home, but himself remained in the Peloponnese, to discuss the present situation with the Achaeans and concert plans for the future.

55. At the same time Cleomenes had noted that Antigonus had dismissed his Macedonian troops, and kept only his mercenaries under arms while he spent his time at Aegium, which is three days' march from Megalopolis. He knew that on account of its size and of the fact that its inhabitants were scattered over a large area the city was difficult to defend, that at that moment it was very carelessly guarded because of Antigonus' presence in the Peloponnese, and above all, that most of its citizens of military age had been killed in the battles at the Lycaeum and Ladoceia. He made contact with a number of Messenian exiles who happened to be living in Megalopolis at that time, and with their help he contrived to get inside the walls at night undetected. However, when daylight dawned the Megalopolitans fought back with such courage that Cleomenes was not only in danger of being driven out again, but came near to having his whole force annihilated. The townsfolk had in fact defeated and repulsed him three months earlier when he had forced his way into the quarter known as the Colaeum. But on the

present occasion he had the advantage of superior numbers and of having had the time to seize the commanding positions beforehand, and so his plan succeeded, and in the end he drove out the Megalopolitans and took complete possession of the city. Once it was in his power, he destroyed it in so savage and vindictive a manner as to leave no prospect that it could ever be inhabited again. I believe that he did this because Megalopolis and Stymphalia were the only cities in which, throughout all the vicissitudes of fortune that they experienced, he never succeeded in suborning a single citizen or finding a supporter or associate to take part in his schemes. In the case of the people of Cleitor their noble passion for liberty was dishonoured by only one man, Thearces, and, as one might expect, they refused to acknowledge him as a native of their city and insisted that he was a changeling, the son of one of the foreign soldiers who were then garrisoning Orchomenus.

56. One of the writers who lived in the times of Aratus is Phylarchus. His accounts of events often contradict and his opinions differ from those of the Achaean statesman, but he is nevertheless regarded by some readers as a trustworthy witness. Accordingly, since I have chosen to follow Aratus' narrative for the history of the Cleomenean Wars, it will, I think, be useful and indeed necessary for me to examine the question of the two writers' relative credibility; in this way we shall ensure that falsehood shall not be allowed to enjoy equal authority with truth in their respective writings. Speaking generally, there are many statements scattered throughout Phylarchus' work which have been made at random and without discrimination. There is no need for me on the present occasion to criticize him for lapses which concern other parts of his work, or to study these minutely, but it is essential that I should investigate in detail those which relate to the period I am describing, namely, the Cleomenean War. Such an examination will in fact be quite sufficient to enable us to judge the general purpose and character of his work.

For example, since it was his purpose to emphasize the cruelty of Antigonus and the Macedonians and also that of Aratus and the Achaeans, he tells us that the Mantineans, when they fell into the hands of their enemies, were subjected to terrible sufferings, and that the calamities which befell this city, the most ancient and the most populous in Arcadia, were so dreadful as to horrify all the Greeks and move them to tears. In his eagerness to arouse the pity of his readers and enlist their sympathy through his story he introduces graphic scenes of women clinging to one another, tearing their hair and baring their breasts, and in addition he describes the tears and lamentations of men and women accompanied by their children and aged parents as they are led away into captivity. Phylarchus reproduces this kind of effect again and again in his history, striving on each occasion to recreate the horrors before our eyes. Let us ignore for the moment the ignoble and unmanly nature of his treatment of the subject, and consider the nature and use of history itself. It is not a historian's business to startle his readers with sensational descriptions, nor should he try, as the tragic poets do, to represent speeches which might have been delivered, or to enumerate all the possible consequences of the events under consideration; it is his task first and foremost to record with fidelity what actually happened and was said, however commonplace this may be. For the aim of tragedy is by no means the same as that of history, but rather the opposite. The tragic poet seeks to thrill and charm his audience for the moment by expressing through his characters the most plausible words possible, but the historian's task is to instruct and persuade serious students by means of the truth of the words and actions he presents, and this effect must be permanent, not temporary. Thus in the first case the supreme aim is *probability*, even if what is said is untrue, the purpose being to beguile the spectator, but in the second it is *truth*, the purpose being to benefit the reader. Apart from these considerations, Phylarchus merely relates most of the catastrophes in his history, without suggesting why things are done or to what end, and in the absence of such an analysis it is impossible to feel either pity or an anger which matches the circumstances. Everybody, for example, regards it as an outrage for a free man to be beaten, but if anyone provokes this action because he was the first to resort to violence, then he is regarded as having been rightly punished. Again, if this punishment is imposed for a reformatory or disciplinary purpose, then those who strike free men are considered worthy of praise and of gratitude. Or again, to kill a citizen is considered to be the greatest of crimes and therefore the one which carries the supreme penalty, but it is well-known that the man who kills a thief or an adulterer is left untouched, and the slayer of a traitor or a tyrant is rewarded in every country with honours and preeminence. It follows that our final judgement of good and evil is decided in every case not by the actions themselves, but by the different motives and purposes of those who perform them.

64. At the beginning of the spring which followed the capture of Megalopolis [1] Cleomenes assembled his troops, while Antigonus was still in his winter quarters at Argos. He addressed them with a speech that matched the occasion, and then led out his army and invaded the territory of the Argives. Many people consider that this was an unduly dangerous, even a foolhardy step, because the passes which gave access to Argive territory were strongly fortified, but to any qualified observer it was both a safe and a wise course of action. Cleomenes had already discovered that his opponent had sent his forces home,[2] and it was clear to him that there would be no danger of a counter-attack, and further that if the countryside were ravaged up to the city walls the Argives would be enraged at the sight and would lay the blame on Antigonus. If the Macedonian King had found himself unable to bear the reproaches of the populace and had then marched out and risked a battle with the troops which he had available, the odds would certainly have been in favour of an easy victory for Cleomenes. On the other hand, if Antigonus continued to follow out his plan and remained inactive, Cleomenes would have succeeded both in frightening his enemies and putting fresh heart into his own troops, after which he could still, so he calculated, withdraw safely into Laconia. In the event this is exactly what happened. As the countryside was laid waste, crowds gathered in the city and heaped abuse on Antigonus. But he, playing his proper part both as a general and as a king, allowed no consideration to distract him from the rational conduct of the war, and so he remained on the defensive. Cleomenes for his part carried out his plan to devastate the country,

1. 222 B.C. Megalopolis had fallen in the autumn of the preceding year.
2. The Macedonian troops were needed at home during the winter to work in the fields. This was a normal feature of Greek military life, and especially in Macedonia.

and having thus struck terror into the enemy and raised the spirits of his own troops in preparation for the coming struggle, he returned home unmolested.

65. Early in the summer, when he had been reinforced by the return of the Macedonians and Achaeans from their winter quarters, Antigonus advanced with his army and the allied contingents into Laconia. His Macedonian troops consisted of 10,000 infantry for the phalanx, 3,000 *peltasts*[1] and 300 cavalry. Besides these he had 1,000 Agrianians,[2] 1,000 Gauls,[3] a detachment of mercenaries numbering 3,000 infantry and 300 cavalry, an Achaean contingent also numbering 3,000 picked infantry and 300 cavalry, and 1,000 infantry from Megalopolis[4] armed in the Macedonian style and under the command of Cercidas. The allied troops consisted of 2,000 Boeotian infantry and 200 cavalry, 1,000 Epirot infantry and 50 cavalry, the same number of Acarnanians, and 1,600 Illyrians under the command of Demetrius of Pharos. Antigonus' combined forces amounted to 28,000 infantry and 1,200 cavalry.

Cleomenes, who had expected this invasion, had blocked the other passes which gave access to Laconia by posting garrisons, digging trenches and constructing barricades of trees. He himself took up position with an army of 20,000 men at a place named Sellasia, as he calculated that this was the approach the invaders were most likely to choose, and this was in fact what happened. The pass is overlooked by two hills, one named Evas and the other Olympus, and the road to Sparta runs between them following the bank of the river Oenous. Cleomenes fortified both these hills with a trench and a palisade. On the hill of Evas he posted the Perioeci[5]

1. A crack force of Macedonian mobile infantry, equipped with smaller shields but sufficiently heavily armoured to fight alongside the phalanx.
2. This tribe lived around the Rhodope mountains and the source of the Strymon. Their weapons were the javelin, sling or bow, and they were a versatile corps, often used for special operations.
3. Probably Gallic infantry from Europe, not from Galatia in Asia Minor.
4. Antigonus had armed the Megalopolitans because they had lost their own resources. Their arms would have included the *sarissa*, the twenty-one-foot infantry pike.
5. The Perioeci, originally Spartan colonists of the hills and coastal districts of Laconia, had free status and formed the second class in the Spartan hierarchy, below the Spartiates. Within the state only the latter had political rights, but in foreign relations the Perioeci counted as Spartans and shared the obligation

and the allied troops under the command of his brother Eucleidas,[1] while he himself held Olympus with the Lacedaemonians and mercenaries.[2] On the level ground by the river on each side of the road he posted his cavalry and a part of the mercenary force. When Antigonus arrived, he at once perceived the strength of the position, and the skill with which Cleomenes had posted each of the various parts of his army to the best advantage in relation to the ground, so that the whole appearance of his dispositions resembled that of a trained soldier poised and ready to fight. No preparation had been omitted, either for attack or defence, so that the Spartan array constituted at the same time a battle line ready for action and a fortified camp which was hard to approach.

66. Antigonus therefore decided against any hasty attempt to engage the enemy and storm the position. Instead he pitched his camp a short distance away with his front protected by the river Gorgylus. There he waited for several days, making use of the time to reconnoitre the special features of the country and the character of the troops opposed to him, while he also tried a number of feints in the hope of enticing the enemy into showing his hand. But he never succeeded in finding a weak or unguarded spot, since on every occasion Cleomenes parried his thrusts with a counter-movement. So Antigonus abandoned these tactics and in the end by apparent consent both Kings decided to put the issue to the test of battle.[3] And indeed these two commanders whom Fortune had ranged opposite one another were at once exceptionally gifted and evenly matched. To face the enemy's left flank, posted on the hill of Evas, Antigonus placed his Macedonian infantry, equipped with bronze shields, and the Illyrians, the two drawn up in alternate

---

to bear arms. After his coup of 227 B.C. Cleomenes had formed a special corps of 4,000 Perioeci whom he armed in the Macedonian style.

1. Another feature of Cleomenes' coup had been to make his brother Eucleidas co-ruler. Hitherto there had never been two Spartan Kings at once from the same family.

2. The Lacedaemonians constituted the Spartan phalanx of 6,000 men; the mercenary contingent probably numbered about 5,600.

3. cf. p. 176. Cleomenes' decision to fight was no doubt influenced by the news which had reached him only ten days before that his Egyptian subsidies had been cut off.

units,[1] and this wing was commanded by Alexander the son of Acmetus and Demetrius of Pharos. Behind these were placed the Acarnanians and Epirots, and in the rear 2,000 Achaeans, who were held in reserve.[2] His cavalry were drawn up opposite that of the enemy, under the command of Alexander and supported by 1,000 Achaean and the same number of Megalopolitan infantry. Antigonus decided that he himself would lead the mercenaries and the rest of the Macedonians against Cleomenes' position on Olympus. The mercenaries were posted in front, and behind them the Macedonians were drawn up in a double phalanx with no space between the two units;[3] he was compelled to adopt this formation because of the narrowness of his front. It was agreed that the Illyrians would begin the fighting by attacking the hill of Evas as soon as they saw a flag of linen waved from the direction of Olympus. They had already on the previous night succeeded in occupying a position right at the foot of the slope of Evas in the bed of the river Gorgylus.[4] The signal for action for the Megalopolitans and the cavalry was to be a scarlet flag which would be raised by the King.

67. When the moment for the assault arrived, the Illyrians were given their signal, the officers passed the word to the men to do their duty, and all the Illyrians at once sprang into view of the enemy and launched their attack on the hill. At this point the light-armed mercenaries who had been stationed in the valley to support the Spartan cavalry noticed that the Achaean units were not covered by any troops behind them, and so they launched a

1. This was a more flexible formation than the phalanx, and comparable to the Roman maniple.

2. The Achaeans formed a second line behind the Acarnanians and were evidently intended to close the gap between right and centre when the left wing advanced up the hill.

3. The normal depth of the phalanx, which numbered 10,000 men, was sixteen ranks; here the width was halved and the depth increased to thirty-two ranks.

4. Polybius consistently omits to mention the Acarnanians' part in the action, but according to Plutarch's account they would have been grouped with the Illyrians and took part in the advance up the hill. These troops were in hiding in the river bed, and together were sufficiently numerous to outflank the Spartan left.

charge from the rear. This move threatened the whole of Antigonus' right wing, which was pressing the attack up the hill of Evas, since they were facing Eucleidas' troops above them and were being strongly attacked by the mercenaries from behind and below. At this critical moment Philopoemen of Megalopolis saw what was happening, and at the same time what was likely to happen. At first he tried to point out the danger to the senior commanders, but as he was still quite a young man[1] and had never before held a command, nobody took any notice of him. Finally he called upon his fellow-citizens to rally round him and boldly charged the Spartan cavalry. His action quickly created a diversion. The mercenaries, who had been harassing the rear of the troops advancing up Evas, heard the commotion and, seeing that their own cavalry were engaged, broke off their action and ran back to their original positions to support the cavalry. Meanwhile the Illyrians and Macedonians and the rest of the assault force found themselves freed from the threat to their rear, and hurled themselves with fresh courage upon the enemy. And so, as became clear afterwards, it was Philopoemen's action which was principally responsible for the success of the attack on Eucleidas' position.

68. The story goes that after the battle Antigonus, who was disposed to chaff Alexander, the commander of the cavalry, asked him why he had ordered an attack before the signal had been given. Alexander denied the accusation and retorted that the attack had been begun by a boy from Megalopolis who had acted against his orders. The King's reply was that the boy had grasped the situation and acted like a good general; it was Alexander, the so-called general, who had acted like a boy.

However this may be, Eucleidas' troops threw away the advantages of their strong position when they saw the enemy advancing on them. What they should have done was to charge immediately while the enemy was still some way down the slope. In this way they would have broken up their formation and thrown them into confusion, and they could themselves have withdrawn slowly step by step and safely regained their positions on the higher ground.

1. Philopoemen was to become one of the most brilliant commanders of the Achaean League. At this date he was thirty-one, and was serving in the Achaean cavalry under Alexander.

If they had at the outset wrested from their opponents the special advantages which the Illyrians derived both from their armour and their close-knit formation, they could easily have put them to flight because of the more favourable position which they occupied on the hill. As it was, they acted as if victory were already assured and did exactly the opposite of all these things. That is to say, Eucleidas' troops remained in their original positions on the crest with the object of meeting the enemy as high up the slope as possible, so that when the latter were repulsed their flight would be all the longer and would take place over steep and precipitous ground. But, as might have been expected, it was the reverse which happened. The Spartans had left themselves no room for withdrawal, and when they received the charge of the Macedonians, who were comparatively fresh and still in unbroken order, they found themselves at the disadvantage of having to fight along the very summit of the hill. From this point whenever the Spartans were forced to give ground through the weight of their opponents' armour and their close-packed formation, the Illyrians immediately occupied the place where they stood, but each time that Eucleidas' men took a step backwards, they were thrust on to lower ground, because they had left themselves no room to fall back or to change formation. The result was not long delayed. They were compelled to turn and begin a withdrawal which proved disastrous, as it lay for a long distance over difficult and rocky ground.[1]

69. At the same time the cavalry action was also being decided, and here Philopoemen and the Achaean horsemen rendered magnificent service; indeed it was for their liberty that the whole battle was being fought. Philopoemen's horse was killed under him, whereupon he continued to fight on foot and was severely wounded by a thrust which pierced both thighs. Meanwhile the forces of the two Kings became involved in the fighting on Olympus, and the battle began with a clash between their light-armed troops and mercenaries, of which each had about 5,000. Some of these attacks took place between separate units and others along the whole line, but both sides fought with great bravery – all the more so because the contest took place in full view of the Kings and of the opposing

1. Polybius, as so often, introduces a note of dramatic irony: this was the fate which Eucleidas' men had planned for their opponents.

armies, so that both regiments and individual antagonists vied
with one another to prove their courage. At length Cleomenes
saw that his brother's troops had been routed and that his cavalry
on the low ground were about to give way. He feared that he
might find himself attacked from all directions at once, and so he
was compelled to break down part of his protecting palisade and
lead out his whole force in line from one side of his fortifications.
At this point both commanders ordered their trumpeters to sound
the retreat for the light-armed troops, and withdrew them from
the space between the armies. Then the two phalanxes shouted
their war-cry, levelled their pikes and met in a head-on charge.
A fierce struggle followed. At one point the Macedonians were
forced to retire, and gave ground for a considerable distance before
the resolute onslaught of the Lacedaemonians, and at another the
tremendous weight of the Macedonian phalanx compelled their
adversaries to fall back. At last Antigonus ordered his pikemen to
mass in close order, and taking advantage of the peculiar formation
of the double phalanx they launched a charge which finally dislodged the Lacedaemonians from their positions. The whole
Spartan army was routed and the troops were cut down as they
fled, but Cleomenes, surrounding himself with a small detachment
of horsemen, reached Sparta in safety.[1] Then as night fell he went
down to Gythium, where preparations had been made some time
before for him to escape by sea if the need arose, and set sail with
his friends for Alexandria.

70. Having become master of Sparta at a single stroke, Antigonus
went on to treat the Lacedaemonians in a generous and humane
spirit. He restored the traditional constitution,[2] and a few days
later marched his army away, as he had received news that the
Illyrians had invaded Macedonia and were ravaging the country.

1. The breakthrough when it came was overwhelming because Antigonus'
heavy infantry was concentrated to an extraordinary extent. The double
phalanx massed 10,000 men behind a 300-yard line. According to Plutarch's
account all but 200 of the Spartan phalanx died on the field. The contrast
between the slaughter of the Spartan troops and the King's escape, so alien to
Spartan tradition, is intentional.

2. Antigonus restored the ephors and abolished Cleomenes' programme of
'Lycurgan' reform. In this sense he was putting the clock back to an aristocratic, rather than encouraging a democratic regime.

So it is that Fortune always decides the greatest issues in human affairs in an arbitrary fashion. In this instance, if Cleomenes had put off the battle for a few days, or if even after his return to Sparta he had waited for a little while to take advantage of the change in the situation, he would have saved his crown.

As it was, Antigonus marched to Tegea and likewise restored the ancient constitution there, and two days later arrived in Argos at the moment when the Nemean Games were being celebrated. There he was awarded every kind of honour and distinction to immortalize his memory, both by the Achaean League and by the individual states, after which he hurried back to Macedonia where he found the Illyrians. He compelled them to fight a pitched battle and won a victory, but while he was shouting to encourage his troops in the fighting, he exerted himself so violently that he took to vomiting blood, fell into the morbid condition of which this is a symptom, and died soon afterwards. He had aroused great hopes among all the Greeks, not only because of the services he had rendered them in the field, but rather because of his high principles and standards of conduct. His successor upon the throne of Macedon was Philip, the son of Demetrius.[1]

71. I owe a word of explanation as to why I have written of the Cleomenean War at such length. This period immediately precedes the times which will be the subject of my main history, and I therefore thought that it would be useful – indeed the original plan of my work obliged me – to give a clear picture of the relations between the Macedonians and the Greeks at that time. At about the same date to which I am referring Ptolemy Euergetes fell ill and died, and was succeeded by Ptolemy surnamed Philopator.[2] Seleucus III, the son of the Seleucus who was surnamed Callinicus or Pogon, also died at about this time,[3] and was succeeded on the throne of Syria by his brother Antiochus.[4] The same phenomenon

1. Philip V, son of Demetrius II, was born in 238 and was seventeen at his accession.

2. Ptolemy III, known as Euergetes I, reigned from 246–221; Ptolemy IV, Philopator, from 221–204.

3. Seleucus III, Soter, reigned from 227–223, when he was assassinated in his camp.

4. Antiochus III, known as the Great, reigned from 223–187, and later plays a prominent part in this history.

occurred with these three rulers, Antigonus, Ptolemy and Seleucus, as with the three first successors of Alexander the Great, namely that their deaths all fell within a single Olympiad, in the case of the earlier Kings the 124th and of the later the 139th.

I have thus completed this introduction or preamble to my history. In it I have shown in the first place, when and by what means and for what reason the Romans, after making themselves supreme in Italy, first took a hand in affairs outside that country and challenged the Carthaginians for the command of the seas; and secondly, I have sketched the situation of Greece, of Macedonia and of Carthage at that time. I have now in accordance with my purpose arrived at the point when the Greeks were on the eve of the Social War, the Romans of the Hannibalic, and the Kings of Asia of the war for Coele Syria. The termination of the events which I have described above as immediately preceding these wars, and the deaths of the three Kings who had directed affairs up to this point mark a fitting close to this book.

BOOK III

Introduction

1. In the first book of my history I explained that I had fixed as my starting-point the Social War in Greece, the Hannibalic War and the war for Coele Syria.[1] In the same book I also set forth the reasons why I devoted my first two books to a review of the period which preceded these events. I shall now attempt to give a complete account of these wars, of their causes and of the reasons why they were fought on so grand a scale, but first of all I have a few words to say concerning my work as a whole.

The subject on which I have undertaken to write, the theme, that is, of how, when and why all the known parts of the world were brought under the domination of Rome, is to be seen as a single action and a single spectacle, which has an identifiable beginning, a fixed duration and an acknowledged end.[2] I propose to preface this by a short survey of the principal phases in this process from start to finish, since it is in this way, I believe, that I can best convey to the student of my history a clear conception of my plan. A preliminary grasp of the whole is of great service in enabling us to master the details, while at the same time some previous acquaintance with the details helps us towards the comprehension of the whole. So in the conviction that a preliminary survey which combines the two will provide the best preparation, I shall arrange the introductory summary to my history on this principle. I have already explained the general scope and the limits of my theme. As to the particular events with which it deals, these begin with the above-mentioned wars and end with the destruction of the Macedonian monarchy. From the beginning to the end of my chosen period there is a span of fifty-three years, which embraces a greater

1. For the definition of this area, see p. 291, and note 1.
2. The critical terminology for the Aristotelian doctrine of the unity of a *dramatic* work is here applied to *history*.

number of momentous events than any other period of comparable length in past history. In recounting these I shall begin from the 140th Olympiad, and shall arrange my exposition in the following order.

2. First I shall identify the causes of the above-mentioned war between Rome and Carthage, known as the Hannibalic War, and relate how the Carthaginians invaded Italy, broke up the dominion of Rome over the whole country, brought the Romans to a state of near panic both for their own safety and for the possession of their native land, and contrary to all expectation conceived great hopes of capturing Rome itself.

Next I shall try to explain how at the same period King Philip of Macedon, after he had concluded his war with the Aetolians and subsequently settled the affairs of Greece, conceived the design of forming an alliance with the Carthaginians.[1] Then I shall describe how Antiochus and Ptolemy Philopator first quarrelled and finally went to war with one another for the possession of Coele Syria, and how the people of Rhodes, together with Prusias, the ruler of Bithynia, declared war on the Byzantines and forced them to cease levying tolls on ships bound for the Black Sea.

At this point I shall interrupt my narrative to introduce a description of the Roman constitution. Then, as a sequel to this study, I shall describe how the peculiar character of this constitution contributed very largely not only to the restoration of Roman rule over the Italians and the Sicilians, but also to the acquisition of Spain, to the recovery of Cisalpine Gaul, and finally to the victorious conclusion of the war with Carthage and to the idea of attaining the dominion of the whole world.

Next I shall introduce another digression to relate the fall of the power of Hiero of Syracuse, and from this I shall pass on to the disturbances which took place in Egypt. Here I shall report how, after the death of Ptolemy, Antiochus and Philip of Macedon entered into a compact to partition the territories of Ptolemy's infant son, and I shall describe their acts of injustice in the course of which Philip set about annexing Egypt and also Samos and Caria, while Antiochus took possession of Coele Syria and Phoenicia.

3. The next phase in my plan will be to round off the dealings

1. See p. 298.

between the Romans and the Carthaginians in Spain, Africa and Sicily, after which, in accordance with the pattern of events at that time, I shall shift the scene of my narrative and give my whole attention to Greece and its neighbourhood. There I shall report the naval battles which Attalus and the Rhodians fought against Philip of Macedon, and then deal with the war between Philip and the Romans,[1] describing how this came about, and what was the outcome. From this I shall turn to the grievances harboured by the Aetolians, and how in consequence of these they called in the help of Antiochus from Asia, and thus kindled the war from Asia against the Achaeans and the Romans. Then, having explained the causes of this war and how Antiochus crossed over to Europe, I shall relate first of all how he was driven out of Greece, secondly how after his defeat in this campaign he relinquished all his territories in Asia up to the Taurus mountains, and thirdly how the Romans, after crushing the aggression of the Gallic tribes in Galatia, established undisputed rule over the whole of Asia Minor and delivered all its inhabitants west of the Taurus from the fear of barbarian invasions and the lawless actions of the Gauls.

After this I shall draw the reader's attention to the misfortunes suffered by the Aetolians and the Cephallenians and touch on the war fought by Eumenes against Prusias and the Gauls, and that between Ariarathes and Pharnaces. I shall also give a description of the unity and settled condition of the Peloponnese, and mention the growth of the island state of Rhodes. Lastly I shall bring the whole narrative to its conclusion with an account of the expedition of Antiochus Epiphanes against Egypt, and of the war between the Romans and Perseus and the destruction of the Macedonian monarchy. All these events will serve to illustrate the manner in which the Romans dealt with each crisis as it arose, and thus established their rule over the whole world.

4. Now if it were possible to form an adequate judgement as to how far states and individuals deserved praise or blame simply on the evidence of their successes or failures, I ought to have stopped here and concluded both the narrative and my whole historical study with an account of these last-mentioned events, and this, in fact, was my original intention. The period of fifty-

1. The Second Macedonian War, 200–197 B.C.

three years ended at this point, and the growth and advance of Roman power was by then complete.[1] Moreover it was by then universally recognized that the whole world must accept the authority of Rome and obey her commands. And yet judgements concerning either the victors or the vanquished which are based on nothing more than the outcome of battles cannot possibly be final; for what have appeared to be the most striking successes have often, if they are not rightly used, brought the most overwhelming disasters in their train, and conversely the most terrible calamities have, if bravely endured, actually turned out to benefit the sufferers. I feel bound therefore to add to my account of the events just mentioned a survey of the policy which the conquerors subsequently pursued, and of how they exercised their world-wide supremacy, and likewise of the impressions and judgements which the rest formed concerning their rulers. Besides this I must also describe the driving forces and the dominant preoccupations of the various peoples concerned, both in their public and their private life. In this way our contemporaries will be enabled to see clearly whether the rule of Rome is something to be welcomed or to be avoided at all costs, and future generations to judge whether they should praise and admire or condemn it. It is in this respect above all that my book may be considered useful for the present and the future. For neither the rulers themselves nor the historians who judge them should see the act of conquest or the subjection of others to their authority as the sole object of a policy, just as no man of good sense goes to war simply for the sake of overwhelming his opponents or sails over the sea simply for the sake of crossing it. In fact nobody applies himself even to the arts or the crafts simply for the sake of learning them, but everyone pursues these activities for the sake of the pleasure, honour or advantage which he may derive from them.

It follows, then, that the final achievement of this work will be to ascertain what was the situation of each people after they had all been subdued and brought under the authority of Rome up to the period of general disturbance and upheaval which ensued.

1. This was, in fact, far from being the case, but Polybius had committed himself to the theory that the power of Rome had ceased to expand after 167 B.C.

Because of the importance and the unexpected character of these later events, and above all because I not only witnessed the greater number of them but also took part in some and directed the course of others, I was persuaded to write about them and to make them the starting-point of what amounts almost to a new work.[1]

5. This period of disturbance embraces the wars of Rome against the Celtiberians and the Vaccaei,[2] that of Carthage against Masinissa, the King of Libya, and of Attalus of Pergamum against Prusias of Bithynia in Asia. Meanwhile Ariarathes, the King of Cappadocia, was driven out of his kingdom by Orophernes through the agency of Demetrius, the King of Syria, and recovered his ancestral throne with the help of Attalus; and subsequently Demetrius, the son of Seleucus, after holding power in Syria for twelve years, lost both his throne and his life when the other Kings joined forces against him.[3] Shortly before this last event the Romans, having cleared the Greeks who had been accused of complicity in the war against Perseus of Macedon of the slanders that had been made against them, allowed these exiles to return to their homes.[4]

Not long afterwards[5] the Romans turned their arms against

1. Polybius had originally planned his history to cover fifty-three years (220–168 B.C.), but in the foregoing chapter he argues that a proper judgement on conquerors and conquered can only be formed by a study of their subsequent relations and conduct. Hence his decision to extend his history down to at least 146 B.C. This raises a number of problems as to when Polybius took this decision, what was the scope of his revised plan, and to what extent this involved revision of the earlier books. Such evidence as we possess suggests that it was only after 146 B.C. that Polybius conceived his new plan, and that this was partly determined by the wish to record events in which he himself had played a considerable part. These included, for example, his presence in Carthage at the time of the Third Punic War (Books XXXI and XXXVI) and his participation in the settlement of Achaean affairs.

2. These wars do not follow the sequence in which Polybius refers to them. The Celtiberian War lasted from 153 to 151; the Carthaginian began in 151; Ariarathes was expelled in 158 and restored in 156; the war between Attalus and Prusias lasted from 156 to 154; Demetrius ruled Syria from 162–150; the return of the Greek exiles took place in 151.

3. He was killed in battle against Alexander Balas, a usurper supported by Attalus and Ptolemy.

4. These were the survivors of the 1,000 Achaeans who had been kept in Italy without trial ever since the battle of Pydna (168 B.C.).

5. The Third Punic War lasted from 149–146 B.C.

Carthage; first of all they had intended that the city should be removed to some other site, but later they made up their minds to destroy it completely, for reasons which I shall explain in due course. At the same time the Macedonians renounced their pact of friendship with Rome and the Lacedaemonians seceded from the Achaean League, and these events brought about the beginning and the end of the disaster which then overtook the whole of Greece.

This, then, is the general plan of my work. Its fulfilment must depend on whether Fortune grants me a sufficiently long span of life. But even if the common human destiny should overtake me, I am convinced that my subject will not languish for want of men who are quite capable of continuing it; there are many who will pledge themselves to carry on the task to its appointed conclusion.

Accordingly, now that I have provided a summary of the most important events so as to convey to my readers an impression of the work as a whole and of its contents in detail, it is time for me to resume my original plan and return to the point at which my history begins.

The Second Punic War

6. Some of those writers who have recorded the history of Hannibal and his times and have tried to identify the causes of this war between Rome and Carthage have cited as its first cause the Carthaginian action in laying siege to the city of Saguntum, and as its second their crossing of the river Ebro in contravention of their treaty with the Romans. I could concede that these events might be described as the *beginnings* of the war, but should by no means agree that they constituted its causes. On the same analogy one might as well say that Alexander the Great's crossing into Asia was the cause of his war against Persia, and Antiochus' landing at Demetrias the cause of his against Rome, neither of which assertions is correct or even plausible. For how could anyone maintain that these actions were the causes of the war in question, when in the case of the Persian war many of the plans and preparations had been made by Alexander, and some even in the lifetime of his

father Philip, and in that of the war against Rome, by the Aetolians long before Antiochus arrived? Such theories are put forward by those who cannot grasp the distinction – still less its magnitude – between a *beginning*, a *cause*, and a *pretext*, and overlook the fact that the cause comes first in a given chain of events and the beginning last. The word *beginning* I shall use to refer to the first attempt to execute and put into action plans which have already been decided; and the word *cause* to those events which influence in advance our purposes and decisions, that is to say our conceptions of things, our state of mind, our calculations about them and the whole process of reasoning whereby we arrive at decisions and undertakings.

The nature of these factors is clearly enough indicated from the examples quoted above. The true causes and the origins of the war against Persia are easy enough for anyone to recognize. The first of these was the retreat of the Greeks under Xenophon[1] from the Upper Satrapies, a march during which although they traversed the whole of Asia and were constantly passing through hostile territory, none of the barbarians dared to stand in their way. The second was the invasion of Asia carried out by the Spartan King Agesilaus, during which he encountered no opposition worth mentioning in any of his campaigns, and was only compelled to return without achieving his aims because of the outbreak of troubles in Greece.[2] These events convinced Philip of the cowardice and indolence of the Persians compared with his own military efficiency and that of the Macedonians; they also opened his eyes to the size and the magnificence of the prizes to be gained from such a war. Accordingly, no sooner had he obtained the avowed support of the rest of the Greeks for his enterprise than he found a suitable pretext in his ardent desire to avenge the injuries which the Persians had previously inflicted on Greece. Thereafter he lost no time in deciding to go to war, and put in hand all possible preparations for this purpose. We must therefore consider the

1. The famous retreat of the Ten Thousand, described in Xenophon's *Anabasis*, which took place in 401–400 B.C.

2. In 396 B.C. Agesilaus invaded Asia Minor and for two years carried on campaigns against the satraps of the western provinces of the Persian Empire. He was recalled when a coalition consisting of Thebes, Athens, Corinth and Argos began to wage war against Sparta.

first set of factors [1] I have mentioned as the *cause* of the war against Persia, the second as its *pretext*, and Alexander's crossing into Asia as its *beginning*.

7. In the same way it is clear that the cause of the war between Antiochus and the Romans was the anger felt by the Aetolians, who considered that they had been slighted by the Romans in a number of ways in respect of the conclusion of the war with Philip; not only did they invite Antiochus over to Greece, but they were ready to do and to suffer anything on account of the resentment which the events of that time had aroused in them. The pretext for the war was the so-called liberation of Greece, which the Aetolians proclaimed, though quite in defiance either of reason or of truth, as they went around from city to city with Antiochus. Finally, the beginning of the war was Antiochus' descent upon Demetrias.

My purpose in dwelling upon this subject at such length is not to criticize earlier writers, but rather to set the student of history on the right path. A physician cannot help the sick if he is ignorant of the causes of certain conditions of the body, nor can a statesman help his fellow-citizens if he cannot follow how, why or by what process each event has developed. The first is hardly likely to institute proper treatment for the body, or the second to be able to deal with the exigencies of the situation, unless he possesses a knowledge such as I have described of each event as it occurs. There is nothing therefore to which we should be more attentive or search out more carefully than the causes of each event as it takes place, for the most important consequences often stem from mere trifles, and it is the initial impulses and decisions which are the easiest to remedy.

8. Now Fabius, the Roman historian, maintains that apart from the injury inflicted on the Saguntines, one of the causes of the war was Hasdrubal's ambitious spirit and love of power. He relates how, after obtaining a command of great importance in Spain, he arrived in Africa and tried to dissolve the Carthaginian constitution and convert the form of government into a monarchy. The other political leaders, however, foresaw his plan and united to

---

1. It was the march of the Ten Thousand and Agesilaus' campaigns which caused Philip and Alexander to conceive the idea of going to war. The pretext was the programme of avenging the wrongs suffered by Greece.

oppose him, whereupon Hasdrubal, suspecting their intentions, left Africa and from that time onward governed Spain as he chose without paying any attention to the Carthaginian Senate. Now Hannibal had both shared and admired Hasdrubal's principles and policy ever since his earliest youth, and when he succeeded Hasdrubal in the supreme command in Spain, he brought the same approach to his handling of affairs. And so, according to Fabius, Hannibal undertook this war against Rome on his own initiative and in defiance of Carthaginian opinion; and not one of the leading men in Carthage upheld his conduct towards Saguntum. Fabius then goes on to tell us that after the city had been captured a Roman delegation presented the demand that the Carthaginians should either hand over Hannibal to them or accept war. Now suppose that the following question were put to this writer: what better opportunity could the Carthaginians have found to achieve what they wanted, or how could they have acted at once more justly and more in their own interest than by granting the Romans' demand? They had, according to Fabius' own evidence, disapproved of Hannibal's actions from the start. By surrendering the man who had committed the offence they could eliminate this common enemy of the state on a plausible pretext, and without the odium of doing it themselves ensure the safety of their territory, stave off the impending war, and give satisfaction to the Romans – and all this could have been achieved simply by passing a resolution. The question is of course unanswerable. So far from doing any of these things, they continued to carry on the war in accordance with Hannibal's policy for seventeen years, and they did not abandon the struggle until finally, after every hope of success had been exhausted, their own city and persons stood in imminent danger of destruction.

9. Why then, it may be asked, have I made any mention of Fabius and his theory? Certainly not through any fear that some readers might find it plausible enough to accept: its inherent improbability is self-evident to anyone who studies it, and needs no comment on my part. My real concern is to caution those who may read the book not to be misled by the authority of the author's name, but to pay attention to the facts. For there are some people who are apt to dwell upon the personality of the writer rather than

upon what he writes. They look to the fact that Fabius was a contemporary of Hannibal and a member of the Roman Senate, and immediately believe that everything he says must be trusted. My personal opinion is that we should not treat his authority lightly, but equally should not regard it as final, and that in most cases readers should test his assertions by reference to the facts themselves.

But I must return to the war between Rome and Carthage, from which this digression has carried me away. The first cause, we must recognize, was the anger of Hamilcar, surnamed Barca,[1] the father of Hannibal. His spirit had never been broken by the outcome of the war in Sicily: he appeared to have maintained quite unimpaired among his troops at Eryx that martial spirit with which he himself was imbued; he had only agreed to peace when compelled by circumstances after the Carthaginian defeat at the naval battle of the Aegates Islands,[2] and so he never weakened in his resolve, but waited for his chance to strike again. If the revolt among the mercenaries had not taken place he would very soon, so far as it lay within his power, have found some other occasion and created the resources to renew the war. But as events turned out, he was completely absorbed in the civil disturbances of that time, and was obliged to devote all his attention to these.

10. After the Carthaginians had put down the rebellion, the Romans announced their intention of making war on them. At first the Carthaginians were willing to negotiate on all points, in the conviction that as the right was on their side, their country's interests would prevail through the sheer justice of her cause. The subject has been dealt with in my earlier books, to which it is necessary to refer in order to understand what I am now saying and what is to follow.[3]

However, as the Romans refused to discuss the question, the Carthaginians had no choice but to yield to circumstances; they deeply resented the injustice, but were powerless to prevent it, and so they evacuated Sardinia and agreed to pay 1,200 talents

1. This theory, which became the established Roman tradition, does not account for the fact that no hostile action against Rome is recorded as having been taken by Hamilcar at the relevant period, nor that he allowed the Carthaginian fleet to become dangerously weak between the wars.

2. See p. 107.

3. It is in fact only briefly touched on at p. 204.

in addition to the sum which had already been demanded, so as not to be forced to accept war at that moment. Here then we have the second and most important cause of the war. For Hamilcar, the anger provoked by this latest injustice – which all his compatriots now shared – was added to the grievance he already nursed from the past; then as soon as he had secured his country's safety by suppressing the rebellion of the mercenaries, he at once threw all his energies into the conquest of Spain with the object of using these resources to prepare for a war against Rome. The success of the Carthaginian enterprise in Spain must be regarded as the third cause of the war, for it was the assurance which they drew from this increase in their strength which enabled them to embark on the war with confidence.

It would be easy enough to produce evidence that Hamilcar played an important part in bringing about the second war between Rome and Carthage, despite the fact that he died ten years before it began, but the following anecdote will be sufficient to confirm the argument.[1]

11. After his final defeat at the hands of the Romans, Hannibal had left his native land and was staying at the court of King Antiochus.[2] Meanwhile the Romans, who were already aware of the designs of the Aetolians, sent an embassy to Antiochus in order to inform themselves as to what policy the King was likely to follow. The Roman envoys saw that Antiochus was treating the Aetolians with favour and seemed disposed to go to war with Rome, and so they made a point of paying attention to Hannibal in the hope of planting suspicion against him in the mind of the King – which in fact was exactly what they achieved. As time went on the King became more and more distrustful of Hannibal, and a moment arrived when they met to talk about the estrangement which had developed between them. During this conversation Hannibal defended himself at length, and then finally, being at a loss for further arguments, he told the following story.

At the time when his father was about to set off with his army on his expedition to Spain, Hannibal, who was then about nine

1. The story does not provide any evidence of Hamilcar's war plans but merely of the fact of his hatred of Rome.
2. In 196 B.C.

years old, was standing by the altar where his father was sacrificing to Zeus. The omens proved favourable, Hamilcar poured a libation to the gods and performed the customary ceremonies, after which he ordered all those who were present at the sacrifice to stand back a little way from the altar. Then he called Hannibal to him and asked him affectionately whether he wished to accompany the expedition. Hannibal was overjoyed to accept and, like a boy, begged to be allowed to go. His father then took him by the hand, led him up to the altar and commanded him to lay his hand upon the victim and swear that he would never become a friend to the Romans.

He then impressed upon Antiochus, now that the latter knew these facts, that so long as the King's policy was hostile to Rome he could rely upon Hannibal implicitly and regard him as his most whole-hearted supporter. But if ever he should come to terms or make a pact of friendship with Rome, he need not wait to hear of any slanders against the Carthaginians, but should immediately distrust and be on his guard against him, for there was nothing that lay in his power that he would not do to harm the Romans.

12. When Antiochus heard this story, he was convinced that Hannibal was expressing his genuine feelings and speaking the truth, and so put aside all his former mistrust. For our part we should regard this as an unmistakable proof of Hamilcar's hostility and of his general attitude towards Rome, and indeed this was confirmed by the facts, for he succeeded in instilling into his son-in-law Hasdrubal and his son Hannibal an enmity towards Rome which it would be impossible to surpass. Hasdrubal in fact died before these intentions could be fully demonstrated, but events gave Hannibal the opportunity to prove only too clearly the hatred of Rome which he had inherited from his father. For this reason it is of the greatest importance for statesmen to make sure that they understand the true reasons whereby old enmities are reconciled or new friendships formed. They should observe when it is that men come to terms because they are yielding to circumstances, and when because their spirit has been broken. In the former case they must consider such people as merely biding their time for a favourable opportunity, and be on their guard against them, while in the latter they may trust them as genuine friends and subjects, and not hesitate to command their services as the occasion may require. And so we

may now pronounce the *causes* of the Hannibalic War to have been those which I have stated. Its *beginnings* were as follows.

13. The Carthaginians bitterly resented their defeat in the war for Sicily, as I mentioned above, and they were further provoked by the affair of Sardinia and the size of the increased indemnity which they had finally been compelled to agree to pay. Accordingly, after they had subdued the greater part of Spain they were ready to seize any opportunities that presented themselves for retaliating against Rome. After the death of Hasdrubal, to whom they had entrusted the supreme command in Spain in succession to Hamilcar, at first they waited to discover how the army would respond. Then, when the news arrived that the troops had chosen Hannibal by universal acclaim as their commander, they made haste to summon an assembly of the people, which unanimously confirmed the soldiers' choice. After taking over the command, Hannibal at once set out to subdue the tribe known as the Olcades.[1] He arrived before their most important city, Althaea, pitched camp there, and after a series of vigorous attacks which terrified the inhabitants, he quickly captured the town, with the result that the rest of the tribe were overawed and submitted to the Carthaginians. After imposing a tribute upon the towns and taking possession of a large sum of money, he withdrew into winter quarters at New Carthage. He proceeded to treat his troops with great generosity, distributing a bounty to them at once and promising further payments later, and in this way he established great goodwill towards himself and inspired high hopes for the future.

14. In the following summer[2] he set out again, took the offensive against the Vaccaei,[3] and captured the town of Hermandica at his first attempt. Arbocala, however, proved to be a large city, and because of the size and the courage of its population, he was forced to lay siege to it. It was only after much trouble that he was able to take it by storm. Later, on his return march, he suddenly found himself in a position of great danger. The Carpetani,[4] who were the

1. A tribe inhabiting the district now known as La Mancha.

2. 220 B.C.

3. A tribe inhabiting the territory on the middle waters of the Douro, around the borders of Leon and Old Castile.

4. They inhabited the mountainous region north of the Tagus, the modern Sierra di Guadarrama.

strongest tribe in the neighbourhood, gathered to attack him, and were joined by the neighbouring tribes. They had been incited to this action by the refugees of the Olcades, and also urged on by those who had escaped from Hermandica.[1] If the Carthaginians had been compelled to meet this combined host in a pitched battle, they would certainly have been defeated. As it was Hannibal, combining skill with caution, faced about and retreated until he had placed the Tagus between himself and the enemy. There he halted to oppose the crossing of the river, and took advantage both of the water-barrier and of his elephants, of which he had about forty, in such a way that the whole action turned out just as he had calculated and as no one else would have dared to expect. For when the barbarians tried to force a crossing at various points, the greater number of them were killed as they left the water by the elephants, who followed the river's edge and attacked them as soon as they struggled up the bank. Many men were also cut down in the stream itself by the cavalry, as the horses could keep their footing better in the current, and the mounted men had the advantage of height over the infantry whom they were attacking. Finally Hannibal moved over to the offensive, crossed the river, attacked the barbarians, and put to flight a force of more than 100,000. After this defeat none of the other tribes south of the Ebro ventured lightly to face the Carthaginians, with the exception of the people of Saguntum. For his part Hannibal was at pains to keep his hands off this city for as long as he could. He was anxious not to give the Romans any explicit pretext for a war until he had secured possession of the rest of the country; in this he was following his father Hamilcar's precepts and advice.

15. Meanwhile the people of Saguntum sent one embassy after another to Rome, partly because they foresaw what was coming, and partly because they were anxious that the Romans should be kept informed of the growing power of the Carthaginians in Spain. For a long while the Romans had disregarded their appeals, but this time they sent out some commissioners to investigate the Saguntines' reports. At the same time Hannibal, having completed the conquests he had intended for that season, returned with his troops to winter in New Carthage,[2] the city which was in a sense

1. The modern Salamanca.   2. In the winter of 220–219 B.C.

the chief ornament and the centre of the Carthaginian empire in Spain. There he found a delegation from Rome, granted them an audience and listened to the message they had to deliver. The Romans called upon Hannibal to leave Saguntum alone, which they claimed lay within their sphere of influence, and to refrain from crossing the Ebro, according to the undertaking given in the agreement made with Hasdrubal.[1] Hannibal responded as might have been expected from a man who was young,[2] full of martial spirit, confident in the success of his enterprises and spurred on by his long-standing hatred of Rome. In replying to the delegates he claimed to be protecting the interests of the Saguntines. Not long before, party strife had broken out in Saguntum and the Romans had been called in to arbitrate, and Hannibal now accused them of having caused some of the leading citizens to be unjustly put to death. The Carthaginians, he warned them, would not overlook this treacherous act of seizure, for it was an ancestral tradition of theirs always to take up the cause of the victims of injustice. At the same time, however, he sent home to Carthage asking for instructions on how he was to act, in view of the fact that the Saguntines were relying on their alliance with Rome to commit wrongs against some of the peoples who were subject to Carthage.

In his dealings with the Romans he was in a mood of unreasoning and violent anger, and so did not cite the true reasons for what had happened, but resorted to a number of groundless pretexts, as is apt to happen to men who disregard the proper course of action because they are obsessed by passion. How much better it would have been if he had demanded that the Romans should hand back Sardinia, and at the same time remit the indemnity which they had unjustly extorted when they took advantage of Carthage's misfortunes to threaten her with war if their ultimatum was rejected. As it was, by saying nothing about the real cause of his country's grievances and inventing a non-existent one about Saguntum, he gave the impression that he was embarking on the war not only in defiance of reason but even of justice. The Roman delegates concluded that war was clearly inevitable and so sailed to Carthage to

1. Hannibal was still far to the south of the Ebro; Polybius may here be citing a warning rather than a protest from the Romans.
2. He was now twenty-seven.

communicate the same protest to the authorities there. They never expected, however, that the war would take place in Italy, but assumed that they would fight in Spain, with Saguntum as their base for operations.

The Second Illyrian War

16. The Senate, in adapting their plans to this assumption, now decided that they must secure their position in Illyria, since they expected that the war with Carthage would be both long and hard-fought. It so happened that at that time[1] Demetrius of Pharos was sacking and destroying the Illyrian cities subject to Rome, and had broken his treaty with the Republic by sailing beyond Lissus with fifty boats and pillaging many of the islands in the Cyclades. He had quite forgotten the various services the Romans had rendered him, and felt contemptuous of their power when he saw it threatened first by the Gauls and now by Carthage. Instead he rested all his hopes upon the royal house of Macedon, because he had taken the side of Antigonus and fought with him in his campaigns against Cleomenes. In view of these events and of the flourishing fortunes of the Macedonian kingdom, the Romans were anxious to secure their position in the lands to the east of Italy; they felt confident that they would have time to curb the reckless folly of the Illyrians and to rebuke and punish Demetrius for his audacity and ingratitude. However, in these calculations they were deceived, for Hannibal outstripped their plans by the speed with which he captured Saguntum, and in consequence the war was fought not in Spain but at the very gates of Rome and throughout the whole of Italy. But it was with these considerations in mind that the Romans dispatched Lucius Aemilius with an army just before the summer in the first year of the 140th Olympiad.[2]

1. The chronology of this section is somewhat uncertain. No senatorial decision occasioned by the return of the envoys from Carthage could have been taken before the winter of 220–219. Demetrius had sailed into the Cyclades in the summer of 220.

2. The summer of 219 B.C.

The Second Punic War

17. At the same time Hannibal had started with his army from New Carthage and was on the march towards Saguntum. The city lies on the seaward side of the range of mountains which connects Iberia with Celtiberia[1] and is a little under a mile from the sea. The territory which its inhabitants cultivate yields every kind of crop and is the most fertile in the whole of Spain. Hannibal pitched camp in front of the town and set to work with energy to begin a siege, since he foresaw that there were many advantages to be gained from its capture. He believed first of all that in this way he could deny the Romans any prospect of fighting a war in Spain, secondly that by this action he would inspire such terror throughout the country as to make those tribes which had already submitted more obedient, and the rest who were still independent more cautious, and most important of all, that he would be able to advance in safety towards Italy without leaving an enemy in his rear. Besides these advantages he reckoned that the capture of the city would provide him with ample funds and supplies for his proposed expedition, that he would raise the spirits of his troops by the booty that would be distributed among them, and earn the goodwill of the Carthaginians at home by the spoils he would send there.[2] With these considerations in mind he threw all his energies into pressing forward the siege. At one moment he would set an example to his troops by taking part personally in the hazards of manning the siege-works, at another by cheering on his men and exposing himself recklessly to danger in the fighting. At last, after enduring every kind of hardship and anxiety, he succeeded in capturing the city in the eighth month of the siege. An immense quantity of booty in the form of money, slaves and property fell into his hands. The money he set aside for his own expedition, as he had previously determined, the slaves he distributed among his troops according to their deserts, and the miscellaneous property was at once sent off entire to Carthage. The results of the operation in no way disappointed his expecta-

1. The mountains between the modern New Castile and Aragon.
2. These consisted of miscellaneous property; the rewards for the troops came from the money raised by the sale of slaves.

tions: on the contrary his original plans were all fulfilled. He had succeeded in making his men more enthusiastic for future action and the Carthaginians better disposed to grant his requests, and now that he found himself in possession of such abundant resources he was able to take many steps to further his expedition.

The Second Illyrian War

18. While these events were in train, Demetrius, who had obtained intelligence of the Romans' plans, at once dispatched a strong garrison to the city of Dimale,[1] with the necessary supplies to maintain such a force. In the other Illyrian cities he put to death those who opposed his policy, and installed his supporters in power; at the same time he himself selected 6,000 of his bravest troops and quartered them in Pharos.[2] When the Roman consul arrived in Illyria with his army he found the enemy full of confidence in the natural strength of Dimale and the arrangements which had been made for its defence. He received the impression that the place was generally considered to be impregnable, and accordingly determined to attack it before anywhere else, so as to strike terror into the enemy. Next he gave the necessary instructions to his officers, had siege-works erected at various points and invested the city. Seven days later he captured the place by storm and at one blow broke the spirit of the whole of the enemy, with the result that envoys appeared from all the neighbouring towns and offered to place themselves unconditionally under the protection of Rome. Having accepted their submission and imposed such conditions as appeared suitable in each case, the consul then sailed to Pharos to attack Demetrius himself. There he learned that the capital of the island was strongly fortified, that a large body of picked troops had been assembled inside it, and that it was well-stocked with supplies and munitions of war. Accordingly, as he was beginning

1. This city has been identified as the modern Krotina, situated in the hills north-west of Berat.
2. The modern town of Starigrad on the island of Hvar.

to grow anxious that the siege would prove long and difficult, he devised the following stratagem. He sailed up to the island at night with his whole force and disembarked the greater part of it in a number of well-wooded valleys, and then at daybreak sailed quite openly with a squadron of twenty ships to the harbour nearest to the town. When Demetrius saw this naval force, he was filled with contempt at its apparent weakness and led a sortie from the town to the harbour to prevent the enemy from landing.

19. When the two forces met they became involved in heavy fighting and more and more troops were drawn out of the city, until at last the whole garrison had poured out to take part in the action. Then the Roman force, which had landed in the night and had marched by a concealed route, arrived at the crucial moment in the battle, seized a steep hill between the town and the harbour, and cut off the troops which had sallied out. When Demetrius discovered what had happened, he at once broke off his attack on the troops who were landing; then after rallying his men he addressed them and led them forward to fight a pitched battle against the enemy force which had occupied the hill. The Romans watched the Illyrian troops advancing upon them resolutely and in good order, and then fell upon their formations, while at the same time their comrades, who had landed from the ships and seen how the battle had developed, charged the enemy from the rear. The Illyrians were thus attacked on all sides and were thrown into great disorder and confusion. Finally, when Demetrius' troops found themselves under pressure from both front and rear, they turned and fled, some of them escaping to the town, but the greater number scattering across country to the various parts of the island. Demetrius himself had kept some boats at a lonely spot on the coast in readiness for such a contingency, and he now made his way there. He went on board, sailed under cover of darkness and arrived unexpectedly at the court of King Philip of Macedon, where he remained for the rest of his life. He was a man of a bold and adventurous spirit, but completely deficient in reasoning power and in judgement, and these weaknesses brought him to an end which was in keeping with the rest of his career. He embarked with Philip's approval on an ill-planned and reckless attempt to capture Messene and was killed in the fighting, as I shall relate in detail when

we reach that period. Aemilius, the Roman consul, immediately followed up his victory by taking the town of Pharos by storm, after which he razed it to the ground. He proceeded to subdue the rest of Illyria, and after settling the affairs of the province as he considered best, he returned towards the end of the summer to Rome. There he celebrated a triumph amid the acclamations of the whole people, for he was considered to have handled the campaign with great skill and even greater courage.

The Second Punic War

20. Now when the news of the fall of Saguntum was received in Rome, there was no debate on the question of whether or not to go to war. Some historians maintain that this took place, and even go to the absurd lengths of setting down the speeches alleged to have been made on both sides. The Romans had already given warning a year before that if the Carthaginians entered the territory of Saguntum this would be treated as an act of war. So now that the city had been taken by assault, how could they possibly assemble to debate whether they should declare war or not? And how is it that these writers paint a dramatic picture of the gloomy appearance of the Senate, while in the same breath they tell us that fathers brought their sons from the age of twelve upwards to the Senate House, and that these boys attended the debate but did not divulge a word of what was said to their nearest relatives? All this is as unlikely as it is untrue, unless we are to believe that Fortune, among its other blessings, had bestowed upon the Romans the gift of being wise from their cradles. I need not waste any more words upon compositions such as those of Chaereas or Sosylus:[1] they possess none of the elements of order or of authority which are proper to history, but are pitched at the level of the common gossip of the barber's shop.

What the Romans did on hearing of the disaster which had

1. Nothing is known of Chaereas. Sosylus of Lacedaemon accompanied Hannibal on his campaigns and taught him Greek.

befallen Saguntum was to appoint ambassadors and send them post-haste to Carthage.[1] They were instructed to give the Carthaginians two alternatives, one of which, if it was accepted, would humiliate as well as harm the Carthaginian state, while the other would prove the beginning of a great struggle and great dangers. In short, they must either surrender Hannibal and the members of his council, or war would be declared. When the Roman envoys arrived, appeared before the Senate and delivered their message, the Carthaginians listened with indignation to this choice of alternatives, but nevertheless they selected their most able orator to speak, and proceeded to justify their action as follows.

21. They declined to discuss the agreement between Hasdrubal and the Romans on the grounds that it had never been made, or that if it had, it was not binding upon them, having been concluded without their approval. Here they claimed to be following the precedent established by the Romans themselves, since the treaty which had been drawn up during the war for Sicily when Lutatius was in command had been accepted by Lutatius himself, but later repudiated by the Romans because it had been made without their approval. Throughout the statement of their case the Carthaginians rested their argument and indeed insisted upon the last treaty which had been made at the end of the war for Sicily. Here they pointed out that there was no clause relating to Spain, but that there was one which expressly laid down that the allies of each power should be secure from attack by the other. They argued that the Saguntines were not allies of Rome at the time of the treaty, and to prove their point they several times read out aloud the terms of the agreement.

For their part the Romans categorically refused to discuss the justification of the Carthaginians' action at Saguntum. They contended that so long as Saguntum stood unharmed the situation permitted a plea of justification, and it was possible to settle the points at issue by discussion, but that now the treaty had been broken by the seizure of the city the Carthaginians must either hand over the culprits, which would make it clear to all that they

1. The delegation could not have left Rome before March, 218 B.C., and possibly not until June, on receipt of the news that Hannibal had crossed the Ebro.

had no share in the crime and that it had been committed without their approval, or if they refused to do this and admitted their complicity, they must accept war.

During this debate the question of treaties between Rome and Carthage was dealt with more or less in general terms, but it seems to me necessary to study it in rather greater detail. It will be useful – both to practical statesmen whose duty and interest it is to possess accurate information on these matters so as to avoid mistakes in any critical debates,[1] and also to students of history to prevent their being led astray by the ignorance or bias of historians – for there to be a survey which is generally recognized as accurate of the treaties concluded between Rome and Carthage from the earliest times to the present.[2]

22. The first treaty between Rome and Carthage was made in the consulship of Lucius Junius Brutus and Marcus Horatius;[3] they were the first consuls who were appointed after the expulsion of the Etruscan Kings and who dedicated the temple of Jupiter Capitolinus, and these events took place twenty-eight years before Xerxes' invasion of Greece. I give below as accurate a translation as I can of this treaty, but the modern language has developed so many differences from the ancient Roman tongue that the best scholars among the Romans themselves have great difficulty in interpreting certain points, even after much study. The treaty, then, runs more or less as follows:

'There shall be friendship between the Romans and their allies and the Carthaginians and theirs on these conditions:

The Romans and their allies shall not sail beyond the Fair Promontory[4] unless compelled to do so by storm or by enemy action. If any one of them is carried beyond it by force, he shall not

---

1. The reference to 'critical debates' is probably to those of the Senate in the years preceding the Third Punic War.

2. In fact up to 218 B.C.

3. The first year of the Republic was 509/8 B.C. Polybius records three treaties made before the First Punic War. The second (p. 201) is undated; the third is synchronized with Pyrrhus' invasion of Italy (218 B.C.).

4. Polybius takes this to be the modern C Bon, probably rightly; but it could also be C. Farina, in which case the area from which the Romans were to be excluded would be west of that cape, and not in the Syrtes as Polybius believes.

buy or carry away anything more than is required for the repair of his ship or for sacrifice, and he shall depart within five days.[1]

Those who come to trade shall not conclude any business except in the presence of a herald or town-clerk. The price of whatever is sold in the presence of these officials shall be secured to the vendor by the state, if the sale takes place in Africa or Sardinia.[2]

If any Roman comes to the Carthaginian province in Sicily, he shall enjoy equal rights with others. The Carthaginians shall do no injury to the peoples of Ardea, Antium, the Laurentes and the peoples of Circeii, Tarracina or any other city of those Latins who are subject to the Romans.

As regards those Latin peoples who are not subject to the Romans, the Carthaginians shall not interfere with any of these cities, and if they take any one of them, they shall deliver it up undamaged. They shall build no fort in Latin territory. If they enter the region carrying arms, they shall not spend a night there.'

23. The Fair Promontory referred to is the cape immediately to the front of Carthage to the north. The Carthaginians forbid the Romans to sail south of this with warships,[3] the reason being, as it seems to me, that they did not wish them to become acquainted with the coast around Byzacium or the Lesser Syrtes, which they call Emporia because of the great fertility of that region.[4] If anyone has been carried there by a storm or driven by enemy action and needs anything for the purpose of sacrificing to the gods or repairing his ship, he may take this but nothing more, and those who touch there must leave within five days. The Romans may come for trading purposes to Carthage itself, to all parts of Africa on this side[5] of the Fair Promontory, to Sardinia and to the Cartha-

1. Similar restrictions were imposed at about the same time by Naucratis of Egypt. In general the Carthaginians were concerned at this date with safeguarding their commercial interests and regulating trade, the Romans with establishing the recognition of their political rights over Latium.

2. This does not mean that the state underwrites the debt, but merely that it compels the defaulter to pay if he has means to do so.

3. Polybius seems to be in error in restricting this to warships.

4. The coastline for some two hundred miles south of Carthage, including the modern Gulf of Hammamet and the Gulf of Gabes (Lesser Syrtes).

5. An ambiguous phrase. If the Fair Promontory is C. Bon it must mean *west of*, but if it is C. Farina it must mean *east of*. Polybius thinks it is the former.

ginian province of Sicily, and the Carthaginian state undertakes to secure payment of their just debts.

The wording of this treaty shows that the Carthaginians consider Sardinia and Africa as belonging absolutely to them; in the case of Sicily they use different language to define their interests, and refer in the treaty only to those parts of it which are under their rule. In the same way the Romans only make stipulations concerning Latium, and do not refer to the rest of Italy, since it was not under their authority.

24. Later on a second treaty was made, in which the Carthaginians include Tyre and Utica, and mention besides the Fair Promontory the place-names of Mastia and Tarsium as the points beyond which the Romans may not make raiding expeditions or trade or found cities. This treaty runs more or less as follows:

'There shall be friendship on the following conditions between the Romans and their allies, and the Carthaginians, Tyrians, people of Utica and their respective allies. The Romans shall not make raids, or trade or found a city on the farther side of the Fair Promontory, Mastia or Tarsium.[1]

If the Carthaginians capture any city in Latium which is not subject to Rome, they shall keep the goods and the men, but deliver up the city.

If any Carthaginians take prisoner any of a people with whom the Romans have a treaty of peace in writing, but who are not subject to Rome,[2] they shall not bring them into Roman harbours, but if one be brought in and a Roman claims him, he shall be set free.[3] The Romans shall not do likewise.

If a Roman obtains water and provisions from any place which is under Carthaginian rule, he shall not use these supplies to do harm to any member of a people with whom the Carthaginians enjoy peace and friendship. Neither shall a Carthaginian act in this way. If either party does so, the injured person shall not take private

1. The location of these places is uncertain. Although Polybius seems to regard them as near the Fair Promontory they were perhaps in Spain.

2. In particular the towns of Tibur and Praeneste, with which the Romans had separate treaties.

3. This clause suggests a parallel practice to the Roman ceremony of manumission, whereby a slave could be touched and set free.

vengeance, and if he does so, his wrongdoing shall be a public offence.

No Roman shall trade or found a city in Sardinia or in Africa, or remain in a Sardinian or African port longer than he needs to obtain provisions or to repair his ship. If he is driven there by a storm, he shall depart within five days.

In the Carthaginian province of Sicily and at Carthage he may transact business and sell whatever is permitted to a citizen. A Carthaginian in Rome may do likewise.'

Once more in this treaty the Carthaginians place especial emphasis upon Africa and upon Sardinia; they insist with great stringency on this claim and forbid all approaches to the Romans. They refer to Sicily in different terms however, and mention the part which is subject to them. In the same way the Romans when referring to Latium forbid the Carthaginians to wrong the peoples of Ardea, Antium, Circeii and Tarracina. These are the cities which lie on the sea-board of that Latin territory with which the treaty is concerned.

25. A third and final treaty was made with Carthage by the Romans at the time of Pyrrhus' invasion of Italy and before the Carthaginians embarked on the war for the possession of Sicily.[1] This treaty retains the terms of all the previous agreements and adds the following:

'If the Romans or the Carthaginians make a written alliance against Pyrrhus they shall both conclude it in such a way that they may help each other in the land of the party on whom he is making war.

Whichever party may need help, the Carthaginians shall provide the ships both for transport and for operations, but each shall provide the pay for its own men.

The Carthaginians shall also give help to the Romans by sea if need arises, but no one shall compel the crews to disembark against their will.'

1. The most likely explanation of the historical context of this treaty is that the Carthaginians feared the possibility that the Romans would conclude a peace with Pyrrhus after the latter's defeat at Asculum in 280 B.C., and would have preferred to keep the war going in Italy. Pyrrhus was reputed to cherish ambitions to invade Africa.

The oaths which had to be sworn to the various treaties were as follows. In the case of the first the Carthaginians swore by their ancestral gods, and the Romans, in accordance with an old custom, by Jupiter Lapis, and in the case of the second treaty by Mars and Quirinus. The oath by Jupiter Lapis is taken as follows. The man who is swearing to the treaty takes in his hand a stone, and when he has taken the oath in the name of his country, he says:

'If I abide by this oath, may all good be my lot: but if I do otherwise in thought or act, let all other men dwell safe in their own countries enjoying their own laws and in possession of their own property, temples and tombs, and may I alone be cast out even as this stone is now.' Then having spoken these words, he throws the stone from his hand.

26. Now since such treaties exist and are preserved on bronze tablets to this day in the treasury of the Aediles beside the temple of Jupiter Capitolinus, we can only read with astonishment what has been written by the historian Philinus on this subject. It is not the fact of his ignorance which is surprising, since even in our own day those Romans and Carthaginians whose age brought them nearest to the period in question and who were most versed in public affairs did not know of these records. What is extraordinary is how and on what authority he ventured to maintain the opposite – namely that there was a treaty between Rome and Carthage, according to which the Romans were bound to keep away from the whole of Sicily and the Carthaginians from the whole of Italy, and that the Romans broke both the treaty and their oath at the time when they first crossed to Sicily – when in fact no such document exists nor ever has done. Yet Philinus asserts this in so many words in his second book. I touched upon this subject in the introductory section to my history, but have reserved the more detailed discussion for this place,[1] for the reason that many readers have relied upon Philinus' treatment of this subject and have thus been led astray. As regards the crossing of the Romans into Sicily, if anyone chooses to find fault with them for ever having received into their friendship and afterwards having assisted those Mamertines who treacherously seized possession both of Messana and also

1. The arrival of the Romans at Messana is mentioned on p. 55 and Philinus' unreliability on pp. 55–6, but there is no reference to this alleged treaty.

of Rhegium, he would have good reasons for condemning their action; but if he supposes that they went there in breach of oaths or treaties, then he is obviously ignorant of the truth.

27. At the end of the war for Sicily, then, another treaty was made, the provisions of which were as follows:

'The Carthaginians shall evacuate Sicily and all the islands lying between Italy and Sicily.[1]

The allies of both parties shall be secure from attacks by the other.

Neither party shall impose any contribution upon nor erect any public buildings nor enlist soldiers in the dominions of the other, nor form alliances with the allies of the other.

The Carthaginians shall pay 2,200 talents to the Romans within the period of ten years, and a sum of 1,000 talents forthwith.

The Carthaginians shall surrender to the Romans all prisoners of war free of ransom.'

Later, at the end of the civil war in Africa, and after the Romans had gone to the lengths of passing a decree declaring war on Carthage, the following clause was added to the treaty, as I mentioned above. 'The Carthaginians shall evacuate Sardinia and pay a further sum of 1,200 talents.'

The last agreement after the above-mentioned treaties was the one made with Hasdrubal in Spain, which provided that: 'The Carthaginians shall not pass the Ebro in arms.' These, then, were the mutual obligations which existed between the Romans and the Carthaginians from the earliest times down to the period of Hannibal.

28. In the light of the above, while we may conclude that the crossing of the Romans into Sicily was not in breach of any treaty, as regards the second war which resulted in the imposition of the clauses concerning Sardinia, it is impossible to discover any reasonable ground or pretext for the Romans' action. In this instance it must be acknowledged that the Carthaginians were compelled through the sheer necessity of their situation, and contrary to all justice, to evacuate Sardinia and pay the added indemnity which I have mentioned.

To justify their demand the Romans claimed that in the course of

1. i.e. the Aegates and Liparean Islands.

the civil war in Africa the Carthaginians had committed wrongs against the crews of ships sailing from Rome, but they had in fact exonerated them from this charge when they received back all the Roman sailors who had been taken to Carthage, and in return released all Carthaginian prisoners of war as an act of grace and without ransom. I have related these events in an earlier book.[1]

Having established these facts, then, it remains for us to decide after a thorough investigation which of the two states should be regarded as the originator of the Hannibalic War.

29. I have already recorded what the Carthaginians had to say in their defence, and will now give the Romans' reply. It is true that they did not use these arguments at that particular moment, because of the general indignation provoked by the fall of Saguntum, but they have been stated on many subsequent occasions and by many different people in Rome. First they insist that the agreement with Hasdrubal cannot be left out of the question, as the Carthaginians had the audacity to suggest, for it contained no proviso, as the treaty drawn up by Lutatius did, to the effect that, 'this treaty shall be valid if it is accepted by the Roman people'. On the contrary, Hasdrubal gave the undertaking absolutely and unconditionally that: 'The Carthaginians shall not cross the Ebro in arms.' Again, the treaty concerning Sicily contained the clause, as the Carthaginians admit, that 'The allies of each party are to be secure from attack by the other,' and this does not apply only, as the Carthaginians interpreted it, to those who were allies at that time. If that had been the case, a further clause would have been added either excluding both parties from entering into alliances other than their existing ones, or else providing that those who were subsequently received into alliance should not participate in the benefits of the treaty. However, since neither of these clauses were added, it is clear that each party guaranteed that all the allies of the other, both those then existing and those to be admitted later, should be immune from attack. This seems perfectly reasonable, for surely the two parties would never have made a treaty whereby they deprived themselves of the power to admit into alliance, as occasion might demand, any peoples whose friendship seemed to be of advantage to them; nor again, if they had taken any such peoples

1. Book 1, chapter 83.

under their protection, would they ignore injuries done to them by any other nation whatever. On the contrary, the main point present in the minds of both parties when they made the treaty was that each should abstain from attacking the existing allies of the other, and on no account admit any of these into alliance with themselves. As regards subsequent alliances, to which this clause especially applies, they engaged that they would not enlist soldiers or levy contributions in the provinces of each or in territories allied to each, and that all allies of each party should be immune from attack by the other.

30. This being so, it is a fact beyond dispute that the Saguntines had placed themselves under the protection of Rome many years before Hannibal's time.[1] The most important proof of this, and one which the Carthaginians themselves accepted, is that when political strife broke out in Saguntum, the people did not turn to the Carthaginians to mediate, even though they were close at hand and were already playing an active part in Spain, but appealed to the Romans, and with their help restored the political situation to order. Accordingly, if we regard the destruction of Saguntum as the cause of the Hannibalic War, then the Carthaginians must be judged to have been in the wrong in starting the conflict, both from the point of view of the treaty of Lutatius, which provided that the allies of each power should be secure from attack by the other, and from that of the agreement with Hasdrubal, whereby the Carthaginians engaged not to cross the Ebro in arms. If, on the other hand, we identify the cause of the war with the Roman annexation of Sardinia and with the added indemnity which they extorted from the Carthaginians, then we must certainly agree that the latter had good reason to embark on the war. Just as they had yielded to circumstances earlier, so they now took advantage of circumstances to retaliate against those who had wronged them.

31. Now some uncritical readers might think that it is unnecessary for me to discuss considerations of this kind in such minute detail. My answer is that if there were any man who believed

1. The date is uncertain but it probably preceded the Ebro treaty (225): perhaps between 230 and 228 B.C. However, Saguntum lay south of the Ebro, and hence an alliance with Rome, if this implied in the last resort armed assistance, was irreconcilable with the Ebro treaty.

himself so self-sufficient as to be able to deal with any eventuality, I should accept that knowledge of the past might benefit him, but would not be indispensable. However, if there is no one to be found who could claim such omniscience in conducting either his private life or his country's affairs – since no man of sense, even if all is well with him now, will ever reckon with certainty on the future – I shall insist that a knowledge of past events such as I have described is not merely an asset but is absolutely essential.

Let us consider three situations such as must often arise. Imagine the case of a statesman who is wronged either in his private capacity or through an injustice suffered by his country; or of one who is anxious to acquire some possession, or to anticipate the attack of an enemy; or finally, one who is content with things as they are. In each of these situations it is past history which can instruct him; in the first case how to find supporters and allies; in the second how to rouse to action those whose cooperation he wishes to enlist; and in the last how to give the right stimulus to others to ensure the success of his own principles and preserve the *status quo*. All men are inclined to adapt themselves to present circumstances and to assume whatever character may be demanded by the necessities of the moment, so that it is difficult to distinguish the real principles of each, and all too often the truth is obscured. But men's past actions can be subjected to the test of actual facts so as to reveal the true nature of their policies and intentions, and then we discover where we can turn for gratitude, kindness and help, and where for the contrary. In this way we shall have many opportunities to learn who is likely to comfort us in our distress, share our anger and join us in retaliating against our enemies, all of which is of great assistance to us throughout human life, whether public or private. It follows therefore that neither writers nor readers of history should confine their attention to the narrative of events, but must also take account of what preceded, accompanied and followed them. For if we remove from history the analysis of why, how and for what purpose each thing was done and whether the result was what we should reasonably have expected, what is left is a mere display of descriptive virtuosity, but not a lesson, and this, though it may please for the moment, is of no enduring value for the future.

32. For this reason I wish to correct the misapprehension of those who think my work is hard to obtain and difficult to read because of the number of books it contains. It is infinitely easier to read forty books, all of which are woven together as it were thread by thread in a series of unbroken texture, and which thus present a clear picture of events in Italy, Sicily and Africa from the time of Pyrrhus to the capture of Carthage, and those in the rest of the world by means of a continuous account from the flight of Cleomenes of Sparta up to the batrle between the Romans and the Achaeans at the Isthmus, than it is to read or procure the books of those writers who deal with separate episodes. Apart from their being many times as long as my history, the reader cannot establish any facts with certainty from them. The reasons for this are, first, because most of them provide different accounts of the same event; secondly, because they omit those *parallel occurrences*, by comparing and evaluating which we arrive at a far more reliable general picture than is possible if everything is judged in isolation; and finally because many of the most important factors of all evidently lie beyond their grasp. For it is my contention that by far the most important part of historical writing lies in the consideration of the consequences of events, their accompanying circumstances, and above all their causes. Thus I regard the war with Antiochus as having originated from that with Philip, the war with Philip from that with Hannibal, and the Hannibalic War from the one fought for the possession of Sicily, while the intermediate events, however many and diverse they may be, all converge upon the same issue.[1] All these tendencies can be recognized and understood from a general history, but this is not the case with histories of separate wars, such as the one fought against Perseus or Philip, unless indeed anyone imagines that by simply reading the reports of pitched battles contained in these works he has gained a clear understanding of the plan and the conduct of the war. This, however, is by no means the case, and I consider that my history is as much superior to these episodic compositions as learning is to mere listening.

1. Polybius regards the wars fought against Philip and Antiochus as acts of Roman expansion following upon the war with Hannibal. The latter is some-

33. I digressed from my narrative at the point where the Roman ambassadors had been received at Carthage. After they had heard the Carthaginians' statement of their case, they spoke no word in reply, but the senior member of the delegation pointed to the bosom of his toga and declared to the Senate that in its folds he carried both peace and war, and that he would let fall from it whichever they instructed him to leave. The Carthaginian Suffete answered that he should bring out whichever he thought best, and when the envoy replied that it would be war, many of the senators shouted at once, 'We accept it!' It was on these terms that the Senate and the Roman ambassadors parted.

Meanwhile Hannibal, who was wintering at New Carthage, first of all dismissed the Spanish troops to their own cities, in the hope of thus leaving them ready and well-disposed towards his next campaign. Next he gave instructions to his brother Hasdrubal as to how to carry on the administration of Spain, and what preparations to make for the defence of the province against the Romans, if he should happen to be absent. Besides this he made arrangements for the security of Africa: here he adopted the effectual and far-sighted measure of posting soldiers from Spain to Africa and vice versa, helping in this way to cement the loyalty of each province towards the other. The troops who crossed to Africa came from the tribes of the Thersitae,[1] Mastiani,[2] the Iberian Oretes[3] and Olcades,[4] and numbered 1,200 cavalry and 13,850 infantry. Besides these there were 870 Balearians. They call them by the word which means 'slingers', and from this skill of theirs they give the same name both to this people and to their native islands. Most of these troops were stationed at Metagonium[5] on the northern African coast and some in Carthage itself.

4,000 infantry were sent from the cities of Metagonium to Carthage to serve both as reinforcements for the defence of the capital and

---

times seen as the first step in the Roman plan for world dominion (p. 44), and sometimes as the event which led them to conceive the idea (p. 43).

1. The origins of this people are unknown.
2. A tribe from Andalusia.
3. Their territory lay on the Guadalquivir river, near Castulo.
4. See p. 190.
5. A bay on the coast of Spanish Morocco, east of Cape Melilla.

also as hostages. For a naval force he left with his brother Hasdrubal fifty quinqueremes, two quadriremes and five triremes, thirty-two of the quinqueremes and all the triremes being fully manned. He also provided him with a contingent of cavalry consisting of 450 Libyans and Libyo-Phoenicians, 300 Ilergetes, and 1,800 Numidians drawn from the tribes of the Massyli, Masaesyli, Maccaei and Maurusii who inhabit the coastal districts of Africa. His infantry strength consisted of 11,850 Libyans, 300 Ligurians and 500 Balearians, together with twenty-one elephants.

The accuracy of these details concerning Hannibal's war establishment need not surprise the reader, even though anyone actually engaged in mobilizing the troops would have found difficulty in matching it. At the same time I need not be condemned as if I were imitating those historians who try to make their inaccuracies convincing. The fact is that I discovered on Cape Lacinium[1] a bronze tablet which Hannibal himself had had inscribed with these details while he was in Italy, and since I considered this to be an absolutely trustworthy piece of evidence, I had no hesitation in following it.

34. After Hannibal had put in hand all the necessary measures for the security of Africa and Spain, he still waited anxiously for the messengers he was expecting from the Celts. He had thoroughly informed himself concerning the fertility of the regions at the foot of the Alps and near the river Po, the density of the population, the bravery of its men in war, and above all their hatred of Rome, which had persisted ever since the earlier war, which I described in my last book in order to enable my readers to follow what I am now about to relate. Hannibal therefore harboured great hopes of these tribes, and had been at pains to send envoys who bore lavish promises to the Celtic chieftains, both those living south of the Alps and those who inhabited the mountains themselves. He was convinced that he could only carry the war against the Romans into Italy if, after having overcome the difficulties of the route, he could reach the territory of the Celts and engage them as allies and partners in his campaign.

At last his messengers returned with the news that the Celts

1. A cape in the extreme south-east of Italy, near Croton, the modern Cape Colonna.

were ready to cooperate and eagerly awaited his arrival; they also reported that the passage of the Alps was arduous and difficult but by no means impossible, and so at the approach of spring he assembled his troops from their winter quarters. At the same time he received the news of the reception of the Roman embassy in Carthage, which served to raise his spirits, and so, trusting that he would be supported by popular feeling at home, he openly appealed to his men to join him in the war against Rome.[1] He impressed upon them how the Romans had demanded that he and all the senior officers of his army should be handed over to them, and at the same time he told them of the wealth of the country they were about to invade and of the friendly feelings and active support of the Gauls. When he saw that the soldiers were as eager as himself to start, he praised their spirit, ordered them to be ready on the day fixed for their departure, and dismissed the assembly.

35. After completing during the winter the arrangements I have already described, and having thus provided for the security of Africa and Spain, he began his march on the appointed day with an army of about 90,000 infantry and 12,000 cavalry. Having crossed the Ebro, he set about subduing the tribes of the Ilergetes, Bargusii, Aerenosii and Andosini as far as the Pyrenees. He made himself master of all this territory, took several cities by storm, and completed the campaign with remarkable speed, but he was involved in heavy fighting and suffered some severe losses. He left Hanno in command of the whole territory north of the Ebro and placed the Bargusii under his brother's absolute rule; this was the tribe which he distrusted most on account of their friendly feelings towards the Romans. He detached from his army a contingent of 10,000 infantry and 1,000 cavalry to be commanded by Hanno, and deposited with him all the heavy baggage of the expeditionary force. At the same time he sent home an equal number of troops. In doing this he had two objects: first to leave behind a number of men who would be well-disposed to himself, and secondly to hold out to the rest of the Spaniards a good prospect of returning home, not only for those who were serving with him but for those

1. The Roman ultimatum was not delivered at Carthage until late in March 218 at the earliest and possibly not until June, so that this speech may well be imaginary.

who remained behind, so that if he were ever in need of reinforcements they would all enthusiastically respond. With the rest of his force, which had been disencumbered of its heavy baggage and now consisted of 50,000 infantry and about 9,000 cavalry, he pressed on through the Pyrenees towards the crossing of the Rhône. The army he commanded was formidable not so much for its numerical strength as for its efficiency, since it had been highly trained in a continual series of campaigns against the Spanish tribes.

39. At the time of which we are now speaking the Carthaginians ruled the whole of that part of Africa which faces the Mediterranean, from the Altars of Philaenus[1] on the Greater Syrtes as far as the Pillars of Hercules. The length of this coastline is more than 16,000 stades. They had also crossed the straits at the Pillars of Hercules and made themselves masters of the whole of Spain as far as the promontory on the coast of the Mediterranean known as Emporiae, where the Pyrenees which separate the Celts from the Spaniards meet the sea. This spot is about 8,000 stades from the outlet of the Mediterranean at the Pillars of Hercules. The distances which make up this coastline are: 3,000 stades from the Pillars to New Carthage, from which Hannibal started out for Italy; 2,600 stades from there to the Ebro; 1,600 stades from the Ebro to Emporiae, and about 1,600 stades from Emporiae to the crossing of the Rhône. This last part of the road has now been carefully measured by the Romans and is marked with milestones at every eighth stade. From the crossing of the Rhône, if one follows the bank of the river upstream as far as the foot of the pass from the Alps into Italy, the distance is 1,400 stades. The length of the pass which Hannibal was to cross to bring him down into the plain of the Po is about 1,200 stades. Thus, starting from New Carthage, he had to march in all a distance of some 9,000 stades.[2] By the time that he reached the Pyrenees he had completed nearly half the journey in terms of mileage, but in terms of difficulty the greater part of his task still lay before him.

1. These originally marked the boundary between Carthage and Cyrene; they were situated near the modern El Agheila, south-west of Benghazi.
2. This is a rounded-off total: the distances actually quoted add up to about 8,400 stades, amounting to about 1,000 Roman miles.

40. Hannibal was now engaged in attempting to cross the Pyrenees, where the Celts caused him great anxiety because of the natural
strength of the passes which they occupied. Meanwhile the Romans
had received from the envoys they had sent to Carthage a report
on the speeches that had been made and the decisions taken there.
The news also reached them, sooner than they had expected, that
Hannibal and his army had crossed the Ebro,[1] whereupon they
decided to put the consuls with their legions into the field and to
send Publius Cornelius Scipio to Spain and Tiberius Sempronius
Longus to Africa.[2]

At the same time as they were engaged in enrolling the legions
and making other preparations, they were also pursuing the scheme
which had already been voted in the assembly for establishing two
colonies in Cisalpine Gaul. They took active steps to fortify the
towns and ordered the colonists to present themselves there within
thirty days; 6,000 of them had been assigned to each city. One,
which was founded to the south of the Po, was named Placentia;
the other, which lay north of the river, Cremona. These two colonies
had hardly been established when the Gallic tribe of the Boii rose
in revolt. They had long been waiting for an opportunity to throw
off their allegiance to Rome, but had not found a suitable occasion.
Now, encouraged by the messages they had received telling them
that the Carthaginians were close at hand, they seceded from Rome,
abandoning the hostages they had handed over at the end of the
war which I described in my last book. They appealed to the
Insubres, who readily joined them because of their long-standing
grievance against the Romans; then the two tribes overran the
lands which had been allotted to the colonies, and when the
settlers took to flight, pursued them to Mutina, another Roman
colony, and laid siege to the city.

Among those who were shut up there were three men of high
rank who had been sent out as commissioners to supervise the

1. It is not certain whether this news reached Rome before the return of
the envoys; it may even have preceded their mission to Carthage.

2. Scipio, with an army of 8,000 legionaries, 14,000 allied infantry, 600
Roman and 1,600 allied cavalry was to proceed to Massilia and thence invade
Spain. Sempronius with another 8,600 citizen troops, 16,000 allied infantry
and 1,800 cavalry was to establish a base in Sicily for the eventual invasion of
Africa.

distribution of land: Gaius Lutatius, a former consul, and two former praetors. These men requested a parley, to which the Boii agreed, but when the three officials left the city, the tribesmen treacherously seized them, hoping to use them to recover their own hostages. The praetor Lucius Manlius was in command of a body of troops occupying an advanced position to defend the region, heard of what had happened, and marched to the rescue. The Boii, however, had learned of his approach and prepared ambushes in a forest which lay on his line of march, attacked him from all sides as soon as he entered the woods and killed many of the Romans. The survivors at first took to flight, but when they reached some higher ground they rallied sufficiently to enable them with some difficulty to make an orderly withdrawal. The Boii followed close behind and shut up this force too, at a village named Tannes. When the news reached Rome that the fourth legion was surrounded and closely besieged by the Boii, the people immediately sent off the legions which had been voted to Scipio to relieve it, placed this force under the command of a praetor, and ordered the consul to enrol other legions from the allies.

41. In my second and third books I have now surveyed the course of Celtic affairs and their outcome, from the earliest times up to the moment of Hannibal's arrival.

Meanwhile the Roman consuls, having completed the necessary preparations for their respective assignments, set sail in the summer [1] to carry out the operations which had been planned. Publius Cornelius Scipio was bound for Spain with a fleet of 60 ships, and Tiberius Sempronius Longus for Africa with 160 quinqueremes. The latter appeared to be preparing an armada of an overwhelming size: he collected forces from every quarter and put in hand such ambitious preparations at Lilybaeum as to give the impression that he was about to sail up to Carthage and lay siege to it forthwith. Meanwhile Scipio sailed along the coast to Liguria, crossed from Pisae to the neighbourhood of Massilia in five days, anchored off the first mouth of the Rhône, which is known as the Massiliot mouth, and disembarked his troops. He had heard that Hannibal was already crossing the Pyrenees, but because of the difficulty of the country on his route and the number of Celtic tribes which

1. Actually in August 218 B.C.

lay between, he felt sure that the Carthaginians were still many miles away.

Hannibal, however, had bribed some of the Celts to let him pass, and forced his way through the territory of others. Then he continued his march, keeping the Sardinian Sea on his right, and suddenly appeared with his army at the crossing of the Rhône long before anybody had expected him. When the news of his arrival was reported to Scipio, the general could hardly believe that the enemy could have marched so quickly, but he was anxious to discover the exact truth. He therefore dispatched a reconnaissance party consisting of 300 of his bravest cavalry, and sent with them a number of Celts who were serving with the Massiliots as mercenaries to act as guides, and supporting troops. He himself stayed behind to rest his men after the voyage and to discuss with the military tribunes what was the best ground on which to give battle to the enemy.

42. Meanwhile Hannibal had arrived in the neighbourhood of the river, and immediately set about trying to cross it at a point where the stream is still single, some four days' march from the sea. He used every resource to make friends with the natives living by the bank, and bought up all their canoes and boats, of which there was a large number, since many of the inhabitants of the Rhône valley are engaged in sea-borne trade. He also obtained from them the kind of logs which are suitable for building canoes, so that within two days he had mustered an innumerable quantity of small ferry-boats, for in this situation every soldier was anxious to be independent of his neighbour and relied on his own efforts for his chance of getting across. But in the meanwhile a large force of barbarians had gathered on the opposite bank to prevent the Carthaginians from crossing. Hannibal took note of this and decided that he could neither force a passage in the face of such a large body of the enemy, nor stay where he was, for fear of being attacked on all sides. Accordingly, on the third night he detached a part of his army, gave them native guides and sent them off under the command of Hanno, the son of Bomilcar the Suffete.

This contingent marched upstream following the bank of the river for 200 stades, at which point the river divides, forming an island, and there they halted. They found plenty of timber ready to hand; then, by lashing or nailing a number of logs together they quickly built a large number of rafts strong enough for their immediate purpose, and on these they made the crossing safely and met no opposition. They occupied a naturally strong position and rested there for a day, partly to recover their strength after so much physical effort, and partly to prepare for the movement they had been ordered to carry out. Meanwhile Hannibal was occupied with similar preparations for the main body of the army; the problem which caused him the greatest difficulty was how to get his thirty-seven elephants over the river.

43. On the fifth night[1] the force which had crossed earlier under Hanno started off a little before daybreak marching downstream along the opposite bank towards the barbarian army. Meanwhile Hannibal also had his troops ready and was waiting for the moment he had chosen to cross. He had filled the boats with his light cavalry and the canoes with his lightest infantry. The large boats were placed the furthest upstream and directly against the current and the lighter ones below them, so that the heavier craft should absorb the main force of the water and the canoes be less exposed to risk in crossing. The plan for the horses was that they should swim astern of the boats, with one man on each side of the stern guiding three or four by their leading reins, and in this way a large number of the animals were brought over with the first wave of troops. The barbarians, as soon as they saw what the enemy were attempting, poured out of their camp in scattered groups without any order, since they felt sure they could easily stop the Carthaginians from landing.

As soon as Hannibal saw the column of smoke which was the pre-arranged signal that Hanno's force was close at hand, he ordered all those in charge of the ferry-boats to embark and push out against the stream. This was immediately done, and a most dramatic and thrilling spectacle followed. The men in the boats cheered and shouted as they tried to outstrip one another and strained against the strength of the current. All this time the two armies faced one another at the very edge of the river, the Carthaginians following the progress of the boats with loud cheers and sharing in their comrades' agony of suspense, while the barbarians

1. i.e. after the army had first arrived at the Rhône.

yelled their war-cries and challenged their enemies to battle. But at this moment, when the barbarians had completely deserted their camp, Hanno's force on the far bank suddenly delivered their attack. Some of them set fire to the encampment, while the main body fell upon those who were opposing the crossing. The barbarians were taken completely by surprise; some of them rushed back to save their tents, while others defended themselves against this attack from the rear. Hannibal, when he saw that the battle was proceeding exactly as he had intended, immediately formed up his first division as it landed, addressed a few words to the men, and at once engaged the barbarians. The Celts had no time to form their ranks, they were again taken by surprise by this manoeuvre, and soon turned and took to flight.

44. The Carthaginian commander, having thus won control of the bridgehead and defeated the enemy, immediately set about transporting the men who had been left on the other bank. In a short while he had ferried his whole army across, and encamped for that night beside the river. The next morning he learned that the Roman fleet was anchored off the mouths of the Rhône; whereupon he selected a body of 500 Numidian horsemen, and sent them off to reconnoitre the location and the strength of the enemy and to observe their movements. At the same time he ordered the men who had the charge of ferrying over the elephants to set about their task. Next, he paraded the army, presented to them Magilus and the other Celtic chieftains who had come to him from the plains of the Po, and with the help of an interpreter explained to the troops what had been the decision of the Celtic tribes, as their leaders had reported it. What most encouraged his men was first of all the actual appearance of the envoys who were inviting them to come and promising to join them in the war against Rome, and secondly, the confidence they could feel in the promises of the Gauls to guide them by a route on which they would be abundantly supplied with necessities and which would lead them rapidly and safely to Italy. Besides this, the envoys had much to say of the size and the wealth of the country where they were going, and of the eager spirit of the men who would fight by their side in their battles against the Romans.

After they had addressed the troops to this effect, the Celts withdrew and Hannibal came forward and spoke to his men. He began by recalling their past achievements and reminded them that although they had engaged in many dangerous operations and fought in many a battle, they had never failed in one when they followed his plans and advice. Then he urged them to take heart in the knowledge that the hardest part of their task had already been achieved, since they had already forced the passage of the river and had seen and heard for themselves the evidence of their allies' goodwill and readiness to help them. He appealed to them to have confidence and leave to him those details which were his own business, and to obey orders and show themselves to be men of courage and worthy of their own past record. The army received his words with great enthusiasm and loud applause, whereupon Hannibal praised the men, offered up a prayer to the gods on behalf of all, and then dismissed the assembly. He gave out orders that they should take their rest and make their preparations with all speed, as the march would be resumed on the following day.

45. After the assembly had been dismissed, the Numidian horsemen who had been sent out to reconnoitre returned to camp; the greater number of the party had been killed and the rest arrived in headlong flight. Quite near their camp they had met the detachment of Roman cavalry sent out by Scipio for the same purpose, and the engagement had been fought with such courage and fury that the Romans and Celts lost some 140 horsemen and the Numidians more than 200. After the action the Romans rode on in pursuit right up to the Carthaginian camp, surveyed it, and then galloped back to warn their general that the enemy had arrived. They reached the Roman camp safely and delivered their report, whereupon Scipio immediately had the troops' baggage loaded on to the ships, and marched off with his whole army up the river bank in the hope of meeting the Carthaginians.

At dawn the day after the assembly had been held Hannibal dispatched the whole of his cavalry in the direction of the sea to act as a covering force, and moved his infantry out of camp and set them on the march, while he himself waited for the elephants and the men who had been left with them to cross the river. The method by which they were transported was as follows.

46. A number of solidly built rafts were constructed, and two

THE SECOND PUNIC WAR

of these were lashed together and firmly fixed to the bank at the
point where the raft entered the river,[1] their combined width being
about fifty feet. Other rafts were then attached on the riverward
side so as to form a pontoon which projected into the stream. The
side which faced upstream was made fast to trees growing on the
bank, so that the whole structure should remain securely in place
and not be dislodged by the current. When the whole pontoon had
been extended to a length of some 200 feet, they attached two solidly
built rafts to the far end; these were strongly fastened to one
another, but so connected to the main pontoon that the lashings
could easily be cut. They made fast to the two rafts several towing
lines; these were to be taken up by boats whose task was to tow the
rafts, prevent them from being carried downstream, and hold them
against the current, thus transporting the elephants which would be
on them. Next they piled up quantities of earth along the whole
pier of rafts until they had raised its surface to the same level as the
bank, and made it look like the path on the land which led down to
the crossing. The elephants were accustomed to obey their Indian
mahouts until they arrived at the edge of the water, but they
would on no account venture into it. This time they led the elephants
along the earthen causeway with two females in front, whom the
rest obediently followed. As soon as they were standing on the last
rafts, the ropes holding these were cut, the boats took up the strain
of the tow-ropes, and the rafts with the elephants standing on them
were rapidly pulled away from the causeway. At this the animals
panicked and at first turned round and began to move about in all
directions, but as they were by then surrounded on all sides by
the stream, their fear eventually compelled them to stay quiet.
In this way, and by continuing to attach fresh rafts to the end of the
pontoon, they managed to get most of the animals over on these,
but some became so terror-stricken that they leaped into the river
when they were half-way across. The drivers of these were all
drowned, but the elephants were saved, because through the power
and the length of their trunks they were able to keep these above the
surface and breathe through them, and also spout out any water
which had entered their mouths. In this way most of them survived
and crossed the river on their feet.

1. i.e. the first two rafts rested wholly on land.

47. After the elephants had been put across in this fashion, Hannibal formed them into a rearguard together with the cavalry, and proceeded up the river bank, marching away from the sea in an easterly direction, as though he were heading for the centre of Europe. The Rhône has its source beyond the recess of the Adriatic Gulf[1] on the northern slopes of the Alps and facing the west, and then flowing in a south-westerly direction it falls into the Sardinian Sea. For much of its course it runs through a deep valley, to the north of which lives the Celtic tribe of the Ardyes, while its southern side is entirely enclosed by the northern slopes of the Alps. The plains of the Po, which I have described at length in an earlier passage, are separated from the Rhône valley by a series of peaks of these mountains which, starting from Marseilles, extend to the head of the Adriatic. It was this range which Hannibal now crossed to enter Italy via the Rhône valley.

Now some of the writers who have reported this crossing of the Alps, through their desire to impress their readers with their descriptions of the wonders of these mountains, have fallen into the two vices which are the most alien to the spirit of history, by which I mean distortions of fact and self-contradictory statements. For example, they present Hannibal as a commander of unrivalled courage and foresight, but at the same time show him as totally lacking in judgement. Then elsewhere, since they can find no other way out of the labyrinth of falsehood into which they have strayed, they introduce gods and the sons of gods into what is supposed to be a factual history. They show us the Alps as being so rugged and inaccessible that so far from horses and troops accompanied by elephants being able to cross them, it would be difficult for the most agile of infantrymen to get through, and at the same time they represent the country as so desolate that if some god or hero had not met Hannibal and showed him the way, his whole army would have been lost and perished to a man. Reports of this kind are typical of the two vices I have mentioned – they are at once false and inconsistent.

1. This is one of Polybius' most startling geographical errors. Since he believed that the chain of the Alps ran east and west, and that the Rhône rose to the north of it, it follows that the river would be expected to flow in a westerly direction.

48. In the first place, could anyone imagine a more improvident general or a more incompetent leader than Hannibal would have been if, finding himself in command of such a large army on which all his hopes for the success of the expedition were placed, he had not familiarized himself with the roads or the lie of the country, as these writers suggest, and had no idea of where he was marching or against what enemy, or indeed of whether the whole expedition was practicable at all? In other words, what these authors are suggesting is that Hannibal, who had experienced no setback to mar his high hopes of success, would have committed himself to a plan which not even a general who had suffered a total defeat and was at his wits' end for a solution would have adopted, that is, to take his army into completely unknown territory. In the same way, their description of the desolation of the country and the extreme steepness and inaccessibility of the route is glaringly inaccurate. They have failed to bring to light the fact that the Celts, who live near the Rhône, have not once nor twice before Hannibal's arrival, but on many occasions, and those not in the distant past but quite recently, marched large armies across the Alps and fought side-by-side with the Celts of the Po valley against the Romans, as I related in an earlier book. They have not even discovered that there is a considerable population which inhabits the Alps themselves, but in ignorance of all these facts, they report that some hero appeared and showed Hannibal the road. The natural consequence of this is that they fall into the same difficulties as the tragic dramatists, who all need a *deus ex machina* to resolve their plots, because they are based on false or improbable assumptions. Similarly, these historians have to fall back on apparitions of gods or heroes, because the foundations of their narrative are inaccurate or unconvincing. For how is it possible to build a rational ending on an irrational beginning?

Of course Hannibal did not act as these writers imply, but pursued his plans with sound common sense. He had taken pains to inform himself of the natural wealth of the district into which he planned to descend and of the resentment which its people felt against the Romans, and to overcome the difficulties of the route he engaged as his guides and scouts natives of the country who were about to take part in his campaign. On these matters I can speak with some confidence, as I have questioned men who were actually present on these occasions about the circumstances, have personally explored the country, and have crossed the Alps myself to obtain first-hand information and evidence.

49. The consul Publius Cornelius Scipio arrived at the place where the Carthaginians had crossed the Rhône three days after they had resumed their march. He was astounded to find that the enemy had already pressed on, as he had felt certain that they would never venture to advance into Italy by this route, partly because of their numbers and partly because of the fickle nature of the barbarians who inhabited the region. However, when he learned that they had taken this risk, he hurried back to his ships and immediately began to embark his forces. He then dispatched his brother to carry on the campaign in Spain, while he himself turned back and set sail for Italy; his plan was to march with all speed through Etruria and anticipate the enemy by arriving first at the foot of the pass by which they would descend from the Alps.

Meanwhile Hannibal, after marching for four days after his passage over the Rhône, reached a place which is known as 'The Island'. This is a thickly populated district which produces large quantities of corn and takes its name from its natural situation. It is triangular in shape: the rivers Rhône and Isère form two sides of the figure and meet at its apex. The size and the shape of the triangle are similar to those of the Nile Delta, except that the base of the latter is formed by the sea, into which the branches of the river discharge their waters, whereas here the base consists of a range of mountains which are difficult to approach or to penetrate – indeed, one might say, are almost inaccessible. When Hannibal arrived in this region, he found that the throne was being disputed by two brothers, each of whom confronted the other with an army that was ready to fight. The elder of the two approached Hannibal and appealed to him for his help in securing the throne, a request which Hannibal granted, since it seemed clear in the present circumstances that such action would turn out to his advantage. And indeed, after joining forces with this prince and driving out his rival, Hannibal received some valuable help from the victor. Not only did the new ruler supply the army with large quantities of corn and other provisions, but he replaced all their old and worn-out weapons with new ones, thus re-equipping the whole force at exactly the right moment. He also supplied most of Hannibal's troops with new clothes and boots, which were of the greatest help to them in their crossing of the Alps. But he rendered an even more important service than this: because the Carthaginians were full of anxiety at the prospect of marching through the territory of the Allobroges, he used his troops to guard their rear, and in this way enabled them to reach the foot of the pass in safety.

50. After a march of ten days along the banks of the river,[1] during which he covered nearly 100 miles, Hannibal began his ascent of the Alps and soon found himself beset with great dangers. So long as the Carthaginians had remained in the plains the various chieftains of the Allobroges had left them alone because of their fear both of the Carthaginian cavalry and also of the barbarian troops who were escorting them. But as soon as the latter had set off for home and Hannibal's troops began to advance into difficult country, the Allobrogian chiefs gathered a large force and took up commanding positions alongside the road by which the Carthaginians would have to climb.[2] If they had only kept their plans secret, they would have completely destroyed the Carthaginian army. But in the event their scheme became known, and though the Celts inflicted heavy casualties on Hannibal's troops, they suffered at least as many themselves. Hannibal received intelligence that the barbarians had seized these points of vantage and he pitched camp at the foot of the pass; there he halted while he sent forward some of his Gallic guides to reconnoitre the ground and report on the enemy's dispositions and the general situation. His orders were carried out, and he then discovered that it was the enemy's habit to remain under arms in their positions and guard them carefully during the daytime, but to withdraw at night to a neighbouring town. So Hannibal revised his plans in the light of this report and devised the following stratagem. He advanced with his whole army quite openly,

1. The text refers only to 'the river', but the line of march strongly suggests the Isère.

2. Polybius' account of the passage of the Alps differs in various important details from Livy's because the two authors used different sources. Livy's description can most plausibly be interpreted as bringing the army over by a more southerly route across the Mont Genèvre pass, Polybius' by a more northerly across the Mont Cénis.

and when he approached the part of the road where further movement would be threatened, he pitched camp only a short distance
from the enemy. As soon as it was dark, he gave orders for watch-
fires to be lit and left the greater part of his troops in camp. He then
led forward a picked force of lightly armed men, and passing through
the defile seized the positions which the enemy had just left on
withdrawing into the town according to their usual habit.

51. At daybreak the barbarians saw what had happened, and at
first did nothing to press their attack. But later, as they watched
the long train of pack animals and horsemen slowly and painfully
making their way up the narrow track, they were tempted by this
opportunity to harass the advance. When they went into action
and attacked at several different points at once the Carthaginians
suffered heavy losses, especially of their horses and baggage mules,
and this was not so much at the hands of the enemy as because of
the nature of the ground. The road leading up to the pass was not
only narrow and uneven but flanked with precipices, and so the
least movement or disorder in the line caused many of the animals
to be forced over the edge with their loads. It was chiefly the horses
which brought about this confusion whenever they were wounded:
some of them, maddened by the pain, would wheel round and
collide with the baggage mules, while others, rushing on ahead,
would thrust aside anything that stood in their way on the narrow
path, and so throw the whole line into disarray. When Hannibal
saw this, he realized that even those who survived this ambush
would have no chance of safety if their baggage train were destroyed,
and so he took command of the body of troops which had seized
the enemy's positions on the previous night, and hurried to the
rescue of those at the head of the column. He killed great numbers
of the Allobroges, as he had the advantage of attacking them
from higher ground, but the losses were equally heavy among his
own troops, since the turmoil and the mêlée in his main column
were greatly increased, and now came from both directions at once
on account of the shouts and struggles of those who were fighting
higher up the slope. It was only when he had killed most of the
Allobroges and driven off the rest in headlong retreat towards their
own territory that the horses and the survivors of the mule train
could make their way slowly and with great difficulty over the

dangerous stretch of the path. After this action Hannibal rallied as many of his troops as he could, and attacked the town from which the enemy had made their sortie. He found it almost empty, as all the inhabitants had been lured out by the prospect of easy plunder, and he at once took possession of it. The seizure of this place brought him several immediate as well as future advantages: he recovered a number of his baggage mules and horses, and many of the men who had been captured with them, and found a supply of corn and of cattle to last him for two or three days. But an even more important gain was that his victory inspired such fear among the tribes in the vicinity that none of those who lived near the ascent were likely to dare to attack him again.

52. He proceeded to pitch camp there and rested for a day before resuming his march. For the following three days he led his army safely over the next stretch of their route, but on the fourth he once more found himself in great danger. The tribes which lived near the pass joined forces to lay a treacherous plot against him. They came out to meet him carrying branches and wreaths, which are recognized among almost all the barbarian peoples as tokens of friendship, just as Greeks use the herald's staff. Hannibal, however, was inclined to be suspicious of the good faith of these people, and took especial pains to discover what were their intentions and the meaning of this approach. The Gauls told him that they were well aware of the capture of the city and the destruction of those who had tried to attack him. They explained that this was why they had come to meet him, since they had no desire to do him harm, nor to suffer any themselves, and they promised to deliver up hostages from among their own people. Hannibal was reluctant to believe these assurances and hesitated for a long time; then in the end he decided that if he accepted their overtures he might make them more pacific and less inclined to attack him, but that if he refused, he would only provoke them into open hostility. So he agreed to their proposals and pretended to accept their professions of friendship. The barbarians then handed over their hostages, provided him with large numbers of cattle, and indeed put themselves unreservedly into his hands, whereupon Hannibal trusted them so far as to engage them as guides for the next difficult section of his route. For two days they showed him the way,

but then the same tribe gathered their forces, and coming up behind the Carthaginians attacked them as they were passing through a steep and precipitous defile.

53. This time Hannibal's army would have been wiped out, but for the fact that his fears had not been allayed, and that having some foreboding of what might happen, he had stationed his mule train and his cavalry at the head of the column and the heavy infantry in the rear. The infantry covered his main body and were able to check the onslaught of the barbarians, so that the disaster was less serious than it might have been, but even so, a great number of men, pack animals and horses perished in the attack. The enemy had gained the higher ground and could move along the slopes, and from there some of them rolled down rocks, while others struck down their opponents with stones at close quarters. The Carthaginians were thrown into such confusion and felt so threatened by these tactics that Hannibal was compelled to spend the night with only half his force near a certain bare rock which offered some protection. Here he was separated from his cavalry and from the mule train, and waited to cover their advance, until after a whole night's struggle they slowly and with great difficulty made their way out of the gorge. By the next morning the enemy had broken off contact, and Hannibal was able to rejoin the cavalry and baggage animals and advance towards the top of the pass. He was no longer threatened by any concentration of barbarians, but at a few points on the route he was harassed by scattered groups who took advantage of the ground to launch attacks on his front and rear and carry off some of the pack animals. His best resource in this situation were the elephants, for the enemy were terrified by their strange appearance, and never dared to approach the part of the column in which they were stationed. On the ninth day of his march Hannibal reached the top of the pass, and there he pitched camp and halted for two days to rest the survivors of his army and wait for the stragglers. While he was there many of the horses which had taken fright and run away and a number of the mules which had thrown off their loads unexpectedly rejoined him: they had followed the trail of his march and now wandered back into the camp.

54. By this date it was nearing the time of the setting of the

Pleiades,[1] and snow was already gathering around the mountain crests. Hannibal saw that his men had lost heart because of the sufferings they had already endured and the hardships which they believed still lay ahead. So he called his troops together and strove to raise their spirits, and for this purpose he relied above all on the actual sight of Italy, which now stretched out before them, for the country lies so close under these mountains that when the two are seen simultaneously in a panoramic view, the Alps seem to rise above the rest of the landscape, like a walled citadel above a city. Hannibal therefore directed his men's gaze towards the plains of the Po, and reminded them of the welcome they would receive from the Gauls who inhabited them. At the same time he pointed out the direction of Rome itself, and in this way he did something to restore their confidence. The next day he broke camp and began the descent. During this part of his march he met none of the enemy except for a few prowling marauders, but because of the snow and of the dangers of his route he lost nearly as many men as he had done on the ascent. The track which led down the mountainside was both narrow and steep, and since neither the men nor the animals could be sure of their footing on account of the snow, any who stepped wide of the path or stumbled overbalanced and fell down the precipices. These perils they could endure, because by this time they had become accustomed to such mischances, but at length they reached a place where the track was too narrow for the elephants or even the pack animals to pass. A previous landslide had already carried away some 300 yards of the face of the mountain, while a recent one had made the situation still worse. At this point the soldiers once more lost their nerve and came close to despair. Hannibal's first thought was to avoid this impasse by making a detour, but a fresh fall of snow made further progress impossible and he was compelled to abandon the idea.

55. These conditions were so unusual as to be almost freakish. The new snow lying on top of the old, which had remained there from the previous winter, gave way easily, both because it was soft, having only just fallen, and because it was not yet deep. But

1. Taken literally this would mean early November, but it is possible that Hannibal was on the pass about the third week of September, and that the phrase is used in a general sense to indicate the beginning of the bad season.

when men and beasts had trodden through it and penetrated to the frozen snow underneath, they no longer sank into it, but found both their feet slipping from under them, as happens when people walk on ground which is covered with a coating of mud. What followed made the situation even more desperate. In the case of the men, when they found they could not get a foothold on the lower layer of snow they fell, and then, as they struggled to rise by using their hands and knees, slid downwards even faster on these, no matter what they clutched on the way, since the angle of the slope was so steep.

As for the animals, when they fell and struggled to rise they broke through the lower layer of snow, and there they stayed with their loads, as though frozen to the earth, because of their weight and the congealed state of the old snow. Hannibal was compelled to give up the idea of attempting a detour, and, after clearing the snow away from the ridge, pitched camp there. Then he set his troops to work on the immensely laborious task of building up the path along the cliff. However, in one day he had made a track wide enough to take the mule train and the horses; he at once took these across, pitched camp below the snow-line and sent the animals out in search of pasture. Then he took the Numidians and set them in relays to the work of building up the path. After three days of this toilsome effort he succeeded in getting his elephants across, but the animals were in a miserable condition from hunger. The crests of the Alps and the parts near the tops of the passes are completely treeless and bare of vegetation, because of the snow which lies there continually between winter and summer, but the slopes half-way down on the Italian side are both grassy and well-wooded, and are in general quite habitable.

56. After he had reassembled all his forces Hannibal resumed the descent, and three days after leaving the precipice I have just described he arrived in the plains. He had lost many men at the hands of the enemy, at the various river crossings and in the course of his march, while the precipices and difficult passes of the Alps had cost not only many human lives but even greater numbers of horses and mules. The whole march from New Carthage had taken him five months, and the actual crossing of the Alps fifteen days, and now when he boldly descended into the plains of the Po valley

and the territory of the Insubres, the army that was left to him consisted of 12,000 African and 8,000 Spanish infantry, and not more
than 6,000 cavalry in all; he himself explicitly mentions these figures
in the inscription on the column at Lacinium which records the
strength of his forces.

At about this time, as I mentioned above, Publius Cornelius
Scipio, the consul, had left the greater part of his forces under his
brother Gnaeus to carry on the campaign in Spain and to take the
offensive against Hasdrubal, while he sailed back to Pisae with a
small body of men. He then marched through Etruria and took over
from the praetors the command of the legions stationed on the
frontier which were engaged in fighting the Boii. From there he
advanced into the plain of the Po, pitched camp and waited for the
enemy, whom he was impatient to bring to battle.

57. Now that I have brought my narrative and the generals on
both sides and the war itself into Italy, I wish before beginning my
description of the operations to say a few words about the kind of
material which I believe to be proper to my history.

Some readers may well ask themselves why, since the greater
part of my account of events concerns Africa and Spain, I have
said nothing more about the mouth of the Mediterranean at the
Pillars of Hercules, or about the Outer Sea and its special characteristics, or about the British Isles and the processes of extracting
tin, or about the gold and silver mines of Spain itself, all these being
topics concerning which other writers have provided lengthy and
mutually contradictory reports. I have passed over these subjects
not because I considered that they had no place in my history,
but first of all because I was anxious to avoid constantly interrupt-
ing my narrative and distracting my readers from the main theme;
and secondly because I decided not to refer to them merely in a
haphazard fashion or in passing, but to allot them their due place
and time in my scheme, and thus to provide as true a description
as lies within my power. Let no one be surprised, then, if when I
arrive at such places in the course of my history, I refrain from
describing them for the reasons I have just given. Those readers
who insist on such topographical digressions at every point fail
to understand that they are acting like the type of gourmand at a
dinner party who samples everything on the table, and so neither

truly enjoys any dish at the moment that he tastes it, nor digests it well enough to derive any benefit from it afterwards. Those who treat their study of history in this fashion likewise receive no true pleasure at the moment of reading, nor instruction for the future.

58. No province of historical writing stands in greater need of study or correction than this one;[1] there is plenty of evidence for this conclusion, but I may cite the following in particular. Nearly every writer, or at any rate the great majority, has attempted to describe the situation and the special features of the countries which lie at the extremities of the known world, and most have committed glaring errors at many points. We should, of course, on no account pass over their mistakes, and we should make our comments with due system and method, not haphazardly nor in passing; at the same time we should not find fault, or rebuke them, but rather recognize their achievements while correcting their imperfections, always bearing in mind that they too, if they had lived in our times, would have corrected and modified many of their statements. In the distant past, indeed, it is very rare to find a Greek who undertook to investigate these remote parts of the world; this was because of the practical impossibility of doing so. The sea offered so many dangers that it is difficult to calculate them, while those on land were more numerous still. And even if anyone succeeded, whether by design or by force of circumstances, in reaching the furthest confines of the world, this did not necessarily mean that he was able to accomplish his purpose. Some of these regions were so completely barbarous and others so desolate that it was often difficult to observe phenomena at first hand, and even harder to obtain information about what had actually been seen because of the differences in language. Again, even if a man was able to make himself an eye-witness, it was still more difficult for him to use moderation in his statements, to scorn travellers' tales of marvels and prodigies, to prefer truth for its own sake, and to tell us nothing beyond this.

59. In ancient times these problems made it not merely difficult but almost impossible to give a reliable description of the regions I have mentioned, and so we should not find fault with these writers for their omissions and inaccuracies, but rather, considering the

1. i.e. geographical information and its place in the writing of history.

period at which they wrote, praise and admire them for having at
least discovered something and added to the sum of human knowledge on these subjects. But in our own times, partly because of the
empire which Alexander established in Asia and the Romans in
other parts of the world, almost all regions have become approach-
able either by sea or by land. At the same time our men of action in
Greece have been released from the pressures of political or military ambition, and so have plenty of opportunities to pursue inquiries or research, from which it follows that we ought to be able
to acquire a truer and more accurate picture of those regions which
were once unknown. This, at any rate, is what I shall try to establish when I reach a suitable point in my history to introduce the
subject, and it will be my aim to instruct in full detail those who are
curious about such things. It was, in fact, with this express object
that I underwent the dangers and hardships of making journeys
through Africa, Spain and Gaul, and voyages on the sea which
adjoins these countries on their western side; in other words to
correct the imperfect knowledge of earlier writers, and to make these
parts of the world known also to the Greeks.[1]

After this digression from my narrative, I shall return to the
pitched battles which the Romans and the Carthaginians fought in
Italy.

60. I have already described the strength of Hannibal's forces
when he entered Italy. On his arrival he at once pitched camp at the
very foot of the Alps, and his first concern was to rest his troops.
The whole army had not only suffered terribly from the fatigue of
the climb and the descent and the roughness of the mountain
tracks, but they had undergone great hardships on account of the
shortage of provisions, and the lack of the most elementary bodily
necessities, so that under the pressure of continuous physical effort
and want of food many of the soldiers had fallen into a state of
utter dejection. It had proved impossible to carry enough provisions
for so many thousands of men, and when the pack animals perished,
the greater part of the supplies had been lost with them. The result
was that while Hannibal started after the crossing of the Rhône

1. This passage was evidently written after Polybius' travels in Gaul, Spain
and Africa, approximately between 151 and 146 B.C.

with 38,000 infantry and more than 8,000 cavalry he lost nearly half his force as I have described above in making his way through the passes, while the survivors, because of the ceaseless privations they endured, came in their outward appearance and general condition to look more like beasts than men.

Hannibal therefore concentrated all his attention upon the care of his troops and their horses until they were thoroughly restored both in body and spirit. A little while later, after his army had regained its condition, he learned that the tribe of the Taurini, who lived at the foot of the Alps, had fallen out with the Insubres and were inclined to be suspicious of the Carthaginians. Hannibal first of all approached them to solicit their friendship and alliance, but when they rejected his overtures he pitched camp before their principal city[1] and captured it in three days. He then put to the sword all those who had resisted him, and by this action inspired such fear among the neighbouring tribes of barbarians that they immediately flocked to him to make their submission. The rest of the Celtic tribes who inhabit these plains had been eager to join the Carthaginians from the outset, but the Roman legions had advanced beyond the territory of most of them and now stood between them and their would-be allies; they therefore kept quiet, and some were even obliged to serve with the Romans. It was this factor which persuaded Hannibal not to delay any longer, but to advance and attempt some action to encourage those who were ready to share in his enterprise.

61. This was the scheme which Hannibal had in mind when he learned that Scipio had already crossed the Po with his forces and was close at hand. At first he was unwilling to believe the report when he remembered that he had left the Roman commander only a few days before at the crossing of the Rhône, and that the voyage from Massilia to Etruria was a long and difficult one; moreover he had also been informed that the land route across Italy from the Tyrrhenian Sea to the Alps was likewise long, and involved an arduous march. But when more and more messengers came in, all of whom confirmed this intelligence in greater detail, he was both

1. Probably the modern Turin.

astonished and impressed by Scipio's plan of advance and the way he had executed it. Scipio's feelings were very similar,[1] for he had never expected in the first place that Hannibal would attempt the crossing of the Alps with a foreign army, and had assumed that if he did venture upon it the expedition was certain to perish. Having made these assumptions, when he discovered that Hannibal was safe and was already laying siege to cities in Italy he was astounded at his opponent's audacity and daring.

In Rome itself the news produced a similar effect. The last to be heard of the Carthaginians had been the report of their capture of Saguntum, and the excitement created by this event had only just died down. Steps had been taken to deal with that situation by the dispatch of one consul to Africa, to blockade Carthage itself, and of the other to Spain, to engage Hannibal there; now the news had arrived that Hannibal was already at hand with his army and was actually besieging cities in Italy. This turn of events took the authorities completely by surprise, and in their alarm they at once sent orders to Longus at Lilybaeum informing him of the enemy's arrival in Italy, and instructing him to break off his present operations and return with all possible speed to take part in the defence of his own country. Longus immediately assembled the crews of his fleet and gave orders for it to sail to Italy. As for the land forces, the military tribunes were ordered to administer an oath to the soldiers binding them to present themselves by a fixed date at Ariminum[2] before the hour of rest. This is a town on the Adriatic coast at the southern edge of the plains of the Po. Thus there was great excitement and activity in every quarter, and since the news was so unexpected by Romans and Carthaginians alike, it produced on both sides that single-minded concern for the future which is most dangerous to an adversary.

Scipio, having already crossed the Po, decides to advance beyond the Ticinus and the armies approach one another to the north of the river.

1. These judgements are all thoroughly speculative. Scipio might have been surprised by the speed of Hannibal's arrival, but it would have been far more surprising for Hannibal if he had *not* encountered Roman armies on the enemy's northern frontiers.

2. After forty days (see p. 237).

65. Next day both commanders advanced their troops along the bank of the Po which is nearest to the Alps, the Romans having the river on their left and the Carthaginians on their right. On the following day they learned from their foragers that the two armies were almost in contact, whereupon both sides pitched camp and remained in their positions. The next morning the two generals led out all their cavalry, while Scipio took his javelin-throwers in addition, and both made a rapid advance across the plain to reconnoitre one another's forces. As each force drew near and saw the clouds of dust that were thrown up by the other's movements they quickly formed themselves into battle order. Scipio placed his javelin-throwers and their supporting Gallic cavalry in the van, and drawing up the rest of his troops in line, moved forward at a slow pace. Hannibal stationed his bridled cavalry and all the heavy cavalry units in front and led them straight up to the enemy, keeping his Numidian cavalry on each wing, ready to make an outflanking movement.

Both the generals and their cavalry were so carried away by their ardour to engage that when the two lines met the javelin-throwers had no time at all to discharge their first volley. They turned and immediately retired through the gaps to a position behind their cavalry, in terror of the approaching charge and of being trampled underfoot by the horsemen who were bearing down upon them. The cavalry forces met head on and for some while the battle was evenly balanced; it became a mixed action of cavalry and infantry because of the number of men who dismounted in the course of the fighting. But at length the Numidians outflanked the Romans and fell upon them from the rear; and the javelin-throwers on foot, who had fled from the cavalry charge at the beginning, were now ridden down by the weight of numbers and the furious onslaught of the Numidians. At this point the Roman cavalry, which had been engaged from the outset with the Carthaginian centre and had lost many men, but had inflicted even heavier losses on the enemy, now found themselves being attacked by the Numidians from the rear. At this they broke and fled, many of them scattering in different directions; only a few rallied and remained with the consul.

66. After this action Scipio broke up his camp and marched

across the plains to the bridge over the Po, moving as fast as possible to get his legions over the river before the Carthaginians arrived. He had observed that the country was flat, and since the enemy had the superiority in cavalry and he himself had been severely wounded, he had decided to withdraw his forces to a place of safety. For his part Hannibal had at first expected that the Romans would risk an infantry battle, but when he saw that they had abandoned their camp he followed them as far as the bridge over the Ticinus. There he found that most of the planking of the bridge had been torn up, but that the troops who had been left to guard it were still at their posts on his side of the river. He captured this detachment, which was some 600 strong, and when he learned that the main body of the Roman army was by then far ahead of him, he wheeled about and marched in the opposite direction up the Po, looking for a place where the river would be easy to bridge. After two days' march he halted and built a bridge of boats. He then ordered Hasdrubal to supervise the passage of the army, whilst he himself crossed the river at once and proceeded to give audience to the envoys who had arrived from the neighbouring districts. What had happened was that as soon as he had won the cavalry engagement, all the Celtic tribes in the vicinity made haste, as they had wished from the start, to declare their support for the Carthaginians, furnishing supplies and sending contingents to serve with them. Hannibal received all these adherents warmly, and after his troops had joined him from the other side of the river, he led his men along the Po in the opposite direction to his previous line of march, this time advancing downstream expressly to seek out the enemy.

Meanwhile Scipio had crossed the Po and was encamped at the Roman colony of Placentia; here he occupied himself with having his wounded soldiers nursed and his own injuries tended, and as he believed that his force was securely established in a safe position, he made no move. But two days after Scipio had crossed the river, Hannibal appeared close by, and the next day he drew up his army in battle order in full view of the Romans. Then, as nobody came out to attack him, he pitched camp at a distance of about six miles away.

67. Meanwhile the Celtic contingents who were serving in the Roman army had decided that the Carthaginians' prospects were

now decidedly brighter and had concerted a plot among themselves; for the moment they remained quietly in their quarters, while they watched for an opportunity to attack the Romans. All ranks within the entrenched camp had taken their evening meal and retired to rest; the Celts then waited for the greater part of the night to pass, seized their arms about the time of the morning watch, and fell upon the Romans who were quartered near them. They killed many men outright and wounded not a few, and finally after cutting off the heads of those they had murdered, they went over to the Carthaginians. Hannibal welcomed them enthusiastically: he addressed a speech of encouragement to them, and after promising them all fitting rewards, he sent them off to their own cities to tell their compatriots of what they had done and to urge the rest to join him, for by this time he felt that once the other Celts learned of this act of treachery on the part of their fellow countrymen towards the Romans, they would all have to take his side. At the same time a delegation from the Boii visited him and delivered up the three Roman commissioners who had been sent out from Rome to partition their lands, and whom, as I mentioned earlier, they had seized by an act of treachery. Hannibal responded with gratitude to their goodwill, and gave formal pledges of friendship and alliance to their envoys. The three Romans, however, he handed back to them, advising them to keep the men in order to negotiate the return of their own hostages from Rome, as had been their original intention.

Scipio was deeply concerned at this treacherous attack. He saw the danger that since the Celts had been disaffected for a long time past, this fresh initiative might influence all the Gallic tribes in the neighbourhood to go over to the Carthaginians, and so he determined to take precautions for the future. The following night, just before the morning watch, he broke camp and marched towards the river Trebbia and the high ground near it, where he felt that he could rely both upon the natural strength of the position and the loyalty of the neighbouring allies.

68. As soon as Hannibal discovered that Scipio had left he sent his Numidian horse in pursuit, and soon afterwards the rest of the cavalry, while he and the main body of the army followed close behind. The Numidians, when they found the Roman camp empty,

stopped to set fire to it, and this delay proved to be of great service
to the Romans, for if the Numidians had immediately pressed on
and overtaken the baggage train, many of those accompanying it
would have been killed, so flat was the terrain through which they
were marching. As it was, the greater number succeeded in crossing
the Trebbia, but those who were stationed in the extreme rear of
the column were either cut down or captured by the Carthaginians.

Scipio, having got his men over the Trebbia, encamped on the
first hills that he found, fortified his position with a trench and a
palisade, and waited there for Longus and his army; meanwhile he
paid especial attention to the treatment of his wounds, since he was
eager to take part in the coming battle. Hannibal for his part
pitched camp some four or five miles away, and meanwhile the
Celtic population who inhabited the plain, encouraged by the
favourable prospects of the Carthaginians, supplied them with
abundant provisions and stood ready to play their part in any of
Hannibal's operations or battles.

When the news of the cavalry action was received in Rome, the
people were disconcerted to learn that it had not turned out as they
had expected, but there was no lack of pretexts to persuade them
that this was not really a defeat. Some put the blame on the consul's
excessive ardour, and others upon deliberate ill-will on the part of
the Celts, which it was considered had been proved by their subsequent desertion. But generally speaking, so long as their infantry
forces were still intact, the people's confidence in the ultimate
success of Roman arms remained unaffected. Thus when Longus
and his legions reached Rome and marched through the city, the
people still believed that these troops had only to appear on the
field to decide the battle.

Longus' men then assembled at Ariminum in fulfilment of the
oath they had taken, and their general led them out with all speed to
join forces with Scipio. The two armies duly made contact and
Longus pitched camp close to Scipio, but after this he needed time
to rest his men, who had undertaken a continuous march of forty
days from Lilybaeum to Ariminum. In the meanwhile he prepared
his troops for battle and held many conferences with Scipio, during
which he acquainted himself with recent events and discussed with
his colleague the measures to be taken in the present situation.

69. At about this time Hannibal was able to seize the town of Clastidium and capture both the garrison and the stores of grain, the place having been betrayed to him by a native of Brundisium to whom the Romans had entrusted its defence. Hannibal used the grain for his immediate needs, but he took trouble to do no harm to the prisoners and he paraded them wherever he went; his purpose was to provide an example of his policy, so that those who found themselves overtaken by the chances of war should not give way to panic or abandon hope that he would spare their lives. He gave a generous reward to the man who had betrayed the town, as he was anxious to win over others in positions of authority to the Carthaginian cause.

After this he discovered that some of the Celtic tribes who lived between the valleys of the Trebbia and the Po had made a treaty of friendship with him, but were at the same time negotiating with the Romans, believing that in this way they would make themselves safe from both Romans and Carthaginians alike; and so he sent a force of 2,000 infantry and about 1,000 Celtic and Numidian horsemen with orders to raid the district. The orders were carried out and great quantities of booty were secured, whereupon the Celts promptly appeared in the Roman camp and appealed for help. Longus had for some time been looking for an opportunity to take the offensive, and he immediately seized on this occasion to send out a force which included the greater part of his cavalry and about 1,000 javelin-throwers on foot. They marched quickly so as to overtake the raiders on the far side of the Trebbia; there they engaged the enemy in a struggle for possession of the spoils and compelled the Celts and Numidians to fall back upon their fortified camp. Those who were occupying the advanced positions in front of the Carthaginian camp soon understood what had happened and brought up reserves to support their hard-pressed comrades, whereupon the Romans in their turn were routed and retreated to their own camp. When Longus saw this, he mustered the whole of his remaining cavalry and javelin-throwers, and with these reinforcements the Celts were again repulsed and retired to a position of safety. The Carthaginian commander was not prepared for a general battle and made it a principle never to be drawn into a decisive engagement unless by deliberate choice, and certainly not on a casual impulse. In this situation he acted as a good general should: he checked the troops that were in retreat and compelled them to halt and face about as they approached their own camp. He would not allow them to pursue and engage the enemy, however, but sent out his officers and buglers to recall them. The Romans halted for a short while and then withdrew; they had lost a few of their number, but had inflicted far heavier casualties on the Carthaginians.

70. In his delight and elation at this success Longus was consumed with the ambition to force a decisive battle as soon as possible. Because of Scipio's illness, he was entitled to handle the situation according to his own judgement, but since he wished to obtain his colleague's opinion he consulted him on the subject. Scipio, however, took exactly the opposite view of the situation. He believed that the legions would benefit greatly from a winter spent in training, and also that the Celts, unstable and treacherous as they were, would not remain loyal to the Carthaginians once the latter ceased to win victories and were forced to remain inactive, but would in turn break faith with their latest allies. He also hoped that when his wound was healed he himself could render some real service in partnership with his collague. For all these reasons, therefore, he urged Longus to let the situation remain as it was. Longus was well aware that each of these arguments was true and inescapable. But he was spurred on at once by ambition and by a blind confidence in his good fortune and yearned to deal the decisive blow in the campaign himself: accordingly he was anxious that the battle should take place before Scipio could be present or the new consuls designate could take up their commands, and the moment for this was almost due. And so, since the time he chose for the engagement was dictated not by the facts of the situation but by his personal motives, his judgement was bound to be at fault.

Hannibal's view of the position was very similar to Scipio's, but was based on the opposite reasons: he was anxious to draw the enemy into battle, first to exploit the warlike spirit of the Celts while it was still active, secondly to engage the Roman legions while they were still raw recruits and had little battle experience, and thirdly to come to grips before Scipio had recovered. The most pressing consideration, however, was that he wished to keep the initiative and not let time slip away without achieving a success, for when a general leads his army into a foreign country and embarks on a hazardous campaign, his only chance of safety lies in sustaining the hopes of his allies by continually striking some fresh blow. This was Hannibal's purpose, which he made in the knowledge that Longus cherished the impulse to take the offensive.

71. Hannibal had some time before noticed a piece of ground between the two camps, which, although flat and treeless, was well suited for an ambush; it was crossed by a watercourse with high overhanging banks that were densely overgrown with thorns and brambles, and here he planned to lay a trap for the enemy. He had a good chance of catching them off their guard, for the Romans always suspected wooded ground because the Celts were apt to choose such terrain for their ambushes, but they had no fear of treeless spaces. They overlooked the fact that the latter may offer the concealment and security required for an ambush even more effectively than woods, for the reason that the men who are lying in wait have an excellent view over long distances and in most cases can also find sufficient cover. A watercourse with an overhanging bank and a quantity of reeds or ferns or some kind of thorny plants can serve to conceal not only infantry but even cavalry, if the simple precaution is taken of laying any shields which carry blazons flat on the ground and hiding the helmets underneath them.

Hannibal confided his plan for the coming battle to his brother Mago and the other officers of his staff. They all approved of the scheme, and so after the troops had taken their evening meal Hannibal sent for Mago, who was still quite young, but was full of warlike spirit and had been trained from his boyhood in the art of soldiering; he then put the young man in command of a detachment consisting of 100 infantry and 100 cavalrymen. Earlier in the day he had himself picked out these men as among the most daring soldiers in his army, and told them to come to his tent after supper. There he addressed them in such a way as to rouse their spirits for the occasion, and ordered each to pick out ten of the bravest men from his own company and report to a particular place in the camp which they knew. They carried out his orders, and during the night Hannibal sent out the whole force, which now amounted to 1,000 cavalrymen and the same number of infantry, to the spot selected for the ambush. He provided the detachment with guides and gave his brother instructions for the timing of his attack. At daybreak he himself paraded the Numidian cavalry, all of whom were men of exceptional endurance: he spoke to them, promised rewards to those who distinguished themselves, and then ordered them to ride up to the enemy's entrenchments. They were to gallop across the river and try to draw out the Romans by hurling javelins at them, the object of this manoeuvre being to entice the enemy into action before they had taken their morning meal or made any preparations for battle. He then summoned his other officers, roused their spirits for the coming encounter, and gave orders to the whole army to have breakfast and prepare their arms and horses for action.

72. As soon as Longus saw the Numidian cavalry approaching, he first sent out his own cavalry, unsupported but with orders to engage the enemy. He then dispatched a body of some 6,000 javelin-throwers and proceeded to move his whole army out of the camp. His superiority in numbers and his success in the cavalry action of the previous day had filled him with so much confidence that he imagined the mere appearance of his troops would decide the issue. But the year was now well into December, the day was bitterly cold with occasional gusts of snow, and the men and horses had almost all left the camp without having taken their morning meal. At first they were buoyed up by their natural high spirits and martial ardour, but when they had to ford the Trebbia, which was in full flood because of the rain which had fallen in the previous night on the high ground above the camp, the infantry had great difficulty in wading across, since the water was running breast high. In consequence, as the day wore on the whole army began to suffer intensely both from the cold and from want of food. The Carthaginians, by contrast, who had eaten and drunk in their tents and groomed their horses, were all anointing and arming themselves round their camp-fires. Hannibal had been watching for his opportunity, and as soon as he saw that the Romans had crossed the Trebbia he moved up his pikemen and slingers, numbering some 8,000, as a covering force and then led out his army. He advanced about a mile and then drew up his infantry in a single line 20,000 strong and consisting of Spaniards,

Celts and Africans, while his cavalry, which together with the contingents of his Celtic allies numbered over 10,000, was divided between the two wings. He also divided his force of elephants and stationed them in front of the wings of the infantry phalanx, so that his flanks were doubly protected. At this point Longus recalled his cavalry when he saw that they could not deal effectively with the enemy; for the Numidians easily evaded their attacks by dispersing and withdrawing, after which they would wheel round and charge with great dash, these being the peculiar tactics in which they excelled. Sempronius' infantry were marshalled in the regular Roman order[1] and numbered some 16,000 Romans and 20,000 allies, for this is the strength of a complete Roman army that is mobilized for an important campaign when circumstances cause the consuls to combine their forces. He then posted his cavalry, which totalled 4,000, on either wing, and advanced upon the enemy with measured determination, marching in order at a slow pace.

73. When the two armies came within range the action was opened by the light-armed troops[2] in the forward positions. In this phase of the battle the Romans suffered from many disadvantages and the Carthaginians proved themselves far more effective: the Roman javelin-throwers had been struggling against adverse conditions ever since daybreak, and had used up most of their missiles in the skirmish against the Numidians, while the remainder had been rendered useless by being so long exposed to the wet. The cavalry and the rest of the army were similarly handicapped, whereas the situation of the Carthaginians was exactly the opposite. They waited in their ranks, fresh, braced for action and ready to give support wherever it was required. So as soon as the skirmishers had retired between the gaps in the lines and the heavy infantry had engaged, the Carthaginian cavalry at once attacked both flanks of the enemy; they had the advantages of superiority in numbers and of their men and horses having started completely fresh, as I have explained. The Roman cavalry fell back before the Carthaginian charge, leaving the flanks of the infantry

1. i.e. in the three lines of *hastati*, *principes* and *triarii*. See pp. 320–21.
2. These were the Roman javelin-throwers, who were opposed by Hannibal's pikemen and slingers.

exposed, whereupon the Carthaginian pikemen and the main body of the Numidians raced ahead of the troops in front of them and attacked the Romans on both flanks, causing them heavy losses and hindering them from dealing with the troops on their front. The heavy infantry who formed the front line and the centre of both armies kept up a hard-fought struggle, which for a long while yielded no advantage to either side.

74. At this point in the battle the Numidian infantry and cavalry under Mago emerged from their hiding-place and suddenly charged the enemy's centre from the rear, a manoeuvre which threw the whole Roman army into confusion and dismay. Finally both wings of Longus' infantry, which were being hard-pressed from the front by the elephants and from the flanks by the light-armed troops, gave way and were forced back by their attackers to the river which lay behind them. After this, although the rear of the Roman centre was suffering heavily at the hands of the Numidians who had attacked from their ambush, those in the front who found themselves pushed forward overcame the Celts and a division of Africans, killed great numbers of them and broke through the Carthaginian line. But when they saw that both their wings had been driven from the field they abandoned hope of restoring the situation or of returning to their camp; they were deterred from this partly through their fear of the enemy's cavalry, and partly by the storms of rain which continued to pour down and increased the difficulties of recrossing the Trebbia. This body of troops, which numbered not less than 10,000, therefore closed their ranks and succeeded in withdrawing safely to Placentia. Of the remainder of the Roman army the greater part were killed by the elephants and the cavalry; the survivors among the infantry and most of the cavalry managed to join the troops I have just mentioned, and reached Placentia with them. The Carthaginians pursued the enemy as far as the Trebbia, but were prevented by the storm from advancing any further, after which they returned to their camp. They were all exultant at the outcome of the battle, which they regarded as a decisive success: the losses among the Spaniards and Africans were very small and most of the casualties had been suffered by the Celts. The whole army had been severely

affected, however, by the pouring rain and the snowfall that followed it, with the result that all the elephants died except for one, and large numbers of men and horses perished from the cold.

75. Longus was well aware of what had really happened, but was anxious to conceal the details as far as possible from the authorities in Rome, and he therefore dispatched messengers with the news that a battle had taken place but that a storm had deprived his army of victory. The Romans accepted this version at first, but soon afterwards they learned that the Carthaginians were still in possession of their camp and that all the Celts had joined them, while their own troops had abandoned their camp, retreated from the battlefield, had all now taken refuge in the neighbouring cities, and were drawing their supplies from the sea and by way of the Po. When these facts became known, they understood quite clearly what had been the result of the battle. The news took them by surprise and caused them to put in hand many more preparations for the war, and especially to protect positions which lay in the way of the enemy's advance. They dispatched legions to Sardinia and to Sicily and garrisons to Tarentum and other places of strategical importance, and besides these measures they fitted out a fleet of sixty quinqueremes. The consuls designate, Gnaeus Servilius and Gaius Flaminius, took steps to mobilize the allies, enrol the legions drawn from Roman citizens, and establish depots of stores at Ariminum and in Etruria, which they had chosen as the bases for the campaign. They also appealed for help to Hiero, the ruler of Sicily, who sent a contingent of 500 Cretans and 1,000 light infantry – in short, they hastened their preparations in every direction. It is when the Romans stand in real danger that they are most to be feared, and this principle applies both to their public and to their private life.

77. At the beginning of the following spring[1] Gaius Flaminius marched his army through Etruria and pitched camp before Arretium, while on the east coast Gnaeus Servilius moved up as far as Ariminum to oppose the enemy's advance from that quarter. Meanwhile Hannibal, who was passing the winter in Cisalpine Gaul, kept the Romans he had captured in the battle under guard

1. 217 B.C.

and gave them only just sufficient rations to keep them alive; the prisoners taken from the allies, on the other hand, he treated with great kindness, and later summoned them to an assembly and made a speech to them. He pointed out that he had come to fight not against them but against the Romans on their behalf, and that therefore, if they knew where their interests lay, they would respond to his offers of friendship, for he had come above all to give the Italians back their freedom and to help them recover the cities and the territories which the Romans had taken away. With these words he sent them all back to their homes without demanding a penny of ransom; his object in all this was to win over the inhabitants of Italy to his cause, to alienate them from their attachment to Rome, and to stir up revolt among those who believed that their harbours or cities had suffered decline as a result of Roman rule.

78. During this winter Hannibal also tried a characteristically Punic deception. He was well aware of the fickleness of the Celts, and because it was only very recently that he had established friendly relations with them he was on his guard against attempts on his life. He therefore had a number of wigs made, each of which created the impression of a man of a different age, and these he constantly changed, while at the same time dressing in a style which matched the wig. In this way he made it difficult to recognize him, not only for those who caught no more than a passing glimpse of him, but even for those who knew him well.

Meanwhile he had noticed that the Celts were becoming restive at the fact that the war was still being carried on within their frontiers, and were impatiently looking forward to an invasion of the enemy's territory. They made out that this was because of their hatred of the Romans, but the real reason was their own greed for the spoils of war. At any rate Hannibal decided to resume his advance as quickly as possible and so satisfy the expectations of his troops. Accordingly, as soon as the weather began to grow warmer he set about questioning those who knew the country best, and discovered that the other routes for invading Roman territory were not only long but were thoroughly familiar to the enemy, whereas the road which led through the marshes to Etruria was both short and likely to take Flaminius by surprise. Hannibal was always inclined by temperament to favour the unexpected solution and so this was the line of march which he chose. But when the news began to circulate among his troops that their general was going to lead them through marshy country there was a decided lack of enthusiasm to start, since everybody imagined that they would be passing through deep swamps and quagmires.

79. However, Hannibal had taken pains to inquire into the nature of the terrain and had made sure that the water lying on the ground they would have to cross was shallow and the bottom solid. When he broke camp and began his march, he placed the Africans, the Spaniards and all the best fighting troops in the forward part of his column and interspersed the baggage train among them, so as to make sure that all the army's necessities would be available for the immediate future. As for looking further ahead, he made no provision for the pack animals, since he reckoned that once within the enemy's territory he would have no need for them if he were defeated, but that if he gained control of the open country he would have no problems of supply. The Celts were stationed behind the troops I have just mentioned, and the cavalry brought up the rear of the army, the command of the rearguard being entrusted to his brother Mago. He made these dispositions for a number of reasons, but chiefly because of the lack of endurance and the aversion to hard physical effort of the Celts: his idea was that if because of the hardships of the march they should try to turn back, Mago could intercept them with the cavalry and forestall any such attempt. The Spaniards and the Africans succeeded in traversing the marshes while the ground was still firm, and because they were already hardened to such exertions they did not suffer too severely. The Celts, on the other hand, could only struggle through with great difficulty, since not only had the marshy soil been softened and trampled down by those who had gone before, but the men themselves found the whole effort of the march exhausting and demoralizing since they were quite unaccustomed to hardship of this kind. They were prevented from turning back, however, by the cavalry posted behind them. The whole army was affected above all by lack of sleep, since they were obliged to keep moving for four days and three nights, during which time they were continuously marching through water, but the Celts suffered far more from fatigue than the rest and lost many more

men. Most of the pack animals fell and perished in the mud, the only service which they rendered consisting in the fact that, as they fell, the men piled the packs on their carcasses and lay on them, and in this way could stay out of the water and snatch a little sleep during the night. Also, many of the horses became lame because of the prolonged march through the mud. Hannibal himself, who was riding on the one surviving elephant, had great difficulty in making the crossing: he suffered intense pain from a severe attack of ophthalmia, which finally caused him to lose the sight of an eye, as the situation made it impossible for him to halt and have treatment for it.

80. After he had accomplished this crossing of the marshes contrary to everybody's expectations, he found Flaminius encamped in Etruria before the city of Arretium. Hannibal's first action was to pitch his own camp at the edge of the swamps, his object being to rest his troops while he reconnoitred the region in front of him and collected intelligence about the enemy. He learned first that the surrounding country promised a wealth of plunder, and secondly that Flaminius possessed a rare talent for the arts of demagogy and playing to the gallery, but very little for the practical conduct of the war, and yet was absurdly over-confident about his own resources. Hannibal calculated that if he marched past his opponent's army and advanced into the region in front of him Flaminius would be far too sensitive to the jeers of his rank and file to be able to look on while the country was devastated; at the same time he would be so provoked by the sight that he would follow wherever he was led, and could also be lured by the prospect of winning the coming battle himself without waiting for his colleague. All these factors led him to conclude that Flaminius would give the Carthaginian army plenty of opportunities to attack him.

81. This reasoning on Hannibal's part was both far-sighted and strategically sound. The truth is that there is no more precious asset for a general than a knowledge of his opponent's guiding principles and character, and anyone who thinks the opposite is at once blind and foolish. When individuals or ranks of soldiers are matched against one another the one who means to conquer must search out relentlessly how best to achieve his object, and in particular the point at which his enemy appears most vulnerable or least

protected. In the same way the commander must train his eye upon the weak spots of his opponent's defence, not in his body but in his mind. There are many men who have allowed not only the welfare of the state but their own private fortunes to go to ruin through their own indolence and lack of energy. Some are so addicted to wine that they cannot even go to sleep without making themselves befuddled with drink, and others so abandoned to the pleasures of sex and their judgement consequently so undermined that they have not only ruined their countries and their careers, but have brought their own lives to a disgraceful end. Now when an individual shows himself to be a coward or a fool, the humiliation is at least personal and private, but when a general shows these qualities the effect is universal and produces the most damaging public consequences of all, for not only does he render those under his command inefficient, but he often involves in the greatest dangers those who have trusted him.

On the other hand, rashness, excessive audacity, blind impetuosity, vanity or foolish ambition are all easily exploited by the enemy and are most dangerous to any allies, for a general with such defects in his character will naturally fall victim to all kinds of stratagems, ambushes and trickery. And so the leader who will most quickly gain a decisive victory is the man who can recognize his enemy's mistakes and choose precisely that spot to attack which takes full advantage of the opposing commander's weaknesses. For just as a ship, if it is deprived of its pilot, will fall with its whole crew into the hands of the enemy, so the general who can outwit or outmanoeuvre his opponent is liable to capture his entire army. And so on this occasion, since Hannibal had correctly appreciated and anticipated Flaminius' actions, his plan achieved the results he intended.

82. Hannibal had hardly left the vicinity of Faesulae, advanced a short way beyond the Roman camp and made a raid upon the neighbouring district, before Flaminius exploded into a fury of rage, imagining that the enemy were treating him with contempt. And a little later, when the Carthaginians began to ravage the countryside and the columns of smoke rising on all sides bore witness to the devastation, the consul became still more indignant and regarded this as an intolerable affront. Some of his officers

advised him not to risk a headlong pursuit of his opponents in the effort to bring them to battle, and considered that he should stay on the defensive and beware of their superiority in cavalry; above all they urged him to wait for his colleague to arrive, and not to engage until they could do so with their combined forces. But Flaminius not only ignored the advice, but could not bear to listen to the officers who advanced such arguments; he asked them to imagine what would be said in Rome if the army were to remain in its encampment in the rear of the enemy, while the whole Italian countryside was ravaged almost up to the walls of the capital. This was his point of view when he finally struck camp and led his army forward; he paid no attention to the timing or the direction of his march but pressed on blindly, intent only upon meeting the enemy, as though there could be no doubt that victory already belonged to him. Indeed, he had even created such over-confidence among the populace that the soldiers were outnumbered by crowds of camp-followers who accompanied his march in the hope of finding plunder, and carried chains, fetters and other such gear with them.

Meanwhile Hannibal continued his advance towards Rome, passing through Etruria and keeping the city of Cortona and its hills on his left and Lake Trasimene on his right, and as he marched he went on burning and devastating the countryside, always with the object of luring the enemy into action. When he saw that Flaminius was almost in contact with him, the Carthaginian, who had already selected the ground which would best suit his purpose, made his dispositions for battle.

83. The road at this point passed through a narrow and level valley enclosed on both sides by an unbroken line of lofty hills. At the eastern end of this defile rose a steep eminence with sheer slopes that were difficult to climb; at the western end lay the lake, from which the only access to the valley was a narrow passage which ran along the foot of the hillside. Hannibal led his troops along the edge of the lake, and then through the valley. He himself occupied the hill at the eastern end with his African and Spanish troops. His slingers and pikemen were ordered to make a detour and march round from the front under cover of the hills, and were then posted

in extended order to the right of the valley.[1] The Celts and the cavalry were moved round to the left of the valley and likewise stationed in a continuous line under the hills, the last of them being posted at the entrance to the defile between the hillside and the lake.

All these dispositions were effected during the night, and having surrounded the valley with his troops posted in ambush Hannibal made no further move. Meanwhile Flaminius was following close behind, impatient to overtake the enemy. He had pitched camp very late the night before near the edge of the lake, and next day in his eagerness to engage he led his advance guard at first light along the shore to the entrance of the valley which I have already described.

84. That morning a thick mist still hung over the lakeside. Then, as soon as the greater part of the Roman army had entered the defile and was already in contact with the Carthaginians, Hannibal gave the signal for battle, passed the word to the troops who were lying in ambush, and fell upon the Romans from all sides at once. This sudden appearance of the enemy took Flaminius completely by surprise. The mist blotted out all visibility, and with the attack being launched from higher ground and from so many points at once, the centurions and military tribunes were not only unable to issue any of the necessary orders but even to grasp what was happening. They found themselves under attack simultaneously from the front, the flanks and the rear. In consequence most of the troops were cut down while they were still in marching order and without the least chance of defending themselves, delivered up to slaughter, so to speak, by a complete lack of judgement

1. The terms right and left are used from the point of view of Hannibal as he advanced. Thus the slingers and pikemen were placed to the south and south-west of the Roman column, the Celts and cavalry to the north, except for the last contingent. Flaminius' situation became increasingly difficult the further he advanced into the defile. His army, which in column extended for some six or seven kilometres, could easily be split up in an attack, the narrow strip of land between his men and the lake offered too little margin either to retreat or to rally, and the rising ground hindered the chances of breaking through to the north. The battle provides one of the rare instances in history in which a general lies in ambush with the whole of a large army and accounts for almost the whole of the troops opposed to him.

on the part of their commander; in a word, death took them unawares while they were still wondering what to do. Flaminius himself, demoralized and thrown into utter despair by what had happened, was attacked and killed by a band of Celts. Some 15,000 Romans perished in the valley. In this situation they could do nothing to help themselves, and yet they would not yield to circumstances; they considered it their supreme duty, as all their training had taught them, never to turn tail or to leave their ranks. As for those in the rear who had been trapped between the hillside and the lake, they suffered an even more humiliating, or rather pitiable fate. They found themselves herded into the lake, whereupon some lost their heads, tried to swim away in their armour and were drowned, while the greater number waded out as far as they could. There they stood with only their heads above the water; then, when the cavalry rode in after them and death stared them in the face, they raised their hands, uttering the most piteous pleas for mercy and begging to be spared. In the end they were either killed by the horsemen or steeled themselves to self-destruction. About 6,000 of those in the valley succeeded in defeating the enemy immediately in front of them, but although they might have been of great service, they were unable to go to the rescue of their comrades or work round to the rear of their opponents, because they could see nothing of what was happening. So they continued to press ahead, convinced that they must sooner or later encounter the enemy, until they discovered that, without noticing it, they had broken through to the higher ground. As they reached the crest of the hills the mist dispersed and they could see the full extent of the disaster, but by then it was too late to help, since the enemy were now victorious on all sides and in complete possession of the battlefield. They therefore closed their ranks and retreated to a certain Etruscan village. After the battle Hannibal dispatched Maharbal with the Spaniards and pikemen to surround the place, whereupon the Romans, seeing themselves threatened on every side, laid down their arms and surrendered on condition that their lives should be spared.

Such was the final outcome of the battle fought in Etruria between the Romans and the Carthaginians.

85. When the soldiers who had surrendered on terms were

brought before Hannibal as well as the others, he had the entire body of prisoners assembled, a total of more than 15,000 men. He began by telling them that Maharbal had no authority to spare their lives without first consulting him, and he went on to attack the Romans. Finally he distributed the Roman prisoners among his army to be kept under guard, but released the allies and sent them all back to their homes, reminding them, as he had done on a previous occasion, that he had not come to fight against the Italians, but on behalf of the Italians against Rome. He then gave his own troops time to rest, and buried those of the dead who were of the highest rank. These numbered about thirty, while his total losses amounted to 1,500, most of them Celts. After this he began to discuss with his brother and his friends where and how they should next take the offensive, for by this time he felt confident of his ultimate success.

When the news of the defeat reached Rome, the sheer size of the catastrophe made it impossible for the leaders of the state either to conceal or to tone down the facts, and they were obliged to summon an assembly of the people and announce it. So when the praetor declared from the Rostra, 'We have been defeated in a great battle', the words left his audience so stunned that for those who were present on both occasions the disaster seemed far greater at that moment than it had done even at the time of the battle itself. And this was not surprising. For so many years the people had had no experience of either the report or the fact of an acknowledged defeat that they could not now accept such a reverse with moderation or with dignity. This was not the case, however, with the Senate, which continued to exercise its proper judgement, taking thought for the future and considering what it was the duty of all classes to do, and how to set about this.

86. At the time of the battle the other consul, Gnaeus Servilius, had been at his post in the district of Ariminum, which is situated on the coast of the Adriatic where the plains of Cisalpine Gaul join the rest of Italy, near the mouths of the river Po. When he learned that Hannibal had invaded Etruria and encamped near Flaminius his intention had been to join his colleague with his whole force. But since the size of his army made this impossible, he at once dispatched Gaius Centenius with a force of 4,000 cavalry. These

troops were to advance ahead of his main body and to support Flaminius if the situation became critical. After the battle Hannibal received reports that these reinforcements were approaching, and dispatched Maharbal with the pikemen and a contingent of cavalry to meet them. Maharbal found Centenius and killed half his force in his first attack; then he pursued the rest to a hill in the vicinity and succeeded in capturing them all on the following day.

The news of the battle at Lake Trasimene was only three days old, so that the fever of agitation it had caused throughout the city was still at its height, when the report of the new disaster arrived; and this time not only the people but even the Senate were dismayed. It was therefore resolved to set aside the normal process of government through annually elected magistrates and adopt more radical measures to meet the crisis; there was a general feeling that the situation of Rome and the circumstances which now threatened the people demanded the appointment of a single commander with absolute powers.

Meanwhile Hannibal, who by this time felt completely confident of success, decided against the idea of approaching Rome for the present and began to march towards the Adriatic; there he met no opposition and proceeded to ravage the country as he went. He passed through Umbria and Picenum and reached the coast on the tenth day of his march.[1] During his advance he amassed so much plunder that his army could neither drive it nor carry it with them, and he also killed a number of the inhabitants on his route. He had given the order, which is customary when a city is taken by storm, that all adults whom his troops found there should be killed, and he had done this because of his inborn and inveterate hatred of the Romans.

87. He then pitched camp near the Adriatic in a region which was extraordinarily rich in all kinds of produce, and he made it his first care to rest his army and restore the health both of his men and of their horses. As a result of the cold to which they had been exposed while spending a winter in Cisalpine Gaul, the absence of the oil massage to which they were accustomed, and the hardships of their subsequent march through the swamps, almost all his men

1. The battle of Lake Trasimene had taken place on 21 June; Hannibal arrived at the coast about a fortnight later.

and their horses were suffering from scurvy and its attendant consequences. So now that he was the master of a rich countryside he brought his horses back into good condition, and restored the health of his men both in body and in spirit. He also rearmed his African troops with Roman equipment, selecting the best weapons for the purpose, since he was now in possession of huge stores of captured arms. At the same time he sent messengers by sea to give the Carthaginians at home a full report of what had happened, for this was the first time that he had reached the sea since he invaded Italy. The news aroused tremendous rejoicing in Carthage and the authorities lost no time in taking steps to give every possible support to the conduct of the war both in Italy and in Spain.

The Romans had appointed as their dictator Quintus Fabius, a man of great natural gifts, and outstanding for his steadiness of judgement, so much so, indeed, that even in my own time the members of his family, because of his success and achievements, are known as Maximi, or The Greatest. A dictator differs from the consuls in the following respects: namely, that while each of the consuls is attended by twelve lictors the dictator has twenty-four, and while the consuls are obliged on many occasions to refer to the Senate to carry out their plans, the dictator is a general with absolute powers. Thus when he is appointed all the other magistrates in Rome cease to hold power, with the exception only of the tribunes of the people.[1] I will return to this subject in greater detail in a later book.[2] At the same time the people appointed Marcus Minucius as master of the horse. The master of the horse is subordinate to the dictator, but becomes his successor in authority if the dictator is engaged in other matters.

88. Hannibal now moved his camp from time to time, but remained close to the Adriatic. During this period by bathing his horses with old wine, of which there was plenty to hand, he succeeded in restoring their coats to good condition. At the same time he ensured that his wounded were healed, and that the rest of his troops regained their health and spirits for the tasks which lay before them. He marched through and devastated the territories

1. This statement is incorrect. The magistrates in office, including the consuls, carried on under the orders of the dictator.
2. This passage has not survived.

of Praetuttia, Hadriana, Marrucina and Frentana, and then advanced towards Iapygia. This province is divided between three peoples, each of whom give their name to a district, that is the Daunii, the Peucetii, and the Messapii, and it was the territory of the Daunii[1] which Hannibal first invaded. His first objective was the Roman colony of Luceria, and there he ravaged the surrounding territory. He went on to encamp near Vibinum, overran the territory of Arpi, and plundered the whole region of Daunia without meeting any resistance.

Meanwhile Fabius, after offering sacrifice to the gods following his appointment, also took the field, with his second-in-command and the four legions which had been conscripted for the emergency. He joined forces near Narnia with the army which had been on its way from Ariminum to reinforce Flaminius, and there he relieved Gnaeus Servilius, the present general, of his command on land; he then sent him to Rome with an escort, and with orders to hold himself ready to give support wherever necessary if the Carthaginians should attempt any operations from the sea. Together with his master of the horse he then took over the command of the whole army and encamped opposite the Carthaginians and about six miles away, at a place called Aecae.

89. As soon as Hannibal learned of Fabius' arrival he decided to unnerve the enemy by attacking him at once, and so he led out his army, approached the Roman camp and drew up his men in battle order. There he waited for some time, but as nobody came out to meet him he finally retired to his own camp. For his part Fabius had decided not to take any risk, still less to venture a pitched battle, but to make the safety of his men his first and principal aim, and having chosen such a strategy, he resolutely followed it. At first he was despised for this, and his action gave people the excuse to say that it was inspired only by cowardice, and that he was terrified of an engagement. But as time went on he compelled everyone to admit that it would have been impossible for anybody to have acted with more prudence in the existing circumstances. It was not long before events themselves

---

1. Daunia is the district which extends from Mount Garganus southward. The Peucetii lived in the district inland from Bari, the Messapii in the hinterland of Brundisium and Tarentum.

bore witness to the wisdom of his policy, and this was natural enough.

The facts were that the enemy's forces had undergone a continuous training in war which had begun in their earliest youth, they had a general who had been brought up with them and had been accustomed from childhood to operations in the field, they had won many battles in Spain, and had twice in succession defeated the Romans and their allies; and above all they had cast aside any alternative course of action, so that their only hope of survival rested in victory. On the Roman side the situation was exactly the reverse: his army's comparative lack of experience made it impossible for Fabius to face the enemy in a pitched battle, and so on consideration he decided to fall back upon those resources in which the Romans were superior. These were an inexhaustible supply of provisions and manpower, and to these advantages he clung, and devised his strategy accordingly.

90. During the ensuing months he continued to move on a parallel line to the enemy, while he occupied in advance all those positions which he knew from his experience of the country to be most advantageous. Since he could always count on an abundance of supplies in his rear, he never allowed his soldiers to forage or to become separated from the camp on any pretext. Instead, his forces were kept continually concentrated, while he watched intently for whatever opportunities time or place might provide. By these methods he contrived to kill or capture many groups of the enemy who had strayed from their camp on foraging expeditions. In following these tactics he had two aims: first, to keep on reducing the enemy's limited manpower, and secondly, by means of these minor successes to rebuild the spirit of his own troops, whose confidence had been shattered by their earlier defeats. But as for fighting a pitched battle, which was what his opponent purposed, nothing would induce him to accept the challenge. However, this policy was far from satisfying his subordinate, Marcus Minucius, who shared the popular opinion. He constantly disparaged Fabius for his feeble and dilatory conduct of the campaign, which he contrasted with his own eagerness to take the offensive and risk a battle.

After the Carthaginians had ravaged the districts I have mentioned they crossed the Apennines and descended into the territory of the Samnites. These lands were very fertile and had been untouched by war for many years past, so that here they found themselves among such an abundance of supplies that they could neither use up their plunder nor destroy it. They also overran the territory of the Roman colony of Beneventum and captured the city of Venusia, which was filled with a great quantity of all kinds of property. All this while the Romans followed the Carthaginian rearguard, keeping one or two days' march behind them but taking care never to approach any closer and engage the enemy. From these manoeuvres Hannibal understood that Fabius, while clearly determined to avoid a battle, had no intention at all of abandoning the open country, and so he made a bold advance into the region known as Falernum, in the plain of Capua. This move, he was convinced, would bring one of two results: either he would compel the enemy to fight, or he would prove beyond doubt that he was the master of the field and that the Romans were abandoning the country to him. This demonstration, he hoped, would cause alarm among the cities and persuade them to throw off their allegiance to Rome. For until this moment, even though the Romans had been defeated in two battles, not a single Italian city had gone over to the Carthaginians: all of them had kept faith with Rome, although some of them were suffering severely. Such was the awe and the respect with which the allies regarded the Roman state.

91. Yet in spite of this fact Hannibal had good reasons for calculating as he did. The plains which surround Capua are the most celebrated in all Italy for their fertility, their beauty, their proximity to the sea, and the fact of their being served by those ports which are frequented by travellers to Italy from almost every part of the world. The region also contains the finest and the most celebrated cities in Italy. On its coast lie Sinuessa, Cumae and Dicaearchia,[1] and to the south of these, Neapolis and finally Nuceria. Inland and to the north are Cales and Teanum, and to the east and south the territory of the Daunii and Nola. In the centre of the plain is Capua, once the richest of all the cities in this area. The myth which has come down to us concerning this and the other celebrated plains which are likewise called Phlegraean is surely one of

1. Also known as Puteoli, the modern Pozzuoli.

the most plausible, for it seems entirely natural that they should have proved a particular cause of strife among the gods because of their beauty and fertility.

Besides these advantages the plain is strongly protected by nature and is hard to approach. One side is bounded by the sea and the rest by a lofty and unbroken chain of mountains, through which there are only three passes from the interior, all of them narrow and difficult of access: one leads from Samnium, the second from Latium and the third from the country of the Hirpini. So by establishing their camp in this plain the Carthaginians transformed it into a kind of theatre, where they could surprise all the inhabitants by their unexpected arrival, make a spectacle of the cowardice of their enemies, and prove beyond dispute that they were the masters of the open country.

92. It was with these considerations in mind that Hannibal left Samnium, crossed the pass near the hill known as Eribianus, and pitched camp by the river Volturnus, which divides the Campanian plain almost exactly in half. His camp was on the side of the river which is nearer to Rome, but he was able to ravage the whole plain with foraging parties which met no resistance. But although Fabius was astonished by the audacity of this move he continued to follow all the more strictly his chosen plan of campaign. However, his colleague Minucius and all the centurions and military tribunes in the army were convinced that the enemy were well and truly trapped, and urged him to make haste to reach the plain, and not allow the finest part of the country to be devastated. Fabius did indeed exert himself to get there and made a pretence of showing the same eagerness as the more aggressive and adventurous spirits. But when he drew near to Falernum he confined his operations to showing himself on the hills and moving parallel to the enemy. He did this to avoid giving the impression to the Italian allies that he was abandoning the open country, but he did not bring his army down into the plain, and he avoided an open engagement both for the reasons I have mentioned and because the Carthaginians were superior in cavalry.

By ravaging the whole plain Hannibal had by now done his utmost to lure the Romans into action and he had also amassed an immense quantity of plunder. He therefore decided to withdraw, as he was anxious not to waste his booty, but to store it in a place which would be suitable for his winter quarters, so that his army should not only live well for the present but be assured of abundant supplies throughout the winter. Fabius guessed that his opponent planned to return by the same route as he had entered the plain. He discovered that because of its narrow shape this egress offered an excellent opportunity for an attack by ambush, and so he posted 4,000 men at the pass itself, and left them with orders to make full use of the advantage of the ground and attack with spirit when the right moment arrived. He himself with the main body of his troops encamped on the hill which faced the pass and overlooked it.

93. When the Carthaginians arrived and pitched camp on the level ground under these heights Fabius hoped that he could at least carry off their plunder without a battle; he might even be able to put an end to the whole campaign by exploiting the commanding position which he now occupied. In consequence his whole attention was now concentrated upon considering where and how he could take advantage of the lie of the ground, and which troops he should use to attack the enemy. While the Romans were intent upon these preparations, Hannibal, who had anticipated how they would probably act, gave them neither the time nor the respite to concert their plans. He sent for Hasdrubal, who was in command of the army's pioneers, and ordered him to have as many faggots as possible of dry wood made up with all speed, to select from the plundered herds some 2,000 of the strongest ploughing oxen, and to mass them in front of the camp. When this was done he assembled the pioneers and showed them a ridge which was situated behind his camp, and the pass by which he intended to march. When they received the order, they were to drive the oxen towards this high ground as fast and as furiously as they could until they reached the top. Next he ordered the whole army to take their evening meal and to retire to rest early. Towards the end of the third watch of the night he led the pioneers out of the camp and ordered them to fasten the faggots to the horns of the oxen. There were plenty of men available and the task was quickly carried out, after which he ordered them to light all the faggots and drive the oxen up to the ridge. The light-armed pikemen, who were stationed immediately behind, were ordered to help the drivers for a certain distance up

the slope. Once the animals were well on the move, the soldiers should run along behind them and keep them together as they made for the higher ground. They were then to occupy the ridge, so that if the Romans advanced on to any part of it, they should engage and attack them. At the same time Hannibal himself made off with his main body towards the narrow entrance of the pass; his order of march consisted of the heavy infantry in front, next the cavalry, then the captured herds, and finally the Spaniards and Celts.

94. The Romans who were guarding the gorge, as soon as they saw the burning torches moving up the heights, concluded that Hannibal was making a rapid advance in that direction, and so they abandoned the entrance to the pass and marched to the hill to meet the enemy. But as they approached the oxen they were completely mystified by the moving lights and imagined they were about to meet something far more formidable than was really the case. When the pikemen arrived on the scene the two sides skirmished for a short while, and then as the oxen rushed through between them they broke off contact and remained on the heights waiting for daybreak, for they were quite unable to understand what had happened. Fabius himself, partly because he too was baffled by the situation, and in the words of Homer 'suspected some deep design',[1] and partly because he stuck firmly to his original plan of refusing a general engagement, remained in his camp, made no move and likewise waited for daybreak. Meanwhile Hannibal, whose plan had been successfully carried out in every detail, brought both his army and his plunder safely through the gorge, since the force which had been posted to guard the defile had left their position. When daylight came, he saw the Romans drawn up and facing his light-armed pikemen and sent up a contingent of Spaniards to reinforce them. These troops attacked the Romans, killed about 1,000 of them, easily rescued their own light-armed troops, and brought them down to join the main body.

Having successfully accomplished this withdrawal from Falernum, Hannibal encamped safely and began to consider where and how he should establish his winter quarters,[2] for by this time he had

1. *Odyssey*, X, 232.
2. The date was probably about the beginning of September.

inspired great fear and uncertainty among all the cities and peoples of Italy. In the meanwhile, although Fabius was reviled by the populace for his feebleness in allowing the enemy to escape from an apparently hopeless situation, he still refused to depart from his original policy in any respect. A few days later, however, he was obliged to leave for Rome to perform certain sacrifices, and handed over the command to his master of the horse. As he took his leave he left strict instructions with Minucius that he should pay less attention to inflicting damage upon the enemy and more to avoiding disaster for himself. Minucius, however, paid no heed to these warnings and even as Fabius was uttering them, he was completely engrossed in his schemes for embarking on a decisive battle.

100. Such was the state of affairs in Spain. In Italy we had left Hannibal looking for winter quarters after his withdrawal from the Falernian plain. He had discovered meanwhile from his scouts that the region around Luceria and Gerunium possessed abundant supplies of corn and that Gerunium was the best place in which to collect and store it. He decided to make it his winter quarters and advanced into this district, marching by way of Mount Liburnus. When he arrived at Gerunium, which is some twenty-four miles from Luceria, he first appealed to the inhabitants to make an alliance and offered pledges for the advantages he could confer upon them, but when they rejected his overtures he laid siege to the city. He quickly captured it and proceeded to put the inhabitants to the sword, but was careful not to damage the walls or the majority of the houses, since he intended to use them as granaries during the winter. He then encamped his army in front of the town and fortified the position with a trench and a palisade. When this work was completed he dispatched two divisions of the army to fetch in the corn; each division had orders to bring in daily for its own use the quantity specified by the officers in charge of the commissariat. The remaining third of the army was detailed to guard the camp and to cover the foraging parties on their local expeditions. Since most of the surrounding country was flat and easily accessible, the foragers almost innumerable, and the weather favourable for harvesting the grain, the result was that immense quantities were collected every day.

101. When Minucius took over the command from Fabius, he at first followed the Carthaginians along the line of the hills, since he felt sure that he would meet them as they attempted to cross. But when he learned that Hannibal had already occupied Gerunium, was foraging in that district and had established himself in a fortified camp in front of that city, he altered his line of march and came down from the hills by way of a ridge which slopes down towards Gerunium. He was resolved to engage the enemy upon any terms whatsoever, and when he reached the mountain which is known as Calene, in the territory of Larinum, he pitched camp there. Hannibal now took note of the enemy's approach. He left a third of his army to forage, and taking the other two divisions, pitched camp on some high ground; his purpose was both to give protection to his foragers and to overawe the Romans. Between the two armies there was another hill, which as Hannibal noticed, not only lay close to the Roman camp, but also overlooked it, and so after dark he dispatched a contingent of 2,000 pikemen to occupy it. When it grew light Minucius sighted this force, led out his own light-armed troops and attacked the position. There was a short skirmishing engagement in which the Romans were victorious, and later they transferred their whole camp to this hill. For some while Hannibal kept the greater part of his army within their lines, because the enemy was so close at hand, but after some days he was compelled to send out some of his men to find pasture for the animals and others to bring in the corn. He was anxious, according to his original plan, to keep his captured herds alive and also to garner as much corn as possible so as to ensure sufficient supplies to last the whole winter; this was to feed not only his men but also his horses and pack animals, for the cavalry was the arm on which he relied above all others.

102. Minucius had noticed that large numbers of the Carthaginians were scattered all over the country to carry out these tasks, and so he chose the hour when the sun was at its height to lead out his forces. When he arrived near the enemy's camp he drew up his heavy infantry in battle order, divided the cavalry and light infantry into several groups, and sent them out to attack the foragers, with orders to take no prisoners. This move placed Hannibal in a difficult position, since he was neither strong enough to accept

battle with his main body drawn up outside his camp, nor could he march out to the rescue of those who were scattered about the country. The Romans who had been sent to hunt down the foraging parties killed large numbers of them, and the troops drawn up in front of Hannibal's entrenchments finally became so contemptuous of the enemy that they began to pull down the palisade and came near to storming the whole Carthaginian camp. It was a critical moment for Hannibal, but in spite of this storm of trouble which had descended on him he managed to repulse the attackers and by a supreme effort to hold his camp. Finally his situation was relieved by the arrival of Hasdrubal with a force of some 4,000 men, who had fled from the open country where they had been foraging and had taken refuge at the camp near Gerunium. This reinforcement restored Hannibal's confidence a little, and he made a sortie, drew up his troops a little way in front of the camp and launched an attack, which after hard fighting relieved the pressure on his defences. Minucius had inflicted heavy losses on the Carthaginians in his assault on the camp and even more in his attacks on the foraging parties, and he left the field with great hopes for the future. The next day the Carthaginians evacuated their camp and he promptly occupied it himself. This happened because Hannibal had become alarmed that the Romans might approach the camp at Gerunium by night, find it undefended and capture his baggage and stores, and so he decided to return and establish himself there again. After this the Carthaginians showed far more care and took stricter precautions for their foraging expeditions, while the Romans on the contrary grew more confident and took greater risks.

103. Minucius' success was reported in Rome in terms which went far beyond the true facts, and so delighted the people; their confidence rose first because there was at last a change for the better to relieve their previous pessimism concerning the war, and secondly because they could now believe that the former inertia and lack of spirit which had prevailed in the army did not spring from any lack of courage among the soldiers, but from the excessive caution of their commander. Everybody, accordingly, united in blaming Fabius, and he was accused of supinely allowing his opponent to pass him by. Minucius' reputation on the other hand

rose so high on account of this achievement that the people took a completely unprecedented decision: they conferred absolute power both upon the master of the horse and upon the dictator, in the belief that the former would quickly put an end to the war. Accordingly two dictators were actually appointed for the same campaign, something which had never before happened in the history of Rome. When Minucius was informed of his popularity among the people and of the authority which had been conferred upon him by this decree, his desire to take risks and to launch some daring initiative against the enemy was redoubled.

Fabius on the other hand returned to the army not in the least changed by recent circumstances, and more than ever convinced of the correctness of his original judgement. It did not escape him, however, that Minucius, who was now puffed up with pride, was jealously opposing him at every turn and was wholeheartedly set upon risking a battle. He therefore offered his colleague two alternatives, either to command the army on alternate days, or to divide it in half and use his own legions in any way that he thought fit. Minucius readily agreed to the division of the army, whereupon this arrangement was put into effect, and the two halves of the army encamped at a distance of about a mile and a half from one another.

104. Meanwhile Hannibal had obtained intelligence of the rivalry between the two generals and of Minucius' ambitious and impulsive nature, partly through information provided by prisoners, and partly through his own observation of what was happening. He concluded that these factors should work in his favour rather than against him, and he thereupon turned his attention to Minucius, for he was anxious to curb the latter's aggressive inclinations and anticipate his offensive. Between his camp and that of Minucius there was a small hill which could be used against either position, and he decided to occupy this point of vantage. He knew full well that as a result of his previous success Minucius would at once rush out to counter the move, and so he devised the following stratagem. The country surrounding the hill was bare of trees, but contained plenty of broken ground and hollows of every kind. He therefore sent out after dark a contingent of 500 cavalry and about 5,000 light-armed and other infantry. This body was divided

into groups of 200 or 300 men each, who had orders to occupy the most favourable positions for an ambush; then, to make sure that these troops should not be seen in the morning by the Roman foraging parties, Hannibal himself occupied the hill at daybreak with his light-armed troops. As soon as Minucius saw this move he thought it an excellent opportunity for a counter-attack, and immediately sent out his light infantry with orders to engage the enemy and contest the position of the hill. After these he sent out his cavalry, followed by the legions, which he led in person, marching in close order; this was what he had done in the previous battle, and he intended to follow the same tactics.

105. The day was just breaking and the Romans had their eyes and their attention concentrated upon the fighting on the hill, with no suspicion of the troops who were waiting in ambush. Hannibal kept sending reinforcements to his men on the heights, and when soon afterwards he appeared with his cavalry, followed by the rest of his army, the cavalry on both sides quickly came into action. The result of this clash was that the Roman light infantry were forced to give ground by the great numbers of the Carthaginian horse, and fell back upon the legions, throwing their formation into confusion. At the same time the signal was given to the troops lying concealed in ambush; they appeared from all directions at once and launched an attack, with the result that suddenly not only the light infantry but the whole of Minucius' force found itself in a critical position. It was at this moment that Fabius, who had watched the progress of the battle and was now seriously alarmed that the Romans might suffer a total defeat, moved up his army in haste to rescue his colleague. At his approach the Romans took heart once more, and although their whole battle line had been broken, they rallied again round their standards, and with Fabius' army to cover their retreat, succeeded in withdrawing to safety. In the meanwhile, however, many of the light infantry had been killed, while the losses among the legionaries were even heavier and included many of their bravest troops.

The freshness and the perfect discipline of the relieving troops caused Hannibal some alarm, and he promptly abandoned his pursuit and broke off the fighting. To those who were engaged in the action it was clear beyond doubt that Minucius' rashness had almost brought about a total defeat, and that, as before, the situation had only been saved by Fabius' prudence. Those in Rome, on the other hand, had been given a clear demonstration of how the foresight, logical thinking and cool calculation of a general differ from the rashness and bravado of a mere soldier. The Roman army, at any rate, had been taught a practical lesson, and they now proceeded to fortify a single camp and unite their forces inside it. Henceforward they paid all due attention to Fabius and to his orders. The Carthaginians built a palisade around the hill which was now in their hands, and dug a trench between it and their own camp. They garrisoned the hill, and then proceeded unmolested to make their preparations for the winter.

106. The season for the consular elections was now approaching and the Romans elected Lucius Aemilius Paullus and Gaius Terentius Varro. When they were installed in office, the dictators laid down their powers and the consuls of the previous year, Gnaeus Servilius and Marcus Atilius Regulus, who had been appointed after the death of Flaminius, were invested with proconsular authority by Paullus. These officers then took command in the field and directed the movements of their forces as they thought best. After consulting the Senate, Paullus at once set about enrolling the soldiers who were still needed to bring the legions up to strength for the campaign and sent them into the field. He gave strict orders to Servilius that he must on no account be drawn into a pitched battle, but that he should seek out frequent and vigorous minor operations with the object of training the recruits and build-in up their confidence for a major engagement, for the Senate was convinced that one of the principal causes of their recent defeats lay in their having used newly raised and untrained conscripts. The consuls also placed an army under the command of the praetor Lucius Postumius, and sent him to Cisalpine Gaul to create a diversion.

At the same time they arranged to recall the fleet, which was wintering in Lilybaeum, and dispatched to the generals in Spain all the necessary supplies for their campaigns in that theatre. These and other preparations for the war were the duties with which the consuls occupied themselves, and on receiving their instructions Servilius carried out all such minor operations as they required.

I shall not describe these in any greater detail, since no decisive or noteworthy results ensued, partly because of the circumstances of the time, and partly because of the very nature of the orders. All that took place was a large number of skirmishes and minor clashes in which the Roman commanders distinguished themselves and were generally considered to have conducted the campaign with courage as well as good sense.

107. Throughout the winter and the spring the two armies thus remained encamped opposite one another, and it was only when the season had advanced far enough to allow his supplies to be collected from the year's crops[1] that Hannibal began to move from the camp at Gerunium. By that time it would be in his interest, he considered, to use every means in his power to force the enemy to fight, and so he occupied the citadel of a town named Cannae, where the Romans had collected the corn and other supplies from the district around Canusium. The town itself had previously been reduced to ruins, but the capture of the citadel and the stores caused some alarm in the Roman army. Its fall was a blow to them, not only because of the loss of the stores but because its position commanded the surrounding district. The generals therefore sent frequent messages to Rome to request instructions, pointing out that if they approached the enemy it would be impossible to avoid a battle, for the country was being pillaged and the attitude of the allies was beginning to waver.

The Senate decided that the army should fight, but they ordered Servilius to wait and dispatched the consuls to the front. It was to Paullus that all eyes were turned and upon his abilities and experience that the most confident hopes were founded, because of the high reputation he had earned in his earlier career, and also because a few years before he was considered to have shown courage and rendered great service to the state in the Illyrian campaign.[2] It was now decided to put eight legions into the field, a step which the Romans had never taken before, each legion consisting of 5,000 men, not counting the allies. The Romans, as I have previously explained,[3] regularly employ four legions, each consisting

1. The date was early June.
2. See pp. 193, 195–7.
3. See p. 57.

of about 4,000 infantry and 200 cavalry, but on occasions of exceptional need they raise the strength of the infantry in each legion to 5,000 and of the cavalry to 300. They make the number of the allied infantry equal to that of the Roman citizens in the legions, but as a rule the allied cavalry are three times as numerous as the Roman. To each of the consuls they assign two legions and half of the allied troops when they send them into the field. Most of their wars are decided by one consul, an army of two legions and the normal quota of allied troops, so that it is only on rare occasions that they employ all their forces at the same moment and in the same battle. But this time they were so alarmed and apprehensive that they decided to bring not just four but eight legions into action.

110. Next day the consuls broke camp and led their troops towards the position in which they had heard the enemy was entrenched. On the second day they arrived within sight of the Carthaginians and pitched camp about five miles away. Paullus noted that the surrounding country was flat and treeless, and his view was that they should not attack the enemy there, since the Carthaginians were superior in cavalry, but should try to lure them on by advancing to a terrain where the battle could be decided by the infantry. Gaius Terentius Varro, in consequence of his small military experience, held the opposite opinion, with the result that disputes and differences of view broke out between the two commanders, the most dangerous situation which can arise. Now when two consuls are present, the custom is that each commands on alternate days, and as Varro happened to be in command on the following day, he broke camp and ordered an advance with the object of approaching the enemy; he did this in spite of strong protests and active opposition on the part of Paullus. Hannibal moved out his light-armed troops and cavalry to meet him, took him by surprise while he was still on the march and threw the Roman formation into confusion. However, they succeeded in containing the first charge of the Carthaginians by moving up some of their heavy infantry to the front; then later, by bringing into action their javelin-throwers and the cavalry, they began to get the better of the fighting. This was because the Carthaginians had no substantial reserves, while on the Roman side some of the light-

armed troops were strengthened by the presence of units from the legions, who fought in the midst of their ranks.

The approach of darkness compelled them to break off the action in which the Carthaginians had been less successful than they had hoped. The next day Paullus, who still did not consider the situation favourable for a battle but could not safely withdraw his army, pitched camp with two-thirds of his force on the bank of the river Aufidus. This is the only river which flows right through the Apennines, that long chain of mountains which forms the watershed of all Italian rivers, those on the west descending to the Tyrrhenian Sea and those on the east to the Adriatic. The Aufidus, however, pierces this range, since it has its source on the Tyrrhenian side and flows into the Adriatic. For the remaining third of his army Paullus fortified a position on the far side of the river to the east of the ford.[1] This was situated nearly a mile and a quarter from his main encampment and rather further from that of the enemy; his object was to protect the foraging parties from his principal camp west of the river, while harassing those of the Carthaginians.

112. The next day Hannibal ordered all his troops to prepare themselves and their equipment for action, and the day after he drew up his army along the bank of the river and made it plain that he wished to give battle at once. Paullus, however, was still dissatisfied with the ground on which he found himself; he saw that the Carthaginians would soon be obliged to move their camp to obtain supplies, and after strengthening his two camps with additional guards he made no further move. Hannibal waited for some time, and then as he found no response from the Roman side he marched his troops back to their entrenchments, but he sent out his Numidian cavalry to attack the enemy's water-carriers from the smaller Roman camp. The Numidians then rode up to the actual palisade of the camp and prevented the men from drawing water. Not only did this action serve as an added provocation to Varro, but the soldiers who had shown themselves eager for battle became more and more impatient at the delay. Generally speaking there is nothing that men find harder to bear than a prolonged suspense,

1. i.e. on the right bank of the Aufidus.

but once the decision has been taken, they find means to endure even what would otherwise seem the very worst that could happen.

When the news reached Rome that the armies were encamped opposite one another, and that clashes between the outposts were occurring daily, the mood of the city became one of intense excitement and fear. Most people dreaded the outcome, because of the reverses they had suffered on more than one occasion, and in their mind's eye they anticipated and pictured to themselves the consequences of total defeat. All the oracles that had ever been pronounced to them were upon men's lips, each temple and house was beset with signs and prodigies, and the city became one great scene of supplicatory processions and prayers. In times of danger the Romans will go to astonishing lengths to propitiate both gods and men, and there is no ceremony of this kind which they regard as unbecoming or beneath their dignity.

113. On the next day Varro took over the command, and immediately after sunrise he moved his forces simultaneously out of both camps. He crossed the river with the troops from the main camp[1] and immediately drew them up in order of battle, followed by those from the other camp who were ranged next to them in the same line, the whole army facing south. The Roman cavalry were stationed next to the river on the right wing, and the infantry next to them in the same line. Here the maniples were grouped more closely than in their normal formation, so that the depth of each was several times greater than its width.[2] The allied cavalry was placed on the left wing, and the light-armed troops a little way in front of the whole army. The total strength of the Roman forces including the allies amounted to some 80,000 infantry and a little over 6,000 cavalry. At the same time Hannibal brought his slingers and pikemen over the river and placed them in the forward positions. Then he led the rest of his troops out of their camp, crossed the river at two points and drew them up opposite the enemy. On the left flank close to the river he stationed his Spanish

1. Varro crossed to the right bank, below Cannae, and it was there that the battle took place, the Romans fighting with their backs to the sea.

2. The object of this grouping was to break through the enemy's centre and win the battle before the weight of the Carthaginian cavalry could decide the issue.

and Celtic horse opposite the Roman cavalry. Closer to the centre were placed half of his African heavy infantry, then the Spanish and Celtic infantry, next to them the other half of the Africans, and finally on his right wing the Numidian cavalry. At this stage his whole army was drawn up in a straight line, but he then moved forward the central contingents of the Spaniards and Celts, keeping the flanking units in contact with them to suit his plan; this formation produced a crescent-shaped bulge, with the line of the flanking companies thinning out as it was extended. The object of this arrangement was to begin the battle with the Spaniards and Celts and use the Africans as a reserve to support them.

114. The Africans were equipped with Roman armour and weapons, for Hannibal had fitted them out with the finest of the arms he had captured in previous battles. The shields used by the Spaniards and Celts were very similar to one another, but their swords were quite different. The point of the Spanish sword was no less effective for wounding than the edge, whereas the Gallic sword was useful only for slashing and required a wide sweep for that purpose. The troops were drawn up in alternate companies, the Celts naked, the Spaniards with their short linen tunics bordered with purple – their national dress – so that the line presented a strange and terrifying appearance.

The Carthaginian cavalry was about 10,000 strong, and their infantry, including the Celts, not much above 40,000. The right wing of the Roman army was commanded by Paullus, the left by Varro, and the centre by the consuls of the preceding year: namely Marcus Atilius Regulus and Gnaeus Servilius. Hasdrubal commanded the Carthaginian left, Hanno the right, and Hannibal with his brother Mago the centre. The Romans, as I have mentioned, faced the south and the Carthaginians the north, so that neither was put at a disadvantage by the rising sun.

115. The battle opened with a clash between the advance guards, and at first, while only the light infantry were engaged, the fighting was evenly balanced. But as soon as the Spanish and Celtic horse on the left wing came into contact with the Roman cavalry, the action began in earnest and the fighting which developed was truly barbaric. There was none of the usual formal advance and withdrawal about this encounter: once the two forces had met they

dismounted and fought on foot, man to man. Here the Carthaginians finally prevailed, and although the Romans resisted with desperate courage, most of them were killed in the hand-to-hand fighting. Their opponents drove the rest remorselessly along the river bank, cutting them down as they retreated, and it was at this point that the heavy infantry took the place of the light-armed troops and came to close quarters. For a while the Spaniards and Celts held their formation and fought with great gallantry, but then they turned tail, forced back by the sheer weight of the legions, and the convex centre of the Carthaginian line was driven in. The Roman maniples surged forward triumphantly and easily pierced the enemy's front, since the Celts were extended in a thin line, whereas the Romans had thrust their way in from the wings towards the centre where the heaviest fighting was taking place. The Carthaginian centre and wings did not go into action at the same moment – it was the central units which were engaged first because the Celts were drawn up in a crescent-shaped formation which placed them ahead of the wings – and thus it was the convex curve of the crescent which was closest to the enemy. However, because the Romans were pursuing the Celts and pressing inwards against that part of the front which was giving way, they penetrated the enemy's line so deeply that they then had both contingents of the African heavy infantry on their flanks. At this point the African infantry on the right wing turned inwards so as to face left, and then charged the enemy's flank beginning from the right, while those on the left wing likewise turned inwards and attacked in similar fashion, the action in each case responding to the needs of the moment. The result was exactly what Hannibal had planned: the Romans by pressing too far ahead in pursuit of the Celts were trapped between the two divisions of Africans. They could no longer hold their maniple formation, but were compelled to turn either singly or rank by rank to defend themselves against the enemy who were attacking their flanks.

116. Meanwhile Paullus, although he had been on the right wing since the beginning of the battle and had taken part in the cavalry action, was still safe and unwounded. But he wished to translate the words he had uttered in the address to his soldiers into deeds and to take part in the fighting. He saw that the outcome of the

battle was likely to be decided by the legions, and so he rode into the centre of the line; there he threw himself into the thick of the fighting, exchanging blows with the enemy, and cheering on and encouraging his men. Meanwhile Hannibal, who had taken his place in this part of the field since the beginning of the battle, was doing the same.

While this was going on the Numidians on the Carthaginian right were attacking the cavalry opposite them on the Roman left; they did not inflict many casualties, however, nor did they suffer any serious losses themselves because of their peculiar methods of fighting. Nevertheless, they kept the Roman cavalry effectively out of the battle by drawing them off and attacking them now from one quarter and now from another. By this time Hasdrubal had virtually destroyed all the enemy's cavalry by the river, and rode up to support the Numidians. The cavalry of the Italian allies, seeing that he was about to charge them, broke and fled. At this point Hasdrubal seems to have handled his forces with rare skill and judgement. He saw that the Numidians had the superiority in numbers and knew that they were at their most effective and formidable when they had the enemy on the run. He therefore left them to deal with the retreating Romans, while he led his own squadrons to the part of the battlefield where the infantry were engaged, and galloped up to support the Africans. He fell upon the Romans from the rear, and by launching a number of charges from several directions he at once put fresh heart into the Africans and dealt yet another blow to the sinking spirits of the Romans. Here Paullus was killed in the thick of the fighting after receiving several terrible wounds. This was a man who had discharged his whole duty to his country throughout his life, and not least at the end of it.

Now so long as the Romans could keep an unbroken front and turn to meet the successive attacks of the encircling enemy they were able to hold out. But as their outer ranks were continually cut down and the survivors were forced to pull back and huddle together, they were finally all killed where they stood. Among them were Marcus Atilius Regulus and Gnaeus Servilius, the consuls of the preceding year; both had conducted themselves in the battle as brave men who were worthy to be citizens of Rome.

While this hand-to-hand fighting and slaughter were still going on, the Numidians pursued the fleeing Roman cavalry, killing many of them and tearing others from their horses. A handful of men escaped to Venusia, among whom was the consul Varro, who thus matched a tenure of office which had proved disastrous to his country with an equally disgraceful flight.

117. So ended the battle between the Romans and the Carthaginians at Cannae, a struggle in which both victors and vanquished fought with indomitable courage. The proof of this is the fact that out of the 6,000 cavalry on the Roman side only seventy escaped with Varro to Venusia, while about 300 of the allied horse took refuge in different cities in scattered groups. Of the infantry, some 10,000 were captured fighting, although not in the actual battle, and only about 3,000 got away from the field to the towns of the neighbourhood. All the rest to the number of about 70,000 died gallantly. At Cannae, as in previous encounters, it was the superior numbers of the Carthaginian cavalry which contributed most to the victory, and the battle demonstrated to posterity that it is more effective to have half as many infantry as the enemy and an overwhelming superiority in cavalry than to engage him with absolutely equal numbers. On Hannibal's side about 4,000 Celts were killed, together with 1,500 Spaniards and Africans and about 200 horsemen.

The 10,000 Romans who were captured did not take part in the battle for the following reason. Paullus had left a reserve of 10,000 in his camp with the intention that if Hannibal had neglected to protect his own quarters and committed his whole army to the field, these men might force their way in during the fighting and capture the enemy's baggage. On the other hand if Hannibal had foreseen this danger and left a sufficient force on guard, then his strength would have been correspondingly diminished. The Romans were taken prisoner in the following circumstances. Hannibal had left a strong enough detachment to guard his camp, and at the same time as the main battle commenced the Romans carried out their orders and attacked this force. At first the defenders held out, but as they were beginning to be hard-pressed, Hannibal, who had meanwhile gained the upper hand in every part of the field, came to their rescue, put the Romans to flight, and shut them up in their own camp. He killed 2,000 of their number and captured all the rest. The Numidians likewise stormed the various strongholds in the district which had given shelter to the beaten enemy, and rounded up the fugitives, who consisted of about 2,000 cavalry.

118. After the battle had been decided as I have described, the consequences which both sides expected soon followed. The Carthaginians as a result of their victory became masters of almost all the rest of the coast. The Tarentines immediately surrendered to them, Arpi and a number of other Campanian towns invited Hannibal to come to them, and all eyes were now turned upon the Carthaginians, who for their part cherished great hopes that they could even capture Rome by assault. As for the Romans, after this defeat they gave up all hope of maintaining their supremacy over the Italians, and began to fear for their native soil, and indeed for their very existence, since they expected Hannibal to appear at any moment. And in fact the next event made it seem as though Fortune herself had taken sides against them in their struggle, and had filled their cup of tribulation to overflowing. Only a few days later, while the city was still aghast at the news of Cannae, Lucius Postumius, the general whom they had sent to Cisalpine Gaul, was surprised by the Celts in an ambush and his army wiped out. In spite of these blows the Senate left nothing undone that was in its power to do. It encouraged the people, strengthened the defences of the city, and considered the facts of the situation in a brave and manly spirit; and the events that were to follow bore witness to its steadfastness. For although the Romans had beyond any dispute been worsted in battle and their military reputation annihilated, yet through the peculiar virtues of their constitution and their ability to keep their heads they not only won back their supremacy in Italy and later defeated the Carthaginians, but within a few years had made themselves masters of the whole world.

Since I have now described the events which took place in Italy and in Spain during the 140th Olympiad, I shall now bring this book to a close here. Then, after I have related the history of Greece during the same Olympiad down to the same date, I shall give a separate account of the Roman constitution before proceeding with the rest of my history. I believe that a description of this not only has an important bearing upon the whole scheme of my work, but will also prove of great service both to students of history and to practical statesmen in the task of reforming or of drawing up other constitutions.

BOOK IV

Affairs in Greece

CIVIL WAR IN CYNAETHA

The events described in this passage took place during the 140th
Olympiad (220–216 B.C.). Cynaetha was a city of Arcadia on the
site of the modern Kalavryta. About 240 B.C. the city had been
captured by the Achaeans during the generalship of Aratus, and was
thereafter governed by a pro-Achaean party. The class conflicts
which later broke out there were connected with the social reforms
introduced into Sparta by Cleomenes III after his seizure of power in
227 B.C.; in fact the confiscation and redistribution of land which was
effected in Sparta made a popular appeal throughout the Peloponnese.
The Aetolians, who were then at war with the Achaeans, took the
opportunity to encourage these revolutionary sentiments among the
allies of the latter.

17. The people of Cynaetha are Arcadians, and their city had
for many years been torn by interminable and irreconcilable
struggles between their political parties. The two factions had time
and again retaliated upon one another with massacres, banishments,
confiscations of goods and re-division of lands, and at the time of
which I am writing the pro-Achaean party had gained the upper
hand and were in possession of the city, and the Achaeans had
provided them with a military governor and a garrison to defend
the walls. This was the state of affairs when, shortly before the
invasion by the Aetolians, the exiled faction appealed to their
compatriots in the city, begging that there should be a general
reconciliation and that they should be allowed to return home. The
party in power granted this request, and sent a delegation to the
Achaean League since they wished to obtain the agreement of
their allies to any settlement they might make. The Achaeans
willingly accepted this proposal, believing that both sides would

regard them with goodwill, since those who were in power had all their hopes centred on the Achaeans, while those who were about to return would owe their safe restoration to the consent of the League. The Cynaethans then dismissed the commandant and the garrison and recalled the exiles, who numbered about 300, having first obtained from them such pledges as are generally considered by all men to be completely inviolable. The returning exiles had no cause or pretext after their readmission to make them suppose that any further strife was about to arise; but for their part, from the very first moment of their restoration they began to plot against the city and their benefactors. It seems likely to me that even at the very moment when they were exchanging oaths and pledges over the sacrifice, their thoughts were concentrated upon the impious conspiracy to break faith with the gods and with those who had trusted them. For no sooner were they associated with the government than they approached the Aetolians and offered to betray the city to them; they could not wait a moment to bring about the destruction of those who had saved them or of the city which had bred them.

18. The bold stroke by which they carried out their plan was effected as follows. Some of the exiles had been appointed to the office of polemarch. It is the duty of these officials to close the city gates, to keep the keys while the gates remain closed, and to be on guard during the day in the gate-houses. The Aetolians had provided themselves with scaling-ladders and lay in wait for the predetermined moment to attack. The polemarchs belonging to the party of the exiles killed their colleagues in one of the gate-houses and then opened the gate, whereupon some of the Aetolians rushed in through this entrance, while others planted their ladders against the walls and seized the fortifications. The whole population of the city was overcome with panic and confusion at this turn of events, and was completely at a loss what to do. They could not give their whole attention to the attackers who were pouring in through the gate because of the assault which was also taking place on the walls, nor could they deal effectively with the struggle on the walls because of those who had forced their way in through the gate. In these circumstances the Aetolians quickly gained possession of the town, and then, amid the rest of their outrages, they performed one

act of summary justice. This was to kill before anyone else the traitors who had admitted them to the city, after which they plundered their property. Then all the rest of the citizens were massacred in the same way. Finally they quartered themselves in their victims' houses, systematically looted all their property, and tortured many of the Cynaethans whom they suspected of having concealed money, plate, or other valuables.

After inflicting these outrages on the Cynaethans the Aetolians removed their troops, leaving a garrison to guard the walls, and marched towards the town of Lusi. When they arrived at the temple of Artemis, which is situated between Cleitor and Cynaetha and is regarded as sacrosanct by the Greeks, they threatened to drive away the sacred herds and plunder the other property in the precincts of the temple. But the people of Lusi acted with excellent sense. They gave the Aetolians some of the sacred furniture of the temple, and in this way persuaded them to abandon their impious plan and to refrain from committing any outrage. The Aetolians accepted this gift, immediately left the place and pitched camp in front of the town of Cleitor.

19. Meanwhile Aratus, the commander of the Achaean League, had sent word to Philip of Macedon to appeal for help. He also took steps to mobilize those Achaeans who had been selected for service, and sent for the troops which the Messenians and the Lacedaemonians had agreed to provide according to the arrangements made between these two states and Achaea.

The Aetolians at first urged the people of Cleitor to abandon their alliance with the Achaeans and make one with themselves in its place. When the Cleitorians refused this proposal outright, they attacked the city and tried to capture it outright by assaulting the walls. The inhabitants, however, put up a gallant and spirited resistance, and so the Aetolians yielded to force of circumstances, broke up their camp and marched once more against Cynaetha. On their way they raided and drove off the sacred herds at Lusi in spite of their earlier promise to respect them. At first they offered to hand over Cynaetha to the Eleans, but when this people declined to accept the city, they determined to hold it for themselves and appointed Euripidas as the military governor. Later, when they became alarmed at the reports which reached them that a relieving force was on its way from Macedonia, they burned the city and abandoned it. They then marched to Rhium, the port on the Corinthian Gulf, intending to cross from there to the mainland.

20. Now the people of Cynaetha, who had undergone these cruel sufferings at the hands of the Aetolians, were nevertheless regarded as having preeminently deserved their fate. And yet it is also a fact that the Arcadian nation as a whole enjoys a high reputation for virtue among the Greeks, and this is not only because of the hospitality and humanity which its people display in their character and their customs, but in particular because of their piety towards the gods. It therefore seems worthwhile to digress for a moment to consider the savage character of the Cynaethans, and to ask ourselves why, although they are indisputably of Arcadian stock, they so far surpassed all the other Greeks of that period in cruelty and lawless behaviour.

My own opinion is that they were the first and indeed the only people among the Arcadians to have abandoned an institution which had been nobly conceived by their ancestors, and was studied by all the inhabitants of Arcadia in their relation to their natural conditions. I am referring here to the special attention given to music, and by this I mean true music,[1] which is a blessing to all peoples, but in the case of the Arcadians, a necessity. We should certainly not accept the suggestion of Ephorus,[2] who threw into the preface to his history a sentence that was quite unworthy of him, to the effect that music was introduced among men merely for the purpose of beguiling and deceiving one another. Nor should we imagine that the Cretans and the Lacedaemonians did not have good reason for substituting the use of the flute and of rhythmic movement in place of the trumpet in their military operations.[3] In the same way the early Arcadians knew what they were about when they gave music such an important place in their

1. This includes poetry sung to music, but does not denote music in the much broader educational context given it by Plato.

2. Ephorus of Cyme in Aeolis was the leading Greek historian of the fourth century B.C. His history in thirty books ends in 365 B.C. In the passage referred to, Ephorus was probably contrasting music with history and claiming that the one was designed to thrill, the other to instruct.

3. The trumpet was primarily intended for giving signals, and was unsuited for marching in step.

public life that not only boys but young men up to the age of thirty were obliged to study it constantly, even though in other respects they lived under the most austere conditions. For it is a fact that is well-attested and familiar to all that Arcadia is almost the only nation in which the boys are taught from their earliest childhood to sing in measure the hymns and paeans in which they commemorate, according to their traditions, the gods and heroes of particular localities. Later they learn the measures of Philoxenus[1] and Timotheus,[2] and every year in the theatre there are keenly contested competitions in choral singing to the accompaniment of professional flute-players, the boys taking part in the events which are suitable to their age and the men in what is called the men's festival. And in addition to these occasions, it is their custom all through their lives to entertain themselves at their banquets: they do not listen to hired performers but create their own music, each man being called upon for a song in turn. They are not at all ashamed to admit that they are completely ignorant of other studies, but in the case of singing nobody can claim to be untaught because everybody is obliged to learn; nor can they say that they know how to sing, but excuse themselves from performing, for this would be considered a disgrace among them. Besides this, the young men practise marching strains on the flute while they are on parade, perfect themselves in dances, and give annual displays in the theatres, all these activities being carried on through the patronage of the state and at the public expense.

21. In introducing these practices I do not believe that the ancestors of the Arcadians thought of them as luxuries or extravagances. On the contrary, they saw that personal manual labour was the general lot, that the life of the people was toilsome and hard, and that as a natural consequence of the country's cold and gloomy climate the character of its inhabitants was correspondingly austere. The fact is that as mortal men we adapt ourselves by sheer necessity to climatic influences, and it is this reason and no other which causes separate nations and peoples dwelling widely apart to differ so

1. Philoxenus of Cythera (435–380 B.C.), a writer of dithyrambic verse, lived in Syracuse during the reign of Dionysius the younger.
2. Timotheus of Miletus (450–360 B.C.) was famed for having added four new strings to the seven-stringed lyre.

markedly in their circumstances, their physique and their complexion, as well as in most of their customs. So it was with the intention of softening and tempering the stubbornness and harshness of nature that the early Arcadians introduced the practices I have described. Besides this, they inculcated the habit for men and women alike of holding frequent social gatherings, sacrificial ceremonies, and dances performed by young men and girls, and exerted themselves by every possible means to humanize the hardness of the national character through the softening and civilizing influence of such institutions.

The Cynaethans, on the other hand, entirely neglected these efforts, although they stood in even greater need of them than their compatriots, because their country is more rugged and their climate harsher than that of any other part of Arcadia. And so by concentrating all their attention upon their domestic problems and political rivalries they finally became so brutalized that there was no city in Greece in which such atrocious or such frequent outrages were committed. I mention the following episode to illustrate the depths to which the Cynaethans had sunk in this respect, and the abhorrence which was felt by the rest of the Arcadians for their actions. After the great massacre of their people the Cynaethans sent a delegation to Sparta, but on their way there every Arcadian city which the envoys entered immediately ordered them by public proclamation to depart, while the Mantineans, after the visitors had gone, carried out a solemn purification from this taint of blood by offering sacrifices and carrying the victims round their city and the altars of their territory.

Byzantium and the Black Sea

38. The position of Byzantium in relation to the sea affords greater advantages for its security and prosperity than that of any other city in our quarter of the world, but in relation to the land the situation is exactly the opposite. On the seaward side it commands the entry to the Black Sea so completely that no one can sail in or

out without the consent of the Byzantines. The result of this is that they exercise absolute control over the supply of those numerous products which the rest of the world requires for its everyday life, and in which the Pontus is particularly rich. As regards the necessities of life, there is no disputing the fact that the lands which surround the Pontus provide both cattle and slaves in the greatest quantities and of the highest quality; and as for luxuries, the same regions not only supply us with honey, wax and preserved fish in great abundance, but they also absorb the surplus produce of our own countries, namely olive oil and every kind of wine. In the case of corn there is a two-way traffic, whereby they sometimes supply it when we need it, and sometimes import it from us. If the Byzantines had adopted a deliberately hostile attitude to the Greeks, or if in the past they had allied themselves with the Gauls, or, particularly at the present time, with the Thracians, or again if they had abandoned their city altogether, the Greeks would have been completely shut out from this trade, or else it would have become quite unprofitable for them. The reason for this is that because of the narrowness of the straits, and of the number of barbarians who live along their shores, it would have been impossible for Greek ships to sail into the Pontus. It is, no doubt, the Byzantines themselves who draw the greatest financial benefit from the location of their city, since they can easily export all their surplus produce and import whatever they need at a profit to themselves, and yet, as I have pointed out, they perform great services to other peoples. And so, since they are the common benefactors of all Greece, it is not only gratitude they ought to receive but the universal support of the Greek peoples whenever they are threatened by the barbarians.

Now the great majority of Greeks are quite unfamiliar with the peculiar natural advantages of Byzantium's situation, since it lies far away from those parts of the world which are most frequently visited. And yet we are all curious to be informed upon such matters and to visit in person places which possess a special or exceptional interest, or, if they are out of our reach, to form as accurate an impression or idea of them as we can. This being so, I ought to set down the facts of the case and explain what it is that makes this city so extraordinarily prosperous.

39. The sea which is known as the Pontus is a little over 2,500 miles in circumference, and has two mouths which are situated diametrically opposite to one another. The one opens into the Propontis and the other into the Maeotic Lake,[1] which has a circumference of about 930 miles. Many large rivers flow into these two basins from the Asiatic side, while those on the European side are even larger; thus the Maeotic Lake as it fills up flows into the Pontus, and the Pontus into the Propontis. The mouth of the Maeotic Lake is known as the Cimmerian Bosphorus, and is about three and a half miles in width and seven in length, and this stretch of water is shallow throughout. The mouth of the Pontus is called the Thracian Bosphorus, and it is about fifteen miles long, but is not of a consistent width. At the end which leads into the Propontis, that is, the southern extremity, the channel between Byzantium and Calchedon is about a mile and three-quarters wide. At the mouth of the Pontus it begins at the so-called Holy Place,[2] where according to legend Jason first sacrificed to the twelve gods on his return voyage from Colchis. The Holy Place is situated on the Asiatic side and is about a mile and a half distant from the opposite point in Thrace, which is known as the temple of Sarapis.

There are two causes of the constant flow which takes place from the Maeotic Lake and the Pontus. The first, which is obvious to all, arises from the fact that where many streams discharge their waters into basins of limited circumference, the water continually increases in volume, and if there were no outlets would be bound to rise higher and fill up a larger area in the basin. But as outlets do exist, the surplus water flows away and is continually carried through the channels which are there to receive it. The second cause is that after heavy rains the rivers wash down into these basins large quantities of alluvial deposits of all kinds; the water in the seas is displaced by the banks which are thus created and is forced up to a higher level, and then carried out in the same way through the existing outlets. And so just as this influx of water with deposits of alluvial matter from the rivers is a continuous

1. The modern geographical equivalents are the Black Sea (Pontus), the Sea of Marmara (Propontis), and the Sea of Azov (Maeotic Lake).
2. A temple dedicated to Zeus.

process, so the outflow through the mouths must also be continuous.

These, then, are the two reasons why the current flows through the Pontus, and their credibility rests not on the tales of traders but on the principles of natural science; it is not easy to find a more accurate approach than this.

40. However, since we have now pursued this subject so far, I must not leave any point unexplained or baldly asserted, as so many writers are accustomed to do, but rather present a description which is duly supported by argument so as to leave no doubts in the reader's mind. This is the special characteristic of the present age, in which, since every sea and every land can be visited by travellers, we can no longer seriously put forward the testimony of poets and mythographers on topics of which we are ignorant, as my predecessors have done on most subjects, or offer, as Heracleitus puts it, 'untrustworthy witnesses to disputed facts'; instead I must do my best to lay before my readers an account which will carry conviction on its own merits.

My contention here is that the silting up of the Pontus has been in progress from time immemorial, and is still continuing, and that in the course of time both this sea and the Maeotic Lake will be completely filled up, assuming that the local conditions remain the same and that the factors which produce the alluvial deposits continue to operate.[1] For since time is infinite and the volume of these basins is undoubtedly finite, it is clear that even if the influx were quite insignificant, the seas must be filled up sooner or later. For by the law of nature, if a finite quantity continually increases or decreases over an infinite period, then even if the increase or decrease be infinitesimal (for this is what I am now assuming), the hypothesis requires that the process will eventually be completed. But when, as in this case, the influx is by no means infinitesimal, but in fact large quantities of soil are being washed down, it becomes clear that the transformation I have forecast will come to pass not at some remote date, but in the near future. And in fact it is even now visibly taking place. The Maeotic Lake is already so

1. The fact that this forecast has not materialized is no doubt due to Polybius' having underestimated the speed of the constant rush of water out of the Black Sea, which is strong enough to carry away the alluvial deposits.

much silted up that the greater part of it is no more than five or seven fathoms deep, so that large ships can no longer sail in it without a pilot. And from having been at one time, as all ancient authorities agree, a sea which continued into the Pontus, it is now a fresh-water lake.[1] The reason for this is that the salt water has been forced out by the silting up of the bottom, and the inflow from the rivers has taken its place. The same thing will happen to the Pontus, and indeed this transformation is already being brought about. It is not yet obvious to most observers, because of the size of the basin, but to those who examine the evidence a little more carefully it is already clear enough what is happening.

41. For example, in the area where the Danube flows out of Europe into the Pontus through several mouths a bank has been formed opposite the river by the mud which has been discharged from the mouths; it is nearly 120 miles in length, and a day's voyage out to sea, so that ships which are navigating the Pontus and are far away from the shore may easily, if they are sailing unwarily, run aground on certain parts of these shoals, which sailors call 'the Breasts'. The fact that these deposits are not formed close inshore but are driven so far away from the land must be accounted for as follows. In so far as the currents of the rivers are stronger than those of the sea and force a way through it, the earth and other matter washed down by the stream must continue to be thrust forward, and cannot be allowed to come to rest or subside. But when the impetus of the current has become spent amid the increasing depth and volume of the sea, then the earth sinks by reason of its natural weight and settles. This is why in the case of large and swift rivers where the sea near the coast is deep, the deposits build up at some distance away, but in the case of small and sluggish streams, the sand-banks are formed close to their mouths. This fact is clearly demonstrated when heavy rains occur, because at such times even quite small streams, when they have overpowered the waves at their mouths, force their mud out to sea to a distance which corresponds to the strength of their currents. We must certainly not refuse to believe in the extent of the sandbank formed by the Danube or in the quantity of the stones, timber and earth which are washed down by the other rivers; indeed it

1. This statement is incorrect.

would be foolish to do so when we often see with our own eyes some insignificant winter torrent [1] quickly swell into a flood, scoop out a bed, and force its way through high ground, sweeping down with it every variety of wood, soil and stones, and forming deposits of such a size that in a short time the area may so change its appearance as to become unrecognizable.

42. Accordingly, we should not be surprised if the continuous flow of such great rivers produces an effect of the kind I have described and finally fills up the Pontus; in fact, logic would appear to make this process not merely a probability but a certainty. The following is a symptom of what is likely to happen. The Maeotic Lake is at present sweeter than the Pontus, while the Pontus in its turn is distinctly sweeter than the Mediterranean. From this it is clear that when the time required to fill the Maeotic Lake shall have been extended in proportion to the size by which the Pontus basin exceeds the Maeotic, the Pontus will likewise become a shallow fresh-water lake.[2] In fact we may expect that this will happen more quickly, since the rivers which flow into the Pontus are both larger and more numerous.

What I have said above is intended for those who are inclined to disbelieve that the Pontus is now filling up and will continue to do so, or that so vast a sea can ever become a lake or marsh. Besides this, I also have in mind the prodigies and fabrications which are related to us by returning merchants. My purpose is that we should not be obliged by sheer ignorance to listen with the credulity of children to everything that we are told, but that being in possession of some elements of the truth, we may use them to test the reliability or the opposite of whatever is reported to us.

43. I now return to my description of the peculiar excellence of the situation of Byzantium. The channel which connects the Pontus and the Propontis, is, as I have mentioned, about fifteen miles in length. The so-called Holy Place marks the northern end, and the Strait of Byzantium the southern, while half-way between

1. The typical Greek stream, dry in summer and swollen in winter, is contrasted with the constantly flowing rivers.

2. To illustrate Polybius' involved proposition: if the basin of the Pontus were three times that of the Maeotic Lake and it were to take 1,000 years to fill the latter, then in 3,000 years' time the Pontus would likewise become a fresh-water lake.

these on the European side stands the Hermaeum:[1] this is situated on a headland which projects into the channel and marks its narrowest point, a distance of barely half a mile from Asia. It is here that Darius is said to have had his bridge of boats constructed, when he crossed to attack the Scythians. Above this point the strength of the current flowing from the Pontus is uniform, because of the similarity of the country on each shore of the channel. But when it reaches the Hermaeum on the European side, which is, as I remarked, the narrowest point of the straits, the water being thus confined and sweeping strongly against the headland, rebounds as if from a blow, and hurls itself against the Asiatic shore opposite. From there it again recoils and strikes the promontory on the European coast, which is known as 'the Hearths', and from here its force is again diverted to the point on the Asiatic side named 'the Cow', where according to legend Io first set foot, after having swum the strait. Finally the current flows rapidly from 'the Cow' to Byzantium itself; in front of the city it divides into two streams, the smaller entering the inlet which is known as 'the Horn',[2] while the latter is again deflected. By this time it no longer has sufficient strength to reach the opposite shore on which stands Calchedon. It has now several times crossed and recrossed the channel, which is here appreciably wider, and so it slackens and no longer rebounds from shore to shore at an acute angle, but is deflected at an obtuse angle, misses Calchedon, and flows out through the middle of the strait.

44. It is this fact which gives Byzantium such a favourable situation and Calchedon the opposite. At first sight one might think that each was equally conveniently placed, but in practice it is not easy to sail up to Calchedon, if you wish to do so, whereas the current carries you to Byzantium whether you like it or not, as I have just explained. The proof of this is that those who wish to cross from Calchedon to Byzantium cannot sail there on a straight course because of the current which separates them. Instead they steer obliquely for 'the Cow' and the place known as Chrysopolis

1. Now the site of the Ottoman castle of Roumeli Hisar, built by Mohammed II.

2. The so-called Golden Horn, the long creek which in the modern city separates Istanbul from Galata.

on the Asiatic shore.[1] It was this town which the Athenians once occupied on the advice of Alcibiades when they first attempted to levy toll on ships sailing into the Pontus, and from here the passengers entrust themselves to the current, which carries them willy-nilly to Byzantium. The approaches to Byzantium on the other side are equally favourable from either direction. For a vessel running before a south wind from the Hellespont, or from the Pontus to the Hellespont with the Etesian winds, the course from Byzantium along the European coast to the beginning of the narrows of the Propontis at Sestos and Abydos is a direct and easy one, and so is the return voyage to Byzantium.

But for the route from Calchedon along the Asiatic coast the case is exactly the opposite, because the coastline is broken by several deep bays, and the promontory formed by the territory of Cyzicus juts out a long way into the sea. Again, it is not easy for a vessel bound for Calchedon from the Hellespont to follow the European coastline as far as the vicinity of Byzantium, and then tack and make for Calchedon, since the current and the other factors I have mentioned would hamper such a manoeuvre. In the same way it is impossible for a ship leaving Calchedon to steer straight for Thrace, since not only the intervening current but also the northerly and southerly winds hinder both attempts: the south wind will carry a vessel towards the Pontus and the north wind away from it, and these are the winds which must be made use of for the voyage from Calchedon to the Hellespont or for the return journey. These, then, are the advantages which Byzantium enjoys in relation to the sea: I shall now describe its disadvantages in relation to the land.

45. These arise from the fact that on the landward side it is completely blocked in from sea to sea by the territory of Thrace, and that the Byzantines maintain a perpetual and insoluble state of war with the Thracians. It is impossible to make a carefully prepared attack, gain a decisive victory and so terminate the fighting, on account of the great number of Thracian chieftains and their followers. If the Byzantines overcome one chieftain, three others still more formidable invade his territory. Nor do they improve matters at all if they give way and agree to make terms

1. The modern Scutari.

and pay tribute, for if they make concessions to one chief, this action brings down five times as many enemies upon them. In consequence, as I explained, they find themselves involved in a war of exceptional difficulty and endless duration, for what can be more dangerous or more alarming than a war with barbarians who also live on your borders?

These, broadly speaking, are the trials and hazards with which the Byzantines have to contend on land, but apart from the other evils attendant upon war, they are condemned to suffer a fate which resembles the torments of Tantalus,[1] as Homer describes them. They find themselves the owners of a most fertile territory, but having lavished infinite labour on their land and been rewarded with a superb harvest, the barbarians then sweep down, burn some of the crops and carry off the rest, so that apart from the lost toil and expense, the very beauty of the harvest adds to their misery and anguish, as they see it wantonly destroyed before their eyes.

1. Tantalus was punished by being forced to stand forever in water which he could not drink, and with fruit trees out of reach over his head.

BOOK V

Affairs in Egypt

THE DEATH OF CLEOMENES

The young Ptolemy Philopator took possession of the throne of Egypt early in 221 B.C. Seleucus, King of Syria, had died in 223, and Antigonus in the summer of 221; their successors, Antiochus and Philip, were nineteen and seventeen respectively. Cleomenes III, the King of Sparta, had taken refuge in Egypt after his decisive defeat by the Macedonians at the battle of Sellasia in the summer of 222 B.C. (see pp. 170–75).

34. As soon as his father Euergetes had died, Ptolemy IV, who was surnamed Philopator, had his brother Magas and those who supported him executed, and himself took possession of the throne of Egypt. He supposed that by destroying his rivals in this way he had through his own action rid himself of dangers at home, and that Fortune had delivered him from dangers abroad, for it so happened that Antigonus and Seleucus had just died, and their successors, Philip and Antiochus, were quite young, indeed almost boys. At any rate, these considerations made him feel secure in his situation, and he began to conduct his reign as if it were a perpetual festival. He neglected the business of state, made himself difficult to approach, hardly deigned to receive the members of his court or the officials responsible for internal affairs, and treated with contempt or indifference those who handled his country's interests abroad, to which his predecessors had given more attention than to the administration even of Egypt itself. Because they ruled the territories of Coele Syria[1] and of Cyprus the earlier Ptolemies had

1. This term originally signified the long depression which begins between the mountain ranges of Lebanon and Anti-Lebanon and runs through the valleys of the Litani, the Jordan and the Dead Sea, down to the modern Aqaba and the Red Sea; it was later associated with the territory of Phoenicia, so as to include the area between Egypt and Cilicia.

always been able to put pressure on the Kings of Syria both by sea
and by land. Their sphere of control included the principal cities,
fortresses and harbours all the way along the coast of the eastern
Mediterranean from Pamphylia to the Hellespont and the region
around Lysimacheia, which gave them a commanding influence
over the islands and the smaller kingdoms of Asia Minor; while
their occupation of Aenus, Maroneia and other cities even further
afield enabled them to keep an effective watch upon the affairs of
Thrace and Macedonia. Since they had extended their power to
such remote regions and had long ago established such a far-flung
system of client states to protect them, the Kings of Egypt had
never felt anxiety concerning their rule at home, but had naturally
attached great importance to the handling of foreign affairs.
Philopator, however, neglected all these areas of his authority,
and gave his whole attention to ignoble love affairs, and to senseless and continuous drinking. And so, as might have been expected,
it was not long before conspiracies began to be formed, against
both the King's life and his throne. The first of these came from
Cleomenes, the exiled King of Sparta.

35. Now so long as Ptolemy Euergetes was alive, Cleomenes
had kept quiet: he had committed his fortunes and pledged his
loyalty to the Egyptian King, and lived in the constant belief that
he would be given the necessary help to recover his ancestral
kingdom. But after Euergetes' death,[1] as time slipped by, the situation in Greece seemed almost to cry out for Cleomenes' return.
Antigonus was dead, the Achaean League was engaged in a war,
and the Spartans by this time, as Cleomenes had planned and intended from the beginning, shared the hatred which the Aetolians
felt for the Achaeans and the Macedonians. For all these reasons,
then, Cleomenes felt the moment demanded that he should act at
once and do his utmost to leave Alexandria. So first of all he sought
an audience with the King, and pleaded on more than one occasion
that he should be provided with sufficient troops and supplies
to launch an expedition against Sparta. Then, as Ptolemy would
not listen to this, he made an earnest appeal to be allowed to leave
with his own household, since the situation held out sufficiently
good prospects that he could recover his ancestral throne. But

1. The new King had begun his reign in 221 B.C.

Ptolemy, for the reasons I have mentioned above, showed himself completely indifferent to such questions, took no thought for the future, and continued with extraordinary thoughtlessness and folly to turn a deaf ear to Cleomenes.

Meanwhile Sosibius, who at that time exercised the chief influence upon affairs, conferred with his friends and came to the following conclusion about Cleomenes. They decided against the idea of sending him out with a fleet and supplies, because as a result of the death of Antigonus they considered that foreign affairs mattered little to Egypt, and that expenditure on such enterprises would be a waste of money. Moreover, now that Antigonus was no more, none of the remaining rulers could be considered a match for Cleomenes; they therefore feared that he would have little difficulty in making himself the master of Greece, and would then prove a serious and formidable rival to themselves. This seemed all the more likely because Cleomenes had been in a position to observe Egyptian affairs, had come to despise the King, and had discovered that there were many parts of the kingdom which were only loosely held, were far removed from the seat of government and thus afforded plenty of scope for revolutionary intrigue. There were, for example, a number of ships based on Samos and a considerable army stationed at Ephesus. These were the reasons which made Ptolemy's advisers reject the idea of sending off Cleomenes with an expedition and supplies; at the same time they judged that it would be by no means in their interests first to humiliate such an eminent man and then to let him go: such a course of action was certain to make an enemy of him. The other alternative was to keep him in Egypt against his will, but this they immediately dismissed without discussion, on the principle that there was no safety in putting the lion into the same fold as the sheep. It was Sosibius himself who was particularly opposed to any such possibility, and for the following reason.

36. At the time when he and his supporters were plotting the murder of Magas and Berenice,[1] they were tormented by fears that their project would fail, the main reason for this being the exceptional courage of Berenice. In this situation they were obliged to conciliate all the courtiers and entice them with the prospect of

1. The widow of Ptolemy Euergetes and mother of Magas and Philopator.

favours to come if the conspiracy succeeded. It was then that Sosibius, since he knew that Cleomenes needed help from the King and that he was a man of judgement who had a real grasp of the situation, confided the whole plot to the Spartan and held out great hopes of what he might gain from it. Cleomenes saw that Sosibius was in a state of great anxiety and was particularly nervous about the attitude of the foreign mercenaries, and so he urged him to pluck up his courage and promised that so far from doing him any harm, the troops would support him. When Sosibius showed his surprise at these assurances, Cleomenes replied: 'Don't you see that 3,000 of these men are from the Peloponnese[1] and 1,000 from Crete? I have only to nod to them, and they will come over to you as one man. With these troops united in one body what have you to fear? Not the Syrians and the Carians, by any chance?' At that time, Sosibius was delighted to hear these words, and returned with redoubled confidence to resume his conspiracy against Berenice. But later, as he observed the total passivity displayed by the King, Cleomenes' words echoed in his mind, and the recollection of the Spartan's daring and of his popularity with the mercenaries tormented him. And so on this occasion he took the lead in urging the King and his friends to imprison Cleomenes before it was too late. Then, in order to lend more urgency to his advice, he made use of the following circumstance.

37. There was a certain citizen of Messenia named Nicagoras, who had been a family friend of Archidamus, the King of Sparta. Earlier in Archidamus' life they had seldom met, but when the King fled from Sparta through fear of Cleomenes and came to Messenia, Nicagoras not only readily received him into his house and supplied all his needs, but from the close association that followed, there grew up between them a relation of warm affection and good-will. So when Cleomenes later held out hopes to Archidamus that he could return home, and that their differences could be reconciled, Nicagoras devoted himself to the task of negotiating and concluding an agreement between them. When this had been confirmed, Archidamus left for Sparta trusting to the conditions of the pact which

1. The phrase 'from the Peloponnese' probably refers to the recruiting centre at Taenarum in the extreme south of the peninsula, a depot which was no doubt controlled by Sparta.

had been arranged through Nicagoras; but Cleomenes came to meet them and had Archidamus put to death,[1] though he spared Nicagoras and the rest of his companions. To the outside world Nicagoras pretended to be grateful that his life had been spared, but in his heart he nursed a bitter hatred against Cleomenes for what had happened, since all the appearances suggested that he had been responsible for the King's death.

This Nicagoras had arrived at Alexandria with a cargo of horses a short while before the events I have been describing, and when he disembarked he met Cleomenes with his friends Panteus and Hippitas, who were strolling on the quay. When Cleomenes saw Nicagoras, he came up, greeted him warmly, and asked what business had brought him there. When he replied that he had come with a cargo of horses to sell, Cleomenes said, 'You would have done much better to bring one of male prostitutes and girls to play the harp; that is the kind of cargo to please this King!' At the time Nicagoras smiled and said nothing, but a few days later, when he had had several meetings with Sosibius because of the business with the horses, he quoted Cleomenes' words against him. He noticed that Sosibius listened with satisfaction to what he was saying, and thereupon he told him the whole story of his earlier grievance against Cleomenes.

38. When Sosibius understood that this man bore Cleomenes a grudge, he persuaded him, with the help of a bribe on the spot and the promise of a further sum to follow, to write a letter accusing Cleomenes and to leave it sealed; then a few days after Nicagoras had sailed, his servant was to bring Sosibius the letter, as though it had been sent by his master. Nicagoras played his part in the plot and when, after he had sailed, the letter was duly delivered, Sosibius at once took it and the servant to the King. The servant said that Nicagoras had left the letter with instructions that it should be handed to Sosibius, and in it the writer asserted that Cleomenes, if he were not provided with a properly equipped expeditionary force, intended to raise a rebellion against the King. Sosibius at once took advantage of this opportunity to urge the King and his other friends not to delay, but to take the precaution

1. Plutarch in his *Life of Agis and Cleomenes* represents Cleomenes as privy to the murder of Archidamus, but not responsible for it.

of putting Cleomenes under house arrest. This was done and a huge house was put at his disposal in which he spent his time under guard, the only real difference between his situation and that of other prisoners being that he had a bigger gaol to live in. In this situation, and with nothing but the bleakest hopes for the future, Cleomenes determined to make a dash for freedom at any cost; not that he really believed that he could recover it – for he had none of the elements of success on his side for such an attempt – but rather because he was resolved to die nobly and not to submit to any situation that was unworthy of the mettlesome courage he had always shown in the past. Perhaps also those words of Hector, spoken before his last fight with Achilles, which have always commended themselves to men of dauntless spirit, came back into his mind and helped to inspire him:

> Let me then sell my life dearly at least, not perish ignobly:[1]
> Die in some valiant attempt, that men yet unborn shall remember.

39. He therefore waited for a day when Ptolemy made an excursion to Canopus. Then he set a rumour going among his guards that the King was about to release him, and made this the excuse to give a banquet for his own suite of attendants, and to send presents of meat, wine and garlands to the guards. The soldiers suspected nothing, treated themselves generously to his hospitality, and before long became quite drunk. Cleomenes then gathered his friends and servants together, and at about midday they slipped out of the house armed with daggers and unnoticed by the guards. Going forward into the street they met Ptolemy, the governor, who had been left by the King in charge of the city, and the sheer audacity of their attack so overawed his attendants that they were able to drag him out of his chariot and lock him up. Then they went out and began to call upon the people to rise and seize their freedom. But the attempt had taken the whole city so completely by surprise that not a soul responded to their appeal or showed any sign of joining the uprising. Thereupon they turned back and made for the citadel, in the hope of forcing the gates and persuading the prisoners to join them. But this attempt also collapsed, as the guards of the prison had been warned of their intention and had

1. *Iliad*, XXII, 304–5.

secured the gates. So at last they turned their weapons upon themselves, and died like brave men and Spartans. Such was the end of Cleomenes, a man of outstanding gifts, both in his social dealings and in his capacity for affairs; one who was, in a word, formed by nature both to lead and to rule.

Affairs in Greece

PHILIP AND THE GREEKS

This passage describes events in Greece in the summer of 217 B.C. Polybius notes the effect of the news of the crushing defeat suffered by the Romans at the battle of Lake Trasimene in June of that year.

101. It was at the moment when Philip was besieging Thebes[1] that the Romans were defeated by Hannibal at Lake Trasimene, but the report of this battle had not yet reached Greece. Philip arrived too late to attack the Illyrian galleys off Cape Malea,[2] and so he anchored off Cenchreae[3] and sent off his decked ships with orders to sail round the Peloponnese towards Aegium and Patrae. At the same time he had the rest of his ships dragged across the Isthmus of Corinth and ordered them all to anchor at Lechaeum on the Corinthian Gulf, while he himself hurried off with his friends to Argos to attend the opening of the Nemean Games. But no sooner had he taken his seat to watch the festival than a courier arrived from Macedonia with the news that the Romans had been defeated in a great battle and that Hannibal had gained control of the open country. The only man to whom he showed the dispatch at first was Demetrius of Pharos, and he ordered him to keep the news strictly to himself. Demetrius seized this opportunity to urge Philip to disengage himself from the Aetolian War as soon as possible and to concentrate his efforts first of all on subduing Illyria and then on invading Italy. 'The whole of Greece is ready

1. This is Phthiotic Thebes in Thessaly, not the Boeotian city.
2. The south-easterly cape of the Peloponnese.
3. The port of Corinth on the Saronic Gulf.

to do your bidding even now,' he told Philip, 'and it will remain obedient to you in future. The Achaeans are inclined to support Macedonia in any case and the Aetolians have lost heart because of the reverses they have suffered in the recent war. But to go beyond Greece and invade Italy is the first step towards the conquest of the world, and there is no man who has a better claim to undertake it than yourself. This is the moment to strike a blow, when the Romans have suffered a disastrous defeat.'

102. With such arguments as these Demetrius found it easy to arouse Philip's ambition, and this was natural enough in a king who was so young, who had proved so successful in his undertakings, who already possessed a reputation for daring, and who in addition to these qualities claimed descent from a family which beyond all others was inclined to cherish ambitions to rule the world.

First of all then, as I have said, Philip confided the contents of the dispatch to nobody but Demetrius, and next he summoned a council of his friends to discuss the question of making peace with the Aetolians. Aratus was inclined to support the idea of opening negotiations: he thought it a good moment to discuss a settlement now that the Macedonians had gained the upper hand in the war. So Philip, without waiting to receive the joint delegations which were already discussing peace terms, immediately sent Cleonicus of Naupactus to Aetolia; he had found this statesman still waiting for the meeting of the assembly of the Achaean League after his capture by the naval commander of the Achaeans. Then he advanced from Corinth with his ships and his land forces as far as Aegium. From there he marched northwards to Lasion, captured the fortress of Perippia, and in order not to appear too ready to bring the war to an end, he gave it out that he was planning an invasion of Elis. By this time Cleonicus had paid two or three visits to Aetolia, and the Aetolians begged the King to meet them personally at a conference. This Philip agreed to do, and he thereupon called for a cessation of all hostilities, and dispatched couriers to all the allied cities inviting them to send delegates to take part in the negotiations. He himself crossed over with his army, pitched camp at Panormus, which is a harbour on the north coast of the Peloponnese lying exactly opposite Naupactus, and there waited for the delegation from the allies. While they were assembling he sailed across to Zacynthus, settled the affairs of the island on his own initiative, and then returned to Panormus.

103. When the delegates had gathered, Philip sent Aratus, Taurion and some of those who had accompanied these commanders to visit the Aetolians. They found the latter in full assembly at Naupactus, held a short discussion at which they were left in no doubt as to the Aetolians' desire for peace, and then sailed back to inform Philip. For their part the Aetolians, who were most anxious to bring the war to an end, sent envoys to Philip urging him to sail across and meet them with his army; they could then arrange a personal conference and a satisfactory settlement of all the matters in dispute. The King agreed to this request and crossed with his army, landing at the so-called Hollows of Naupactus, which are situated about two and a half miles west of the town. There he pitched camp, surrounded his ships and troops with a palisade, and waited for the conference to begin. The Aetolians arrived with their whole force but without their arms, settled themselves a quarter of a mile away from Philip's camp, and proceeded to send messages and open the discussions. The King's first move was to send delegates from all the allied states, whom he instructed to offer peace to the Aetolians, on the condition that both sides should retain what they held at that moment. The Aetolians were glad to accept peace on these terms, after which there were continuous discussions between the two sides on various matters of detail. The great majority of these I shall pass over, since they contained nothing which is worth recording, but I propose to report the speech made by Agelaus of Naupactus at the first conference in the presence of the King and the allies. He spoke as follows:

104. 'It would be best if the Greeks never went to war with one another, if they could regard it as the greatest gift of the gods for them all to speak with one voice, and could join hands like men who are crossing a river; in this way they could unite to repulse the incursions of the barbarians and to preserve themselves and their cities. But if we have no hope of achieving such a degree of unity for the whole country, let me impress upon you how important it is at least for the present that we should consult one

another and remain on our guard, in view of the huge armies which have been mobilized, and the vast scale of the war which is now being waged in the west. For it must already be obvious to all those who pay even the slightest attention to affairs of state that whether the Carthaginians defeat the Romans or the Romans the Carthaginians, the victors will by no means be satisfied with the sovereignty of Italy and Sicily, but will come here, and will advance both their forces and their ambitions beyond the bounds of justice. I therefore beg you all to be on your guard against this danger, and I appeal especially to King Philip. For you the safest policy, instead of wearing down the Greeks and making them an easy prey for the invader, is to take care of them as you would of your own body, and to protect every province of Greece as you would if it were a part of your own dominions. If you follow this policy, the Greeks will be your friends and your faithful allies in case of attack, and foreigners will be the less inclined to plot against your throne, because they will be discouraged by the loyalty of the Greeks towards you. But if you yearn for a field of action, then turn your attention to the west, keep it fixed on the wars in Italy, and bide your time, so that when the moment comes, you may enter the contest for the sovereignty of the whole world. Now the present moment is by no means unfavourable to such hopes. But you must, I entreat you, put aside your differences with the Greeks and your campaigns against them until times have become more settled, and concern yourself first and foremost with this aspect of the situation which I have just mentioned, so that you retain the power to make peace or war with them as you think best. For if you wait until the clouds which are now gathering in the west settle upon Greece, I very much fear that these truces and wars and games at which we now play may have been knocked out of our hands so completely that we shall be praying to the gods to grant us still this power of fighting or making peace with one another as we choose, in other words of being left the capacity to settle our own disputes.'

105. This speech of Agelaus' strongly swayed the allies in favour of peace, and none of them more than Philip, since the speaker's arguments reinforced the inclination which he had already formed as a result of Demetrius' advice. Accordingly the two sides reached

agreement on all the matters of detail, and after ratifying the settlement the conference dispersed, each delegation carrying home with it peace instead of war.

All these events took place in the third year of the 140th Olympiad, that is, the battle of Lake Trasimene in Etruria, that of Antiochus in Coele Syria, and the treaty between Philip and the Aetolians and Achaeans.

It was at this time and at this conference[1] that the affairs of Greece, of Italy and of Africa first became involved with one another. From this point both Philip and the leading statesmen in Greece ceased to make wars, truces and treaties with one another in the light of events in Greece alone, but fixed their attention upon the issues at stake in Italy. And soon afterwards the same process took effect among the islanders of the Aegean and the inhabitants of Asia Minor. Those who were displeased with Philip, and some of the opponents of King Attalus of Pergamum, no longer turned to the south or the east – that is to Ptolemy or to Antiochus – but henceforward looked to the west, some of them sending diplomatic missions to Carthage and some to Rome. The Romans followed suit by sending embassies to Greece, since they were disturbed by the audacious nature of Philip's policy, and wished to take precautions against an attack from him now that they were themselves in difficulties.

And so, now that I have, as I believe, given a clear indication, as I promised, of how, when and why Greek affairs became involved with those of Italy and of Africa, I shall continue my account of Greek history down to the date of the battle of Cannae, in which the Romans were defeated by the Carthaginians. This disaster marked the point to which I had already brought my narrative of the war in Italy, and there too I shall close the present book.

1. The battles of Lake Trasimene and of Paphia in Coele Syria took place in June 217, and the conference at Naupactus in August. However, in interpreting this conjunction of events as a turning-point in Mediterranean history Polybius was forcing the evidence. There is no record of an appeal to Rome from the islanders or the Greeks of Asia Minor for many years, no delegation from the opponents of Attalus is reported as having approached Carthage, and no Roman embassy crossed the Aegean until 200 B.C.

BOOK VI

From the Preface

2. Some of my readers, I know, will be wondering why I have postponed until this moment my study of the Roman constitution and thus interrupted the flow of my narrative. I have, however, already made it clear at a number of points that I have always regarded this analysis as one of the essential parts in my design. I touched on this subject in particular at the beginning and in the preliminary survey of this history; there I remarked that the best and most useful aim of my work is to explain to my readers by what means and by virtue of what political institutions almost the whole world fell under the rule of one power, that of Rome, an event which is absolutely without parallel in earlier history. Having made this my purpose, I could find no more suitable occasion than the present to direct attention to what I am about to say and to test the truth of my remarks. In private life, if you wish to pass judgement on the characters of good or of bad men, you would not, assuming that your opinion is to be subjected to a genuine test, examine their actions only at periods of unclouded tranquillity, but rather at times of conspicuous success or failure. The test of true virtue in a man surely resides in his capacity to bear with spirit and with dignity the most complete transformations of fortune, and the same principle should apply to our judgement of states. And so, since I could find no greater or more violent changes of fortune in our time than those which befell the Romans, I have reserved this place in my history for my study of their constitution.

The particular aspect of history which both attracts and benefits its readers is the examination of causes and the capacity, which is the reward of this study, to decide in each case the best policy to follow. Now in all political situations we must understand that the principal factor which makes for success or failure is the form of a state's constitution: it is from this source, as if from a fountain-head, that all designs and plans of action not only originate but reach their fulfilment.

On the Forms of States

3. In the case of those Greek states which have time and again risen to greatness and then experienced a complete change of fortune, it is an easy enough task both to chronicle their past and to pass judgement upon their future. There is no difficulty in reporting the known facts, nor is it hard to guess what is to come from our knowledge of what has preceded it. However, in the case of the Romans it is by no means easy either to explain the present situation, because of the complicated nature of their constitution, or to predict the future, because of our ignorance of the characteristic features both of their private and of their public life in the past. The subject demands an exceptional measure of attention and of study if we wish to obtain a clear view of the distinctive qualities of their constitution.

Most of those writers [1] who have attempted to give an authoritative description of political constitutions have distinguished three kinds, which they call *kingship, aristocracy* and *democracy*. We are, I think, entitled to ask them whether they are presenting these three to us as the only types of constitution or as the best, for in either event I believe that they are wrong. It is clear that we should regard as the *best* constitution one which includes elements of all three species; this has been proved not only in theory but in practice by Lycurgus, who was the first to construct a constitution, that of Sparta, on this principle. But we cannot admit that these are the only three varieties of constitution, for we have seen examples of monarchical and tyrannical governments which differ very

1. Polybius is not necessarily referring here to the classic authors on this subject, such as Herodotus, Plato and Aristotle, but more probably to authors of the second rank who wrote nearer to his time.

widely from kingship,[1] even though they possess certain points of resemblance to it, and this is the reason why one-man rulers usurp and employ, so far as they can, the title of *king*. There have also been several oligarchic constitutions which bear certain superficial resemblances to aristocracies, though here again the difference is as wide as it is possible to be, and the same generalization applies to democracies.

4. The truth of what I have just said may be illustrated by the following arguments. We cannot say that every example of one-man rule is necessarily a kingship, but only those which are voluntarily accepted by their subjects, and which are governed by an appeal to reason rather than by fear or by force. Nor again can we say that every oligarchy is an aristocracy, but only those in which the power is exercised by the justest and wisest men, who have been selected on their merits. In the same way a state in which the mass of citizens is free to do whatever it pleases or takes into its head is not a democracy. But where it is both traditional and customary to reverence the gods, to care for our parents, to respect our elders, to obey the laws, and in such a community to ensure that the will of the majority prevails – this situation it is proper to describe as democracy.

We ought thus to name six kinds of government: the three commonly spoken of which I have just mentioned, and those which have certain elements in common with these, by which I mean one-man rule, minority rule and mob rule. The first of these to come into being is one-man rule, which arises unaided and in the natural course of events. After one-man rule, and developing from it with the aid of art and through the correction of its defects, comes kingship. This later degenerates into its corrupt but associated form, by which I mean tyranny, and then the abolition of both gives rise to aristocracy. Aristocracy by its very nature degenerates into oligarchy, and when the populace rises in anger to avenge the injustices committed by its rulers, democracy is born; then in due course, out of the licence and lawlessness which are generated by this type of regime, mob rule comes into being and completes the cycle. The truth of what I have just said will become

1. Polybius refers, for example, to Cleomenes of Sparta as a tyrant and despot (see p. 159).

perfectly clear to anyone who makes a careful study of the beginnings, origins and changes which are natural to each of these forms of government. For it is only by observing how each of these constitutions comes into being that one can see when, how, and where the growth, the perfection, the change and the end of each is likely to recur. I believe that the Roman constitution is a better subject than any other for this method of analysis, because its origin and growth have from the very beginning followed natural causes.

5. Now the process whereby the different forms of government are naturally transformed into one another has been discussed in the greatest detail by Plato and certain other philosophers. But as these analyses are complex and are developed at great length, they are beyond the reach of all but a few. I shall therefore try to give a brief summary of the theory so far as I think it applies to serious history and appeals to the common intelligence of mankind. If my exposition appears to leave out certain factors because I am speaking in generalities, the detailed discussion which follows should sufficiently compensate the reader for any difficulties which for the present I have left unsolved.

What then are the origins of a political society, and how does it first come into being? From time to time, as a result of floods, plagues, failures of crops or other similar causes, there occurs a catastrophic destruction of the human race, in which all knowledge of the arts and social institutions is lost. Such disasters, tradition tells us, have often befallen mankind, and must reasonably be expected to recur. Then in the course of time the population renews itself from the survivors as if from seeds, men increase once more in numbers and, like other animals, proceed to form herds. Because of their natural weakness it is only to be expected that they should herd with their own kind, and in this situation it is inevitable that the man who excels in physical strength and courage should lead and rule over the rest. This phenomenon can be seen at work among those animals which lack the faculty of reason, such as bulls, boars, cocks and the like, among which the strongest are indisputably the masters, and we must regard it as the teaching of nature in the truest sense. Originally, then, it is probable that men lived in this fashion, herding together like animals and following the strongest and the bravest as their leaders; in this situation the limits of the leader's rule are defined by his strength, and the name which we should apply to this system is monarchy. But when in the course of time families and social relationships begin to develop in such communities, the idea of kingship is born, and then for the first time mankind conceives the notions of goodness, of justice, and of their opposites.

6. The manner in which these concepts originate and evolve is as follows. The intercourse of the sexes is a universal instinct of nature, and the birth of children is the result. But suppose that one of those who have been thus reared grows to manhood, and then so far from showing gratitude or helping to protect those who have brought him up deliberately injures them by word or deed; he will certainly displease and offend all those who have been associated with his parents, and have witnessed the care and the trouble they have spent in tending and feeding their children. Men differ from the other animals in that they are the only creatures to possess the faculty of reasoning, and it is certain that such a difference of conduct will not escape them as it does the animal species; they will notice what is done and be displeased at it, for they will look to the future and reflect that they might suffer the same treatment. Again, when a man who has been helped, or rescued from some difficulty, so far from showing gratitude to his benefactor actually tries to do him harm, it is clear that those who hear of the affair will naturally be displeased and offended at his behaviour, will share the resentment of their neighbour, and will imagine themselves to be placed in his position. In this way each individual begins to form an idea of the theory and meaning of duty, which is the beginning and end of justice.

In the same way, when one man stands out among all his companions in defending them from danger, and confronts or awaits the onslaught of the most powerful wild beasts, it is natural that he should receive marks of favour and of preeminence from the people, while a man who does the opposite will suffer their disapproval and contempt. Here again it is reasonable to suppose that some theory will develop among the people as to what is noble and what is base, and what constitutes the difference between them, with the result that one type of conduct will be admired and imitated because of its advantages, and the other avoided. And so when the most prominent and most powerful man among the people constantly uses the weight of his authority to support the views of the majority on the matters I have just mentioned, and when in the opinion of his subjects he rewards or punishes each according to his deserts, then they will do his bidding not through fear of violence, but because their judgement approves him. They will join in supporting his rule, however old he may be, and will rally round him as one man, and resist all those who conspire against his rule. In this way, and almost imperceptibly, the monarch develops into a king when reason becomes more powerful than ferocity or force.

7. It is in this way, then, that the first ideas of goodness and of justice and of their opposites are naturally formed among men, and this is the origin and the genesis of true kingship. The people ensure that the supreme power remains in the hands not only of the original leaders but of their descendants, since they are convinced that those who are descended from and educated by such men will cherish principles similar to their own. But if they ever become dissatisfied with the descendants, they no longer choose their kings and rulers for their physical strength, but on the merits of their judgement and of their powers of reasoning, for they have come to understand from practical experience the difference between the one set of attributes and the other.

In ancient times, then, those who had been singled out for royal authority continued in their functions until they grew old; they built imposing strongholds, fortified them with walls, and acquired lands to provide for their subjects both security and an abundance of the necessities of life. While they were pursuing these aims they were never the objects of envy nor of abuse, because they did not indulge in distinctions of dress or of food or drink at the expense of others, but lived very much in the same fashion as the rest of their subjects, and kept in close touch with the people in their daily activities. But when rulers received their power by inheritance, and found that their safety was well provided for and their food more than sufficient, this superabundance tempted them to indulge their appetites. They assumed that rulers should be distinguished from their subjects by a special dress, that they should enjoy additional luxury and variety in the preparation and serving of their food, and that they should be denied nothing in the pursuit of their love affairs, however lawless these might be. These vices provoked envy and indignation in the first case, and an outburst of passionate hatred and anger in the second, with the result that the kingship became a tyranny. In this way the first step was taken towards its disintegration, and conspiracies began to be formed. These did not originate from the worst men in the state, but rather from the noblest, the most high-minded and the most courageous, because such men find it hardest to endure the insolence of their rulers.

8. Once the people had found their leaders they gave them their support against their rulers for the reasons which I have stated above, with the result that kingship and monarchy were swept away and in their place the institution of aristocracy came into being and developed. The people, as if discharging a debt of gratitude to those who had overthrown the monarchy, tended to place these men in authority and entrust their destinies to them. At first the aristocrats gladly accepted this charge, made it their supreme concern to serve the common interest, and handled both the private and public affairs of the people with the greatest care and solicitude. But here again the next generation inherited the same position of authority as their fathers. They in turn had no experience of misfortunes and no tradition of civil equality and freedom of speech, since they had been reared from the cradle in an atmosphere of authority and privilege. And so they abandoned their high responsibilities, some in favour of avarice and unscrupulous money-making, others of drinking and the convivial excesses that go with it, and others the violation of women and the rape of boys. In this way they transformed an aristocracy into an oligarchy, and soon provoked the people to a pitch of resentment similar to that which I have already described, with the result that their regime suffered the same disastrous end as had befallen the tyrants.

9. The truth is that whenever anybody who has observed the hatred and jealousy which are felt by the citizens for tyrants can summon up the courage to speak or act against the authorities, he finds the whole mass of the people ready to support him. But

after they have either killed or banished the oligarchs, the people do not venture to set up a king again, for they are still in terror of the injustices committed by previous monarchs, nor do they dare to entrust the government to a limited class, since they still have before their eyes the evidence of their recent mistake in doing so. At this point the only hope which remains unspoiled lies with themselves, and it is in this direction that they then turn: they convert the state into a democracy instead of an oligarchy and themselves assume the superintendence and charge of affairs. Then so long as any people survive who endured the evils of oligarchical rule, they can regard their present form of government as a blessing and treasure the privileges of equality and freedom of speech. But as soon as a new generation has succeeded and the democracy falls into the hands of the grandchildren of its founders, they have become by this time so accustomed to equality and freedom of speech that they cease to value them and seek to raise themselves above their fellow-citizens, and it is noticeable that the people most liable to this temptation are the rich. So when they begin to hanker after office, and find that they cannot achieve it through their own efforts or on their merits, they begin to seduce and corrupt the people in every possible way, and thus ruin their estates. The result is that through their senseless craving for prominence they stimulate among the masses both an appetite for bribes and the habit of receiving them, and then the rule of democracy is transformed into government by violence and strong-arm methods. By this time the people have become accustomed to feed at the expense of others, and their prospects of winning a livelihood depend upon the property of their neighbours; then as soon as they find a leader who is sufficiently ambitious and daring, but is excluded from the honours of office because of his poverty, they will introduce a regime based on violence. After this they unite their forces, and proceed to massacre, banish and despoil their opponents, and finally degenerate into a state of bestiality,[1] after which they once more find a master and a despot.

Such is the cycle of political revolution, the law of nature according to which constitutions change, are transformed, and finally revert to their original form. Anyone who has a clear

1. This process is illustrated by the case of Cynaetha (see pp. 277–9).

grasp of this process might perhaps go wrong, when he speaks of the future of a state, in his forecast of the time it will take for the process of change to take place, but so long as his judgement is not distorted by animosity or envy he will very seldom be mistaken as to the stage of growth or decline which a given community has reached, or as to the form into which it will change. Above all, in the case of the Roman state this method of examination will give us the clearest insight into the process whereby it was formed, grew, and reached the zenith of its achievement as well as the changes for the worse which will follow these. For this state, if any ever did (as I have already pointed out), takes its foundation and its growth from natural causes, and will pass through a natural evolution to its decay. At any rate the reader will best be able to judge of the truth of this assertion from the narrative which follows.

10. At this point I propose to give a brief account of the legislation of Lycurgus, which has an important bearing upon my present theme. For Lycurgus understood very well that the changes which I have described came about through an inevitable law of nature, and he took the view that every type of constitution which is simple and founded on a single principle is unstable, because it quickly degenerates into that form of corruption which is peculiar to and inherent in it. For just as rust eats away iron, and wood-worms or ship-worms eat away timber, and these substances even if they escape any external damage are destroyed by the processes which are generated within themselves, so each constitution possesses its own inherent and inseparable vice. Thus in kingship the inbred vice is despotism, in aristocracy it is oligarchy, and in democracy the brutal rule of violence, and it is impossible to prevent each of these kinds of government, as I mentioned above, from degenerating into the debased form of itself. Lycurgus foresaw this, and accordingly did not make his constitution simple or uniform, but combined in it all the virtues and distinctive features of the best governments, so that no one principle should become preponderant, and thus be perverted into its kindred vice, but that the power of each element should be counterbalanced by the others, so that no one of them inclines or sinks unduly to either side. In other words, the constitution should remain for a long

while in a state of equilibrium thanks to the principle of reciprocity or counteraction. Thus kingship was prevented from becoming arrogant through fear of the people who were also given a sufficiently important share in the government, while the people in their turn were restrained from showing contempt for the kings through their fear of the Senate. The members of this body were chosen on grounds of merit, and could be relied upon at all times to take the side of justice unanimously. By this means that part of the state which was at a disadvantage because of its attachment to traditional custom gained power and weight through the support and influence of the senators. For that very reason the result of the drawing-up of the constitution according to these principles was to preserve liberty for the Spartans over a longer period than for any other people of whom we have records.

Now Lycurgus through his powers of reasoning could foresee the direction in which events naturally move and the factors which cause them to do so, and thus constructed his constitution without having to learn the lessons which misfortune teaches. The Romans, on the other hand, although they have arrived at the same result as regards their form of government, did not do so by means of abstract reasoning, but rather through the lessons learned from many struggles and difficulties; and finally, by always choosing the better course in the light of experience acquired from disasters, they have reached the same goal as Lycurgus, that is, the best of all existing constitutions.

On the Roman Constitution at its Prime

11. From the time of the crossing of Xerxes to Greece, and more especially from a date some thirty-two years after that, the details of the Roman political system continued to pass through even more satisfactory modifications, and had arrived at its best and most perfect form at the time of the Hannibalic War.

I can well believe that to those who have been born under the Roman Republic my account of it may seem somewhat incomplete because of the omission of various details . . .

Now the elements by which the Roman constitution was controlled were three in number, all of which I have mentioned before, and all the aspects of the administration were, taken separately, so fairly and so suitably ordered and regulated through the agency of these three elements that it was impossible even for the Romans themselves to declare with certainty whether the whole system was an aristocracy, a democracy or a monarchy. In fact it was quite natural that this should be so, for if we were to fix our eyes only upon the power of the consuls, the constitution might give the impression of being completely monarchical and royal; if we confined our attention to the Senate it would seem to be aristocratic; and if we looked at the power of the people it would appear to be a clear example of a democracy. The powers of these three elements over the various parts of the state were, and with a few modifications still are, as follows.

12. The consuls, until such time as they are required to lead out the legions,[1] remain in Rome and exercise supreme authority over all public affairs. All other magistrates with the exception of the tribunes[2] are subordinate to them and are bound to obey them, and it is they who present foreign embassies to the Senate.[3] Besides these duties they refer urgent business to the Senate for discussion and are entirely responsible for implementing its decisions. It is also their duty to supervise all those affairs of state which are administered by the people; in such cases they summon meetings of the popular assembly, introduce measures and execute the decrees of the people. As for preparations for war and the general conduct of operations in the field, their power is almost absolute. They are entitled to make whatever demands they consider appropriate

1. At the time of which Polybius is writing the consuls normally left Rome for their military duties shortly after entering on their year of office.
2. The tribunate was specifically designed as a check upon the consular power, and a motion proposed in the Senate by a tribune could not be vetoed by a consul. The powers of the tribunate gradually widened into a judicial control of the magistracy, so that they became the principal means that the state possessed of enforcing criminal responsibility upon the executive – in other words the tribunate could prosecute officials who had been at fault.
3. These were heard early in the consular year, before each consul left for his province.

upon the allies,[1] appoint military tribunes,[2] enrol soldiers and select those who are suitable for service. They also have the power to inflict punishment when on active service upon anyone under their command, and authority to spend any sum they think fit from the public funds; in this matter of finance they are accompanied by a quaestor, who complies wholly with their instructions. Thus if anyone were to consider this element in the constitution alone, he could reasonably say that it is a pure example of monarchy or kingship. Here I may add that any changes which may take place now or in the future in the functions I have just described, or am about to describe, do not alter the truth of my analysis.

13. Let us now consider the Senate. This body has control of the treasury and regulates the flow of all revenue and expenditure; the quaestors require a decree of the Senate to enable them to authorize expenditure on any given project, with the exception only of payments made to the consuls. The Senate also controls what is by far the largest and most important item of expenditure – that is, the programme which is laid down by the censors every five years to provide for the repair and construction of public buildings – and it makes a grant to the censors for this purpose. Similarly any crimes committed in Italy which require a public investigation, such as treason, conspiracy, poisoning and assassination, also come under the jurisdiction of the Senate.[3] Again, if any private person or community in Italy requires arbitration for a dispute, or is in need of formal censure, or seeks help or protection, it is the Senate which deals with all such cases. It is also responsible for dispatching embassies or commissions to countries outside

1. The obligations of each of the allies were laid down in their respective treaties of alliance, and each was required to keep a register of its effective strength. Extraordinary demands might be made in an emergency.

2. The first four legions enrolled in each year had their tribunes elected by the tribal assembly, twenty-four in all. The tribunes for the other legions were nominated by the consuls.

3. The Italian allies were nominally and originally independent states, and the Senate's competence to intervene arose out of its role in foreign affairs, and in particular its duty to secure the confederation. Many cases of treason and of conspiracy arose out of the Second Punic War, because of Hannibal's efforts to encourage the allies to secede or revolt: e.g. in the regions of Campania, Tarentum, Bruttium, etc.

Italy, either to settle differences, to offer advice, to impose demands, to receive submissions, or to declare war; and in the same way whenever any foreign delegations arrive in Rome, it decides how they should be received, and what answer should be given them. All these matters are in the hands of the Senate and the people have nothing to do with them.

Thus to anyone who happened to be living in Rome when the consuls were away from the city the constitution might well appear to be completely aristocratic, and this is the impression which prevails among many of the Greek states and of the kings of other countries, since the Senate handles almost all the business of state which concerns them.

14. So when we consider that the Senate exercises authority over all the detailed functions which I have described, and, most important of all, has complete control of expenditure and revenue, and that the consuls hold absolute power in respect of military preparations and operations in the field, we are naturally inclined to ask what place in the constitution is left for the people. The answer is that there is undoubtedly a role for the people to play, and a very important one at that. For it is the people alone who have the right to award both honours and punishments,[1] the only bonds whereby kingdoms, states and human society in general are held together. The fact is that in states where the distinction between these is not recognized, or is recognized in theory but ill-applied in practice, none of the business in hand can be properly administered, for how can this be done if the good and the wicked are held in equal estimation? The people, then, are empowered to try many of the cases in which the offence is punishable by a fine, when the penalty for an offence is a serious one and especially when the accused have held the highest offices of state; and they are the only court which may try on capital charges. As regards this last, they have one custom which is particularly praiseworthy and deserves mention. This allows men who are on trial for their lives, if they are in the process of being condemned, to leave the country openly and thus to inflict a voluntary exile upon themselves – so long as one of the tribes which pronounce the verdict has not yet

1. In other words, the people controlled the law courts, and the election of holders of public office.

voted. Such exiles may take refuge in the territories of Neapolis, Praeneste, Tibur and certain other towns, with which this arrangement has been made by treaty.

On the same principle it is also the people who bestow offices on those who deserve them, and these are the noblest rewards of virtue the state can provide. Besides this, the people have the power to approve or reject laws, and most important of all, they deliberate and decide on questions of peace or war. Furthermore, on such issues as the making of alliances, the termination of hostilities and the making of treaties, it is the people who ratify or reject all of these. And so from this point of view one could reasonably argue that the people have the greatest share of power in the government, and that the constitution is a democracy.

15. I have described how political power is divided between these three elements in the state, and I shall now explain how each of the three can, if it chooses, work with or against the other. The consul, when he sets out with his army, equipped with the powers I have mentioned, appears to hold absolute authority for the execution of his purpose, but in practice he needs the support both of the people and of the Senate and cannot bring his operations to a successful conclusion without them. It is obvious, for example, that the legions require a constant flow of supplies, but without the approval of the Senate neither corn nor clothing nor pay can be provided, so that a commander's plans can be completely frustrated if the Senate chooses to be antipathetic or obstructive. It also rests with the Senate to decide whether a general can execute all his plans and designs, since it has the right either to send out another general when the former's term of office has expired, or to retain him in command for another year. Again, it is in the power of the Senate either to celebrate a general's successes with pomp and magnify them, or to obscure and belittle them. For the processions which they call triumphs, in which the spectacle of what they have achieved in the field is actually brought before the eyes of their fellow-citizens, cannot be properly staged, or in some cases enacted at all, unless the Senate agrees and grants the necessary funds. As for the people, it is a matter of prime necessity for the consuls to consider their interests, however far away from home they may be, for as I have explained above, it is the sovereign

people which ratifies or rejects the suspension of hostilities and the making of treaties. But most important of all is the fact that on laying down their office the consuls are obliged to account for their actions to the people; so under no circumstances is it safe for the consuls to neglect to cultivate the goodwill both of the Senate and of the people.

16. The Senate, again, although it possesses such great power, is obliged first of all to pay attention in public affairs to the views of the people and to respect their wishes. Besides this, it cannot carry out inquiries into the most serious and far-reaching offences against the state – such as involve the death penalty – and take steps to control them, unless its decree is confirmed by the people. The same is the case in matters which directly concern the Senate itself. For if anyone introduces a law which aims to remove from the Senate some of its traditional authority, or to abolish the precedence or other dignities of the senators, or even to reduce some of their property,[1] in all such cases it is the people alone who are empowered to pass the measure or to reject it. It is also a fact that if a single one of the tribunes interposes his veto, the Senate is not only prevented from reaching a final decision on any subject, but cannot even meet and hold sittings. Now the tribunes are always bound to carry out the decrees of the people, and above all, to pay attention to their wishes. For all these reasons, therefore, the Senate stands in awe of the masses and takes heed of the popular will.

17. On the same principle, however, the people also have obligations towards the Senate and must take its wishes into account both individually and collectively. All over Italy an immense number of contracts, far too numerous to specify, are awarded by the censors for the construction and repair of public buildings, and besides this the collection of revenues from navigable rivers, harbours, gardens, mines, lands – in a word every transaction which comes under the control of the Roman government – is farmed out to contractors. All these activities are carried on by the people, and there is scarcely a soul, one might say, who does not have some interest in these contracts and the profits which are derived from them. Some people actually purchase the contracts from the

1. This may refer to the legislation introduced by Gaius Flaminius concerning the public lands in Gaul (see p. 132).

censors for themselves, others act as their partners, others provide security for the contractors, while others may pledge their property to the treasury for this purpose. All these transactions come under the authority of the Senate. It can grant an extension of time, it can lighten the contractor's liability in the event of some unforeseen accident, or release him altogether if it proves impossible for him to fulfil his contract. There are in fact many ways in which the Senate can either inflict great hardship or ease the burden for those who manage public property, for in every case the appeal is referred to it. More important still is the fact that the judges in the majority of civil trials where the action involves large interests are drawn from the Senate.[1] The result is that all citizens, being bound to the Senate by ties which ensure their protection, and being also uncertain and afraid that they may need its help, are very cautious about obstructing or resisting its will. In the same way, people would think twice about opposing the projects of the consuls, since they will come both individually and collectively under their authority while on a campaign.

18. These, then, are the powers which each of the three elements in the system possesses to help or to harm the others; the result is a union which is strong enough to withstand all emergencies, so that it is impossible to find a better form of constitution than this. For whenever some common external threat compels the three to unite and work together, the strength which the state then develops becomes quite extraordinary. No requirement is neglected, because all parties vie with one another to find ways of meeting the needs of the hour, and every decision taken is certain to be executed promptly, since all are cooperating in public and in private alike to carry through the business in hand.

The consequence is that this peculiar form of constitution possesses an irresistible power to achieve any goal it has set itself. The time then comes when the people are freed from these external threats and reap the good fortune and prosperity which their successes have earned them, and then as they enjoy this affluence they are corrupted by flattery and idleness and become insolent and overbearing. This happens often enough, and yet it is at such

1. In smaller actions the parties probably dispensed by agreement with the enrolment of a senatorial judge.

moments above all that the constitution reveals its power to correct such abuses. Whenever one of the three elements swells in importance, becomes overambitious and tends to encroach upon the others, it becomes apparent for the reasons given above that none of the three is completely independent, but that the designs of any one can be blocked or impeded by the rest, with the result that none will unduly dominate the others or treat them with contempt. Thus the whole situation remains in equilibrium since any aggressive impulse is checked, and each estate is apprehensive from the outset of censure from the others.

The Roman Military System

19. After they have elected the consuls, they proceed to appoint military tribunes; fourteen are drawn from those who have seen five years' service and ten from those who have seen ten. As for the rest, a cavalryman is required to complete ten years' service and an infantryman sixteen before he reaches the age of forty-six, except for those rated at less than 400 *drachmae* worth of property who are assigned to naval service. In periods of national emergency the infantry are called upon to serve for twenty years and no one is permitted to hold any political office[1] until he has completed ten years' service.

When the consuls are about to enrol soldiers they announce at a meeting of the popular assembly the day on which all Roman citizens of military age must report for service, and this is done every year. On the appointed day, when those who are liable for service have arrived in Rome and assembled on the Capitoline Hill, the fourteen junior military tribunes divide themselves into four groups, according to the order in which they have been appointed by the people or the consuls; this is because the main and original division of the Roman forces is into four legions. The four

1. The arm in which a young nobleman would normally serve was the cavalry; this meant that nobody could stand for political office until he had completed his twenty-seventh year.

tribunes first appointed are assigned to the first legion, the next
three to the second, the next four to the third and the last three to
the fourth. Of the ten senior tribunes the first two are appointed
to the first legion, the next three to the second, the next two to the
third, and the last three to the fourth.

20. When the tribunes have been posted in such a way that each
legion has the same number of officers, those of each legion take
up a position apart, draw lots for the tribes one by one, and call
up each in the order of the lottery. From this tribe they first of all
select four youths, who are as similar to one another as possible in
age and physique. When these four are brought forward the
officers of the first legion have first choice, those of the second
legion second choice, those of the third third, and those of the
fourth last. When the next batch of four is brought forward, the
officers of the second legion have first choice, and those of the
first choose last. With the next four the tribunes of the third legion
have first choice, those of the second last, and so on. In this way
by giving each legion the first choice in turn, all the legions receive
men of approximately the same standard. After they have selected
the total number required, that is, when the strength of each legion
has been brought up to 4,200, or in times of especial danger 5,000,
it was the custom in earlier times to choose the cavalrymen; but
in our day these are enrolled first of all. The censor selects them
on a property basis, and 300 are posted to each legion.

21. When the enrolment has been carried out in this fashion, the
tribunes who have been assigned to this duty then parade the
conscripts, and each of them selects from the whole body one man
whom they consider the most suitable; he is then ordered to take
the oath that he will obey his officers and carry out their commands
to the best of his ability. Then the rest of the conscripts come
forward, and each swears that he will do the same as the first man.

At the same time the consuls send out orders to the magistrates
of the allied cities in Italy from which they wish to raise troops,
stating the numbers required and the day and the place at which
the men selected for service must appear. The authorities then
choose the men and administer the oath by means of a similar
procedure, appoint a commanding officer and a paymaster and
dispatch the contingent to Rome.

After the conscripts have been sworn in, the military tribunes at Rome announce for each legion a day and a place for the men to present themselves without arms, and then dismiss them. When they report on the given date, the youngest and those with the lowest property qualification are posted to the *velites*, the next group to the *hastati*, those in the prime of life to the *principes*, and the oldest to the *triarii*. These are the names used by the Romans for the four classes in each legion which are distinguished from one another both in age and in equipment. They are divided so that the senior, the *triarii*, number 600, the *principes* 1,200, and the *hastati* 1,200, the remainder being made up of *velites*. If the strength of the legion exceeds 4,000, the numbers of each of these classes are increased in proportion, except for the *triarii*, whose strength remains constant at 600.

22. The youngest soldiers, the *velites*, are ordered to carry a sword, javelins and a target. This last is circular, three feet in diameter, strongly made and large enough to protect a man. They also wear a plain helmet[1] which is sometimes covered with a piece of wolf's skin or something similar, which serves both to protect and to identify the soldier; this enables the officers to recognize the man and to observe whether or not he shows courage in the face of danger. The wooden shaft of the javelins which they carry is about three feet in length and a finger's breadth in diameter. The head is a span[2] in length and is hammered out thin and so finely sharpened that it is inevitably bent at the first impact, thus making it useless for the enemy to hurl back; otherwise the weapon would be equally serviceable for both sides.

23. The next age group, known as the *hastati*, are ordered to wear a complete panoply. The Roman panoply consists in the first place of a long shield (*scutum*). The surface is convex; it measures two and a half feet in width and four in length, and the thickness at the rim is a palm's breadth. It consists of two layers of wood fastened together with bull's hide glue; the outer surface is then covered first with canvas and then with calf-skin. The upper and lower edges are bound with iron to protect the shield both from the cutting strokes of swords and from wear when resting on the

1. i.e. without a crest.   2. About nine inches.

ground. In the centre is fixed an iron boss, which turns aside the heavy impact of stones, pikes and weighty missiles in general. Besides the shield they also carry a sword which is worn on the right thigh and is called a Spanish sword.[1] This has a sharp point and can deal an effective blow with either edge, as the blade is very strong and unbending.

In addition, the *hastati* carry two throwing spears (*pila*), a bronze helmet and greaves. The spears are of two kinds, the slender and the thick. Of the thicker kind some are round and a palm's breadth in diameter, others are a palm square.[2] The slender spears which they carry as well as the thicker variety are like medium-sized hunting spears, the length of the wooden shaft being about four and a half feet. The iron head is barbed and is of the same length as the shaft. They take great pains to ensure the utility of this weapon by attaching the iron firmly to the shaft. It is fastened into the wooden shaft half-way up its length and riveted with a series of clasps, so that in action it will break rather than come loose, although its thickness at the socket where it meets the wood measures only a finger and a half.[3] Finally, the *hastati* wear as an ornament a plume of three purple or black feathers standing upright about a foot and a half in height. These are placed on the helmet, and the general effect combined with the rest of the armour is to make each man look about twice his real height, and gives him an appearance which strikes terror into the enemy. Besides this armament the private soldiers also wear a brass breast-plate a span square, which is placed in front of the heart, and called a heart-protector (*pectorale*). This item completes their panoply, but those who are rated at a property qualification of above 10,000 *drachmae* wear instead a coat of chain-mail (*lorica*). The *principes* and *triarii* are armed with the same weapons, except that instead of the throwing-spear, the *triarii* carry long thrusting-spears (*hastae*).

24. The *principes*, *hastati* and *triarii* each elect ten centurions

1. Polybius refers to this as having been employed during the Second Punic War, but it may well have been adopted from Spanish troops fighting for the Carthaginians during the First.

2. i.e. some had a circular and some a square cross-section.

3. The breadth of the shaft was about three inches, and that of the iron head fitted into it about one inch.

according to merit, and then a second ten.[1] All these have the title of centurion, and the first man elected is a member of the military council. The centurions in their turn appoint an equal number of rear-rank officers (*optiones*).[2] Together with the centurions these officers then divide each of the classes into ten companies, leaving out the *velites*, each company being allotted two centurions and two *optiones*. The *velites* are then divided into equal groups among all the companies, 120 of them to each company. These companies are known as orders (*ordines*), maniples[3] (*manipuli*), or standards (*signa*), and their officers as centurions (*ordinum ductores*). These officers then choose from the ranks two of their bravest and most soldierly men to be the standard-bearers (*signiferi*) for each maniple. There is nothing unreasonable in appointing two centurions for each maniple, for it is impossible to be sure what a commander may be called upon to do or what may happen to him, and since the exigencies of war do not allow of any excuses, they are anxious that the maniple should never be without a leader and commander. When both centurions are present the senior commands the right half of the maniple and the junior the left; otherwise the one who is present commands the whole. In choosing their centurions the Romans look not so much for the daring or fire-eating type, but rather for men who are natural leaders and possess a stable and imperturbable temperament, not men who will open the battle and launch attacks, but those who will stand their ground even when worsted or hard-pressed, and will die in defence of their posts.

25. On similar principles they divide the cavalry into ten squadrons (*turmae*), and from each of these they select three officers (*decuriones*), who in turn appoint three quartermasters (*optiones*). The first to be chosen commands the squadron, the other two carry the rank of *decuriones* and all three bear this title. If the first of these is not present, the second takes command of the

---

1. The first ten of these officers were known as *centuriones priores*, the second as *posteriores*.

2. The *optio* relieved the centurion of various administrative duties and may be described as a kind of quartermaster.

3. The maniple therefore consisted on average of 420 men, a tenth of a legion.

squadron. The armour worn by the cavalry is now very similar to that which is used in Greece. In earlier times they had no breast-plates, and fought in tunics which allowed great ease and agility in mounting and dismounting, but exposed them to great danger in hand-to-hand fighting, as their bodies were almost completely unprotected. Besides these disadvantages their lances were also unserviceable in two ways. In the first place they made them so slender and pliant that it was impossible to take a steady aim, and the shaking of the weapon from the motion of the horse caused many of them to break before the iron tip became fixed in anything. Secondly, the butt end was not fitted with a spike, so that they could only deliver the first thrust with the point, and if the weapon then broke it became quite useless. The cavalry shield was made of ox-hide and was somewhat similar in shape to those round cakes with a boss in the middle which are used at sacrifices. These shields were of little value in attack as they were not hard enough, and when the leather cover peeled off and rotted after exposure to rain they became not merely awkward, as they had been before, but quite useless. Since this equipment proved so unsatisfactory in use, the Romans lost no time in changing over to the Greek type. The advantage of this was that in the case of the lance the horseman could deliver the first thrust with a sure and accurate aim, since the weapon was designed to remain steady and not quiver in the hand, and also that it could be used to deliver a hard blow by reversing it and striking with the spike at the butt end. The same may be said of the Greek shields, which, since they are firmly and solidly made, render good service against both attack[1] and assault. As soon as they made these discoveries the Romans began to copy Greek arms, for this is one of their strong points: no people are more willing to adopt new customs and to emulate what they see is better done by others.

26. When the tribunes have formed the conscripts into these units and given orders for them to arm themselves in this fashion, they dismiss them to their homes. Then when the day comes on which they have all sworn to assemble at the place named by the consul, all those whose names have been entered upon the roll appear without fail, for no excuse is accepted barring adverse

1. 'Attack' probably signifies missiles thrown from a distance.

omens, or some accident which makes attendance completely impossible. It is normal on these occasions for each consul to name a separate assembly-point for the troops under his command, since each will have been allotted two Roman legions and his due share of the allied troops.

At the same time the allies also assemble with the Roman citizens, and the organization and command of their units is supervised by officers appointed by the consuls; these are twelve in number and are known as the prefects of the allies. These men select for the consuls from the whole allied forces that have been mobilized those infantry and cavalrymen who are best fitted for service, and who are known as *extraordinarii*, that is, picked troops. The total of allied infantry usually equals that of the Romans, while the cavalry is three times as many. Out of these they select about one-third of the cavalry and one-fifth of the infantry to serve as *extraordinarii*. The rest they divide into two corps, one known as the right wing and the other as the left.

After making these arrangements, the military tribunes take both the Romans and the allies and proceed to pitch their camp. No matter where this is done, one simple formula for a camp is employed, which is adopted at all times and in all places. I think therefore that this is the right moment for me to try to explain to my readers, in so far as this can be done in words, the dispositions which the Romans use for their troops when they are on the march, when they are encamped and when they are in action. There is surely nobody so indifferent to excellence in performance as to refuse to take a little extra trouble to understand matters of this kind; if once he has read of these technicalities, he will be well-informed on a subject which certainly deserves his attention.

27. The Roman method of laying out a camp is as follows. Once the site has been chosen, the position which affords the best view of the whole area, and is most convenient for giving out orders, is reserved for the general's tent (*praetorium*). They plant a standard on the spot where they intend to pitch the tent, and measure off round this a square plot of ground, each side of the square being 100 feet distant from the standard, so that the whole area of the square is four *plethra*.[1] Along one side of this square,

1. 10,000 square feet.

whichever offers the best facilities for watering and foraging, the Roman legions are stationed as follows. As I have explained, there are six military tribunes in each legion, and since each consul always has two Roman legions with him, it follows that there are twelve tribunes in a consular army. They pitch the tents of these officers all in one straight line running parallel to the selected side of the square and fifty feet from it, so as to leave space for the horses, mules and baggage of the tribunes. These tents are pitched with their backs to the square of the *praetorium* and facing the outer side of the camp, in the direction which I shall henceforth refer to as the front. The tents of the tribunes are sited at an equal distance from one another, so that they extend along the whole breadth of the space occupied by the legions.

28. They next measure another distance of 100 feet from the front of all these tents. At that distance another line parallel to that of the tents is drawn, and here they begin to mark out the quarters for the legions, which they arrange as follows. They bisect the last-mentioned straight line, and from that point draw another line at right angles to it. Along this line, on either side of it and opposite one another they encamp the cavalry of each legion. There is a space of fifty feet between the two sides, which is exactly bisected by the line last mentioned. The manner of encamping the infantry is similar to that employed for the cavalry. The space allotted forms the complete figure of a square, alike for the maniples and for the squadrons. This square faces one of the roads (*viae*) which run through the camp; the side facing the road is of a fixed length of 100 feet, and they normally try to make the breadth the same, except in the case of the quarters for the allies. When they have to accommodate legions of a greater strength, they increase the length and breadth of the squares proportionately.

29. The cavalry camp is thus laid out so as to occupy as it were the two sides of a street which starts from the middle of the tribunes' tents, and runs at right angles to the line along which these tents are pitched and to the thoroughfare in front of them. The whole arrangement of the streets in fact resembles a system of crossroads which run on either side of the blocks of tents, those of the cavalry on one side, and those of the infantry on the other. The spaces assigned to the cavalry and to the *triarii* in each legion

are back-to-back: the company adjoins the troop but faces in the opposite direction and there is no space between them. The depth allowed to each company of *triarii* is only half of its frontage, because as a rule the strength of a company of *triarii* is only half that of the other classes. However, although the maniples may be of unequal strength, the length of frontage allotted to them is always the same, because of the reduced depth of their quarters. Next and parallel with the spaces assigned to the *triarii* they place the *principes*, opposite them and with a space of fifty feet between. As both classes face the intervening space, two more streets are formed at right angles to the 100-feet wide thoroughfare which runs in front of the tents of the tribunes, both issuing on the side of the camp which is opposite the tribunes' quarters, and which we agreed to call the front. After the *principes* and back-to-back against them with no intervening space, they encamp the *hastati*. As each class, according to the original establishment of the army, consists of ten maniples, the streets are all equal in length and they all finish in a straight line on the front side of the camp, the last maniples in the lines being placed so as to face the front.

30. Beyond the *hastati*, and again separated by a space of fifty feet, they encamp the allied cavalry, beginning from the same line, that of the road which runs in front of the tribunes' tents, and ending on the same line in the front of the camp. As I mentioned above, the strength of the allied infantry units is the same as that of the Roman, but from the former we have to deduct the contingents of *extraordinarii*. The strength of the allied cavalry units, however, is double that of the Roman, after we have deducted the one-third who serve as *extraordinarii*. Thus in laying out the camp they proportionately increase the depth of the space allowed to the allied cavalry so as to make it equal to that occupied by the Roman legions. By this time five streets have been completed, and next they quarter the allied infantry, increasing the depth of their position in proportion to their larger numbers.[1] They are placed back-to-back with the cavalry with no intervening space, so that

1. This is because without the *extraordinarii*, who number one-fifth of the allied contingent, there are 2,400 men to get into ten spaces, instead of 3,000 into thirty spaces.

the infantry face the rampart which runs along the outer sides of the camp. In each maniple the first tent at either end of the row is occupied by the centurions. In laying out the camp in this fashion, they always leave a space of fifty feet between the fifth unit and the sixth, thereby forming another road which traverses the whole camp. This runs parallel to the tents of the tribunes and at right angles to the others, and is called the *via quintana*, as it borders the fifth squadrons and maniples.

31. The spaces behind the tribunes' quarters are used as follows. On the right of the general's quarters (*praetorium*) is the market, and on the left the office of the quaestor and the supplies of which he is in charge. Behind the last of the tribunes' tents on either side, and more or less at right angles to these, are the quarters of the cavalry picked out from the *extraordinarii*, and also those of a number of volunteers[1] who serve out of personal friendship for the consul. These are all encamped parallel to the ramparts along the sides of the camp, the one set of quarters facing the quaestor's depot and the other the market. For most of the time these troops are placed near the consul not only in camp but also on the march, and on other occasions too they are constantly in attendance on the consul and the quaestor. Back-to-back with them and looking out towards the rampart are stationed the picked infantry, who perform the same service as the cavalry I have just described. Beyond these quarters is left another space 100 feet in breadth which runs parallel to the tents of the tribunes, skirts the *praetorium*, the market-place and the *quaestorium*, and stretches from rampart to rampart. On the farther side of this thoroughfare are placed the rest of the *extraordinarii* cavalry, so as to face the market, the *praetorium* and the *quaestorium*. Between these lines of the cavalry and exactly opposite the centre of the *praetorium* runs a passage fifty feet wide; this leads to the rampart at the rear of the camp, and runs at right angles to the 100-feet wide road at the back of the *praetorium*. Back-to-back with these cavalry quarters, and facing the rampart and the rearward side of the whole camp, are placed the rest of the *extraordinarii* infantry. Finally, the empty

[1] These were veterans who re-enlisted on special terms and formed a bodyguard for the general.

spaces to the right and left of these and next to the rampart on each side of the camp are assigned to foreign troops and to any allied troops who may enter the camp.

The result of these dispositions is that the whole camp is laid out as a square, and the arrangement both of the streets and the general plan gives it the appearance of a town. The rampart is dug on all sides at a distance of 200 feet from the tents, and this empty space serves a number of important purposes. In the first place it provides the proper and necessary facilities for marching the troops in and out; it ensures that they all march into this space by way of the road which passes their own quarters, and thus do not enter any one street in a mass, and so hustle or jostle one another. Also all cattle which are brought into the camp and all plunder captured from the enemy are collected in this precinct and safely guarded during the night. But the most important use made of this space is that if the camp is attacked by night it prevents the tents from being set on fire and keeps the soldiers out of range of the enemy's missiles, or if a few of them do carry so far, they are almost harmless because of the distance and of the margin which has been left in front of the tents.

32. Given the numbers of cavalry and infantry, and on the assumption that the strength of each legion is either 4,000 or 5,000 men, and given likewise the depth and length and the number of the maniples and squadrons, and besides these the dimensions of the passages and roads and all other details, it is possible, for any-body who wishes, to calculate the area and the perimeter of the camp. If an exceptionally large number of allies should happen to be present, either of those who were on the original strength or of those who have been attached for a special occasion, space is made for the latter in the area on either side of the *praetorium* by reducing the market and the quaestor's depot to the smallest size possible which will still meet urgent needs, while for the former, if the excess over the normal happens to be large, they add two streets, one at each side of the quarters of the Roman legions, and facing the ramparts on each side of the camp.

On occasions when the two consuls with their four legions are united in one camp, all we need to do is to imagine two camps similar to the one I have described placed back to back, the two adjoining at the point where the *extraordinarii* infantry are quartered, the troops whom we described as facing the ramparts to the rear of each camp. In this case the shape of the camp becomes oblong, its area is doubled, and the perimeter of the entire rampart measures half as much again. Whenever the two consuls happen to encamp together, this is the formation they adopt; when they are apart the only difference is that the market, the quaestor's depot and the *praetorium* are placed between the two legions.

33. After the camp has been laid out the military tribunes parade all those present, and administer an oath to each man separately, both freemen and slaves. Each individual swears that he will steal nothing from the camp, and that if he should find anything, he will bring it to the tribunes. Next they issue their orders to the maniples of the *hastati* and the *principes* of each legion. The maniples are detailed to take responsibility for the ground in front of the tents of the tribunes. This is the space where much of the business of the camp is transacted in the daytime, and so they make sure that it is swept and watered with great care. Of the remaining eighteen maniples, three are assigned by lot to each of the tribunes, of whom there are six in each legion, and each of these maniples takes its turn of duty in waiting upon the tribune. The following are some of the services they render him. When the army encamps, they pitch his tent for him and level the ground around it, and if it is necessary to take any special precautions to fence off his baggage they attend to this. They also provide two guard rotas for him, each guard consisting of four men, one being posted in front of his tent and the other behind it next to the horses. As each tribune has three maniples assigned to him, and there are more than 100 men in each maniple, not counting the *triarii* or the *velites*, who are not liable for this service, the duty is a light one, since it only comes round to each maniple on every third day. This arrangement amply provides the necessary well-being for the tribune, and also maintains the seriousness and dignity of his office. The maniples of the *triarii* are exempt from this personal service for the tribunes, but each of their maniples provides a guard every day for the squadron of cavalry which adjoins its quarters. This guard, besides maintaining a general look-out, pays special attention to the horses to prevent them from injuring or

incapacitating themselves by getting entangled in their tethers, or from breaking loose and creating confusion or disturbance in the camp by running against other horses. Finally, every maniple in turn mounts guard each day outside the consul's tent, both to protect him from plots and to enhance the dignity of his rank.

34. As regards the construction of the ditch and the stockade around the the camp,[1] this work is undertaken by the allies for the length of the two sides along which their wings are quartered; the other two sides are assigned to the Romans, one to each legion. Each side of the camp is divided into sectors according to the number of maniples, and the centurions stand by and supervise the work of each maniple; at the same time two of the tribunes superintend the construction of the side as a whole and ensure that the work is thorough, and it is also these officers who supervise all other work connected with the camp. They work in pairs and each pair is on duty in turn for two months out of six. They draw lots for their turn, and the pair on whom the lot falls is responsible for supervising all active field operations. The prefects of the allies divide their duties on the same system. Every day at first light the Roman cavalry parade at the tents of the tribunes, and the tribunes then report to the consul. He gives the necessary orders to the tribunes, they to the cavalry officers and centurions, and these pass them on to the other ranks when the proper time comes.

The procedure whereby they ensure the safe passing round of the watch-word for the night is as follows. One man is selected from the tenth maniple of each class of infantry and cavalry which occupies the position at the end of the road between the tents nearest the front of the camp. This soldier is relieved from guard duty, and he reports each day at sunset to the tent of the tribune on duty; there he is given the watch-word, that is, a wooden tablet with the word inscribed on it, and takes his leave. On returning to his quarters he hands over the watch-word and tablet in the presence of witnesses to the commander of the maniple next to his own, who in turn passes it on to the one next to him, and so on. All repeat this procedure, until the tablet reaches the first maniples,

1. In Roman military terminology *agger* is the rampart and *vallum* the stockade on top of it. Polybius often uses the word *charax* or *charakoma* to represent the whole structure.

which are stationed near the tents of the tribunes, and these men are obliged to deliver the tablets to the tribunes before dark. If all the tablets issued are handed in, the tribune on duty knows that the watch-word has been delivered to all the maniples and has passed through every one of them on the way back to him. If any of the tablets are missing, he investigates the matter immediately, as he knows by the marks on the other tablets from which part of the camp the missing one has failed to return, and the man who is responsible for its non-appearance is appropriately punished.

35. The keeping of night watches is arranged as follows. The consul's tent is guarded by the maniple on duty, and those of the tribunes and the cavalry squadrons by the men appointed from the maniples according to the system which I have explained above. Each unit, whether maniple or squadron, also posts a guard composed of its own men for its own security. The remaining guards are appointed by the consul. As a general rule there are three pickets at the *quaestorium* and two at the tents of each of the legates[1] and members of the military council. The whole outer perimeter of the camp is guarded by the *velites*, who are posted every day along the stockade. This is their special duty, and they also guard the entrances to the camp, a guard of ten men being assigned to each. Of those who are posted on picket duty, the man from each maniple who is to take the first watch is brought to the tribune in the evening by one of the *optiones* from his unit. The tribune hands over a tablet to each of these men, one for each guard post; the tablets are quite small and have a sign written on them, and on receiving this, each man returns to the post assigned to him.

The duty of going the rounds is entrusted to the cavalry. The first *decurio* of the first squadron in each legion must issue orders early in the morning to one of his *optiones* so as to give notice before the morning meal to four young men of his squadron that they have been detailed to go the rounds. The same man must also give notice in the evening to the *decurio* of the next squadron that it is his duty to make arrangements for going the rounds on the following day. On receipt of this instruction the *decurio* must carry

1. These were senior officers often recruited from the Senate and attached to the consul's staff as advisers. Their rank was perhaps between that of quaestor and military tribune.

out the identical procedure on the next day, and so on throughout the cavalry squadrons. The four men from the first squadron, who have been selected by the *optiones*, draw lots for the watch they are to take. Then they report to the tribune and receive from him written orders specifying which posts they are to visit and at what time. Next all four take up their positions for the night next to the first maniple of the *triarii*, for it is the duty of the centurion of this maniple to have a bugle sounded at the beginning of each watch.

36. When the appointed time comes, the man who has drawn the first watch by lot makes his rounds, taking some friends with him as witnesses. He visits the posts which are detailed in his orders, not only along the stockade and the gates, but all the guard posts of the infantry maniples and the cavalry squadrons. If he finds the guards of the first watch awake, he takes over their tablet, but if he finds any one of them asleep or absent from his post, he calls upon those with him to witness the fact, and continues on his rounds. The same procedure is repeated by those who go the rounds on the other watches. The responsibility for having a bugle sounded at the beginning of each watch so that those who are going the round should visit the various posts at the right time, belongs, as I mentioned, to the centurions of the first maniple of the *triarii* in each legion, each of whom takes this duty for a day.

Each of the men who have made the rounds returns the tablets at daybreak to the tribune. If all are handed in, the men are dismissed without question, but if any one of them delivers a smaller number of tablets than the number of posts he has visited, the signs on the tablets are checked so as to discover to which post the missing one belongs. When this has been ascertained, the tribune sends for the centurion of the maniple; he brings the men who were on picket-duty and they are then confronted with the patrol. If the fault lies with the picket, the patrol can quickly make this clear by calling the witnesses who accompanied him, indeed he is obliged to do this. But if nothing of this kind has happened, then the blame recoils upon the patrol.

37. A court-martial composed of the tribunes immediately sits to try him, and if he is found guilty, he is punished by beating (*fustuarium*). This is carried out as follows. The tribune takes a cudgel and lightly touches the condemned man with it, whereupon

all the soldiers fall upon him with clubs and stones, and usually kill him in the camp itself. But even those who contrive to escape are no better off. How indeed could they be? They are not allowed to return to their homes, and none of their family would dare to receive such a man into the house. Those who have once fallen into this misfortune are completely and finally ruined. The *optio* and the *decurio* of the squadron are liable to the same punishment if they fail to pass on the proper orders at the proper moment to the patrols and the *decurio* of the next squadron. The consequence of the extreme severity of this penalty and of the absolute impossibility of avoiding it is that the night watches of the Roman army are faultlessly kept.

The ordinary soldiers are answerable to the tribunes and the tribunes to the consuls. A tribune, and in the case of the allies a prefect, has power to inflict fines, distrain on goods, and to order a flogging. The punishment of beating to death is also inflicted upon those who steal from the camp, those who give false evidence, those who in full manhood commit homosexual offences, and finally upon anyone who has been punished three times for the same offence. The above are the offences which are punished as crimes. The following actions are regarded as unmanly and dishonourable in a soldier: to make a false report to the tribune of your courage in the field in order to earn distinction; to leave the post to which you have been assigned in a covering force because of fear; and similarly to throw away out of fear any of your weapons on the field of battle. For this reason the men who have been posted to a covering force are often doomed to certain death. This is because they will remain at their posts even when they are overwhelmingly outnumbered on account of their dread of the punishment that awaits them. Again, those who have lost a shield or a sword or any other weapon on the battlefield often hurl themselves upon the enemy hoping that they will either recover the weapon they have lost, or else escape by death from the inevitable disgrace and the humiliations they would suffer at home.

38. If it ever happens that a large body of men break and run in this way and whole maniples desert their posts under extreme pressure, the officers reject the idea of beating to death or executing all who are guilty, but the solution they adopt is as effective as it

is terrifying. The tribune calls the legion on parade and brings to the front those who are guilty of having left the ranks. He then reprimands them sharply, and finally chooses by lot some five or eight or twenty of the offenders, the number being calculated so that it represents about a tenth of those who have shown themselves guilty of cowardice. Those on whom the lot has fallen are mercilessly clubbed to death in the manner I have already described. The rest are put on rations of barley instead of wheat, and are ordered to quarter themselves outside the camp in a place which has no defences. The danger and the fear of drawing the fatal lot threatens every man equally, and since there is no certainty on whom it may fall, and the public disgrace of receiving rations of barley is shared by all alike, the Romans have adopted the best possible practice both to inspire terror and to repair the harm done by any weakening of their warlike spirit.

39. The Romans also have an excellent method of encouraging young soldiers to face danger. Whenever any have especially distinguished themselves in a battle, the general assembles the troops and calls forward those he considers to have shown exceptional courage. He praises them first for their gallantry in action and for anything in their previous conduct which is particularly worthy of mention, and then he distributes gifts such as the following: to a man who has wounded one of the enemy, a spear; to one who has killed and stripped an enemy, a cup if he is in the infantry, or horse-trappings if in the cavalry – originally the gift was simply a lance. These presentations are not made to men who have wounded or stripped an enemy in the course of a pitched battle, or at the storming of a city, but to those who during a skirmish or some similar situation in which there is no necessity to engage in single combat, have voluntarily and deliberately exposed themselves to danger.

At the storming of a city the first man to scale the wall is awarded a crown of gold. In the same way those who have shielded and saved one of their fellow-citizens or of the allies are honoured with gifts from the consul, and the men whose lives they have preserved present them of their own free will with a crown; if not, they are compelled to do so by the tribunes who judge the case. Moreover, a man who has been saved in this way reveres his rescuer as a father for the rest of his life and must treat him as if he were a parent. And so by means of such incentives even those who stay at home feel the impulse to emulate such achievements in the field no less than those who are present and see and hear what takes place. For the men who receive these trophies not only enjoy great prestige in the army and soon afterwards in their homes, but they are also singled out for precedence in religious processions when they return. On these occasions nobody is allowed to wear decorations save those who have been honoured for their bravery by the consuls, and it is the custom to hang up the trophies they have won in the most conspicuous places in their houses, and to regard them as proofs and visible symbols of their valour. So when we consider this people's almost obsessive concern with military rewards and punishments, and the immense importance which they attach to both, it is not surprising that they emerge with brilliant success from every war in which they engage.

For his pay the infantryman receives two *obols* a day, the centurion twice this amount, and the cavalryman a *drachma*. The infantry receive a ration of wheat equal to about two-thirds of an Attic *medimnus* a month, and the cavalry seven *medimni* of barley and two of wheat.[1] Among the allies, the infantry receive the same and the cavalry one and one-third *medimni* of wheat and five of barley. These rations are provided free to the allies, but in the case of the Roman troops the quaestor deducts from their pay the price of the wheat and their clothes, and any additional arms they may need.

40. The procedure adopted whenever the Romans break camp is as follows. As soon as the first signal is given, the men strike their tents and assemble their baggage, but no soldier may strike his tent or set it up until this has first been done for the tribunes and the consul. At the second signal they load the baggage on to the pack animals, and at the third the leading maniples must advance and set the whole camp in motion. As a rule the *extraordinarii* are placed at the head of the column; after them come the right wing of the allies and behind them their pack animals. Next in the order is

---

1. The infantryman received about half a bushel of wheat per month, the Roman cavalryman one and a half bushels of wheat and six of barley, and his allied counterpart three to four bushels of barley and one of wheat.

the first of the Roman legions with its baggage behind it, after which comes the second followed by its pack animals, together with the baggage train of the allies, who bring up the rear, the left wing of the allies providing the rearguard. The cavalry sometimes ride in the rear of their respective divisions, sometimes along with the baggage animals, so as to keep them together and protect them. When an attack is expected from the rear the same general formation is maintained, but the allied *extraordinarii* drop back and form the rearguard instead of the advanced guard. Of the two legions and wings, each takes it in turn to occupy the front or the rear position on alternate days; the purpose of this change of formation is to give all ranks an equal opportunity to find a fresh water-supply and fresh foraging ground.

If a situation of unusual danger threatens, however, they adopt a different order of march, assuming that there is sufficient open ground. In this case the army advances in three parallel columns, consisting of the *hastati*, *principes* and *triarii*. The baggage trains of the leading maniples are placed in front, those of the second immediately behind, and so on, the baggage trains being interspersed between the bodies of fighting troops, With this formation, if the column should be threatened, the troops face to the right or left, according to the direction from which the attack comes, and can then quickly get clear of the baggage and confront the enemy. Thus the infantry can take up its order of battle very rapidly and in a single movement – except that it might be necessary to wheel the *hastati* round the others[1] – while the mass of pack animals and their drivers are in their proper place during a battle, that is covered by a line of troops.

41. Whenever the army on the march draws near the place of encampment, one of the tribunes and those of the centurions who are in turn selected for this duty go ahead to survey the whole area where the camp is to be placed. They begin by determining the spot where the consul's tent should be pitched, according to the considerations I have described above, and on which side of

1. If the *hastati* were advancing in the right-hand column and the attack came from the left, the fighting troops would turn left and form three lines; the *hastati* would then be in the rear and would have to wheel around the rest to get into the front line.

this space to quarter the legions. Having decided this, they first measure out the area of the *praetorium*, next they draw the straight line along which the tents of the tribunes are set up, and then the line parallel to this, which marks the starting-point of the encampment area for the troops. In the same way they draw the lines on the other side of the *praetorium*, according to the plan which I have already described in detail. All this is done with little loss of time and the marking-out is an easy task, since all the distances are regulated and are familiar. They then proceed to plant flags: the first on the spot where the consul's tent is to stand, the second on that side of it which has been chosen for the camp, a third at the central point of the line on which the tribunes' tents will stand, and a fourth on the parallel line along which the legions will encamp. These latter flags are crimson, but the consul's is white. The lines on the other side of the *praetorium* are marked sometimes with flags of other colours, sometimes with plain spears. After this they proceed to lay out the streets between the various quarters, and plant spears to mark each street. The result is that when the legions on their march have arrived near enough to get a good view of the site, the whole plan quickly becomes familiar to everyone, as they can reckon from the position of the consul's flag, and get their bearings from that. Everyone knows exactly in which street and in which part of that street his tent will be situated, since every soldier invariably occupies the same position in the camp, and so the process of pitching camp is remarkably like the return of an army to its native city. When that happens, the troops leave their ranks at the city gate and each man makes straight for his home from there, and reaches it without difficulty because he knows both the quarter and the exact spot where his house is situated. The same thing happens in a Roman army's camp.

42. It is because the Romans in laying out a camp aim above all at ease of movement that their approach to the problem seems to me the exact opposite to that of the Greeks. The latter, when they choose, think above all of the security they can achieve by exploiting the natural strength of the position, first because they grudge the labour involved in entrenching, and secondly because they think that man-made defences are inferior to those provided by the natural features of the site. And so as regards the plan of the camp

as a whole they are compelled to adopt all kinds of shapes so as to conform to the lie of the ground, and to move the various parts of the army to unsuitable locations, with the result that everyone is uncertain as to the details of the camp and his own position in it. The Romans, on the other hand, prefer to undergo the fatigue of digging and other defensive preparations for the sake of having a consistent and uniform plan for a camp which is familiar to everybody. These are the most important facts concerning Roman military theory, and in particular concerning their method of encampment.

The Roman Republic Compared with Others

43. Almost all historians have commended to us the reputation for excellence of the constitutions of Sparta, Crete, Mantinea and Carthage, and several have also mentioned those of Athens and Thebes. I can agree with the praise of the first category, but I believe that little need be said of the systems of Athens and of Thebes. The rise of both of these states was abnormal; neither remained for long at the zenith of their power, and the decline which they suffered was on no modest scale. It was by a sudden stroke of chance that they obtained a spectacular predominance, but then, while still apparently flourishing and likely to remain so, they experienced a complete reverse of fortune. When they attacked the Lacedaemonians the Thebans were exploiting the senseless errors committed by their opponents, and the hatred which these had aroused among their allies; moreover, the reputation for superiority which they gained among the Greeks was due to the valour of one or at most two men who had observed these weaknesses. And indeed, Fortune soon proved that the successes which the Thebans gained at the time were due to the heroism of her leading men, not to the form of her constitution. It is well-known that the predominance of Thebes took its rise, attained its height and ceased with the lives of Pelopidas and Epaminondas, and we must conclude that the hegemony which she enjoyed at that time

was the work of her citizens and not of her system of government.

44. Much the same verdict must be passed on the Athenian constitution. It is true that the Athenians enjoyed more frequent periods of success, but the most glorious of all was the one which coincided with the admirable leadership of Themistocles.[1] Thereafter she experienced a complete reversal of fortune, which was due to the instability of the national character. For the Athenian populace is always more or less in the situation of a ship without a commander. So long as fear of the state of the sea or the occurrence of a storm obliges the sailors to behave sensibly and to obey the orders of the captain they do their duty admirably. But before long they become overconfident and begin to treat their superiors with contempt and to fall out with one another. Some are anxious to continue the voyage, while others urge the captain to bring the ship to anchor, some let out the sheets, while others hinder them and order the sails to be furled; and not only does the whole spectacle of their disunity and bickering appear disgraceful to any outside observer, but the situation is positively dangerous for all those who are taking part in the same voyage. The result which all too frequently follows is that after escaping the dangers of the wildest seas and the most violent storms, they succeed in wrecking the ship when it is within harbour and within reach of the shore.

This is precisely the fate which has more than once befallen the Athenian system of government. After warding off the greatest and most terrible dangers through the heroism of her people and their leaders, the state has passed into periods of unclouded tranquillity, and then quite gratuitously and senselessly suffered complete breakdown. For this reason I need say no more about this constitution[2] or that of Thebes, since both are states in which the

1. Themistocles' period of leadership lasted from about 489 to 480 B.C. and culminated in the victory over the Persian fleet at Salamis.

2. Polybius condemns the Athenian constitution compared with the Roman for two reasons: first, that it was not 'mixed' and so did not contain adequate checks and balances, and secondly, that it failed to keep an empire. But the power of Athens of which Themistocles laid the foundation was, at any rate in modern eyes, consolidated by Pericles. Thus Polybius seems to regard as a period of decline the very years which modern readers would regard as the golden age of Athens, i.e. the period between the Persian and the

masses take all decisions according to their random impulses. In the case of Athens the populace is headstrong and spiteful; in that of Thebes it has been trained to grow up with habits of violence and ferocity.

45. When we turn to the constitution of Crete, there are two points which particularly call for attention. How could the most learned of the writers of earlier times, namely Ephorus, Xenophon, Callisthenes and Plato, claim in the first place that it resembled the constitution of Sparta, and secondly that it was worthy of admiration? I do not believe that either of these assertions is true, and I base my opinion on the following facts. Let me deal first with its dissimilarity to the Spartan constitution. We may name three distinguishing features of the latter. First of all, there are the land laws according to which no one citizen may own more land than another, but all are to possess an equal share of the public land. The second concerns the acquisition of money: since money is a commodity which was quite discredited among the Spartans, it follows that any rivalry which might arise from the possession of more or less of it is completely eliminated from the constitution. The third is the fact that of those officials by whom or with whose cooperation the whole administration is carried on, the kings hold a permanent office, while the members of the Senate are appointed for life.

46. Among the Cretans the practice in these matters is exactly the opposite. Their laws permit the citizen to acquire land without any restriction – the sky is the limit, as the saying is – and money is held in such high regard among them that the possession of it is regarded as not merely necessary, but also as most honourable. And indeed, avarice and greed are so much ingrained in the Cretan character that they are the only people in the world who consider no form of gain to be shameful. Again, their public offices are held on an annual tenure and through democratic election. In view of all this I have often felt at a loss to understand how the authors mentioned above can maintain that two constitutions which embody such diametrically opposed characteristics possess common

---

Peloponnesian Wars (480–434 B.C.). His criticisms of the democracy refer in the main to the late fifth and the fourth century B.C.

features and are akin to one another. Besides overlooking such differences, these writers make lengthy comments into the bargain on the work of Lycurgus, claiming that he was the only legislator who grasped the essentials of the problem.

Now every state relies for its preservation on two fundamental qualities, namely bravery in the face of the enemy, and harmony among its citizens; and Lycurgus, by eliminating the desire for wealth, eliminated at the same time civil discord and strife. And so the Lacedaemonians, since they have been delivered from these evils, excel all the other Greeks both in the conduct of their internal affairs and in their spirit of unity. Having made this assertion, these writers observe at the same time that the Cretans, because of their ingrained craving for wealth, are involved in frequent seditions, public and private, murders, massacres and civil wars; yet this fact they consider immaterial, and still have the audacity to argue that the two political systems have much in common. Ephorus, indeed, apart from the names, uses the same terms to explain the political complexion of the two states, so that if one did not note the proper names, there would be no means of knowing which of the two he was describing.

The above are the points in which I believe these two political systems differ, and I shall now explain why I think the Cretan constitution should neither be praised nor imitated.

47. In my opinion there are two basic elements in every political system, by virtue of which its true form and quality are either desirable or the opposite. By these I mean its customs and its laws. The desirable ones are those which make men's private lives virtuous and well-disciplined and the public character of the state civilized and just; the undesirable are those which have the opposite effect. So when we see that the customs and laws of any given people are good, we can conclude with confidence that the citizens and their constitution will likewise be good; and on the same principle when we see a community in which private life is characterized by greed and avarice and public conduct by injustice, then clearly we have good reason to pronounce their laws, their particular customs and their constitution in general to be bad. Now with a few rare exceptions it would be impossible to find private conduct more deceitful nor public policy more unjust than that which

prevails in Crete. Accordingly, since I cannot regard the Cretan constitution as being either similar to the Spartan or as in any way deserving praise or imitation in itself, I dismiss it from the comparison which I have proposed to make.

As for Plato's celebrated republic, which is highly praised by certain philosophers, I do not think it admissible that this should be brought into the argument about constitutions. For just as we do not allow artists or athletes who are not duly registered[1] or have not been in training to take part in festivals or games, so we should not admit the Platonic constitution to this contest for the prize of merit, unless some example can be provided of it in action. Up to the present, at any rate, the idea of comparing it with the constitutions of Sparta, Rome or Carthage would be like bringing forward some statue and then comparing it with living and breathing men. For even if the statue were absolutely perfect in respect of its workmanship, the comparison of a lifeless object with a living being would strike the spectators as quite inadequate and incongruous.

48. I shall therefore omit constitutions of this kind, and continue with my account of that of Sparta. It seems to me that from the point of view of ensuring harmony among the citizens, keeping Spartan territory intact, and preserving the liberty of his country, Lycurgus' legislation and the foresight which he displayed were so admirable that one can only regard his wisdom as something divine rather than human. The equal division of landed property together with the simple diet and the practice of eating it communally which he instituted were well-calculated to create a temperate and disciplined private life, and to protect the community as a whole from dissensions and civil strife, as was his training in the endurance of hardships and dangers to produce a breed of noble and courageous men. Now when both these virtues, courage and self-discipline, are combined in one soul or one state, evil will not easily spring from such a soil, nor will such men easily be overcome by their neighbours. And so by constructing his constitution in this spirit and out of these elements, Lycurgus ensured the absolute safety of the whole territory of Sparta and bequeathed to the Spartans

1. This refers to the associations or guilds of performers who competed at such festivals, especially actors and singers.

their freedom as a lasting inheritance. But as regards the annexation of neighbouring territories, or the assertion of their supremacy in Greece, or the pursuit of a wider policy of aggrandizement, he seems to have made no provision whatever, either in particular legislation or in the general constitution of the state. What he had still to do was to impose on his countrymen either some necessity or else an established principle whereby just as he had made them simple and contented in their private lives, so the spirit of the city should be rendered similarly moderate and contented in its public policy. But as it was, while he made them into disinterested and sensible individuals in their private activities and their internal institutions, as regards their attitude to the rest of the Greeks he left them ambitious, eager for supremacy, and acquisitive in the highest degree.

49. It is notorious, for example, that the Spartans were among the first of the Greeks to cast a covetous eye upon the territory of their neighbours, and that they made war upon the Messenians out of greed and for the purpose of enslaving them. Besides this, all the historians are at one in recording how out of sheer obstinacy they bound themselves by an oath never to break off the siege of Messene until they had captured the place.[1] And finally it is common knowledge that because of their craving for supremacy they were obliged to take orders from the very people whom they had conquered in battle. For when the Persians invaded Greece, the Spartans overcame them as champions of the freedom of Greece, yet after the invaders had retired and fled, the Spartans betrayed the Greek cities of Asia Minor to them through the Peace of Antalcidas, to obtain the money which would enable them to establish their supremacy over the rest of the Greeks.[2] And it was then that an important defect in their constitution revealed itself.

So long as their ambitions extended only to ruling over their neighbours or the inhabitants of the Peloponnese, they found the

1. Probably towards the end of the eighth century B.C.
2. As a result of Lysander's agreement with Cyrus in 407, Persia made money available to Sparta to assist her in the Peloponnesian War against Athens. The Peace of Antalcidas was negotiated in 387 B.C., and the Greek cities in Asia Minor, which the Spartan King Agesilaus had freed during his invasion of Persian territory, reverted to Persian rule.

supplies and resources which their own country could provide were sufficient, since all the provisions needed for their campaigns were at hand, and they could quickly return home to revictual or else send supplies to the army. But once they had begun to make expeditions by sea or to fight campaigns outside the Peloponnese, it became clear that neither their iron currency nor the exchange of their crops for the commodities they lacked could provide for their needs so long as they remained confined by Lycurgus' economic legislation, since these enterprises required a currency which was in universal circulation and a supply of goods from foreign sources. The result was that the Spartans were compelled to become petitioners to the Persians, to impose tribute on the Greek islanders, and to exact contributions from the rest of the Greeks. They were compelled to recognize that if they retained the Lycurgan system, it would be impossible to exert any important influence on affairs, let alone achieve the hegemony of Greece.

50. What then is the object of this digression? I wished to show in the light of historical fact that for the purpose of guarding a nation's territory securely and maintaining its liberty Lycurgus' constitution is perfectly adequate to its task. Thus from the point of view of those who hold that this is the supreme end of a constitution, we must admit that there is not and never was a preferable constitution or political system. But if a statesman aspires to larger ambitions than these, and finds greater prestige and honour in putting himself at the head of multitudes, becoming the ruler of vast areas and populations and causing the eyes of the whole world to be turned towards him, then we must admit that the Spartan constitution is deficient, and that the Roman is superior and certainly better devised for the attainment of power. The proof of this is that when the Lacedaemonians attempted to win supremacy in Greece it was not long before they were in danger of losing their own liberty, whereas the Romans, who had aimed in the first place merely at establishing their dominion over the Italians, went on in a very short time to bring the whole world under their rule, and in this achievement the abundance of supplies which they had at their disposal played no small part.

51. The constitution of Carthage seems to me to have been well-designed at the outset in its most important features. The

Carthaginians had kings, the assembly of elders had the powers of an aristocracy, and the people were supreme in such matters as were appropriate, so that the general framework of the state was similar to that of Rome and Sparta. But at the time when the Hannibalic War began, the political state of Carthage was in decline, while that of Rome was growing better. Every organism, every state and every activity passes through a natural cycle, first of growth, then of maturity and finally of decay, and since the component parts are at their strongest when it reaches its zenith, it was for this reason that the difference between the two states displayed itself at this moment. The power and prosperity of Carthage had developed far earlier than that of Rome, and in proportion to this her strength had begun to decline, while that of Rome was at its height. at least so far as her system of government was concerned. Accordingly, at Carthage the influence of the people had already become predominant in the councils of state, while at Rome the Senate still had the decisive voice. This meant that in the one case the deliberations were conducted by the masses, and in the other by the most eminent men, with the result that the decisions on public policy made by the Romans proved superior; in other words, although they suffered several overwhelming disasters in the field, the wisdom of their counsels finally enabled them to overcome the Carthaginians in the war.

52. Let us now consider differences of detail, such as, in the first place, the conduct of the war. Here we find that in operations at sea the Carthaginians, as might be expected, were better trained and equipped, because seamanship had long been their national calling and they occupy themselves with the sea more than any other people; but in military campaigns the Romans train themselves to an altogether higher standard. In fact they devote their whole energies to this aspect of war, whereas the Carthaginians largely neglect their infantry, though they do show some degree of interest in their cavalry. The reason for this is that they employ foreign and mercenary troops, whereas those of the Romans are citizens and natives of their own country; so in this respect too we must judge the Roman political system to be superior to the Carthaginian. The Carthaginians depend at all times on the courage of mercenaries to safeguard their prospects of freedom, but the

345

Romans rely on the bravery of their own citizens and the help of their allies. The result is that even if they happen to be defeated at the outset, the Romans carry on the war with all their resources, but this is impossible for the Carthaginians. For the Romans, knowing themselves to be fighting for their country and their children, can never weaken in the fury of their struggle, but continue to fight with all their heart and soul until the enemy is overcome. It follows that although the Romans are, as I have mentioned, much less skilled in the handling of their naval forces, they nevertheless prove successful in the end, because of the gallantry of their men; for although skill in seamanship is of great importance in naval battles, it is the courage of the marines which proves the decisive factor in winning a victory. The fact is that Italians in general have a natural advantage over Phoenicians and Africans both in physical strength and in personal courage, but at the same time their institutions contribute very powerfully towards fostering a spirit of bravery in their young men. I quote just one example to illustrate the pains taken by the Roman state to produce men who will endure anything to win a reputation for valour in their country.

53. Whenever one of their celebrated men dies, in the course of the funeral procession his body is carried with every kind of honour into the Forum to the so-called Rostra, sometimes in an upright position so as to be conspicuous, or else, more rarely, recumbent. The whole mass of the people stand round to watch, and his son, if he has left one of adult age who can be present, or if not some other relative, then mounts the Rostra and delivers an address which recounts the virtues and the successes achieved by the dead man during his lifetime. By these means the whole populace – not only those who played some part in these exploits, but those who did not – are involved in the ceremony, so that when the facts of the dead man's career are recalled to their minds and brought before their eyes, their sympathies are so deeply engaged that the loss seems not to be confined to the mourners but to be a public one which affects the whole people. Then after the burial of the body and the performance of the customary ceremonies, they place the image of the dead man in the most conspicuous position in the house, where it is enclosed in a wooden shrine. This image consists

of a mask, which is fashioned with extraordinary fidelity both in its modelling and its complexion to represent the features of the dead man. On occasions when public sacrifices are offered, these masks are displayed and are decorated with great care. And when any distinguished member of the family dies, the masks are taken to the funeral, and are there worn by men who are considered to bear the closest resemblance to the original, both in height and in their general appearance and bearing.[1] These substitutes are dressed according to the rank of the deceased: a toga with a purple border for a consul or praetor, a completely purple garment for a censor, and one embroidered with gold for a man who had celebrated a triumph or performed some similar exploit.

They all ride in chariots with the fasces, axes, and other insignia carried before them, according to the dignity of the offices of state which the dead man had held in his lifetime, and when they arrive at the Rostra they all seat themselves in a row upon chairs of ivory. It would be hard to imagine a more impressive scene for a young man who aspires to win fame and to practise virtue. For who could remain unmoved at the sight of the images of all these men who have won renown in their time, now gathered together as if alive and breathing? What spectacle could be more glorious than this?

54. Moreover, the speaker who pronounces the oration over the man who is about to be buried, when he has delivered his tribute, goes on to relate the successes and achievements of all the others whose images are displayed there, beginning with the oldest. By this constant renewal of the good report of brave men, the fame of those who have performed any noble deed is made immortal, and the renown of those who have served their country well becomes a matter of common knowledge and a heritage for posterity. But the most important consequence of the ceremony is that it inspires young men to endure the extremes of suffering for the common good in the hope of winning the glory that waits upon the brave. And what I have just said is attested by the facts. Many Romans have volunteered to engage in single combat so as to decide a whole battle, and not a few have chosen certain death, some in war to save the lives of their countrymen, others in times

1. The man chosen was normally a member of the family, but there are instances of the deceased having been represented by an actor.

of peace to ensure the safety of the Republic. Besides this, there have been instances of men in office who have put their own sons[1] to death, contrary to every law or custom, because they valued the interest of their country more dearly than their natural ties to their own flesh and blood. Many stories of this kind can be told of many men in Roman history, but one in particular will serve as an example and a proof of my contention.

55. The story goes that while Horatius Cocles[2] was engaged in combat with two of the enemy at the far end of the bridge over the Tiber which gives entrance to the city on the west, he saw a large body of reinforcements approaching. Fearing that they would succeed in forcing the passage and entering the city, he turned round and shouted to those behind him to retire at once and make haste to break down the bridge. His comrades obeyed, and all the time that they were demolishing it Horatius stood his ground. He suffered many wounds, but he held back the enemy's attack and astounded them not so much by his physical strength as by his endurance and courage. Once the bridge was cut the enemy's advance was halted, whereupon Cocles threw himself into the river still wearing his armour and weapons. He deliberately sacrificed himself because he valued the safety of his country and the glory which would later attach itself to his name more than his present existence and the years of life that remained to him. This is a typical example, it seems to me, of the spirit of emulation and the ambition to perform deeds of gallantry which the customs of the Romans help to implant in their young men.

56. Again, the Roman laws and customs which concern money transactions are superior to those of Carthage. In the latter country no activity which results in a profit is seen as a cause for reproach, but to the Romans nothing is more disgraceful than to receive bribes or to seek gain by improper means. Just as they whole-heartedly approve the acquisition of money if the methods are

1. e.g. Lucius Junius Brutus for conspiracy (Livy, *Early History of Rome*, II. 5), and Titus Manlius Torquatus for indiscipline (Livy, op. cit., VIII. 7).
2. Polybius treats this famous legend as a historical event, and probably places it in the context of the wars against Lars Porsenna and the Tarquins. According to Livy's version (op. cit., II. 10), which is the source of Macaulay's poem, Horatius swam safely to land.

reputable, so they condemn it absolutely if the sources are forbidden. An illustration of this is the fact that among the Carthaginians bribery is openly practised by candidates for office, whereas at Rome it is a capital offence. And so, as the rewards offered to merit are precisely the opposite in the two countries, it is natural that the methods employed to obtain them should be equally dissimilar.

However, the sphere in which the Roman commonwealth seems to me to show its superiority most decisively is in that of religious belief. Here we find that the very phenomenon which among other peoples[1] is regarded as a subject for reproach, namely superstition, is actually the element which holds the Roman state together. These matters are treated with such solemnity and introduced so frequently both into public and into private life that nothing could exceed them in importance. Many people may find this astonishing, but my own view is that the Romans have adopted these practices for the sake of the common people. This approach might not have been necessary had it ever been possible to form a state composed entirely of wise men. But as the masses are always fickle, filled with lawless desires, unreasoning anger and violent passions, they can only be restrained by mysterious terrors or other dramatizations of the subject. For this reason I believe that the ancients were by no means acting foolishly or haphazardly when they introduced to the people various notions concerning the gods and belief in the punishments of Hades, but rather that the moderns are foolish and take great risks in rejecting them. At any rate the result is that among the Greeks, apart from anything else, men who hold public office cannot be trusted with the safe-keeping of so much as a single talent, even if they have ten accountants and as many seals and twice as many witnesses, whereas among the Romans their magistrates handle large sums of money and scrupulously perform their duty because they have given their word on oath. Among other nations it is a rare phenomenon to find a man who keeps his hands off public funds and whose record is clean in this respect, while among the Romans it is quite the exception to find a man who has been detected in such conduct.

1. In particular among the Greeks.

Conclusion

57. The fact, then, that all existing things are subject to decay is a proposition which scarcely requires proof, since the inexorable course of nature is sufficient to impose it on us. Every kind of state, we may say, is liable to decline from two sources, the one being external, and the other due to its own internal evolution. For the first we cannot lay down any fixed principle, but the second pursues a regular sequence. I have already indicated which kind of state is the first to evolve, which succeeds it, and how each is transformed into its successor, so that those who can connect the opening propositions of my argument with its conclusion will be able to make their own forecast concerning the future. This, in my opinion, is quite clear. When a state, after warding off many great perils, achieves supremacy and uncontested sovereignty, it is evident that under the influence of long-established prosperity life will become more luxurious, and among the citizens themselves rivalry for office and in other spheres of activity will become fiercer than it should. As these symptoms become more marked, the craving for office and the sense of humiliation which obscurity imposes, together with the spread of ostentation and extravagance, will usher in a period of general deterioration. The principal authors of this change will be the masses, who at some moments will believe that they have a grievance against the greed of other members of society, and at others are made conceited by the flattery of those who aspire to office. By this stage they will have been roused to fury and their deliberations will constantly be swayed by passion, so that they will no longer consent to obey or even to be the equals of their leaders, but will demand everything or by far the greatest share for themselves. When this happens, the constitution will change its *name* to the one which sounds the most imposing of all, that of freedom and democracy, but its *nature* to that which is the worst of all, that is the rule of the mob.

Now that I have described the formation of the Roman state, its rise, the attainment of its zenith, and its present condition, and likewise the differences for better or worse between it and the other constitutions, I will bring this study to an end.

58. I return, then, to the period which follows immediately after the date at which I began this digression, but first I propose to single out one episode for brief mention. My purpose in doing this is to give an illustration, not just in theory but in practice, of the perfection and the strength of the Roman constitution as it then existed, as though I were exhibiting one work as a specimen to reveal the skill of a fine artist.

After his victory at Cannae Hannibal captured the 8,000 Roman soldiers who had been left to guard their camp, but he then allowed them to send a deputation to Rome to discuss the matter of their ransom and release. The troops selected ten of their leaders, whom Hannibal sent off, after exacting an oath that they would return to him. One of these men, just as he was going beyond the palisade of the camp, said that he had forgotten something, and after collecting what he had left behind, once more set out, imagining that since he had returned he had kept his promise and released himself from his oath. On their arrival in Rome, the delegates begged and entreated the Senate not to grudge the prisoners their release, but to allow each to pay three *minae* and return to his people, for Hannibal, they said, had granted this concession. They pleaded further that the men deserved to be released, for they had not been guilty of cowardice in the fighting, nor had they done anything unworthy of Rome. They had been left behind to guard the camp, and after all the rest of the army had perished, they had been compelled by circumstances to surrender to the enemy. Yet although the Romans had suffered crushing reverses in the war, had lost virtually all their allies and expected from day to day that their city itself would be threatened, still, after listening to this plea they neither forgot their dignity under pressure of calamity nor allowed themselves to lose sight of what had to be done. They recognized that Hannibal's object was at once to lay his hands on some money and to sap the fighting spirit of the troops opposed to him by suggesting that even when they were beaten they still had a chance of safety. Therefore the Senate, so far from granting this request refused to allow either pity for their compatriots or any consideration of the service those men might render in future to prevail. They frustrated Hannibal's calculations and all the hopes he had built on these by declining to ransom the prisoners. At the same time they established the rule for their own men that they must either conquer or die on the field, since if they were beaten no hope of safety remained for them. After they had passed this resolution they dismissed the nine delegates, who then returned to Hannibal of their own free will, because they were bound by their oath. As for the man who had tried to free himself from his pledge by a trick, they put him in chains and sent him back to the enemy. In this way Hannibal experienced less joy from his victory than disappointment, when he saw with amazement the unshaken resolve and the lofty spirit which the Romans showed in their resolutions.

BOOK VII

Affairs in Sicily

2. After the plot against King Hieronymus[1] of Syracuse and the
departure of Thraso, the young King's uncles, Zoippus and
Adranodorus, persuaded him to lose no time in sending ambassadors to Hannibal. He accordingly selected Polycleitus of Cyrene
and Philodemus of Argos and sent them to Italy with instructions
to discuss a joint plan of action with the Carthaginians. At the
same time he sent his brothers to Alexandria. Hannibal received
Polycleitus and Philodemus hospitably, held out encouraging
prospects to the young King, and sent back the ambassadors without delay accompanied by his namesake, Hannibal, who commanded the Carthaginian squadron of triremes in Italy, together with
the Syracusan Hippocrates and his younger brother Epicydes. It so
happened that both these men had been serving for some time under
Hannibal; they had adopted Carthage as their country since their
grandfather had been exiled because he was believed to have
assassinated Agatharchus, one of the sons of Agathocles. The
ambassadors duly returned to Syracuse; there Polycleitus presented his report and the Carthaginian delegate delivered the
message entrusted to him by Hannibal, whereupon the King immediately showed his willingness to make an agreement with the
Carthaginians. He urged that this Hannibal who had come to him
should proceed at once to Carthage, and promised to send delegates
of his own to negotiate with the Carthaginians.

3. Meanwhile the Roman praetor at Lilybaeum had received
reports of these events, and sent envoys to Hieronymus to renew
the treaty which had been made with the King's ancestors. In the
presence of the Carthaginian delegation Hieronymus declared that
he felt sorry for the Romans on account of the resounding defeats

1. Hieronymus had succeeded his grandfather, Hiero II, with whom the
Romans had had a treaty of alliance, in 216 B.C.

353

they had suffered at the hands of the Carthaginians in the fighting in Italy. The Roman envoys were dumbfounded at his want of tact, but nevertheless inquired what was his source of information, whereupon the King pointed to the Carthaginians who were present and invited the Romans to refute the report if it were untrue. The Romans retorted that it was not their custom to accept the word of their enemies, and advised him to do nothing to infringe the existing treaty. Such a policy would not only be correct in itself, but would work in his own best interests. Hieronymus replied that he would consider the matter and inform the delegation, but he also inquired why before his grandfather's death a Roman squadron of fifty ships had sailed as far as Cape Pachynus and then returned again. The fact was that a short while before, the Romans had received a report that Hiero had died. They feared that some elements in Syracuse might take advantage of the youth of his heir to overrun the government, and so had ordered this cruise, but as soon as they had learned that Hiero was still alive, the ships had returned to Lilybaeum. The Romans therefore admitted that the ships had sailed, their purpose being to protect him in view of his youth and to help him maintain his authority, but on receipt of the news that his grandfather was still alive, they had sailed back again. At this the young man exclaimed, 'Then allow me too, my Roman friends, to maintain my authority by "sailing back" to see what I can get from Carthage!' The Romans saw clearly enough where his sympathies lay and did not prolong the discussion; they returned to Lilybaeum where they reported the outcome of the meeting to the praetor who had sent them. From that time on the Romans kept watch on the King and regarded him as an enemy.

4. Hieronymus then chose Agatharchus, Onesigenes and Hipposthenes as his envoys and sent them to Carthage with Hannibal, instructing them to make a treaty on the following terms. The Carthaginians were to assist him with land and sea forces and after expelling the Romans from Sicily, they were to partition the island so that the boundary of their respective provinces would be the river Himera, which almost exactly divides the island in half. On arriving in Carthage the delegates opened negotiations and pursued the discussions, in which they found the Carthaginians prepared to meet them on every point. But meanwhile Hippocrates

and his brother had brought the young Hieronymus entirely under their influence. They began by exciting his imagination with their accounts of Hannibal's marches and tactics and pitched battles in Italy, and then went on to tell him that nobody had a better right to rule over the whole of Sicily than himself. In the first place he was the son of Nereis, the daughter of King Pyrrhus of Epirus, the only man whom all the Sicilians had accepted as their leader and king, by their free choice and out of affection for him, and secondly he was the heir to the sovereign rights of his grandfather Hiero. In the end the two so won over the young man through their talk that he paid no attention to anyone else; this was partly because he possessed a naturally unstable character, but still more because they had raised his ambitions to giddy heights. And so while Agatharchus and his colleagues were still negotiating in Carthage along the lines of their original instructions, Hieronymus sent off another delegation whose members claimed that the sovereignty of the whole of Sicily was his by right, demanded that the Carthaginians should help him to recover the island, and promised to support them in their Italian campaign. The Carthaginians now clearly perceived the full extent of the young man's instability and unbalanced condition, but they still considered that it would be in many ways against their interests to abandon Sicilian affairs. They therefore agreed to all of Hieronymus' demands, and having previously made ready a number of ships and troops, they set about arranging to transport their forces to Sicily.

5. As soon as the Romans learned of this, they dispatched envoys to Hieronymus to protest against his violation of the treaty made with his ancestors. The King then summoned his council and asked their advice as to what action he should take. The Sicilian members remained silent since they feared for their ruler's lack of judgement, but Aristomachus of Corinth, Damippus of Lacedaemon, and Autonous of Thessaly all advised him to adhere to his treaty with the Romans. Adranodorus was alone in urging him not to let the opportunity slip, on the ground that this was his only chance of establishing his sovereignty over the whole of Sicily. After he had spoken, the King asked Hippocrates and his brother for their opinion, and when they replied that they took the same view as Adranodorus, the meeting of the council was terminated.

This was how the decision was taken to go to war against Rome. Hieronymus was anxious to leave the impression that he had dealt adroitly with the Roman envoys, but in the event he mishandled the interview so badly as to make it certain that he would not only fail to conciliate them but would cause them most serious offence. He declared that he would abide by the treaty on condition first that the Romans repaid him all the gold they had received from his grandfather Hiero; secondly that they returned the corn and other gifts they had received during the whole of Hiero's reign; and thirdly that they acknowledged that all the towns and the country lying east of the river Himera belonged to Syracuse. It was on these terms that the Roman envoys and the Syracusan council parted, and from that moment Hieronymus pressed forward his preparations for war, mobilizing and arming his forces and making ready his other supplies.

7. Some of the historians who have described the fall of Hieronymus have written at great length, and introduced an element of the supernatural into the story by reporting the various prodigies that preceded his reign and the misfortunes that befell the Syracusans. They have painted in dramatic colours the cruelty of his character, and the impious nature of his actions, and finally the strange and terrible circumstances that attended his death, so that to judge from their accounts neither Phalaris[1] nor Apollodorus[2] nor any other tyrant would seem to have been more ferocious than he. The fact remains, however, that he was a mere boy when he came to power, and that he lived for no more than thirteen months after his accession. In this space of time it is possible that one or two men may have been tortured and some of his friends or other Syracusans executed, but it is hardly likely that his rule can have been extravagantly wicked or his impiety outrageous. It must be admitted that his character was exceptionally erratic and violent, but it cannot be compared with that of the other tyrants I have named. The truth

1. Phalaris, the tyrant of Agrigentum from 571–555 B.C., was notorious for his cruelty, and is alleged to have roasted his enemies alive in a brazen bull.

2. Apollodorus was a democratic leader in the city of Cassandreia in the Chalcidice peninsula (in the time of Thucydides the place was known as Potidaea). Apollodorus seized power with the help of a band of Gaulish mercenaries and ruled from about 279–76 B.C.

of the matter, as it seems to me, is that those who write the history of particular episodes, whenever they have to deal with a subject which is narrowly limited in its interest, are compelled by sheer lack of subject-matter to exaggerate the importance of trivial incidents and to write at great length on matters which are scarcely worth mentioning at all. There are some also who make the same kind of mistake through sheer lack of judgement. How much more to the point it would be if the space given by such a writer to those topics which at present merely fill up and spin out his books were devoted to the reigns of Hiero and of Gelo without even mentioning Hieronymus! This would at once be more enjoyable for the curious reader and more useful to the student of history.

8. Hiero is in the first place a more interesting subject because he established himself as the ruler of Syracuse and her allies entirely through his own abilities, for he owed neither wealth, nor reputation nor anything else to Fortune. Most remarkable of all, he achieved his position by his own efforts, without killing, banishing or injuring a single citizen, and not only acquired but also maintained his power in the same fashion. During a reign of fifty-four years he kept his country at peace and his authority undisturbed by conspiracies, and he even contrived to escape envy, which all too often pursues a man of superior abilities; indeed on more than one occasion when he tried to lay down his power, he was prevented from doing so by the united action of the citizens. He not only conferred great benefits on the Greeks, but took trouble to win their good opinion, and at the end he left behind him a great personal reputation and a legacy of universal goodwill towards the Syracusans. And although he lived throughout his reign in the midst of affluence, luxury and lavish expenditure, yet he survived for more than ninety years and retained all his faculties, as well as keeping every part of his body unimpaired – the strongest testimony, as it seems to me, of the balance and sobriety of his life.

Gelo, his son, who lived to the age of over fifty, made it his highest object in life to obey his father and not to consider wealth or royal power or anything else as more valuable than affection and loyalty to his parents.

Affairs in Greece

THE TREATY BETWEEN HANNIBAL AND PHILIP OF

MACEDON

9. 'This is a sworn treaty between Hannibal the general, Mago, Myrcan, Barmocar, such other members of the Carthaginian Senate as were present with him, and all Carthaginians serving under him on the one side, and on the other side Xenophanes, son of Cleomachus the Athenian, the envoy whom King Philip of Macedon, son of Demetrius, sent to us to represent him, together with the Macedonians and their allies.

The oath is taken in the presence of Zeus, Hera and Apollo; in the presence of the god of Carthage, of Hercules and of Iolaus; in the presence of Ares, Triton and Poseidon; in the presence of the gods who fight on our side, and of the sun, the moon and the earth; in the presence of rivers, harbours and waters; in the presence of all the gods who rule Carthage; in the presence of all the gods who rule Macedonia and the rest of Greece; in the presence of all the gods of war who preside over this oath.

Hannibal the general and those with him and all the Carthaginian senators with him and all the Carthaginians serving in his army propose that in respect of what seems good to you and to us we should make this sworn treaty of friendship and goodwill and become as friends, kinsmen and brothers on the following conditions.

First, that King Philip and the Macedonians and those of the rest of the Greeks who are their allies should protect the Carthaginians, the sovereign people, Hannibal their general and all those peoples who live under Carthaginian rule and observe the same laws; likewise the people of Utica and all cities and tribes that are subject to Carthage, and our soldiers and allies: likewise all cities and tribes in Italy, Cisalpine Gaul and Liguria with whom we are in alliance, and with whomsoever in this country we may hereafter enter into an alliance.

Second, that King Philip and the Macedonians and those of the rest of the Greeks who are their allies shall be protected and guarded by the Carthaginians who are serving with us, by the people of Utica, and by all cities and tribes that are subject to Carthage, by our allies and soldiers and by all peoples in Italy, Cisalpine Gaul and Liguria who are our allies, and by such others as may hereafter enter into alliance with us in Italy and the adjacent regions.

Third, that we shall form no plots, nor set ambushes against one another, but with all sincerity and goodwill, and without subterfuge or secret design we shall be the enemies of those who make war against the Carthaginians, always excepting those kings, cities and nations with whom we have sworn treaties and friendships.

Fourth, that we shall likewise be the enemies of those who make war against King Philip, always excepting the kings, cities and peoples with whom we have sworn treaties and friendships.

Fifth, that you will be our allies in the war in which we are now engaged against the Romans, until such time as the gods grant victory to us and to you, and you will give us such help as we may need or as we shall mutually determine.

Sixth, that when the gods have granted us victory in the war against the Romans and their allies, if the Romans shall request the Carthaginians to make terms of peace, we shall make such an agreement as shall include you too, and on the following conditions:

That the Romans shall never be permitted to make war on you;

That the Romans shall no longer rule over Corcyra, Apollonia, Epidamnus, Pharos, Dimale, the Parthini, or Atintania,[1] and that they shall hand back to Demetrius of Pharos those of his friends who are at present in territory under the rule of Rome.

Seventh, if the Romans ever make war upon you or upon us, we shall give help to one another in this conflict as may be required on either side.

Eighth, the same action shall follow if any other nation makes war upon you or upon us, always excepting those kings, cities, or peoples with whom we have sworn treaties of alliance.

Ninth, if we decide to remove from or add to this sworn treaty, we shall remove or add only such clauses as both of us may determine.'

1. These were all towns and islands on the Adriatic coast ruled over by Demetrius of Pharos before he was driven out by the Romans. See p. 195.

THE CHARACTER OF PHILIP

11. I propose to interrupt my narrative here to say a few words on the subject of Philip, since it was this point in his career which marked the beginning of the change and deterioration in his character. This, it seems to me, is a most striking example, which deserves the attention of any practical statesman who wishes to profit from the study of history, to however small a degree. The prominence of his position and the brilliance of his genius ensured that both the good and evil impulses of this King were equally conspicuous and widely known throughout all Greece; and so too were the practical consequences of these impulses when they were contrasted with one another. At the time of his accession to the throne the provinces of Thessaly and Macedonia and indeed all the other parts of his kingdom were more loyal and well-disposed towards him than they had been to any of his predecessors, even though he had succeeded to the crown at such an early age, and this fact is easily proved by the following evidence. Although he was frequently called away from Macedonia on account of the war between the Lacedaemonians and the Aetolians, not only did none of these peoples revolt, but none of the barbarian tribes who lived on the frontier ventured to touch Macedonia.

Again, it would be impossible to speak too highly of the affection and devotion which Alexander, Chrysogonus and his other friends showed towards him, nor is there any doubt that within a short space of time the Peloponnesians, Boeotians, Epirots and Acarnanians all benefited greatly from his actions. Indeed, to use a somewhat extravagant phrase, it could be said very aptly of Philip that his benevolent policy made him the darling of Greece. For example there is a most conspicuous and striking proof of the value of high principles and good faith in the fact that the Cretans, after they had reached an understanding with one another and formed a general alliance, proceeded to elect Philip the protector of the whole island, and that this settlement was reached without any recourse to fighting or violence, something for which it would be difficult to find a precedent in the whole history of Crete. And yet, after his attack on the Messenians all these beneficent tendencies suffered a total change, and this transformation was quite logical. For as he completely reversed his own principles, so it was inevitable that he should also transform other men's opinion of him, and that he should meet with completely different results in his various undertakings. At any rate this was what happened, and the events I am about to relate will make this transformation quite clear to those who follow me with care.

12. When Philip decided to seize the citadel of Messene he told the magistrates of the city that he wished to visit the place to offer a sacrifice to Zeus. He climbed the acropolis with his attendants, and when, as is the usual custom, he was offered the entrails of the slaughtered victim, he took them in his hands, and stepping to one side he held them out to Aratus and those who were with him, and asked the question, 'What does this sacrifice signify? Should I withdraw from the citadel or stay in possession of it?' Demetrius of Pharos answered him on the spur of the moment, 'From the point of view of a diviner, the message is to withdraw at once; from the point of view of a practical ruler it is to keep it, so that you do not let this opportunity slip and afterwards search in vain for a better one. Remember that it is only by holding both his horns that you can keep the ox down.' The horns, so-called, referred to the strongholds of Mount Ithome in Messenia and the Acrocorinth, and the ox to the Peloponnese. Philip then turned to Aratus and asked him, 'Is your advice the same?' When Aratus did not reply Philip asked him to say exactly what he thought; the other hesitated for a moment and then replied, 'If you can keep this place without breaking your word to the Messenians, then I advise you to keep it. But if, by the act of seizing and garrisoning it, you put yourself in a position to lose all the other citadels and the garrison which stood guard over the allies when you inherited your kingdom from Antigonus (by this Aratus meant the confidence of the Greeks in the King's good faith) then think carefully whether it would not be better to take your troops away, and leave men's confidence in you to stand guard over the Messenians as well as the other allies.' Philip's personal inclination was to break his word, as he made clear by his subsequent conduct, but only a little while before he had been sharply rebuked by the younger Aratus for causing so much loss of life, and so now, when the elder Aratus

spoke out frankly and with authority, and urged him not to ignore his advice, the King felt ashamed, took him by the hand, and said, 'Let us go back by the way that we came.'

13. When Aratus saw that Philip was now deliberately embarking upon a war with Rome and had entirely changed his policy towards his allies, he had the greatest difficulty in dissuading the King, and only achieved his purpose by impressing upon him the many difficulties that he would have to face and making a number of pleas.

At this point I wish to remind my readers of a statement which I made in my fifth book, which was then quite unsupported, but has now been confirmed by events; I do this so as not to leave any proposition of mine unproved or open to question. In my account of the Aetolian War, I remarked that Philip behaved with excessive barbarity in his destruction of the porticoes and other sacred objects at Thermum, but I added that in view of his youth at that time we ought not to blame the King so much as the friends with whom he was then associated.[1] I went on to say that Aratus' conduct throughout his life made it inconceivable that he would ever have committed such an outrage, and that the action was much more characteristic of Demetrius of Pharos. I promised that I would make good this assertion in the sequel, and I reserved the proof for this moment in my narrative. For this is the point, as I explained in my description of Philip's treatment of the Messenians, when the King committed the first of his great crimes; and all this happened through the accident of one day on which Demetrius happened to be present and Aratus arrived too late. From that moment it was as if Philip had for the first time had a taste of human blood and of the massacre and betrayal of his allies; he did not change from a man into a wolf, as in the Arcadian fable which is quoted by Plato,[2] but from a king into a ferocious tyrant. A still more striking proof of the contrasting attitudes of Demetrius and Aratus is provided by the advice which each of them gave

1. The reference is to Book V.9, not included in this abridgement. The episode occurred in 218 B.C. when the Macedonians destroyed the colonnades, statues and dedicatory offerings at Thermum in Aetolia in reprisal for the desecration of Dium and Dodona by the Aetolians.

2. *Republic*, VIII.565d.

about the citadel of Messene, which I have just quoted: this leaves no room for doubt concerning the matter of the responsibility for the outrage in Aetolia, that is, the ravaging of Thermum.

14. Once we admit this, it is easy enough to judge the extent to which their principles differed. For just as Philip on the former occasion took Aratus' advice and kept his word to the Messenians concerning the fate of their citadel, and thus, as the saying is, brought a little balm to the terrible wound which his massacres had caused, so in Aetolia by following Demetrius' advice he sinned not only against the gods by destroying the objects which had been consecrated to them, but also against men by showing himself a bitter and implacable foe to all who opposed him. The same is true of his behaviour in Crete. There too, so long as he employed Aratus as his principal adviser, not only did he treat the Cretans fairly as a people, but he did not commit an injustice against a single individual; in this way he kept all the Cretans under his control, and through the integrity of his rule he won the goodwill of all the Greeks. Conversely, by following the lead given him by Demetrius and inflicting on the Messenians the sufferings I have described above, he lost both the goodwill of his allies and the confidence of the rest of the Greeks. So important for the young ruler is the choice of the friends who surround him, since it may lead either to disaster or to the firm establishment of his rule, and yet this is a matter to which the majority pay no attention at all, but treat with an inexplicable indifference.

BOOK VIII

Affairs in Sicily

THE SIEGE OF SYRACUSE

In the summer of 214 Hieronymus was ambushed in the city of Leontini and assassinated. The regicides, who were pro-Roman, also killed Adranodorus, Hieronymus' uncle, but in the ensuing elections the pro-Carthaginian leaders Epicydes and Hippocrates were returned as generals. The subsequent capture and sack of the neighbouring city of Leontini by the Romans enabled Epicydes and Hippocrates to enlist popular support for the Carthaginian cause.

3. After Epicydes and Hippocrates had seized power in Syracuse, they managed to transfer the friendship and allegiance which their compatriots had previously cherished for Rome to the side of Carthage. Meanwhile the Romans, who had already been informed of the fate which had befallen Hieronymus, the tyrant of Syracuse, appointed Appius Claudius Pulcher as pro-praetor to command the land forces, and Marcus Claudius Marcellus to take charge of the fleet. These officers then took up a position not far from the city and decided to assault it with their land forces at the quarter known as the Hexapyli;[1] the fleet was to attack at the so-called Portico of Scytice in Achradina, where the city wall extends to the quay-side. The Romans' wicker screens, missiles and other siege apparatus had been made ready beforehand, and they felt confident that with the number of men at their disposal they could within five days bring their preparations to a point which would give them the advantage over the enemy. But here they failed to reckon with the talents of Archimedes or to foresee that in some cases the genius of one man is far more effective than superiority in numbers. This lesson they now learned by experience.

1. A gate built in the city wall on the north edge of the Epipolae plateau.

The strength of the defences of Syracuse is due to the fact that the city wall extends in a circle along high ground with steeply overhanging crags, which are by no means easy to climb, except at certain definite points, even if the approach is uncontested. Accordingly Archimedes had constructed the defences of the city in such a way – both on the landward side and to repel any attack from the sea – that there was no need for the defenders to busy themselves with improvisations; instead they would have everything ready to hand, and could respond to any attack by the enemy with a counter-move. For his part Appius Claudius Pulcher, who was equipped with penthouses and scaling-ladders, brought these into operation to attack the part of the wall which adjoins the Hexapyli gate to the east.

4. Meanwhile Marcellus was attacking the quarter of Achradina from the sea with sixty quinqueremes, each vessel being filled with archers, slingers and javelin-throwers, whose task was to drive the defenders from the battlements. Besides these vessels he had eight quinqueremes grouped in pairs. Each pair had had half of their oars removed, the starboard bank for the one and the port for the other, and on these sides the vessels were lashed together. They were then rowed by the remaining oars on their outer sides, and brought up to the walls the siege engines known as *sambucae*.[1] These are constructed as follows. A ladder is made, four feet in width and high enough to reach the top of the wall from the place where its feet are to rest. Each side is fenced in with a high protective breastwork, and the machine is also shielded by a wicker covering high overhead. It is then laid flat over the two sides of the ships which are lashed together, the top protruding a considerable distance beyond the bows. To the tops of the ships' masts are fixed pulleys with ropes, and when the *sambuca* is about to be used, the ropes are attached to the top of the ladder, and men standing in the stern haul up the machine by means of the pulleys, while others stand in the bows to support it with long poles and make sure that it is safely raised. After this the oarsmen on the two outer sides of the ships row the vessels close inshore, and the crews then attempt to prop the *sambuca* against the wall. At the top of the

1. The *sambuca* was a musical instrument, a kind of many-stringed harp, triangular in shape.

ladder there is a wooden platform which is protected on three sides by wicker screens; four men are stationed on this to engage the defenders, who in the meanwhile are struggling to prevent the *sambuca* from being lodged against the battlements. As soon as the attackers have got it into position, and are thus standing on a higher level than the wall, they pull down the wicker screens on each side of the platform and rush out on to the battlements or towers. Their comrades climb up the *sambuca* after them, the ladder being held firm by ropes which are attached to both ships. This device is aptly named, because when it is raised the combination of the ship and the ladder looks remarkably like the musical instrument in question.

5. This was the siege equipment with which the Romans planned to assault the city's towers. But Archimedes had constructed artillery which could cover a whole variety of ranges, so that while the attacking ships were still at a distance he scored so many hits with his catapults and stone-throwers that he was able to cause them severe damage and harass their approach. Then, as the distance decreased and these weapons began to carry over the enemy's heads, he resorted to smaller and smaller machines, and so demoralized the Romans that their advance was brought to a standstill. In the end Marcellus was reduced in despair to bringing up his ships secretly under cover of darkness. But when they had almost reached the shore, and were therefore too close to be struck by the catapults, Archimedes had devised yet another weapon to repel the marines, who were fighting from the decks. He had had the walls pierced with large numbers of loopholes at the height of a man, which were about a palm's breadth wide at the outer surface of the walls. Behind each of these and inside the walls were stationed archers with rows of so-called 'scorpions', a small catapult which discharged iron darts, and by shooting through these embrasures they put many of the marines out of action. Through these tactics he not only foiled all the enemy's attacks, both those made at long range and any attempt at hand-to-hand fighting, but also caused them heavy losses.

Then, whenever the enemy tried to work their *sambucae*, he had other engines ready all along the walls. At normal times these were kept out of sight, but as soon as they were needed they were hoisted above the walls with their beams projecting far over the battlements, some of them carrying stones weighing as much as ten talents, and others large lumps of lead. As soon as the *sambucae* approached, these beams were swung round on a universal joint, and by means of a release mechanism or trigger dropped the weight on the *sambuca*; the effect was not only to smash the ladder but to endanger the safety both of the ships and of their crews.

6. Other machines invented by Archimedes were directed against the assault parties as they advanced under the shelter of screens which protected them against the missiles shot through the walls. Against these attackers the machines could discharge stones heavy enough to drive back the marines from the bows of the ships; at the same time a grappling-iron attached to a chain would be let down, and with this the man controlling the beam would clutch at the ship. As soon as the prow was securely gripped, the lever of the machine inside the wall would be pressed down. When the operator had lifted up the ship's prow in this way and made her stand on her stern, he made fast the lower parts of the machine, so that they would not move, and finally by means of a rope and pulley suddenly slackened the grappling-iron and the chain. The result was that some of the vessels heeled over and fell on their sides, and others capsized, while the majority when their bows were let fall from a height plunged under water and filled, and thus threw all into confusion. Marcellus' operations were thus completely frustrated by these inventions of Archimedes, and when he saw that the garrison not only repulsed his attacks with heavy losses but also laughed at his efforts, he took his defeat hard. At the same time he could not refrain from making a joke against himself when he said: 'Archimedes uses my ships to ladle sea-water into his wine-cups, but my *sambuca* band have been whipped out of the wine-party as intruders!' So ended the efforts to capture Syracuse from the sea.

7. At the same time Appius Claudius Pulcher found himself faced with similar difficulties when he attacked by land, and finally he abandoned the attempt. While his troops were still at a distance from the walls they suffered many casualties from the mangonels and catapults. This artillery was extraordinarily effective both in the volume and the velocity of its fire, as was to be expected when

Hiero had provided the supplies, and Archimedes designed the various engines. Then, even when the soldiers did get close to the wall, they were so harassed by the volleys of arrows and darts which continually poured through the embrasures, as I described above, that their advance was effectually halted. Alternatively, if they attacked under cover of their penthouses, they were crushed by the stones and beams that were dropped on their heads. The defenders also killed many men by means of the iron grappling-hooks let down from cranes, which I mentioned earlier: these were used to lift up men, armour and all, and then allow them to drop. In the end Pulcher withdrew to his camp and summoned a council of the military tribunes, at which it was unanimously decided to use any other methods rather than persist in the attempt to capture Syracuse by storm. And this resolution was never reversed, for during the eight months' siege of the city which followed, although they left no stratagem or daring attempt untried, they never again ventured to mount a general assault. So true it is that the genius of one man can become an immense, almost a miraculous asset, if it is properly applied to certain problems. In this instance, at any rate, the Romans, having brought up such numerous forces both by sea and by land, had every hope of capturing the city immediately, if only one old man out of all the Syracusans could have been removed; but so long as he was present they did not dare even to attempt an attack by any method which made it possible for Archimedes to oppose them. Instead they concluded that in view of the large population of the town, the best way to reduce it was by starvation; they therefore cut off supplies from the sea by means of the fleet, and by land by means of the army, and rested their hopes on this solution. But as they were anxious to achieve some useful results outside, and not waste all the time during which they would be blockading Syracuse, the two commanders separated and divided their forces. Pulcher took command of two-thirds and invested the city, while Marcellus with the remaining third made raids on those parts of Sicily which were supporting the Carthaginians.

Affairs in Greece

PHILIP OF MACEDON

8. When he arrived at the city of Messene Philip set about ravaging the place with a malevolence that showed he was indulging his anger rather than acting sensibly, for he seems to have expected that however much damage he caused, his victims would never feel resentment or hatred towards him. Now, I have been impelled to give a more detailed account of these events both here and in the preceding book for another reason, besides those I have already mentioned: namely, the inadequacy of my predecessors' treatment of the subject. Some of our historians have made no mention whatever of events in Messenia at this time; others, perhaps influenced by their favourable opinions of kings or else by their fear of them, have argued that the outrages committed by Philip against the Messenians in defiance both of divine and of human law, so far from being regarded as wrong, should on the contrary be praised and justified as worthy actions. And indeed, it is not only in regard to the Messenians that the chroniclers of Philip's life have written in this fashion: they have done much the same in other instances too, with the result that their compositions bear little resemblance to history, but much more to panegyric. My own opinion is that we should neither praise kings nor blame them without due regard for the truth (as has so often been done), but should always write of them consistently in the light of our previous statements, and in accordance with their conduct and policy. It may be argued that this is easy enough to profess, but extremely difficult to practise, because the situations and circumstances of life are so many and so various that men may sometimes be obliged to give way to these, and so be prevented from saying or writing what they really believe. Making allowance for all this, we may excuse some writers in some instances, but not others.

9. In this respect I consider that the writer most to be blamed is Theopompus.[1] At the beginning of his history of Philip, son of

---

1. Theopompus of Chios was born in 378 B.C. He was an admirer of Sparta, and wrote a history of Greece centred on the period of Spartan hegemony.

Amyntas,[1] he says that the main consideration which impelled him to undertake this work was the fact that Europe had never before produced such a man as this Philip. However, immediately afterwards, both in his preface and throughout the book, he portrays Philip first of all as having been so promiscuous in his relations with women that he did everything in his power to ruin his own household by his passionate and ostentatious cravings in this direction; secondly, as having behaved with the utmost injustice and lack of scruple in his schemes for forming friendships and alliances; thirdly, as having treacherously seized and enslaved a great number of cities by deceit and by force; and finally, as having been so addicted to strong drink that he was often seen by his friends openly drunk even during the hours of daylight. Anyone who chooses to read the beginning of his forty-ninth book will be astonished at the extravagance of this writer, who, apart from his other statements, has ventured to express himself as follows – I quote the passage in his own words:

'Anyone in Greece or among the barbarians whose character was thoroughly lascivious or shameless could be expected to gravitate to Philip's court in Macedonia, where he would earn the title of one of "the King's companions". For Philip made it his custom to turn away men of good reputation who took care of their property, but to honour and promote those who were spendthrifts and passed their time drinking and gambling. The result was that he not only confirmed them in their weaknesses but made them past masters in every kind of wickedness and vice. Was there indeed any shameful or infamous attribute which they lacked, or any good or honest one which they possessed? Some of them used to shave and depilate their bodies, although they were men, while others made love to their companions although they were bearded. They habitually took two or three minions about with them, and themselves provided the same service for others, so that it would be quite fair to call them courtesans rather than courtiers and male prostitutes rather than men at arms; in this way after being by

---

This took up the record of events after Thucydides and continued down to 394 B.C.

1. The father of Alexander the Great.

nature man-eaters, they became through their practices man-whores.'

'In a word,' Theopompus goes on, 'and not to drag out the subject, particularly since I have a mass of other topics to deal with, I consider that those who were styled Philip's friends and companions were more brutish and bestial in their natures and characters than the Centaurs who inhabited Mount Pelion, or the Laestrygones who lived in the plain of Leontini, or any other monsters.'

10. Everyone will surely join in condemning such a display of embittered feeling and intemperate language on the part of this author. He deserves blame not only for writing in terms which wholly contradict the stated purpose of his book, but also for falsely accusing the King and his companions, and above all for expressing his accusation in such coarse and repellent language. Even if he had been writing of Sardanapalus or one of his courtiers, he would hardly have dared to set down such obscenities, and to testify to the lascivious character and debauched way of life of that ruler, we still have the epigram inscribed on his tomb, which ran as follows:

> All the delights of my table, all the delights of my bed
> Still I enjoy . . .

But when we come to speak of Philip and his friends, the problem is not merely that we should hesitate to accuse them of cowardice, effeminacy and shameless immorality. It is rather that when we set ourselves the task of honouring their achievements we might well fail to find words adequate to describe their courage, their perseverance, and, in a word, the manly virtue of their character. For there can be no doubt that by their indefatigable energy and daring they raised Macedonia from the status of a petty kingdom to that of the greatest and most glorious monarchy in the world. And apart from what was accomplished during Philip's lifetime, the successes that were achieved by Alexander after his father's death won for them a reputation for valour which has been universally recognized by posterity. Despite his extreme youth, we should perhaps give a great share of the credit to Alexander as the commander-in-chief of the expedition, but we should attribute no less to his friends and comrades, who overcame the enemy in many battles against all expectation, and endured many extraordinary toils, dangers and hardships. Later, even though they came into possession of vast wealth and enjoyed unlimited opportunities to satisfy every desire, none of them suffered any deterioration of their physical strength for that reason, nor did they commit any unjust or licentious actions to gratify the demands of passion. On the contrary, all those who were associated with Philip and later with Alexander showed themselves by their magnanimity, their daring and their self-discipline to be truly royal. We need not mention any of these men by name. But after Alexander's death, when they became rivals for the possession of an empire which covered the greater part of the earth, the glory of their achievements was such as to fill chronicle after chronicle with the record of their exploits.

To sum up, we might allow that the bitter attack which Timaeus the historian wrote against Agathocles, the tyrant of Sicily, however excessive it may appear, possesses some justification, since it is directed at a personal enemy, a wicked man and a tyrant, but that of Theopompus does not deserve serious consideration.

11. For the latter, after proclaiming at the outset that he intends to write about a king most richly endowed by nature with every quality that makes for virtue, proceeds to accuse him of everything that is disgraceful and abominable. It follows, then, that the author has shown himself to be either a liar and a flatterer in the remarks at the beginning of his history, or else to be a fool and a simpleton in the statements made throughout the main body of the work. What else can we suppose if he imagined that he would both enhance his reputation by indulging in senseless and far-fetched abuse, and at the same time make good his enthusiastic estimate of Philip? Again, it is impossible to approve of the general scheme which Theopompus chose to adopt. For having undertaken to write a history of Greece from the point at which Thucydides left off, as soon as he approaches the date of the battle of Leuctra and the most brilliant period of Greek history he abandons Greece and her various enterprises in the middle of his work, changes his theme, and decides to write the history of Philip. Surely it would have been more dignified as well as more just to have included Philip's

achievements in the general history of Greece rather than the history of Greece in that of Philip? It seems inconceivable that even a man preoccupied by his devotion to a royal dynasty would hesitate, if he were granted the power and the opportunity, to transfer the title and the principal role in his work to Greece, or that anyone in his senses who had already begun to write the history of Greece and made some progress with the work would have exchanged it for the showy pomp of a royal biography. What then can have induced Theopompus to overlook such glaring inconsistencies? The explanation is surely that in writing the first history his motive was to pursue an ideal, but in the second, his own interests. It is possible that as regards his error in altering the scheme of his history he might have produced some justification if anybody had questioned him, but as for the disgraceful language which he uses about the King's friends, I do not think he could have excused himself, but would have had to admit that he had offended gravely against propriety.

12. Although Philip was now[1] openly treating the Messenians as his enemies he did not succeed – in spite of attempting to ravage their territory – in inflicting any serious damage on them, but towards some of those who had been his most intimate friends he behaved with the most abominable cruelty. For example, when the elder Aratus showed his disapproval of Philip's treatment of the Messenians, the King contrived not long afterwards to have him poisoned through the agency of Taurion, his commissioner in the Peloponnese. This fact was not generally known at the time, because the drug was not one of those which immediately kill the victim, but was a slow poison which created a morbid condition of the body. But Aratus himself was aware of the King's crime, as the following circumstance shows. While he concealed his condition from the rest of the world, he could not refrain from revealing it to one of his servants named Cephalon, who knew him very well. This man took great care of Aratus during his illness, and on one occasion pointed out some of his master's spittle on the wall, which was tinged with blood. At this Aratus said to him, 'That, Cephalon, is the reward I have received for my friendship with Philip.' Such a great and noble quality is self-control that the victim of this

1. 213 B.C.

crime was actually more ashamed than the perpetrator, to feel that after having taken part with Philip in so many great enterprises in the King's interests he should have received so vile a return for his loyalty.

After his death Aratus received the honours he deserved both from his native city and from the Achaean League as a body, in consequence both of his having so often held the office of commander-in-chief,[1] and of having performed such great services to the nation. They voted him sacrifices and honours of the kind that are paid to heroes and, in a word, everything that could contribute to make his name immortal. If the dead can experience any feeling, then we may believe that Aratus takes pleasure in the gratitude of the Achaeans and in the recollection of the dangers and hardships which he endured in his life.

Affairs in Italy

THE SIEGE OF TARENTUM

The opening paragraph of this chapter belongs to a passage of general reflections about politics, and there is a gap between this and the beginning of the succeeding narrative. Pyrrhus had originally been called in by the democratic regime which then (281 B.C.) controlled the city. The situation at the time of the Second Punic War was quite different. The Romans had taken a number of hostages from Tarentum, who in 212 attempted to escape from Rome; the men were caught and summarily executed. This action provoked a number of their friends and relatives, thirteen young men of noble birth, to form the conspiracy which is described in the ensuing chapters.

24. It was the arrogance that is so often induced by prosperity which persuaded the Tarentines to call in King Pyrrhus of Epirus to help them. For every democracy which has enjoyed property for a considerable period first develops through its nature an attitude of discontent towards the existing order, and then looks

1. This office was the chief magistracy in Achaea.

around for a master. When it has found one, it soon begins to hate him again, once it becomes clear that the change of system is for the worse. Such was the experience of the Tarentines on this occasion . . .

The Tarentines who had decided to approach Hannibal left the city as though they were making a foraging raid, and reached the neighbourhood of Hannibal's camp under cover of darkness. Most of the party hid themselves in a wood by the side of the road, but Philemenus and Nicon then went up to the camp. There they were seized by the guards and brought before Hannibal, for they had said nothing about who they were or where they had come from, but had simply announced that they wished to see the general. They were soon led into Hannibal's presence, whereupon they explained that they wished to speak to him in private. Hannibal readily granted them the interview, and the two men then explained who they were and what was the situation in Tarentum; at the same time they uttered a whole catalogue of accusations against the Romans, as they did not wish to give the impression of having undertaken their mission without good reason. Hannibal thanked them, listened courteously to their proposals and then dismissed them, at the same time arranging that they should return and visit him again in the near future. For the present he told them that as soon as they had put some distance between themselves and the camp they should round up and drive off the first herds of cattle that they saw being taken out to pasture, and carry off the herdsmen with them. They should then make their way home without fear, for he would make sure of their safety. Hannibal did this first of all to gain time, so that he could test the reliability of what the young men had told him, and secondly to create confidence among the Tarentines, by making it appear that the conspirators had really left the city on a foraging expedition. Nicon and his companions then proceeded to carry out their instructions to the letter. The immediate result was that Hannibal was well-pleased to have found a way of carrying out his plans to capture the city. For their part, Philemenus and the rest became all the more eager to pursue their attempt when they reflected that their first interview had been successfully accomplished, that they had found Hannibal amenable, and that the quantity of the plunder they had brought back had firmly established their credit with their countrymen. Some of the captured cattle they sold and some they slaughtered, so as to give entertainments, and in this way they not only won the confidence of the Tarentines, but encouraged quite a number more to follow their example . . .

25. After this they made a second expedition to Hannibal which they arranged in the same fashion. This time they pledged their word to him, and they received Hannibal's promise that the Carthaginians would neither exact tribute of any kind nor impose any other burdens on them; in return the Carthaginians would be allowed to plunder the houses and lodgings of the Romans after the capture of the city. They also settled on a watch-word which would allow the Carthaginian sentries to admit them into the camp without delay whenever they came. In this way they were enabled to have several more meetings with Hannibal; sometimes they pretended to be leaving the city to forage, sometimes for a hunting expedition.

Once they had laid these plans for the future, the majority of the conspirators were content to bide their time until the moment of action, allowing Philemenus to play the part of the huntsman. This sport was his dominating passion, and he had the reputation of regarding it as the most important activity in life. Accordingly he was told to make use of the game he killed to make friends first with Gaius Livius, the military commandant of the city, and also with the guards of the towers which protected what is known as the Temenid gate.[1] Philemenus undertook this task and managed to bring in game at frequent intervals, either killing it himself or procuring it from Hannibal. Some of this he presented to Livius and some to the sentries on the tower, so as to accustom them to being ready to open the gate to him at any time. He made a habit of going out and returning from his expeditions after dark, supposedly because he was afraid of the enemy, but in reality to prepare the way for the attempt he was planning. In this way he gradually brought about an arrangement whereby the sentry on the gate would open the postern for him at night immediately and

1. The gate used by Philemenus was a little way south of the Temenid gate; it was through the latter that Hannibal entered the city.

without a challenge whenever he whistled as he approached the wall. Finally, the conspirators learned that on a certain day the Roman commandant would be present at a large entertainment which was to be given early in the day at the building known as the Museum, which is near the market-place; and they agreed with Hannibal that the plot should be carried out on that day.

26. Hannibal had for some time given out that he was sick, so the curiosity of the Romans should not be aroused when they learned that he had spent so long in the same place, and he now pretended that his illness had become more serious. His camp was three days' march from Tarentum, and as the appointed day approached he got ready a picked body of about 10,000 men. These had been selected from his infantry and cavalry for their fighting spirit, and also for their ability to march quickly. They were ordered to take rations for four days, and at dawn the force set off and marched at their fastest speed. A group of eighty Numidian horsemen was ordered to keep some four miles ahead and to spread out on both sides of the road. The purpose of this manoeuvre was to prevent the enemy from getting a glimpse of the main body. Hannibal calculated that any whom they encountered would either be taken prisoner or, if they escaped, would carry a report to the city that a party of Numidians was raiding the district. When the Numidians were about fifteen miles from Tarentum, Hannibal halted his troops for their evening meal on the banks of a river which flowed through a ravine and offered excellent cover at that point, and there summoned a meeting of his officers. He did not explain to them the details of his plan, but dwelt on three points. First of all, he appealed to them to fight bravely, since the prize for success had never been greater; secondly, each of them was to keep the men under his command in close order on the march, and severely punish any who left the ranks on any pretext whatsoever; and lastly, they were to carry out his orders to the letter and not attempt anything on their own initiative. With these words he dismissed the officers and resumed the march just after dusk, his aim being to reach the city walls by about midnight. He had Philemenus with him to show the way, and had procured a wild boar to enable him to play his part as a huntsman.

27. The young conspirators had been well-informed, and Gaius

Livius had been present with his friends at the public celebration since the early morning. At about the hour of sunset, when the drinking was at its height, a report came in that Numidian cavalry were scouring the vicinity. Livius acted to meet this incursion and nothing more. He summoned some of the officers and ordered them to take half his cavalry force and ride out to prevent the enemy from devastating the countryside; having made this decision he was all the less suspicious that anything more serious was afoot. Meanwhile Nicon and Tragiscus and their confederates gathered together at nightfall in the city and lay in wait for Livius to return home. The banqueters rose from the table somewhat early in the evening as the drinking had begun in the afternoon. Most of the conspirators withdrew to a chosen spot where they waited, but a few of the younger men went to meet Livius and his friends, and by their noisy progress and the uproarious jests which they exchanged they created the impression that they too were returning from a carouse. As Livius and his party were even more fuddled with wine, they were soon sharing loud laughter and horseplay. Finally they turned back and escorted Livius to his house, where he lay down to rest quite overcome with wine, as might be expected after a party which had begun so early in the day. He was quite unaware that anything unusual or disturbing was impending and lay there relaxed and full of good cheer.

Meanwhile, when Nicon and Tragiscus had rejoined their companions, they divided themselves into three groups, and took up position in the streets which gave most convenient access to the market-place. There they kept watch so that they would be the first to learn of any news from outside the walls or of any movement inside the city. Some of them posted themselves near Livius' house, since they knew that if any suspicion should arise as to what was about to happen, he would be the first to receive the news and that whatever measures were taken would originate from him. At last the commotion caused by the returning guests subsided, all other noise of the same kind died away, and the great majority of the townsfolk returned to bed; meanwhile the night wore on, nothing happened to dash their hopes of success, and so the young men gathered again and proceeded to carry out their part of the plot.

28. The arrangements between the young Tarentines and Hannibal were as follows. Hannibal was to approach the city from an easterly direction, that is, to arrive at the quarter which faces inland. He was to advance towards the Temenid gate, and there light a fire on the spot which some people call the tomb of Hyacinthus and others the tomb of Apollo. Tragiscus, as soon as he saw this, was to light an answering fire from within the walls. After this exchange of signals Hannibal was to put out the fire and advance slowly towards the gate. Following these plans, the young men crossed the inhabited quarter of the city and reached the cemetery. I should explain here that the whole of the eastern part of Tarentum is occupied by tombs, since up to this day the inhabitants bury all their dead within the walls in obedience to the command of an ancient oracle. The god, so the legend goes, gave this answer to the Tarentines – that they would fare better and more prosperously if they shared their dwelling-place with the majority. They interpreted the oracle as meaning that they would be better-off if they kept both the departed and themselves within the walls, and so the Tarentines up to this day bury their dead inside the gates.

The young men reached the tomb of Pythionicus, where they waited to see what would happen. Presently Hannibal's force approached and gave the expected signal. The moment they saw the fire Nicon and Tragiscus and their companions felt their courage revive, and they lit their own beacon in reply. Then as soon as Hannibal's signal was put out, they ran at full speed to the gate-tower; they had to make their way there in time to surprise and kill the guards, since it had been agreed that the Carthaginians should advance at a slow pace. Everything went according to plan. The guards were taken completely by surprise, and while some of the conspirators cut them down, others slashed through the bolts. The gates were quickly thrown open and Hannibal's troops arrived at the appointed hour; he had advanced at precisely the right speed, so that there was no occasion for him to halt along the road approaching the city.

29. Having got his troops into Tarentum according to his prearranged plan, not only without any danger but without having made the slightest noise, Hannibal felt that he had accomplished

379

the most important part of his scheme, and he therefore advanced confidently towards the market-place along the street which leads up from what is called the Batheia or Deep Road. He left his cavalry force, which numbered 2,000, in reserve outside the walls, to protect him against any attack by the enemy from outside, and to guard against any unforeseen contingency, such as often arises in operations of this kind. When he arrived near the market-place he halted his troops in marching order and waited for Philemenus to appear, since he was also anxious to see how this part of his plan would succeed. When he had first lit the fire signal and was about to advance towards the Temenid gate, he had sent off Philemenus carrying the wild boar on a stretcher and followed by a contingent of 1,000 Africans to the next gate, for he was anxious, in accordance with his original plan, that the success of the operation should not depend entirely on one chance, but on several.

Philemenus came up to the wall, whistled in his accustomed fashion, and the guard immediately appeared and came down to the postern gate. Philemenus called to him from outside to open it quickly because they were carrying a wild boar and were tired. The guard was delighted and made haste to open, hoping that there would be something for him from Philemenus' bag, since he was always given a share of whatever game was brought in. Philemenus then entered first, carrying the front end of the stretcher; with him was a man dressed like a shepherd, as though he were one of the country folk, and after him came two other men carrying the dead beast from behind. When all four had passed through the postern, they first struck down and killed the guard, as he was unsuspectingly touching and examining the boar, and then quietly and unhurriedly let in the next group of thirty Africans who were immediately behind them but in advance of the main body. Next they proceeded to cut the bolts, while others of the party killed the remaining guards, and others gave a pre-arranged signal which summoned the rest of the Africans who had been waiting outside. When these had also passed through the gate, the whole contingent marched to the market-place in accordance with their orders. Here they joined Hannibal, who, delighted that the whole operation was being carried out just as he had intended, proceeded to the next stage of his plan.

30. He detached a contingent of 2,000 Celts, divided them into three companies, and assigned two of the young Tarentines who had managed the conspiracy to command each group. He also sent several of his own officers to accompany these troops, with orders to occupy the streets which gave the most convenient access to the market-place. When this had been done, he told the young Tarentines to pick out and save any of their fellow-citizens they might happen to meet, and to shout out from a distance that the citizens of Tarentum should stay where they were, since they were in no danger. At the same time the Carthaginian and Celtic officers were ordered to kill at sight all the Romans they met. The three bodies of troops then separated and began to carry out these orders.

As soon as it became known to the Tarentines that the enemy were within the walls, a babel of shouting broke out, and confusion reigned everywhere. As for Gaius Livius, when he heard that the Carthaginians had broken in, he understood that in his drunken condition he was incapable of dealing with the situation, and rushed out of his house with his attendants to make for the gate which leads to the harbour. There the guards opened the postern for him, and escaping through this he seized one of the boats which were anchored there, went on board with his servants, and was conveyed along the coast to the citadel. Meanwhile Philemenus and his companions had provided themselves with some Roman bugles and some men who had learned how to blow them, and stood in the theatre and sounded the call to arms. The Romans rallied to the summons carrying their weapons, and according to their usual custom ran towards the citadel, which was exactly what the Carthaginians had intended. They came on to the streets in groups that were scattered and too small to take up a formation. There they encountered the Carthaginians and the Celts, and in this way many of them were killed.

As day began to break the Tarentines remained quietly in their houses, since it was impossible for them to form a clear idea of what was happening. Because of the sounds of the bugle-calls, and of the fact that no looting or acts of violence were taking place inside the city, they imagined that the commotion had been caused by the Romans. But when they saw that many Romans were lying dead in the streets and that the Gauls were stripping some of their bodies the suspicion dawned upon them that the Carthaginians had entered the city.

31. Meanwhile Hannibal had encamped his force in the market-place and the Romans had withdrawn into the citadel where they had always kept a garrison; and as it was by then broad daylight, he summoned all the Tarentines by herald to assemble without arms in the market-place. The conspirators also went round the city calling upon the people to rally to the cause of freedom, and to take heart since it was for their sake that the Carthaginians had come. The Tarentines who supported the Romans retired to the citadel as soon as they realized what had happened; the rest obeyed the summons and arrived without arms in the market-place, where Hannibal addressed them in friendly terms. The Tarentines loudly applauded every word, for they were delighted at this unexpected turn of events, whereupon Hannibal dismissed the meeting and ordered everyone to hurry back to his house and write over the door the words 'A Tarentine's'. He warned them, however, that anyone who wrote these words on the house of a Roman would be put to death. He then selected the most suitable of his officers and sent them out with orders to plunder the houses which belonged to the Romans. All houses which had no inscription on them were to be regarded as enemy property, and meanwhile he kept the rest of his men drawn up as a reserve to support the pillagers if necessary.

32. An immense quantity of possessions of various kinds was collected in this way, and the plunder was no less than the Carthaginians had expected. They bivouacked that night under arms, and on the next day Hannibal summoned another general assembly which included all the Tarentines. At this he decided to cut off the citadel from the rest of the town by means of a wall, so that the Tarentines should no longer have anything to fear from the Roman garrison occupying that stronghold. His first measure was to build a palisade, which ran parallel to the wall of the citadel and the moat in front of it. He knew very well, of course, that the enemy would not watch this operation passively, but would certainly make some effort at resistance, and so for this encounter he held some of his best troops ready, as he considered that it was of the

greatest importance for the future that he should inspire the Romans with fear and the Tarentines with confidence.

And indeed, no sooner had the work of constructing the palisade been begun than the Romans launched a bold and furious attack on it. After resisting for a little while, Hannibal made his men retire in order to lure his opponents forward, and then when they advanced beyond the moat, he ordered up his reserves, counter-attacked, and fell upon the enemy. A desperate struggle followed, since the fighting took place in a confined space between two walls, but in the end the Romans were repulsed and put to flight. Many of them were killed where they fought, but a large number lost their lives by being driven back and forced over the edge into the moat.

33. After he had safely completed the palisade, Hannibal was content to remain quiet for a while, since his plan had achieved the desired effect. He had shut up the enemy, confined them within their own walls, and made them fear for themselves as well as for the safety of the citadel, while he had made the townspeople so confident that they now considered themselves a match for the Romans even without the help of the Carthaginians. His next move was to make a trench parallel to the palisade and the wall of the citadel, but this was dug a little way behind the palisade and closer to the city. In this instance the earth was thrown up all along the trench on the side nearer to the town, and a second palisade was erected on top of this, thus creating a fortification almost as effective as a wall. After this he began to build a wall at an appropriate distance from the second palisade and still closer to the city, extending from the street named Saviour to the Deep Road, these fortifications being strong enough to protect the Tarentines adequately even without men to defend them. He then left a garrison sufficient to defend the city and the wall, together with a detachment of cavalry to support them, and he himself pitched camp some five miles outside Tarentum on the banks of a river which some people call the Galaesus, but which is more generally known as the Eurotas, taking its name from the river which flows through Sparta. The Tarentines have many names of Spartan origin, both in their city and in the neighbouring countryside, for they are acknowledged to be a colony established by the Lacedaemonians

and connected with them by blood. Thanks to the energy and enthusiasm of the Tarentines and the help given them by the Carthaginians the wall was soon finished, and Hannibal next turned his mind to the problem of capturing the citadel as well.

34. After these preparations for the siege had been completed, the Romans received some reinforcements by sea from Metapontum. This measure of relief did something to restore their spirits; they made a night attack on the siege-works, and succeeded in destroying all of Hannibal's machines and apparatus. After this setback he abandoned the idea of taking the citadel by storm, but as the new wall had been finished, he summoned a meeting of all the Tarentines and pointed out that the most important step under present circumstances was to gain control of the sea. The citadel, as I have already mentioned, commanded the entrance to the harbour, and this meant that the Tarentines could neither use their ships inside it nor sail out of it, whereas the Romans could safely receive all the supplies they needed from the sea; thus so long as this situation prevailed, it was impossible for the city to make its newly won freedom secure.

Hannibal saw this clearly, and explained to the Tarentines that if the garrison of the citadel were deprived of the facility of its seaborne supplies, they would quickly come to terms of their own accord, abandon the fortress and surrender the place. The Tarentines listened to him and saw the force of his argument, but could think of no way of putting it into effect, unless a fleet were to appear from Carthage, which at that time was impossible. They therefore replied that they could not understand what Hannibal was leading up to in bringing up this subject. When he went on to say that it was clear that they themselves, even without the help of the Carthaginians, were very nearly in command of the sea at that moment, they were even more astonished and quite unable to guess his meaning. But Hannibal had taken note of the street which lay just inside the cross-wall and ran parallel to it, leading from the harbour to the outer sea; this thoroughfare, he realized, could easily be used for his purpose, which was to convey the ships along it from the harbour to the southern side of the city. As soon as he disclosed this scheme to the Tarentines they not only agreed entirely with what he said, but immediately felt an unbounded admiration for the man, for they were convinced that his courage and ingenuity could surmount every obstacle. They quickly constructed wheeled trucks and the whole operation was no sooner proposed than accomplished, since there was unlimited manpower and enthusiasm to undertake the work. Once they had transported their ships to the outer sea, the Tarentines were able to blockade the Romans without any danger to themselves and cut off their supplies from outside. Hannibal then withdrew with his army, leaving a garrison in the city, and after three days returned to his old camp, where he remained for the rest of the winter . . .

BOOK IX

Introduction

1. In composing my history I have deliberately followed a uniform plan and this, I recognize, imposes a certain austerity upon the whole work, with the result that there is only one type of reader who is likely to judge it favourably and find that it suits his taste. Most other authors, if not every one, can appeal to a wide and diverse public by including all the various modes of historical writing in their work. Thus those who enjoy a story are attracted by the genealogical treatment of history; the curious and those with antiquarian interests by a recital of the planting of colonies, of the foundation of cities and of their ties of kinship; and the statesman by the actions of nations, cities and rulers. Now as I have concentrated my attention strictly upon this last category and made it the exclusive object of my whole composition, the work has been shaped, as I explained, to appeal only to one type of reader, and thus will scarcely make attractive reading for the majority. I have set forth elsewhere at length the factors which impelled me to exclude other modes of historical writing and to limit myself to the recording of actions alone, but there is no reason why I should not recapitulate them briefly so as to impress the principle upon the minds of my readers.

2. The topics of genealogies and myths, the planting of colonies, the foundation of cities and their ties of kinship have already been treated by many authors in many different styles. It follows then that a writer who sets out to deal with these matters at the present time must either commit the disreputable act of claiming as his own what is really the work of others, or else must clearly be wasting his labour, since there is no denying the fact that the material which is the object of his research and composition has already been adequately recorded and handed down to posterity by his predecessors. For these and other reasons I decided to pass

over such themes, and instead to write a history of actual events. I did this first of all because new occurrences constantly present themselves which require novel treatment – since it was obviously impossible for the ancients to describe matters which took place after their own times – and secondly, because such a history possesses the greatest practical utility of all. This was always the case in the past, and is preeminently so in the present, when the progress of the arts and sciences has been so rapid that the student of history is equipped with a method for dealing scientifically, one might say, with any contingency that may arise. My purpose, therefore, was not so much to give pleasure to my readers as to benefit those who devote their attention to history, and hence I passed over other topics and was led to compose a history of this kind. The thoroughness with which my readers apply themselves to it will provide the best evidence of the truth of what I have just said.

Affairs in Italy

THE SIEGE OF CAPUA

The year was 211. Tarentum had fallen to the Carthaginians in the winter of 213/12, and with the capture of Thurii, Metapontum and Heracleia Hannibal held all the Greek cities of the south except for Rhegium. In 212 Appius Claudius Pulcher and Quintus Fulvius Flaccus planned to besiege Capua, and in that summer Hanno was heavily defeated by Flaccus in an attempt to relieve Capua.

3. Hannibal now surrounded the palisade which Appius Claudius Pulcher had erected outside Capua, and began by launching a series of skirmishing attacks in the hope of provoking his opponent to come out and give battle. When the Romans did not respond to these manoeuvres, Hannibal's assault developed into something very like an attempt to storm the position. The cavalry rode up in squadrons, and with loud cries hurled their javelins into the fortifications, while the infantry attacked in their regular companies and tried to tear down the palisade. But even by these methods he

was unable to make the Romans alter their tactics. They used their light-armed troops to beat off the attack on the palisade and kept the heavy infantry drawn up near their standards, where they protected themselves with their shields against the hail of missiles.

Hannibal's efforts were thus frustrated, since he could neither force his way into Capua, nor lure the Romans out of their camp, and he began to consider what was the best course of action in the circumstances. And indeed in my opinion the situation just then was such as to baffle not only the Carthaginians but anyone else who heard of it. It must have seemed almost incredible that the Romans, who had been defeated in so many pitched battles by the Carthaginians, and who even now could not venture to meet them in the field, at the same time refused to withdraw or to abandon the command of the open country. Before this the Romans had done no more than dog the enemy's movements along the hills, but now they had established themselves on the plains in the most prosperous district of Italy, and were besieging the strongest city in it. Yet at the same time they were surrounded and being attacked by the enemy whom they could not even bear the thought of meeting in battle, while the Carthaginians, in spite of having won an unbroken series of victories, found themselves at times in no less difficulty than the very troops they had defeated. Both sides, it seems to me, now adopted this course of action because each had grasped the fact that Hannibal's cavalry was the cause of the Carthaginians' victories and of the Romans' defeats. Thus the earlier tactics of advancing parallel to the enemy which the Roman armies had adopted after their reverses were entirely logical, since they were then marching through country in which the enemy had no chance of harming them, and similarly, the actions of both sides before Capua were exactly those that were to be expected.

4. The position was, then, that the Roman army did not dare to leave their camp and give battle because of their fear of the enemy's cavalry, but they remained with complete confidence behind their entrenchments, secure in the knowledge that these same horsemen who had defeated them in pitched battles could not touch them there. The Carthaginians, on the other hand, could not stay encamped in that position with their cavalry, be-

cause all the forage in the surrounding countryside had been systematically destroyed by the Romans with that very end in view, and it was impossible to transport over such long distances sufficient hay and barley to feed so many horses and mules. For the same reasons the Carthaginians did not dare to attack an enemy protected by a trench and a palisade without the support of their cavalry, since if they lacked this decisive arm, an engagement fought on equal terms would be an extremely doubtful and dangerous venture. Besides this, they were also afraid that the newly elected consuls[1] might suddenly arrive, establish themselves in their rear, and cause them great difficulties by cutting off their supplies. For these reasons Hannibal concluded that it would be impossible to raise the siege by launching a direct assault, and accordingly changed his plan. It occurred to him that if he could make a secret march and suddenly appear before Rome, he might achieve some worthwhile advantage against the city through the surprise and alarm he would inspire among the inhabitants; failing that, he would at least put pressure upon Pulcher either to abandon the siege of Capua and hasten to the rescue of his native capital, or else to divide his forces. In this event both the force detached to relieve Rome and the one which was left behind would be easier for him to defeat.

5. With this purpose in mind he dispatched a man with a letter to Capua. He arranged this by persuading one of the Libyans in his army to desert to the Roman camp and from there make his way into the city. He took especial trouble to ensure the security of the letter because he was very much afraid that the Capuans, when they saw him leaving, might suppose that he was abandoning them, and in their despair might surrender to the Romans. He therefore wrote to explain what his purpose was in breaking camp, and sent off the Libyan, so that when they learned of his departure they should continue to endure the siege as resolutely as ever.

When it was learned in Rome that Hannibal had pitched camp alongside the Roman lines surrounding Capua and was besieging them in turn, the citizens were filled with excitement and alarm,

---

1. The consuls for 211 were Gnaius Fulvius Centumalus and Publius Sulpicius Galba.

for they sensed that the impending decision was crucial to the whole war. As a result the people's whole attention was concentrated upon the preparation and dispatch of resources to that quarter. As for the Capuans, once they had received the letter brought by the Libyan and grasped the Carthaginian plan, they continued their resistance to the siege and determined to put this prospect of deliverance to the test. And so Hannibal, on the fifth day after his arrival outside Capua, arranged for his men to take their evening meal and leave their camp-fires burning, and contrived to withdraw his troops in such a way that the enemy knew nothing of what was happening. He made a succession of forced marches through the territory of Samnium and each day sent his advance guard ahead to reconnoitre and occupy positions near the road; by these means he managed, while the Romans were still thinking only of events in Capua, to cross the Anio unobserved and finally reach a point no more than five miles from the walls of Rome, where he established his camp.

6. When the arrival of his army was reported, a wave of fear and panic swept through the city, so sudden and completely unexpected was this development; for never before had Hannibal approached so close to the capital. Apart from this, the suspicion also entered the Romans' minds that the enemy would never have advanced so far nor shown such audacity unless the army at Capua had already been destroyed. The men therefore immediately manned the walls and occupied the commanding positions outside the city, while the women made the round of the temples and besought the gods to protect them, sweeping the pavements of the shrines with their hair, as is their custom at moments when extreme peril threatens the country. But just after Hannibal had pitched his camp and was planning his attack on the city for the following day, a stroke of luck intervened to save Rome.

The consuls Gnaeus Fulvius Centumalus and Publius Sulpicius Galba had already completed the enrolment of one legion, and had bound the conscripts on oath to present themselves with their arms at Rome on the very day that Hannibal had chosen for his attack; moreover they were also engaged in selecting and enrolling the recruits for a second legion. The result was that a large body of men had by coincidence been assembled at the very moment when they were needed.[1] The consuls then boldly led out these troops, drew them up in battle order in front of the city, and thus checked Hannibal's intended attack. The Carthaginians had at first pressed forward eagerly with the alluring hope that they might even succeed in capturing Rome by assault; but when they saw the enemy drawn up in battle formation and soon afterwards discovered from a prisoner what had happened, they abandoned the idea of attempting a direct attack, and turned instead to ravaging the surrounding country and setting fire to the houses. In these first raids they rounded up and drove into their camp an enormous number of animals, since they were now in a territory which nobody had ever expected the enemy to enter; but later, when the consuls ventured to pitch camp less than a mile and a half from him, Hannibal withdrew.

7. He did this for three reasons. First, he had by now collected a huge quantity of plunder; secondly, he had abandoned all hope of capturing Rome; lastly, and most important of all, he reckoned that the time had now come by which, according to his original plan, Pulcher would have heard of his threat to Rome and would then either abandon the siege of Capua and bring his army to save the capital, or else leave a part of it behind while he hastened to the rescue with the main body. In either event he considered that he would have achieved his purpose, and so he broke camp and marched out before daylight.

In the meanwhile Publius Sulpicius Galba had destroyed the bridges over the Anio and thus obliged Hannibal to get his troops across by using a ford; he then attacked the Carthaginians as they were attempting the crossing and caused them great difficulty. He could not make this a decisive action because of the large numbers of the enemy's cavalry, and the ease with which the Numidians were able to ride over every part of the field. But he succeeded in wresting back a large proportion of the plunder from the enemy,

1. According to Livy, *The War with Hannibal*, XXVI, Hannibal's approach had already been reported to Rome. Fabius Maximus maintained that the forces available in Rome were sufficient for the city's defence, and that to recall part of the army from Capua would be playing into Hannibal's hands. In Livy's version, the Senate left the decision to the generals at Capua, whereupon Fulvius marched back to Rome with a force of 15,000 infantry and 10,000 cavalry.

and after killing some 300 of them he withdrew to his camp. Later, as he formed the opinion that the Carthaginians were now retreating in haste out of fear, he followed in their rear, keeping to the line of the hills. Hannibal at first marched at great speed, since he was in a hurry to reach his objective.[1] But at the end of the fifth day he received a report that Pulcher was still engaged in besieging Capua. At this he halted and waited for the pursuing force to come up; then he launched a night attack on the Romans, killed a large number of them, and drove the rest out of their camp. However, when day broke and he saw that the Romans had retired and taken up a strong position on a steep hill, he decided not to continue his attack. Instead he directed his march through Daunia and Bruttium, and descended on Rhegium so unexpectedly that he came very near to capturing the city. As it was, he cut off all those of the inhabitants who had left for the country, and took prisoner a large number of the citizens.

8. It is right, I think, on this occasion to single out for our admiration the courage and resolution which both the Romans and the Carthaginians displayed in this campaign. There was a similar episode for which Epaminondas of Thebes earned universal praise by acting as I shall now describe.

When he reached Tegea with his allies,[2] he discovered that the Lacedaemonians had arrived at Mantinea with their whole army, and had gathered their allies in order to bring the Thebans to battle. He thereupon ordered his troops to take their evening meal at an early hour, and a little while after dark he led them out on the pretext that he was anxious to occupy some points of vantage before the coming battle. He gave this impression to the rank and file, but then continued his advance and made straight for Sparta, which he reached at about the third hour of the day.[3] He achieved complete surprise, and finding no one to defend the city, he forced his way right up to the market-place and occupied all that quarter

1. i.e. to reach Capua, from which he hoped that most of the Roman troops would have been withdrawn.

2. In 362 B.C.

3. The distance is about thirty-eight miles. It has been calculated that Epaminondas left Tegea towards 7 p.m. and reached Sparta between 8 and 9 on the following morning.

which faces the river. But here he encountered a stroke of bad luck. A deserter had escaped to Mantinea during the night and had informed King Agesilaus of what was happening, so that a Spartan relief force arrived just as the city was about to be occupied, and so frustrated Epaminondas' hopes. However, after giving his men their morning meal on the banks of the Eurotas, and allowing them a short rest to recover their strength after their hard march, he set off back at once by the same road, for he reckoned that since the Lacedaemonians and their allies had hurried to the rescue of Sparta, Mantinea would now be left without defenders in its turn, and this proved to be the case. So he called upon the Thebans to make yet another effort, and pressing ahead by forced marches through the night, he reached Mantinea by about midday and found it almost completely undefended. But just then the Athenians, who were vigorously supporting the Lacedaemonians in their struggle against the Thebans, arrived to help the former, in accordance with the terms of their treaty. And so at the very moment when the vanguard of the Theban army reached the temple of Poseidon, which is a little under a mile from the city, it so happened that the Athenians appeared as if by design on the hill which overlooks Mantinea. When they saw these troops, the few Mantineans who had been left behind summoned up enough courage to man the walls and drive off the Theban attack.

So when it comes to assigning the blame for the failure of these operations, the correct analysis is the one we are given by those historians who say that the commander did everything which a good general ought to do, and that Epaminondas got the better of his opponents, but was himself defeated by Fortune.

9. Much the same verdict may be passed in this instance on Hannibal, for we can hardly withhold our praise or admiration for a general who achieved all that he did. He began by taking the offensive against the enemy, and trying to force him to raise the siege with a series of harassing attacks. When this attempt failed, he made straight for Rome itself; then, when his plan to capture the city was frustrated by a turn of events which was beyond human calculation, he turned and both carried the pursuing enemy along with him and also kept watch so that in the likely event of the forces besieging Capua making some move, he could take advantage of it. Then

finally, and still in pursuit of his original plan, he applied himself to the destruction of the enemy, and all but depopulated Rhegium.[1]

As for the Romans, we must conclude that they dealt with this crisis better than the Lacedaemonians. The latter flocked off to rescue their native city the moment the news first reached them, but in so far as it depended on them they threw away Mantinea. The Romans, on the other hand, not only saved their own city, but so far from relaxing pressure on the Capuans, they held firmly and immovably to their purpose, and afterwards pursued the siege with greater determination than ever.

I have made these remarks not to pronounce a panegyric upon the Romans or the Carthaginians, whose qualities I have praised on many other occasions, but rather for the sake of the leaders of both these peoples, and of all those whose task it is to direct the affairs of states in times to come,[2] so that by recalling or picturing to themselves these events, they may be inspired to emulate them. In this way I hope they will acquire the nerve to undertake plans which may appear to be fraught with risk and danger, but which, on the contrary, are bold without being reckless, are admirable in their conception, and will deserve to live in men's memories whether they succeed or fail. The essential condition is that whatever is undertaken should be based upon sound reasoning.

1. Polybius' account of the fall of Capua has not come down to us. The end of the story is recorded in Livy, op. cit., XXVI. 12–16. In the same year (211) Capua fell, and Hannibal lost the Carthaginian garrison and his officers Hanno and Bostar who commanded it. Of the Capuan senators who had supported the city's secession from Rome, twenty-seven committed suicide and some seventy were executed by the Romans.

2. The wording of this sentence suggests that this book was written before the destruction of Carthage in 146 B.C.

On Generalship

The context of this discussion is unknown, but it is to be regarded as supplementary to Polybius' lost book on Tactics.

12. The hazards which are inseparable from military operations demand great vigilance, but it is possible to achieve success in any of these situations, provided that the measures taken in the execution of a given plan are soundly thought-out. Now it is easy to deduce from the history of former wars that far fewer operations are carried out openly and by employing direct force than by stratagem and the use of opportunity. On the other hand, experience also shows that in those actions which depend on the choice of the right moment, failure is more frequent than success. Nor can there be any doubt that the majority of these failures are due either to error or to negligence on the part of the commander. We may now consider how the competence I have referred to above can be attained.

I believe in the first place that all those events which occur in war and fall outside the scope of human calculation should be described not as *actions* but as *accidents* or *coincidences*. Accordingly, since they fall under no fixed rules nor form any part of a system, I propose to leave them aside: my subject is the conduct of a campaign according to a settled plan, which I shall now proceed to describe.

Every operation requires a fixed time for its commencement and a period and place for its execution. It also demands secrecy, recognized signals, known persons by whom and through whom it is to be carried out and a detailed operational plan. It is clear that the man who has correctly provided for all these factors will not fail in the final result, but on the other hand, the neglect of any one of them may wreck the whole scheme. So true is it that nature makes a single trivial error sufficient to cause the failure of a plan, and yet absolute precision in every detail is barely enough to ensure success.

13. It follows then that in such enterprises commanders cannot afford to overlook a single item. The first and most essential require-

ment is silence. A man must under no circumstances reveal his plan to anyone who is not involved in it, neither from joy if some unexpected hope should materialize, nor from fear, nor familiarity with nor affection for any individual; he must impart the knowledge of it only to those without whom it cannot be put into execution, and even then, not a moment sooner than is necessary, and only when the need for the services of each one demands it. Moreover, it is imperative to keep a check not only upon our tongues but even more so upon our minds, for many who have not opened their mouths have nevertheless betrayed their thoughts either by the expressions on their faces or by their actions.

The second requisite is a wide experience of the possibilities of movement by night and day, in other words an accurate knowledge of how long a march or a voyage will take, not only on land but also by sea. The third and most important is to have an appreciation of time derived from the observation of the heavens, and to make successful use of this for one's design.

Again, the choice of ground for the proposed operation is a matter of great importance, since this often proves the apparently impossible to be possible and vice versa. Finally, we must pay great attention to the matter of signals and counter-signals, and to the choice of individuals by whom or in whose company the scheme is to be carried out.

Of these essentials some are learned by routine experience, some by inquiry, and some by experience scientifically acquired. Ideally the commander should have a first-hand knowledge of the roads by which he is to march, of the place he is bound for, and of the nature of the ground, as well as of the people by whose agency and in whose company he intends to act. Failing this, the next best thing is that he should make careful inquiries and not rely on chance informants; it is also essential that the pledges of good faith given by his guides should always be in the hands of those who are following their guidance.

14. A commander may gain the requisite knowledge of these and similar matters in the course of his normal experience as a soldier, partly by practice and partly by inquiry. But the kinds of problem which involve scientific principles demand a scientific education, particularly in astronomy and in geometry, and although

the work involved in this is not extensive, at least for military purposes, the study itself is important, and potentially of great use in the kind of operations we are discussing. The most important aspect of astronomy from our point of view is that which concerns the principles which govern the length of nights and days. Obviously if day and night were always of equal length, the matter would give us no trouble and the knowledge involved would be common property. But since nights and days differ not only from one another, but also so to speak within themselves, it is clear that we must acquaint ourselves with the increase and decrease of both; for it is impossible to calculate correctly a day's march and the distance travelled in it without knowing the different lengths of day and night. In fact it is impossible to time any operation correctly without such knowledge: it will inevitably take place either too late or too soon. And here let me add that it is only in warlike enterprises that it is a worse fault to be ahead of time than behind it. For the commander who arrives later than the hour which has been determined only misses his opportunity, for he becomes aware of the fact before he arrives and so can get safely away, but he who arrives too early, approaches the enemy and is discovered, not only fails in his attempt, but runs the risk of being wiped out altogether.

15. It is the choice of the right moment which controls all human action, and above all the operations of war. This means that a general must have an exact knowledge of the dates of the summer and winter solstices and of the equinoxes, and of the increase and decrease of the days and nights in between, for only in this way will he be able to calculate proportionately the distances he can cover by sea or by land. He must also be familiar with the subdivisions of day and of night, so as to know at what hour to order the reveille or when to be on the march, for it is impossible to bring an operation to a successful end unless one has begun it correctly. The time of day may be calculated by observation either of the shadows of objects, or of the sun's course, or of its position in the sky. At night, however, it is difficult to be sure of the hour, unless one is familiar with the twelve signs of the zodiac and their system and order in the visible heavens; this knowledge is easy enough to acquire through a study of the constellations. Nights

are, naturally, of unequal length, but during the course of each one, whether long or short, six out of the twelve signs of the zodiac must rise above the horizon: it follows then that during the same portions of each night equal portions of the twelve signs must become visible. Now, as it is known which position in the zodiac the sun occupies each day, it is clear that as it sets in the west that part of the zodiac which is diametrically opposite must rise above the eastern horizon. Accordingly, the subdivisions of the night which follow the rising of the sign opposite the sun correspond to the rising and the passage across the heavens of the various signs in their successive order.[1] On cloudy nights, however, we must rely upon observation of the moon, because, generally speaking, on account of her size her light is always visible in whatever part of the heavens she may be. And so provided that we have sufficient knowledge to be acquainted with the daily variation in the time of her rising, we can guess the hour by noting the time and place sometimes of her rising and sometimes of her setting. In this case too the method of observation is simple enough, for the limit of the lunar cycle is generally speaking one month, and all the months are perceptibly alike.

16. We may therefore praise Homer's judgement because he represents Odysseus, the man fitted above all others for leadership, as observing the stars so as to guide not only his course at sea but also his enterprises on land. The fact is that those accidents which arise unexpectedly and defy accurate forecasting – such events as sudden rains and floods, exceptional frosts and snowfalls, foggy or cloudy weather and the like – are quite enough to cause great and frequent difficulties for us. But if we omit to provide even for those things which can be foreseen, then we are almost certain to fail in the majority of enterprises, and we shall have only ourselves to blame. None of these factors, then, can be neglected, if we are to avoid those errors into which many other generals are said to have fallen, as well as the particular instances which I shall quote.[2]

1. The important point in this formula is that different zodiacal signs rise at different speeds: thus in the short nights of summer six swiftly rising, and in the long nights of winter six slowly rising signs become visible.

2. There follows a series of examples of such errors, committed by Aratus, Cleomenes, Nicias and others, which has been omitted from this selection.

The Character of Hannibal

22. Everything that befell both peoples, the Roman and the Carthaginian, originated from one effective cause – one man and one mind – by which I mean Hannibal. It was he who beyond any doubt was responsible for the Italian campaign in Italy and who directed that in Spain, first through the elder of his brothers, Hasdrubal, and later through Mago: these were the generals who killed the two Roman commanders in that country, Publius and Gnaeus Scipio. Besides this he also managed affairs in Sicily first through Hippocrates[1] and later through Myttones the African.[2] He was also active both in Greece and in Illyria, where he succeeded in stirring up trouble and causing alarm to the Romans, and creating a threatening diversion through the pact which he made with Philip of Macedon.[3] So great and extraordinary a product of nature is a man who possesses a mind equipped by its original constitution to carry out any project that lies within the reach of human endeavour.[4]

However, since the course of events has led us to consider the character of Hannibal, I think it is incumbent upon me to give my opinion concerning those qualities which have aroused most controversy; and here I am thinking especially of the charges which have been levelled at him of excessive cruelty and excessive greed. And yet it is no easy matter to state the truth either about Hannibal in particular, or about other men in general who are engaged in public affairs. Some people hold that it is the force of circumstances which puts men's natures to the test, and that some are seen in their true character when they come into possession of power – even if they have hitherto managed to disguise it completely – and when they suffer misfortune. Personally I do not think this judgement is soundly based, for it seems to me that it is by no means the exception but rather the rule that men should

1. See pp. 353–5.
2. Myttones was sent by Hannibal to Sicily after the fall of Syracuse. After some early successes as a cavalry commander, he came to terms with the Romans.
3. See pp. 358–9.
4. Compare the phrase used of Archimedes, p. 368.

find themselves obliged to contradict their real principles in what they say or do, and this may be forced upon them either by the complexity of a situation or by the suggestions of their friends.

23. Past history will provide us with many examples of what I am saying. Consider first of all the case of Agathocles of Sicily. All the historians agree that he began by showing great cruelty in executing his early enterprises and establishing his power, but that later, as soon as he became convinced that his authority over the Sicilians was secure, he was regarded as the gentlest and most humane of men. Was not Cleomenes of Sparta at once a most excellent king, a most harsh tyrant, and again, in his private dealings a most considerate and courteous man? And yet it is not reasonable to suppose that such completely contradictory temperaments can exist side by side within the same natures. The truth is rather that some rulers are obliged to adapt their conduct to the demands of circumstances and to display towards others a disposition which is contradictory to their real natures, so that so far from men's characters being revealed by such situations, they are much more often disguised. The same kind of impression is often created as a result of the suggestions made by friends, and this applies not only to generals, rulers and kings, but also to states. Thus, for example, we find that in Athens while Aristides and Pericles were in power, the state was responsible for very few cruel actions, whereas at the period when Cleon and Chares wielded influence, the situation was just the reverse.[1] Again, at the time when Sparta became the most powerful state in Greece, King Cleombrotus[2] continually acted in the spirit of a policy of friendly alliance, while his contemporary King Agesilaus behaved in the opposite fashion, from which we must note that the character of states themselves is apt to vary with that of their rulers. So it was

1. Aristides' period of influence was between 490 and 477, though he was in exile during 483/2 and 480. Pericles was in office from 461–429. His opponent Cleon was at the height of his power from 429–422. Chares' political career lasted from 366 for thirty years, when he was active in opposing the power of Macedonia.

2. Of Sparta's two Kings during this period Cleombrotus, representing the Agiad dynasty, ruled from 380 until his death at the battle of Leuctra in 371. Agesilaus, the Eurypontid King, ruled from 399–360.

with King Philip of Macedon,[1] who acted most wickedly and impiously when Taurion and Demetrius were his agents, but in a far more humane fashion when he was associated with Aratus and Chrysogonus.

24. Hannibal, it seems to me, was faced with very similar conditions. The circumstances he had to deal with were at once extraordinary and continually changing; moreover, his closest associates differed so widely in character that it is extremely difficult to judge his real character on the evidence of the actions he carried out in Italy. As for what he did under pressure of circumstances, this is easy enough to trace from what I have already written and what is to follow, but we should not ignore the influence of his friends, especially as we know of one piece of advice which gives us a sufficient indication in this direction. At the time when Hannibal was considering the idea of taking his army to invade Italy from Spain, it was foreseen that he would meet extraordinary difficulties in feeding his troops and keeping them regularly supplied; indeed, the difficulties of the march appeared almost insuperable, both because of its length and because of the numbers and the savage nature of the barbaric inhabitants of the countries which lay between. It appears that these problems were discussed on several occasions at Hannibal's war council, and that one of his friends, a certain Hannibal who was surnamed Monomachus (The Gladiator), remarked that as far as he could see there was only one way by which they could manage to reach Italy. When Hannibal asked him to explain what he meant, Monomachus replied that they must teach the army to eat human flesh and accustom themselves to this. Hannibal could say nothing against either the audacity or the practicality of the idea, but he could not persuade himself or his friends to entertain it. It has been said that the acts of cruelty in Italy which were attributed to Hannibal were really the work of this man, but of course the pressure of circumstances played an equally important part.[2]

1. See p. 361 (Aratus) and p. 373 (Taurion).
2. Polybius attributes the tales of atrocities committed in Italy either to the actions of Monomachus (but did Hannibal lend them his authority?), or to force of circumstances in which Hannibal acquiesced. He does not discuss whether they were the inventions of propaganda.

25. Hannibal does appear to have been particularly fond of money, as was his friend Mago, who commanded in Bruttium. This account I obtained in the first place from the Carthaginians themselves, for the local inhabitants know best not only which way the wind lies, as the proverb says, but also the character of their compatriots. I also heard a more detailed version from Masinissa,[1] who spoke at length on the love of money, which is a general characteristic of the Carthaginians, and which was especially marked in the case of Hannibal and of his friend Mago, who was also known as the Samnite. Among other things, he revealed to me that these two men had generously shared out all kinds of operations with one another from their earliest youth. Each of them had captured many cities in Spain and in Italy, some by force of arms and some by treachery, but they had never actually taken part in the same enterprise. Indeed, they had taken greater pains to outmanoeuvre one another than the enemy; this was to ensure that the one should never be present when the other captured a city, so as to avoid any conflict of interest between them on such occasions, or any problem of having to share the spoils, since they were both of equal rank.

26. However, it was not only the suggestions of friends which changed and did violence to Hannibal's natural character. The pressure of circumstances played an even more important part, as my narrative will clearly show, both in the earlier and the succeeding chapters. When the city of Capua fell into the hands of the Romans, all the other cities began, not surprisingly, to falter in their attachment to the Carthaginians, and to look around for opportunities and pretexts for returning to their allegiance to Rome. In this crisis Hannibal was evidently plunged into a most difficult dilemma. If he established himself in one place, he might be threatened by several hostile armies seeking to intercept his movements, and it would be impossible for him to keep watch over all the cities, which were widely separated from one another. On the other hand, he could not split up his forces, for in that event he

1. The ruler of Numidia in Polybius' time. He belonged to the Massyli, a Numidian tribe, and commanded a Numidian contingent in Spain from 212 to 206. Later he joined Scipio and fought with him in Africa. The Romans recognized him as king and increased his territory at the expense of Carthage.

would fall an easy prey to the enemy: he could not personally command in several places at once, and each of his divisions would be outnumbered by their opponents. He was therefore forced to abandon some of the cities quite openly and to withdraw his garrisons from others, for fear that if they turned against him he would lose his own troops as well. In some instances he allowed himself to break the treaties he had made, removing the inhabitants to other towns and confiscating their property for plunder, and in this way he aroused great indignation, so that some peoples accused him of impiety and others of cruelty. These measures were inevitably accompanied by thefts of money, murders and pretexts for the use of violence, both by the departing and the incoming troops, since everyone acted on the assumption that the inhabitants who were left behind were on the point of going over to the enemy. All these factors make it exceptionally difficult to pass judgement on Hannibal's real nature, since we have to allow both for the influence of his friends and for the force of circumstances. At any rate the impression which prevailed about him was that to the Carthaginians he was notorious for his love of money, and to the Romans for his cruelty.

BOOK X

The Character of Scipio

2. Now that I am about to describe Scipio's exploits in Spain, and indeed the whole record of his achievements throughout his career, I think I must first of all draw my readers' attention to his character and qualities. The fact that he won greater fame than almost anyone before him makes the whole world curious to know what kind of man he was, and what were the natural gifts and the training which enabled him to succeed in so many great enterprises. And yet mankind at large can hardly avoid being led astray and forming a false opinion on these matters, since the description provided by those who have written about him departs so widely from the truth. The soundness of my claim will become clear to all those who are capable of appreciating through my narrative the most glorious and the most adventurous of his achievements. Now all other writers represent him as a man favoured by Fortune who usually succeeded in his undertakings against all the odds and with the help of mere chance, for they apparently consider that such men are more godlike and more worthy of our admiration than those who always act upon rational calculation. They do not seem to recognize that these are two quite different categories of achievement, the one being merely enviable, while the other is in the highest degree praiseworthy. The former is commonly encountered among quite ordinary men, while the latter can be achieved only by those of sound judgement and mental ability, and it is these whom we should regard as most godlike and most beloved by the gods.

Personally I consider that Scipio's character and principles were remarkably similar to those of Lycurgus, the Spartan law-giver. On this analogy, we should not assume that Lycurgus was unduly influenced by superstition, nor that he was constantly prompted by the Pythian priestess when he drew up the constitution of

Sparta,[1] nor in Scipio's case that he won so great an empire for his country by following the guidance of dreams and omens. Both men, no doubt, saw clearly that the majority of mankind are not easily persuaded of anything that is strange to them, nor will they venture upon great risks without the hope of some divine aid. And so Lycurgus made his scheme for society both more acceptable and more credible by constantly invoking the support of the Delphic oracle for what were really his own ideas, while Scipio likewise strengthened the confidence of the men under his command and their readiness to face dangerous enterprises by instilling into them the faith that his plans were divinely inspired. The fact remains, however, that his actions were invariably governed by calculation and foresight, and this will become clear from what I am about to say.

3. It is widely acknowledged that Scipio was a man of humane and generous disposition, but the testimony that he was also astute and discreet and possessed a mind which was always concentrated upon the purpose he had in view, comes only from those who were closely associated with him, to whom his character stood revealed as if by the light of day. One of these was Gaius Laelius,[2] who had been the witness of almost every word and deed of Scipio's from his boyhood until the end of his life, and who convinced me of the truth of his evidence, because what he had to say seemed probable in itself and corresponded to the record of Scipio's achievements. Scipio's first exploit on the battlefield, he told me, took place on the occasion of the cavalry action between his father's forces and Hannibal's in the neighbourhood of the Po.[3] He was at that time seventeen years old[4] and was taking part in his first campaign. The elder Scipio had put his son in command of a picked troop of horse to ensure the boy's safety, but when the latter caught sight of his father in the thick of the action sur-

1. Both Xenophon and Plato had contributed to the theory that Lycurgus derived his institutions from Delphi, or at least obtained approval from that quarter. Polybius praises Lycurgus for his foresight in recognizing 'the political cycle' and devising his mixed constitution to withstand it (see p. 303).

2. He was consul in 190, and must have survived Scipio by some twenty years to have been able to give information to Polybius.

3. The battle of the river Ticinus, described in Book III. 64.

4. Eighteen according to Livy, who is probably correct.

rounded by the enemy, dangerously wounded and with only two or three horsemen near him, he at first tried to urge the rest of his troop to ride to the rescue. Then, when he found they were hanging back because of the overwhelming number of the enemy around them, he is said to have charged by himself with reckless daring against the encircling cavalry. After this his comrades felt obliged to attack in support, whereupon the enemy were thrown into confusion and their formation broken up; and the general, finding himself thus unexpectedly saved, was the first to salute his son as his rescuer in front of the whole army. After this exploit had won him a reputation for bravery which all were bound to recognize he was careful to refrain from exposing himself to danger when his country's entire hopes rested upon his safety. Such conduct is not the mark of a general who trusts to luck, but of one who possesses intelligence.

Affairs in Spain

THE CAPTURE OF NEW CARTHAGE

These events took place in the spring of 209. Scipio's father Publius and his uncle Gnaeus had been defeated and killed in 212. In the following year Scipio, although only twenty-four, had volunteered in Rome to fight in Spain, and had immediately been appointed to the command.

6. To resume my narrative, on the occasion I am now describing Scipio called his men together and addressed them before crossing the Ebro. He urged them not to be disheartened by their recent defeats. 'The Romans,' he told them, 'have never been beaten by the Carthaginians in a trial of valour. We failed on this last occasion because of the treachery of the Celtiberians and of the rash action of our generals in allowing themselves to become separated from one another, on account of their trust in the alliance they had with the tribesmen.[1] But now the enemy themselves are suffering from

1. The Carthaginians had bribed the Celtiberians, who were serving as auxiliaries with the Roman forces, to desert.

the same disadvantages. Their armies are encamped far apart from one another, and because of their overbearing treatment of their allies, they have alienated them and turned them into enemies. The result is that some of them are already negotiating with us, while the rest, as soon as they can pluck up the courage and when they see that we have crossed the river will gladly take our side, and that is not so much out of any affection for us as because they long to take revenge on the Carthaginians for the outrages they have suffered. But most important of all is the fact that the enemy's commanders are quarrelling among themselves and are not willing to fight as a single army, while if they attack us separately it will be all the easier to defeat them.'

He called upon his soldiers to remember all these facts and to cross the river with confidence. After that it was his task and that of the other commanders to decide what should be the next step. When he had made this speech, he left his colleague Marcus Silanus with a detachment of 3,000 infantry and 500 cavalry to guard the ford and protect the allies to the north of the river, while he himself began to take the main body across. Meanwhile he did not confide his plans to anyone. The truth was that he had decided not to do any of the things he had given out in public, but to lay siege suddenly to the city to which the enemy had given the name of New Carthage.

I consider this action to be the first and strongest proof of the opinion which I expressed earlier. Scipio was at that time a mere twenty-seven years old, yet not only had he first of all grappled with a situation which because of the magnitude of the recent disasters had been generally regarded as hopeless, but having set himself the task, he rejected those solutions which were plain and obvious to everybody, and devised one which took his friends and the enemy equally by surprise. None of this was achieved without the most careful calculation.

7. The fact is that Scipio, right at the outset and while he was still in Rome, had made detailed inquiries about the treacherous action of the Celtiberians and the separation of the two Roman armies, and had come to the conclusion that these were the causes of his father's defeat. The result was that he was not weighed down, as most of his compatriots had been, either by fear of the Cartha-

ginians or by the general feeling of dismay. So when he learned later that the allies of Rome north of the Ebro were still loyal, and that the Carthaginian generals were quarrelling with one another and treating the Spaniards oppressively, he felt increasingly confident for the prospects of his expedition, and this was not because he trusted to Fortune, but from deliberate calculation. At any rate, as soon as he arrived in Spain he began to question everybody and to explore all sources of information, and he thus learned that the enemy's forces were divided into three groups. Mago, he heard, was occupying an area east of the Pillars of Hercules in the country of the tribe known as the Conii;[1] Hasdrubal, the son of Gisco, was in Lusitania near the mouth of the Tagus;[2] the other Hasdrubal[3] was engaged in besieging a city in the territory of the Carpetani; and, most important of all, each of them was at least ten days' march from New Carthage. Accordingly Scipio's appreciation was that if he decided to engage the enemy, it would be extremely dangerous to risk a battle with all three at once, bearing in mind that they had already defeated his predecessors and greatly outnumbered his own forces. On the other hand, if he made a forced march to attack one of the three, and the enemy refused battle, he might find himself surrounded if the other forces came up to help, in which case he feared a repetition of the disaster which had befallen his father and uncle.

8. He therefore ruled out these alternatives, but when he received intelligence that New Carthage was the most important base for supplying the enemy and a source of great damage to himself in the present war he took pains during the winter to gather information about the city from the people who knew it best. He discovered first of all that it was virtually unique among the cities of Spain in possessing a harbour which could accommodate a fleet and naval forces, and that it was also conveniently situated for the Carthaginians to make the direct sea crossing from Africa. He also learned that it was there that the Carthaginians kept the greater part of their money, all the baggage of their army and their mercenaries, the hostages they had taken from the whole of Spain, and,

1. In southern Portugal.
2. i.e. on the Atlantic coast of Portugal.
3. Hannibal's younger brother.

most crucial of all, that the fighting troops who garrisoned the citadel were only 1,000 strong. The reason for this was that so long as the Carthaginians controlled almost the whole of Spain, the possibility that anyone would think of besieging the city had never been foreseen. The rest of the population was large, but was composed of artisans, tradesmen and sailors, none of whom possessed any military experience. All these factors, Scipio considered, would tell against the city's security if he were suddenly to appear before it. Besides this he had familiarized himself with the topography of New Carthage, the general plan of the city and the character of the lagoon which encircled it. In particular he had learned from a number of fishermen who plied their trade there that the whole lagoon was shallow and could be forded at many points, and that the tide which covered it receded far enough every evening to make this possible. After weighing up all these factors, he came to the conclusion that if he could accomplish his plan he would at once deal a tremendous blow to the enemy and gain a decisive advantage for Rome. Moreover, even if his plan failed, he could still ensure the safety of his men because of his command of the sea, once he had secured his camp; this in itself presented no great problem because all the enemy's forces were still so far away. Scipio therefore put aside all other projects and devoted the whole of the time spent in winter quarters to preparing for this operation.

9. Now although he had conceived such an ambitious scheme and was still only, as I have explained, in his twenty-eighth year, he concealed all the details from everybody except Gaius Laelius, until the moment came when he thought it right to make the plan public. And yet while other authors agree that Scipio made these calculations, when they describe how the whole operation was carried out they give the credit not to the man himself and to his foresight but to the gods and to Fortune; they do this in spite of all probability, of the evidence of those who lived with Scipio, and of the fact that he wrote a letter to King Philip of Macedon, in which he explained that it was only after making the calculations I have just mentioned that he embarked on the Spanish campaign in general and on the operations at New Carthage in particular.

However that may be, he next issued secret orders to Laelius, who commanded the fleet, and who was, as I have explained, the only man who knew the details of the plan, to sail to New Carthage while Scipio himself advanced with his army by forced marches. He had with him about 25,000 infantry and 2,500 cavalry. He arrived at New Carthage on the seventh day of his march[1] and pitched his camp to the north of the town; it was protected by a trench and a double palisade which extended from the sea to the lagoon. He did not construct any defences on the side facing the town, as his position was well enough protected by the lie of the ground. But now that I am about to describe the siege and capture of the city, I must first give my readers a sketch of its geographical position and its surroundings.

10. New Carthage is situated about half-way down the eastern coast of Spain, in a gulf which faces south-west and is approximately two and a half miles long and a little over a mile wide. This gulf can be used as a harbour for the following reason. At its mouth lies an island with only a narrow passage on either side; this has the effect of breaking the sea-waves, so that the whole bay is extremely calm, except that the south-west wind sometimes blows through both the channels and raises a swell. This, however, is the only wind that ruffles the surface, since from other directions the bay is completely land-locked. From its innermost corner a peninsula crowned by a hill juts out, and on this height the city stands. On the east and south it is surrounded by the sea, and on the west by a lagoon. The latter extends so far to the north that the remainder of the peninsula, which is bordered by the sea on the other side and connects the city to the mainland, is only a quarter of a mile in breadth. The city itself has a depression in the centre, and on its southern side the approach to the sea is across level ground. On the other side it is surrounded by hills, two of which are high and rugged; the other two, although lower, are rocky and difficult to climb. The largest of the three rises to the east of the city, jutting out into the sea, and on it is built a temple of Asclepius. The second hill occupies a corresponding position on the western side, and has on it a splendid palace, which is said to have been built by Hasdrubal when he was aiming at establishing royal power.

The other three smaller eminences are situated to the north of

1. As the distance from the Ebro to New Carthage is nearly 500 miles, this seems an impossible estimate of his speed.

the city, the most easterly being known as the hill of Vulcan, the next as the hill of Aletes (who according to legend was granted divine honours for having discovered the silver mines) while the third is called the hill of Saturn. A canal has been cut to join the lagoon and the neighbouring sea for the convenience of shipping, and a bridge built over this channel, so that carts and beasts of burden can bring in supplies from the country.

11. Such is the nature of the city and its surroundings. The Roman camp was protected on its inner side both by the lagoon and by the outer sea, and so at this point needed no fortification. The intervening sector of the peninsula which joins the city to the mainland Scipio also left unfortified, even though it abutted upon the middle of his camp. He may have done this either to intimidate the enemy, or to accommodate the plan of the camp to his own purposes – so that for example there should be no obstacle to the passage of troops, when either making a sortie or withdrawing into the camp. The perimeter of the city was at that time no more than two and a half miles in circumference. I know that some authorities describe it as five or so, but this is incorrect, as I know from personal observation, not just from hearsay, and at the present day it has contracted still further.

When the fleet had taken up its station at the appointed date, Scipio decided to assemble the army and address his men; he intended to encourage them by using exactly the same arguments as those with which he had convinced himself and which I described above. He began by demonstrating to them that the operation was perfectly feasible, summed up briefly the damage which its success would inflict on the enemy and the advantages the Romans would gain from it, and went on to promise crowns of gold to the first men to scale the walls, and the usual rewards to those who showed conspicuous bravery. Finally he told them that it was Neptune who had first suggested the plan to him: he had appeared to Scipio in a dream and had promised to give the Romans such a spectacular sign of aid when the time for action arrived that his support would be unmistakably visible to the whole army. This shrewd combination of accurate calculation with the promise of gold crowns and the assurance of the help of Providence created great enthusiasm among the young soldiers and raised their spirits.

12. On the following day Laelius' ships, equipped with many different kinds of missiles, encircled the city on the seaward side, while on land Scipio sent forward 2,000 of his strongest men together with parties carrying the scaling-ladders, and at about the third hour he began the assault. Mago, the Carthaginian commandant, divided his garrison of 1,000 men into two groups, one being posted in the citadel and the other on the eastern hill. As for the rest of the inhabitants, he armed 2,000 of the most able-bodied with such weapons as he could find in the city, and posted them near the gate which faced the isthmus and the enemy's camp; the others he ordered to man the walls and defend them to the best of their ability. As soon as the bugles of Scipio's troops gave the signal for the assault to begin, Mago opened the city gate and launched a charge of the armed citizens; he believed that he could in this way create a panic among the enemy and upset their plan of assault. The citizens attacked with spirit the Roman troops who were drawn up outside their camp on the isthmus, and a furious battle developed, with the townspeople and the men in the camp shouting and cheering to encourage their comrades. But the strength of the two sides was far from equal: the Carthaginians issued through a single gate and had to cover nearly a quarter of a mile, while the Romans had their reserves close at hand and could enter the battlefield from many different points, and so the odds were heavily in their favour.

For his part Scipio had deliberately stationed his men close to the camp so as to draw the enemy out as far as possible, for he knew very well that if he could destroy these men, who represented as it were the steel edge of the civil population, he would so dishearten the rest that none of them would have the courage to venture beyond the gate. For the time being, however, the battle was stubbornly fought, since both sides had picked out their best men. But finally, as reinforcements continued to come up from the Roman camp, the Carthaginians were forced back by sheer weight of numbers, and then broke and fled. Many of them were killed in the fighting and the rout, but the greater number were trampled down by one another in panic as they crowded back through the gate. At this the inhabitants of the city were thrown into such dismay that even the defenders of the walls deserted their posts.

The Romans all but succeeded in forcing their way through the gate with the fugitives, and meanwhile were able to fix their scaling-ladders in place without opposition.

13. All this time Scipio himself had by no means remained aloof from the fighting, but had also taken all possible precautions for his safety. He had with him three men carrying large shields, which they held so as to cover him completely on the side which was exposed to the wall, and thus protected him from missiles. In this way he could pass along the lines, or survey the battle from higher ground, and so contributed a great deal to the needs of the moment, for not only could he see how the battle was developing, but the fact that he was in full view of his men inspired them to fight with redoubled spirit. The result was that nothing which could contribute to the success of Roman arms was left undone, and as soon as the situation suggested that some fresh measure was required, the need was quickly and effectively supplied.

When the Roman front ranks boldly stepped forward to mount the scaling-ladders, the danger of the operation arose, they found, not so much from the numbers of the defenders as from the height of the walls. Then the defenders themselves began to pluck up courage, as they saw the difficulties which threatened their opponents. Some of the ladders broke under the weight of the many men who had to climb them simultaneously because of the height of the walls, while on others the leading attackers became dizzy because they had climbed so far, so that very little effort was needed on the part of the besieged to throw them off the rungs. Again, whenever the defenders countered by hurling beams or other missiles from the battlements, all the men clinging to the ladders would be swept off and dashed to the ground. And yet in spite of these setbacks, nothing could check the ardour of the Roman assault, and whenever the leading attackers fell, their places were instantly taken by those behind them. But by this time the day was already far advanced, and as the soldiers were suffering badly from fatigue, Scipio ordered the assault force to be recalled.

14. The spirits of the garrison rose when they saw that they had, as they believed, beaten off the attack. Scipio, on the other hand, was now waiting for the tide to fall. He had mustered 500 men with scaling-ladders by the shore of the lagoon and had brought up

fresh reserves at the isthmus and in front of the eastern gate. Then after addressing his troops, he issued them with even more ladders than before, so that the whole stretch of the wall would be covered with men clambering up it. When the signal for the assault was again sounded and the attackers propped their ladders against the walls and swarmed up them with undaunted courage, a feeling of dismay swept over the defenders and their spirits sank. They had imagined themselves delivered from their ordeal, but now they were threatened by a fresh assault. Besides this, they were beginning to run short of missiles and were greatly disheartened by the number of men they had lost. And so it was only with difficulty that they met the attack, although they held out with such courage as they could muster.

Then, just as the struggle on the walls was at its height, the tide began to ebb. The water began to recede from the edges of the lagoon, and the outgoing current flowed so swiftly through the channel into the neighbouring sea that to those who were not familiar with this phenomenon the sight appeared incredible. Meanwhile Scipio had his guides ready and ordered all the men he had selected for this operation to step into the water and to have no fear, and indeed he possessed a special gift for instilling confidence and imparting his own enthusiasm to his men whenever he called upon them. At the moment when they obeyed and raced through the shallow water the whole army was imbued with the feeling that this enterprise must be the work of some god. When they remembered Scipio's words about Neptune and the promise he had made them in his speech, their ardour was redoubled; they locked their shields above their heads, forced a passage to the city gate, and strove to hack their way through it with axes and hatchets.

Meanwhile the force which had crossed the lagoon arrived at the city wall. They found the battlements deserted, and so not only set up their ladders unopposed, but swarmed up them and seized possession of the wall without striking a blow, for the defenders had been called away to other points, in particular to the isthmus and the eastern gate. Nobody had thought it possible that the enemy could reach the wall from the side of the lagoon, and most demoralizing of all there was such a babel of shouting and such scenes of confusion that it was impossible for the townspeople to hear or see to any purpose.

15. As soon as they had seized the wall, the Romans began to advance slowly along the top of it and to hurl off any of the enemy they met on their way, their weapons being particularly well-suited for fighting of this kind. When they reached the gate, some of them climbed down and began to slash through the bolts, whereupon their comrades outside began to force their way in. Meanwhile those who were attacking the walls on the side of the isthmus had by now overcome the defenders and gained a footing on the battlements. Finally, when they had seized possession of the walls in this fashion, the troops who had fought their way through the city gate dislodged the defenders of the eastern hill and captured it.

Scipio, when he judged that a large enough number of troops had entered the town, let loose the majority of them against the inhabitants, according to the Roman custom; their orders were to exterminate every form of life they encountered, sparing none, but not to start pillaging until the word was given to do so. This practice is adopted to inspire terror, and so when cities are taken by the Romans you may often see not only the corpses of human beings but dogs cut in half and the dismembered limbs of other animals, and on this occasion the carnage was especially frightful because of the large size of the population.

Scipio himself with about 1,000 men pressed on towards the citadel. Here Mago at first put up some resistance, but as soon as he knew for certain that the city had been captured he sent a message to plead for his safety, and handed over the citadel. Once this had happened the signal was given to stop the slaughter and the troops then began to pillage the city. When darkness fell, those of the Romans who had been detailed to guard the camp remained there, while Scipio with his 1,000 men bivouacked in the citadel. He then recalled the rest of his troops from the private houses of the city and ordered them through the military tribunes to collect all the spoils in the market place, each maniple bringing its own share, and then to mount guard over the plunder and sleep by it. He also summoned the *velites* from the camp and posted them to guard the eastern hill.

16. This was how the Romans gained possession of the city of New Carthage in Spain. Next day all the booty, both the baggage of the troops who had been serving with the Carthaginians, and the household possessions of the townsfolk and artisans, was collected in the market-place, where the military tribunes divided it among their respective legions, according to the Roman custom. After a city has been captured, the Romans adopt the following procedure with the spoils. Sometimes a proportion of the soldiers from each maniple and sometimes the whole maniple itself – the precise number depending on the size of the city – are detailed to collect plunder. They never use more than half the army on this task, and the rest remain in their ranks, it may be inside or outside the city, as the occasion may demand. The army is normally divided into two legions of Roman citizens and two of allies, and it is only on rare occasions that all four legions are assembled together. All those who have been detailed to collect the plunder then bring it back, each man to his own legion, and after it has been sold, the tribunes distribute the proceeds equally among all, including not only those who have been left behind in the protecting force, but also those who are guarding the tents or tending the sick, or who are absent on any special duties.

SCIPIO AND THE SPANIARDS

It was now the winter of 210, the year in which Scipio had captured New Carthage. He had already made a deep impression on the Spaniards by his generous treatment of the hostages he found there, and he now proceeded to build upon these foundations.

34. In Spain Publius Scipio, the Roman commander, was spending the winter at Tarraco, and there his first achievement was to win the trust and friendship of the Spaniards by restoring the hostages to their various families. In this undertaking he gained by chance the help of Edeco, the chief of the Edetani. This prince, as soon as he learned that New Carthage had been taken and that his wife and children were in Scipio's hands, at once foresaw that the Spaniards were likely to change sides, and was anxious to take the lead in

any such movement. He believed that by acting in this way not only did he stand the best chance of recovering his wife and children, but he would also appear to have attached himself to the Romans of his own free will and not by compulsion. And this was how events turned out. As soon as the troops had been dismissed to their winter quarters, Edeco presented himself at Tarraco with his relatives and friends. There, when he obtained an interview with Scipio, he said that he thanked the gods most fervently that he was the first of the Spanish chieftains to meet the Roman commander. The others, he explained, were still sending envoys to Carthage and looking for help from that quarter even while they were also stretching out their hands to the Romans, but he had come to entrust not only his own person but his friends and relatives to the good faith of Rome. If he were regarded as a friend and an ally he would be able to render the greatest service to the Romans both now and in the future. For as soon as the Spaniards saw that he had been admitted to friendship with the Roman general and that his requests had been granted, they would all rally to Scipio with a similar end in view – to have their relatives restored to them and to enjoy the alliance of Rome. If they were treated with such honour and consideration, their loyalty would be so firmly secured that they would give him their full support throughout the rest of his operations. He therefore asked that his wife and children should be restored to him, and that before he returned to his kingdom he should be declared a friend of Rome; he asked for these two concessions to give him the chance to demonstrate by every means in his power the goodwill which he and his friends felt for the Roman cause.

35. These were the points which Edeco made, and when he had finished speaking, Scipio, who had been thinking along much the same lines and who was already inclined to grant his request, returned Edeco's wife and children and declared him to be his friend. Indeed he went further than this, and in the course of their conversation he charmed the Spaniard in a number of ways: he held out high hopes for the advantages that all those who were associated with Edeco would enjoy in the future, and finally sent them back home. The outcome of this meeting was soon reported

far and wide, and all the Spanish tribes living north of the Ebro who had not previously been on friendly terms with the Romans now, as if with one accord, came over to their side.

Scipio's affairs were now developing as favourably as he could wish, and so after the Spanish envoys had left he disbanded his naval force, seeing that there was nothing to challenge his command of the sea. He picked out the best of the crews, distributed them among the maniples, and in this way increased the strength of his land forces.

Now at this time Andobales and Mandonius, two of the most powerful chieftains in Spain, were generally believed to be among the most loyal supporters of the Carthaginians. The truth was, however, that they had for a long time been disaffected and were only awaiting the right moment to revolt. This had been the case ever since Hasdrubal, as I mentioned in an earlier chapter, had demanded that they should pay a large sum of money and hand over their wives and daughters as hostages – all this on the pretext that he mistrusted them. They decided that the present moment provided a good opportunity and so they collected all their forces, left the Carthaginian camp by night, and withdrew to some high ground which offered a strong enough position to ensure their safety. Thereupon the majority of the other Spaniards also deserted Hasdrubal. They had long resented the arrogant behaviour of the Carthaginians, and they seized the first opportunity that presented itself to show their feelings.

36. The same thing has happened in the past to many other peoples. For, as I have had occasion to remark before, it is a great feat to steer a policy to a successful conclusion or to overcome one's enemies in a campaign, but it requires a great deal more skill and caution to make good use of such triumphs. Thus we find that those who have won victories are far more numerous than those who have used them well, and this is precisely what happened to the Carthaginians at that time. After they had defeated the Roman forces and killed their two commanders, Gnaeus and Publius Scipio, they imagined that their position in Spain had been secured beyond any possible doubt. They went on to treat the native population in an overbearing manner, with the result that their subjects, instead of being their allies and friends, became their

enemies. This process was perfectly natural, because the Carthaginians had assumed that the method by which power should be acquired is quite different from that by which it should be maintained, and they had not discerned that the people who preserve their supremacy best are those who uphold the same principles by which they originally won it. And yet it is evident enough and has been observed over and over again that men gain power by acting humanely towards their neighbours and by holding out the prospect of a better life for the future. But if, after they have achieved the desired supremacy, they then maltreat their subjects and govern them tyrannically, it is only natural that when the policy of the rulers has changed, the attitude of their subjects should follow suit. This is what now befell the Carthaginians.

37. In this situation Hasdrubal was exposed to many different anxieties concerning the dangers that threatened him. First he was disturbed by the revolt of Andobales, secondly by the opposition of the other commanders and their hostility towards him, and thirdly by the presence of Scipio in the vicinity, for he expected that the Roman would very soon arrive with his army. So when he found he was being deserted by the Spaniards, who were all with one accord going over to the enemy, he decided upon the following plan. He would make all possible preparations and then engage the enemy in battle. If Fortune were to give him the victory, he could safely consider what his next action should be, but if he were defeated he would retreat with the survivors into Gaul; there he would recruit as many of the natives as possible, and then march into Italy to share the fortunes of his brother Hannibal.

After deciding on this course of action Hasdrubal continued his preparations. Meanwhile Scipio was rejoined by Gaius Laelius,[1] who reported to him the instructions of the Senate. Scipio then collected his troops and marched them out of their winter quarters; on his way he was joined by the Spaniards who welcomed him with enthusiasm when their forces met. Andobales had for some time already been in communication with Scipio, and when the latter drew near the district in which he was encamped he gathered his friends together and paid a visit to the Roman commander. When the two men met, Andobales explained how he had once

1. In March 208. Laelius had just visited Rome.

been on friendly terms with the Carthaginians, and dwelt on the various services he had rendered them and on his loyalty to their cause. Then he went on to describe the various injustices and insults he had suffered at their hands. He therefore appealed to Scipio to judge for himself the truth of all he had said. If it appeared that he was accusing the Carthaginians unjustly, then it would be clear to Scipio that he would not keep faith with Rome. But if after taking into consideration all the wrongs he had suffered, it were proved that he had no choice but to abandon his former friendship with them, then Scipio could rest assured that once he had chosen to side with the Romans he would be steadfast in his attachment to them.

38. Andobales had more to say on this subject, and when he had finished Scipio replied that he fully accepted all the Spaniard had told him. He himself had the clearest evidence of the arrogance of the Carthaginians' behaviour, and in particular of their licentious treatment of the wives and daughters of the chieftain and his friends, whom he had found in the situation of captives and slaves rather than hostages. He added that he had honoured his obligations towards them with a strictness which their own fathers could scarcely have equalled. Andobales and his companions acknowledged that they knew this, and they all did obeisance to him and saluted him as king. Everyone who was present applauded their words, whereupon Scipio, who was much moved, told them to take heart, for they would meet with nothing but kindness at the hands of the Romans. He then at once handed over the Spaniards' daughters, and next day made a treaty with them, the principal condition of the agreement being that they should follow the Roman commanders and obey their orders. After these arrangements had been concluded the Spaniards went back to their own camp, gathered their forces and returned to Scipio. There they were quartered in the Roman camp[1] and joined the advance against Hasdrubal.

The Carthaginian commander was then encamped in the district of Castalon, near the town of Baecula and not far from the silver

1. Allies were not always quartered in a Roman camp; in view of the earlier defeat of Scipio's father by the Spanish tribes, this perhaps represented a special gesture of confidence.

mines. When he learned of the arrival of the Romans, he moved his camp to a new site in which his rear was shielded by a river and his front by a stretch of level ground: this was wide enough to enable him to deploy his troops and was bounded by a ridge sufficiently steep for effective defence. Here he remained in position, keeping his covering force on the ridge in advance of his main body. Scipio when he came up was eager to give battle, but felt uncertain as to how to proceed when he saw what a strong and advantageous position the enemy had chosen. However, after waiting for two days he became alarmed at the possibility that Mago and Hasdrubal, the son of Gisco might arrive, in which case he would find himself surrounded by the enemy on all sides, and he therefore determined to venture an attack and try the enemy's strength.

39. Having prepared his army for battle, he kept the main body within his camp but sent forward the *velites* and a picked force of infantry with orders to climb the ridge and attack the enemy's covering force. They carried out the order with great gallantry, and at first the Carthaginian commander made no move and waited for the outcome of this action; however, when he saw that his men were being hard-pressed and were suffering heavy losses from the fury of the Roman attack, he led out his troops and drew them up along the brow of the hill, relying on the natural strength of the position. Scipio responded by sending forward his light-armed troops, ordering them to reinforce the *velites* who had begun the attack:[1] then, having the rest of his army ready for action, he took half of the main body and working his way round the ridge attacked the Carthaginians from the left flank. The other half under the command of Laelius were ordered to proceed in similar fashion and attack from the right. While this manoeuvre was in progress Hasdrubal was still engaged in leading his troops out of the camp. Up to this moment he had waited there, trusting to the natural strength of his position and feeling confident that the enemy would never venture to attack him, and so because the flank assault took him by surprise, he was too late in deploying his troops. The Romans were now attacking the wings of the Carthaginian position

1. The distinguishing feature of these tactics is the holding attack by the light-armed troops in the centre, while the heavy infantry are used to attack on both flanks.

where their opponents had not yet occupied the ground, and they not only succeeded in scaling the ridge without loss, but as the enemy were still moving into their positions when they charged, they killed some of them by attacking on the exposed flank, and forced others to turn and flee while they were still attempting to form their line.

When Hasdrubal saw his troops retreating and thrown into confusion, he fell back on his original plan and decided not to fight it out to the death. Instead he gathered together his elephants and his war-chest, and collecting as many as possible of the fugitives, he retreated along the valley of the Tagus and made for the pass which led over the Pyrenees and towards the Gallic tribes who inhabited that part of the country. Scipio thought it unwise to follow Hasdrubal, for fear of being attacked by the other Carthaginian generals; instead he gave up the enemy's camp to his soldiers to plunder.

40. The next day he collected the prisoners, who numbered some 10,000 infantry and more than 2,000 cavalry,[1] and occupied himself with making the necessary arrangements for them. All the Spaniards living in the region I have described[2] who were still allies of the Carthaginians now came to make their submission to the Romans, and when they encountered Scipio, they saluted him as king. Edeco had been the first to do this and make obeisance to him, and later Andobales had followed suit. On those occasions Scipio had passed over the salutation without taking any particular note of it, but after the battle when all the tribes hailed him as king, he began to give the matter his attention. He therefore summoned the Spaniards to a meeting and told them that he was willing to be spoken of by them all as kingly, and indeed to act in a truly kingly manner, but that he did not wish to be a king or to receive this title from anyone.[3] After he had explained this, he told them to call him *imperator*.

1. These numbers sound exaggerated, as Hasdrubal's army totalled some 25,000 in all.

2. i.e. near Castulo, in the vicinity of the modern town of Linares.

3. Scipio could of course never forget the hatred with which the word 'king' was regarded in Rome. Polybius evidently took the title to be used in the Hellenistic sense of a man with military, moral and intellectual qualities of a kingly character. This may also be the earliest recorded instance of the acclamation of a general by his troops as *imperator*.

Perhaps even at this early stage of his career it would be right to take note of Scipio's greatness of mind. The proof of this is that although he was still quite a young man, and had been so conspicuously blessed by Fortune that all those who came under his authority were moved of their own accord to pay him this tribute and speak of him as a king, he nevertheless kept his self-control and moderated this popular impulse and the accompanying show of dignity. But this exceptional greatness of mind is even more to be admired during the closing scenes of his life, when in addition to his exploits in Spain he had defeated the Carthaginians, subdued the largest and most prosperous regions of Africa from the Pillars of Hercules to the Altars of Philaenus to his country's rule, conquered Asia and overthrown the Kings of Syria, brought the greatest and richest area of the known world under the sway of Rome, and enjoyed the opportunity of exercising royal power wherever he chose to stretch out his hand for it. Such achievements indeed might have tempted not only a man but even a god, if the expression is permissible, to display arrogance; yet Scipio so far excelled all other men in this quality of magnanimity that when the prize of kingship, the highest ambition for which a man would even dare to pray to the gods, was often placed within his grasp by Fortune, he declined it and set a higher value upon his country and his loyalty to her than the status of kingship, which is the object of universal admiration and envy.

Scipio then proceeded to pick out all the Spaniards from among his prisoners, and released them to return to their homes without ransom. He also gave orders that Andobales should choose for himself 300 of the captured horses; the rest he distributed among those who had none. After this he moved his troops into the Carthaginian camp because of its excellent situation. He himself remained there, waiting to see what the other Carthaginian generals would do, but he also dispatched a body of men to the pass leading over the Pyrenees so as to keep watch on Hasdrubal's movements. Finally, as it was by now late in the season, he withdrew with his army to Tarraco to spend the winter in that district.

BOOK XI

Affairs in Italy

THE BATTLE OF THE METAURUS

Hasdrubal had wintered in Gaul in 208/7, crossed the Alps in the spring of 207, and perhaps arrived in the Po valley in May. To prevent the junction of his army with Hannibal's, one consul, Gaius Claudius Nero, had been sent to watch the latter in the south, the other, Marcus Livius Salinator, to oppose Hasdrubal in the north. Hasdrubal's messages to his brother were intercepted, and revealed that the hoped-for meeting of the two armies was to take place in Umbria. Livius had encamped close to Hasdrubal, and Nero, leaving a covering force to watch Hannibal, detached 6,000 infantry and 1,000 cavalry and succeeded in joining forces with Livius. When Hasdrubal learned that the consular army facing him had been reinforced, he tried to withdraw northwards, but missed his way and was overtaken by the Romans at the river Metaurus.

1. Hasdrubal's arrival in Italy was far easier and more rapid than had been expected.

Never before had Rome been so tense with excitement and dread as the citizens awaited the outcome of the battle ...

None of these factors pleased Hasdrubal, but the situation gave him no time for delay since he could see that the Romans were already in battle order and were advancing upon him; he was therefore compelled to draw up the Spaniards and the Gauls who were serving with him. He proceeded to station his elephants, which were ten in number, in advance of his line, and he increased the depth of his ranks so that the whole army covered only a narrow front. Then he himself took up position in the centre behind the elephants and attacked the enemy's left; he had already determined that in this battle he would either conquer or die. At the same time Salinator and his troops moved forward against the enemy with a confident and measured step, and when the two lines met his troops fought with great courage. The other consul, Gaius Claudius Nero, who was stationed on the right wing, could not advance and outflank the enemy because of the difficult nature of the ground in front of him, and Hasdrubal had relied on this fact when he attacked the Roman left. At first the consul was in a quandary at being thus immobilized, but presently circumstances showed him what needed to be done. He regrouped his men, and transferring some of them from the rear of the right wing, he passed round the Roman battle line to the left, and attacked the Carthaginians on their right flank where the elephants were stationed. Up till then the issue had hung in the balance, the soldiers on both sides fighting with desperate courage, for there was as little hope of safety for the Romans if they were defeated as there was for the Spaniards and the Carthaginians. The elephants too had proved of no more service to the one side than to the other, for as they were hemmed in between the two armies and exposed to a hail of missiles, they threw both the Roman and the Spanish ranks into disorder. But as soon as Nero's troops worked their way round and charged from behind the enemy, the balance was changed, as the Spaniards now found themselves being attacked from front and rear, and most of them were cut to pieces on the battlefield. Six of the elephants were killed with their mahouts, and the other four forced their way through the lines and were later captured alone, as their drivers had abandoned them.

2. Hasdrubal had shown himself to be a brave man throughout his life; now in his last hour he died in the thick of the fighting, and I must not take leave of him without paying the tribute that is his due. I have already mentioned that he was Hannibal's brother and that when Hannibal left Spain he had placed him in command of the province. I have also described how in his many battles against the Romans and amid the various difficulties with which he had to contend because of the character of the generals who were sent from Carthage to serve with him, he had endured all these reverses and changes of fortune with a fortitude and a nobility of spirit that were worthy of a son of the great Barca. I will now explain how in his last battle he set an example which in my opinion deserves both to be noted and to be emulated. It is

especially noticeable that most generals and kings, when they embark upon a decisive battle, all the time have in their mind's eye the glory and the advantages they will win if they succeed. Their whole attention is concentrated upon how they will manage affairs assuming that everything goes in their favour, but it does not occur to them to envisage the possibility of failure, or to make plans about what they should do or how they should behave in the event of defeat. Yet the truth is that the first course presents few difficulties, whereas the second requires great foresight. The result is that most of them, because of their lack of spirit or of resource in such an eventuality, render their defeat positively humiliating. Such commanders, although their men may have fought bravely for them, tarnish the memory of their former exploits, and make themselves objects of reproach for the rest of their lives. It is easy to see that many leaders fall into this error, and since history affords us so many examples of the fact, it follows that herein lies the most important difference between the quality of one commander and another. By contrast, Hasdrubal, so long as there was a reasonable prospect that he could accomplish something worthy of his past achievements, treated his safety in battle as a matter of the greatest importance. But when Fortune had deprived him of all hope for the future and driven him to the last extremity, then, while he used every resource which might bring him victory both in his preparations for the battle and on the field itself, he gave equal thought as to how in the event of total defeat he should face that eventuality and suffer nothing unworthy of his past career.

These remarks may serve as a warning to all those who direct public affairs that they should neither betray the hopes of those who trust in them by recklessly exposing themselves to danger, nor by clinging to life when duty has shown them another path add shame and disgrace to the disasters which have already befallen them.

3. The Romans, having won the battle, proceeded to pillage the enemy's camp. There they found many of the Celts lying drunk and asleep on their litter beds, and slaughtered them like so many sacrificial victims. They then rounded up the rest of the prisoners, and this part of the spoils yielded them more than 300 talents to the treasury. No less than 10,000 Carthaginians and

Gauls were killed in the battle;[1] the Roman losses amounted to 2,000. Some of the Carthaginians of high rank were captured, but the rest of them were killed. When the news of the victory arrived in Rome, the people at first could not believe it, for the very reason that they had been so anxious for it to happen. But when more messengers arrived, not only announcing the fact but elaborating the details, then the whole city was plunged into transports of joy. Every sanctuary was decorated and every temple loaded with sacrificial offerings or victims. The Romans experienced a mood of such hope and confidence that it was as though Hannibal, whom they had so much dreaded until now, was no longer in Italy at all.

The Character of Hannibal

19. It is impossible to withhold our admiration for Hannibal's leadership, his courage and his ability in the field, when we consider the duration of his campaigns, and take note of the major and minor battles, the sieges, the defections of cities from one side to the other, the difficulties he encountered at various times, and in short, the whole scope of his design and its execution. For sixteen years he waged ceaseless war against the Romans in Italy, and throughout that time he never released his army from service in the field, but, like a good pilot, kept those great numbers under his control and free from disaffection either towards himself or one another. He succeeded in this despite the fact that he was employing troops who belonged not only to different countries but to different races. He had with him Africans, Spaniards, Ligurians, Celts, Phoenicians, Italians and Greeks, men who had nothing naturally

1. Polybius' figures are much more convincing than Livy's, who gives the Carthaginian dead as 56,000 and the Roman as 8,000. Modern scholars estimate Hasdrubal's strength at 30–35,000 men, approximately the same as Livius' army. Some of these escaped or never reached the battlefield: it is reckoned that about 10,000 were taken prisoner. Livy, in *The War with Hannibal*, at the end of XXVII. 51, relates the story that the first news which Hannibal received of the disaster was when the head of his brother was flung on to the ground in front of his outposts.

in common, neither in their laws, their customs, their language, nor in any other respect. None the less the skill of their commander was such that he could impose the authority of a single voice and a single will even upon men of such totally diverse origins. And all this he achieved under conditions which were by no means consistent but perpetually changing, with the gale of fortune often blowing in his favour, but also at times in the opposite direction. There are excellent reasons, therefore, for admiring Hannibal's ability in these respects, and we can say with confidence that if only he had subdued other parts of the world first and finished with the Romans, not one of his projects would have eluded him. But as it was, since he turned his attention first to those whom he should have dealt with last, his career began and ended with them.

BOOK XII

Criticisms of Timaeus and His Approach to History

ERRORS ON THE FAUNA OF AFRICA AND CORSICA

3. It is impossible not to be impressed by the richness of the soil of Africa, and therefore one is inclined to say of Timaeus' account not only that he was unacquainted with Africa but that he was childish, deficient in judgement and a slave to those ancient traditions which have been handed down to us to the effect that the whole of Africa is sandy, dry and barren. The same is true regarding its animal life, for the total of horses, oxen, sheep and goats which inhabit the country is so immense that I doubt whether an equal number can be found in all the rest of the world. The reason for this is that many of the African tribes make no use of cereals, but live among the flocks and herds and eat their flesh. Again, who has not read of the great numbers and the strength of the elephants, lions and panthers of Africa, or the beauty of its antelopes, or the size of its ostriches? These creatures do not exist at all in Europe, while Africa is full of them. Timaeus had made no inquiries into this fact, and indeed seems to have set out deliberately to record the opposite of the actual truth.

In the case of Corsica he again gives us the same kind of haphazard account as he does of Africa. In the description which he includes in his second book he says that the island contains many wild goats, sheep and cattle, as well as deer, hares, sheep, wolves and certain other animals, that the inhabitants spend their time hunting these creatures, and that this is their sole occupation. But in fact not only is there not a single wild goat or wild ox on the island, but also no hares, wolves, deer, or similar creatures, except for a number of foxes, rabbits and wild sheep. The rabbit, when seen from a distance, looks like a small hare, but when you catch it it differs a great deal from a hare, both in appearance and in taste, and it lives for the most part underground.

4. The impression that all the animals on the island are wild arises from the following cause. The island is thickly wooded and the countryside so rocky and precipitous that it is impossible for the shepherds to follow their flocks and herds about as they graze. So whenever they wish to collect them they take up position in some convenient place; from there they summon them by horn, and all the animals respond without fail to the instrument which they recognize. Now if any travellers who may touch at the island see goats and cattle grazing unattended and try to catch them, the animals will not come near them because they are not used to them and take to flight. Again, if the shepherd sees the strangers disembarking and sounds his horn, the herd will run off at full speed and gather round the horn. For this reason the animals give the appearance of being wild, and Timaeus, after making some careless and perfunctory inquiries, has set down this random statement.

There is nothing surprising in the fact that the animals should obey the sound of a horn, for in Italy those who are engaged in herding swine use exactly the same method. The swineherd does not follow the animals, as he does in Greece, but walks in front and sounds a horn at intervals, while the animals keep behind him and respond to the call. Indeed the pigs have become so accustomed to answering the particular instrument belonging to their herd that those who witness this practice for the first time are amazed and can hardly believe their ears. The fact is that because of the great size of the population and the abundance of food the droves of swine in Italy are very large, especially among the inhabitants of Tuscany and the Gauls, so that a single farrowing of a single herd may produce a thousand or even more piglets. The peasants therefore drive them out from their night sties to feed according to their litters and ages. Then if several droves are taken to the same place, they cannot keep the various groups apart, and so they become mixed up, either while they are being driven out, or as they are feeding, or on the way home. So the swineherds invented the horn call as the simplest method of separating them without labour or trouble when the litters had become mixed. And in practice whenever one of the swineherds leads off in one direction sounding his horn, and another turns away in another direction, the animals separate of their own accord and follow with such eagerness the sound of the individual horn which they know that it is impossible to check them or turn them back.

In Greece, on the other hand, if different herds belonging to different owners meet one another in the oak forests in their search for acorns, whichever swineherd has the most assistants with him and the best opportunity is apt to take his neighbours' pigs when he drives his own away. Alternatively, a thief may lie in wait and drive off some of the animals without the swineherd knowing how he lost them; this is because the pigs are inclined to wander off a long way from their masters in their eagerness to find the acorns at the time when they are beginning to fall.

ERRORS CONCERNING SICILY

4c. It is clear from the evidence I have quoted that Timaeus' descriptions of Africa, of Sardinia, and above all of Italy[1] are unreliable, and that speaking generally he has quite neglected the business of making first-hand inquiries, which is the historian's most important duty. For since many events occur simultaneously in different places and it is impossible for the same man to be everywhere at once, and likewise impossible for him to have seen with his own eyes all the different places in the world and observed their peculiar features, the only course which remains to a historian is to question as many people as possible, to believe such witnesses as are trustworthy, and to prove himself a good judge of the reports that reach him.

4d. Yet although Timaeus dwells at great length upon the need for accuracy, he seems to me to fall a long way short of the truth. So far from making a thorough investigation of the facts by questioning others, he cannot give us reliable information even about things which he has seen with his own eyes or places he has visited in person. This will become sufficiently clear if we demonstrate his ignorance of the facts in respect of some of the statements which he has made about Sicily. It will surely require little more evidence of his inaccuracy if we find that he was ignorant or wrongly informed about even the most celebrated places in the country where

1. No examples of Timaeus' inaccuracies concerning Sardinia or Italy have survived.

he was born and bred. Thus he tells us that the fountain of Arethusa in Syracuse has its source in the Peloponnese in the waters of the river Alpheius, which flows through Arcadia and past Olympia. This river, he says, then plunges into the earth, flows for nearly 500 miles[1] under the Sicilian Sea, and then reappears in Syracuse. This, he maintains, is proved by the fact that once upon a time after heavy rains had fallen at the time of festival at Olympia and the river had flooded the sanctuary there, the fountain of Arethusa threw up a quantity of dung from the beasts which had been sacrificed at the festival, and even a golden bowl which the Syracusans recognized as one of the vessels used at Olympia, and kept for themselves.

INTENTIONAL AND UNINTENTIONAL FALSEHOODS

11a. Timaeus remarks that the greatest offence in the writing of history is falsification; he therefore advises all those whom he has convicted of making false statements to find some other name for their books, and call them anything they may choose, but not history.

12. Taking as an analogy the case of a carpenter's rule, he argues that it may be too short or too narrow for one's purpose, but that so long as it possesses the essential attribute of a rule, namely straightness, it must still be called a rule. On the other hand if it lacks straightness or fails to conform at all to that quality, it must be called anything rather than a rule. The same principle applies to historical works: those which are faulty in style or in treatment or any other particular, yet still keep a grasp upon the truth, are entitled to be called histories, while those which fall away from the truth must no longer be called by that name. I would agree with him that truth must play the dominant role in works of this kind, and I made a similar statement elsewhere in this work[2] to the effect that just as a living creature, if it is deprived of its eyesight, is rendered completely helpless, so if history is deprived of the truth, we are left with nothing but an idle, unprofitable tale.

I have also remarked, however, that there are two kinds of falsehood, the one being the result of ignorance and the other

1. In fact some 330 miles.　　　　2. See p. 55.

intentional, and that we should pardon those who depart from the truth through ignorance, but unreservedly condemn those who lie deliberately. So much being agreed, I maintain that there is a great difference between the kinds of falsehood which arise from ignorance and from intention respectively. The one is pardonable and deserves kindly correction, but the other outright condemnation, and it will be seen that Timaeus himself is a prime offender in this latter respect, as I shall now proceed to show.

TIMAEUS ON CALLISTHENES, DEMOCHARES OF ATHENS, AGATHOCLES OF SICILY

12b. We are certainly entitled to criticize and ridicule the wild outpourings of those authors who dream dreams and write like men possessed. But those who have themselves produced a great deal of such nonsense should, so far from attacking others, think themselves lucky if they escape blame. This indeed is Timaeus' own position. He condemns Callisthenes as a flatterer for writing in the style that he did, contends that he was far from being a philosopher since he paid so much attention to ravens[1] and raving women, and concludes that Alexander was fully justified in punishing him, since he had corrupted the young King's mind as far as was in his power. He praises Demosthenes and the other orators who were active at that time, and says that they were men worthy of Greece because they spoke against the granting of divine honours to Alexander; the philosopher, on the other hand, he argues, thoroughly deserved the fate that befell him, since he had invested

---

1. In 331 Callisthenes accompanied Alexander on his journey across the Libyan desert to visit the shrine of Zeus Ammon at the Siwa Oasis. Hence the reference to the ravens: these birds are said to have guided the march when the tracks across the desert had been obliterated. 'What was most remarkable of all,' according to Callisthenes, 'was that if any of the company went astray in the night, the birds would croak and caw over them until they had found their way back to the track.' Timaeus alleges that Callisthenes flattered Alexander by representing him as the son of Zeus in consequence of the visit to the oracle. See Plutarch, *Life of Alexander*, 27. Later Callisthenes fell out of favour because he criticized Alexander's adoption of certain Persian customs, especially the act of receiving obeisance from the Macedonians. He was tutor to Hermolaus and thus became implicated in the conspiracy of the pages, and is said to have been executed or died in prison in 327. See *Life of Alexander*, 55.

a mere mortal with the aegis and the thunderbolt of Zeus, and so was rightly visited by divine retribution.

13. Elsewhere Timaeus alleges that Demochares[1] was guilty of unnatural lust, that he was thus unworthy to blow the sacred flame, and that in his erotic practices he went far beyond the writings of Botrys, Philaenis and other pornographic authors. Indeed Timaeus has uttered scurrilous charges and abuse such as one would scarcely hear from the inmates of a brothel, let alone a man of culture. And in order to make his habit of launching foul accusations and his total lack of decency more credible he has libelled Demochares even further, dragging in the evidence of an obscure comic poet. You will ask on what grounds I conclude that the charge was false? In the first place because Demochares was a man of good family and upbringing, being the nephew of Demosthenes, and secondly because he was considered by the Athenians to be worthy not only of being elected general[2] but of holding other offices as well, none of which would have come his way if he had had such acts of shame to combat. So Timaeus, as it seems to me, is accusing not so much Demochares as the Athenian people for advancing such a man and entrusting their lives and their country to his charge. But in fact none of this is true. If it were, then not only Archedicus the comic poet would have said this about Demochares, as Timaeus alleges; it would have been repeated by many of Antipater's friends, for Demochares had ventured to speak with great licence against him and to say many things that were likely to annoy not only the Macedonian general[3] but his successors and friends, one of whom was Demetrius of Phalerum.[4] The same charge would also have been exploited by

1. Demochares of Leuconoe (c. 350–275), the son of Demosthenes' sister, was a democratic statesman of Athens who was well-known for the outspoken character of his oratory. He was active at Athens after the expulsion in 307 B.C. of the Macedonian regency set up by Cassander under Demetrius of Phalerum. The city was liberated from its Macedonian occupiers by a sudden invasion led by Demetrius Poliorcetes, the son of Antigonus.

2. Perhaps during the years 306 and after, when he took an active part in Athens's wars against King Cassander of Macedon.

3. Antipater died in 319 B.C. When Alexander set off for Persia he had left Antipater in charge of Macedonia and Greece.

4. The philosopher who was appointed by Cassander as governor of

many of Demochares' political opponents, which again included Demetrius of Phalerum. In his history Demochares makes a number of weighty accusations against Demetrius, arguing that his position as the leading man in the state and the achievements on which he prided himself were just such as a petty tax-gatherer might have boasted of; his pretensions, according to Demochares, amounted to the fact that the city was abundantly supplied, the cost of living was small, and the necessities of life were available to everybody at a low price. He also recalls of Demetrius that a mechanical snail, which emitted slime as it crawled along, went in front of his procession, and after it a string of donkeys were led through the theatre.[1] This was as if to signify that Athens had surrendered to others all the glory of Greece and was obeying the commands of Cassander, but Demetrius, according to Demochares, was in no way ashamed of this. Yet in spite of such provocation neither Demetrius nor anyone else brought any accusation resembling that of Timaeus against Demochares.

14. Accordingly, since I regard the evidence provided in his own country as more reliable than Timaeus' malice, I declare with confidence that Demochares' life was innocent of these accusations. But even supposing that he was guilty of any such disgrace, what occasion or what event compelled Timaeus to record it in his history? Men of good sense, when they decide to retaliate against their enemies, consider first of all not what the other party deserves to suffer but how it is proper for them to act. In the same way when we use the language of reproach the first consideration should be not what our enemies deserve to be called but what it is proper for us to say. If writers make all their judgements according to the measure of their own anger and jealousy, we inevitably come to suspect their statements and to be on our guard against their

Athens. He held this position from 317 to 307, when he was unseated by the invasion of Demetrius Poliorcetes.

1. Both the economic situation and the procession are held up as symbolic of Demetrius' administration, a regime of bread and circuses. The procession was given during the theatrical festival of the Dionysia in 309/8 B.C. But it is Demochares who interprets the donkeys and other details as representing the degradation of Athens; they were merely part of the show, which in itself had no special significance.

exaggerations. So in the present instance I can claim that there are good grounds for rejecting Timaeus' slanders against Demochares; he, on the other hand, can claim neither pardon nor credit from anyone, since in giving his native virulence scope to abuse its object he has allowed himself to be carried beyond the bounds of decency.

15. I disapprove just as much of his vilification of Agathocles of Sicily,[1] even admitting that that ruler was the most impious of men. I am referring here to the passage at the end of his history where he alleges that Agathocles in his early youth was a common prostitute, one willing to associate with the most licentious characters, a jackdaw, a buzzard, a man who would face in any direction on request. Besides all this Timaeus says that when Agathocles died, his wife, as she was lamenting him, cried out: 'Ah, what have I not done to you! What have you not done to me!' In this instance one might well repeat what has already been said in the case of Demochares, but it is also astonishing to find Timaeus speaking with such extraordinary rancour. And yet Timaeus' description of Agathocles makes it clear that the man must have possessed some remarkable natural advantages. Consider his career, how at the age of eighteen he escaped from the potter's wheel, the kiln and the clay, and found his way to Syracuse, and how within a short time he advanced from these humble beginnings, made himself master of Sicily, became the terror of the Carthaginians, and finally grew old in royal office and died with the title of king. All these facts surely prove that there were great and wonderful qualities in him, and that he was endowed with rare gifts and an exceptional capacity for public affairs. In view of all this it is the historian's duty to record for posterity not only those details which tend to confirm slanderous accusations, but also everything which redounds to Agathocles' honour, for that is the proper function of history. However, since Timaeus is blinded by his own malice, he has given us a hostile and exaggerated report of all Agathocles' defects but has failed to mention any of his virtues. He apparently does not understand that in the writing of history it is just as misleading for an author to conceal what actually happened as to report what did not. I myself have avoided such

1. Agathocles was an especial object of dislike to Timaeus.

excessive criticism as would tend to make Timaeus hated, but have not omitted anything that had a bearing upon my purpose.

TIMAEUS' CRITICISMS OF OTHER WRITERS

23. Timaeus makes a violent attack upon Ephorus, but is himself guilty of two serious errors: in the first place he bitterly accuses others of the same mistakes that he has made himself, and secondly he shows a complete lack of moral sense in publishing these allegations in his works and trying to implant such ideas in the minds of his readers. For if we have to admit that Callisthenes deserved to die as he did under torture, then what punishment ought Timaeus to have suffered, for it would be far more just for the anger of the gods to have descended upon him than upon Callisthenes? The latter wished to make a god of Alexander, but Timaeus exalts Timoleon above the most illustrious of the gods. Callisthenes praised a man whose spirit, by common consent, had in it something superhuman. Timaeus, by contrast, honoured Timoleon, who appears not only never to have carried out any great enterprise, but never even to have attempted one. In his whole career he accomplished one single move,[1] and that not a very important one considering the size of the world, namely the voyage from Corinth to Syracuse.[2] The truth is in my opinion that Timaeus believed that if Timoleon, who had sought fame in a mere saucer of a place such as Sicily, could be shown to stand comparison with the most famous of the world's heroes, then he himself, who had written only of the affairs of Italy and Sicily, could stand comparison with those writers whose books had dealt with world-wide events and with universal history. These remarks should suffice to defend Aristotle, Theophrastus, Callisthenes, Ephorus and Demochares against the attacks of Timaeus; they are

1. Literally *line*: the metaphor refers to the game Five Lines, played in ancient Greece on a board with pieces and dice, and somewhat resembling backgammon.

2. Timoleon sailed to Sicily from Corinth at the age of sixty-seven in 344 B.C. and delivered Syracuse from the tyranny of Dionysus II. In 341 he decisively defeated the Carthaginians and liberated a large portion of Sicily. See Plutarch's *Life of Timoleon*.

also addressed to those who believe Timaeus to be truthful and unprejudiced.

24. Let us now consider the character of Timaeus according to his own principles. He tells us that poets and prose-writers reveal their true natures in their works by dwelling repeatedly on certain topics. For example he remarks that Homer is constantly describing banqueting scenes, and that this suggests the poet was something of a glutton. In the same way Aristotle, since he frequently describes rich food, must have been a gourmet and a lover of delicacies. On the same analogy he draws conclusions about the tyrant Dionysius' love of luxury because of his interest in the decoration of his dining couches and the attention he constantly gave to the varieties and special characteristics of different fabrics. This inevitably leads us to apply the same principle to Timaeus himself and to pass unfavourable judgements on his character. For while he shows great ingenuity and audacity in attacking others, his own statements continually draw upon dreams, prodigies and unlikely stories: in a word he is a prey to ignoble superstition and old wives' tales. At any rate it emerges clearly from what I have just said that many men, although they may be present at an event, might just as well not be there, and likewise may be eye-witnesses yet actually see nothing; this fact arises from their ignorance and defective judgement, and Timaeus is a case in point.

TIMAEUS ON THE BULL OF PHALARIS

25. Let me take the well-known story of the brazen bull, which runs as follows. It was made by Phalaris at Agrigentum where he was tyrant, and it was his custom to punish his subjects by shutting men up in it and lighting a fire underneath. As the brass grew red hot and the man inside was scorched and roasted to death, because of the construction of the machine the sound as it reached the ears of those present resembled the roaring of a bull. At the time of the Carthaginian conquest[1] the bull was taken from Agrigentum to Carthage. The trap-door at the joint of its shoulder-blades through which the victims were lowered into it is still preserved, and it is impossible to find any reason why such a bull should have been

1. The Carthaginian general Himilco captured Agrigentum in 406/5.

made in Carthage. However Timaeus set out to demolish the familiar story and to refute the accounts given by the poets and historians. He insisted that the bull which was in Carthage did not come from Agrigentum and that no such appliance had ever existed there, and he has devoted a long disquisition to the subject.[1]

What language, then, are we to use in speaking of Timaeus and what name can we find for him? My own opinion is that he has earned for himself all the harshest criticisms which he applies to others. From what I have already said it has been clearly enough established that he is a quarrelsome, misleading and irresponsible writer, but from what I am about to add it will also be evident that he lacked any knowledge of philosophy and was, to put it bluntly, quite uneducated. For example towards the end of his twenty-first book he makes Timoleon say in the course of an address to his troops, 'The earth lying beneath the heavens being divided into three parts named Asia, Africa and Europe ...'[2] Is it believable that such a phrase could ever have been used on an occasion of this kind, even by the celebrated Margites,[3] let alone by Timoleon?

TIMAEUS' METHODS IN COMPOSING SPEECHES

25a. There is a proverb which tells us that a single drop, taken from even the largest vessel, is enough to reveal to us the nature of the whole contents, and the same principle may be applied to the subject we are now discussing. Accordingly when we find one or

1. According to a scholiast's note on Pindar, *Pythian Odes* I, Timaeus stated that the Agrigentines threw the bull into the sea after Phalaris' death, and that the bull shown in the city in his own time represented the river Gela. Diodorus Siculus, *History*, XIII.90.4, reports that a bull was taken to Carthage at the time of the city's capture in 406 B.C. A bull was found at the sack of Carthage in 146 and Scipio restored it to Agrigentum. This is presumably the bull with a trap-door which Polybius testifies to having seen at Carthage. In the present state of our knowledge neither Timaeus nor Polybius can be proved to be wrong.

2. This was a familiar geographical expression. The point of Polybius' criticism is that it is totally out of place to introduce such a pedantic utterance into an eve-of-battle speech.

3. A proverbial name for a fool; also the hero of the comic epic of that name, traditionally attributed to Homer.

two false statements in a book and they prove to have been deliberately made, we know that we can no longer treat anything that is said by such an author as reliable or trustworthy. However if I am to convince those who are inclined to be captious, I must say something of the principle which Timaeus applies in composing the speeches of politicians, the addresses of generals, and the discourses of ambassadors, in short all such kinds of public utterance which summarize events and bind the whole history together. Can any of Timaeus' readers have failed to observe that his reports of these pronouncements disregard the truth and that this is done deliberately? The fact is that he has neither set down what was said, nor the real sense of what was said.[1] Instead, after first making up his mind what ought to have been said, he catalogues all these imaginary speeches and the accompanying details, just as if he were exercising on a set theme in the schools: in other words he tries to show off his rhetorical powers, but provides no account of what was actually spoken.

25b. Now the special function of history, particularly in relation to speeches, is first of all to discover the words actually used, whatever they were, and next to establish the reason why a particular action or argument failed or succeeded. The mere statement of a fact, though it may excite our interest, is of no benefit to us, but when the knowledge of the cause is added, then the study of history becomes fruitful. For it is the ability to draw analogies between parallel circumstances of the past and of our own times which enables us to make forecasts as to what is to happen: thus in some cases where a given course of action has failed, we are impelled to take precautions so as to avoid a recurrence, while in others we can deal more confidently with the problems that confront us by repeating a solution which has previously succeeded. On the other hand, a writer who passes over in silence the speeches which were actually made and the causes of what actually happened and introduces fictitious rhetorical exercises and discursive speeches in their place destroys the peculiar virtue of history. In this respect Timaeus is a persistent offender, and we all know that his books are full of faults of this kind.

25c. I may perhaps be asked how, if he is the kind of writer I

1. i.e. neither a transcript nor a résumé.

am now proving him to be, he has enjoyed such ready acceptance and credit from some of his readers. The reason is that his works are so full of criticism and abuse of his competitors that his readers do not judge him in the light of his own treatment of history or of his own statements, but rather by his capacity for attacking others; and here he seems to me to have shown an extraordinary industry and an outstanding talent. Indeed in this respect he very much resembles Strato of Lampsacus, the writer on physical science. He, too, is apt to shine most when he sets out to expound and refute the theories of others, but when he puts forward any original proposition or explains his own ideas, he appears to men of science to be far more stupid and dull than they had expected. For my part I think the same principle applies to literature as to human life in general, for here too it is easy enough to find fault with others, but difficult to behave impeccably ourselves. Certainly one sees often enough that those who are most ready to find fault with their neighbours are the most blameworthy in their own lives.

COMPARISON OF HISTORY AND MEDICINE

25d. Besides the matters which I have dealt with above, there is another point to be mentioned about Timaeus. Because he had resided in Athens for nearly fifty years,[1] where he could consult the works of earlier authors, he assumed that he was in possession of the most important resources for the writing of history, but here, in my opinion, he was much mistaken. History and the science of medicine are similar in this respect, that each of them may be said to be divided, broadly speaking, into three different departments, which correspond to the different dispositions of those who embark upon these callings. There are in the first place three departments of medicine: one is concerned with the theory of disease, the second with diet, and the third with surgery and pharmaceutics. Now the study of the theory of disease, which takes its rise chiefly from the schools of Herophilus[2] and of Calli-

1. The dates of Timaeus' stay are uncertain, either about 339–289, or 315–265 B.C.
2. Herophilus of Calchedon (fl. early third century) discovered the rhythm of the pulse and was especially interested in the causes of disease; he and his

machus of Alexandria, is certainly a proper part of medical science, but there goes with it a certain air of ostentation and pretentiousness, and its practitioners give themselves such an air of superiority as to suggest that no one else is master of the subject. But when you apply the test of reality by bringing a patient to one of them, you find them just as incapable of dealing with the needs of the situation as those who have never read a medical treatise at all. Indeed there have been a number of patients who had nothing serious the matter with them, but were impressed by a mere verbal display and actually endangered their lives by entrusting themselves to the care of such physicians, for these men are just like pilots who steer a ship by the book. And yet they travel from city to city with great éclat, and when they have collected a crowd they reduce skilled doctors to confusion, virtually singling them out by name. These may be men who have given proof of their skill in actual practice, but in spite of that the persuasive power of eloquence often prevails over the testimony of practical experience.

The third branch of medicine, which is concerned with producing genuine skill in each professional treatment of the several cases, is not only rare in itself, but is often eclipsed by sheer volubility and audacity because of the lack of judgement of the general public.

TIMAEUS' LACK OF POLITICAL AND MILITARY EXPERIENCE AND UNWILLINGNESS TO TRAVEL

25e. In the same way political history is also made up of three parts. The first consists of the industrious study and collation of documents; the second is topographical and includes the survey of cities, places, rivers, harbours, and in general the special features of land and sea and the distances of one place from another; while the third is concerned with political activity. And just as in the case of medicine, many people aspire to write history because of the

---

later followers came to be regarded as more concerned with aetiology than with cure. They tended to align themselves with the philosophy of Stoicism, while the empiricists, who were more concerned with treatment, inclined towards the Sceptic philosophy. Polybius believed that one should study the causes of disease so far as this was necessary for cure, but not for the sake of a mere display of theoretical knowledge.

high opinion in which political history has been held; but most of them bring to the undertaking nothing to justify their claim to write it except irresponsibility, recklessness and roguery. They court favour like vendors of drugs and will always say whatever the occasion may require for the sake of scraping together a living by this means. I need say no more about authors of this kind.

There is, however, another category of authors, who appear to be justified in undertaking the writing of history, but who in fact are just like the theoretical doctors. They haunt the libraries and become thoroughly versed in memoirs and records, and then convince themselves that they are properly equipped for the task;[1] but while they may appear to outsiders to bring everything that is needed to the writing of political history, yet in my opinion they provide no more than a part. Certainly the study of the memoirs of the past has its value for discovering what the ancients believed and the ideas which people formerly entertained about conditions, places, nations, states and events, and also for understanding the circumstances and eventualities with which each nation in earlier times had to deal. And certainly past events are relevant in making us pay attention to the future, provided that a writer inquires in each case into the facts as they actually occurred. But to persuade oneself, as Timaeus did, that the resources of documentary research alone can equip one to write an adequate history of recent events is naïve beyond words. It is as though a man were to imagine that he was a capable painter, indeed a master of the art, merely by virtue of having looked at the works of the past.[2]

25f. I can illustrate this point even more clearly through the passages which I propose to discuss, in particular those taken from certain parts of Ephorus' history. When this historian writes about war he seems to me to show some understanding of naval operations, but to be completely ignorant about battles on land. Thus if we look closely at his descriptions of the naval battles near Cyprus and Cnidus, in which the Persian King's commanders were fighting, in the first instance against Evagoras of Salamis

1. It is in this category that Polybius places Timaeus, as distinct from the quacks.

2. Polybius' point is that it is recent history in particular which demands some experience of public affairs.

and in the second against the Spartans,[1] we are bound to admire the writer for his descriptive power and for his knowledge of tactics, and we gain from these much information which is useful for similar circumstances. But this is certainly not the case when he reports the battle of Leuctra between the Thebans and the Spartans, or the battle of Mantinea between the same opponents, in which Epaminondas lost his life.[2] If we examine the details of these engagements and the battle formations and changes which took place during the actual fighting, Ephorus merely excites our ridicule because he gives the impression of being completely inexperienced in these matters and of never having seen a battle. The battle of Leuctra was, it is true, a simple operation and only one portion of the opposing forces was engaged, so that the writer's ignorance is not so very glaringly exposed. On the other hand his version of the fighting at Mantinea gives the illusion of being composed with a wealth of technical virtuosity, but in fact the description is quite imaginary, and the writer completely failed to understand what happened in the battle. This becomes clear if we establish an accurate picture of the ground and then check the movements which he describes as being carried out on it. The same criticism applies to Theopompus and above all to Timaeus, who is the subject of the present argument. When these authors provide only a summary account of such events their errors escape notice, but whenever they offer a minute and detailed description they show that they are in the same class as Ephorus.

25g. It is in fact equally impossible for a man who has had no experience of action in the field to write well about military operations as it is for a man who has never engaged in political affairs and their attendant circumstances to write well on those topics. And since the writings of mere book-worms lack both first-hand experience and any vividness of presentation, their work is completely without value for its readers. For if you remove from

1. The Persians defeated Evagoras, King of Cyprus, off Citium in 381 B.C. In 394 Sparta's naval supremacy, which she had established over Athens at the close of the Peloponnesian War, was ended at the battle of Cnidus, where the Spartans were defeated by a Persian fleet commanded by Conon the Athenian and largely manned by Greek crews.

2. The battle of Leuctra, July 371, put an end to the Spartan hegemony of Greece. The battle of Mantinea was fought in the early summer of 362.

history the element of practical instruction, what is left is insignificant and without any benefit to them. Again, when writers try to provide details about cities and places without possessing firsthand experience of this kind, the result is bound to be very similar, since they will leave out many things which ought to be mentioned and deal at great length with other details which are not worth the trouble. Timaeus often falls into this error because he does not rely upon the evidence of his own eyes.

25h. In his thirty-fourth book Timaeus remarks that he lived in Athens continuously for fifty years as a foreigner, and admits that he had no experience of fighting and never visited places to observe them at first hand. Accordingly, when he has to deal with such matters in his history he makes many errors and misstatements, and if he ever gets near the truth, it is rather in the manner of those animal painters who make their sketches from stuffed dummies. In these cases the draughtsman sometimes catches the correct outline, but there is none of the vividness and animation of real living creatures which it is the special function of painting to capture. This is just what happens with Timaeus, and generally speaking with all those who start out from this bookish approach. What is lacking is the vivid realization of the actual objects, since this element can only be created by the personal experience of the writer, and accordingly those who have never themselves participated in public life fail to arouse the interest of their readers.

For this reason the writers of the past believed that historical memoirs should possess such vividness that they would make the reader exclaim whenever the narrative dealt with political events that the author must have taken part in politics and had experience of public affairs; or when he dealt with war that he had known active service and risked his life; or when he turned to domestic matters that he had lived with a wife and brought up children, and similarly with the various other aspects of life. Now this quality can only be found in the writing of those who have played some part in affairs themselves and made this aspect of history their own. Of course it is difficult to have been personally involved and played an active role in every kind of event, but it is certainly necessary to have had experience of the most important and those of most frequent occurrence.

251. The proof that what I am saying is by no means impossible to achieve is offered us by Homer, for in his poetry we find much of this kind of vividness. At any rate it would, I think, be generally agreed from the foregoing arguments that the study of documents is only one of the three elements which contribute to history, and stands only third in importance. The truth of this proposition can best be demonstrated from the various kinds of public utterance which Timaeus introduces: that is, the debating speeches of politicians, the harangues of commanders, and the discourses of ambassadors. There are few situations which allow scope for every possible argument to be set forth, and most leave room merely for the few brief statements which naturally present themselves. And even among these there are some which are appropriate for the present and others for the past; others again may be suitable for Aetolians, or for Peloponnesians or for Athenians. But what is quite untrue to the facts, besides being full of affectation and pedantry, is to expand a speech without point or occasion so as to include every possible argument, and this is what Timaeus with his trick of inventing arguments does to every subject. This practice has indeed caused many statesmen to fail and be brought into contempt, whereas the essential principle, on the contrary, is to select those arguments which are relevant and suitable to the occasion. But since there is no fixed rule as to which or how many of the possible arguments should be used in a particular instance, an unusual degree of attention and clarity of principle is called for on the part of the historian, that is if we intend to benefit rather than mislead our readers. It is never easy to formulate exactly what the situation demands, but it is not impossible to be guided towards it through precepts based upon personal experience and practice.[1] For the present, the best way of conveying my meaning is as follows. If historians first clearly describe the situation, the aims and the circumstances of those who are discussing it, and next report what was actually said, and finally explain to us the reasons why the speakers succeeded or failed, we shall arrive at a true picture of what happened. We shall also, by distinguishing what was success-

1. i.e. the precepts are offered to the statesman by the historian whose works he reads, these precepts being based on the historian's own experience and practice.

ful from its opposite, and by drawing analogies from this have good prospects of success in dealing with any future situation that may confront us. However, it is difficult in my opinion to trace causes, but all too easy to string together phrases in books. And in the same way, while it is given only to a few to speak briefly and to the point and to discover the rules which govern this facility, to write at great length and to little purpose is a very common accomplishment indeed.

THE CAUSES OF TIMAEUS' FAULTS AND THE QUALITIES OF THE GOOD HISTORIAN

27a. The political part of Timaeus' history combines all his faults of composition which I have already described. I shall now explain the prime cause of his errors, one which many people will find improbable, and yet it will prove to be the truest explanation of the charges that have been brought against him. He seems to me to have developed a talent for detailed research together with a certain competence based on inquiry, and in a word to have approached the task of writing history in a painstaking spirit, and yet in certain respects I can think of no historian who appears to have been less experienced or to have taken less trouble. The following considerations will illustrate my point. Nature has provided us with two instruments, so to speak, with the help of which we make all our inquiries and obtain our information. I mean by these the faculties of hearing and of sight, and of the two, according to Heracleitus, that of sight is by far the more trustworthy. 'The eyes are more accurate witnesses than the ears,' he informs us. Now Timaeus has pursued his inquiries through the medium which although the more agreeable is also the inferior, that is he has refrained completely from employing his eyes and preferred to employ his ears.[1] Moreover even the ear may receive its information in two ways, either by reading or by the examination of witnesses, and with the second of these, as I have indicated above, Timaeus took very little trouble.

The reason for his preference is easy enough to understand. You can busy yourself among books with very little danger or

1. i.e. by reading, here regarded as a function of the ears, not the eyes.

hardship, provided only that you have taken care to have access to a city which is well supplied with records[1] or to have a library close at hand. After that you need only pursue your researches while reclining on your couch, and you can compare the mistakes of earlier historians without undergoing any hardship. Personal investigation, on the other hand, demands much greater exertion and expense, but it is of prime importance and makes the greatest contribution of all to history. This is evident from the expressions used by historians themselves. Ephorus, for example, declares that if writers could be personally present at all events as they happen this would be the best of all modes of experience. Theopompus says that the best military historian is the man who has been present at most battles, and the best writer of speeches the man who has taken part in most debates, and that the same principle applies to the sciences of medicine and navigation. And Homer has been even more emphatic on this subject than the others. When he wishes to set before us the qualities that the man of action should possess, he presents the image of Odysseus in these words:

> Muse, let us sing of that man of many resources, the rover
> Far over land and sea . . .

and a little further on

> Many the cities of men he observed and the manners he noted,
> Many the hardships he bore in his wanderings over the ocean[2]

and again

> One who had suffered the shocks of the battlefield and of the tempest,[3]

28. It seems to me that the dignity which belongs to the art of history also demands a man of this kind. Plato contends that human affairs will go well when either philosophers become kings or kings study philosophy, and for my part I should say that it will be well with history when one of two conditions is fulfilled. Either the task should be undertaken by men of action, in which case they

---

1. Athens, where Timaeus worked, had little to offer as regards records concerning the western Mediterranean countries.
2. *Odyssey*, I, 1–3.   3. *Odyssey*, VIII, 183.

must approach it not in the fashion of the present, when it is treated as a matter of secondary importance, but in the conviction that this is their most necessary and honourable employment, and apply themselves to it with undivided attention throughout their lives. Alternatively those who set out to write history must understand that the experience of affairs is an essential qualification for them. Until that day comes, there will be no respite from the errors that historians will commit.

Now Timaeus never gave the least thought to these considerations. He spent all his life in one place of which he was not even a citizen, and he seems almost deliberately to have cut himself off from any active participation in war or politics, or any personal experience gained from travel and observation; and yet for some unknown reason he has acquired the reputation of being an eminent historian. The proof that this is a fair characterization of Timaeus can easily be found in his own words, for in the preface to his sixth book he remarks that some people suppose that it requires more talent, hard work and training to write rhetorical speeches than it does to write history. He points out that Ephorus had in his time disagreed with this view, but because he had been unable to reply adequately to those who held it, Timaeus himself undertakes to draw a comparison between history and rhetorical writing. But this is really quite out of place, because to begin with his statement about Ephorus is untrue. Throughout his work Ephorus is admirable in his phraseology, his treatment, and the working-out of his argument; he is most eloquent in his digressions and in the expression of his personal reflections, and in a word whenever he enlarges on any subject, and besides this it so happens that his remarks on the difference between historians and speech writers are particularly persuasive and convincing. Timaeus, however, is anxious to avoid giving the impression that he is echoing Ephorus, and so besides making an inaccurate statement about him, he has also condemned all other historians. And so when he comes to discuss at great length and in a confused manner subjects which others have handled quite correctly, he imagines that not a living soul will notice what he is doing.

28a. His purpose in this passage is to glorify history, and so he says that the difference between this and declamatory writing is as great as that between real buildings and furniture and the land-scapes and compositions which we see in painted scenery.

Secondly he says that the collection of the materials required for writing a history is a more laborious task than the whole course of study for the business of declamatory speaking. He himself, he says, took such pains and incurred such expense in collecting his notes from Tyre[1] and in conducting research into the customs of the Celts, Ligurians and Iberians that he could scarcely expect either his own testimony or that of others to be believed. One would like to ask this writer which plan of research he considers the more laborious – to sit quietly in a town collecting notes and inquiring into the manners and customs of the Ligurians and Celts, or to obtain personal experience of the majority of places and peoples and see them at first hand? Or again, which requires the greater effort, to question those who were present at the various operations about the details of the order of battle, the sea-fights and the sieges, or to be present at the actual scene and experience the dangers and changes of fortune of these actions as they occurred? My own view is that the difference between real buildings and those depicted in stage settings, or between the composition of history and of speeches is not so great as the difference in all historical writing between a narrative which is based on participation or first-hand experience, and one which is derived from hearsay and the tales of others.

However Timaeus, since he has had no experience of the first mode of writing, naturally supposes that the task which is really of least consequence, and easiest to carry out, namely that of collecting records and questioning those who have knowledge of the various events, is the most important and most difficult. And yet even in this field men who have no first-hand experience are bound to make serious mistakes, for how is it possible for a man to examine a witness about a battle or a siege or a naval action, or to grasp the details of his narrative effectively if he has no clear conception of the subject himself? The truth is that the interrogator contributes as much to the narrative as his informant, since the recollection of the accompanying details leads on the narrator from one point to the next. On the other hand the man who lacks the

1. For his writings on Carthage.

experience of action is neither equipped to question those who have taken part in one, nor, even if he is present himself, can he understand what is happening: consequently even if he is on the spot, he might just as well not be there.

BOOK XIV

Affairs in Africa
SCIPIO'S CAMPAIGNS

The date at the opening of this chapter is the winter of 204/3. Scipio had returned from Spain to Rome in 206, been elected consul in 205, and crossed to Africa as proconsul in 204. At the beginning of 203 his command was extended until he should have finished the war. In Italy the consuls Gnaeus Servilius Caepio and Gaius Servilius Geminus were in Etruria and Bruttium respectively.

1. While the two consuls were engaged in operations in Italy, Scipio, who was in winter quarters in Africa,[1] received information that the Carthaginians were fitting out a fleet. He therefore put in hand his own naval preparations, and he was at the same time involved in besieging Utica. He still cherished some hope of winning over Syphax[2] and sent him a succession of messages, for the two armies were not far apart, and Scipio believed that he could detach the prince from his alliance with Carthage. He suspected that Syphax was already tired of the girl on whose account he had chosen to side with the Carthaginians, and that his friendship with them had lost its warmth, for he was well aware that the Numidians were by nature quick to become satiated with whatever pleased them, and were for this reason fickle towards gods and men alike. At this moment Scipio's mind was much distracted by various anxieties for the future; he was afraid to risk a battle in the open field because of the enemy's superiority in numbers, and he readily seized upon the following opportunity which now presented itself.

1. He was encamped outside Utica, some twenty-five miles north-west of Carthage.

2. Sophonisba, the daughter of Hasdrubal, had been given in marriage by her father to Syphax to win the latter's support for Carthage (see Livy, *The War with Hannibal*, XXIX. 23).

Some of the messengers whom he sent to Syphax reported that the Carthaginians had built their huts in their winter camp entirely out of various kinds of wood and boughs without using any earth, while in the case of the Numidians the first troops to arrive had made theirs of reeds, while the reinforcements who kept coming in from the cities had likewise for the time being used nothing but boughs. Some of the latter were encamped inside the trench and palisade, but the majority were outside. Scipio therefore concluded that the method of attacking the camp which would take the enemy most completely by surprise would be to set it on fire, and he began to make plans for such an attempt. Now Syphax, in the communications which had passed between him and Scipio, kept harping upon the idea that the Carthaginians should evacuate Italy and the Romans follow suit as regards Africa, while each side should continue to occupy the possessions which they held between the two countries. Scipio had hitherto refused absolutely to listen to this suggestion, but he now began to drop hints to the Numidian prince that the course he wished to see adopted was not out of the question. Syphax's mind was greatly relieved, and as a result his exchanges with Scipio became bolder than before. This meant that the messengers passing between them became more numerous and their visits more frequent, so that on some occasions each party spent several days in their adversaries' camp without any precautions being taken about their movements. For these missions Scipio would include a number of men of tried experience and others of military capacity; they would be humbly and shabbily dressed, disguised in fact in the clothes of slaves, and their task was to examine and explore the approaches and entrances to both camps without interference. There were two camps, one of them occupied by Hasdrubal which contained 30,000 infantry and 3,000 cavalry, and another less than a mile and a half away which belonged to the Numidians and accommodated 50,000 infantry and 10,000 cavalry.[1] The latter was the easier to approach and its huts were particularly vulnerable to fire, since the Numidians, as I have just said, used neither wood nor earth for their building materials, but only reeds and matting.

1. These figures look improbably large. A more likely estimate is that the combined forces amounted to 30,000 infantry and 5,000 cavalry.

2. By the beginning of the spring Scipio had carried out all the reconnaissance he needed for this attempt against the enemy. He also launched his ships and built siege-engines for them, as though he were about to blockade Utica from the sea. He once again occupied the high ground above the town with his infantry, who numbered about 2,000, and spared no expense in fortifying this position and digging a moat around it. He wished to give the enemy the impression that these preparations were made for the purpose of carrying on the siege, but his real intention was to guard himself against the risk of anything happening at the time of his incendiary operation. He was afraid that once the legions had left their camp the garrison at Utica might pluck up courage to make a sortie, attack the palisade which was near the city, and surround the troops he had left to defend it.

While he was making these preparations he also sent a message to Syphax to ask whether, assuming that Scipio agreed to the prince's proposals, the Carthaginians would accept them too, and not repeat that they must have time to consider the terms. He also gave orders to his envoys not to return until they had received an answer on this point. When the legates arrived and Syphax heard their message, he felt sure that Scipio was ready to conclude the treaty, partly because the Romans had said that they would not leave without obtaining an answer, and partly because of their evident anxiety to secure the agreement of the Carthaginians. He immediately sent word to Hasdrubal explaining what had happened and urging him to accept the offer of peace. Meanwhile he himself let the time go by without taking any further precautions, and allowed the Numidians who kept joining him to encamp outside his lines. Scipio to all appearances continued to act in the same way, but in reality he was making every preparation for an attack. As soon as Syphax received confirmation from the Carthaginians that he should conclude the peace treaty he was overjoyed, and passed on the news to the envoys, who immediately returned to their camp to inform Scipio of Syphax's action. At this the Roman commander at once sent another mission to explain to Syphax that for his part Scipio was well-satisfied and was making every effort to secure the peace, but that some members of his military council took a different view and argued that matters should remain as they were. The envoys duly arrived and delivered this message to Syphax. Scipio had dispatched them in order not to appear to be breaking the truce if he should carry out any warlike action while the negotiations for peace were still in progress between the parties. He considered that once he had made this statement he was free to act as he chose without laying himself open to blame.

3. Syphax was greatly disappointed when he learned this news, since he had convinced himself in advance that peace was assured, but he arranged a meeting with Hasdrubal at which he told him of the message from the Romans. They discussed it at length and debated how they should deal with the situation, but in all their thinking and the plans which arose from it they had no suspicion of what was about to happen. They showed no foresight whatever concerning their own security or the possibility that any disaster might threaten them; on the other hand, they were all eagerness to take some offensive action and challenge the enemy to fight on level ground. Throughout this time Scipio continued to make preparations and issue orders so as to give his own troops the impression that he was about to attempt the capture of Utica. Then suddenly he summoned the ablest and most reliable of his military tribunes to a conference at noon. At this meeting he confided his plan to them, and ordered them to take their evening meal early and lead the legions out of the camp after all the trumpeters had sounded the retreat at the usual hour of the day; at supper-time it is the custom for the trumpeters to sound this call outside the general's tent, so as to give notice that the night watches should then take up their positions. Next he sent for the spies whom he had sent at various times to the enemy's camps, questioned them and compared the details they gave concerning the approaches and entrances. He called in Masinissa to evaluate their reports and followed his advice because of his personal knowledge of the locality.

4. When all preparations had been completed for the expedition Scipio left behind a sufficiently strong force to guard the camp, and towards the end of the first watch he led out his troops, the enemy being about seven miles away. He arrived in their vicinity towards the end of the third watch and proceeded to divide his force, placing half of his legionaries and all the Numidian troops

under the command of Gaius Laelius and of Masinissa. Their orders were to attack Syphax's camp, and Scipio appealed to his troops to acquit themselves like brave men, but not to act impetuously; they knew very well that since a night attack hinders a soldier from enjoying normal vision, he needs a combination of daring and a cool head to take its place. He took command of the rest of the army himself and advanced against Hasdrubal's camp. He had decided not to deliver his assault until Laelius had set fire to the other camp, and so with this plan in mind he advanced at a slow pace.

Laelius and Masinissa had meanwhile divided their force into two parts which attacked Syphax's camp simultaneously. The enemy's huts, as I mentioned above, might have been expressly constructed to catch fire. As soon as the front ranks of the Roman troops had set light to them, the flames instantly spread along the first row, and because the huts were placed so close to one another and contained so much inflammable material the blaze quickly became uncontrollable. Laelius remained in the rear to cover the operation, while Masinissa knew exactly the points at which the men who were trying to escape from the flames would have to leave the camp, and posted his men to cover these exits. None of the Numidians, not even Syphax, had any idea of what had really happened. Instead everybody supposed that the camp had caught fire by accident and so, all unsuspecting, some men starting up out of their sleep, and others taken by surprise while they were still carousing, cup in hand, they rushed out of their huts. Many were trampled by their own comrades in the exits from the camp, many were surrounded by the flames and burned to death, while all those who escaped from the blaze ran straight into the enemy and were slaughtered before they knew what they were doing or what fate had overtaken them.

5. While all this was happening, the Carthaginians on seeing the extent of the fire and the huge conflagration that rose into the sky, supposed that the Numidian camp had caught fire by accident. Some of them hurried to give assistance, while all the rest rushed out of their camp unarmed and stood in front of it gazing with horror at the spectacle. Thereupon Scipio, finding that the whole operation had gone precisely as he had planned, attacked the troops

who had wandered out. He killed some, pursued others, and proceeded to fire their huts, so that the general conflagration and destruction which I have described in the Numidian camp was now repeated in the Carthaginian. Hasdrubal at once abandoned any idea of fighting the fire, as he knew from what had just happened to him that the disaster which had overtaken the Numidians owed nothing to chance, but was the result of the enterprise and daring of the enemy. He now thought of nothing but saving himself, and indeed there was little enough hope of doing even this. For the fire spread with great speed and soon engulfed the whole area of the camp. The passages which intersected it were filled with horses, mules and men, some of them half-dead and devoured by the flames, and others in a state of frantic terror and excitement. Thus even those who had the determination to rally and defend themselves were hindered by these obstacles, and amid the general uproar and confusion which prevailed all hope of safety disappeared.

The case of Syphax and the other commanders was very similar. The two generals contrived to make their escape with a small body of cavalry; but of all the rest, thousands upon thousands of men, horses and mules perished miserably and piteously in the flames, while others of their comrades died a disgraceful and dishonourable death at the hands of the enemy as they strove to escape the fury of the fire, for they were cut down naked and defenceless, not only without their arms but without even their clothes to cover them. The whole place was filled with wails of dismay, confused shouting and cries of terror which mingled in an unspeakable din, while above all this rose the roar of the raging fire and of flames which overcame all resistance. It was the combination and the unexpectedness of these elements which made them so frightful, for indeed any one of them alone would have been enough to strike terror into the human heart. Indeed it is impossible for any man alive to give a true picture of this appalling scene, no matter how much he might exaggerate, so much did it exceed in horror any event that has hitherto been recorded. For this reason, of all the many brilliant operations carried out by Scipio, this seems to me the most spectacular and the most daring.

6. When the day broke and he found that the enemy had all either been killed or were in headlong flight, Scipio issued further orders

to the military tribunes and at once started in pursuit. At first Hasdrubal remained in the town where he had taken refuge, since in spite of receiving warning of Scipio's approach he still felt confidence in the strength of the place. But later, when he found that the inhabitants were in a mutinous frame of mind, he shrank from the prospect of resisting Scipio's advance, and so continued his retreat with the survivors, who consisted of not less than 500 cavalry and about 2,000 infantry. After this the inhabitants of the town surrendered unconditionally to the Romans. Scipio spared them, but allowed his soldiers to plunder two of the neighbouring towns, and then returned to the camp from which he had set out.

Now that all the hopes and plans upon which they had originally based their campaign had been frustrated, the Carthaginians felt deeply despondent. They had counted upon shutting up the Romans on the promontory near Utica which the latter had chosen for their winter quarters, and had made all their preparations with a view to blockading them with their armies from the landward side and with the fleet from the sea. Now they found that through a sudden and unforeseen disaster they had been forced to give up the command of the open country to the enemy. Worse still, they felt that they and the capital might now be attacked at any moment, and so their mood was one of panic verging upon despair. Nevertheless the situation made it imperative that they should consider the future and decide what measures to take; however, when the Senate assembled, it was full of perplexity, and the most surprising and confused suggestions were put forward. Some senators urged that they should send word to Hannibal and recall him from Italy, since they believed that Carthage's one remaining hope lay with that general and his army. Others were for sending an embassy to Scipio to ask for a truce and to open negotiations with him for concluding a peace. Others again argued that they should summon up their courage, get in touch with Syphax, who had retired to the town of Abba nearby, and collect those survivors of his army who had escaped the disaster. This in fact was the opinion which finally prevailed. Accordingly, the Carthaginian government began to reassemble their forces. They sent out Hasdrubal to supervise this task, and they also sent word to Syphax appealing to him to help

them and to abide by his original undertaking, and assuring him
that Hasdrubal would shortly join him with his army.

7. Meanwhile Scipio had in the first place occupied himself with
the preparations for the siege of Utica. Then when he learned that
Syphax was still in the field and that the Carthaginians were again
mobilizing an army, he led out his own troops and encamped in
front of the city. At the same time he distributed among the soldiers
the booty won during the recent operations, and sent away the
merchants after they had made their profit.[1] Scipio's victory had
inspired high hopes among his soldiers for the rest of the campaign, and accordingly they attached no great value to the present
spoils and were willing to dispose of them to the dealers for a low
price.

Now Syphax and his friends had at first planned to continue
their retreat and return home, but it so happened that near the town
of Abba they met a contingent of Celtiberians over 4,000 strong
who had been hired by the Carthaginians, and the sight of these
reinforcements raised their spirits sufficiently to persuade them to
halt their retreat. At the same time the young girl Sophonisba, who,
as I have mentioned, was Hasdrubal's daughter and was married
to Syphax, implored her husband to stay and not desert the Carthaginians at such a critical moment in their affairs. In the end the
Numidian prince allowed himself to be persuaded and yielded to
her entreaties. The arrival of the Celtiberians also put fresh heart
into the Carthaginians. Their numbers were reported in the capital
as 10,000 instead of 4,000, and it was said that their courage and the
excellence of their weapons made them irresistible in the field. What
with these rumours and the vulgar gossip of the rabble the spirits
of the Carthaginians suddenly rose, and their confidence that they
could once more take the field against the enemy was redoubled.
Finally, within thirty days the Carthaginian troops pitched camp
and fortified their position together with the Numidians and the
Celtiberians in the region known as the Great Plains; their combined strength amounted to not less than 30,000 men.

8. When the news of these events reached the Roman camp

1. After a city had been plundered and the spoils distributed among the
soldiers, the latter disposed of it to dealers who followed the army to carry
out these transactions.

Scipio immediately decided to move against the enemy, and after issuing orders to the forces which were besieging Utica by land and sea on how to pursue their operations, he started on his expedition, the whole army being equipped in light marching order with a minimum of baggage. On the fifth day he reached the Great Plains, and once he had arrived in the vicinity of the enemy, he pitched camp for the first day on a hill some four miles away. The next day he came down and drew up his army less than a mile from the enemy, his cavalry being stationed in front to protect the infantry. For the next two days both armies remained in their positions and tested one another's strength in some minor skirmishing operations; then on the fourth day both generals led out their forces and drew them up for battle. Scipio simply adopted the regular Roman formation, placing the maniples of *hastati* in the front rank, then behind them the *principes* and last of all the *triarii*. Of his cavalry he stationed the Italians on the right and the Numidians under Masinissa on the left. For their part Syphax and Hasdrubal placed the Celtiberians in the centre opposite the Roman maniples, the Numidians on the left and the Carthaginians on the right.

In the first charge Syphax's Numidians were driven back by the Italian horse and the Carthaginians by Masinissa, for their spirit had been broken by the earlier defeats they had suffered. The Celtiberians, on the other hand, fought splendidly and held their ground against the Roman centre; their ignorance of the country ruled out any hope that they could escape by flight, and their treachery to Scipio any chance that their lives would be spared if they were taken prisoner. Scipio had never committed any act of hostility towards them during any of his Spanish campaigns, and so they were regarded as having broken faith with him in coming to fight on the Carthaginian side. At any rate, when the wings gave way, the whole of their contingent was quickly encircled by the *principes* and *triarii* and cut down where they stood, except for a few survivors. Thus perished the Celtiberians, but they nevertheless rendered the greatest service to the Carthaginians not only during the fighting but also in the rout, for if the Romans had not encountered their resistance but had immediately pursued the fugitives, very few of the enemy would have got away. As it was, thanks to this last stand Syphax accomplished his withdrawal to his own territory in safety, and Hasdrubal was also able to reach Carthage with the remnants of his army.

9. After making the necessary arrangements for the disposal of the spoils and of the prisoners of war, Scipio called a meeting of his military council to consider what his next action should be. It was decided that he should remain in the region of the Great Plains with a part of the army and visit the various settlements of the area; meanwhile Laelius and Masinissa should take the Numidians and part of the Roman infantry and pursue Syphax so as to give him no time to stop and organize resistance. After settling these arrangements the two forces separated, Laelius and Masinissa marching in pursuit of Syphax, while Scipio made the round of the neighbouring townships. Some of these were frightened into offering their surrender to the Romans, while others were besieged and taken by assault. The whole country in fact was ripe for a change of government, for the people had suffered a continuous period of hardship and heavy taxation on account of the war in Spain, which had dragged on for so many years.

In Carthage itself the general feeling of insecurity had been serious enough before, but now the state of unrest among the citizens was even more disturbing, and the impression prevailed that after suffering a second defeat on such a crushing scale the Carthaginians had lost all confidence in themselves and despaired of their cause. In spite of this, those who were believed to be the most manly spirits in the Senate urged that the Carthaginians should sail with the fleet against the besiegers of Utica and try to raise the siege and engage the enemy's ships, which were quite unprepared for an attack. They also demanded that Hannibal should be recalled, and that this prospect of salvation should be put to the test without delay. In these courses of action there remained, so far as could be calculated, great hopes of saving the country. Others argued, however, that the time for such expedients was past and that what they must do now was to fortify the city and prepare for a siege. If they could agree to act as one people, chance would still offer them many opportunities to strike a blow. The same counsellors also recommended that they should consider the possibility of suing for peace and make up their minds on what conditions and by what means they could find an escape from their present sufferings. After several speeches had been made, they adopted all these proposals together.[1]

10. As soon as these matters had been decided, those senators who were to sail for Italy went immediately from the council chamber to the harbour, and the admiral went directly on board his ship. The remainder occupied themselves with securing the defences of the city and frequently met to discuss matters of detail.

Scipio's camp was by now overflowing with plunder, as he encountered no resistance and everybody gave way to his incursions. He therefore decided to transfer the greater part of his booty to his original base, and with the army thus relieved of its encumbrance, his plan was to seize the entrenched position before Tunis and then encamp in full view of Carthage. He reckoned that such a move would do more than anything to strike terror into the Carthaginians' hearts and fill them with dismay. Meanwhile the enemy had already within a few days manned and provisioned their ships and were about to put to sea to carry out their plan; but at that moment Scipio arrived at Tunis, the garrison took to flight, and he at once occupied the place. Tunis is only some fifteen miles from Carthage and is visible from almost every point in the capital. It is, as I have mentioned earlier, a city of great natural strength which has been reinforced by its man-made fortifications.

11. By the time that the Romans pitched their camp there, the Carthaginian fleet was already on its way to Utica. As Scipio watched the approach of the enemy's ships, he became alarmed at the danger to his own vessels, for nobody aboard had expected to be attacked and they were quite unprepared for such an eventuality. He therefore immediately broke camp and hurried back to protect his naval forces. There he found that his decked ships were well-equipped to carry siege-engines and move them up to the walls and were ready to support siege operations, but were in no state to fight a sea battle, whereas the Carthaginian fleet had been making ready throughout the winter for this very purpose. Accordingly he abandoned any idea of putting to sea and giving battle to the enemy. Instead he anchored his warships in a line and moored the

1. i.e. the proposals for resistance, not for surrender.

transports round them in a ring three or four vessels deep. Then he had the masts and yard-arms taken down and the transports lashed securely together, leaving only a small space between each through which the light craft could sail in and out.[1]

1. Livy, op. cit., XXX. 10, describes the Punic attack on this fleet, after which nearly sixty Roman transports were towed away to Carthage.

BOOK XV

Affairs in Africa

THE FINAL CAMPAIGN

After the battle of Cirta and the capture of Syphax in 203 the Carthaginians had sued for peace. Scipio had been authorized to propose terms, the Carthaginians had accepted these and sent envoys to Rome. Then early in 202 a Roman convoy sailing from Sicily was driven ashore by a gale on to the island of Aegimurus at the entrance to the Bay of Carthage. Before the negotiations in Rome could be concluded the convoy had been wrecked, attacked and captured.

1. As the result of a storm off the African coast the Carthaginians captured a fleet of Roman transports and with them a great quantity of stores. Scipio was much vexed at this turn of events, since he had not only lost the supplies for his own army but the enemy were now abundantly provided with their necessities; what angered him even more, however, was that the Carthaginians had broken the recently sworn articles of truce and that another cause had been found for renewing the war. He therefore immediately chose Lucius Sergius, Lucius Baebius and Lucius Fabius to remonstrate with the Carthaginians about what had occurred, and at the same time to notify them that the Roman people had ratified the proposed peace settlement, for a dispatch had just reached him from Rome informing him of this fact. On their arrival at Carthage, the envoys were first heard by the Senate and later were presented to the popular assembly, to whom they spoke freely and frankly about the present state of affairs. They began by reminding their audience that when the Carthaginian delegates arrived in Tunis and were received by Scipio's advisory council, not only did they do reverence to the gods and make obeisance to the earth, but they abased themselves by falling prostrate upon the ground and kissing the feet of the assembled officers; then afterwards, when they had

risen, they accused themselves of having broken the original treaty between the Romans and the Carthaginians. For this reason they acknowledged, so they said, that the Romans would have good cause to inflict whatever penalties they chose, but they begged them to remember the vicissitudes of human fortune and not to proceed to extreme measures; in this way the folly of the Carthaginians could serve as testimony to the generosity of their opponents. And so, the Roman envoys continued, when Scipio and the rest of his colleagues who had been present recalled that scene, they could only ask themselves with amazement how the Carthaginians could now ignore what they had then said and venture to break the sworn articles of the agreement. It was clear beyond doubt that they only dared to behave in this way because they had put their trust in Hannibal and his forces. But, if so, their action was thoroughly ill-advised, for it was common knowledge that for two years past Hannibal and the best of his troops, after being driven out of the rest of Italy, had retreated into the Lacinian promontory. There they had been closely pent up, indeed almost blockaded, and had only with difficulty managed to save themselves and escape to Africa. 'And yet', the Romans went on, 'even if they had left Italy victorious and intended to engage our army which has just defeated yours in two successive battles, your hopes for the future would amount to no more than an even chance, and you ought to consider the prospect of another defeat quite as seriously as that of a victory. If that should happen, which gods can you call to your aid and what argument can you use to implore the victors to take pity upon your misfortune? Through your own treachery and folly you will surely have cut yourselves off from all hope of mercy at the hands of gods or men.'

2. After delivering this speech the envoys took their leave. As for the Carthaginians, only a few considered that they should feel bound by the terms of the treaty. The majority both of the politicians and of the members of the Senate were angered by the conditions which it imposed, and found it difficult to tolerate the blunt language of the envoys. Besides this they were not at all inclined to hand over the ships and the supplies they had captured with them. Above all, they believed that there was not merely a remote chance but a strong probability that with the aid of Hannibal's

forces they could overcome the enemy. Accordingly the popular assembly voted simply to dismiss the envoys without returning them an answer, but those of the politicians who were resolved to use every means to stir up the war again held a meeting and devised the following stratagem. They announced that every precaution must be taken to ensure the safe conduct of the Roman envoys to their camp, and at once ordered two triremes to be made ready to escort them. They also sent a message to Hasdrubal, the admiral, and asked him to have some vessels ready not far from the Roman camp; then, as soon as the escorts took leave of the Romans, the other vessels were to bear down and sink them, for the Carthaginian fleet was at this moment anchored close to Utica. After making these arrangements with Hasdrubal, they then sent off the Romans.

In the meanwhile they had ordered the commanders of the triremes to leave the envoys in the strait as soon as they had passed the mouth of the river Macar, and then to sail away, since at this point the Roman camp was already within sight. The escort followed these instructions, and no sooner had they passed the river mouth than they put about and sailed home. Lucius Baebius and his colleagues felt somewhat affronted, since they regarded it as an act of disrespect that the escort should have quitted their company so soon, but they did not suspect any danger. Then, as they sailed on alone, three Carthaginian triremes suddenly bore down upon them from their hiding-place. When they came up to the Roman quinquereme they were unable to ram her as she avoided all their attempts, nor could they board her as the crew put up a brave resistance. Instead they ran alongside and continued to circle round her, shooting at the marines and killing many of them. At last the Romans saw that soldiers from their own camp were running down to the beach to help them, and managed to run the ship ashore. Most of the marines were killed, but the envoys, surprisingly, came off safe.

3. The result of this action was that the war was resumed, but this time the cause of its renewal was more serious and the struggle even more bitter than before. The Romans considered that they had been treacherously attacked, and they were determined to overcome the Carthaginians, while the latter, who were well aware

of what they had done, were ready to go to any lengths rather than fall into the power of their enemies. Since the feelings on both sides were so inflamed, it was clear that the issue must be decided by a battle, and in consequence not only all the inhabitants of Italy and of Africa but also the peoples of Spain, Sicily and Sardinia were kept in a state of suspense and anguished excitement while they awaited the outcome.

Hannibal's forces had by this time become weak in the cavalry arm, and he sent to a certain Numidian named Tychaeus, who was a relative of Syphax and who enjoyed the reputation of possessing the best cavalry in Africa. Hannibal appealed to this man to lend his help and come to the rescue of Carthage; Tychaeus, he felt sure, must know that if the Carthaginians won he would be able to maintain his rule, but that if the Romans were victorious then his life would be in danger as well as his possessions, because of Masinissa's greed for power. Tychaeus was persuaded by this appeal and joined Hannibal with a body of 2,000 horse.

4. Meanwhile Scipio, after he had provided for the security of his fleet and delegated the command of it to Baebius, set out on a series of operations against the Carthaginian cities. He no longer accepted the submission of those who offered to surrender, but took each place by storm and sold the inhabitants into slavery, to demonstrate the anger he felt against the enemy because of the treacherous action of the Carthaginians. He also sent message after message to Masinissa explaining how the Carthaginians had violated the treaty, and urging him to mobilize as strong a force as possible and make haste to join him. Masinissa, as I have explained above,[1] started out with his own troops reinforced by ten cohorts of Roman infantry and cavalry together with officers provided by Scipio.[2] His purpose was not only to recover his ancestral kingdom, but with the help of the Romans to annex that of Syphax as well, and in this aim he eventually succeeded.

It so happened that at about this time the envoys sent from Rome to complete the peace negotiations in Carthage arrived at the

1. This refers to a part of the history which has been lost. Masinissa had acted as soon as the truce mentioned on p. 464 had been made, in order to win back his kingdom from Syphax.
2. i.e. Masinissa's campaign had the full support of the Romans.

Roman camp. Baebius at once sent on the Roman officials to Scipio but detained the Carthaginian delegates. The latter were deeply despondent and supposed that their lives must be in great danger, for as soon as they heard of the impious treatment of the Roman envoys by the Carthaginians, they thought it certain that the Romans would take vengeance upon them for this outrage. But when Scipio learned from the Roman commissioners that the Senate and people had accepted the settlement he had made with the Carthaginians and were ready to grant all his requests, he was delighted at the news and instructed Baebius to treat the Carthaginian delegates with every courtesy and send them home. In this, as it seems to me, he acted both generously and wisely. He knew that his own countrymen attached great importance to the practice of keeping faith with ambassadors, and so in deciding his action he considered first and foremost the obligations of the Romans rather than the deserts of the Carthaginians. And so he made a point of curbing his personal indignation and the resentment he felt at the recent events, and set himself to uphold 'the noble traditions of our fathers', as the saying is. The result was that he gained a moral advantage over the whole Carthaginian people and over Hannibal too, by rising above their baseness with his own generosity.

5. When the Carthaginians saw their provincial cities being sacked, they sent word to Hannibal, entreating him not to delay but to come to grips with the enemy and put the issue to the test by fighting. He listened to the messengers and then told them in reply that they should confine their attention to other matters and rest assured about this one, for he himself would choose the right moment to fight. A few days later he moved his camp from the neighbourhood of Hadrumetum,[1] advanced and then established himself near Zama, a town which lies about five days' journey[2] to the west of Carthage.

From there he sent out three spies to discover the whereabouts of the Romans and the nature and dispositions of their camp. When these men were captured and brought before Scipio, so far from following the usual practice of punishing them, he actually detailed

1. Now known as Sousse, about seventy-five miles south of Tunis.
2. About eighty miles.

a military tribune to accompany them and show them exactly how the camp was laid out. When this had been done, he asked them whether the officer had explained everything to them sufficiently thoroughly. When they confirmed that he had, he gave them provisions and an escort, and told them to make a careful report to Hannibal of everything they had seen. On their return Hannibal was deeply impressed by the courage and the lofty spirit which Scipio had shown, so much so that he conceived the surprising idea that the two should meet and talk with one another. Having made this decision, he sent a herald to announce that he wished to discuss the whole situation with Scipio, and on receiving this message the Roman commander replied that he would send word to Hannibal appointing a time and a place for the interview. On the next day Masinissa arrived with a force of 6,000 infantry and 4,000 cavalry. Scipio received him warmly and congratulated him on having brought under his rule all of Syphax's former subjects. He then broke up his camp and after reaching a town named Naragara encamped there; he chose a position which was conveniently situated in other respects and which provided him with water within the range of a javelin's throw.

6. From there Scipio sent word to the Carthaginian commander, saying that he was ready to meet and discuss matters with him. On hearing this Hannibal broke up his camp and advanced to a point less than four miles distant from the Romans. There he encamped on a hill, which seemed in most respects well-suited to his present intention, but was rather too far away from water, so that his men suffered much hardship from this disadvantage. On the next day both generals rode out of their respective camps escorted by a few horsemen, and then leaving these behind, met in the intervening space by themselves, each being accompanied by an interpreter. Hannibal first saluted Scipio and then began to speak as follows.[1]

He only wished, he told Scipio, that the Romans had never coveted any possessions outside Italy, nor the Carthaginians any outside Africa. Both peoples had built up noble empires, and Nature,

1. This meeting is also reported in Livy, *The War with Hannibal*, XXX. 30–31, and is not inherently improbable. Hannibal may well have wanted to avoid the battle or sought the opportunity to meet and assess his adversary.

469

it might be said in a word, had marked out their proper limits. 'But first of all,' he continued, 'we went to war to decide the possession of Sicily and afterwards that of Spain, and both of us have ignored the lessons of Fortune. Finally we have reached the point at which one of us has risked the safety of his native soil in the past, while the other is doing so at this moment. What remains for us, then, but to consider by what means we can avert the wrath of the gods and reconcile our present rivalry? I myself am ready to make the attempt, since I have learned by actual experience how fickle is Fortune, how by a slight shift of the scale she brings about changes of the greatest moment to either side, and how she sports with mankind as if her victims were little children.

7. But I fear that you, Scipio, partly because you are very young and partly because the whole course of events in Spain and in Africa has favoured your plans, so that you have never yet experienced the ebb-tide of Fortune, will not be influenced by my words, however much truth they may contain. But consider the facts in the light of one example, which is taken not from far-off times but from our own. I am that Hannibal who after the battle of Cannae became master of almost the whole of Italy, who later advanced up to Rome itself, pitched camp within five miles of her walls, and there took thought as to how I should deal with you and your country. Today I am here in Africa, on the point of negotiating with you, a Roman, concerning my country's very existence and my own. Remember this change of Fortune, I beg you, and do not be over-proud, but keep your thoughts at this moment upon the human scale of things; in other words, follow that course which will produce the most good and the fewest evil consequences. For what man of sense would choose to rush into the danger which confronts you now? If you are victorious, you will add little of importance to your own reputation or to the glory of your country, but if you are defeated you will wipe out through your own action the memory of all the fame and the honours you have already won. What then is my object in telling you these things? I propose that all the territories whose possession we have disputed in the past, that is Sicily, Sardinia and Spain shall belong to Rome, and that Carthage shall never go to war with her on their account. All the other islands lying between Italy and Africa shall

likewise belong to Rome. Such terms of peace would, I am certain, prove in the future the most secure for the Carthaginians and the most honourable for you and all the Romans.'[1]

8. After this speech of Hannibal's, Scipio replied as follows. He pointed out that in neither of the wars fought for the possession of Sicily and of Spain had the Romans been the aggressors: the Carthaginians had indisputably initiated both, as no one knew better than Hannibal himself. The gods had borne witness to this by granting the victory not to those who had struck the first unjust blow, but to those who had taken up arms to defend themselves. He himself constantly kept before his eyes the fickleness of Fortune, and he also took into account, so far as it lay within his power, the uncertainty of human affairs.

'But as for those conditions you propose,' he went on, 'if you had yourself withdrawn from Italy and then made such an offer before the Romans had crossed to Africa, I do not think your hopes would have been disappointed.[2] But since you only quitted Italy through force of circumstances, while we in the meanwhile have crossed to Africa and gained control of the open country, it is clear that the situation now stands on a very different footing. In fact this is the most important question of all – what is the position we have now reached? After your countrymen had been defeated and had sued for peace, we drew up a written treaty in which it was provided, in addition to your proposals, that the Carthaginians should give back their prisoners without ransom, that they should surrender their ships of war, pay us 5,000 talents, and finally provide hostages for the performance of these conditions. These were the terms upon which they and I agreed with one another. We sent envoys from both sides to Rome to submit these proposals to the Senate and the people, we Romans confirming that we agreed to the terms, and you Carthaginians begging that they should be granted. The Senate consented and the people

1. These terms offered substantially less than those agreed before the Carthaginian breach of the truce and Scipio could hardly have expected that there would be any chance of persuading the Roman people to accept them.
2. It is difficult to understand why the Carthaginian government never offered to evacuate Italy during all the years when such a proposal could have been used as a bargaining point.

471

ratified the treaty. But once the Carthaginians had obtained what they asked for, they treacherously violated the peace. What course then is left to me to take? Put yourself in my position and tell me. Are we now to strike out the harshest clauses of the treaty? In that case we should be rewarding your countrymen for their lawless actions, and teaching them to betray their benefactors on another occasion. Or should we grant their present request in the hope of earning their gratitude in the future? Remember that just now they first of all obtained what they had begged for as suppliants, and then the moment your return gave them the slightest hope of success, they at once treated us as foes and enemies. In view of this, if we were to add some even harsher conditions, there would be some reason to refer the treaty once more to our popular assembly, but if we were to withdraw any of the concessions, it would be useless even to mention this discussion of ours to them. What further purpose, then, does our conference serve? The fact is that you must either put yourself and your country unconditionally into our hands, or else fight and conquer us.'

9. After this exchange, which offered no prospect of a compromise, Hannibal and Scipio parted, and the next morning both generals led out their forces and engaged. The Carthaginians were fighting for their very survival and the possession of Africa, the Romans for the empire and sovereignty of the world.[1] Is there indeed anyone who, once he has grasped the situation, can remain unmoved when he reads the story of this battle? It would be impossible to find more warlike soldiers, or generals who had been more successful or were more thoroughly versed in the art of war, nor had Fortune ever offered the opposing armies a greater prize than this, since the victors were destined to become the masters not only of Africa and of Europe but of all parts of the world known to history. And this, indeed, proved to be the outcome.

Scipio drew up his army in the following formation. In the front line he placed the *hastati* with regular intervals between the maniples, and behind them the *principes*. However the *principes* were not positioned in the usual Roman fashion, that is, covering each of the gaps between the maniples of the front line, but at some

1. See especially p. 43 and p. 300 for Polybius' view of the importance of the battle of Zama in shaping the course of world history.

distance *directly behind* the maniples themselves; he adopted this formation because of the large number of the enemy's elephants.[1] Last of all the *triarii* were drawn up in the rear rank. On his left wing he stationed Gaius Laelius with the Italian cavalry, and on the right Masinissa with the whole of his Numidian contingent. The spaces between the maniples of the front rank were filled with companies of *velites*. These troops were ordered to begin the battle, and if they were forced back by the charge of the elephants to withdraw; those who could move quickly enough were to escape down the straight lanes left between the formations, and those who were overtaken to move either to the right or the left into the spaces between the lines.

10. After he had made these dispositions Scipio rode along the ranks and delivered to his troops an address which, though short, was well-matched to the occasion. 'Remember the battles you have fought in the past,' he told them, 'and bear yourselves like brave men who are worthy of your reputation and of your country. Keep this fact before your eyes: that if you overcome the enemy not only will you be the complete masters of Africa, but you will win for yourselves and for Rome the unchallenged leadership and sovereignty of the rest of the world. If the battle should turn out otherwise, those of you who fall will meet a death that is made for ever glorious by this sacrifice for your country, but those who save themselves by flight will be left with a life that brings them nothing but misery and disgrace. There will be no place in Africa that can give you safety, and if you should fall into the hands of the Carthaginians, no one who faces the facts can doubt what treatment will await you. I pray that none of you may live to suffer that fate. And so now that Fortune has given us the choice of the most glorious of prizes according to which way the battle is decided, we should be the most mean-spirited, and in a word the most witless of all mankind if we were to reject the most splendid of rewards and choose the worst of misfortunes merely in order to cling to life. So when you go to meet the enemy, there are two objects only to keep before you, to conquer or to die. When men

1. i.e. to allow the elephants to pass unopposed through the ranks. Normally the gaps were roughly equal to the width of the maniples themselves, so that the conventional formation resembled a chess-board.

are inspired by that spirit, they will always master their adversaries, for when they enter the battle they have already chosen to sacrifice their lives.'

11. This was how Scipio appealed to his men. Meanwhile Hannibal had also drawn up his army. In front of the whole force he stationed his elephants, of which he had over eighty, and behind them the mercenaries,[1] whose strength was about 12,000, consisting of Ligurians, Celts, Balearians and Mauretanians. Behind these he placed the native Libyans and Carthaginians, and in his last line, some 200 yards behind the rest, the troops he had brought with him from Italy. His wings were protected by cavalry, with the Numidian allies on the left and the Carthaginian horsemen on the right. He ordered the commanders of each contingent to address their own men, and told them they had a sure foundation for victory in the presence of himself and the troops he had brought back from Italy. As for the Carthaginians, he told their officers to picture to them what would be the consequences of defeat, and to leave them in no doubt as to what would be the fate of their wives and children. They carried out his orders and Hannibal then passed along the lines of his own troops. He spoke to them at some length and called upon them to remember the seventeen years during which they had been comrades in arms, and the many battles they had fought against the Romans. 'In all those actions,' he told them, 'you proved yourselves invincible and you never gave the Romans the smallest hope that they could defeat you. Let us forget for the moment the scores of minor engagements; I ask you to remember above all the battle of the Trebbia which you fought against the father of this Scipio who commands the Romans today, the battle of Lake Trasimene, when our opponent was Flaminius, and of Cannae when we defeated Paullus. The struggle which awaits us today bears no comparison with any of those battles, whether you consider the numbers of our adversaries or their

1. It is likely that all of these had been recently recruited. It is not certain whether the Balearians and Mauretanians were slingers and light cavalry respectively or whether they had been hastily trained as infantry, as the description of the fighting on p. 476 implies. Hannibal's tactics suggest that he regarded the front-line troops as expendable and hoped to weary the Romans and blunt their swords before the Carthaginian veterans came into action (see p. 478).

courage.' Having said this he told them to look up and take note of the enemy's ranks that were ranged against them. Not only was this a smaller army but it contained not even a fraction of the soldiers who had fought them in the past; and as for their courage, the Romans were no longer the men they once had been. For in those earlier contests the Romans' strength had still been unbroken and they had never known defeat, while the soldiers of today were in some cases the sons and in others the mere remnants of those legions which he had time and again defeated and put to flight in Italy. And so he called upon them not to let slip the glory and the renown of their earlier achievements and their general's, but to fight bravely and to uphold the proud reputation they had earned as an army that had never known defeat.

12. These were the addresses that the two commanders delivered. By the time that the dispositions had been completed on both sides the two opposing contingents of Numidian horse had both been skirmishing for some while, and it was then that Hannibal ordered the drivers of his elephants to charge the enemy. But when the sound of trumpets and bugles pierced the air all around them, some of the animals panicked, turned tail and stampeded to the rear, colliding with the squadrons of Numidian cavalry which had come up to support the Carthaginians, and then as Masinissa attacked at the same time, the Carthaginian left wing was quickly left exposed. The rest of the elephants charged the Roman *velites* in the space between the two armies and killed many of them, but also suffered heavy losses themselves. Then finally all the beasts took fright: some of them escaped by way of the gaps between the maniples through which the Romans allowed them to pass, while others fled towards the right wing where they were met with volleys of javelins from the cavalry, and in the end stampeded clean off the battlefield. It was at this moment that Laelius, taking advantage of the confusion caused by the elephants, launched a charge against the Carthaginian cavalry, drove them back in headlong flight and pressed the pursuit, as also did Masinissa on the right wing. Meanwhile the two opposing bodies of heavy infantry were advancing upon each other at a slow and resolute pace, except for the troops whom Hannibal had brought with him from Italy, who remained in their original positions. When the two armies arrived within

striking distance, the Roman troops charged the enemy uttering their war-cry and clashing their swords against their shields as is their custom, while from the mercenaries on the Carthaginian side there arose a strange babel of shouts and yells, for they did not all speak with one voice but, as Homer says of the Trojan army,[1]

> Here there was no common language;
> Many and strange were the tongues of this host
> Many and far-off their homelands

as appears from the composition of Hannibal's army, which I described just now.

13. The whole battle then became a hand-to-hand struggle of man against man.[2] In this contest the courage and skill of the mercenaries at first gave them the advantage and they succeeded in wounding great numbers of the Romans. Even so the steadiness of their ranks and the superiority of their weapons enabled Scipio's men to make their adversaries give ground. All this while the rear ranks of the Romans kept close behind their comrades and cheered them on, but the Carthaginians by contrast shrank back in cowardly fashion and failed to support the mercenaries. The result was that at last the barbarians themselves gave way; it seemed to them that they had been abandoned by their own side, and so as they retreated they turned upon the soldiers in their rear and began to cut them down. This action forced the Carthaginians to die bravely in spite of themselves, for when they found they were being slaughtered by the mercenaries, they were obliged quite against their will to fight both the barbarians and the Romans at the same time: when they had been brought to bay they defended themselves with desperate courage and killed a great number both of the mercenaries and of the enemy. This counter-attack by the Carthaginians even threw some of the maniples of the *hastati* into confusion, but as soon as the officers of the *principes* saw what was happening, they held their own ranks firm, and most of the mercenaries and the Carthaginians were cut down where they stood, either by their own side or by the *hastati*. Hannibal then barred

1. *Iliad*, IV, 437.
2. i.e. the fighting was in the Roman fashion as distinct from the collective impact of the Greek phalanx.

the fleeing survivors from entering the ranks of his veterans; he ordered his rear ranks to level their spears and hold the men off when they approached, and they were obliged to take refuge on the wings or in the open country.

14. The space between the two corps which still remained on the field was by now covered with blood, corpses and wounded men, and the physical obstacle created by the enemy's rout presented a difficult problem to the Roman general. Everything combined to make it hard for him to advance without losing formation: the ground slippery with gore, the corpses lying in blood-drenched heaps, and the spaces between encumbered with arms that had been thrown away at random. However, Scipio first arranged for his wounded to be carried to the rear, and next for those of the *hastati* who were pursuing the enemy to be recalled by bugle. Then he regrouped the *hastati* in the forefront of the ground where the battle had just been fought, and opposite the enemy's centre, and ordered the *principes* and *triarii* to deploy and, picking their way over the dead, to take up position in close order on both the wings and in line with the *hastati*.[1] When they had made their way over these obstacles and the line had been formed, the two main bodies hurled themselves upon one another with the greatest ardour and fury. Since they were equally matched not only in numbers but also in courage, in warlike spirit and in weapons, the issue hung for a long while in the balance. Many fell on both sides, fighting with fierce determination where they stood, but at length the squadrons of Masinissa and of Laelius returned from their pursuit of the Carthaginian cavalry and arrived by a stroke of fortune at the crucial moment. When they charged Hannibal's troops from the rear, the greater number of his men were cut down in their ranks, while of those who took to flight only a few escaped, since the cavalry were close upon their heels and the ground was level. The Romans lost over 1,500 men, but of the Carthaginians more than 20,000 were killed and almost as many were taken prisoner.

15. This was the result of the final battle between these two commanders, which decided the war. When the fighting was over Scipio moved forward in pursuit of the enemy, plundered the

1. This was done not by reducing the distance between the individual soldiers, but by closing the gaps between the maniples.

Carthaginian camp and then returned to his own. Hannibal, who was escorted by a few horsemen, did not draw rein until he had arrived safely at Hadrumetum. During the battle he had used every resource which a good general of long experience could be expected to employ. First of all, at his meeting with Scipio he had done his utmost by his own single-handed efforts to find a solution before the battle; in this way he had shown that even while he acted as a man who expected to succeed, he yet remained mistrustful of Fortune and was well aware of the part which the unexpected plays in war. Then, once he had committed himself to battle, he handled the action in such a way that it would have been impossible for any commander with the troops equipped as Hannibal's then were to make better dispositions against the Romans. The order of battle used by the Roman army is very difficult to break through, since it allows every man to fight both individually and collectively; the effect is to offer a formation which can present a front in any direction, since the maniples which are nearest to the point where danger threatens wheel in order to meet it. The arms they carry both give protection and also instil great confidence into the men, because of the size of the shields and the strength of the swords which can withstand repeated blows. All these factors make the Romans formidable antagonists in battle and very hard to overcome.

16. Nevertheless in countering each of these advantages on the Roman side and in applying at the critical moment every resource that could reasonably be expected to succeed, Hannibal displayed a skill that could scarcely have been surpassed. He had massed that large force of elephants and stationed them in front of his army with the express purpose of throwing the enemy into confusion and breaking their ranks. He had also drawn up the mercenaries in front with the Carthaginians behind them in the hope that the enemy would become physically exhausted, and their swords lose their edge through the sheer volume of the carnage before the final engagement took place. Besides this, by keeping the Carthaginians hemmed in on both sides he compelled them to stand fast and fight, so that in Homer's words,[1]

Even those loth to fight should be forced to take part in the battle.

1. *Iliad*, IV, 300.

Meanwhile he kept the most warlike and the steadiest of his fighting troops at some distance in the rear. He intended that they should watch the battle from a distance, leaving their strength and their spirit unimpaired until he could draw upon their martial qualities at the critical moment. And so if, after having taken every measure that lay within his power to secure victory, this commander who had never before suffered defeat failed in the final outcome, we must excuse him. There are times when Fortune thwarts the plans of the valiant, and others when, as the proverb says,

A brave man meets one stronger than himself.

This, we may say, is what befell Hannibal on this occasion.

17. Sometimes men give vent to their feelings in a manner which goes far beyond the normal customs of their nation, and then if this expression of emotion appears to be genuine and springs from the magnitude of their misfortune, it excites the pity of those who see or hear it. On the other hand, when such a demonstration appears to be a mere piece of posturing and play-acting, it does not arouse pity but rather anger and hostility. This is what happened on this occasion in the case of the Carthaginian envoys.

Scipio made a short preliminary statement to their embassy.[1] He said that the Romans had no obligation to treat them kindly for their own sakes, since on their own admission they had begun the war against Rome by the act of taking Saguntum in defiance of the treaty, and enslaving its inhabitants; and more recently, they had been guilty of treachery in breaking the terms of a treaty they had signed and sworn to observe.[2] 'But for our own sake,' he went on, 'and in consideration of the vicissitudes of Fortune and the dictates of humanity, we have decided to show clemency and treat you magnanimously, and this will be clear to you yourselves if you recognize the facts as they are. Certainly you ought not to find it strange if we compel you to suffer some penalty or follow some line of action or give up this or that possession; on the

1. Livy, op. cit., XXXVI. 10–11, states that in spite of a general feeling of anger among the Romans and a desire to destroy Carthage, Scipio decided at this point to offer peace terms. He gives as the reason the possibly large effort which would have been involved in besieging Carthage and the fear that his successor might take the credit.

2. i.e. by the attack on the Roman envoys (see pp. 466–7).

contrary, you should think it an unexpected concession if we grant you any favours at all, since it is through the wrongs which you yourselves have committed that Fortune has deprived you of any claim to pity or pardon and placed you at the mercy of your enemies.' After this preamble he explained the concessions which were to be made to them and the penalties to which they would have to submit.

18. The following were the heads of the terms proposed by the Romans. Carthage was to retain all the cities which she possessed in Africa before she commenced the late war against Rome, all her former territory together with flocks, herds, slaves and other property. From that day forward the Carthaginians should suffer no further injury,[1] they should be governed by their own laws and customs, and would not have a Roman garrison quartered on them. These were the concessions made; the clauses of the opposite character were as follows.

The Carthaginians were to pay reparations to the Romans for all acts of injustice committed during the truce; prisoners of war and deserters who had fallen into their hands at any time were to be handed over; all their elephants[2] and all ships of war with the exception of ten triremes were to be surrendered; they were not to make war on any people outside Africa at all, and on none in Africa without consent from Rome;[3] they were to restore to Masinissa all the houses, territory, cities and other property which had belonged to him or to his ancestors within the boundaries which would later be assigned to that king; they were to provide the Roman army with sufficient corn for three months and with pay until a reply should be received from Rome concerning the treaty; they were to pay an indemnity of 10,000 talents of silver over a period of fifty years in instalments of fifty Euboic talents

1. e.g. ravaging of their territory. The effective date was probably that on which Scipio put the terms to the Carthaginian envoys.

2. Livy reports that they were forbidden to train any more elephants.

3. This clause refers specifically to offensive war outside Carthaginian territory: i.e. it was assumed that if Carthage went to war outside Africa, she would be the aggressor. Livy's account forbids war to be carried on within Africa against a Roman ally. This clause covered Carthaginian action against, for example, Masinissa, and resulted in repeated provocations against Carthage which finally led to the Third Punic War.

each year;[1] and they were to hand over as a guarantee of good faith 100 hostages. These were to be chosen by the Roman commander from among the young men of the country between the ages of fourteen and thirty.

The End of the Second Punic War

19. These were the terms which Scipio announced to the envoys, who as soon as the communication was complete hastened back to explain them to their fellow-countrymen in Carthage. On this occasion it is said that one of the senators decided to speak against the acceptance of the terms, and was actually beginning to do so when Hannibal came forward and forcibly pulled him down from the platform. When the other members showed their anger at such a breach of the traditions of the Senate, Hannibal rose to his feet and confessed that he had been at fault; if he acted in any way contrary to their customs, they must pardon him, since they knew that he had left Carthage when he was only nine, and had only now returned when he was past forty-five. He therefore appealed to them not to confine their attention to the question of whether he had violated the procedure of the house; they should rather consider whether or not he was genuinely concerned for his country, for this was the real reason why he had committed this misdemeanour. 'It seems to me amazing,' he told them, 'and indeed quite beyond my comprehension that anyone who is a citizen of Carthage and has full knowledge of the policies which we have both individually and collectively adopted against Rome should not thank his stars that now that we are at their mercy we have obtained such lenient terms. If you had been asked only a few days ago,' he continued, 'what you expected your country would suffer in the event of a Roman victory, the disasters which threatened us then appeared so overwhelming that you would not even have been able to express your fears. So now I beg you not even to debate the question,

[1] The time span of fifty years was intended to prolong the period of subjection and prevent the paying-off of the indemnity in advance.

but to declare your acceptance of the proposals unanimously, to offer up sacrifices to the gods, and to pray with one voice that the Roman people may ratify the treaty.'

All the senators considered that this advice was as well-conceived as it was timely, and so they passed a resolution to conclude the treaty on the conditions set out above. The Senate then immediately sent out the envoys with instructions to accept the terms.[1]

Affairs in Macedonia, Syria and Egypt

20. It is a remarkable fact that so long as Ptolemy Philopator was alive and had no need of help from the Kings of Macedonia and Syria, these rulers were very ready to provide it, but no sooner had he died, leaving as his heir a mere child whom it was their natural duty to help in preserving his dominions, than they at once hastened to divide his kingdom, encouraging one another to ruin the defenceless orphan. They did not even, as is customary among tyrants, trouble themselves to invent some paltry pretext for their shameful deed, but proceeded at once to act in a manner so brutal and so predatory that one can only liken their behaviour to that of fishes, among which it is said that – although they all belong to the same species – the larger live by annihilating the smaller. The treaty which they drew up between them reflects, as if in a mirror, the very image of impiety towards the gods and savagery towards other men, not to mention the unbounded rapacity of the two kings. And yet though a man might feel that he had good cause to blame Fortune for her handling of human affairs in this instance, yet he could almost forgive her when he learns how she afterwards made them pay a just penalty for their actions, and how by making these kings an example, she set up an unforgettable lesson for posterity.

1. The envoys returned first to Scipio, and the Carthaginians were then granted a three months' truce during which they were to send envoys to Rome. The hearing of the envoys in Rome and the decision to make peace on the terms recommended by Scipio are described in Livy, op. cit., XXX. 42–3.

For even while they were in the act of breaking faith with one another and dismembering the child's kingdom, she brought the Romans upon them and justly and fittingly visited them with the very wrongs which they had wickedly tried to practise against others. For both kings were soon conquered in battle, and were not only prevented from coveting the possessions of others, but were forced to pay tribute and submit to the commands of Rome. Finally, within a short space of time Fortune raised up again the kingdom of Ptolemy, while as for the rival dynasties she dealt them in the one case total destruction, and in the other a series of misfortunes almost as crushing.

Affairs in Egypt

A PALACE REVOLUTION

Ptolemy IV (Philopator) had proved a weak ruler, who adopted an indolent and dissipated life-style and conducted his reign, which lasted from 220–204 B.C., 'as if it were a perpetual festival' (p. 291). The country was administered by his cunning and unscrupulous adviser Sosibius, who could not, however, prevent a serious decline both in the external and the internal strength of the kingdom. A son was born to Ptolemy in 210, who was at once proclaimed joint ruler. About 207 Philopator separated from his able and virtuous Queen Arsinoë, and fell more and more under the odious and unpopular influence of his favourite, Agathocles, his mistress Agathoclea, (Agathocles' sister) and Oenanthe (their mother). Meanwhile revolts and secessions in the Delta and Upper Egypt had begun to undermine the security of the kingdom. In 204 Philopator died, whereupon Sosibius and Agathocles seized power, had Arsinoë murdered, and forged a will appointing themselves guardians of the seven-year-old heir, Ptolemy Epiphanes. Sosibius in his lifetime, according to Polybius, had brought about the deaths of Lysimachus (Philopator's eldest son), Magas (Philopator's brother), Berenice (Philopator's mother), Cleomenes of Sparta and Arsinoë (Philopator's wife). He himself died in 203, leaving the regency in the nerveless hands of Agathocles. The popular uprising against the latter took place in 202. Tlepolemus, the military commander of the region of Pelusium, succeeded Agathocles as regent and survived in power till 196. Meanwhile Philip of Macedon and Antiochus the Great of Syria had concerted their unscrupulous pact to partition a number of the Ptolemaic possessions outside Egypt. Philip seized Samos in 201, while Antiochus invaded Coele Syria in 201 and later penetrated as far as the Sinai desert.

26. Agathocles' first action was to summon a meeting of the Macedonian guards[1] and appear before them accompanied by Agathoclea and the boy-king Ptolemy Epiphanes. At first he pretended that he was unable to speak because of the flood of tears that choked him. But after wiping his eyes again and again with his cloak and then ostentatiously mastering his emotion, he lifted the boy in his arms and exclaimed, 'Take this boy, whom his father Philopator on his death-bed placed in the arms of this woman,' here he pointed to his sister Agathoclea, 'and entrusted to your loyalty, soldiers of Macedon. Her affection, alas, does not command the power to ensure his safety, so it is upon you and your strength that his fate depends. It must have been clear for a long while to all of you who have eyes to see that Tlepolemus[2] is intriguing for a position which is far above his station, and now he has even named the day and the hour at which he intends to assume the crown. You need not rely on my word alone to judge the truth of this; you can ask those who know the facts and have just come from the scene of these events.' As he said this he brought forward Critolaus, who confirmed that he had himself seen the altars being erected and the sacrificial victims being prepared in front of the people for the coronation ceremony.

When the Macedonian guards heard this, so far from being moved to pity by what Agathocles had told them, they paid no attention whatever to his words and showed their contempt for him so plainly by booing and murmuring to one another that he hardly knew himself how he escaped from the assembly. Scenes

1. The Macedonians owned land and constituted the most important part of the Egyptian army.
2. An able soldier belonging to a distinguished Persian family which had emigrated to Egypt.

very similar to this took place at the meetings of the other regiments of the army. Meanwhile numbers of men kept arriving by boat from the garrisons stationed in Upper Egypt, and all of them appealed to their friends and relatives to help them in the present situation and not to stand by and let them be subjected to a monstrous tyranny at the hands of such unworthy men. But the factor which most strongly incited the soldiers to revenge themselves on the government was that any delay was potentially dangerous to them, since Tlepolemus controlled all the means of importing provisions into Alexandria.

27. Besides this there was one action of Agathocles and his supporters which particularly angered the populace and Tlepolemus besides. Tlepolemus' mother-in-law Danae was taken from the temple of Demeter, dragged unveiled through the middle of the city, and thrown into prison, and this was done expressly to demonstrate Agathocles' hostility to the general. This outrage so infuriated the people that they no longer spoke of it privately or secretly. Some expressed their detestation of the men in power by covering all the walls of the city with inscriptions at night, while others began to meet quite openly in groups for the same purpose.

As he watched these signs of growing hostility, Agathocles began to fear for his own safety and at one point considered fleeing the country, but as he had been too lacking in foresight ever to have prepared for an escape, he soon abandoned this idea. His next step was to draw up lists of men who would be ready to take part in a conspiracy; this would involve the immediate execution of a number of his enemies, the arrest of others and the seizure of absolute power for himself. While he was busy with this plot, one of the King's personal staff named Moeragenes was accused of reporting everything that went on in the palace to Tlepolemus and of working on his behalf; he did this, it was alleged, because of his friendship with Adaeus, the governor of the neighbouring province of Bubastis. Agathocles at once ordered Nicostratus, his secretary of state, to arrest Moeragenes and give him a searching interrogation, threatening him with every kind of torture. Moeragenes was promptly arrested and taken to a remote part of the palace; there he was first questioned directly in the normal fashion about these accusations, and when he refused to confess to any of them, he was stripped. Some of his captors began to prepare the instruments of torture, while others with whips in their hands were taking off their cloaks, when at that moment a servant ran up to Nicostratus, whispered something in his ear and hurried out again. Nicostratus immediately followed him, did not utter a word but repeatedly slapped his thigh with his hand.

28. The situation in which Moeragenes now found himself was so extraordinary that it almost defied description. Some of his captors stood close by on the point of raising their whips to strike him, while others were preparing the instruments of torture before his eyes. When Nicostratus hurried out all of them were left looking at one another as though struck dumb, and expecting him to return at any moment. Then, as time dragged on, they all one by one slipped away and Moeragenes was left entirely by himself. After this he was able, much to his astonishment, to make his way across the palace until he burst half-clothed into a tent close by, which was occupied by the Macedonian guards. When he came upon them they happened all to be sitting together taking their morning meal, and so he told them his story and the strange fashion in which he had escaped. Some of them at first refused outright to believe his story, but when they looked at him without his clothes, they were compelled to accept it. Moeragenes took advantage of this complete change of circumstances to appeal with tears in his eyes to the Macedonians, not only to help save him but also to consider the King's safety and above all their own. He impressed upon them that they faced certain destruction if they did not seize the present opportunity when the resentment of the populace was at its height and everyone was ready to punish Agathocles. Now was the time to act, he reminded them, when the people's emotions were at boiling-point, and it only needed someone to make the first move.

29. These words at last aroused the Macedonians to action and they agreed to do as Moeragenes advised. They began by making an immediate tour of the tents belonging to the Macedonian guards, after which they visited those of the other troops, which were all close together and faced the same quarter of the city. The populace had for a long while been in the mood to revolt, and it needed only one man with the courage to call them out; then, once the attempt had begun it spread like wildfire. Within a bare four hours peoples

of all nationalities in the city, civilians as well as soldiers, had agreed to rebel against the government.

At this moment chance also played a great part in helping them to achieve their purpose. A letter had fallen into Agathocles' hands, and at the same time some of his spies were brought to him. The letter turned out to be addressed by Tlepolemus to the army informing them that he would shortly be in Alexandria, and the spies reported that he had actually arrived. This news threw Agathocles into such a state of panic that he became incapable of taking any action at all, or even of thinking about the dangers that surrounded him. Instead he went off to drink at the usual hour and behaved at the dining-table with his customary self-indulgence. His mother Oenanthe went in great distress to visit the Thesmophorium,[1] since the temple was open for the annual sacrifice. There she first of all fell on her knees and with eloquent gestures implored the help of the goddesses, and then seated herself near the altar and remained silent. Most of the women who were present found a certain pleasure in seeing her so despondent and distressed; they said nothing, but the relatives of Polycrates and some other women of the nobility, who were not yet aware of the imminent danger, came up to console her. But Oenanthe screamed at them, 'Do not come near me, you monsters! I know only too well how your hearts are set against us and how you are praying to the goddesses that the worst shall overtake us. But for all that, if it is the will of heaven, I trust that you shall one day taste the flesh of your own children.' With these words she called upon the attendants of the festival to drive the women away and strike them with their staves if they refused to leave. For their part they availed themselves of this excuse to quit the shrine in a body; at the same time they raised their hands to the goddesses and uttered a prayer that Oenanthe herself might suffer the fate she had threatened to bring upon others.

30. The male inhabitants of the city had already decided to rise in revolt, but now that in every household the anger of the women was added to their own, the popular hatred against Agathocles

1. This temple was situated outside the city a little way to the east. The Thesmophoria was a fertility ceremony held in honour of Demeter and Persephone, usually at the time of sowing in October/November.

flared up with redoubled fury. As soon as night fell the whole city
was filled with uproar, the blaze of torches and the sound of hurry-
ing feet. Some of the people were gathering with shouts in the
stadium, others encouraging one another, while others again were
running to and fro trying to hide themselves in places which were
unlikely to be suspected. The stadium, the wide avenues which
surrounded the palace, the main street of the city and the area in
front of the theatre of Dionysus were now packed with a multitude
of all nationalities. Meanwhile Agathocles, when he learned what
was happening, roused himself from his state of drunken stupor,
for he had only just dismissed his drinking-party, and taking the
whole of his family with the exception of Philo, he went to visit
the King. After addressing a few words to the boy in which he
lamented his own misfortunes, he took him by the hand and went
up to the covered gallery which runs between the water-garden
known as the Maeander and the wrestling arena, and leads to the
entrance to the theatre. There he made fast the first two doors and
then passed through the third with a few of the palace bodyguard,
the King, and the members of his own family. The doors were each
secured by two bars, but were only made of lattice-work, so that it
was possible to see through them.

By this time the mob had gathered from every quarter of the
city in such immense numbers that not only the open spaces but the
roofs and steps were thronged with people, and from them there
arose a continual confused clamour and uproar, such as might be
expected from a crowd in which women and children are mingled
among the men; for in Carthage and in Alexandria too the children
play as prominent a part in these disturbances as the adults.

31. As the day began to break, the general hubbub made it
difficult to distinguish individual cries, but one phrase stood out
above the rest, the words 'Bring the King!' The first positive
action came from the Macedonian guard, who advanced and seized
the gate of audience of the palace. Soon afterwards, once they had
discovered where the King was, they went round, removed the
first door of the gallery from its hinges, approached the second, and
demanded with loud shouts to see the King. Agathocles, who was
now concerned for his own safety, besought the bodyguards to
carry a message on his behalf to the Macedonians, telling them that

he now resigned the office of regent together with its various powers and dignities, as well as his emoluments, and asked for nothing but his life and a bare subsistence: all that he desired was to retire to his original station in life, where he could not, even if he wished it, cause harm to anyone. All the other bodyguards refused, but Aristomenes, who later became the chief minister, agreed to carry the message. This man was an Acarnanian by birth, and although he was well on in years when he obtained the chief power in the state, he is considered to have proved himself a most admirable and scrupulous guardian of the interests of the King and of the Egyptian kingdom. The excellence of his performance of that office is all the more remarkable because he had been equally conspicuous as a flatterer of Agathocles when the latter was at the height of his prosperity: he was the first man who, after having invited Agathocles to a banquet, singled him out among all the guests and presented him with a crown of gold, an honour which it was the custom to render only to the King. He was likewise the first who ventured to wear a ring with Agathocles' portrait engraved on it, and when a daughter was born to him he named her Agathoclea.

Enough of this man's character; to return to my story. After undertaking this mission for Agathocles, he went out by a wicket gate to the Macedonians. No sooner had he spoken a few words and explained Agathocles' proposal than the Macedonians tried to run him through. However, a few of the soldiers interposed their hands and appealed to the others to spare him. Aristomenes then went back to the palace, having been told that he should either return bringing the King with him or not come out at all. After sending him back with this message the Macedonians then came up to the second door and broke this down as well. Agathocles and those with him now recognized both from the Macedonians' actions and the tone of their demands that they were in a mood to stop at nothing. They therefore tried to plead with the soldiers for mercy, and left no word unsaid which might stir their pity, at least to the extent of sparing their lives; Agathocles went so far as to put his hands through the lattice and Agathoclea her breasts, with which she said she had suckled the King.

32. But at last, when they saw that no amount of lamentation

of their fate was of any avail, they sent out the young King with the bodyguard. The Macedonians took the boy with them, straight away placed him on a horse, and escorted him to the stadium. His appearance there was greeted with loud cheers and applause, whereupon they stopped the horse, and lifting the boy down, led him forward and seated him in the royal stall. As for the crowd, their feelings were now divided between joy and vexation. They were delighted that the King had been brought to them, but also angry that the guilty parties had not yet been arrested and punished as they deserved. And so they continued to raise an uproar, and demanded that those responsible for all the ills the people had suffered should be brought out and made an example of. By this time the day was well advanced, but still the people had found no one who could serve as the scapegoat for their anger. At this point Sosibius, who was the son of the statesman of that name, and who as a member of the bodyguard was particularly mindful of the security both of the King and of the state, came to the conclusion that there was no prospect of appeasing the fury of the mob. He also saw that the young King was distressed, partly by the unfamiliar faces of those who now surrounded him and partly by the commotion of the crowd, and so he asked the King whether he would agree to deliver up to the people those who had in any way wronged him or his mother. The boy nodded his head, whereupon Sosibius told some of the bodyguard to announce the royal decision; then he raised the boy from his seat, and took him away to look after him in his own house which was close by. When the message from the King was made public, a tremendous roar of cheering and applause burst out all over the stadium. Meanwhile Agathocles and Agathoclea had separated and each returned to their own household. Immediately a number of soldiers, some of their own accord and others urged on by the crowd, started out to search for them.

33. The murders and bloodshed which ensued originated from a chance incident. One of Agathocles' attendants and flatterers named Philo left the palace and entered the stadium in a drunken state, and as he observed the turbulent mood of the soldiers, he remarked to those who were standing next to him that if Agathocles came out, they would have reason to repent their behaviour, as had happened a short while before. When the bystanders heard this,

some of them began to abuse him and others to push him about. Then when he tried to defend himself, some of them instantly tore the cloak off his back, while others levelled their spears and stabbed him. He was ignominiously hauled into the midst of the stadium while he was still breathing, and having once tasted blood the people waited eagerly for the arrival of the other victims. Before long Agathocles was led along in fetters, and as soon as he appeared some of the crowd ran up and immediately stabbed him. This in reality was a compassionate rather than a hostile act, for the consequence was to save him from the hideous death which he deserved. Next Nicon was brought in, and then Agathoclea, who with her two sisters had been stripped naked, and after them all the rest of her relatives. Last of all they dragged Oenanthe from the Thesmophorium, placed her on a horse and led her naked to the stadium. All of them were then handed over to the fury of the mob, whereupon some began to tear them with their teeth, others to stab them, others to gouge out their eyes. As soon as any of them fell, the body was torn limb from limb until they had dismembered them all, for the savagery of the Egyptians is truly appalling when their passions have been roused. At the same time a company of young girls, who had been the companions of Queen Arsinoë, learned that Philammon, who had been responsible for her murder, had arrived from Cyrene three days before. They then rushed to his house, forced their way in, killed Philammon with clubs and stones, strangled his son who was scarcely more than a boy, and to crown their work dragged his wife naked into the street and killed her on the spot. Such was the end of Agathocles, Agathoclea and their families.

34. I am well aware that some of the authors who have chronicled these events have resorted to elaborate and sensational descriptions simply to produce a striking effect upon their readers, and have amplified the narrative far more than is necessary to give an adequate account of what happened. Some attribute the whole course of events to Fortune, and stress her fickle character and the inability of mankind to guard against her vicissitudes, while others strive to give a rational account of the unexpected and try to assign reasons or probable causes for everything. It was never my purpose, however, to treat the subject in that way. My reasons were that as a soldier Agathocles was in no way remarkable either for ability or

for courage, as a statesman he was not favoured by Fortune and was certainly not a model in his handling of affairs, while as a courtier he possessed neither the astuteness nor the capacity for intrigue which made Sosibius and many others so successful throughout their lives in the art of managing one king after another. Indeed in this role his situation was the opposite to that of the men I have just mentioned, for it was because of Ptolemy Philopator's weakness as a ruler that Agathocles achieved an un-expectedly high position. But having got there, although after the King's death he was most favourably placed to maintain his power, he lost both his position and his life through his own cowardice and inertia, and in a short while came to be universally despised.

35. For such subjects, as I have already explained, it serves no purpose to amplify the narrative with comment and analysis, but it is a different story in the case of the Sicilians, Agathocles and Dionysius, and of certain other rulers of distinction. Of these two the second started from an obscure and humble position, while Agathocles, as Timaeus tells us with a disparaging allusion, was originally a potter and left the wheel, the clay and the smoke to come to Syracuse as a young man. To begin with they both became in their time tyrants of Syracuse, a city which at that period ranked the highest of all in dignity and prosperity, and later they were recognized as Kings of the whole of Sicily,[1] and even exercised sway over some parts of Italy. Moreover, Agathocles not only made an attempt to conquer Africa, but at the time of his death was still in possession of all the domains that he had previously acquired. It is for this reason that when Publius Scipio, the first man to defeat the Carthaginians, was once asked whom he thought the most successful statesman and the one who best combined the virtues of courage and wisdom, he replied 'Agathocles and Dionysius, the Sicilians.'[2] It is certainly right to single out the careers of such men for the attention of our readers, to make some reference to the vicissitudes of Fortune and the instability of human affairs and to

1. This is not strictly true. Dionysius never used the title of king nor did he strike coins in his own image.

2. Polybius is inconsistent here. There is no reason to suppose that Scipio greatly admired such an autocratic type of ruler; he is more likely to have been thinking of these men as successful adversaries of the Carthaginians.

point a moral to the story, but in the case of the Egyptian Agathocles all this would be out of place.

36. For this reason, then, I have rejected the idea of enlarging on the story of Agathocles of Egypt. One good reason for not doing so is the fact that all such striking reversals of Fortune only hold our attention when they are presented to us for the first time. Thereafter not only does it become unprofitable to read about them or to keep them in mind, but in fact the vivid representation of such events even produces a certain repulsion.

For those who intend to study any subject by using their eyes and ears there are two prime objects, namely their betterment and their pleasure, which should be kept in the forefront of the mind; this principle applies most of all to the study of history where neither of these ends will be achieved if sensational events are disproportionately emphasized. In the first place, abnormal reversals of Fortune arouse no desire in the reader to emulate them himself, and secondly, nobody receives any lasting pleasure from witnessing or reading of things which are contrary to nature and to general human experience. It is true that we are interested in seeing or hearing of them once and for all and for the first time, simply in order to discover that the apparently impossible can actually happen; but having been satisfied on that point nobody takes pleasure in dwelling on the unnatural, and indeed would rather not encounter this kind of thing more often than is necessary. It follows then that what we are told should either give pleasure or arouse the desire to emulate it, and hence that the elaborate treatment of an event which produces neither of these effects is more suitable to the art of tragedy than to history.

But perhaps we should excuse those writers who do not dwell upon themes which follow the pattern of nature or the course of general experience in the world. For they are inclined to think that the most important and most wonderful events in past history are those which they happen to have met in their own experience, or which made a particular impression when they heard about them from others. The result is that they devote far more space than they should to material which is neither original, since others have related it before, nor capable of giving instruction or pleasure. I have now said enough on this subject.

BOOK XVIII

Affairs in Greece

FLAMININUS AND PHILIP

Philip's campaigns from 200–198 B.C. against the Romans had resulted in a number of reverses and he had asked for a conference to negotiate. Flamininus also found this a useful move to gain time while the question of his future appointment was being discussed in Rome. The conference took place in November 198.

1. When the time that had been fixed for this conference came round, Philip set out from the port of Demetrias for the Malian Gulf. He himself travelled in a beaked ship together with five galleys, and was accompanied by the Macedonians Apollodorus and Demosthenes who were his secretaries, by Brachylles[1] from Boeotia, and by Cycliadas the Achaean,[2] who had been driven out of the Peloponnese for the reasons I have already described. With Flamininus[3] came King Amynander of Athamania[4] and Dionysodorus, the representative of King Attalus of Pergamum, while the various Greek nations and city states were represented by Aristaenus and Xenophon from Achaea, the admiral Acesimbrotus from Rhodes, and the general Phaeneas together with several other statesmen from Aetolia. Flamininus and those who accompanied him arrived at the sea shore at Nicaea,[5] gathered on the beach and stood waiting there. Philip, however, after bringing his ship close

1. The officer commanding the Boeotians serving with Philip's army.
2. He had led the pro-Macedonian faction in Achaea, had been elected general in 200, but had resisted Philip's attempt to involve Achaea in the war against Rome. He was exiled when the Achaeans changed their allegiance from Macedon to Rome.
3. Titus Quinctius Flamininus was consul in 198 B.C.
4. A district in north-western Greece between the river Arachthos and the western slopes of the Pindus.
5. A port on the Malian Gulf near Thermopylae.

to the land, remained on board and when Flamininus asked him to come ashore, he rose from his place on the ship and refused to disembark. Flamininus again addressed him, this time to ask what he was afraid of, to which Philip retorted that he was afraid of nothing except the gods, but that he distrusted the majority of those who were present and above all the Aetolians. When the Roman general showed his surprise and remarked that the same danger applied to all those present and that the odds were equal, Philip answered that he was mistaken, for if anything were to happen to Phaeneas there were plenty of men to take command of the Aetolians, but if Philip were to lose his life there was no one at that moment to succeed him on the throne of Macedonia.

All those who were present thought that in opening the conference in this way the King had shown a singular lack of tact, but Flamininus urged him to speak on whatever topics had persuaded him to come. Philip said that it was not for him to speak first, but rather for Flamininus, and went on to invite him to explain what he, Philip, should do to have peace. The Roman general replied that his duty dictated an answer which was both simple and clear. He demanded that Philip should withdraw from the whole of Greece, restore to each of the states the prisoners and deserters he was holding, hand over to the Romans the region of Illyria which he had seized after the treaty that had been made in Epirus,[1] and on the same principle give back to Ptolemy all the towns he had taken from him since the death of Ptolemy Philopator.[2]

2. After saying this Flamininus made no further comment, but turned to the rest of the delegates and asked them to speak according to the instructions of those who had sent them to the conference. Dionysodorus, the representative of King Attalus of Pergamum, was the first to rise. He declared that Philip must surrender those of the King's ships he had taken at the battle of Chios, together with the crews captured in them, and must restore to their original condition both the temple of Aphrodite and the sanctuary of Athena Nicephorus near Pergamum which he had destroyed. He was followed by the Rhodian admiral Acesimbrotus, who

1. The peace of Phoenice, made in 205, which had ended the First Macedonian War.
2. The towns in Thrace taken by Philip in 200.

requested that Philip should evacuate the Peraea which he had seized from the Rhodians, withdraw his garrisons from Iasus, Bargylia and Euromus,[1] allow the Perinthians to resume their political union with Byzantium, and evacuate Sestos and Abydos and all the commercial ports and harbours in Asia Minor. When the Rhodian delegate had finished, the Achaeans demanded that Corinth and Argos should be restored to them undamaged. After them the Aetolians began by insisting, as the Romans had done, that Philip should evacuate the whole of Greece, and went on to require that he should hand back to them undamaged those cities which were formerly members of the Aetolian League.

3. After Phaeneas the Aetolian had put forward these demands, a man named Alexander of Isus,[2] who had the reputation of being both an experienced statesman and an able orator, rose to speak. He attacked Philip on the grounds that he was neither sincere at the present moment in proposing a peace settlement, nor courageous in his manner of waging war when this was required of him. When he attended assemblies and conferences he was constantly setting traps, watching his opportunity and generally behaving as if he were at war, but in war itself he pursued a policy which was both unjust and ignoble. Instead of meeting his enemies face to face, his practice was to retreat before them burning and plundering cities as he went, and by this course of conduct, though he was defeated himself, he spoiled the prizes of the victors. The earlier kings of Macedonia had behaved in precisely the opposite fashion, for they constantly fought one another in the open field, but very seldom razed or devastated cities. This practice was made clear to all in the war which Alexander waged in Asia against King Darius, and again in the long-drawn-out struggle between Alexander's successors in which they all took the field against Antigonus for the mastery of Asia. And the successors of these rulers down to the time of Pyrrhus had followed the same principle. They had always been eager to give battle in the open field, and had done everything in their power to conquer one another by force of arms, but they had spared the cities, so that whoever proved the victor should rule

1. Towns in the province of Caria on the mainland of Asia Minor, north of Rhodes.
2. A town in southern Aetolia, north-east of Naupactus.

over them and be honoured by his subjects. But for a man to abandon war, yet at the same time destroy the very objects for which a
war is waged, was not just madness but the height of madness. Yet
this was exactly what Philip was now doing, for when he made his
forced march back from the pass in Epirus[1] he destroyed more
cities in Thessaly, in spite of being a friend and ally of that country,
than anyone who had actually made war on the Thessalians. Then,
after he had elaborated his case at length with many more examples,
Alexander finally used the following argument. 'Why,' he asked
Philip, 'when the city of Lysimachia was a member of the Aetolian
League and was under the rule of a military governor provided by
them, had he expelled this officer and installed a garrison of his
own? And why had he sold into slavery the people of Cius, which
was also a member of the Aetolian League, when he himself was on
friendly terms with the Aetolians? And finally, on what pretext
was he now occupying the cities of Echinus, Phthiotic Thebes,
Pharsalus and Larissa?'[2]

4. When he had made these points Alexander concluded his
harangue, whereupon Philip had his ship manoeuvred closer to the
shore and stood up on the deck to reply. He told his audience that
Alexander had delivered a speech in the typically theatrical and
Aetolian style. 'We all know,' he said, 'that nobody willingly
destroys his own allies, but that through changes of circumstance
commanders are obliged to do many things which are contrary to
their choice.' While the King was still speaking, Phaeneas, who
suffered from particularly weak eyesight, interrupted him and told
him that he was talking nonsense. 'The truth is,' he said, 'that
you must either fight and conquer, or else obey those who are
stronger than you.' At this, weak though his position was, Philip
could not refrain from indulging his special line in sarcasm, and
so he turned to Phaeneas and said, 'Yes, even a blind man can see
that', for he was quick at repartee and had a special knack for
making his opponents look small. Then addressing Alexander again,
he said, 'You ask me why I annexed Lysimachia. The reason was to
prevent it from being depopulated by the Thracians because of

1. A pass from which Philip had been driven out by Flamininus.
2. These four cities had earlier belonged to the Aetolians and been taken
by the Macedonians.

your own neglect; and indeed this is what happened, since the present war has forced me to withdraw the soldiers who according to you were acting as a garrison, but who were really there to protect the place. As for the people of Cius, it was not I who made war on them, but when Prusias did so I merely helped him to capture the city, and this was your fault as well. Time and again both I and the other Greek states sent envoys to ask you to remove from your statutes the law which allows you to take "plunder from plunder", and you always replied that you would rather remove Aetolia from Aetolia than repeal this law.'[1]

5. When Flamininus remarked that he did not know what the King meant, Philip tried to explain to him that it is a custom among the Aetolians to plunder not only the persons and the territory of those with whom they themselves are at war, but if any other peoples are at war with one another and are at the same time friends and allies of theirs, the Aetolians are allowed to give help to both parties and likewise to plunder the territory of both without any public decree having been passed to that effect. In other words, in the eyes of the Aetolians there are no properly defined limits either of friendship or of hostility, but they are ready to treat as enemies and make war upon all states which are in dispute about anything.

'So what right have they,' Philip went on, 'to condemn me now, if when I was on friendly terms with the Aetolians and in alliance with Prusias I acted against the people of Cius in order to help my own allies? But what is most outrageous of all is that they should attempt to put themselves on the same footing as the Romans and demand that the Macedonians should withdraw from the whole of Greece. To use such language is arrogant enough in the first place, but while we may endure this from the Romans, it is quite intolerable coming from the Aetolians. In any case,' he continued, 'what is this Greece which you demand that I should evacuate, and how do you define Greece? Certainly most of the Aetolians themselves are not Greeks! The countries of the Agraae, the

1. The Aetolians licensed their citizens, in the same manner as various European governments licensed privateers in the eighteenth century, to carry on independent hostilities against countries with whom they were not officially at war.

Apodotae and the Amphilochians cannot be regarded as Greek.[1]
So do you allow me to remain in those territories?'

6. At this Flamininus could not repress a smile, whereupon
Philip added, 'That is all I have to say to the Aetolians. So far
as the Rhodians and King Attalus are concerned, I believe a fair-
minded judge would consider it more just for them to give up the
captured ships and the crews than for me to restore them. It was
not I who first took up arms against Attalus and the Rhodians,
but they against Macedon, as everybody acknowledges. However,
since you have requested this, Titus, I agree to cede the Peraea to
the Rhodians, and the ships and the surviving members of their
crews to Attalus. As for the damage that was done to the sanctuary
of Athena Nicephorus and the shrine of Aphrodite, it is not in my
power to do anything else towards restoring them, but I will send
plants and some gardeners to tend the place and see to the growth
of the trees that were cut down.' Flamininus smiled once more at
the irony in the King's words, and Philip then turned to the
Achaeans. He began by recounting all the favours that they had
received from Antigonus and later from himself; then he quoted
the exceptional honours which the Achaeans had conferred on the
rulers of Macedon, and finally he read out the decree according to
which they had abandoned him and transferred their alliance to
Rome, and he made this the occasion to enlarge upon the fickleness
and ingratitude of the Achaeans in general. In spite of their action,
however, he undertook to restore Argos to them, but in the case
of Corinth he said he would consult with Flamininus.

7. When he had concluded his address to the other envoys,
he turned to Flamininus, remarking that the discussion now rested
between himself and the Romans, and asked whether it was the
general's wish that he should retire from these towns and places in
Greece which he himself had conquered, or whether the withdrawal should also include those he had inherited from his ancestors.
At this Flamininus remained silent, but Aristaenus was primed and
ready to speak on behalf of the Achaeans, and Phaeneas for the
Aetolians, and they were only prevented from doing so by the fact

1. Allowing for a measure of Macedonian rhetoric, it is quite true that
Thucydides had regarded the Amphilochians, who lived at the eastern end
of the Ambracian Gulf, as barbarians.

that the hour was growing late and the day was drawing to a close. Thereupon Philip requested that they should all provide him with written statements setting out their terms for a peace settlement; he pointed out that he was alone and had no advisers to consult, and so wished to reflect upon their various demands. Flamininus was by no means displeased at the evident mockery in Philip's tone, but he did not wish the others to see this, and so made fun of Philip in his turn by saying, 'Of course you are alone by this time, Philip: you have killed off all the friends who could give you the best advice.' At this the Macedonian King smiled sardonically and said nothing. All the envoys then handed their demands in writing to Philip, the terms of which corresponded to those I have already described, and after arranging to resume the conference the next day at Nicaea, they separated. The next morning Flamininus and all the others came punctually at the appointed time, but Philip did not appear.

8. Near the end of the day, by which time Flamininus had almost given up hope, Philip arrived towards dusk, accompanied by the same suite as on the day before. He made out that he had spent the time poring over the envoys' demands in a state of great perplexity and uncertainty as to how to meet them. The other delegates were convinced, however, that his purpose was to prevent the Achaeans and Aetolians from delivering their accusations by reducing the time available for discussion; for on the previous day, just as he was leaving, he had noticed that both these delegations were on the point of attacking him and stating their grievances. So this time as he came up to the meeting-place, he requested that the Roman general should discuss the situation with him in private. The object of this meeting was that they should stop carrying on a mere skirmishing with words on both sides, and arrive at some definite solution of the matters in dispute.

When he repeated this request several times and pressed the idea strongly, Flamininus asked the rest of the delegates who were present what he should do. They urged him to meet Philip and hear what he had to say. Thereupon Flamininus called upon Appius Claudius, who was at the time military tribune, to join him; then he told the other members of the conference who had retired a little way from the sea shore to remain where they were, while he invited Philip to come ashore. The King then disembarked accompanied by Apollodorus and Demosthenes, met Flamininus, and held a private conference with him for a long time. It is difficult to say what passed between them on this occasion, but after they had parted Flamininus set about explaining the King's proposals to the rest of the delegates. He told them that Philip was prepared to give back Pharsalus and Larissa but not Thebes to the Aetolians, that he would restore Corinth and Argos to the Achaeans and the Peraea to the Rhodians, but would not withdraw from the Carian cities of Iasus and Bargylia. To the Romans he would surrender all his possessions in Illyria together with all prisoners of war, and to Attalus he would return his ships and all the survivors of the crews who had been captured in the naval battles.

9. All those who were present immediately declared their dissatisfaction with the peace terms offered and insisted that Philip must begin by complying with their common demand, namely to withdraw from the whole of Greece; without this action all the rest of the concessions had neither value nor meaning. Meanwhile Philip could see that an animated discussion was going on, and as he was afraid of the accusations that would be launched against him, he asked Flamininus, as the hour was getting late, to adjourn the conference to the following day; at their next session, he said, he would either win the others over to his point of view or accept the justice of theirs. Flamininus agreed to this request, and after arranging to meet on the beach at Thronium they parted company.

The next day the whole conference arrived in good time at the appointed place. This time Philip made a short speech in which he appealed to all the envoys and above all to Flamininus not to break off the negotiations for peace now that the majority were in a conciliatory mood, but if possible to reach an agreement among themselves on the points which were still in dispute. If that proved impossible, he would then send an embassy to the Senate and either persuade that body to accept the various controversial issues, or else carry out its decision.[1] The response of all the Greek envoys

1. This was an unprecedented proposal, for hitherto consultation with the Senate had *followed* a preliminary agreement with the Roman general in charge on the spot. Flamininus hoped to obtain an extension of his command in Greece, or failing that to be entrusted with the task of making peace.

was that they should continue the war and disregard Philip's offer. However, the Roman general's view was that while he was well aware of the unlikelihood of Philip's agreeing to any of their demands, still, as his request in no way interfered with their freedom of action, it was quite possible to grant it. None of the proposals which were being discussed at this conference could in fact be ratified without reference to the Senate, and apart from the necessity of ascertaining its opinion, the present moment was in various ways a convenient one. The winter would prevent the armies from taking the field, so that not only would no time be lost by using this period to consult the Senate, but it would be in the interests of all concerned to do so.

10. When the Greeks noticed that Flamininus was by no means averse to referring the matter to the Senate, they quickly agreed to his plan. It was decided that Philip should be allowed to send an embassy to Rome, and that the other states should also send envoys to speak before the Senate and put their case against him.

The conference had thus produced a result which Flamininus could approve and which corresponded closely enough to his original forecasts,[1] and so he hastened to put together the fabric of his own plan, taking care to secure his position and allowing no undue advantage to Philip. For although he was granting him a truce of two months, he insisted that the King must complete his mission to the Senate within that period, and must immediately withdraw his garrisons from Phocis and Locris. He acted vigorously on behalf of the allies by impressing on Philip that no hostile act was to be committed against them by the Macedonians during this period. He put these requirements into writing, and then proceeded to act on his own authority in carrying out his policy. In the first place he sent Amynander to Rome; he chose him partly because he was amenable and could easily be persuaded by Flamininus' friends there to follow any course they might propose,[2] and secondly because his royal title would lend some glamour to the occasion and stimulate people's interest in meeting him.[3] Next,

1. This suggests that the proposal to send an embassy could have been devised by Flamininus himself.
2. i.e. whether to press for a settlement or to continue the war.
3. He was the first king to visit Rome.

as his personal representatives he sent Quintus Fabius, who was his wife's nephew, Quintus Fulvius and Appius Claudius Nero. The delegates from Aetolia were Alexander of Isus, Damocritus of Calydon, Dicaearchus of Trichonium, Polemarchus of Arsinoë, Lamius of Ambracia, Nicomachus, an Acarnanian previously exiled from Thyrreum who had settled in Ambracia, and Theodotus of Pherae, an exile from Thessaly living in Stratos. The Achaeans were represented by Xenophon of Aegium, while Attalus sent Alexander and the Athenians Cephisodorus[1] as their respective delegates.

11. When these envoys arrived in Rome the Senate had not yet decided whether it would be necessary to send both the consuls for the year to Gaul or one of them against Philip. However, when Flamininus' friends were assured that both consuls were to remain in Italy because of the threat of an attack by the Celts, all the Greek envoys appeared before the Senate and stated their grievances against Philip in outspoken terms. In general their accusations dealt with the same matters as they had raised with the King at their previous meeting, but the point which they especially emphasized for the benefit of the Senate was that so long as the cities of Chalcis, Corinth and Demetrias remained under Macedonian rule, it was impossible for the Greeks to entertain any thought of liberty. When Philip himself described these places as 'the fetters of Greece', his words, the Greeks insisted, were only too true. The Peloponnesians could not breathe freely while a royal garrison was stationed in Corinth, the Locrians, Boeotians and Phocians could have no confidence while Philip held Chalcis and the rest of Euboea, nor could the Thessalians or the Magnesians ever enjoy liberty with the Macedonians in possession of Demetrias. Philip's offer to evacuate the other places was nothing but a concessionary gesture to extricate himself from his immediate difficulties, and so long as he retained his hold on these strategic points, he could easily reduce the Greeks to subjection on any day he chose. The envoys therefore urged the Senate either to compel Philip to withdraw from these cities, or to stand by the agreement to which they were a party and continue the war against him with all their strength. The fact was that the hardest part of the struggle was already behind

1. The leading Athenian statesman of the period.

them, for the Macedonians had twice been defeated and had expended the greater part of their resources on land.

They wound up their case with an appeal to the Senate not to cheat the Greeks out of their hopes of liberty, nor to deprive themselves of the noblest claim to renown.[1] This, or something very similar, was the gist of the speeches delivered by the Greek envoys. Philip's representatives had prepared a lengthy statement in reply, but they were prevented at the very outset from delivering it; for when the question was put to them as to whether they would withdraw from Corinth, Chalcis and Demetrias they answered that they had no instructions on that subject.

12. When Philip's delegates were cut short in this way, they made no further statement. Thereupon the Senate, as I have mentioned above, proceeded to dispatch both consuls to Gaul and voted to continue the war against Philip. At the same time they placed Flamininus in charge of affairs in Greece. These decisions were quickly reported there, so that the whole business turned out very much as Flamininus had wished. In the event chance had played only a very small part: the outcome was very largely due to his own skill and foresight in handling the problem. If ever a Roman had proved himself to be thoroughly astute it was he, for both in the management of public affairs and in his private concerns[2] he had exercised a degree of judgement and of practical capacity which could not be surpassed, and all this he had achieved as a young man, for he was still under thirty. He was the first Roman who had crossed to Greece in command of an army.

On Treachery

There has been much discussion of the context of this digression in Polybius' narrative, since it is not clearly indicated in any surviving fragment. The most likely theory is that it refers to the action of the Argive leaders, who in 198 B.C. seceded from the Achaean League

1. i.e. as the liberators of Greece.
2. i.e. the plan which lay behind the dispatch of the embassies to Rome.

and admitted Macedonian troops into Argos. They met a swift retribution when Philip handed them over to Nabis, the tyrant of Sparta.

13. I have often found myself marvelling at many of the mistakes which men make in the conduct of their lives, and particularly in the case of traitors. I wish therefore to say a few words on the subject in connection with the times of which I am writing. I am, however, well aware that this is no simple matter to investigate or even to define, since it is far from easy to say what kind of man we can properly regard as a traitor. We cannot, for example, consider as traitors men who of their own free will engage in combined action with certain kings and princes;[1] nor again those who in times of danger cause their country to shift its existing attachments to other friendships or alliances. Far from it, since in practice such men have often proved to be outstanding benefactors of their country. There is no need for me to go back to the distant past for illustrations, since what I have to say can easily be observed in the times of which I am writing. Thus, for example, if Aristaenus had not in good time persuaded the Achaeans to abandon their alliance with Philip and exchange it for one with Rome, it is clear that his whole nation would have been utterly destroyed. As it was, this action not only ensured the safety of each of the members of the League in the immediate crisis, but it was soon recognized that Aristaenus and his policy were responsible beyond all doubt for the growth in the power of the League which followed. The result was that he was in no sense regarded as a traitor, but universally honoured as the benefactor and saviour of his country. The same principle often applies to others who conduct their policy in a similar fashion and shape it according to the circumstances of the hour.

14. From this point of view while Demosthenes, the Athenian statesman, deserves our praise on a great many counts, we must find fault with him on one: I am speaking here of his rash and ill-considered action when he bitterly attacked the most distinguished men in Greece, accusing Corcidas, Hieronymus and Eucampidas in

1. A reference to the Peloponnesians who cooperated with Philip II and whom Demosthenes denounced as traitors.

Arcadia for betraying the Greek cause when they joined Philip, saying the same thing of Neon and Thrasylochus, the sons of Philiadas, in Messene, of Myrtis, Teledamus and Mnaseas in Argos, of Daochus and Cineas in Thessaly, of Theogeiton and Timolaus in Boeotia and of various other public figures whom he named city by city. Yet all these men had good and explicit reasons to uphold the interests of their states in this way, and especially the inhabitants of Arcadia and Messene. It was these peoples who by their action in encouraging Philip to invade the Peloponnese and break the power of the Lacedaemonians enabled all its inhabitants to breathe freely once again and to harbour the idea of liberty; they undoubtedly increased the power of their own states by winning back the territories and the cities which the Lacedaemonians in their own period of prosperity had annexed from the Messenians, Megalopolitans, Tegeans and Argives.

In return for this it was not their business to make war against Philip and the Macedonians, but to do everything in their power to promote his honour and prestige. If, in taking such a course they had consented to have their towns garrisoned by Philip, or abolished their own constitutions or deprived their fellow-citizens of freedom of action or of speech for the sake of private gain or to win power for themselves, then indeed they would have deserved to be branded as traitors. But if, while continuing to uphold the rights of their individual states, they merely differed in their judgement of the situation because they believed that the interests of Athens did not coincide with their own, then Demosthenes had no right, in my opinion, to call them traitors. Thus in so far as in all his calculations Demosthenes considered only the interests of his own state, assumed that the whole of Greece should have its eyes fixed on Athens, and branded people who did not do this as traitors, he seems to me to have been badly mistaken and to have strayed a long way from the truth. What actually happened to Greece proves that it was not Demosthenes who showed genuine foresight,[1] but rather Eucampidas, Hieronymus, Cercidas and the sons of Philiadas. Indeed all that the Athenians' opposition to Philip brought them was the crowning disaster of their defeat at the battle

1. Polybius is here exercising the privilege of hindsight and judging Demosthenes' policy by the criterion of success rather than of principle.

of Chaeronea. And if it had not been for Philip's generosity and concern for his own reputation, they would have suffered far worse misfortunes; all this was the consequence of Demosthenes' policy. By contrast the states of Arcadia and Messene at once made themselves secure and won a respite from the attacks of the Lacedaemonians, not to mention many private benefits for their citizens, and these advantages were the work of the men whose names I have mentioned above.

15. Hence it is difficult to define those upon whom we can properly lay the name of traitor. Perhaps the situation which comes nearest to it is one in which men at a time of public danger, for reasons either of personal safety or profit, or because of their differences with the opposing party put their city into the hands of the enemy, or who by admitting a garrison or calling in foreign assistance to further their personal aims and policies bring their countries under the domination of a foreign power. All those who commit actions of this kind may fairly be regarded as traitors. And yet, as everybody agrees, the treachery practised by such men has never brought them any real profit or advantage – in fact precisely the opposite – so much so that we ask ourselves with amazement what their original motives can have been, or what calculations can possibly have impelled them to rush into such a fatal situation. For no one has ever yet betrayed a city or an army or a fortress without being found out: if this did not happen at the moment of the action, still in the course of time the whole business has been brought to light. None of these agents, once detected, has ever led a happy life thereafter, but in most cases they meet an appropriate punishment at the hands of the very people whose favour they have tried so hard to win. For generals and rulers often employ traitors to further their interests, but as soon as they have no more use for them it is precisely as traitors, as Demosthenes has remarked, that they treat them. They conclude quite naturally that a man who has betrayed his country and his former friends to the enemy can never prove loyal nor keep faith with them. And even if these men do not suffer punishment at the hands of their masters, it is not easy for them to escape the vengeance of those they have betrayed. Or if they ever contrive to slip out of the clutches of both parties, their evil reputation among

other men still pursues them for the rest of their lives. It creates many terrors for them, both real and imaginary, by day and by night, it helps and encourages all those who harbour designs against them, prevents them even when they are asleep from forgetting their crimes,[1] and makes them dream of every kind of plot and disaster, since they are constantly reminded of their alienation from the rest of mankind, and of the universal hatred which they inspire. And yet, although all these facts are undeniable, it has never, with very rare exceptions, proved impossible to find a traitor whenever one was needed. All this might lead us to conclude that man, who is reputed to be the most cunning of animals, may with good reason be considered the most foolish. For the other animals, which are the slaves of their bodily needs, only suffer misfortune through being led astray by these, while man, though he has reason to guide him, goes astray as much from want of thought as from physical appetite. I have now said enough on this subject.

On the Phalanx

28. In my sixth book I mentioned that when a suitable occasion arose I would attempt a comparison between Roman and Macedonian military equipment and tactical formations, showing how they differ from one another for better or worse. Now that we have seen the two systems opposed to one another in the field, I shall try to fulfil my promise. In the past the Macedonian formation was proved by operational experience to be superior to the others which were in use in Asia and Greece, while the Roman system overcame those employed in Africa and among all the peoples of Western Europe. In our own times we have seen both the two formations and the soldiers of the two nations matched against one another, not just once but on many occasions. It should prove a useful exercise, and one well worth the trouble, to study the differences between them, and to discover the reason why on the battlefield the Romans have always proved the victors and carried off the

1. Compare Shakespeare's *Richard III*, I, iv – Clarence's dream.

prize. If we examine the matter in this way we shall not, like the ignorant majority of mankind, speak merely in terms of chance, and congratulate the victors without giving the reasons, but shall be able to pay them the praise and admiration they deserve because we have come to understand the causes of their success.

There is no need for me to enlarge upon the battles which the Romans fought and lost against Hannibal, for the defeats they suffered had nothing to do with weapons or formations, but were brought about by Hannibal's cleverness and military genius. This point I made sufficiently clear in my descriptions of the battles in question, and there are two pieces of evidence which support my conclusion. The first is the manner in which the war ended, for as soon as a general of ability comparable to Hannibal's appeared on the Roman side it was only a short while before victory was theirs. The second is provided by Hannibal himself, who as soon as he had won his first battle discarded the equipment with which he had started out, armed his troops with Roman weapons, and continued to use these till the end of the war. As for King Pyrrhus of Epirus, he employed not only Italian weapons but also Italian troops and alternated maniples and units of the phalanx in drawing up his battle order against the Romans. But even with the help of these methods he did not succeed in winning a victory, and the outcome of all his battles was somewhat indecisive.[1]

It was necessary for me to deal with these points before beginning my comparison, so that nothing may go unnoticed which could contradict my statements. I shall now proceed to the comparison itself.

29. There are a number of factors which make it easy to understand that so long as the phalanx retains its characteristic form and strength nothing can withstand its charge or resist it face to face. When the phalanx is closed up for action, each man with his arms occupies a space of three feet.[2] The pike he carries was earlier

---

1. This verdict is less than fair to Pyrrhus, who scored victories over the Romans at Heracleia (280) and Ausculum (279), though he certainly suffered heavy losses.

2. This formation assumes a space of three feet not only laterally, i.e. from right shoulder to right shoulder, but from front to rear, i.e. three feet from chest to chest.

designed to be twenty-four feet long, but as adapted to current practice was shortened to twenty-one, and from this we must subtract the space between the bearer's hands and the rear portion of the pike which keeps it balanced and couched. This amounts to six feet in all, from which it is clear that the pike will project fifteen feet in front of the body of each hoplite when he advances against the enemy grasping it with both hands. This also means that while the pikes of the men in the second, third, and fourth ranks naturally extend further than those of the fifth rank, yet even the latter will still project three feet in front of the men in the first rank. I am assuming of course that the phalanx keeps its characteristic order, and is closed up both from the rear and on the flanks, as Homer describes it in these verses:[1]

Shield was pressed close against shield, each man standing shoulder to shoulder;
Over their glittering helmets the horse-hair plumes touched as they nodded,
So tightly packed were the ranks . . .

At any rate if my description is true and exact, it follows that each man in the front rank will have the points of five pikes extending in front of him, each point being three feet ahead of the one behind.

30. From these facts we can easily picture the nature and the tremendous power of a charge by the whole phalanx, when it advances sixteen deep with levelled pikes. Of these sixteen ranks those who are stationed further back than the fifth cannot use their pikes to take an active part in the battle. They therefore do not level them man against man, but hold them with the points tilted upwards over the shoulders of the men in front. In this way they give protection to the whole phalanx from above, for the pikes are massed so closely that they can keep off any missiles which might clear the heads of the front ranks and strike those immediately behind them. Once the charge is launched, these rear ranks by the sheer pressure of their bodily weight greatly increase its momentum and make it impossible for the foremost ranks to face about.

1. *Iliad*, XIII, 131–3. The phalanx was of course unknown to Homer and these lines make no reference to it.

I have described both in general terms and in detail the composition of the phalanx. I must now for purposes of comparison explain the special features of Roman equipment and tactical formation, and the differences which distinguish the two. With the Romans each soldier in full armour also occupies a space three feet wide. However, according to the Roman methods of fighting each man makes his movements individually: not only does he defend his body with his long shield, constantly moving it to meet a threatened blow, but he uses his sword both for cutting and for thrusting. Obviously these tactics require a more open order and an interval between the men, and in practice each soldier needs to be at least three feet from those in the same rank and from those in front of and behind him if he is to perform his function efficiently. The result of these dispositions is that each Roman soldier has to face two men in the front rank of the phalanx, and so has to encounter and fight against ten spear points. It is impossible for one man to cut through all of these once the battle lines are engaged, nor is it easy to force the points away; moreover, in the Roman formation the rear ranks do not support the front, either in forcing the spears away or in the use of their swords. It is easy to understand then, as I mentioned at the beginning, how nothing can withstand the frontal assault of the phalanx so long as it retains its characteristic formation and strength.

31. What then is the factor which enables the Romans to win the battle and causes those who use the phalanx to fail? The answer is that in war the times and places for action are unlimited, whereas the phalanx requires one time and one type of ground only in order to produce its peculiar effect. Now if the enemy were compelled to position themselves according to the times and places demanded by the phalanx whenever an important battle was imminent, no doubt those who employ the phalanx would always carry off the victory for the reasons I have given above. But if it is quite possible, even easy, to evade its irresistible charge, how can the phalanx any longer be considered formidable? Again, it is generally admitted that its use requires flat and level ground which is unencumbered by any obstacles such as ditches, gullies, depressions, ridges and watercourses, all of which are sufficient to hinder and dislocate such a formation. There is general agreement that it is almost impossible,

or at any rate exceedingly rare, to find a stretch of country of say two or three miles or more which contains no obstacles of this kind. But even assuming that such an arena could be found, if the enemy refuses to come down into it, but prefers to traverse the country sacking the towns and devastating the territories of our allies, what purpose can the phalanx serve? If it remains on the ground which suits it best, not only is it unable to assist its allies, but it cannot even ensure its own safety, for the transport of its supplies will easily be stopped by the enemy when they have undisputed command of the open country. On the other hand, if it leaves the terrain which favours it and attempts an action elsewhere, it will easily be defeated. Or again, supposing that the enemy does decide to descend into the plain and fight there, but, instead of committing his entire force to the battle when the phalanx has its one opportunity to charge, keeps even a small part of it in reserve at the moment when the main action takes place, it is easy to forecast what will happen from the tactics which the Romans are now putting into practice.

32. The outcome indeed does not need to be demonstrated by argument: we need only refer to accomplished facts. The Romans do not attempt to make their line numerically equal to the enemy's, nor do they expose the whole strength of the legions to a frontal attack by the phalanx. Instead they keep part of the forces in reserve while the rest engage the enemy. Later in the battle, whether the phalanx in its charge drives back the troops opposed to it or is driven back by them, in either event it loses its own peculiar formation. For either in pursuing a retreating enemy or falling back before an oncoming one, the phalanx leaves behind the other units of its own army; at this point the enemy's reserves can occupy the space the phalanx has vacated, and are no longer obliged to attack from the front, but can fall upon it from flank and rear. When it is thus easy to deny the phalanx the opportunities it needs and to minimize the advantages it enjoys, and also impossible to prevent the enemy from acting against it, does it not follow that the difference between these two systems is enormous?

Besides this, those who rely on the phalanx are obliged to march across and encamp on ground of every description; they must occupy favourable positions in advance, besiege others and be besieged themselves and deal with unexpected appearances of the enemy. All these eventualities are part and parcel of war, and may have an important or a decisive effect on the final victory. In all these situations the Macedonian formation is sometimes of little use, and sometimes of none at all, because the phalanx soldier cannot operate either in smaller units or singly, whereas the Roman formation is highly flexible. Every Roman soldier, once he is armed and goes into action, can adapt himself equally well to any place or time and meet an attack from any quarter. He is likewise equally well-prepared and needs to make no change whether he has to fight with the main body or with a detachment, in maniples or singly. Accordingly, since the effective use of the parts of the Roman army is so much superior, their plans are much more likely to achieve success than those of others. I have felt obliged to deal with this subject at some length, because so many Greeks on those occasions when the Macedonians suffered defeat regarded such an event as almost incredible, and many will still be at a loss to understand why and how the phalanx proves inferior by comparison with the Roman method of arming their troops.

Affairs in Greece

FLAMININUS AND THE PEACE SETTLEMENT

This passage describes the peace settlement that was drawn up after the Romans' decisive victory over Philip at Cynoscephalae in 197 B.C.

44. At this time the ten commissioners who had been appointed to handle the affairs of Greece arrived from Rome bringing the decree of the Senate concerning the peace settlement with Philip. Its principal features were the following. All the rest of the Greeks both in Asia and in Europe were to be free and to enjoy their own laws. Philip was to hand over to the Romans before the beginning of the Isthmian Games [1] those Greeks who were subject to his rule,

1. The Isthmian Games stood third in the order of the great Pan–Hellenic festivals (after the Olympian and the Pythian), and were held in June–July of each alternate year – in June 196 in this case.

and also the towns which he had occupied with garrisons. From the towns of Euromus, Pedasa, Bargylia, and Iasus, as well as Abydos, Thasos, Myrina and Perinthus he was to withdraw his garrisons and leave the inhabitants free. Flamininus was to write to Prusias of Bithynia in accordance with the decree of the Senate concerning the liberation of the city of Cius. Within the same time limit Philip was to restore to the Romans all prisoners of war and deserters and to surrender all his warships, with the exception of five light vessels and his huge flagship, in which the men rowed eight to an oar. He was to pay the sum of 1,000 talents, half of it at once and the other half in instalments spread over ten years.

45. When the contents of this decree became known in Greece all the city states and peoples took heart and were overjoyed, with the solitary exception of the Aetolians. They were disappointed at not having obtained what they expected, and complained bitterly of the decree, which they said was nothing but a verbal arrangement and ignored practical problems. From the actual terms of the decree they put about interpretations of the probable consequences which were calculated to confuse the minds of those who listened to such forecasts. They maintained that there were two distinct pronouncements in the decree which applied to the various cities garrisoned by Philip: one of these ordered him to withdraw his garrisons and hand over the cities to the Romans, and the other to withdraw his garrisons and set the cities free. The cities to be set free were specifically named and were all of them situated in Asia; it was obvious therefore that those to be handed over to the Romans were all in Europe, that is to say Oreum, Eretria, Chalcis, Demetrias and Corinth.[1] This was surely a clear indication that the Romans were taking over from Philip the so-called 'fetters of Greece', and that the Greeks were not being given their freedom, but merely a change of masters.

These arguments of the Aetolians were repeated *ad nauseam*. But in the meanwhile Flamininus left Elateia in Phocis with the ten commissioners, travelled south to Anticyra, and at once sailed across the gulf to Corinth, where he proceeded to confer with the commissioners and consider the settlement of Greece as a whole.

1. For the significance of the last three of these see p. 503.

All this while the slanderous comments of the Aetolians were gaining circulation and were beginning to carry some conviction, so that Flamininus felt obliged to address his colleagues and discuss the terms of the settlement in great detail. The gist of his argument was that if they wished to gain universal renown among the Greeks, and to convince the country as a whole that the Romans had originally crossed the Adriatic not to advance their own interests but to secure the liberties of the Greeks, they must withdraw from every place and set free all the cities which were now garrisoned by Philip. As it happened this was the one subject on which there was room for some uncertainty among the commissioners. Decisions had already been reached in Rome on all other issues and the commissioners had instructions on these from the Senate, but because of misgivings about the intentions of Antiochus, the question of the status of Chalcis, Corinth and Demetrias had been left to their discretion to be decided in the light of the situation on the spot; for it was well-known that for some time past Antiochus had been watching for an opportunity to intervene in the affairs of Greece. In spite of this Flamininus succeeded in persuading his colleagues to set Corinth free immediately and hand it over to the Achaeans, while he continued to occupy the Acrocorinth and the cities of Chalcis and Demetrias.

46. By the time that these decisions had been taken the moment for the celebration of the Isthmian Games had arrived. The expectation of what would happen there had attracted men of the highest rank from almost every quarter of the civilized world, and all kinds of reports and speculations concerning the outcome circulated throughout the festival. Some argued that it was impossible for the Romans to withdraw from certain places and cities, and others that they would give up such places as were considered famous, but keep those which were just as serviceable but happened not to possess the same glamour. Indeed these people went so far as to name the places in question out of their own heads, and vied with one another in the ingenuity of their guesswork. In the midst of this atmosphere of uncertainty, and at the moment when the crowd had assembled in the stadium to watch the games and the trumpeter had called for silence, the herald came forward and delivered the following proclamation:

'The Senate of Rome and Titus Quinctius Flamininus the proconsul, having defeated King Philip and the Macedonians in battle,
leave the following states and cities free, without garrisons, subject
to no tribute and in full enjoyment of their ancestral laws: the
peoples of Corinth, Phocis, Locri, Euboea, Phthiotic Achaea,
Magnesia, Thessaly and Perrhaebia.'

At the very beginning of this announcement a deafening shout
arose, so that some people never heard the proclamation at all,
while others were anxious to hear it again. The greater part of the
crowd could not believe their ears, for what had happened was so
unexpected that it was as if they were listening to the words in a
kind of dream. They clamoured and shouted, each of them moved
perhaps by a different impulse, for the herald and the trumpeter
to come forward into the middle of the stadium and repeat the
proclamation; they wished, no doubt, not only to hear the speaker
but to see him, so difficult did it seem to believe what he was saying.
But when the herald came forward into the centre of the arena,
once more silenced the clamour with the help of his trumpeter, and
read out exactly the same text, such a tremendous outburst of
cheering arose that it is difficult for those who can only read of the
event today to imagine how it sounded. When at last the shouting
died away nobody paid the least attention to the athletic contests;
the cheers of the crowd were replaced by a hubbub of chatter,
people discussing the news with their neighbours or soliloquizing
aloud, all talking like men beside themselves. Indeed, when the
games were over they almost killed Flamininus with the un-
restrained vehemence of their joy and gratitude. Some of them
yearned to look him in the face and hail him as their saviour, others
pressed forward to touch his hand, and the majority threw garlands
and fillets upon him, so that between them they almost tore him to
pieces. But however extravagant their gratitude may appear to
have been, one could say with confidence that it fell far short of the
importance of the event itself. For it was a wholly admirable action
in the first place that the Roman people and their general should
have made the choice to incur unlimited danger and expense to
ensure the freedom of Greece, more remarkable still that they
devoted to this ideal the force sufficient to bring it about, and most
remarkable of all that no mischance intervened to frustrate their

intention. Instead, every factor combined to produce this crowning moment, when by a single proclamation all the Greeks inhabiting both Asia and Europe became free, with neither garrison nor tribute to burden them, but enjoying their own laws.

BOOK XXIV

Affairs in Greece

PHILOPOEMEN AND ARISTAENUS

11. Philopoemen and Aristaenus had little in common either in character or in political outlook. Philopoemen was naturally endowed both mentally and physically for the life of action and of war, Aristaenus for that of politics and debate. In their choice of policy the difference between them may be summed up as follows. During the period of the wars between Philip and Antiochus the supremacy of Rome had become a factor which was inextricably involved in Greek affairs. Accordingly, Aristaenus in his political transactions was always ready to do whatever was required by the Romans, sometimes even to the point of anticipating their demands. At the same time he took pains to keep up the appearance of abiding by the laws, and indeed made a parade of doing so, yet whenever any Greek ordinance was manifestly in conflict with Roman instructions, he gave way at the expense of the law. Philopoemen, on the other hand, readily accepted and unhesitatingly fulfilled all requirements which were in harmony with his country's laws and with the terms of the alliance; however, if a request went beyond these limits, he could never bring himself to comply with it willingly. In the first place, he said, they should argue the point of legality, and after that go on to put their case as a request. Finally, if even this approach failed to persuade the Romans, they should give way under protest, and only then carry out the order.

12. Aristaenus used to justify his policy to the Achaeans by some such argument as this. 'It is impossible,' he said, 'to maintain the friendship with Rome by holding out both the sword and the olive branch [1] at once. If we are resolved to face the Romans and are strong enough to do so, well and good. But if even Philopoemen does not venture to assert this, why should we sacrifice

1. Literally 'the spear and the herald's staff'.

what is possible in striving for the impossible? Every policy embraces two aims, honour and interest. In a situation where honour is within reach the right policy is to aim at this; those who do not possess the necessary strength, however, must take refuge in securing their interest. But to fail in both aims is the supreme proof of mismanagement and this is what is achieved by those who do not explicitly disagree with all that is demanded of them, but comply unwillingly and with reluctance. It follows then that we must either show that we are strong enough to refuse, or if nobody dares to say this, we must do everything we are told with a good grace.'

13. Philopoemen's reply was that people must not imagine he was so ill-informed that he could not appreciate the difference between the Roman and the Achaean state or the superiority of Roman power. 'But it is natural for those who have the upper hand,' he said, 'to press ever harder upon the weaker party; however, this being so, is it really in our interests to fall in at every point with the whims of our masters? And if we put no obstacles whatever in their way, shall we not find the harshest commands being laid upon us in the shortest possible time? Would it not be better to struggle with them to the limits of our power and hold out until we are exhausted? Then, supposing they issue orders which are illegal, if we remind them of this and do something to check their autocratic behaviour, we shall at least soften the harshness of their rule to a certain extent, especially since, as you yourself admit, Aristaenus, the Romans attach great importance to the keeping of oaths, treaties and pledges to their allies. But if we ourselves ignore our rights, and immediately submit ourselves unquestioningly, like prisoners of war, to any order we are given, what difference will there be between the Achaean League and the peoples of Sicily and of Capua? As everyone knows, they have been the virtual slaves of the Romans for years. So either let us admit that the justice of a cause counts for nothing with the Romans, or if we do not go as far as this, we must insist on our rights and not abandon our cause, especially as in the eyes of the Romans we have great and honourable claims upon them. I know very well,' he went on, 'that the time will come when the Greeks will be obliged to give complete obedience to Rome. But do we wish this

to happen as soon or as late as possible? Surely the latter. It is in this sense, then, that my policy differs from Aristaenus'. He is anxious to see the inevitable arrive as soon as possible, while I am striving to the utmost of my power to ward it off.'

From these speeches it becomes clear, I think, that while Philopoemen's policy was honourable and Aristaenus' persuasive, both were founded upon safety. The result was that although great dangers threatened both the Romans and the Greeks in the wars of that time against Philip and Antiochus, yet each of these men protected the rights of the Achaeans vis-à-vis the Romans and kept them unimpaired. All the same, the impression prevailed that Aristaenus was better-disposed towards the Romans than Philopoemen.

BOOK XXXI

Affairs in Rome and Syria

THE ESCAPE OF DEMETRIUS

When Antiochus ·Epiphanes, the ruler of Syria, died in 164 B.C. he left a young son and a daughter. The son, known as Antiochus Eupator, succeeded to the throne under the guardianship of Lysias. His cousin Demetrius, a grandson of Antiochus the Great, had been handed over by his father,·Seleucus IV, Antiochus' successor, to the Romans in 175, when Demetrius was ten, as a pledge of good faith. Thirteen years later the young man could see no good reason why he should continue to be detained as a hostage for the good behaviour of Antiochus' successor, and tried to persuade the Senate to make him the ruler of Syria instead of the boy-king. The Senate, however, preferred to support a puppet rather than an active ruler, and sent out a commission headed by Gnaeus Octavius with instructions to weaken the military forces of Syria. These measures provoked violent resentment and resulted in the murder of Octavius.

11. At this time[1] the report reached Rome of the outrage committed against Gnaeus Octavius and how he had been assassinated, and a delegation sent by Lysias the regent on behalf of Antiochus arrived to give the most solemn assurances that the friends of the young king had been in no way implicated in the deed. The Senate, however, paid little attention to the envoys and had no wish to announce any decision on these matters, or even to make its opinion public.

Demetrius, on the other hand, was greatly excited by the news and immediately sent for Polybius and confided to him his doubts as to whether he should once more raise with the Senate the question of his detention. Polybius advised him 'not to stumble twice on the same stone', but to rely on his own efforts and try his fortune

1. In 162 B.C.

521

in some bold undertaking which might win him a crown, for in the present situation, he hinted, there were plenty of opportunities for action. Demetrius grasped the drift of these remarks and said nothing more at that moment, but soon afterwards he consulted one of his closest friends, Apollonius, on the same subject. This man, who was not only young in years but rather guileless by nature, advised Demetrius to make another appeal to the Senate; he felt confident that since they had unjustly deprived him of his kingdom, they would at least release him from his present detention, for it was absurd that once the young Antiochus had succeeded to the throne of Syria Demetrius should continue to be held as a hostage for him. Demetrius was impressed by these arguments, and so he again appeared before the Senate and appealed to them at least to release him from his obligations as a hostage, since they had decided to guarantee the throne to the young Antiochus. But although he pleaded his cause at length, the Senate decided to uphold its original verdict. And indeed this was only to be expected, since on the previous occasion they had decided to keep the young King on his throne, not because Demetrius had failed to make out a good case, but simply because it suited their interests. And so as the circumstances which had originally influenced their judgement remained the same, it was to be expected that the Senate's decision should be based on the same policy.

12. Thus Demetrius had sung his swan-song (in other words had made his last appeal to the Senate) in vain, and he recognized that Polybius had given him good advice when he warned him not to stumble twice on the same stone. Since he was high-spirited by nature, he regretted what he had done, and as he possessed the natural courage to put his plans into action, he sent for a certain Diodorus who had recently arrived from Syria and took him into his confidence. Diodorus had been Demetrius' foster-father, and was a clever man who had taken great pains to study the course of events in Syria. He pointed out to Demetrius that what with the disturbances created by the murder of Octavius, the mutual distrust which prevailed between the regent Lysias and the people, and the firm belief of the Senate that the responsibility for the outrages against their envoys lay with the King's friends – this com-

bination of events would be most favourable to him if he now appeared upon the scene. The chances were that the Syrians would promptly transfer the crown to him even if he arrived accompanied only by a single slave, while the Senate would not venture to give Lysias any further help or support in view of his recent conduct. The remaining problem, then, was to escape from Rome with such secrecy that nobody would discover his intention. When he had reached this conclusion Demetrius sent for Polybius and confided the plan to him, begging him to lend his help and join him in planning the best way to make his escape.

At that time there happened to be in Rome a man named Menyllus of Alabanda; he had been sent there on a mission from the elder Ptolemy to confront the younger Ptolemy and answer him before the Senate. Polybius had for some time been on friendly terms with Menyllus and had great confidence in him. He thought him exactly the right man for the business in hand, and so introduced him to Demetrius, expressing his regard for him and recommending him warmly. Menyllus agreed to take part in the scheme, and undertook to get a ship ready and provide it with everything required for the voyage. He then found a Carthaginian vessel anchored at the mouth of the Tiber, which had been used to carry sacred offerings, and engaged it. These ships are specially selected at Carthage to carry the traditional offerings of first-fruits which the Carthaginians send to their ancestral gods at Tyre. Menyllus chartered her quite openly for his own voyage home; in this way he could have a month's stock of provisions sent aboard without attracting any suspicion, and could speak freely with the sailors and make his own arrangements with them.

13. When the captain had everything ready and it only remained for Demetrius to complete his own preparations, he first of all sent his foster-father Diodorus to Syria to observe the situation, listen to what people were saying, and so gauge the state of popular feeling. His foster-brother Apollonius had been a partner in the scheme from the beginning, and he also took Apollonius' two brothers, Meleager and Menestheus, into his confidence, but he did not involve any of the other members of his suite, although there were many of them. These three brothers were the sons of

that Apollonius who had held a high position at the court of Seleucus, but had moved to Miletus when Antiochus Epiphanes succeeded to the throne.[1]

The day agreed upon with the sailors was now drawing near, and it became necessary to arrange for one of Demetrius' friends to give a party to serve as an excuse for his going out. It was impossible for him to dine at home, for he had been punctilious in keeping up the habit of sharing his meals with the other members of his suite. Accordingly all those who had been admitted to the plot were to dine at home and then come aboard. Each was to be attended by one slave only; the rest had been sent on to Anagneia and told that their masters would join them there on the next day. Polybius happened at this moment to be ill and confined to bed, but he knew of everything that was in train, as Menyllus was constantly in touch with him. Polybius was worried that if the banquet lasted too long Demetrius might have drunk so much that he would find it difficult to get away, for he was not only young but also by nature fond of his cups. Polybius therefore wrote and sealed a short note and, just as it was growing dark, sent it by one of his servants. This man was told to call out Demetrius' cup-bearer and deliver the note to him; he was not to say who he was, nor where the note had come from, but must tell him to give it to Demetrius at once. This was immediately done and Demetrius received the note and read it. It contained the following maxims:

> The early bird catches the worm[2]
> Night favours all alike, but most the brave[3]
> Be bold, meet danger, act now: lose or win;
> Do anything rather than give yourself away.[4]
> Keep a cool head-piece, and take leave to doubt;
> These are the sinews of the mind . . .[5]

14. When Demetrius read the note he immediately recognized what these quotations referred to and who had sent them; he then

1. In 175 B.C.
2. Literally 'He who *does* gets away with what belongs to him who *intends*' – an anonymous proverb.
3. Euripides, *Phoenissae*, 726.
4. Anonymous.
5. Lines by Epicharmus.

gave it out that he felt unwell, and immediately took his leave escorted by his friends. He then made his way to his lodging and arranged to send to Anagneia all the slaves whom he did not wish to keep with him. He ordered them to bring nets and hunting-hounds and meet him at Cerceii, where he had often been in the habit of going to hunt the wild boar; indeed, it was in this way that his friendship with Polybius had begun. Then he revealed the details of his plan to Nicanor and the rest of his friends, and appealed to them to share his fortunes. They all agreed enthusiastically, whereupon he asked them to return at once to their homes and tell their slaves to travel in the early morning to Anagneia and later to join the huntsmen and the rest of the party at Cerceii. They themselves were to put on travelling clothes and return to him: meanwhile they should give out to their slaves that they were going to fetch Demetrius and would join them the following day at Cerceii.

All these arrangements were duly carried out, after which they went down by night to Ostia at the mouth of the Tiber. Menyllus was already there and had spoken to the sailors. He told them that he had received a message from King Ptolemy; this contained instructions that he himself should remain for the present in Rome, but should send to the King some of the most trustworthy of his young soldiers who would report all the news about his brother. Menyllus told them that he himself would not go aboard, but that the young men who were to sail would arrive about midnight. The ship's officers made no difficulties about this since the charter money had already been paid, and they had completed all their preparations for sailing well before Demetrius and his party arrived at the end of the third watch. There were eight of them in all, besides five adult slaves and three boys. Menyllus greeted them, showed them the provisions in store for the voyage and commended them warmly to the captain and crew. After this they went aboard, and the pilot weighed anchor and set sail just as dawn was breaking. He had no idea of who his passengers really were, but imagined that he was merely giving passage to some soldiers on their way from Menyllus to King Ptolemy.

15. In the meanwhile there was no likelihood that anyone in Rome would be looking the next day for Demetrius or his travelling companions. Those of his household who had been left behind

supposed that he had left for Cerceii, and those in Anagneia who were due to meet him imagined that they would see him there. The result was that his escape went completely unnoticed until one of the slaves who happened to have been beaten at Anagneia ran off to Cerceii. He also supposed that he would find Demetrius there, and when he failed to do so he ran on towards Rome, expecting to meet him on the road. Then, as he could discover no trace of him anywhere, he informed Demetrius' friends in Rome and those members of his household who had been left behind. Four days after his departure people started to look for Demetrius, and it was only then that suspicion dawned on them. Finally on the fifth day, by which time he had already passed the Straits of Messana, a meeting of the Senate was hastily summoned to consider the matter. The Senate gave up all idea of pursuit. In the first place they assumed that Demetrius had by then got a long start on his voyage since the wind was favourable, and secondly they recognized that they would be unable to stop him even if they wished to. A few days later they appointed three commissioners, Tiberius Gracchus, Lucius Lentulus and Servilius Glaucia, to investigate the state of Greece, and next to cross to Asia and observe the results of Demetrius' attempt. They were also to look into the attitude adopted by the other Kings, and act as mediators in the dispute between these rulers and the Galatians. Tiberius Gracchus was appointed because he had special knowledge of these questions. Such was the state of affairs in Italy.[1]

Affairs in Italy

AEMILIUS PAULLUS, SCIPIO AND POLYBIUS

22. The most convincing and the most honourable testimony to the integrity of Lucius Aemilius Paullus was revealed after his death, for the same high reputation which he had enjoyed through-

1. Demetrius' gamble succeeded. He was received with enthusiasm in Syria, seized power, put the young Antiochus to death together with Lysias the regent, and ruled from 162 to 150. He was then in his turn defeated and killed by the usurper, Alexander Balas.

out his life continued unchanged after he had taken leave of it, and this is surely the strongest proof of virtue that can be found. Paullus had brought more gold to Rome from Spain than any of his contemporaries, the whole of the immense treasure of Macedonia had fallen into his hands, and he had wielded complete authority to use this money as he chose. Yet in spite of this he died so poor that his sons could not pay his widow the whole of the estate he had settled on her out of the personalty he had left, and were obliged to sell a part of his real estate. The details of this matter I have dealt with elsewhere.[1] But here we must acknowledge that in the matter of integrity Paullus' example overshadows the reputation even of those whom the Greeks most admired for this quality. For while it is an admirable thing to refuse money which is offered in the interest of the giver, as Aristides of Athens and Epaminondas of Thebes are said to have done, it is far more admirable for a man to have been the master of a whole kingdom and exercised the authority to dispose of it as he chose, and still to have coveted nothing in it.

If this appears incredible to any of my readers, let him remember that the present writer is especially mindful of the fact that it is the Romans above all who are likely to read this book, since the greatest number and the most brilliant of the achievements which it describes belong to them, and that it is impossible that they should either be ignorant of the facts or prepared to pardon an author who utters false statements. It is obvious then that nobody would willingly expose himself to their inevitable disbelief or contempt. This fact should be borne in mind throughout the whole of my history, whenever I may appear to make any surprising statement about the Romans.

23. Now that the progress of my narrative and the period of which I am writing have brought this family of the Aemilii to our notice, I propose for the sake of students of history to carry out a promise which I made in the previous book. I then said that I would tell the story of how Scipio gained such a brilliant reputation at such an unusually early age, and how his friendship and intimacy with the present author became so close that its fame was not confined to Italy and Greece, but their mutual regard and companion-

1. In Book XVIII. 35.

ship became known even in countries beyond. I have already mentioned that their association first began with the loan of some books and the conversations that followed. But as their acquaintanceship became closer, and when the Achaeans who had been summoned to Italy were sent to various provincial cities, then Fabius and Scipio,[1] the sons of Lucius Aemilius Paullus,[2] petitioned the praetor to allow Polybius to remain in Rome. One day when they were all three coming out of Fabius' house, it so happened that Fabius turned off to go to the Forum, while Polybius walked on in another direction with Scipio. As they were strolling along, Scipio asked Polybius in a quiet and gentle tone and blushing slightly, 'Why is it, Polybius, that although my brother and I eat at the same table, you always speak to him, address all your questions and remarks in his direction and leave me out of them? It looks as though you have the same opinion of me that I know the rest of the city has. Everybody thinks that I am a quiet and rather lazy man, and that I have none of the typical Roman urge to action because I do not choose to speak in the law-courts. And they say that the family I belong to has no need of a representative of my sort, but something quite the opposite, and this is what annoys me most of all.'

24. Polybius was somewhat taken aback by the way in which the young man opened the conversation, for he was then only just eighteen years old. 'In heaven's name, Scipio,' he replied, 'you must not talk like that, or get any such idea into your head. I do not speak in this way because I have a poor opinion of you or ignore you – far from it. It is simply that your brother is older than you and so I begin and end my conversations with him, and if I address my remarks or advice to him, it is because I imagine that you share the same ideas. But I am delighted to hear from you that you are vexed at its being thought that your character is milder or softer than is proper for a member of a family such as yours, because this surely proves that you possess a noble spirit. I should be very happy to devote myself to helping you to speak and act in a way that is worthy of your ancestors. Now in the case

1. Of these two sons of Paullus, the elder was adopted by Quintus Fabius Maximus, and the younger was adopted by Publius Cornelius Scipio, the son of the victor of Zama.

2. This was Lucius Aemilius Paullus 'Macedonicus', mentioned on p. 527.

of these studies which it seems to me are beginning to arouse ambition as well as enthusiasm in your brother and yourself, you will find plenty of people to help you both, for there is a whole crowd of learned men whom I can see flooding into Italy from Greece at the present time. But as for the matter which you have just said vexes you so much, I do not think you could find anybody more suitable than myself to help you and encourage your efforts.'

Even before Polybius had finished speaking, Scipio seized his right hand in both of his own, and pressing it affectionately he said: 'I only wish I may see the day when you will give me the first claim on your attention and join your life to mine, for then I shall immediately feel that I am worthy of my family and my ancestors.' Polybius was at once overjoyed at this demonstration of the young man's affection, but also embarrassed when he remembered the exalted position of Scipio's family and the wealth of its members. At any rate from the moment of that conversation, the young man became inseparable from Polybius and preferred his company to any other.

25. From that time onwards they constantly gave one another practical proofs of their attachment, and came to feel a mutual affection which could truly be compared to that of father and son, or of kinsmen of the same blood.

Now the first manifestation of Scipio's desire to lead a noble life was to gain a reputation for self-discipline, and in this respect to rise above the standards observed by his contemporaries. This is a high and normally a difficult aspiration, but at that time it was easy enough because of the deterioration of morals among the great majority. Some young men squandered their energies on love affairs with boys, others with courtesans, and others again upon musical entertainments and banquets and the extravagant expenses that go with them, for in the course of the war against Perseus and the Macedonians they had quickly acquired the luxurious habits of the Greeks in this direction. So far had the taste for dissipation and debauchery spread among young men that many of them were ready to pay a talent for a male prostitute and 300 *drachmae* for a jar of Pontic pickled fish. It was in this context that Cato once declared in a public speech that anybody could see the Republic was going downhill when a pretty boy could cost more than a plot of land and jars of fish more than ploughmen. These extravagances became disgracefully ostentatious at the period which I am describing; the reason was first of all the belief that after the destruction of the Macedonian kingdom the universal supremacy of Rome had been established beyond dispute, and secondly the fact that after the riches of Macedon had been transported to Rome there followed a prodigious display of wealth and splendour both in public life and in private.

Scipio, by contrast, set himself to follow the opposite path. He disciplined all his appetites, and by dint of laying down for himself a consistent and undeviating system of conduct, he built up within the space of five years a reputation in the eyes of the whole people for moderation and self-control.

His next concern was to formulate for his own observance a code of principle and integrity in his handling of financial matters, which again far surpassed the general standard. In this sphere the part of his life which he spent with his real father gave him an excellent foundation, and his natural impulses also led him in the right direction, but besides this, chance also helped him to attain this particular ideal.

26. His first opportunity in this direction arose from the death of Aemilia, the mother of his adoptive father.[1] She was the sister of his real father, Lucius Aemilius Paullus, and the wife of his grandfather by adoption, Scipio Africanus, the victor of Zama. She left her nephew a large fortune, and his handling of this legacy gave the first proof of the nobility of his principles. Whenever Aemilia had left her house to take part in women's processions, it had been her habit to appear in great state, as befitted a woman who had shared the life of the great Africanus when he was at the height of his success. Apart from the magnificence of her personal attire and of the decorations of her carriage, all the baskets, cups and sacrificial vessels or utensils were made of gold or of silver, and were carried in her train on such ceremonial occasions, while the retinue of maids and men-servants who accompanied her was proportionately large.

Immediately after Aemilia's funeral Scipio handed over all her splendid accoutrements to his mother. She had been separated

1. She died in 162 B.C.

from her husband for many years, and her means were far from sufficient to keep her in a state which was suitable for her rank. In previous years she had stayed at home on such ceremonial occasions. But now when a solemn sacrifice had to take place, she drove out in all the state and splendour which had once belonged to Aemilia. All the women who witnessed the sight were moved with admiration for Scipio's goodness and generosity, and lifting up their hands to heaven they prayed that blessings should be granted him. Such conduct would be thought honourable anywhere, but in Rome it was almost miraculous, for there absolutely no one gives away any private property to anyone if he can help it. This was the beginning of Scipio's reputation for nobility of character, and it quickly became widely known, for women are fond of talking, and once they have started a subject they can never have too much of it.

27. After this there arose the matter of Scipio's obligations to the daughters of the great Africanus, who were the sisters of the former's adoptive father. When Scipio came into his inheritance it was his duty to pay each of the daughters half of their portion. Their father had arranged to pay each of them fifty talents. Half of this sum had been paid to the husbands of each by their mother at the time of their marriage, but the other half was still owing when Aemilia died, so that it remained for Scipio to discharge this debt. Roman law laid it down that this part of their dowry that was still due should normally be paid to them over a period of three years, the first payment, consisting of the personal property, being made within ten months, according to the usual custom.[1] Scipio, however, instructed his banker to pay each of the daughters within ten months the entire twenty-five talents. After the ten months had elapsed, the respective husbands, Tiberius Sempronius Gracchus[2] and Scipio Nasica, inquired of the banker whether he had received any instructions from Scipio about the money. At this the banker requested them to accept the payment at once and wrote out a transfer for twenty-five talents to each of them. The husbands,

1. This consisted of clothes, jewels, slaves and other personal property.
2. The younger of the two daughters became the mother of the Gracchi brothers, Tiberius and Gaius, the democratic leaders who lost their lives in the political upheavals of the following generation.

however, told him that he must be mistaken, for according to the
law they were not yet entitled to receive the whole amount, but
only one-third of it. When he assured them that these had been
Scipio's instructions, they still could not believe their ears, and
went to call on the young man, imagining that he had made a
mistake. And indeed this was quite a natural assumption, for in
Rome, so far from paying out fifty talents three years in advance,
nobody would pay one talent before the appointed day, so rigidly
precise is everybody about sums of money, and conscious of time
in their anxiety for profit. At any rate, when they visited Scipio and
asked him what orders he had given the banker, and he replied
'to pay the two sisters the whole amount that was due to them',
they told him he had made a mistake, at the same time insisting
that they were thinking of his interests, since according to the law
he had the right to use the money for a considerable while yet.
Scipio told them that he was well aware of this, but that while in the
case of strangers he observed the letter of the law, he treated relatives and friends, so far as it was in his power, in an informal and
liberal fashion, and he therefore asked them to accept the whole sum
from the banker. When Gracchus and Nasica heard this, they went
away dumbfounded; they were as astonished at Scipio's generosity
as they were embarrassed at their own meanness, although they
were men of as high a character as any in Rome.

28. Two years later, when his real father Paullus died and left
him and his brother Fabius joint heirs to his property, Scipio
again acted with a sense of principle which deserves to be mentioned. Paullus was legally speaking childless: he had allowed two
of his sons to be adopted into other families, while the others, who
had been brought up to succeed him, were both dead,[1] and he
therefore left his property to Scipio and to Fabius. Scipio, since he
knew that his brother was worse off than himself, gave up the whole
of his share of the inheritance, although this was estimated at more
than sixty talents, so that Fabius' estate should become equal to his
own. This became a matter of common knowledge, and he soon
after gave an even more conspicuous proof of his generosity. On
the occasion of their father's funeral Fabius wished to give a

1. Of these two younger sons, one died five days before Paullus' Macedonian triumph in 167 B.C., and the other three days after it.

gladiatorial show, but because of the immense cost of such entertainments, he was unable to meet the expense, whereupon Scipio
provided half the amount out of his own resources. The total cost
of such a show, if it is mounted on such a lavish scale, is not less
than thirty talents.

While this action was still being talked about, Scipio's mother
Papiria died, and he, so far from taking back any of the gifts he
had made to her, transferred all of them together with his mother's
property to his two sisters, even though they had no legal claim
to it. In this way his sisters in their turn came into possession of
the ceremonial ornaments and the retinue which had originally
belonged to Aemilia, and Scipio's magnanimity and devotion to
his family were demonstrated yet again.

Thus Scipio after he had laid the foundations in his early years
for his chosen ideal, never looked back in his progress towards a
reputation for self-discipline and nobility of character. His reputation of generosity was established by his expenditure of some
sixty talents, for this was what he gave away from his own capital;
but it was not so much the size of the sums which he contributed
as the timeliness of the gifts and the graciousness with which he
conferred them. As for his reputation for self control, this cost
him nothing, and by abstaining from the many and varied pleasures
of others he gained a physical health and well-being which remained
with him for the rest of his life. It also brought him many satis-
factions of a different kind, and rewards which amply compensated
for the immediate pleasures he had sacrificed.

29. It remained for him to acquire a reputation for courage,
which may be said to be the most important of all virtues in any
state, but in none more than in Rome, and for this it was necessary
for him to undergo a particularly strenuous training. But here too
Fortune was on his side. The members of the royal family of
Macedon have always been especially devoted to hunting, and the
Macedonians had set aside the most suitable parts of the country
for the breeding of game. During the war against Rome these
districts had been as carefully maintained as ever before, but
because of the succession of national crises they had never been
hunted, with the consequence that there was an abundance of big
game of every kind. When the war had been won, Paullus, who

believed that hunting offered the best training and recreation for young men, placed the royal huntsmen under Scipio's authority and gave him complete control of all matters connected with hunting.

Scipio accepted this commission, and since he could regard himself as being virtually in the position of a king, he devoted his whole time to this activity for as long as the army remained in Macedonia after the battle of Pydna. At that time he was of exactly the right age and physically in his prime, and since he was naturally fitted for it by temperament like a well-bred dog, he developed a great enthusiasm for the sport, a taste which was to last him throughout his life. And so when he returned to Rome and found that Polybius possessed a liking for the chase to match his own, instead of spending the time as most other young men do in the law-courts or on formal visits,[1] haunting the Forum and striving to ingratiate himself with the populace, Scipio devoted his days to hunting. He performed many brilliant feats in the field and there too gained a higher reputation than his contemporaries. Those who dedicated themselves to the law could only win praise by harming one or other of their fellow citizens, since this was the usual result of proceedings in the courts, whereas Scipio, without harming a soul, gained a universal reputation for courage, matching action against eloquence. The result was that in a short space of time he had outstripped his contemporaries more decisively than any Roman is recorded as having done, even though the path he followed in pursuit of fame was quite different to that which all others chose in accordance with Roman tradition and custom.

30. I have dwelt at some length on Scipio's principles and character, beginning from his earliest years, partly because I thought that the story would be enjoyable for my older and profitable for my younger readers, but above all to make what I shall have to write of him in my later books appear credible. I am anxious that none of my readers should find difficulty in accepting anything in Scipio's later life which may sound extraordinary, nor again that he should be deprived of the credit for any of his achievements because these are attributed to chance through ignorance of the true causes of certain events. There were no more than a few occasions of this kind which we can ascribe to chance or good luck.

1. The calls and salutations came first, the legal business later in the morning.

BOOK XXXVI

Affairs in Rome and Carthage

THE THIRD PUNIC WAR

9. A great many different reports were current in Greece on the subject of the final defeat of the Carthaginians by the Romans,[1] and these contrasting versions reflected a wide divergence of opinion. Some people praised the Romans for having pursued a wise and statesmanlike policy to defend their empire. To remove the fear which had constantly hung over them and to destroy the city which had repeatedly disputed the rule of the world with them and was quite capable of doing so again if the opportunity arose, and thus to ensure the supremacy of their own country – these, it was held, were the actions of intelligent and far-sighted men.

But others took the opposite view, and argued that far from upholding the principles by which they had won their supremacy, the Romans were gradually abandoning these and turning towards the same craving for power which had afflicted the Athenians and the Spartans, and that although they had started later than these two states, all the indications were that they would arrive at the same goal. In the past the Romans had made war upon all peoples, but only to the point at which their opponents had been defeated and had acknowledged that they would obey them and execute their commands. But now they had given a foretaste of their future intentions in their behaviour towards Perseus, which had involved the destruction, root and branch, of the Macedonian kingdom, and the new policy had reached its climax in the decision concerning Carthage. The Carthaginians had committed no irretrievable offence against their opponents, yet the Romans had inflicted penalties which were not only harsh but final, even though the enemy had agreed to accept all their conditions and obey all their commands.

Others, however, maintained that the Romans were, generally

1. The reference is the Third and last Punic War.

speaking, a civilized people, and that their national peculiarity on which they prided themselves was that they fought their wars in a straightforward and chivalrous fashion: they did not resort to night attacks or to ambuscades, they scorned any advantage that might be gained by deceit or fraud, and they regarded open and face to face fighting as the only form of combat which was worthy of their character.[1] But latterly throughout their dealings with the Carthaginians they had practised deceit and fraud, coming forward with one set of proposals at one moment and disguising them at the next, until they had deprived the city of all hope of obtaining help from her allies. These methods, it was said, resembled more the kind of intrigues which are carried on by despots than the policy of a constitutional state such as Rome, and could only be described on any honest view as something hardly distinguishable from impiety or treachery.

But there were others, again, who interpreted these actions differently. They maintained that if the Romans had acted in this fashion – offering certain concessions at one moment, and then gradually showing their hand about others – before the Carthaginians had offered to surrender, then the Romans would certainly appear to be guilty of the deceit with which they had been charged. But if the Carthaginians had first thrown themselves upon their enemies' mercy, so that the Romans could act in whatever way seemed best to them, and the latter had afterwards given the orders and imposed the terms on which they had decided, then what had been done bore no resemblance to an act of impiety and very little to one of treachery. Indeed, some would say that it was not even an injustice. For every crime must by its nature fall into one of three categories, and what the Romans did does not belong to any of them. An act of impiety is a wrong committed against the gods or one's parents, or the dead; an act of treachery consists of the violation of sworn or written agreements; and an act of injustice is an offence committed against law and custom. The Romans, however, were not guilty on any of these counts. They had not offended against either the gods, parents or the dead, neither had they broken any sworn oath or treaty – on the contrary,

1. Scipio's incendiary attack upon Syphax (p. 456) hardly accords with this tradition.

they accused the Carthaginians of having transgressed in this fashion. Nor again had they violated laws or customs or their own good faith. They had received a voluntary surrender from a people who had given them the right to do what they chose, and when this people had refused to obey their commands, they had applied force to them.

On Fate and Chance

17. Now since I have criticized those writers who attribute public events and catastrophes in private life to the workings of fate and chance, I wish to set out my views on this subject so far as the limitations of a strictly historical work allow. As regards those phenomena which it is impossible or difficult for a mortal man to understand, it is reasonable enough to escape from the dilemma by attributing them to the work of a god or of chance. Obvious examples are exceptionally heavy or continuous falls of rain or snow, or, on the contrary, droughts or frosts which cause crops to perish, or a persistent outbreak of plague, or other events of this kind, of which it is not easy to discover the cause. In such cases for want of a better explanation it is natural for us to follow public opinion and attempt by prayer and sacrifice to appease the divine powers; we then send to ask the gods what we should say and do to produce a change for the better and to obtain a respite from the evils that oppress us. But as for those events whose causes we can discover and give an explanation as to why they happen, we should certainly not in my opinion regard them as acts of God. Let me give an example of what I mean. In our times the whole of Greece has suffered a shortage of children and hence a general decrease of the population, and in consequence some cities have become deserted and agricultural production has declined, although neither wars nor epidemics were taking place continuously. Now if anyone had proposed that we should consult the gods to find out what we should say or do so as to increase our numbers and repopulate our cities, his advice would have been considered quite futile, since

the cause of this situation was self-evident and the remedy lay within our own power. This evil grew upon us rapidly and overtook us before we were aware of it, the simple reason being that men had fallen a prey to inflated ambitions, love of money and indolence, with the result that they were unwilling to marry, or if they did marry, to bring up the children that were born to them; or else they would only rear one or two out of a large number, so as to leave these well off and able in turn to squander their inheritance. For in cases where there are only one or two children and one is killed off by war and the other by sickness, it is obvious that the family home is left unoccupied, and ultimately, just as happens with swarms of bees, little by little whole cities lose their resources and cease to flourish.

In these circumstances it was of no use whatever to turn to the gods for salvation, for any ordinary man would tell you that the remedy lay in the people's own will, and that it was a question of changing the objects of their ambition or else of passing laws to ensure that the children born to them should also be reared. Here neither prophets nor supernatural powers could provide the solution, and the same principle holds good for similar problems. But where it is impossible or difficult to establish the cause, then the answer must remain in doubt: the recent history of Macedonia is a case in point.

The Macedonians had received a number of considerable benefits from the Romans. The country as a whole had been released from the arbitrary demands and taxes of autocratic rulers and, as was generally admitted, now enjoyed liberty in place of oppression, while the various cities had been delivered, thanks to the Romans, from civil bloodshed and the strife of internal factions. And yet within the space of a few years the Macedonians witnessed the exile, torture and murder of more of their compatriots at the hands of the pretender Philip than had ever happened under any of their legitimate kings. On the other hand, while they were defeated by the Romans when they were led by lawful rulers such as Philip and Perseus,[1] yet now when they were fighting on behalf of a hateful

1. Perseus had been decisively defeated by the Romans at the battle of Pydna in 168. The pretender Philip overcame a Roman legion under the praetor Juventus, but was himself defeated and captured in 148 B.C.

man, they displayed the highest courage in defending his throne and actually overcame a Roman army. Such an outcome can only baffle our intelligence, for it is difficult to discover any rational cause for it. And so in attempting to explain such developments, one would be inclined to call it an infatuation sent from heaven, and to say that the wrath of the gods had fallen upon the Macedonians.

BOOK XXXIX

From the Epilogue

At last, having completed my task, I returned home from Rome. I had been enabled to reap the harvest, it might be said, of my political activity in the past, a favour which I had earned by my loyalty to Rome. And so I offer up my prayers to all the gods that I may continue for the rest of my life in the same course and on the same terms, remembering as I do how Fortune is envious of mortal men, and is most apt to display her power at the very point where a man believes that he has been most blessed and successful in life.

So it has fallen out. But now that I have reached the end of my work, I wish to remind my readers of my starting-point and of the preliminary scheme which I set before them as the ground plan of the whole history, and at the same time to summarize my subject-matter and establish both in general terms and in detail the connection between the beginning and the end. I explained at the outset that I would begin my introductory books from the point at which Timaeus had left off, and then provide a brief review of events in Italy, Sicily and Africa, since Timaeus had confined his attention to those countries in his history. I had then reached the point at which Hannibal took command of the Carthaginian army, Philip the son of Demetrius became King of Macedon, Cleomenes of Sparta was exiled from Greece, Antiochus succeeded to the throne of Syria and Ptolemy Philopator to that of Egypt. There I undertook to make a fresh start, namely at the 139th Olympiad, and from that point to relate the general history of the whole world, marking out the periods of the Olympiads, subdividing these into years, and comparing the history of the various countries by presenting parallel accounts of each down to the capture of Carthage, the battle between the Achaeans and the Romans at the Isthmus of Corinth and the political settlement of Greek affairs which resulted from that event.

It is through this approach, as I said at the beginning, that students of history will obtain the best and the most profitable result from their reading: that is, to discover by what process and under what political system the whole world was subjected to the single rule of Rome, an event completely without precedent in the past. Now that I have accomplished my whole purpose, it remains only for me to specify the periods which are included in my history and to enumerate the contents and divisions of the whole work.

MAPS
CHRONOLOGICAL TABLE
AND INDEX

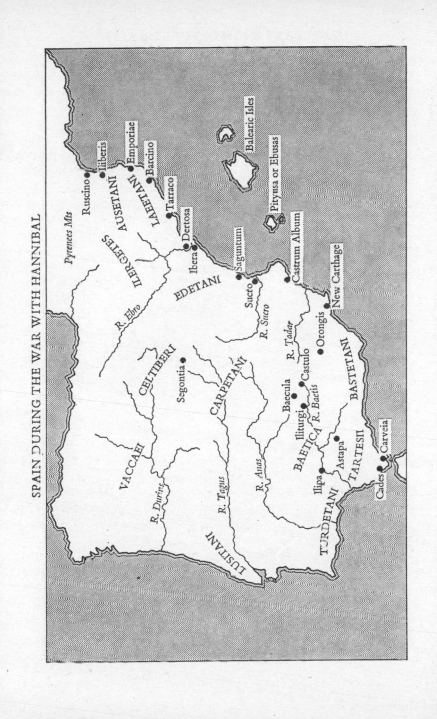

SPAIN DURING THE WAR WITH HANNIBAL

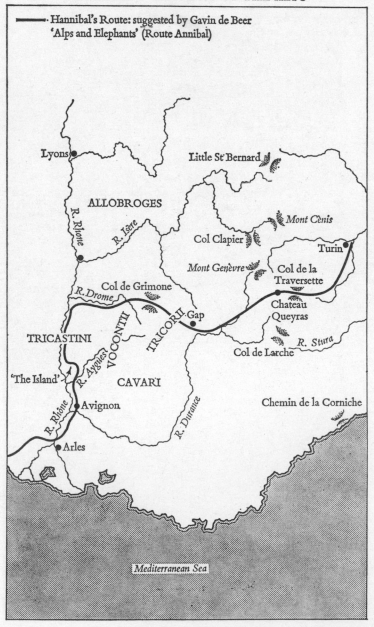

HANNIBAL'S CROSSING OF THE ALPS

Hannibal's Route: suggested by Gavin de Beer
'Alps and Elephants' (Route Annibal)

Lyons

ALLOBROGES

Little St Bernard

R. Rhône

R. Isère

Mont Cènis

Col Clapier

Turin

Mont Genèvre

Col de la
Traversette

Col de Grimone

R. Drome

Gap

Chateau
Queyras

TRICASTINI

R. Aygues

VOCONTII

TRICORII

R. Stura

Col de Larche

'The Island'

CAVARI

R. Durance

Chemin de la Corniche

R. Rhône

Avignon

Arles

Mediterranean Sea

NORTHERN ITALY

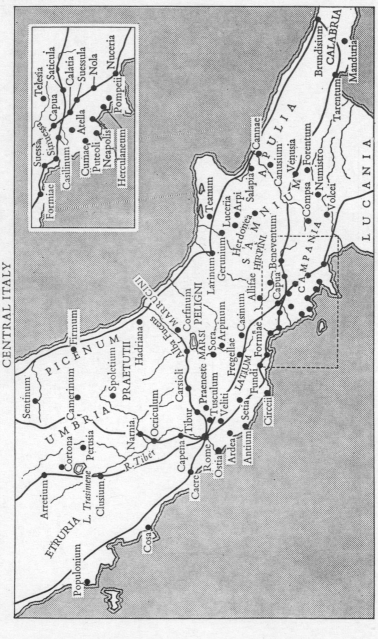

CENTRAL ITALY

SOUTHERN ITALY AND SICILY

APULIA
CALABRIA
Brundisium
Tarentum
Manduria
Metapontum
Heraclea
Volcei
Grumentum
LUCANIA
Thurii
Petelia
Croton
Consentia
C. Palinurus
BRUTTIUM
Caulonia
Locri
Rhegium
Vibo Valentia
Messana
Tyndaris
Tauromenium
Cephalodium
Catana
Thermae
Himeraeae
SICILIA
Henna
Syracuse
Megara Hyblaea
Thapsus
Panormus
Herbesus
Murgantia
Leontini
R. Himera
Acrae
Helorus
C. Pachynus
Segesta
Eryx
Mt.
Camarina
Selinus
Agrigentum
Lilybaeum
Heraclea Minoa
Aegates Isles

AFRICA AND NUMIDIA

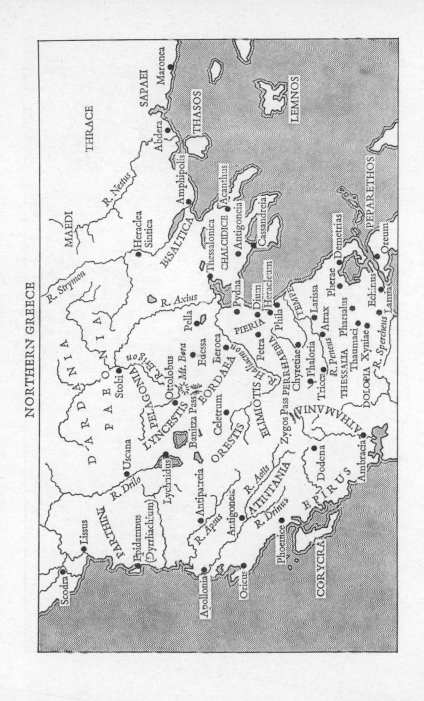

NORTHERN GREECE

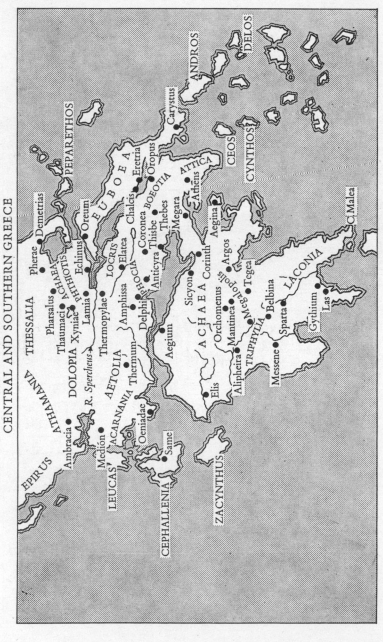

CENTRAL AND SOUTHERN GREECE

PLAN OF HALF A FOUR LEGION CAMP ACCORDING TO POLYBIUS

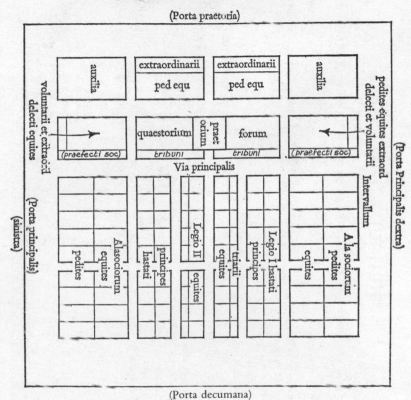

(Porta praetoria)

(Porta Principalis dextra)

(Porta principalis) (sinistra)

(Porta decumana)

auxilia

extraordinarii
ped equ

extraordinarii
ped equ

auxilia

pedites equites extraord delecti et voluntarii

voluntarii et extraord delcti equites

(praefecti soc)

quaestorium

praetorium

forum

(praefecti soc)

tribuni

tribuni

Intervallum

Via principalis

Legio II

principes

hastati

triarii

equites

Legio I hastati

principes

A la sociorum

pedites

equites

Alasociorum

equites

pedites

equites

CHRONOLOGICAL TABLE

The following table lists the main events described or referred to in this selection from Polybius' Histories.

WEST

280	Pyrrhus crosses into Italy
264	First Punic War begins
262	Battle of Mylae
257	Battle of Tyndaris
256	Battle of Ecnomus
247	Hamilcar Barca in Sicily
241	Battle of Aegates Islands: end of First Punic War
240–237	Carthaginian Mercenary War
238	Roman occupation of Sardinia
237–230	Hamilcar in Spain
230–221	Hasdrubal in Spain
226	Ebro river treaty between Rome and Hasdrubal

EAST

280	Achaean League reconstituted
251/50	Aratus frees Sicyon
243/2	Aratus seizes Corinth
235	Cleomenes III accedes at Sparta
229	Antigonus Doson succeeds Demetrius II in Macedonia. Battle of Paxos
229–228	First Illyrian War
227	Cleomenes' *coup d'état.* Earthquake at Rhodes

Date		Date	
225	Gauls defeated at Telamon	225	Seleucus III succeeds Seleucus II
		224	Antigonus in Greece; Hellenic alliance founded
		223	Mantinea razed; Cleomenes takes Megalopolis. Antiochus III succeeds Seleucus III
222	Battle of Clastidium	222	Battle of Sellasia
221	Hannibal succeeds Hasdrubal in Spain	221	Death of Antigonus Doson: accession of Philip in Macedonia.
		220	Accession of Ptolemy IV in Egypt. Outbreak of the War of the Allies in Greece. Beginning of the main part of Polybius' *Histories*
219	Siege and capture of Saguntum	219	Death of Cleomenes in Egypt. Second Illyrian War: Demetrius of Pharos joins Philip
		219–217	Fourth Syrian War
218	Outbreak of Second Punic War. Hannibal leaves Spain, crosses the Alps and reaches Italy. Battle of river Trebbia	218	Philip successful. Thermum sacked
217	Battle of Lake Trasimene. Roman naval victory off the river Ebro	217	Conference of Naupactus; end of the War of the Allies. Battle of Raphia. Peace between Egypt and Syria
216	Battle of Cannae	216	Philip in Illyria
215	Syracuse joins Carthage	215	Alliance between Philip and Hannibal. Beginning of the First Macedonian War
		215 or 214	Philip's intervention in Messenia
214–212	Roman siege of Syracuse		
213/12	Hannibal captures Tarentum		
212	Fall of Syracuse		

	WEST		EAST
211	Hannibal's march on Rome. Fall of Capua. Publius and Gnaeus Scipio killed in Spain	211	Alliance between Rome and Aetolia
210	Publius Scipio (Africanus) lands in Spain		
209	Scipio takes New Carthage		
209–206	Scipio's conquest of Spain		
		206	Aetolians make a separate peace with Philip
		205	Peace of Phoenice. End of the First Macedonian War
204–202	Scipio in Africa	204	Death of Ptolemy IV and accession of Ptolemy V
		203	Downfall of Agathocles in Alexandria
		203/2	Secret pact between Philip V and Antiochus III against Egypt
202	Battle of Zama	201	Philip in Aegean and Asia Minor; fighting against Attalus and Rhodes
201	Peace ending Second Punic War	200	Outbreak of Second Macedonian War
		199	Aetolians join Rome.
		198	Achaeans join Rome. Conference in Locris
		197	Battle of Cynoscephalae. End of Second Macedonian War
		196	Flamininus proclaims the freedom of Greece
		196–193	Antiochus advances in Asia Minor and Thrace
		192–189	Syrian War between Rome and Antiochus
		189	Manlius Vulso attacks the Galatians of Asia Minor
		188	Treaty of Apamea. Settlement of Asia
		186–183	War between Prusias I and Eumenes II

183–179	War between Pharnaces and Eumenes II (allied with Ariarathes IV)
179	Perseus succeeds Philip V in Macedonia
171–168	Third Macedonian War
169	Antiochus IV invades Egypt and withdraws
168	Battle of Pydna. Macedonia divided into four republics. Antiochus invades Egypt again and receives Roman ultimatum to leave. End of Polybius' *Histories* according to the original plan
167	Polybius goes as detainee to Rome
162	Polybius helps Demetrius to escape from Rome to Syria
158	Ariarathes V expelled from Cappadocia
157	Ariarathes restored by Attalus II
156–164	War between Attalus II and Prusias II
150	Return of Polybius and the other detainees to Greece
149	Andriscus' rising in Macedonia
149/8	Sparta secedes from the Achaean League
148	Defeat of Andriscus
147	Roman envoy authorizes the secession of several cities from the Achaean League
146	The Achaean War. Sack of Corinth. Polybius in Greece

153–151	Celtiberian War in Spain
151	Polybius accompanies Scipio to Spain and Africa. Carthage declares war on Masinissa
150	Roman decision to declare war on Carthage
149	Romans invade Africa
146	Sack and destruction of Carthage by Scipio. Polybius' voyage in the Atlantic
145	Polybius visits Rome

End of the extended version of the *Histories*

INDEX

INDEX

Africa, Africans – *contd.*
errors, 429–30; Scipio's campaigns, 452–63, 474–82; Third Punic War, 535–7
Agatharcus, 353–5
Agathoclea, 484, 489–90
Agathocles of Alexandria, 483–93 *passim*
Agathocles of Syracuse, 353, 372, 400, 436, 492
Agelaus, 26, 299
Agesilaus, King of Sparta, 184, 343, 393, 400
agger, 330
Agones, 126
Agraae, 498
Agrianians, 170
Agrigentum, Agrigentines, 66, 68, 71, 88–9, 117, 438–9; capture of, 58–62; temple of Asclepius, 59
Agron, King of Illyria, 112–15
Agyrium, 48
Alba, 129
Albanians, 113
Alcibiades, 289
Alexander the Great, 9, 42, 153, 183, 231, 370–72, 433, 437, 496
Alexander II of Epirus, 157
Alexander, cavalry commander at Sellasia, 172, 360
Alexander, delegate of Attalus I, 503
Alexander Balas, 526
Alexander of Isus, 496–503
Alexandria, 10, 15, 19, 39, 292, 295, 353, 485–8; Maeander water-garden, 488; temple of Demeter (Thesmophorium), 485–7, 491; theatre of Dionysus, 488
Alexon, 88
Allobroges, 223
Alpheius, river, 432
Alps, 14, 125–7, 133–4, 142, 145, 210–12, 220; Hannibal's crossing of, 220–34
Althaea, 190
Amphilochians, 499

Amynander, King of Athamania, 494, 502
Amyntas, 370
anacyclosis, 31
Anagneia, 525–6
Anares, 128, 142, 145
Ancona, 127
Andalusia, 209
Andobales, Spanish chieftain, 418–22
Andosini, 211
Aneroestes, King of the Gaesatae, 133, 137, 141
Anio, river, 390
Antalcidas, Peace of, 46, 343
Antigonus I, King of Macedon, 109, 496
Antigonus II, Gonatas, 153, 156
Antigonus III, Doson, Regent of Macedon, 157, 176–7, 193, 291, 361; alliance with Achaean League, 159–64; campaigns in Peloponnese, 164–9; invades Sparta, 170; wins battle of Sellasia, 170–76
Antiochus III, King of Syria, 43, 176, 179–80, 183–5, 208, 291, 301, 484, 515, 520; dealings with Hannibal, 188–90
Antiochus IV, Epiphanes, 524; death of, 521
Antiochus V, Eupator, 521–26
Antipater, viceroy of Macedon, 153, 434
Antisthenes of Rhodes, 33
Antium, 200
Apennine Mountains, 125–8, 257, 269
Apodotae, 499
Apollo, 358; tomb of at Tarentum, 379
Apollodorus of Cassandreia, 356
Apollodorus, secretary to Philip V, 494, 501
Apollonia, 120–21, 359
Apollonius, the elder, 524
Apollonius, the younger, 522–3
Arachthus, river, 494
Aragon, 194
Aratus of Sicyon, founds Achaean